THIRD AXIS FOURTH ALLY

THIRD AXIS FOURTH ALLY

Romanian Armed Forces in the European War, 1941–1945

MARK AXWORTHY
CORNEL SCAFEŞ
CRISTIAN CRACIUNOIU

ARMS AND
ARMOUR

To my late father, Major 'Bill' Axworthy, who, in what I hope was not the ultimate act of literary criticism, died the day before he was due to read this text. His friendship, tolerance, humour and curry are sorely missed.

Arms and Armour Press
A Cassell Imprint
Wellington House, 125 Strand, London WC2R 0BB

Distributed in the USA by Sterling Publishing Co. Inc.,
387 Park Avenue South, New York, NY 10016-8810.

Distributed in Australia by Capricorn Link (Australia) Pty. Ltd,
2/13 Carrington Road, Castle Hill, NSW 2154.

British Library Cataloguing-in-Publication Data:
a catalogue record for this book is available from the British Library

ISBN 1-85409-267-7

Designed and edited by DAG Publications Ltd.
Designed by David Gibbons; edited by Philip Jarrett;
printed and bound in Great Britain
by Hartnolls Limited, Bodmin, Cornwall

CONTENTS

ABBREVIATIONS

To condense the maximum information into both text and maps, the following abbreviations have been used for Romanian (and German) formations:

I, II, etc.	A Roman numeral indicates an Army Corps.
V T, VI T, etc.	A Roman numeral with the suffix 'T' indicates a Training Corps.
CAV, MT, MECH, etc.	Indicate specialist Cavalry, Mountain and Mechanised Corps.
1, 2, 3, etc.	An Arabic numeral alone indicates an infantry division.
1A, 3M, 6C, etc.	A capital letter suffixed to an Arabic numeral indicates specialist divisions: A = Armoured, C = Cavalry, M = Mountain, G = Guard, F = Frontier, Ft = Fortress, S = Security, R = Reserve, TV = Tudor Vladimirescu.
8c, 4m, 2ft, etc.	A lower case letter suffixed to an Arabic numeral indicates specialist brigades: c = cavalry, m = mountain, ft = fortress.
1ct, 7t, etc.	A lower case 't' indicates training divisions, which were only of brigade strength.
IV, 76, etc.	German formations are underlined where confusion with neighbouring Romanian formations is possible.

ORGANIGRAM ABBREVIATIONS

AA	Anti-Aircraft Gun
AAMG	Anti-Aircraft Machine Gun
AC	Armoured Car
AT	Anti-tank Gun
FG	Field Gun
Fl.Th.	Flamethrower
H	Howitzer
HMG	Heavy Machine Gun
IG	Infantry Gun
LMG	Light Machine Gun
Mr	Mortar
Mt	Mountain Gun
MtH	Mountain Howitzer
1/2 Tk	Half Track

Examples: 2 x 81Mr = Two 81mm Mortars
12 x 47AT = Twelve 47mm Anti-Tank Guns

PREFACE

The Eastern Front is rightly portrayed as a struggle between two gigantic opponents; the USSR and Germany. However, such was its scale that it has swallowed the campaigns of arguably the second Axis army in Europe, that of Romania, almost without trace. That the Romanian Army could claim this status might come as something of a surprise even to close students of the Second World War, who will generally assume that the Italian Army held this position. This disputable assumption has its roots in the fragmentary nature of English-language studies of the Italian war effort and the more understandable absence of a similar work on Romania. This book endeavours to fill the latter void.

The basic contention of the book is that Romania, by virtue of the motivation of Marshal Antonescu and the military and economic resources he put at Axis disposal, was more comparable in importance with Italy than with the minor Axis satellites, and its role in the Second World War is thus deserving of a reappraisal. Indeed, in the absence of any other work on the subject, Romania's role actually needs establishing. The title refers to the fact that Romania was not only the third Axis power in the European war, but also fielded the fourth-largest Allied army in 1944–45. Indeed, in 1943–44 it was the second Axis power on the continent and in 1944–1945 it suffered the third-highest Allied casualties.

Historical circumstances have ensured that Romania's contribution in the Second World War has gone unresearched. In Romania itself, the postwar Communist government forbade investigation into the years 1941–44, when the country was embarrassingly in the Axis camp, and presented a very uncritical, self-promoting official view of the 1944–45 campaign with the Allies. German memoirs have often tended to use the Romanians as scapegoats for their own failures, while Soviet publications have often failed to differentiate Romanian activities from those of the Germans. Both have their own biases, and have tainted many of the few references to Romania in English-language publications, which are generally derived uncritically from German and Soviet sources. This book, for the first time, uses largely Romanian sources to provide a new perspective on the titanic struggle on the Eastern Front. However, in its preparation I have endeavoured to remain critical and detached, for Romanian sources are as prone to special pleading as any other.

ACKNOWLEDGEMENTS

I would particularly like to acknowledge the contribution of my co-authors, who have been invaluable in making this book so comprehensive. Almost all the material relating to Romanian armour, including the whole of Chapter Seven, and the associated photographs, is the result of Cornel Scafeş's researches at the Muzeul Militar over many years. Cristian Craciunoiu is the editor of the magazine *Modelism*, and the leading independent publisher of Romanian naval and air force history. His assistance was fundamental to Chapter Ten. The naval photographs and most of the drawings of aircraft and ships are from his archives, or are derived from them. Both Cornel and Cristian have generously allowed me complete freedom to interpret the facts they laid before me as I saw fit.

Specific recognition must go to Dan Iloiu, Liviu Moroşanu and Ioan Scafeş for their drawings, some of which are so detailed that they defy faithful reproduction in small format. Several original drawings by Constantin Costache have also been redrawn to suit this format. The coarser, unlabelled drawings and all the maps are my own work. I am especially grateful to Adrian Pandea for reviewing Chapters One to Six, and for his many suggested refinements to the text. Similarly, Chapter Ten has benefited enormously from the suggestions and memories of Comandor (Rtd.) Raymond Stanescu and Nicolae Koslinski, whose joint book on the Romanian Navy is due out shortly. Chapters Seven and Eight owe much to Dan Antoniu, who has the finest collection of historical aircraft photographs in Romania, Florin Mihailescu, Neculae Moghior and Ion Taralunga.

My original research for this book was conducted at the Muzeul Militar National, using materials from the Military Archives. The staff of both institutions were enormously helpful. I would particularly mention Jipa Rotaru, Tiberiu Velter, Carol Konig and Horia Şerbanescu at the former, and Mircea Chiriţoiu and the unseen Eftimie Ardeleanu of the latter. Permission to research was obtained through the good offices of the then British Military Attaché to Romania, Colonel Crocker.

My thanks are equally due to the wives and families of all of the above, and most especially to Rodica Scafeş, who put her translator's expertise at my disposal. I would be more than happy to pass on the addresses of any of the above to interested readers.

I must also thank my mother, Lorna Axworthy, who has seen rather more of me during the preparation of this book than is usual, and quite possibly desirable. Others whose assistance and/or tolerance was enlisted include Brigid Hutchinson, Nikki Barrows, Charles Bennett, George Johnston, Ray Hooper, Bill Perceval-Maxwell, David M. Glantz and Nigel Thomas.

Ultimately, the selection of materials for this book and its preparation were my own, and any and all interpretations and opinions derived from them are entirely mine. Any culpable omissions or errors must therefore be laid exclusively at my door. I hope that they are mercifully few.

Mark Axworthy

CHAPTER 1
THE BUILD-UP TO WAR

ROMANIA'S WAR AIMS

Romania's participation in the First World War on the side of the Allies was hugely expensive in both human and material terms, and taught the nation some painful lessons about the limited value of distant allies and the importance of military preparedness and self-sufficiency. It strongly influenced Romania's diplomacy and rearmament in the run-up to the Second World War, and largely predetermined its enemies during that conflict.

Romania delayed its declaration of war until 27 August 1916 in order to secure prior Allied agreement to its over-ambitious claim on large areas of Austria-Hungary, at the core of which was the predominantly Romanian-populated province of Transylvania. However, by that time all four major Allied powers had already exhausted themselves at Verdun, on the Somme, on the Isonzo and during the Brussilov Offensive earlier in the year, and Romania achieved the unfortunate distinction of simultaneously bringing the armies of all four Central Powers down on its large but totally inexperienced and woefully ill-equipped army in their only combined offensive of the war.

The Romanian Army alone had no serious combat experience in either the Balkan or world wars. A French observer over-simplistically described the soldiers as excellent, the officers as lacking all military virtues and the general staff as nearly non-existent. The resulting defeat has been described as the 'Romanian Caporetto' and, by the time the line had been stabilised behind the lower Danube with Russian support, the western half of the country had been overwhelmed from all sides, the capital and much of the Black Sea coast had been lost, and huge troop losses suffered.

Indirect support in the form of an effective Anglo-French offensive from Salonika failed to materialise, and their direct assistance was minimal, essentially being restricted to the British demolition of Romania's oilfields as the Germans approached, and the loan of a Royal Flying Corps squadron which flew across Bulgaria in a prophetic foretaste of United States Army Air Force (USAAF) shuttle missions in the Second World War. The Russians had sent a single corps of dubious quality which sacked the Romanian countryside as enthusiastically as if it was on enemy territory.

In 1917 the Romanian Army was resurrected by expensive purchases of modern French equipment and the assistance of a French Military Mission. In July it launched an attack at Maraşti which achieved local successes and provoked German counterattacks at Mărăşeşti and Oituz over the following two months, both of which were held. These encounters represented the coming of age of the Romanian Army, which had successfully stood up to a great power for the first time. However, by the end of the year it was the last effective Allied force on the whole Eastern Front, as the Bolshevik Revolution brought about the total collapse of the Russian Army in its rear, and the cutting of its always tenuous communications with the Anglo-French. Totally isolated, the Romanians agreed an armistice on 9 December. However, German peace terms were so punitive that, rather than accept them, the Romanian government resigned on 18 March 1918. Only on 7 May could a government be found to accept the terms, albeit grudgingly, and even then it failed to ratify the peace treaty and its acts were later disowned.

On 9 November 1918, with the Central Powers collapsing, Romania was able to re-enter the war and thereby guarantee its seat at the peace table. The collapse of Russia and Austria-Hungary left the area around Romania in a power vacuum, and the predominantly Romanian populations of Basarabia, Bucovina and Transylvania all took advantage of the opportunity to escape foreign control and join Romania during the year. These gains were all recognised by the various peace treaties that settled the First World War. Thus the interwar Romanian state incorporated almost all ethnic Romanians and achieved the borders of the Romania Mare (Great Romania) long desired by nationalists. However, the new borders also included sizeable Slav, German, Hungarian or Bulgarian ethnic minorities, whose mother countries were all anxious to reverse the peace treaties.

ROMANIA, 1940-1945.

In 1919 the Hungarian Communist Government of Bela Kun attacked the new frontier, and Romania promptly occupied Budapest and overthrew his regime. This also heightened the hostility of the new Soviet Union, which launched raids across the Dnestr. In response, in 1921 Romania formed the political and economic Little Entente with Czechoslovakia and Yugoslavia, both newly formed states with similar fears of Hungary. That same year Romania concluded a defensive pact with Poland against attack by the emergent USSR. In a measure that successfully forestalled internal communist subversion, Romania undertook an extensive land reform programme in the 1920s which ensured the country a conservative peasantry and a large food surplus for export.

In 1934 the Balkan Entente was concluded with Yugoslavia, Greece and Turkey, all of whom were suspicious of Bulgaria. As all of this was sponsored by the French, Romania was vocal in urging France to enforce the German demilitarisation of the Rhineland in 1936. However, the French backed down over the issue. Thereafter, each successive Anglo-French diplomatic retreat during the late 1930s progressively undermined the Little and Balkan Ententes, and with them Romanian steadfastness.

Now unsure of western support, Romania and Yugoslavia prudently declined Czech appeals to make the Little Entente a full defensive military alliance in April 1937. Romania gave Czechoslovakia lukewarm diplomatic support against German claims on the Sudetenland until the Anglo-French effectively conceded this territory at the Munich Agreement of 29 September 1938. This completely undermined the residual value of the Little Entente. Romania also objected to the subsequent annexation of more of Czechoslovakia by Poland on 1 October and Hungary on 2 November, and it rejected a German offer to share in the division of Ruthenia, but events were running so consistently in Germany's favour that, in November, King Carol visited Berlin in an effort to mend relations. The failure of Britain or France to act when Hitler occupied Bohemia-Moravia on 15 March 1939 led the Romanian government to conclude the Wohltat economic agreement with the Reich on 23 March 1939. To stop the drift, the Anglo-French responded by giving Romania a unilateral guarantee of its security on 13 April.

The Molotov-Ribbentrop Pact of 23 August 1939 between the USSR and Germany made the Anglo-French guarantee Romania's last lifeline. However, although Britain and France honoured a similar guarantee to Poland by declaring war on Germany on 3 September 1939, they proved powerless to prevent that country being overrun within the month. Romania still had a defensive pact with Poland against the Soviet Union, which also attacked Poland on 17 September, but, recognising the futility of its intervention, the Polish government released Romania from its obligations. Romania facilitated the escape of the Polish Government, its gold reserve, 60,000 troops and 40,000 civilians, but dared do no more.

This initial demonstration of the Wehrmacht's power was instrumental in the conclusion of a major oil protocol between Germany and Romania in late September 1939. However, the fear of Hungarian, Bulgarian, German and/or Soviet invasion persisted. Romania therefore remained fully mobilised to meet every eventuality. More German successes in Scandinavia and the Low Countries led Romania to sign the Oil Pact with Germany on 29 May 1940, under which she agreed to barter oil and food for arms. The defeat of France and the expulsion of Britain from the continent in the following month totally undermined any residual value their guarantees held, and predatory neighbours began to gather against Romania.

The May Oil Pact seriously worried the Soviet Union. On 26 June it demanded the cession of Basarabia and Northern Bucovina, and two days later gave Romania a four-day deadline for withdrawal. Not only were the Western Allies impotent, but Germany had already secretly conceded the former territory to the USSR under the Molotov-Ribbentrop Pact. Isolated, Romania bitterly complied. Basarabia had a large Romanian majority with an overwhelming desire to remain Romanian. In Northern Bucovina, which had never previously been part of Russia, Romanians formed the largest population group, but not an outright majority. Nevertheless, when other non-Ukrainian and non-Russian minorities and anti-Communists are added to them, there was a clear majority preferring Romanian to Soviet rule at the time.

In the year up to the outbreak of war, the new Romanian-Soviet frontier was far from quiet. Shooting was an almost nightly occurrence, as were unexplained overflights by Soviet aircraft. Soviet patrols periodically raided for prisoners, and on 26 October considerable attacks with naval and aerial support were made on Romanian islands in the Danube Delta. Tens of thousands of influential Basarabian Romanians were also deported to Siberia. Thus, psychologically, and often physically, the Romanian Army was at war with the Soviet Union from 26 June 1940. The fact that Northern Bucovina had not been part of the Molotov-Ribbentrop Pact also put Germany increasingly on its guard against the USSR.

On 2 July Romania formally renounced the redundant Anglo-French guarantees and announced that its foreign policy was thenceforward to be determined by Hitler's New European Order. This was apparently well received in Germany. However, before this new relationship could be consolidated by substantive agreements, Hungary, long Germany's informal ally, capitalised on Romania's diplomatic isolation by immediately pressing its long-simmering claim to the whole of Transylvania.

On 15 July Hitler and Mussolini ordered Romania and Hungary to negotiate a peaceful settlement, but the talks immediately became deadlocked. German opinion was that, if the Hungarians attacked Romania, they would be defeated unless Germany intervened, and if that occurred the Romanians, with British help, would sabotage their vital oilfields as they had in the First World War. A peaceful settlement was therefore essential to German interests, so, to reinforce the pressure, Hitler ordered two armoured and ten infantry divisions to concentrate in southern Poland, and sent four armoured and two motorised divisions to Vienna.

The negotiations remained deadlocked, however, so the German and Italian foreign ministers, Ribbentrop and Ciano, eventually had to impose the unsolicited and non-negotiable 'Arbitration' of Vienna on Romania on 30 August. This awarded Northern Transylvania to Hungary, the majority of its claim, and gave Romania a fortnight in which to complete its evacuation. The commanders of the locally raised Romanian divisions were inclined to fight, but Romania was now powerless to resist the dictat effectively, and heavy pressure from Bucharest forced their bitter compliance.

The Transylvanian question was complex. Historically, the Romanian presence long predated the Hungarian. However, centuries of Hungarian rule and an aggressive policy of 'Magyarisation' in the previous century had led to a mixed population. In the whole of Transylvania, which was the original Hungarian claim, there were nearly two Romanians for every Hungarian. Hungarians formed a clear majority in only four isolated counties in the centre of Romania.

In his Vienna Award, Hitler, who favoured the Hungarians as fellow victims of the First World War although he disliked them personally, not only gave Hungary these four counties, but also the intervening Romanian-dominated counties up to the previous Hungarian frontier. Romanian and Hungarian census figures for the area, Northern Transylvania, are directly contradictory, and it can only be said with reasonable confidence that there were between 900,000 and 1,350,000 of each in the territory. However, large numbers of Germans, Jews and Gypsies probably ensured that neither Romanians nor Hungarians formed an absolute majority at the time. The Vienna Award therefore consigned about as many Romanians as Hungarians to Hungary, thereby punishing the former without satisfying the latter, which received only two-thirds of its claim. The dispute rumbled on throughout the war.

The Hungarians immediately began a systematic policy of 'ethnic cleansing' to ensure their contestable majority in Northern Transylvania. By the end of 1940 88,579 registered Romanian refugees had been driven into Romania, and their numbers grew further in 1942 (35,432), 1943 (74,414) and 1944 (5,166). Approximately 80,000 more unregistered refugees stayed with relatives. Particular emphasis was given to expelling academics, professionals, and heads of household likely to give coherence to any resistance. Within Northern Transylvania at least 919 Romanians had been killed and 15,000 arrested by November 1941. Furthermore, 70,000 Romanians were conscripted in labour companies during the war, many of whom were lost with the Hungarian Army in Russia. Another 17,000 were sent as forced labourers to Germany. The Hungarians also collaborated in the deportation of 150,000 Transylvanian Jews to Germany in 1944.

There was passive resistance in Northern Transylvania but, under German pressure, Antonescu officially discouraged an active resistance during the war in order not to antagonise the Germans. He also prudently suspended a plan to re-form two divisions (16 and 17) from Transylvanian refugees to spearhead a postwar return. Between the wars Romania had deliberately built its main aircraft, artillery, mortar and small-arms factories in the secure heart of the country, but the Vienna Dictat now placed the IAR, Astra, Voina and CMC plants within a day's march of the new Hungarian border. The various implications of the Transylvania issue justified the Romanians in keeping their 1st Army of never less than five divisions at home throughout the war, while the Hungarians always had two armies in country. The result was constant tension on the mutual frontier, with 254 armed clashes occurring between September 1940 and August 1944. Hitler held the Hungarians largely responsible.

Throughout their campaigns in the USSR, the Romanian and Hungarian armies would rather have fought each other. This complicated German operational planning and diplomacy considerably. On the other hand, their competition for German favour over Transylvania was a major factor in both countries campaigning deep into the Soviet Union and far beyond their immediate national interests. Whenever Soviet propagandists wanted to undermine the morale of Romanian troops at the front, they would drop leaflets announcing that the Germans had forced further territorial concessions to Hungary behind their backs. Given the events of 1940, most Romanians found this quite plausible. The reverse psychology similarly damaged Hungarian morale.

Lastly, Southern Dobrogea was ceded to Bulgaria under German pressure at the Craiova Accord on 7 September 1940. The Romanians had originally seized Southern Dobrogea in the Second Balkan War of 1913 in order to effect an exchange of the province's ±121,925 Bulgarian population for the similar Romanian minority scattered around Bulgaria. However, little population exchange had occurred, and by 1940 only 15 per cent were Romanian and 38 per cent remained Bulgarian. The legitimacy of Romanian rule depended largely on the unanimous distaste of the large Turkish population (47 per cent) for Bulgaria. The two countries subsequently exchanged the Romanian minority in Southern Dobrogea for the Bulgarian minority in Northern Dobrogea, and the Bulgarian frontier was relatively quiet during the war. On 29 September Romania withdrew from the Balkan Entente, which it had joined to preserve Southern Dobrogea, and thus released itself from military obligations to Yugoslavia, Greece and Turkey. Only when the Vienna Diktat and Craiova Accord had been implemented did Germany guarantee the borders of a reduced Romania.

The German backing for Hungary and Bulgaria in 1940 did not produce all the anticipated dividends. The Hungarians had no territorial grievance against the Soviet Union, and campaigned there only intermittently. The Bulgarians, while willing to undertake a policing role in the occupation of Yugoslavia, could not even be induced to break diplomatic relations with the USSR, let alone declare war. It was the Romanians, who wanted to recover Basarabia, who fought with greater conviction and effect.

However, German policy was governed by the fact that trouble in the resource-rich but volatile Balkans could do more to damage Germany than the wholehearted support of any of its Balkan allies could do to strengthen it. Therefore, throughout the war Germany was more interested in maintaining a peaceful equilibrium in the region than in displaying partiality for its most useful co-belligerent against the Soviet Union. As a result, weapons deliveries appear to have been made with an even-handedness that under-rewarded the much more heavily committed Romanian armed forces.

The effect of Romanian territorial losses in 1940, and Hungarian and Bulgarian gains in 1939–41, was to make Hungary alone potentially as powerful as Romania, and it destroyed Romania's interwar policy of trying to maintain armed forces equal to both combined. In August 1944 the Transylvanian issue allowed the Romanians to switch their allegiance from the Axis to Allied camp with an entirely clear conscience. As a result, Northern Transylvania was the only one of its 1940 losses that Romania was able to recover at the end of the Second World War.

German military memoirs of Romania in the Second World War are often highly coloured by the Romanian defection in 1944, and tend to express an indignant sense of personal betrayal without taking into account the grievous injuries German foreign policy had inflicted on Romania in 1940. As a result, Romania's population had fallen from 19,934,000 in 1939 to an estimated 13,291,434 in September 1940; a loss of 6,758,954 people, half of whom were ethnic Romanians. A similar proportion of its land area was lost. In contrast, Hungary's population had grown from about 9 million in 1939 to an estimated 14,680,000 by 1941, over a million of them probably Romanians.

Thus Romania's war was not Germany's war. In the Second World War Romania had limited objectives of its own: the recovery of the four territories containing about a third of the country's prewar area, population and natural resources lost in 1940. The problem was that these territories were lost to both Axis and Allied powers as a consequence of the Molotov-Ribbentrop Pact. Antonescu attacked the Soviet Union to recover Basarabia and Northern Bucovina in 1941 primarily because this was the first opportunity to present itself, but Transylvania was closest to Romanian hearts and always remained the ultimate goal. Thus, once the retention of Basarabia and Northern Bucovina was no longer possible, Romania changed sides and fought for the recovery of Transylvania in 1944–45. In the Second World War Romania was not consistent in its alliances, but it was consistent in its war aim: the recovery of interwar 'Romania Mare'.

OIL

Romania's main significance in the Second World War was economic, as its oil was the single most vital resource to the German war economy. This alone gave the country an importance in the global struggle out of all proportion to its size. German companies had owned nearly two-thirds of the Romanian oil industry before the First World War, but had been largely excluded from it afterwards. Most oil extraction was undertaken thereafter by British, French, Dutch and American companies. This, and their traditional alliance with Romania, initially gave France and Britain the upper hand in the diplomatic tussle for Romanian oil, but their abandonment of Czechoslovakia in September 1938 began a process that gradually turned Romania from a sympathetic ally into a pragmatic neutral forced to trade its oil with an advancing Germany in exchange for a measure of security. In November 1938, on the back of the Munich Agreement, Hermann Goering negotiated with King Carol the return of German companies to the Romanian oil industry, and the Wohltat Agreement of 23 March 1939, which succeeded Germany's occupation of Bohemia-Moravia by barely a week, guaranteed Germany 25 per cent of Romania's oil output.

However, in the event of war an Allied naval blockade would inevitably force the Reich into additional oil purchases made on the open market in Romania. Consequently, in early September the British and French, with tacit Romanian consent, immediately began to make advance purchases of as much of Romania's oil output as possible at above-market prices. The Germans, reinforced by their early military success in neighbouring Poland and Allied military inertia elsewhere, responded on 28 September by intimidating Romania into guaranteeing oil deliveries at the maximum capacity of transportation facilities. As a sweetener Romania was offered Polish weaponry. On 6 December Romania was pressurised into signing a protocol guaranteeing Germany 130,000 tons of oil a month. This was almost exactly the same rate as the Wohltat Agreement had envisaged, and was intended to confirm existing arrangements. However, winter ice on the Danube, a failure by Germany to provide all necessary rail tankers and the effect of Allied advanced purchases of oil was to continue to depress oil deliveries to Germany well below this level until August 1940.

Nevertheless, by March 1940 it was already obvious to the Allies that oil deliveries to Germany were recovering and that, although the Romanian government remained prepared to evade many of its delivery obligations and to blow up the oilfields if the Germans tried to seize them, this knocked a sizeable hole in Britain's only active strategy at the time – its naval blockade.

The Effect of British Purchases of Romanian Oil on Deliveries to Germany

	Oct. 39	Nov. 39	Dec. 39	Jan. 40	Feb. 40	Mar. 40	Apr. 40	May. 40
To Germany (German Estimate)	98,000t	66,000t	60,000t	28,000t	21,000t	45,000t	52,000t	53,000t
To Britain (British Estimates)	?	35,000t	140,000t	120,000t	75,000t	120,000t	70,000t	75,000t

With both their naval blockade and pre-emptive oil purchase policies being gradually undermined, the British, particularly Churchill at the Admiralty, were soon spurred to more assertive measures. On 25 March 1940 the Royal Navy assembled a sabotage expedition of seven officers and about 110 other ranks from their Mediterranean Fleet at the Romanian Danube port of Braila. They were armed with personal weapons and manned two tugs, four river oil tankers and a lighter, all British owned. Their objective was to block the Danube shipping lane, by which Germany imported most of its Romanian oil, at the vulnerable Iron Gates canal. The four oil tankers, packed with cement, were to be scuttled as block ships in mid-stream. Explosives were also carried to destroy the lock gates and blow the steeply overhanging hillside into the channel, plus fluvial mines to obstruct clearance.

However, the British had yet to develop the commando concept, and the expedition was embarrassingly unclandestine. The Germans had been cultivating the head of the Romanian secret service, who told them of the expedition, and under their diplomatic pressure the Romanian government seized the vessels at Giurgiu on 5 April and expelled the crews. Fortunately for the British there were few repercussions from this outrageous breach of neutrality, because the Romanians were not totally unsympathetic and the Germans easily surpassed it by invading Denmark and Norway a few days later. However, the Romanians were shaken by the unilateral nature of this British adventure and a large increase in suspicious fires in the oilfields, and thereafter put army guards on their oil wells.

The wider Allied position continued to deteriorate with the German invasion of France, and on 29 May Romania signed the Oil Pact with Germany. From June, Romanian oil deliveries to the Reich doubled, and by August they had reached agreed levels. Later in 1940 the British had one last minor success in slightly restricting potential oil deliveries to Germany by acquiring the Belgian, Yugoslav and

French commercial river fleets, and managed to send 75 vessels to Turkey for internment, thus permanently denying Germany their use.

The Germans took a more professional approach to special forces operations in Romania. As early as 15 October 1939 the second company of the élite Brandenburg Battalion had been raised from Romanian Volksdeutsche with a view to safeguarding oil supplies. Under the cover of employment by German shipping companies, its men were stationed in every Danube port, and provided security on barges and trains to the Reich. In June or July 1940 the Germans found details of Allied sabotage plans in Paris, and by August 1940, when it was possible Romania might reject the Vienna Award, the Brandenburgers were covertly in position around Ploieşti to forestall any British attempt to repeat their successful demolition of the Romanian oilfields in the First World War. In the event, the British demolition plans were now too badly compromised to be implemented, and the danger passed when Romania grudgingly accepted the Vienna Award and a 17,561-strong German Army Mission arrived in October to train the Romanian divisions based around the oilfields.

From 1940 to 1943 Germany had only two regular, major sources of oil; its own synthetic production and Romanian natural production. Other sources were finite (prewar reserves and captured stocks), small (Austrian and Hungarian natural production) or irregular (Soviet deliveries in early 1941). At the outbreak of war Germany's synthetic production was insufficient to meet even the minimum domestic needs of its peacetime economy. In 1940 and 1941 Romania supplied 94 per cent and 75 per cent of German oil imports respectively, and it is thus no exaggeration to state that the classic blitzkrieg campaigns of 1941–42 were fundamentally dependent on Romanian oil. By separate arrangement the German forces in the southern USSR purchased their fuel directly from Romania. Thus the main seat of the war from mid-1942 to mid-1944, where its global outcome was predominantly decided by mechanised operations, was entirely dependent on Romanian oil.

Romanian Oil Production and Supply to Germany, 1939–1944

	1939	1940	1941	1942	1943	1944
Production	6,240,000t	5,815,000t	5,577,000t	5,665,000t	5,330,000t	3,525,000t
To Germany[1]	1,556,000t	1,304,800t	3,173,700t	2,302,400t	2,472,700t	1,078,900t
To Others[2]	?	?	±1,000,000t	±1,100,000t	±600,000t	?

[1] Includes deliveries to the Bohemian Protectorate and Wehrmacht.
[2] Italy, minor Axis and Neutrals
Romania tended to be extravagant in its own use of oil.

German oil reserves never rose above 1,500,000 tonnes after 1939. Thus in 1939 and 1940 Germany maintained oil reserves approximately equal to Romanian annual oil deliveries. Once the invasion of the Soviet Union began and consumption rose dramatically, German reserves fell to about six months of increased Romanian deliveries. These time spans therefore represent the approximate duration the Wehrmacht could theoretically have maintained its campaigns uncurtailed without Romanian oil. However, the reality was that it would have had to start cutting back its operations immediately in order to extend the life of its reserves. Given the narrow margins on which German campaigns were already conducted, this would undoubtedly have decided the outcome of the war years earlier.

Italy, which lacked both natural and synthetic production but was engaged in the extraordinarily fuel-hungry North African campaign, was even more heavily dependent on Romanian oil than was Germany. On 8 October 1940 Mussolini, who despised the Romanians as soldiers, even tried to elicit a Romanian request for an Italian Military Mission similar to the German one in order to gain a foothold in the oilfields. However, the Italian Army's chronic weakness made the premise that it had something valuable to teach the Romanian Army implausible, and the idea was rejected by Antonescu, who considered the Italians 'a great people but poor soldiers'. Antonescu was later mischievously able to play off the Italians against the Germans by revealing that the latter were using their monopoly presence in the oilfields to divert some of the former's oil quota.

Most of Axis Europe, except for self-sufficient Hungary, was as dependent on Romanian oil as Italy. This gave Romania some diplomatic leverage within the Axis and enabled it to maintain its own independent intra-Axis foreign policy. Fortunately for the Axis, Romanian production was not decisively disrupted by the early Allied bombing raids of 1941–43.

The Germans had ambitious plans to expand Romanian oil production, but Romanian output had peaked at 8,701,000 tons in 1936 and the Romanians preferred to conserve what was now a declining resource. Deliveries to the Reich peaked in 1941. In June 1942 Mihai Antonescu warned Carl Clodius, the Deputy Director of the Economic Department of the German Foreign Ministry, 'Romania is exhausting her oil reserves ... if oil output is expanded this will exclusively benefit the Reich'. Over-exploitation and increasing Romanian efforts to stem the uncontrolled haemorrhaging of their most valuable natural resource therefore led to a stabilisation of Romanian production and a decline in deliveries after 1941. This was undoubtedly a further spur to Hitler's decision to make the seizure the USSR's Caucasian oilfields the focus of his last strategic offensive in 1942, in support of which the bulk of the Romanian Army went to its doom at Stalingrad. In 1943 Romanian deliveries amounted to only 43 per cent of those planned by the Germans.

However, despite the enormous increase in German synthetic production, and growing Austrian and Hungarian natural production, the increased tempo of fighting ensured that the Reich's oil reserves never grew and Romanian oil remained vital to Germany. This gave great impact to the Allied bombing of the Romanian oilfields and the country's defection in August 1944, which between them contributed significantly to bringing the Wehrmacht to an almost complete standstill by the end of the year. The trail of abandoned German tanks at the Battle of the Bulge was an indirect testimony to this. The loss of Romanian oil even provoked Hitler's first admission that the war was lost.

The Effect of Allied Bombing on Romanian Oil Production, 1944

Month	March 44	April 44	May 44	June 44	July 44
Production	385,000t	176,000t	152,000t	77,000t	63,000t

ECONOMIC RELATIONS WITH THE AXIS

In 1937 Germany had provided 28 per cent of Romania's imports and received 19 per cent of its exports. Thereafter, the Reich's absorption of the Austrian and Czech economies in 1938-39, the Wohltat economic agreement of March 1939, the oil delivery programme of September 1939 and the Oil Pact of May 1940 had all marked a growing German influence which increased Germany's shares to 51 per cent and 44 per cent respectively in 1940. However, these agreements had all been concluded at a time when Romania had still been able to use its neutrality and oil as levers to extract some advantage from the negotiations and, in the two former cases, to evade some of their obligations.

By 4 December 1940 Germany was able to impose on Romania a ten-year treaty of economic collaboration which strongly favoured the former. Thereafter, at least 95 per cent of Romanian trade was with Axis Europe, 88 per cent of it with Germany. Between 1939 and 1944 Germany was able to use this monopoly to inflate the price of its exports to Romania, particularly armaments, by 614 per cent, at the same time as Romanian exports to the Reich grew in price by only 123 per cent. In addition, Germany bought into much of the Romanian petrochemical, metallurgical and wood industries, which were of strategic value to the Reich, and the largest industrial group in the country, Malaxa, was taken over by the Hermann Goering Werke and renamed Rogifer.

Throughout the war, oil revenues meant that Romania had the capacity to pay Germany for all of its reasonable armament requirements despite the inflated prices. However, the Germans were extremely loathe to part with scarce modern armaments. Thus, despite the unfavourable terms of trade the Germans were able to extract for the predominantly captured weaponry they did sell, Romania managed to build up a large balance of payments surplus with the Reich, much of which was covered by gold bullion payments. Romania had accumulated a substantial gold reserve of £88 million by 1944, most of which ultimately fell to the Soviets as reparations.

Romanian agricultural exports to the Reich were also important revenue earners. They helped cushion the German population from the effects of the war in 1940–41, and thereby played a part in perpetuating the complacency that delayed Germany's mobilisation of its war economy. However, once Romania mobilised its own manpower its agricultural output declined, and by 1944 its own cities were suffering food shortages. Food exports to the Reich therefore fell from 979,866 tons in 1940 to only 107,145 tons in 1943. In addition, Romania had to feed all German forces on its soil, a particularly heavy burden in early 1941 and mid-1944.

After Romanian oil, the second key import for the German war economy was Turkish chrome, and Romania was to become embroiled in costly German campaigns in the Kuban and Crimea in 1943–44, partly undertaken to ensure that that country's continued neutrality would perpetuate this vital trade. In August 1944 Romania's defection irrevocably cut off the Reich's access to Turkish chrome supplies as effectively as it cut off oil deliveries. In the war for natural resources that so affected Hitler's military judgements, Romania and its armed forces were a factor of much greater significance than Italy, which had few minerals of its own, and gave

Romania's Marshal Antonescu an importance to Germany that in some ways exceeded that of Mussolini.

INTERNAL POLITICAL DEVELOPMENTS AND THE RISE OF ION ANTONESCU

The dominant figure in Romanian politics before the war was the increasingly autocratic King Carol II. The major political parties were the Liberal Party of Constantin Bratianu and the National Peasants' Party of Iuliu Maniu, which had received 36 per cent and 20.4 per cent of the vote respectively in the last prewar elections in November 1937. Bratianu and Maniu also had huge personal prestige because the former's grandfather had been Prime Minister at the time of Romania's War of Independence against Turkey in 1877–78, and the latter had himself led Transylvania into union with Romania in 1918. The success of the fascistic Iron Guard of Cornelius Codreanu, with 15.4 per cent of the vote, and the National Christian Party, with 9.2 per cent, had pushed the whole spectrum of Romanian politics to the right. All of the major parties therefore had strong nationalist credentials. Only a weak Hungarian party and the internationalist Communist Party, with as few as 800 members before the war, had suspect loyalties.

The Iron Guard, formerly the Legion of the Archangel Michael and colloquially known as the Legionaries or Greenshirts, had its electoral base in Basarabia. It possessed a religious fanaticism lacking in the German and Italian fascist movements, and many Legionaries openly courted martyrdom. The Iron Guard advocated revolutionary terrorism against the State, and as early as 29 December 1933 Legionaries had assassinated the Prime Minister, Ion Duca. In January 1938 its growing electoral power prompted King Carol II to ban it. On 20 February Carol usurped what remained of the 1923 Constitution he had been undermining since 1931 and formed a corporatist regime under which he ruled through a council of personally appointed ministers.

Carol, authoritarian by nature, adopted many of the outward trappings and some of the internal policies of the regimes in Italy and Germany while simultaneously initially resisting their revisionist foreign policies. Codreanu was arrested in April, and on 30 November 1938 Carol had him murdered while allegedly attempting to escape. This occurred barely a week after Carol had left a meeting with Hitler at Berchtesgarten on 24 November, and infuriated the Fuehrer, who appeared either to have approved the assassination of an ideological protétége or to have been outrageously snubbed. This added a personal edge to Hitler's harsh treatment of Romania in 1940. The Iron Guard endured under Horia Sima as a terrorist group, assassinating another of Carol's Prime Ministers, Armand Calinescu, on 21 September 1939.

Romania's wartime leader was to be General Ion Antonescu (1882–1946). He had joined the cavalry in 1904 and his career saw him commanding a regiment (1918), a brigade (1929–31) and a division (1934–37). He had been an outstanding young general staff officer in the First World War, when his influence at the Romanian successes of Maraşti, Maraşeşti and Oituz in 1917 was reportedly out of all proportion to his rank, and again during the successful war with the Communist regime in Hungary in 1919. He thereafter gained diplomatic experience as a military attaché in both Paris (1922–23) and London (1924–26). He also served as commandant of the cavalry school (1920–22) and was twice commandant of the Romanian staff college (1927–29 and 1931–33), where he became widely known and respected by a whole generation of the middle officer corps and established a moral and professional ascendancy over many of his future commanders in the Second World War.

From December 1933 to December 1934 Antonescu was Chief of the Romanian General Staff, and he was made Minister of Defence on 28 December 1937. In these offices he was one of the prime architects of Romania's rearmament. His reputation as a stern disciplinarian, his fiery temper, and his professional ability and personal probity made Antonescu much respected, not to say exceptional, in the army. However, he had an enduring personality clash with the dissolute King Carol, for whom he showed scant respect, and was dropped from the new government formed on 29 May 1938 for not being sufficiently severe on the Iron Guard, to which he initially felt some sympathy for its uncompromising nationalism. Apart from a single month as a corps commander (November 1938) he received no other active appointment for the next two years. In July 1940 his outraged protests at the surrender of Basarabia and Northern Bucovina and his demand for the King's abdication led Carol to dismiss him from the army, and he was detained until 1 September.

The immediate consequence of the successive territorial losses of 1940 was the fall of King Carol's government. Carol was now so discredited that both Bratianu and Maniu refused to form a government, and in his last effective political act he appointed the recently released Antonescu Prime Minister on 4 September. Antonescu promptly forced him into abdication and exile two days later. Although his 19-year-old son was proclaimed King Mihai I in his stead, Carol's authoritarian powers were assumed by Antonescu. Antonescu passed over Bratianu and Maniu and, with German approval, appointed Horia Sima of the Iron Guard his deputy. Their joint regime was proclaimed the National Legionary State, and other Legionaries took over the Foreign, Interior and Labour Ministries. Antonescu kept the Ministry of Defence to himself. Although Antonescu adopted the classic fascist title of 'Conducator' (Leader) while allied to the Iron Guard, he was in fact a more pragmatic nationalist devoid of most of their ideological baggage.

On 23 September 1940 Germany, Italy and Japan signed the Tripartite Pact, and Germany's satellites Hungary, Romania and Slovakia were to adhere to it on 20, 23 and 25 November respectively. In preparation for this, Antonescu's first state visit was to Italy on 14–16 November. It was not a diplomatic success, because he was less than courteous in attacking Mussolini over his role in the imposition of the Vienna Award. It was obvious to Antonescu that Romania had more to offer Italy in oil than Italy had armaments to offer in return, and he thereafter made little attempt to cultivate Mussolini personally. They did not meet again.

Antonescu and Horia Sima visited Germany for the signing of the Tripartite Pact and met Hitler for the first time on 22 November. Antonescu, who had longstanding pro-western sympathies and had bitterly opposed the German peace terms to Romania in 1918, told Hitler frankly at this first meeting that his conversion to the German cause had come late. He also ignored German Foreign Ministry entreaties not to repeat his recent savaging of Mussolini by protesting against the Vienna Award, the reversal of which was always his ultimate foreign policy aim, and promptly lectured the Fuehrer for two hours on the subject. This he repeated at every one of their subsequent meetings, and Hitler often told his regular interpreter, Dr Paul Schmidt, that this performance always impressed him. Such bluntness, and a shared antipathy for Slavs, Hungarians and Jews, led Hitler to believe he knew where he stood with Antonescu.

Antonescu was Romania's most capable soldier, and the Iron Guard were ideologically sympathetic to the Nazis. Hitler's hope was that they would prove the ideal combination to prepare Romania for his coming campaign against the Soviet Union. However, although Antonescu proved pragmatic, efficient and organised, the Iron Guard was congenitally vicious, incompetent and anarchic. It proved a decided liability in power, where its ideologically-driven purges rapidly began to undermine Romania's internal order and led it into conflict with Antonescu. There arose a parallel German rivalry between Ribbentrop's Foreign Ministry, which supported the undoubted practical merits of Antonescu, and Himmler, who had long sponsored the Iron Guard for ideological reasons; it was violently anti-semitic.

To resolve the conflict, Hitler summoned both Antonescu and Sima to Berchtesgarten on 14 January 1941. Much to his irritation Sima failed to attend, either because he was insulted that his invitation arrived via Antonescu or because Antonescu misinformed him that it was a purely military meeting. Hitler therefore had to listen to Antonescu's uncontested litany of complaints about the Iron Guard. As intermediary, Hitler introduced Antonescu to Manfred von Killinger, the new German ambassador to Bucharest, whose first brief was to engineer a reconciliation between him and Sima.

This strengthening of the Foreign Office's position seems to have provoked Himmler's Sicherheitsdienst (SD) into action. It had already armed the Iron Guard with a considerable number of sub-machine guns (a weapon yet to enter Romanian Army service), and on 20 January 1941 it allowed Horia Sima to attempt a coup against Antonescu. The army was easily capable of suppressing the coup, but the issue remained briefly in doubt because the ultimate outcome depended on Hitler's preference. At their meeting the previous week Hitler had been gratified by Antonescu's enthusiastic reception for his first hint at the forthcoming invasion of the USSR. Preferring order to fanaticism in his satellites in the sensitive run-up to the attack, he now pragmatically threw his support behind Antonescu; 'A man of good faith, who is resolved to hold command firmly in his hands, and a very thorough nationalist'.

The Iron Guard were bloodily suppressed by 23 January, but not before German troops had made a token appearance to convince the disbelieving Legionaries that Hitler really was backing Antonescu. Himmler had Horia Sima and 300 leading supporters hidden in various German premises before smuggling them to safety in Germany. In reprisal, Antonescu demanded and received the withdrawal of Himmler's SD from Romania, albeit temporarily. Thereafter, Sima and his supporters were held in Germany as a potential alternative government to Antonescu should his adherence to the Axis falter.

The suppression of the Iron Guard presented Ion Antonescu with a problem. 'I have no party, no political follower; I don't know whom to put in what position or in what department,' he complained. In fact he had one valuable ally, the legal professor Mihai Antonescu, who had been serving as his Justice Minister. A distant cousin of Ion Antonescu, Mihai Antonescu (1904–1946) was to perform the twin roles of Prime Minister and Foreign Minister throughout the war, leaving Ion Antonescu free to concentrate on military matters and the conduct of the war. Indeed, as Ion Antonescu was not in good health, Mihai Antonescu's importance and independence of action often exceeded his official status.

Whereas the fair-complexioned Ion Antonescu struck the Germans as upright and trustworthy, the swarthy Mihai Antonescu always appeared to them shifty and unreliable. Guderian described the latter's friendliness as having a rather slimy quality, and said that he gave an impression of slyness. King Mihai characterised him as 'a sleek, perfumed schemer'. In fact, the two Antonescus were initially in close agreement and their policy differences at first remained superficial. However, the more pragmatic, Anglophile Mihai Antonescu did not feel honour-bound to the Axis cause in the same way as the less flexible Marshal, and when his efforts to make contact with the Western Allies outpaced Ion Antonescu's wishes in 1943–44, furious rows developed. Yet even then Ion Antonescu twice refused to accept Mihai Antonescu's resignation, and even refused Hitler's demand that he be dismissed.

Mihai Antonescu's character differed from that of his master in that he abused his office for personal gain, but he proved indispensable in controlling the civil administration of the country, which, although still widely corrupt, showed a marked ethical improvement over Carol's regime. In the condescending opinion of Count Ciano, the Italian Foreign Minister, he also represented his country quite well as Foreign Minister for a man who only shortly before had been an unknown Bucharest lawyer.

By drawing on fellow soldiers and using Mihai Antonescu's civil contacts, Ion Antonescu was able to announce his new government on 27 January 1941. The new Defence Minister was the academically brilliant General Iosif Iacobici. The sensitive Interior Ministry, which included the Siguranţa secret security police, and the Labour Ministry were given to other army generals. Although Maniu and Bratianu would not join the regime, Mihai Antonescu's drive to recruit a high-quality, technocratic administration led him to employ many of their supporters, especially Liberals, in the economic ministries and diplomatic service. Thus the political opposition was never entirely estranged from Antonescu's regime, which laid Bratianu in particular open to postwar Communist charges of collaboration. Maniu characterised Antonescu as a rival, not an opponent.

While the manner of Antonescu's assumption of power was resented by most civil politicians, his uncompromising nationalism initially gave him widespread political and popular support. This he harnessed in a plebiscite on 2-5 March, which legitimised his government without exposing it to electoral competition. Although Communists were jailed and the Iron Guard leaders sentenced in absentia to hard labour for life – a judgement handed down on 15 June 1941 as part of the cover for Romanian-German preparations against the USSR – Antonescu conducted no systematic purge of the traditional political parties during the war, despite German pressure. However, as the regime's popularity gradually waned, the influence of the Siguranta secret police grew to compensate, 5,463 opponents being imprisoned and 72 people being executed during 1941–44.

The main German military representative in Bucharest throughout the war was General Erik Hansen of the German Military Mission, who also headed the Army Mission in 1940/41. On 22 June 1941 his chief of staff, General Hauffe, took over as head of the German Army Mission when the Romanian army entered the field, but the post reverted to Hansen after Hauffe returned to German Army service in January 1943. General Speidel was the initial commander of the Luftwaffe Mission in 1940/42, but in May 1942 Lieutenant-General Alfred Gerstenberg, formerly air attaché at the German Embassy, took over the post for the rest of the war. Admiral W. Tillesen was head of the Naval Mission from 1940 to 1944. Carl Clodius was charged with German economic relations with Romania throughout the war, including oil and armament deliveries. These became so important that in 1943 he was appointed a virtual supernumerary ambassador to Killinger with similar direct access to both Antonescus.

Thus there was little change in German diplomatic or military representation during the war, and the few replacements appointed were promoted internally from officers who had held subordinate posts in Romania since 1940. As there was also no major change within Antonescu's regime after January 1942, there was a high degree of continuity in Romanian-German relations throughout the war. However, familiarity also bred contempt, and by 1944 all of the resident Germans seriously underestimated the resolution of the opposition to Antonescu and themselves.

Antonescu's training as a staff officer meant that he could meet the leading German generals on equal terms, and he was not easily deceived as to Germany's true military situation. Indeed, in giving him advanced notification of operations Barbarossa, Blau and Citadel, the Germans kept him better informed than any other of their allies. Manstein, Guderian and others were impressed by his obvious professional ability, and this, combined with his head-of-government status, led Hitler to give his opinions a weight he appears to have accorded to those of no other foreigner. Thus his personal influence over Hitler, limited though it was, far outweighed that of the militarily untutored Mussolini. Indeed, by involving Hitler in unwanted adventures across the Mediterranean Mussolini proved a decided handicap, whereas Antonescu proved a decided asset in supporting Hitler in his own dubious adventures around the Black Sea.

Hitler, ever one to reduce matters to an issue of race, attributed the blue-eyed Antonescu's merits to hidden German ancestry. However, behind Hitler's personal regard for Antonescu there lay more pragmatic interests. Goering summed up the German perspective thus; 'One must be very cautious with Antonescu. He is quite a stubborn mule but the only one in Romania who sticks to a pro-German line.' Antonescu considered his word his bond, and there were to be cases where he made onerous commitments on behalf of Romania which arguably put his own honour and the wider interests of the Axis alliance ahead of the specific interests of Romania itself. On the other hand, such prestige as Romania had with Germany was largely dependent on Antonescu's own high standing with Hitler and his generals, which in turn allowed Romania to be probably the least servile of the Axis satellites.

Romania was never occupied by Germany, and it is too much to say that Antonescu's regime was ever supported on German bayonets. However, its endurance once its popular support began to decline from late 1941, and the fortunes of war turned decisively against the Axis in late 1942, was undoubtedly aided by the necessarily familiar relations his regime had with the Germans at the highest level, relations to which there was no viable alternative on either side. Antonescu was irreplaceable to the Germans, while as long as the Allies remained too distant to support a defection and Romania wanted to avoid German occupation he was secure from internal displacement.

The arrival of the first German troops in Romania in October 1940, without prior consultation with Italy, infuriated Mussolini, who, as co-sponsor of the Vienna Award, considered that he had equal interests in the country. Determined to pay Hitler back in his own coin, he therefore attacked Greece on 28 October without consulting the Fuehrer. Within a week the Italian Army was driven back into Albania. In his futile efforts to avoid having to rely on Germany to bail him out, Mussolini tried to enlist Antonescu's support in the event of Yugoslavia intervening. Antonescu refused direct Romanian intervention, but later, when Mussolini had swallowed his pride and asked for German support in late December, he allowed a major German expeditionary force to assemble in Romania. This led the British to withdraw their ambassador in February 1941, but they prudently left a radio transmitter with Maniu.

Bulgaria joined the Axis on 1 March 1941. In April the Germans used Romania and Bulgaria as staging areas for their attacks on both Yugoslavia and Greece, but Antonescu refused to join Italy, Hungary and Bulgaria in dismembering them and declined a specific German invitation to occupy Western Banat, where there was a small Romanian minority. However, he notified Hitler that if the Hungarians occupied Western Banat instead (as had happened earlier, when Romania had turned down Ruthenia), he would feel obliged to move in troops to oppose them. Anxious to avoid such friction in his rear just as his invasion of the USSR was about to be launched, Hitler controlled the area for the rest of the war with three regiments and ten independent battalions of SS Auxiliary Police raised from the local Volksdeutsche. The new satellite Croatia joined the Tripartite Pact on 15 June 1941.

REARMAMENT

Shortly after Antonescu became Chief of the General Staff in December 1933, he conducted a study which revealed that Romania was unable to mobilise more than ten fully equipped divisions for war. The rival Hungarian Army was restricted to only 35,000 men by the Treaty of Trianon, but was believed not only to be exceeding this ceiling but to be modernising rapidly by spending five times as much per man as Romania. This provoked a ten-year rearmament programme, launched on 27 April 1935, designed initially to re-equip the existing 22 infantry divisions, 3 cavalry divisions and 3 mountain brigades, and then to form a motorised brigade and re-equip 9 reserve infantry divisions, a reserve cavalry division, a reserve cavalry brigade and a reserve mountain brigade. This was accompanied by a major expansion in conscription in the run-up to the war, interrupted only by the loss of population accompanying the territorial losses of 1940 which reduced eligible manpower by a third.

Romanian Mobilisation, 1936–1944

	1936/7	1937/8	1938/9	1939/40	15/6/40	22/6/41	15/6/44
Regular Officers	15,341	14,922	13,627	13,663	15,383	16,369	16,850
Regular NCOs	13,216	13,740	15,318	16,089	26,153	29,299	37,073
Active Conscripts	101,792	136,363	157,125	180,411	1,026,135	166,100	189,590
Active Reservists	-	-	-	-		474,490	775,878
New Recruits	-	-	-	-	-	-	154,756

Unlike Czechoslovakia, and to a lesser extent Hungary, which had inherited substantial manufacturing bases from the defunct Austro-Hungarian Empire, Romanian industry was largely related to oil, mineral extraction and the railways, and had to be developed from a low base between the wars. Its manufacturing sector was especially weak, and it was particularly lacking in the capacity to produce the machine tools and power units which would allow it to expand its armaments industry organically. It therefore remained dependent in these key areas on France and Czechoslovakia before the war, and Germany and its Bohemian Protectorate during it. However, Germany was under such pressure that Romania was also obliged to exploit cracks in the Reich's monopolisation of continental industry by making extensive purchases of machinery and equipment from neutral Vichy France, Switzerland and Sweden.

After the First World War Romania possessed about 1,000 Schneider (FF) M1897 75mm, Putilov (RF) M1902 76.2mm and Krupp (KF) M1904/1912 77mm light field guns, and more than 100 captured or reparation Austro-Hungarian Skoda M1914 100mm light howitzers. The mountain artillery emerged with a number of Russian M1909 76.2mm and Skoda M1915 75mm mountain guns, and Skoda M1916 100mm mountain howitzers. Romanian rifles and heavy machine-guns were from the same variety of foreign sources and were likewise of incompatible 8mm, 7.62mm and 6.5mm calibres. By the mid 1930s the essential weaknesses of the Romanian armoury were that it was unstandardised, obsolete and entirely foreign sourced.

The three elements of Romanian rearmament were the upgrading and standardisation of existing equipment using the embryonic local armaments industry, the purchase of plant and production licences for key weaponry, and the import of whatever else could not be produced locally. All was underwritten by oil revenues. Rearmament tentatively began in the early 1930s, but only in 1936 was a concerted effort made to organise local industry, when eight engineering works began conversion to war production. Shell production was divided between UDR Reşita (25 per cent), Malaxa (25 per cent), Astra (21 per cent), Concordia (21 per cent), Wolf (4 per cent) and Lemaitre (4 per cent), which between them could produce most types of standard artillery shells, although not in the quantities required for a sustained campaign.

The most important local development was the unification of field artillery calibres. For this, the Astra factory produced over 1,000 barrel linings for the various

French, Russian and German light field guns inherited from the First World War, allowing them all to fire the same 75mm rounds. The existing Skoda M14 100mm light howitzers were modernised by Astra to the latest Skoda standards to become M14/34s.

For infantry weapons the Czech 7.92mm round was adopted as standard. This was identical to the German 7.92mm round, and led to a fortuitous compatibility in the Second World War. Of the older machine guns in service it only proved possible to convert about 1,000 Schwarzlose 8mm HMGs to fire the new standard 7.92mm ammunition, and they remained in widespread use with the Frontier Guards and Marines, or as light anti-aircraft (AA) weapons on multiple mounts. The old Mannlicher M95 8mm rifles also proved capable of accepting the 7.92mm round, and they and various old, non-standard French and Russian rifles remained in service with the divisional artillery and service troops in the Second World War because insufficient modern Czech replacements were available.

Romanian rearmament was especially closely tied to the allied Czech armament industry, from which 70 per cent of imported weapons were contracted and from which it was intended progressively to assimilate production licences for all 7.92mm infantry weapons and divisional artillery. The CMC small-arms factory was set up by the Czech Zbrojovka factory, and came into full production at Cugir in 1938. By June 1941 the Czechs had delivered more than 18,000 ZB30 LMGs and CMC at least 5,000 – sufficient to equip the whole army. It was intended to licence-build the ZB37 HMG at CMC from July 1940, but the Germans cancelled the deal because they needed the machine tools to supply their own units with the weapon. Instead, 3,500 were imported by June 1941 and another 2,000 by mid-1943. In addition, 700,000 ZB24 rifles were ordered. Sufficient had arrived to re-equip all of the infantry regiments by June 1941, and the mountain and cavalry regiments by early 1942. However, by mid-1943 only 445,640 had been received, and planned local production was never begun because the Germans decided to produce the weapon themselves. Thus its issue never became universal.

It was also decided to replace half of the 75mm, 76.2mm and 77mm divisional artillery with more powerful 100mm light howitzers. To supplement the modernised Skoda M14/34s, 248 Skoda M30 and M34 100mm light howitzers were imported from Czechoslovakia in the mid-1930s, and another 252 were bought from the Germans in 1940–41. Additionally, 180 Skoda M34 150mm medium howitzers were bought in 1936–39 to form half the motorised corps and army artillery. Replacement 100mm and 150mm barrels came to be manufactured by Astra during the war, but not whole guns.

The French were the second major arms supplier. Romania ordered 125 60mm mortars, 188 81.4mm mortars, 160 Schneider 47mm anti-tank (AT) guns, 180 Schneider M36 105mm medium guns and 200 13.5mm and 300 25mm Hotchkiss AA guns directly from France. However, the fall of France interrupted these deliveries after only 144 Schneider M36 105mm guns, 72 25mm Hotchkiss AA guns and all of the mortars, 13.5mm Hotchkiss and Schneider 47mm guns had been delivered. France also sold licences to the Voina factory for 175 Brandt 60mm mortars and 410 Brandt 81.4mm mortars and to the Concordia factory for 140 Schneider 47mm AT guns, all of which were produced throughout the war in numbers far in excess of those specified in the original licences.

To replace the lost French orders the Germans bartered captured Polish weapons under the Oil Pact. These included 45 Schneider M13 105mm guns, 669 Bofors 37mm anti-tank guns (which became the most common such weapon in 1941), 54 Bofors 40mm AA guns, 45 Oerlikon 20mm AA guns and 80 Schneider 75mm M97 light field guns. Of its own weapons, Germany supplied a licence to the Astra factory in 1938 for 360 Rheinmetall 37mm AA guns, 102 of which had been delivered by May 1941, and agreed to sell 300 Gustloff 20mm AA guns in September 1940, the delivery of which had barely begun in May 1941. It also began delivery of 545 Bohler 47mm AT guns in 1941. This was an Austrian weapon virtually identical to the Italian 47mm Breda AT gun, of which 275 were also ordered. Italy also supplied its Pignone M35 flamethrower. Britain's only contribution was a licence for the Reşita factory to build 100 Vickers 75mm AA guns in 1936. A further 100 were begun in July 1941.

Throughout the war, Romanian divisional artillery remained equipped with older, lighter pieces than the Germans or Soviets and, even when armour-piercing rounds were introduced from 1942, their low muzzle velocity did not give them comparable anti-tank potential.

Thus a Romanian infantry division could fire well under half the weight of shell of the similarly sized German infantry division, and could usually only fire about the same weight of shell as the smaller Soviet infantry division. Furthermore, it was consistently outranged by both. In comparison with either Germans or Soviets, the ratio of artillery to infantry was low at divisional level and fell even further behind at corps and army levels.

The best Romanian artillerymen were posted to the seven, later eight, motorised corps heavy artillery regiments. These each possessed modern communications, modern guns (12 Skoda M1934 150mm Howitzers and 12 Schneider M1936

German, Romanian and Soviet Divisional Artillery, 1941–45

	German		Romanian						Soviet			
	1939	1944	1941	1942	1943 [1]	1944 [2]	1944 [3]	1945 [4]	5/41	7/41	7/42	6/44
75mm field gun	-	-	36	24	24	12	24	12	-	-	-	-
76.2mm field gun	-	-	-	-	-	-	-	-	16	16	32	36
100mm howitzer	-	-	16	24	24	24	36	12	-	-	-	-
105mm howitzer	36	34	-	-	-	-	-	-	-	-	-	-
122mm howitzer	-	-	-	-	-	-	-	-	20	8	12	12
150mm howitzer	18	15	-	-	12	12	-	-	-	-	-	-
152mm howitzer	-	-	-	-	-	-	-	-	12	-	-	-
Av. Range (km)	12.7	12.6	11.0	11.0	11.8	12.0	11.0	11.0	12.4	12.8	12.9	12.9
Shell Wt (lb)	2,916	2,562	986	1,069	2,016	1,850	1,444	534	2,916	603	1,014	1,069

1. Only 10 and 19 Infantry Divisions campaigned in 1943 and had this configuration.
2. Theoretical. In fact, there was no 150mm divisional artillery in 1944.
3. Typical. A few divisions also had twelve German 105mm guns, instead of twelve 75mm guns.
4. In 1945 the artillery was so short of guns that twelve 120mm mortars were substituted.

105mm field guns) and modern 4WD artillery tractors. Their standard was high, and they were to earn commendations from both Germans and Soviets. Several independent motorised battalions of the same guns and an assortment of obsolete horsedrawn pieces formed the inadequate army-level artillery, which lacked any of the heaviest guns of 170mm and above possessed by both Germans and Russians. Given the fact that nearly half of all battle casualties on the Eastern Front were from artillery fire, the Romanian Army found itself at a great disadvantage throughout.

Mechanisation

The Romanian Army's mechanisation plans were inevitably compromised by the country's low level of motorisation. In 1938 there were only 35,800 motor vehicles in the entire country, of which 10,400 were commercial types of value to the forces. Romania's prewar motor industry was essentially limited to a single Ford plant with a daily capacity of six to ten vehicles assembled from largely imported components.

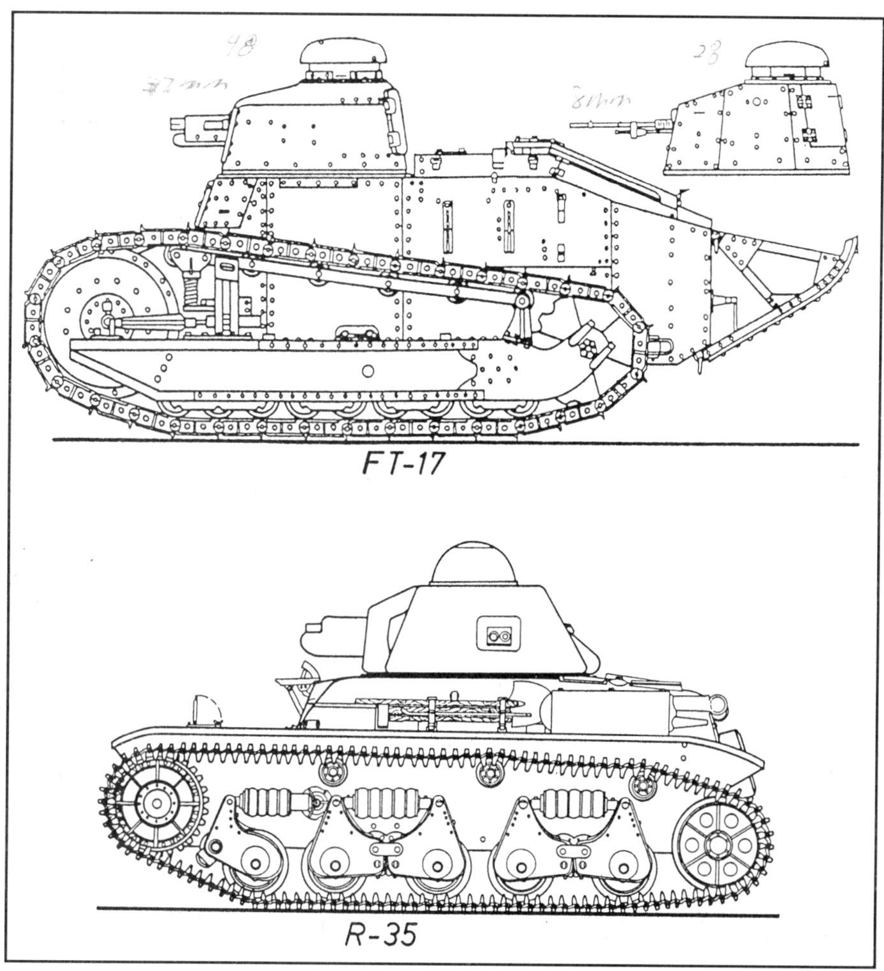

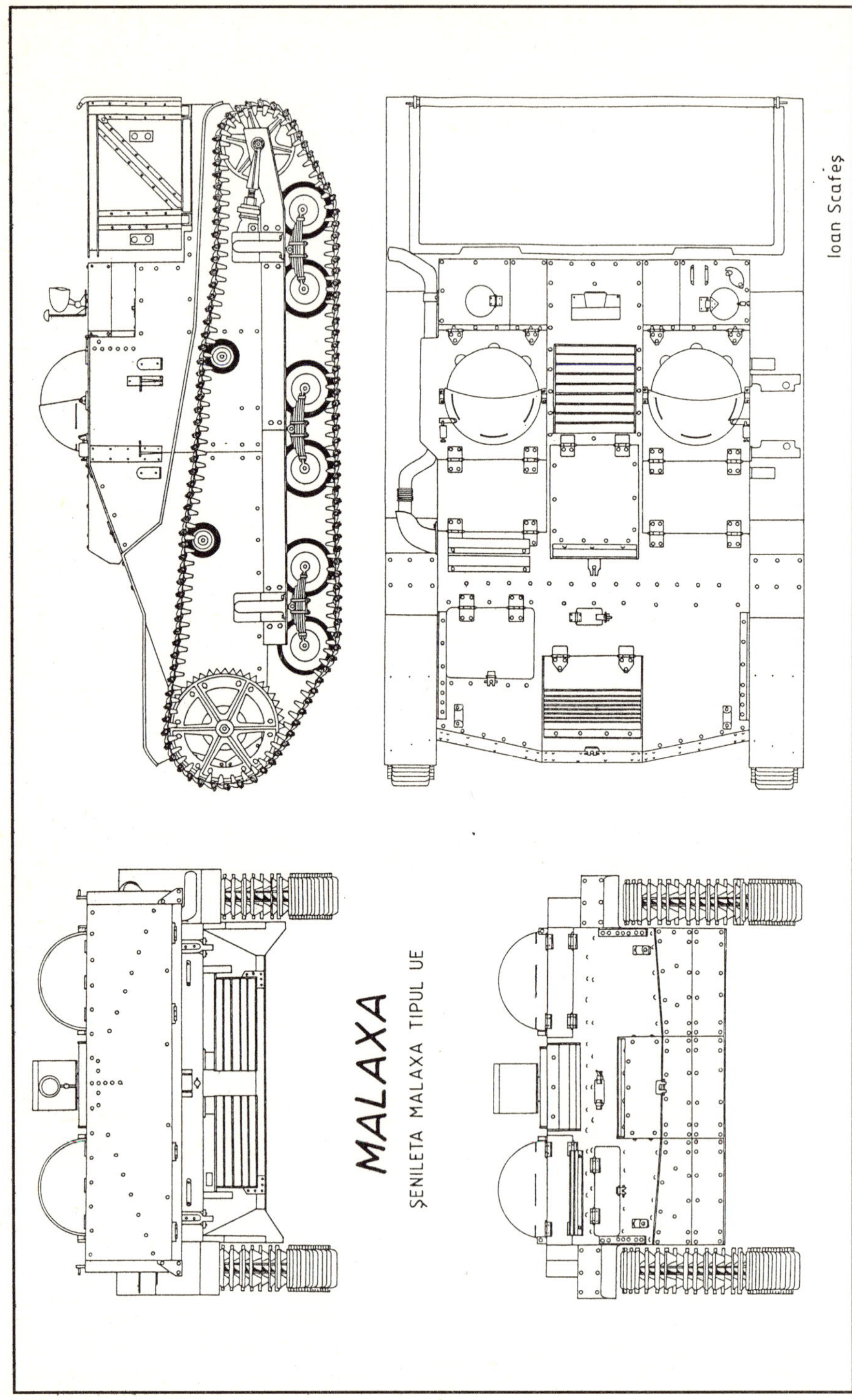
MALAXA
ŞENILETA MALAXA TIPUL UE
Ioan Scafeş

The acquisition of armour was a central theme of Romania's 1935 rearmament plan, so in the autumn of that year a Romanian military commission inspected a range of its traditional allies' tanks in France, Great Britain, Czechoslovakia and Poland. On 30 January 1937 a protocol covering the delivery of tanks, 4WD trucks and heavy artillery was signed with the Czechs, and a similar agreement was made with the French shortly afterwards.

Seventy-six Renault FT-17 light tanks acquired in 1919 were still in Romania's inventory in 1937. Of these, 48 were armed with a Puteaux 37mm gun and 28 with a Hotchkiss 8mm machine gun, but only 20 were serviceable and Skoda was contracted to refurbish them that year. These relics from the First World War were of negligible combat value in the Second World War, but the Romanians managed to keep a battalion of three companies of 25 FT-17s each semi-operational as part of 2nd Armoured Regiment, although their serviceability necessarily remained low. One company was usually retained at the regimental depot in Bucharest, the second was attached to the 18th Security Detachment guarding the oilfields at Ploieşti, and a third was usually divided into independent platoons for security use in other urban centres.

As a first step in the creation of an indigenous AFV industry, the Romanian Ministry of Defence bought a licence to build 300 Renault UE supply carriers in 1937. This was in response to the Hungarian purchase of 151 Italian Ansaldo CV-35 tankettes. The Renault UE supply carrier had been in service with the French army since 1931. It was unarmed and towed a purpose-built caterpillar trailer for cargo. The Romanians particularly wanted it as an all-terrain tractor for the 300 47mm Schneider A/T guns being introduced into the 12-gun divisional anti-tank companies.

The chenillette licence was passed to the Malaxa factory in Bucharest. Consequently it was officially designated the 'Şenileta Malaxa Tipul UE' in Romanian service, but was normally referred to simply as the 'Malaxa'. Malaxa produced almost all of the carrier's components apart from the engine, gearbox and instrument panel, which were imported from Renault. The production of the carrier began during the latter half of 1939, but the German defeat of France cut off the supply of Renault components and production ground to a halt in March 1941 after only 126 carriers (Nos.1-126) and trailers had been built. However, a vehicle return for 22 June 1941 records 178 chenillettes on strength, so it is probable that some further deliveries of Renault UE chenillettes were received from German captured stocks, or that a number of Polish TK and TKS chenillettes had been interned in 1939. The chenillette first saw combat during the Iron Guard coup, when Malaxa's sympathetic proprietor gave the Legionaries two straight off the production line.

MALAXA UE SUPPLY CARRIER

Vehicle Type: Supply carrier / A/T gun tractor. **Manufacturer:** Malaxa, Bucharest (Renault licence). **Designation:** Senileta Malaxa – Tipul UE. **Introduction:** 1940. **No. produced:** 126. **Crew:** 2. **Weight:** 2.74 tons. **Cargo:** 500 kg. **Chassis length:** 2.85m. **Width:** 1.8m. **Height:** 1.26m. **Ground clearance:** 0.3m. **Armament:** Nil (Towed Schneider 47mm A/T Gun or tracked trailer.) **Engine:** Renault, 4 cylinder, watercooled. **Horse power:** 35hp; 2,800 rpm. **Fuel:** Petrol. **Maximum Speed:** 30 kph. **Average road speed:** 15-20 kph. **Vertical obstacle clearance:** 0.4m. **Trench clearance:** 1.22m. **Gradient:** 40°. **Fording depth:** 0.3m. **Range:** ±100 km.

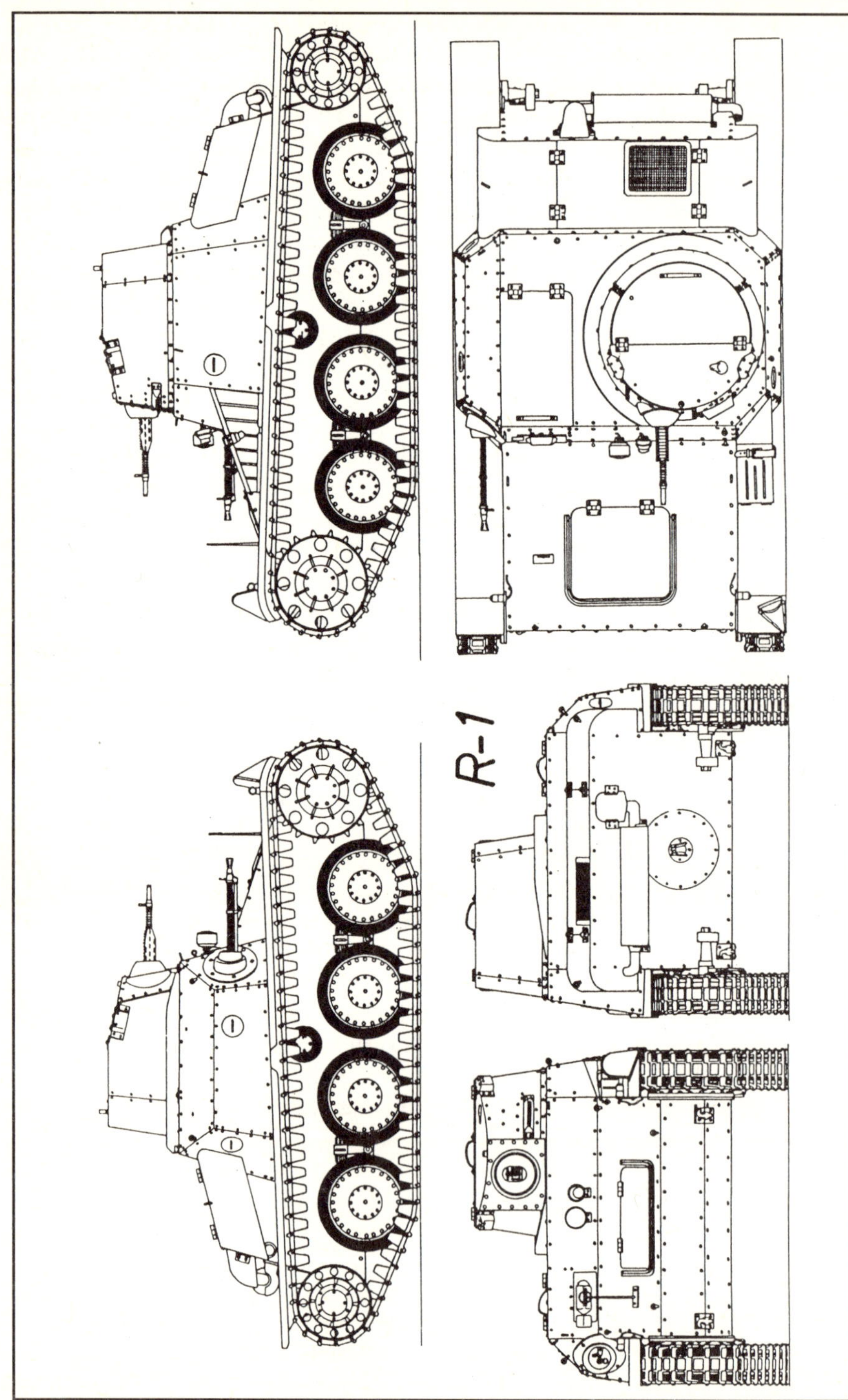
R-1

Romania bought 35 Czech CKD AH-IV light tanks (Nos.1-35) for the cavalry on 18 June 1937. Dubbed the R-1 in Romanian service, the tank weighed 4.2 tons, its main armament was a single 7.92mm heavy machine gun and its thickest armour was 12mm deep. As a modern yet simple vehicle, the R-1 was chosen to become the first tank built in Romania, and a licence was purchased by the Malaxa factory. However, although Malaxa procured a complete set of plans and a sample tank broken down into reference parts (No.301?), its manufacture was delayed by the German takeover of Czechoslovakia and eventually abandoned. This was unfortunate, as the use of its production facilities and the development of its hull would probably have led to the faster production of the more potent Maresal (see below). Although the R-1 was of little combat value on the Eastern Front, it did have some potential in the reconnaissance role, but even this was limited by the lack of a radio.

During 1936-37 Hungary had been negotiating production rights with Sweden for a light tank which it dubbed the Toldi. At the break-up of Austro-Hungary, Hungary had inherited the Manfred Weiss motor company and the MAVAG locomotive works. These companies gave Hungary a local automotive tradition unmatched by Romania and a head start in AFV manufacture. The first Toldis were ordered in 1938, and 190 were delivered during 1940–42. The vehicle weighed 8.7 tons, its main armament was a 20mm gun and its thickest armour was 13mm deep. The Toldi proved a poor tank in service, but it was far superior to the R-1, which Romania could not even get into production. In 1943–44 80 Toldis were rebuilt and 12 new vehicles completed. These weighed 9.4 tons, their main armament was a 40mm gun and their thickest armour was 35mm deep. A final development of the Toldi was the Nimrod self-propelled gun.

In 1937 Romania ordered 126 Skoda S-II-a light tanks (Nos.1-126) from Czechoslovakia. The tank, which received the designation R-2 in Romanian service, weighed 10.5 tons, its main armament was a 37mm gun and its thickest armour was 25mm deep. These characteristics made it superior to the initial Toldis but no more than equal to the later models. The first fifteen R-2s were delivered on 10 June 1937, but the S-II-a was still experiencing serious teething problems and the first R-2s suffered similarly. As a result they were returned to Skoda, where they were modified to Romanian specifications before deliveries resumed. Nevertheless, the R-2 remained a temperamental vehicle requiring careful maintenance. The R-2 could be distinguished from the Czech/German PzKpfw35(t) by differences in the rear of both turret and hull.

The R-2s were formed into the 1st Armoured Regiment, which later became the main component of 1st Armoured Division and had its depot at Tirgovişte. The Germans honoured Skoda's existing contract when they took over Czechoslovakia, but turned down a new Romanian order for another 382 R-2s in mid-1939. However, in order to increase pressure on Romania, they did sell 36 captured Czech S-II-as to Bulgaria in 1940. The R-2 was only of significant operational value in 1941, before the Red Army put substantial numbers of T-34s and KV1s into the field. Yet even at this stage it was vulnerable to Soviet infantry AT rifles.

One further vehicle was developed by the Czechs to Romanian requirements. This was a 5.8-ton tankette armed with a fixed Skoda 37mm gun and protected by

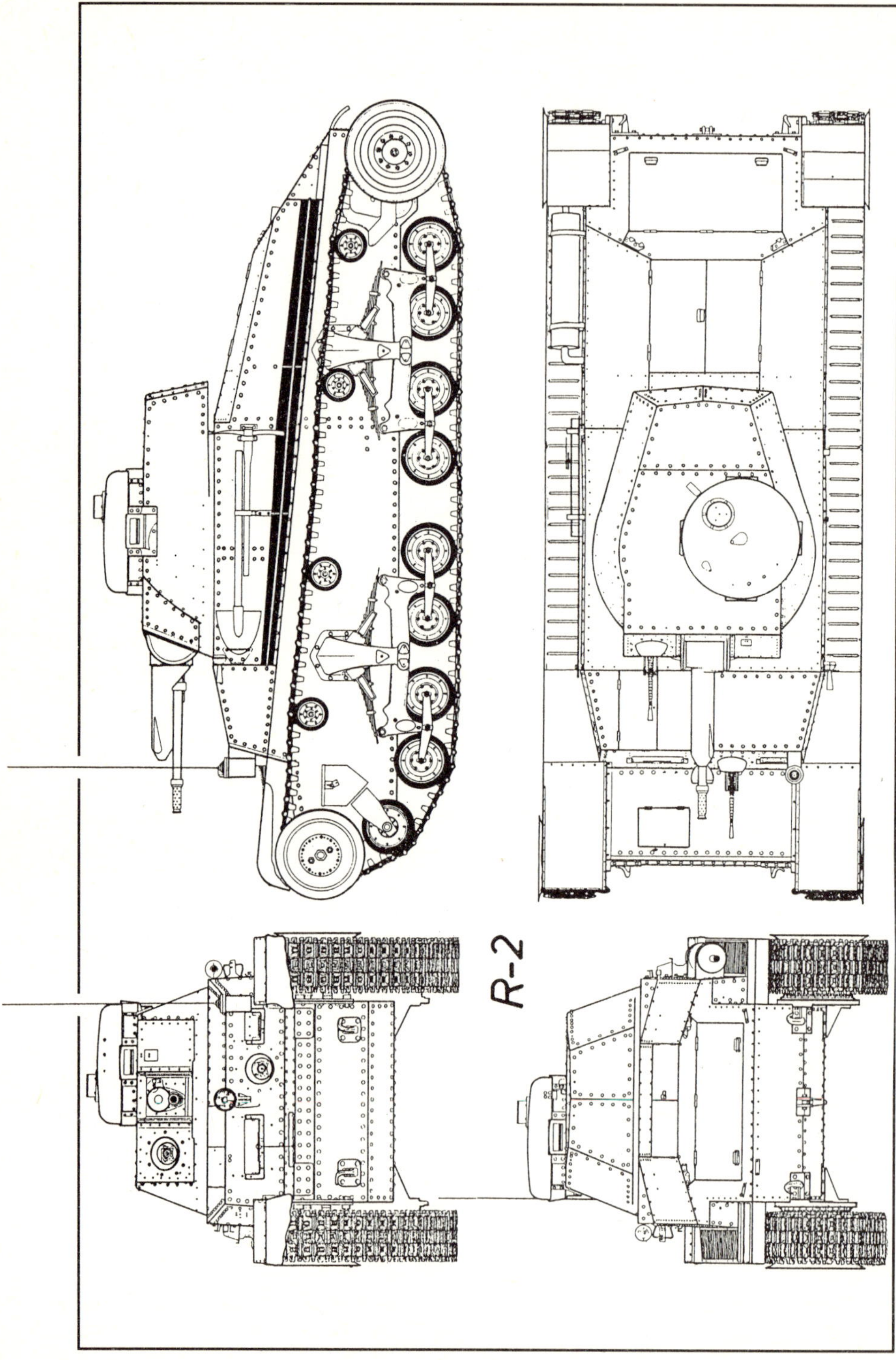
R-2

30mm armour at its thickest. It seems to have combined the chassis of the experimental LKMVP light artillery tractor with the upper works and armament of the T-3-D tankette. An example was certainly demonstrated in Romania, but the project probably died with the German occupation of Czechoslovakia.

By early 1938 negotiations were well advanced for the founding of a tank factory in which to assemble 200 French Renault R-35 infantry tanks, but the French could not complete the deal owing to their own rearmament needs. Consequently, only 41 R-35s were imported for 2nd Armoured Regiment in 1939. In late September 1939 Romania fortuitously interned 34 ex-Polish R-35s, which allowed the expansion of 2nd Armoured Regiment to 75 R-35s in two battalions. The regiment's support services were equipped with French Renault and Laffley trucks. The R-35s were slow, underpowered, undergunned and unreliable infantry tanks without radios and totally unsuited to mobile operations on the Eastern Front. After 1941 they were largely restricted to training and internal security. Some served on anti-partisan operations in Transnistria. Their only redeeming feature was that they were the only Romanian tanks virtually immune to the AT rifles of the Soviet infantry at the outbreak of war.

In 1940 the fall of France cut off the delivery of further R-35s, and Romania applied to the Germans for a licence to build 216 Skoda T-21 medium tanks. This was a development of the R-2 design with which the Romanians were already familiar, and they provisionally designated it the R-3. It weighed 17 tons, its main armament was a 47mm gun and its thickest armour was 30mm deep. However, Romania had yet to join the Axis, and the Germans refused a licence. The Romanians then tried to buy the tanks direct from the Germans but were again rebuffed. This was extremely serious, as the Germans sold Hungary a licence for the similar T-22 in August 1940.

Romania's few armoured cars were allocated to the cavalry for reconnaissance. Two Peugeot and four Austin-Putilov armoured cars of First World War vintage had survived, and in early 1939, when Hungary occupied Ruthenia, a number of ex-Czech armoured cars (described as two unidentified Tatras, eight Tatra M27s and three Skoda M26s) escaped into Romania. A further 103 assorted armoured cars were also to be captured from the Red Army by October 1941. However, none gave significant service in the war. This was probably due to the lack of spare parts. By contrast, Hungary was able to develop the Csaba armoured car on the basis of its existing vehicle industry.

Romania had scrapped four armoured trains of First World War vintage in the mid-1930s. As the Germans were to retain control of all rail lines in Romanian-occupied areas of Russia during the Second World War, Romania did not have to build armoured trains of its own. The *Patria*, Antonescu's official train, was heavily armed with AA guns only.

Before the war, Ford Romana was the army's major source of 2WD trucks, at least 1,600 Ford G198ST and G997T 3-ton trucks being assembled. The bulk of all ambulances (±300) and fuel bowsers (±110) were assembled locally on the same chassis. Probably another ±1,200 Ford 4x2 trucks were delivered to the air force. At the outbreak of war assembly virtually ceased, and Ford Romana thereafter provided mostly repair and maintenance facilities. However, useful as 4x2 trucks were for supply, their lack of a significant cross-country performance inhibited their tactical use.

In 1934, while Antonescu was Chief of the General Staff, a motorised rifle battalion was created within 1st Cavalry Division. In January 1941 this battalion played a key role in suppressing the Iron Guard coup, and Antonescu retitled it the Conducator's Bodyguard Battalion. It was later expanded to a regiment and remained at home throughout the war. In 1936 two infantry battalions were successfully mounted on buses during annual manoeuvres. As a consequence, in the late 1930s the Romanian Army decided to motorise three cavalry regiments (6th and 10th Roşiori, 3rd Calaraşi), two rifle regiments (3rd and 4th Vanatori), its seven regular corps artillery regiments (Nos.1-7), a number of independent army artillery battalions, and divisional signals, AA and AT companies.

The 6x6 vehicles chosen were almost all Czech: ±400 Praga RV 2-ton and ±600 Tatra 93T 3-ton trucks for the motorised rifles and cavalry, and ±150 Skoda 6LTP6L 2-ton and ±1,000 Skoda 6ST6L and 6STP6L 4-ton trucks for the artillery. In addition, ±500 compatible Skoda VL2 2-ton trailers were bought. Romania also imported ±200 Tatra 93C and 93R 6x6 command and reconnaissance cars, and ±200 Stoewer R200 and ±360 Horch 901 4x4 field cars. The latter were used to motorise the remaining divisional Schneider 47mm AT companies when deliveries of the Malaxa chenillette fell short. Before the war, Ford Romana appears to have assembled about 450 Ford Marmon 3-ton 4WD trucks for the air force's 75mm and 37mm AA artillery.

All of these tactical AWD vehicles had significant cross-country capabilitities appropriate to the conditions on the Eastern Front. This stock of specially dedicated military AWD cars and trucks in which Romania had sensibly invested before the war showed a steady decline during the conflict because deliveries virtually ceased in 1941. The Germans, who badly needed these versatile types themselves, would not even supply sufficient replacements to make up natural wastage. The German BMW motorcycle and Zundapp sidecar combination became standard among reconnaissance units, although volunteers for the motorised cavalry often enlisted with their own motorcycles of other types.

The practical repercussions on other pro-western central and southern European countries of the Anglo-French desertion of Czechoslovakia at Munich has gone little remarked. In the case of Romania it made the Germans the major arms and vehicle supplier overnight, and gave them a stranglehold over the Romanian Army's modernisation. They made immediate diplomatic capital by honouring existing Czech contracts. This was a major spur to Romania's transformation from a hawkish western ally into a pragmatic neutral in 1938–40. The fall of France in 1940 completed the process by which the Romanian Army became totally dependent on Germany, even though none of its weaponry was produced within the Reich of early 1938! This was to allow Germany to pitch the Romanian Army into the war without having to divert significant output from Germany's core armament or vehicle industries.

To put Romania's state of motorisation into perspective, it should be noted that the Soviet Union received 427,000 US Lend-Lease trucks and produced that about

300,000 of its own between 1939 and 1945, and the Germans produced 345,914 trucks in the same period and confiscated 290,000 vehicles from occupied territories in 1941–42 alone. It has often been noted how heavily dependent on horsed transport the German army was in comparison with its western adversaries. However, by 1943 it had about twice as many motorised battalions as the Romanian Army could field on foot, and by comparison with its Romanian equivalent the German infantry division was well supplied with vehicles. Furthermore, even in the dark days of 1942, before substantial US aid had been received, the considerably smaller Soviet Rifle Division had a larger proportional allocation of motorised transport.

Motorisation in German, Romanian and Soviet Infantry Divisions, 1939–1944

	German		**Romanian**						**Soviet**		
	1939	1944	1940	1941	1942	1943	1944	1945	5/1941	7/1942	6/1944
Men	17,734	12,772	23,024	16,885	16,097	12,674	15,720	9,193	14,400	10,500	9,600
Motor vehicles	1,009	617	131	178	202	220	181	120	685	165	247
Men per vehicle	18:1	21:1	176:1	95:1	80:1	58:1	87:1	77:1	21:1	64:1	39:1
Horse-drawn vehicles	918	1,365	1,701	1,621	1,615	1,181	1,580	978	888	721	610
Horses	4,842	3,979	9,027	7,595	7,902	5,628	7,258	3,452	?	?	?

The figures in the table represent official allocations. Operational strengths in all cases were normally well below the figures shown. For example, on 25 October 1942 the Romanian infantry divisions had an average of only 102 motor vehicles (including motorcycles) each, and serviceability levels presumably fell well below that. Nevertheless, these figures probably reflect the relative strengths of the three armies fairly accurately.

Although its motor industry was almost non-existent, Romania had 28 workshops turning out thousands of horse-drawn vehicles and was entirely self-sufficient. These included two-wheeled 81mm mortar carriers and their two-wheeled ammunition wagons, a four-wheeled regimental ammunition wagon for the infantry and a larger four-wheeled universal supply wagon. However, existing stocks were far from standardised; there were, for instance, seventeen incompatible types of horse harness in service in 1941.

Thus, even given the generally lower level of mechanisation on the Eastern Front, the problem facing the Romanian Army was of an entirely different order of magnitude to that facing the Wehrmacht or Red Army, and was to be reflected in its limited operational results. The Romanian Army was constitutionally incapable of conducting or exploiting the major breakthrough and encirclement battles which were the decisive feature of both German and Soviet operations. Indeed, the same deficiencies made the Romanian army particularly vulnerable to them. Even in the advances of 1941–42, the Romanian army was usually obliged to conduct a series of frontal infantry actions which had little prospect of resulting in a decisive victory and inevitably resulted in heavy casualties even if they were successful.

Communications

Shortages of communications equipment, not only of radios but of landlines as well, also ensured that no branch of the Romanian Army could be as effective as its German equivalent, however wholeheartedly it adopted German tactics or armament. For example, a Romanian artillery battalion in 1941 had signals equipment inferior to that of a single German battery. As a result, Romanian artillery fire often had to be targeted by the entire battery, rather than by the individual gun, with a consequent heavy over-expenditure of ammunition. Even in prepared positions a Romanian division's heavy reliance on landlines left its communications vulnerable to artillery barrages, but its troubles really began when it was hard-pressed in retreat, because its few radios were inadequate to ensure tactical co-ordination on the move.

ARMY ORGANISATION

On 20 June 1940 Romania was fully mobilised in the face of multiple threats from its neighbours. It fielded four armies (1, 2, 3 and 4), thirteen army corps (GD, I-VIII, X, XI, CAV and MT), twenty-four infantry divisions (1G, 2G, F and 1-21), three cavalry divisions (1C-3C), four mountain brigades (1m–4m), two fortress brigades (1ft and 2ft), an independent cavalry brigade (7c), a motorised brigade (1), a coastal brigade (23), eight reserve infantry divisions (25R-27R, 30R and 32R-35R), a reserve cavalry division (4CR) and five independent Frontier Guard Regiments. Several other reserve divisions remained embryonic. Nearly 1,200,000 men were under arms, and 280,000 horses, 45,300 carts and 3,300 motor vehicles were requisitioned to support them. However, notwithstanding considerable progress in rearmament, this mass of manpower was still chronically underprepared for modern war.

As Romania had achieved all of its territorial ambitions after the First World War, its philosophy of war was defensive. A British intelligence report of 1940 somewhat condescendingly states; 'Romanian strategical and tactical doctrine may be said to follow French lines, with the proviso that a considerable gap exists between French theory and Romanian practice'. Following the French example in disputed Alsace-Lorraine, extensive border fortifications were built in Transylvania, Basarabia, Northern Bucovina and Southern Dobrogea, all of which were lost in the forced territorial concessions of 1940. Huge reserves of munitions had also to be abandoned owing to the severity of Soviet and German/Hungarian deadlines.

Eligible manpower reserves fell from 3.5 million in early 1940 to 2.2 million by the end of the year. A total of 377,967 men already mobilised had to be sent back to the lost territories, and on 1 November 1940 2nd Army, three corps (GD, VIII and X), three infantry divisions (12, 16 and 17) and three reserve divisions (26R, 33R and 34R) had to be disbanded. Several other divisions lost between one and three battalions, and 4th Mountain Brigade had to move its depot out of Northern Transylvania. In effect, a major defeat had been inflicted on the Romanian Army without it being able to fire a shot. The only advantages gained were that, with the loss of most of its minorities, the Romanian Army became a more homogeneous and therefore reliable instrument, and the limited weaponry available could be concentrated more effectively. Another positive factor was the restructuring of the cavalry into six independent brigades (1c and 5c-9c) in October, and the formation of two new horse artillery regiments.

The Romanian Army that fell back within the new state borders between June and September 1940 was bitter in the extreme and thirsting for the opportunity to attack any of its predatory neighbours in revenge. However, it was shackled by twenty years of adherence to a now discredited, French-inspired, static defensive operational philosophy to which all of its organisation, tactics, training, logistics and equipment were attuned. It was thus quite unprepared for the deep-ranging offensive operations now likely to be required of it. Antonescu was partly responsible for perpetuating this situation, because the modernisation programme he promoted in the mid-1930s had mistakenly followed the sterile French example. He now set out to rectify the error.

On 17 September Antonescu made a formal request for a German Military Mission to retrain the Romanian armed forces, and on 12 October 1940 the lead elements of the 22,430-man force entered the country, 17,561 of them being from the German Army. Under their cover, the Germans firstly stationed 13th Motorised Division to protect the Ploieşti oil region from possible Soviet attack and simultaneously converted it into 13th Panzer Division, then prepared the expeditions to Yugoslavia and Greece under the guise of a second training mission (6th Panzer Division) which arrived from mid-December, and finally assembled 11th Army in the spring of 1941 for the invasion of the USSR.

However, notwithstanding the size of the forces in transit, the permanent German presence never amounted to an occupation force. For example, in July 1942 Germany had only 6,000 army, 3,200 naval and 13,000 Luftwaffe personnel in the country. Of these, only the AA crews at Ploieşti were in formed combat units, but they had no internal security application. Although German numbers more than doubled in 1943–44, this was largely due to increased AA deployments and the rear echelons of the Wehrmacht falling back before the retreating Eastern Front. They did not represent an increased German interference in Romanian internal security.

The French artillery practice adopted by the Romanians was conservative, and had proved insufficiently flexible to combat the German blitzkrieg in 1940. Nevertheless, when the German Military Mission began to provide instruction, they found that the Romanian artillery was reluctant to concede the inadequacy of the French techniques in which it was already adept, and the arm proved the most resistant to adopting modern German practice. The Romanians were initially much keener to learn German infantry and tank tactics, and it was only after the horrendous losses in both of these arms at Odessa, partly as a result of inadequate co-ordination with the artillery, that the gunners began to accept German instruction more readily.

The Romanian 5th, 6th and 13th Infantry Divisions and the motorised brigade, all conveniently stationed around Ploieşti, were selected for initial conversion to German training and tactical systems. The remainder of the infantry consisted of the Guard Division, the Frontier Division and fifteen other line divisions (1, 2, 3, 4, 7, 8, 9, 10, 11, 14, 15, 18, 19, 20 and 21). The Frontier Division was the best, as its infantry contained many well-trained, long-service troops experienced in small-unit tactics. The Guard Division, although reliant on conscripts, also had high *esprit de corps*. However, the remaining divisions were full of poorly trained conscripts and reservists.

The Romanian infantry regiments were variously titled Vanatori (1-10), Dorobanţi (1-33) and Infanteria (34–40 and 82-96). Some vanatori (rifle) regiments remained an élite; two belonged to the Guard Division and two more were motorised for the Armoured Division. However, despite their historic titles, the other six vanatori regiments, all but one dorobanţi regiment (6th with the Guard Division) and all of the infanteria regiments comprised the line infantry and were in practice indistinguishable by role or equipment. The reserve infantry regiments were numbered between 41 and 81. There were also eight frontier guard Graniceri Regiments (1–8). Three graniceri regiments made up the Frontier Division, while the other five carried out border patrols and provided the division with the best manpower reserve in the army.

The 1941 infantry divisions were only just beginning to evolve from their French-pattern, First World War structure. They were heavy in poorly trained, reservist infantry who were adequately supplied with modern rifles and heavy and light machine guns, but in March 1941 they still had only 40 per cent of their establishment of 60mm mortars, 60 per cent of 81mm mortars, 70 per cent of 37mm AT guns, 40 per cent of 47mm AT guns, and 20 per cent of AA guns. Worse still, they were totally lacking in sub-machine guns, snipers' rifles, anti-tank rifles, heavy mortars or infantry howitzers. The requirement for heavy anti-tank guns was not yet apparent, and there was never to be any rocket artillery.

The horsedrawn field artillery was better trained, but was still dominated by light field guns of pre-First World War vintage, and although strengthened by increasing numbers of more modern 100mm howitzers, it was compromised by obsolete communications and the lack of an anti-tank round. Co-ordination between the infantry and artillery was poor.

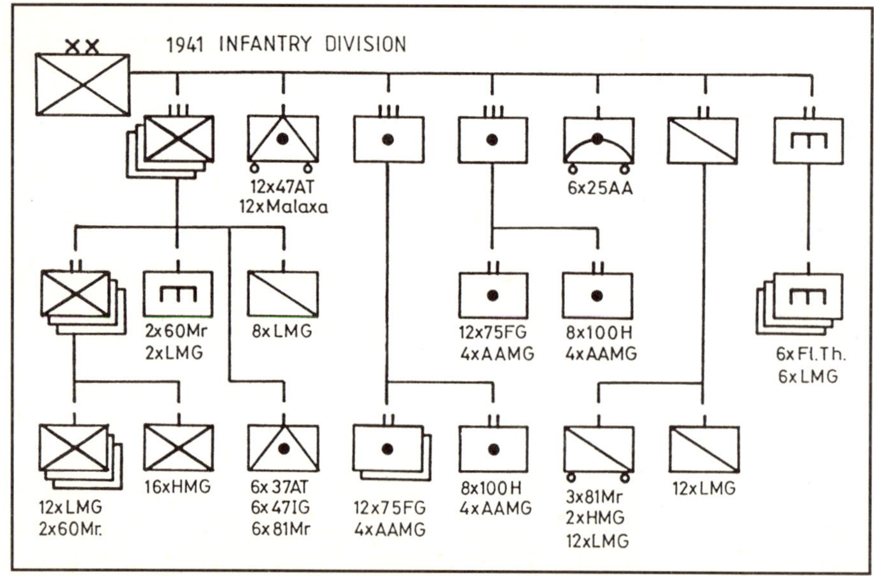

CHAPTER 2

THE FIRST CAMPAIGN June 1941 to June 1942

PREPARATIONS FOR WAR

As early as October 1940, Antonescu had set up a committee drawn from the Defence, Economics and Finance Ministries to prepare Romania for total war. In the interim he ordered partial demobilisation, which reduced the armed forces to 377,957 by December. However, Hitler's hints in January 1941 that war with the Soviet Union was imminent led to a surreptitious partial remobilisation on the eastern borders. By February the six locally raised formations (5c, 8c, 4m, 7, 8, and 21) and two from around Bucharest (G and 6c) were already fully mobilised and in position. In April/May five more divisions, including 1st Armoured, were added from the interior, ostensibly in case the Soviets decided to intervene during the Yugoslav and Greek campaigns. Most received some training from the German 11th Army, which also moved into the area. Romanian intelligence enabled Antonescu to inform Hitler on 5 May that the Soviets had plans to evacuate industry to the east and transfer troops from Siberia to Europe. Both moves were to prove decisive later in the year, but this was not yet apparent.

On 9 or 10 June 1941 Killinger made Antonescu the first of Hitler's allies to be told that the invasion of the Soviet Union would begin on 22 June. Antonescu met Hitler for

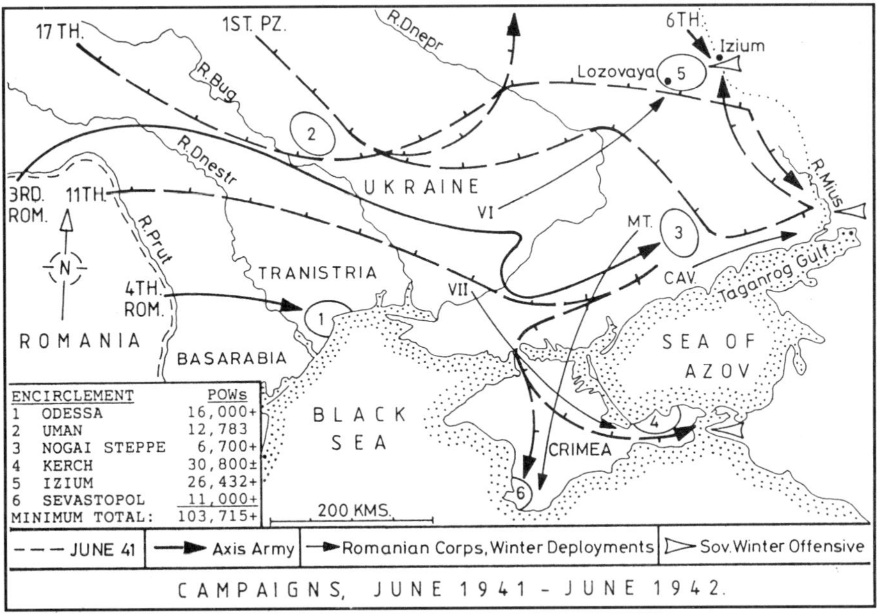

CAMPAIGNS, JUNE 1941 - JUNE 1942.

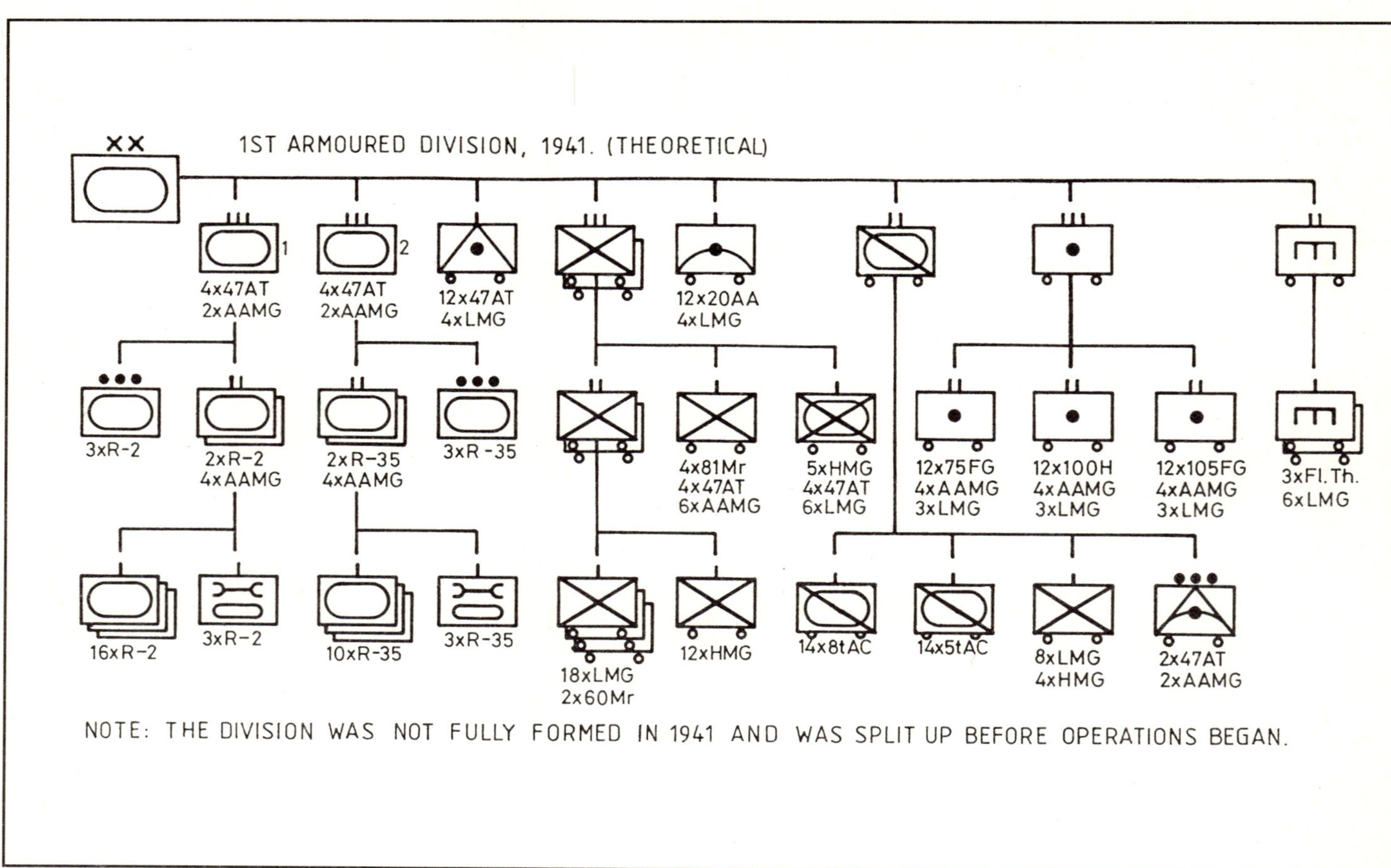
XX
1ST ARMOURED DIVISION, 1941. (THEORETICAL)
1
4x47AT
2xAAMG
2
4x47AT
2xAAMG
12x47AT
4xLMG
12x20AA
4xLMG
3xR-2
2xR-2
4xAAMG
2xR-35
4xAAMG
3xR-35
4x81Mr
4x47AT
6xAAMG
5xHMG
4x47AT
6xLMG
12x75FG
4xAAMG
3xLMG
12x100H
4xAAMG
3xLMG
12x105FG
4xAAMG
3xLMG
3xFl.Th.
6xLMG
16xR-2
3xR-2
10xR-35
3xR-35
18xLMG
2x60Mr
12xHMG
14x8tAC
14x5tAC
8xLMG
4xHMG
2x47AT
2xAAMG
NOTE: THE DIVISION WAS NOT FULLY FORMED IN 1941 AND WAS SPLIT UP BEFORE OPERATIONS BEGAN.

the third time in Munich on 11-12 June 1941, and immediately offered Romania's full support in liberating Basarabia and Northern Bucovina, but was asked to delay full mobilisation until after 22 June to avoid forewarning the Soviet Union. He was appointed head of Army Group Antonescu, comprising the Romanian 3rd and 4th Armies (generals Petre Dumitrescu and Nicolae Ciuperca) and the German 11th Army (General von Schobert), for the duration of the campaign in Northern Bucovina and Basarabia.

The Romanians had very good intelligence about Soviet deployments because Basarabia and Northern Bucovina's population was largely Romanian. The opposing Red Army's Odessa Military District had concentrated thirteen rifle divisions, four tank brigades (700 tanks), two motorised brigades and three cavalry divisions in its 9th and 18th Armies in Basarabia. They totalled 364,700 men. In Northern Bucovina, 12th Army had another six rifle divisions, two tank brigades and a motorised brigade. Also available was an airborne corps, which was being prepared for a quick seizure of the Ploieşti oilfields. In June 1941 a Soviet rifle division was nearly as large and much better armed than its Romanian equivalent, even including tanks. As local Soviet offensive potential was much greater than Romania's, Army Group Antonescu's task was initially to stand on the defensive before the oilfields until German advances elsewhere forced the transfer of significant Soviet forces from the theatre. Only then would an offensive be launched.

Army Group Antonescu's Romanian 3rd Army (MT) was deployed opposite Northern Bucovina. It was initially under the command of the German 11th Army (*LIV*, *XXX*, *XI*, CAV) which lined the River Prut opposite northern Basarabia. The Romanian 4th Army defended the lower Prut opposite central Basarabia with V and III Corps, and also manned the FNB Fortified Line further back on the lower Siret with XI Corps. The independent II Corps (General Macici) defended the lower Danube and its estuary. On 22 June Army Group Antonescu included 325,685 Romanian troops.

As expected, the Soviets made several local attacks across the frontier, the most serious of which was on the Marine Detachment at Chilia Veche in the Danube Delta on 26 June, but no general offensive ensued. The Romanians themselves probed across the Prut, and V Corps' Guard Division seized a small bridgehead opposite Falciu on 22 June. Otherwise combat was light, and the two Romanian armies had suffered only 1,455 casualties by the end of the month. Army Group Antonescu therefore used the time to redeploy in preparation for its own offensive operations, which were due to begin on the night of 2/3 July. Antonescu took the opportunity to replace several inadequate commanders.

Northern Bucovina was to be liberated by 3rd Army, which assembled the Mountain Corps (8c, 1m, 2m, 4m, 7) for the purpose. It became an independent command on 2 July. The main offensive burden was to be borne by the experienced German 11th Army. For this reason it was allocated the Romanian Cavalry Corps (1A, 5c, 6c, 6), which contained most of the Romanian mechanised formations. It and the German XI Corps were to advance on Moghilev. The German XXX and LIV Corps, which included six German infantry divisions and the Romanian 5th, 8th, 13th and 14th Infantry Divisions, were to advance on the Balţi and Dubosari axes. The Romanian 4th Army's III Corps (35R, 15, 11) was to drive directly on the provincial capital of Chişinau, while further south its V Corps (G, F, 21) was to break out of the bridgehead opposite Falciu and head for Tighina. Its XI Corps (1ft, 2ft) remained defensively tasked but had been advanced to the lower Prut. 7th Cavalry Brigade was expected imminently. The independent II Corps (9,10) was to cross the lower Danube and clear the coast when the opportunity arose.

However, the omens for the assault were not particularly propitious. Not only was the strategic surprise that so aided the Germans further north no longer possible, but the assault also lacked sufficient armour to conduct blitzkrieg operations. There were no German mechanised units at all, and 1st Armoured Division had only been created from the motorised brigade on 17 April and was far from fully formed. It consisted of two two-battalion tank regiments (1st with 126 R-2s and 2nd with 75 R-35s), a motorised artillery regiment (12 x 75mm, 12 x 100mm, 12 x 105mm), the two-battalion 3rd Motorised Rifle Regiment, a two-company assault pioneer battalion, three motorcycle companies, an HMG detachment (12 x HMG), a reconnaissance group and a signals company. However, 2nd Armoured Regiment's slow R-35 infantry tanks were totally incapable of rapid mobile operations, so it was subordinated to 4th Army's III Corps. 1st Armoured Division, with 1st Armoured Regiment, 3rd Motorised Rifle Regiment, the 100mm and 105mm artillery battalions and divisional troops was concentrated at Stefaneşti, 70km north-west of Iasi. As a result the Germans and Russians often described the reduced 1st Armoured Division as a tank or motorised brigade in 1941.

THE LIBERATION OF BASARABIA AND NORTHERN BUCOVINA

The assault by 11th Army began on 2 July. On 3 July 1st Armoured Division, supported by its artillery and pioneers, crossed the Prut through a bridgehead created the previous day by the German XI Corps and thrust rapidly towards Mogilev on the Dnestr with the Germans and 5th and 6th Cavalry Brigades. The retreating Soviet 74th and 176th Divisions, supported by elements of 2nd Mechanised Corps, made a stand at Brinzeni on 4/5 July and, in the first tank-versus-tank engagement between a platoon of R-2s and a dozen Soviet tanks, two Soviet T-28s were knocked out for the loss of one R-2. The Dnestr was reached on 8 July and Ataki was taken on the following day, but the division was then called south to assist 4th Army. It therefore cleared the west bank of the Dnestr down to Soroca of the Soviet 176th Rifle Division and then swept back to enter Balţi on 12 July.

Meanwhile, 4th Army's advance further south had first been disrupted by flooding of the Prut and then met fierce resistance. V Corps was contained by heavy counterattacks from elements of 25th, 51st and 150th Rifle Divisions in a small and extremely fiercely contested bridgehead at Ţiganca opposite Falciu, which cost the Guard Division 2,743 casualties and the 21st Division the huge loss of 6,222 men. However, the action at Falciu allowed III Corps (35R, 15, 11) successfully to force the Prut further north against lighter opposition from 95th Rifle Division and 5th and 9th Cavalry Divisions. The Frontier Division and 7th Cavalry Brigade were therefore introduced into III Corps' bridgehead. However, 35th Reserve Division was badly handled by a Soviet counterattack on 8 July, and the rest of III Corps then became bogged down trying to carry the Corneşti Massif against persistent Soviet counterattacks supported by tanks. On 10 July 4th Army suspended the frontal assault in favour of a flank attack from the north.

The deadlock was broken by the German LIV Corps (*50*, *72*, 1A, 5). Spearheaded by 1st Armoured Division, it turned the Corneşti Massif defences from the north and fell on the flank of the Soviet defenders at Calaraşi on 14 July, rapidly unhinging the defences of 5th and 9th Cavalry Divisions and 95th Rifle Division for the loss of only two R-2s to artillery. Soviet losses in counterattacks the following day were prohibitive, and on 16 July 1st Armoured Division was able to force its way into Chişinau from the north, losing one R-2 destroyed and five damaged. It wiped out the Soviet rearguard in the provincial capital before chasing the 95th Rifle Division over the Dnestr at Tighina on 19 July. Three more R-2s were lost in the pursuit, but much of the Soviets' divisional artillery was overrun. This last advance finally forced the stubborn Soviet defenders of southern Basarabia (2C, 25, 51, 150) to withdraw across the Dnestr by 26 July to avoid encirclement, but, in their own words, 'not without loss'.

With its objectives achieved, Army Group Antonescu was dissolved. 4th Army temporarily halted on the Dnestr to regroup pending the political decision to invade the Soviet Union proper. It had already strained its supply lines. The motivation of its largely reservist infantry had been high during the liberation of Basarabia, but its operational results in a series of frontal assaults were meagre, and its casualties of 4,112 dead, 12,120 wounded and 5,506 missing since 22 June were heavy. During 23-27 July, 1st Motorised Artillery Regiment and the pioneer battalion supported

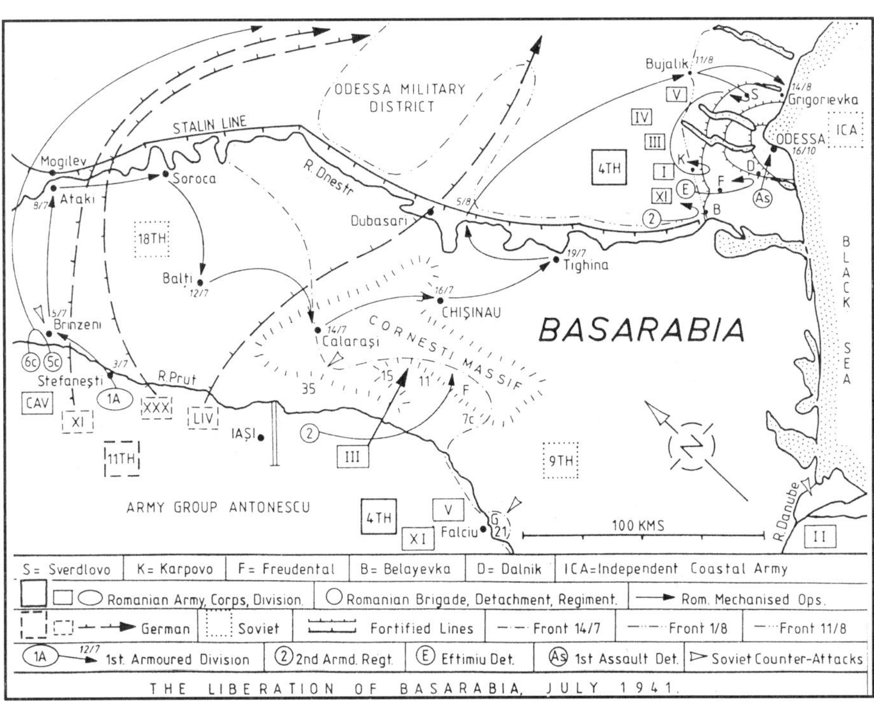

THE LIBERATION OF BASARABIA, JULY 1941.

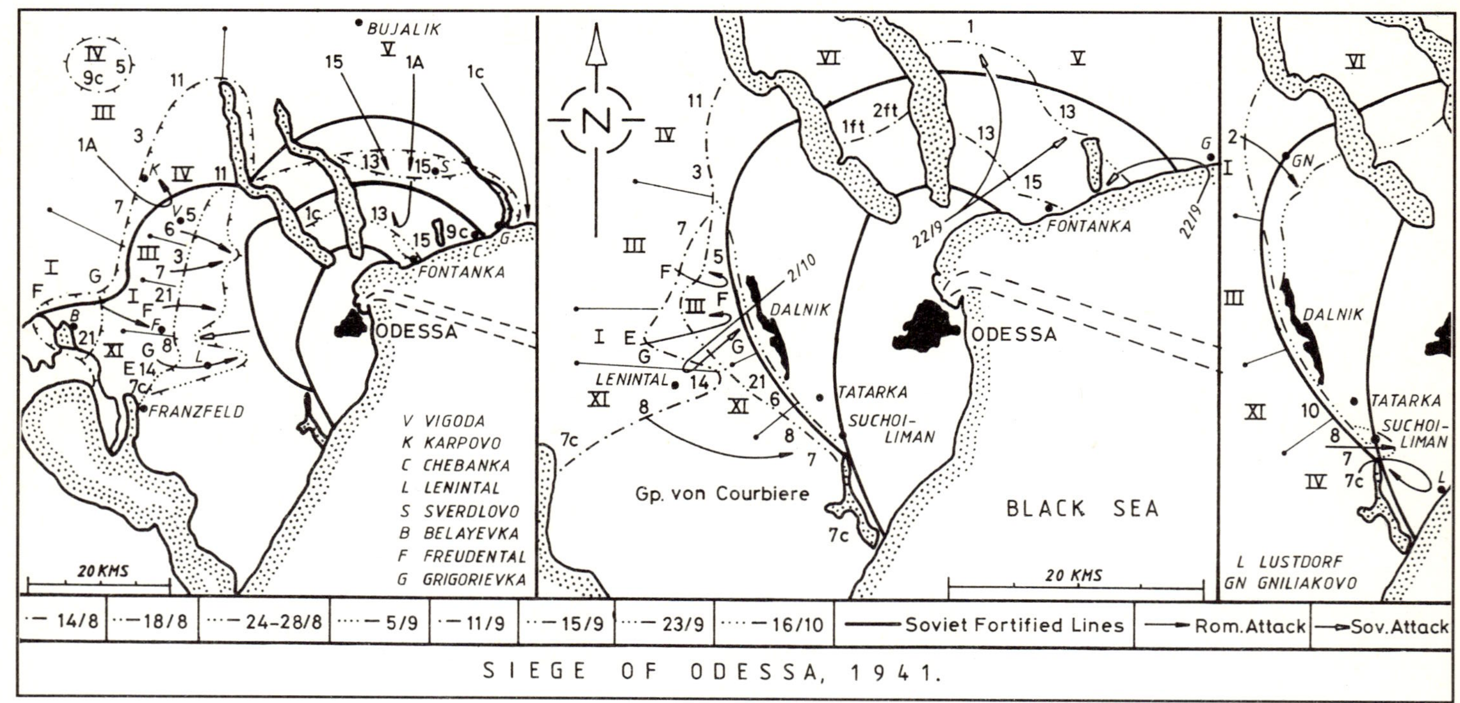

SIEGE OF ODESSA, 1941.

the German LIV Corps' assault crossing of the Dnestr at Dubossary, but the rest of 1st Armoured Division spent the next fortnight repairing its numerous breakdowns. Its combat losses had been very light, but the wear on its vehicles had been heavy. Five Soviet tanks had been captured intact. On 22 August 1941 Antonescu was promoted to the rank of Marshal by the king for his recovery of Basarabia and Northern Bucovina. Both provinces were kept under military administration during the war in order to ensure that any residual communist presence was eliminated.

ODESSA: THE SIEGE IS JOINED, 3–25 AUGUST

The initial German planning for the invasion of the USSR had discounted any possibility of the weak Romanian Army mounting independent offensive operations. However, on 27 July the already overstretched Germans 'urgently desired' Antonescu to use his unengaged 4th Army to capture the important port and railway centre of Odessa, which Schobert later explained was 'of decisive significance to the supply position of 11th Army'. The recovery of Basarabia had been welcomed by every Romanian, but national consensus began to break down at the prospect of the army continuing into the Soviet Union proper. Yet Antonescu informed Hitler; 'I reaffirm that I will pursue operations in the east to the end... I have no conditions and I will consult no one about extending military co-operation into new territory.' However, he attached his 'unconditional' co-operation to a general allusion to Romanian rights in the Carpathians; an oblique reference to Transylvania.

Romania's war now became increasingly Antonescu's war. Unlike most Romanian civil politicians and not a few senior soldiers, Antonescu correctly grasped that Basarabia was only secure as long as the Germans defeated the Russians. This essential logic was to impel him repeatedly to override internal objections and accede to German calls for military assistance at moments of crisis over the next three years. Perhaps more importantly, Antonescu believed that 'the road to Transylvania lies through Russia' and loyal co-operation with Hitler.

Accordingly, on 30 July, Antonescu agreed to Hitler's request, and on 3 August 4th Army began to cross the River Dnestr. The precise objectives and limits of Romanian operations were finalised by Hitler and Antonescu at their fourth meeting, at Berdicev in the Ukraine on 6 August. There Antonescu became the first of sixteen or seventeen Romanian *Ritterkreuz* winners – twice the number the Germans awarded to any other allies. Morale and enthusiasm in 4th Army was still high after the liberation of Basarabia, and it set about its task with determination.

On the night of 5/6 August the armoured division crossed the Dnestr and was subordinated to V Corps (1c, 15). Its mission was to descend on the Black Sea coast in the rear of the Soviet force defending Odessa, thereby cutting the city off from the main Soviet front, which was retreating before the German 11th Army. However, 15th Division's infantry was not trained to co-operate with tanks, and, in the drive from Bujalik to the coast east of Odessa between 11 and 14 August, 1st Armoured Regiment's losses mounted rapidly. Five R-2s were lost or damaged on the 11th, eight on the 12th, nine on the 13th and twenty-five on the 14th.

The opposing Soviet border guard and marine regiments were extremely tough, regular units with a high communist content. Despite heavy casualties and the loss of Sverdlovo on their outer defence line, they were able to inflict considerable damage on 1st Armoured Regiment with artillery and Molotov cocktails, which were effective because inexperienced Romanian infantry often failed to provide close support for its tanks. Nevertheless, the coast east of Grigorievka was reached by 1st Cavalry Brigade on 14 August, the ring round Odessa was closed, and the Soviet 30th Mountain Rifle Division was thereby prevented from reinforcing its garrison.

2nd Armoured Regiment's 74 R-35s were ill-suited to mobile operations and had suffered 50 per cent breakdowns before reaching Odessa, but their heavy armour made them better suited to infantry support than the more flimsy R-2s. From 12 August they were employed in supporting attacks by I Corps (G, F, 21) on the extreme western flank on the Dnestr.

The Soviet Independent Coastal Army defended Odessa behind three concentric rings of defences hurriedly built by nine engineer and thirteen construction battalions raised from the city's civilian population. It possessed two regular rifle divisions (25, 95), one of which had campaign experience against Finland in 1940, and a third (421) was soon formed from regular marine and NKVD regiments. In addition, there were the newly-formed 2nd Cavalry Division and the Tiraspol Fortified Region. The latter, equivalent to a division, consisted of picked troops who had garrisoned the southern end of the Stalin Line, and was particularly strong in heavy machine-guns. These were distributed among the rifle divisions, making them exceptionally well endowed with automatic weapons.

Although much of Odessa's local manpower had already been sent to other fronts, sufficient remained to form eight local defence battalions. There was also a considerable amount of AA and heavy coastal artillery belonging to the naval base, and when this was combined with naval gunfire from the Black Sea Fleet the Soviets had a superiority in the heaviest artillery, which was often to prove decisive. However, only a handful of repairable BT7 and T37 tanks were available. Independent Coastal Army's position was undoubtedly precarious, but it was operating on interior lines, received tens of thousands of reinforcements from the sea, and often had naval gunfire and air support from the Crimea at its disposal.

The city also still had considerable industrial resources which allowed it to construct four armoured trains and convert between 70 and 120 STZ agricultural caterpillar tractors into 'Odessa' tankettes armed with 37mm mountain guns or machine-guns. These primitive tankettes caused the Romanian infantry, who lacked personal anti-tank weapons, considerable problems. Furthermore, Odessa produced 1,500 mortars during the siege. This was more than the entire Romanian Army possessed at the outbreak of hostilities, and so far beyond Odessa's own requirements that it exported to the Crimea.

Independent Coastal Army's strength was to reach at least 86,000, but only some 34,500 were initially front-line combatants. The Romanians estimated it to be 120,000 strong, so in laying siege with the 4th Army initially totalling about 160,000 men they incorrectly believed themselves to be well short of the three-to-one superiority prescribed for a successful attacker. This error undoubtedly affected the confidence of Romanian commanders, and they became so burdened with their own problems that they failed to appreciate how close the Soviet garrison came to collapse on at least two occasions.

On opening the siege on 14 August, General Ciuperca had V Corps (1c, 15), III Corps (7, 11, 3) and I Corps (F, G, 21) in the line, and IV Corps (1A, 9c, 5) in army reserve. On 17 August the Guard and 21st Divisions captured Odessa's water reservoir at Belayevka. During 18-24 August a reinforced III Corps (7, 3, 5, 11, 1A) and I Corps attempted to overwhelm the western perimeter off the march, but with only limited success. 1st Armoured Regiment had been shifted west to spearhead III Corps, but on 18 August it again had to attack with infantry that had had no preparation in co-operating with armour. Its tanks broke clean through the Soviet 95th Rifle Division's front at Karpovo, but the infantry was unable to follow closely. Unsupported, the tanks were caught in the open by Soviet 76.2mm field artillery and 45mm AT guns, and eleven were knocked out and twenty-four damaged – half of the force committed.

By 20 August only twenty of the division's initial 105 R-2s remained serviceable, and the following day 46 damaged R-2s were withdrawn to Chisinau. On 21 August Antonescu had to tell Hitler that, in view of its losses, 1st Armoured Division could not be released to 3rd Army for operations across the Dnepr. That day, Hauffe persuaded Hitler to send an artillery regiment with two independent artillery battalions and a pioneer battalion from 11th Army to 4th Army's support, but Antonescu's request for air support was denied.

The remaining elements of 1st Armoured Division (one tank battalion with 20 R-2s, one motorised rifle battalion, one Schneider 105mm battalion, one Skoda 100mm howitzer battalion, a pioneer company, a Gustloff 20mm AA company, a Rheinmetall 37mm AA battery and a Schneider 47mm AT company) supported I Corps' capture of Freudenthal on 20-24 August. During the same period, III Corps managed to capture Vigoda.

However, important success came only when V Corps (13, 15, 1c) rejoined the assault on the eastern sector on 23 August. For the first time, some artillery support was provided by the Germans. On the following day V Corps captured the coastal artillery positions at Chebanka, and was only halted at Fontanka on 28 August. The three Soviet regiments initially defending against them were virtually annihilated, and a breakthrough into the city was prevented only because the approaches funnelled into a narrow isthmus readily defended by reduced numbers of troops supported by heavy naval artillery fire. This advance also brought Romanian artillery spotters into direct view of Odessa harbour, which was first shelled on 25 August, and resulted in a series of artillery duels with units of the Soviet Black Sea Fleet. Between 2 and 28 August, 4th Army's losses were already 27,307 (5,329 dead, 18,600 wounded and 3,378 missing). The attempt to take Odessa off the march had failed.

ODESSA: THE SECOND ASSAULT, 28 AUGUST TO 5 SEPTEMBER

During a four-day lull in operations on the western sector, from 25 to 28 August, the Romanians brought up fresh divisions and reorganised their dispositions for a more formal assault. On 26 August the remaining armour of both 1st and 2nd Armoured Regiments was amalgamated into the Eftimiu Mechanised Detachment. In the first line were XI Corps (7c, 8, 14, Eftimiu), I Corps (21) and IV Corps (5, 6, 11). In reserve, XI Corps had the Guard Division, I Corps had the Frontier Division and IV Corps had III Corps (3, 7). The main thrusts were to be by XI Corps along the Freudental-Odessa axis and IV Corps along the Vygoda-Odessa axis.

On 28 August the assault resumed, gaining ground across almost the whole length of the western front, and the divisions in reserve were subsequently introduced. The Eftimiu Detachment supported three failed attempts by 7th Cavalry Brigade to break through the extreme left of the Soviet defences at Franzfeld, and was at the forefront of the most successful attack by the Guard Division, which exploited 14th and 8th Divisions' initial assault to drive a dangerous salient into the Soviet line and captured Lenintal on 31 August. This cost a further eleven tanks. IV and III Corps made steady but less spectacular progress.

Despite its loss of ground, Independent Coastal Army had thus far just managed to prevent a breach of its front. However, it had already suffered over 9,000 casualties between 18 and 25 August alone, and by 29 August large additional losses had been suffered in the eastern sector. The shelling of Odessa harbour and the new assault in the west now brought it to the verge of collapse, and Antonescu's target date of 2 September for the fall of Odessa seemed attainable. However, in the nick of time ten battalions totalling 10,000 well-trained reinforcements were landed from Novorosiisk during 30 August to 2 September, under cover of an artillery duel which led to the old cruiser *Komintern* being damaged and the Romanian artillery batteries behind Fontanka being temporarily silenced.

The reinforcements were sufficient to blunt the Romanian offensive and even to launch a counterattack on 2 September. This was repulsed with loss by the Guard and 14th Divisions at Lenintal, but caused the 8th Division to their north to fall back. This division had by now suffered an annihilatory 7,500 casualties in its infantry regiments. The Romanian attacks continued without further significant success until 5 September, when the assault was suspended. Between 28 August and 11 September an additional 31,552 casualties (5,717 dead, 23,731 wounded and 2,100 missing) had been suffered. General Ciuperca reported that 'nearly all our divisions have exhausted their offensive potential, both physically and morally', while the enemy 'takes full advantage of his control of the sea to reinforce Odessa'. As a result he was made the scapegoat for 4th Army's failure and dismissed 'because he lacked offensive spirit and confidence in the battle capacity the Romanian Army'. On 9 September Antonescu replaced him with General Iacobici, the academically brilliant Defence Minister. Antonescu temporarily took over Iacobici's duties as Defence Minister.

The enormous loss of 58,859 men sustained by 4th Army between 3 August and 11 September fell heavily on the best-trained divisions. 4th Army's horse-drawn logistics, geared to positional warfare, had initially proved unable to sustain the troops either with sufficient munitions or food. Thousands of starving soldiers had to forage the rear areas for sustenance, while the attacks relied largely on weight of manpower, some being conducted all too literally 'off the march'. On the positive side, at least 7,000 Soviet prisoners had been taken and they later admitted to over 20,000 wounded.

ODESSA: THE THIRD ASSAULT, 9–21 SEPTEMBER

General Iacobici prepared a new plan which envisaged a preparatory attack to carry a line of hills in front of the second Soviet defence line, a follow-up assault to breach it, and a final thrust into Odessa. Fresh Romanian troops were deployed between 5 and 12 September, bringing 4th Army up to twelve infantry divisions, three cavalry brigades and two fortress brigades. Theoretically these should have contained about 260,000 men, but it is doubtful that there were many more than 200,000, owing to the earlier losses. In many formations heavy casualties had necessitated the amalgamation of sub-units, and divisions with only eight, seven or even six battalions were increasingly common. At Antonescu's request, General Hauffe also managed to secure more substantial German reinforcements under General von Courbiere which were eventually to include an infantry regiment, an assault pioneer regiment and two heavy artillery regiments. They were intended both to train 4th Army in specialist assault tactics and spearhead some attacks themselves. However, requests for Luftwaffe support were again denied. Over exactly the same period the Independent Coastal Army had received 15,350 reinforcements and large ammunition stocks from the sea, during the landing of which a destroyer, a minesweeper and a tug were damaged by Romanian artillery fire. It had also managed to assemble a tank battalion of 'Odessa' tankettes and a few repaired BT7s and T37s.

After a week's respite and better preparation, the assault was renewed on 12 September across the whole western perimeter by XI Corps (7C, 8, 14), I Corps (G, Eftimiu), III Corps (F, 7) and IV Corps (11, 3). Despite heavy losses, I and III Corps ground their way relentlessly towards Dalnik while XI Corps drove steadily southeast on Suchoi-Liman, so that by 14 September 2,000 prisoners had been taken and the Soviet left wing was in imminent danger of being cut off from Odessa.

On the night of 14/15 September, Independent Coastal Army cut its losses and pulled the remains of its left wing back to Suchoi-Liman, abandoning nearly half of its beach head. This precipitated a new crisis, and the fully-trained and equipped 157th Rifle Division (12,600 men) and 18 reinforcement companies were ordered to Odessa from Novorosiisk. The leading elements landed on the night of 17/18 September. The speed of this deployment by sea completely outmatched anything the Romanians could achieve overland.

Anxious to follow-up the collapse of the Soviet left wing, 4th Army attacked the second Soviet defence line along the axis Dalnik-Tatarka-Odessa on 17 September. Von Courbiere's Germans spearheaded the Guard, 21st, 6th and 8th Divisions and the Eftimiu Detachment, which now had only ten tanks left. Dalnik was an already formidable 8km ribbon of buildings lying across the direct route into Odessa which had been integrated into the main Soviet defence line and heavily fortified. It was the key to their whole position on the western perimeter. The news that von Courbiere's force had been repulsed with heavy losses drew little sympathy from the Romanians, who had had to endure weeks of well-intentioned but patronising German criticism of their shortcomings. Von Courbiere put his failure down to the absence of Stuka support and a lack of determination in the jaded Romanian divisions.

Although 4th Army renewed the assault on Dalnik daily until 21 September, inflicting such heavy casualties that Independent Coastal Army had to send 1,700 lightly-wounded men and even firemen to the front, fanatical Soviet resistance backed by strong artillery and aerial support prevented the decisive breakthrough. General Iacobici suspended the assault on Dalnik on 21 September, intending to resume it further south at Tatarka on 23 September. For this purpose IV Corps (7, 8, 7c) was put at the disposal of General von Courbiere.

SOVIET RIPOSTE AND WITHDRAWAL, 22 SEPTEMBER TO 16 OCTOBER

Meanwhile, the damaging Romanian artillery fire on Odessa harbour from beyond Fontanka had proved impossible to suppress indefinitely by naval gunfire, and the Soviets resolved to recapture its positions. On 22 September Independent Coastal Army unexpectedly counterattacked the passive V Corps (13, 15) on the eastern perimeter. While 421st Rifle Division and the newly landed 157th Rifle Division assaulted frontally, the 2,000-strong 3rd Marine Brigade from the Crimea was simultaneously landed by sea at Grigorievka behind 15th Division, and even small groups of paratroops were dropped in rear areas. It was the first truly combined Soviet operation of the war. Air support came from the Crimea.

The two Romanian divisions were in the process of absorbing replacements for their earlier heavy casualties, and 15th Division had thinned its defences near the coast to reduce losses from naval gunfire. Both were caught by surprise, panicked, and were driven back 8-10km in confusion. Owing to the speed of their collapse their losses of 1,300 men were remarkably light, but the vital artillery positions threatening Odessa's sea approaches were lost, although the guns themselves were saved. By the time German Stukas intervened and damaged five supporting Soviet warships, their gunfire was no longer essential to the attack.

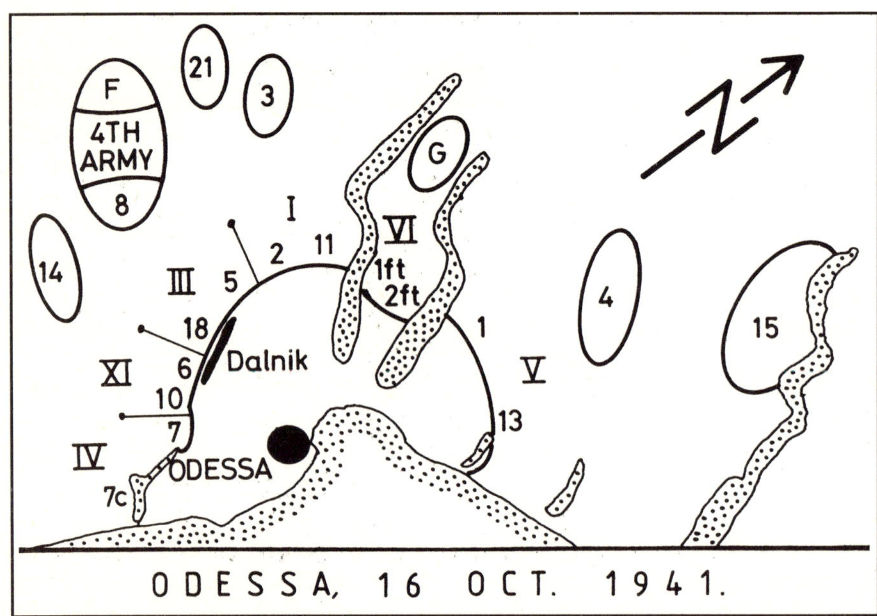

This setback led Antonescu to postpone indefinitely the assault on Tatarka planned for the following day, despite German pleas that it go ahead. A lack of suitable ammunition had already forced 4th Army to repatriate some of its older heavy artillery, and resupply of the army was being disrupted by an unseasonal rise in the Dnestr. Antonescu insisted that 4th Army could not succeed until substantial German ground and air support was received. As this required drawing in an infantry corps from Kiev and artillery from as far away as Denmark, the opening of a proposed third assault was postponed to about 20 October. On 27 September the remnants of the Eftimiu Detachment became the core of 1st Assault Detachment, a specialist unit put under German training to spearhead the next assault. The armoured division contributed a tank battalion (12 R-2s and 10 R-35s), a motorised rifle battalion, four Skoda 100mm howitzer batteries, two Schneider 105mm batteries, a Gustloff 20mm AA company and a special weapons battalion. Other components were the Romanian 21st Assault Pioneer Battalion and the German 50th Assault Pioneer Battalion.

The Soviet counterattack of 22 September had revealed the plummeting morale of many Romanian units, and the Independent Coastal Army began to prepare a frontal assault on its western front. Another 8,300 reinforcements, fifteen tanks and a battalion of Katyusha rocket launchers were landed in preparation. However, on 1 October STAVKA ordered the evacuation of Odessa and the redeployment of its garrison to help defend its supply base in the Crimea, where the German 11th Army had partly overrun the Soviet 51st Army's defences on the Perekop Isthmus during 24-29 September.

The proposed Soviet counterattack on the western sector now had the objective of convincing the Romanians by continued aggression that Odessa was still to be held, when it was actually being evacuated. On 2 September their 2nd Cavalry and 25th Rifle Divisions, supported by units from other divisions, attacked west from Dalnik. Although 2nd Cavalry Division was repulsed, the surprise use of Katyusha rockets allowed the tank battalion (35 mostly 'Odessa' tanks) to break through between the debilitated Guard and Frontier Divisions as far as Lenintal and into the Romanian gun lines. Seven tanks were lost, and as the rest had outrun 25th Rifle Division's infantry they had to withdraw, some towing captured guns. During the afternoon, counterattacks by the Guard and Frontier Divisions chased the Soviets back to their start lines. Soviet casualties had reached 30 per cent in some units, but the attack had the desired effect of convincing 4th Army that no withdrawal was in prospect.

Although successful local attacks over the following fortnight produced prisoners who declared that evacuation was in progress, 4th Army command persisted in this view. On 4 October 7th and 8th Divisions seized Suchoi-Liman and broke right through the southern flank of the Soviet defence system. Released into the breach, 7th Cavalry Brigade almost reached Lustdorf on the coast before a counterattack by 2nd Cavalry Division drove it back. A few days later the fresh 10th Division made inroads at Tatarka, and on 13 October the newly introduced 2nd Division breached the opposite wing of the Soviet second line at Gniljakovo.

Dalnik was now outflanked from both sides, and the prospects for the final assault were promising, but no preparation had been made to exploit these local successes immediately. Instead, new Romanian units were brought forward for the *coup de grâce*. On 16 October IV Corps (7c, 7, 14), XI Corps (6, 10, 21), I Corps (2, 3, 11), VI Corps (G, 1ft, 2ft) and V Corps (1, 4, 13) were preparing for a simultaneous attack. The 14th, 21st, 3rd, Guard and 4th Infantry Divisions were in corps reserve. III Corps (5, 18) was on the defensive opposite Dalnik, while the Frontier, 8th and 15th Infantry Divisions were recuperating in army reserve.

However, the last of the Soviet garrison was skilfully withdrawn on the night of 15/16 October without raising Romanian suspicions. Creditable though it was, this was not the immaculate operation later portrayed by Soviet histories, and a great deal of industrial machinery, transport and weaponry was left on the dockside. 1st Assault Detachment's only operation was to lead the occupation of the conquered city on the following day, and it was disbanded on 24 October. Another 7,000 prisoners were captured by 4th Army, but most of them were local Odessan deserters. Between 12 September and 16 October 4th Army had lost another 7,684 dead, 25,624 wounded and 5,993 missing. However, lessons had clearly been learnt, and the third assault on Odessa was marked by a more economical expenditure of manpower for territory gained than in the first. In addition to having at least 9,000 men taken as prisoners, the Soviets probably suffered well over 20,000 casualties.

ODESSA: LESSONS AND CONSEQUENCES

Including the most distant rear echelons and about 80,000 men brought up for the final assault but never seriously engaged, 340,223 Romanians were deployed for the siege of Odessa at one time or another – a very considerable achievement for the Soviet garrison.

Throughout the siege, 4th Army had lacked the resources to mount a simultaneous assault across the whole perimeter. As a result the Soviets had been able to use their interior lines to concentrate their limited manpower reserves against each successive attack. Where these proved inadequate, they were additionally able use their dominance at sea to call up reinforcements from the Crimea and Caucasus at short notice, owing to the weakness of Axis air interdiction and the Romanian fleet.

The 1941 campaign had cost 1st Armoured Regiment 26 R-2s completely destroyed and 60 seriously damaged but recoverable. Almost all the remainder had suffered lesser damage or major mechanical failure. A similar rate of loss, including about fifteen R-35s completely destroyed, had been suffered by 2nd Armoured Regiment. In 1941 the embryonic Romanian Armoured Division seems to have suffered from repeated mishandling by a high command largely ignorant of mobile operations. Instead of concentrating its already limited force, the division was split up even before the outbreak of hostilities. The rump of the division did manage to conduct mobile operations in Basarabia, and had a leading role in bundling the Red Army out of the province at small loss to itself, but it was twice halted on the Dnestr, and this deprived it of the chance to take a full part in that year's successful blitzkrieg operations.

During the siege of Odessa all Romanian tanks were subordinated to a series of infantry corps which frittered away both armoured regiments in poorly co-ordinated frontal assaults on fortified Soviet positions, ill-supported by unprepared infantry and artillery. Furthermore, the FARR's lack of a dive bomber meant that the full Blitzkrieg formula could never be applied. On the positive side, the German Military Mission was almost gushing in its praise of the persistent bravery of the tank crews.

Odessa revealed that the average Romanian infantry division had very little offensive potential because of inadequate training, armament and leadership. The Soviets found Romanian tactics formulaic and predictable and lacking originality or initiative. Although 1st Armoured Division and 1st and 7th Cavalry Brigades all sought to exploit breakthroughs, infantry commanders were excessively nervous of their flanks and failed to give them close support. Instead they were drawn into direct, mass assaults on Soviet strongpoints which should have been bypassed and mopped up later. For the Romanian infantry, Odessa was therefore a bloodbath reminiscent of the First World War. The losses of the Guard, Frontier, 3rd, 8th and 21st Divisions were heaviest, and they were not fielded again until 1944, spending the intervening period simultaneously rebuilding and watching the Hungarians. This did not reflect a shortage of manpower reserves, but was a political decision based on the fact that the territorial recruitment of Romanian divisions meant that battle casualties tended to fall disproportionally heavily on some districts, with consequent damage to local civilian morale. Seven other less badly hit infantry divisions (5, 6, 7, 11, 13, 14, 15) had to be brought up to strength at their depots over the winter of 1941–42.

Officer losses were even more dreadful. On 22 June 4th Army had 4,821 officers, but had lost 4,599 by 15 October. This was nearly half of those who passed through its ranks during the intervening period – a catastrophic rate in a force that entered the war already desperately short of experienced junior leaders. Even while the war was still in progress, one Romanian military journal had the temerity to highlight one passage on Odessa in bold print; '**Commanders must remember that their men are only flesh and blood**'. The problem of the Romanian infantry divisions was less the lack of moral fibre sometimes alleged by the Germans, than a morale-sapping incapacity to inflict decisive damage on the Soviets, even after the utmost sacrifice.

The real impetus for the assault on Odessa, and much of the responsibility for the high Romanian losses, was Antonescu's. He prudently begun requesting much-needed German assault pioneer, artillery and air support from as early as 21 August because he was well aware of 4th Army's shortcomings. However, little German support was immediately available, and he hoped for reasons of national prestige that 4th Army might take the port before significant German assistance arrived. He therefore drove 4th Army ruthlessly on. His man management style was brutal. On finding an aged reserve officer riding on a cart while his men marched, Antonescu shouted at him, 'If you can't carry out your duties because you are too old and soft, you had best shoot yourself'. Later, on finding the same individual gamely hobbling at the head of his company, Antonescu simply swore at him. Antonescu was not much loved, but he got things done. However, his willpower alone could not compensate for the multiple inadequacies of the Romanian infantry divisions and lack of confidence amongst a number of their commanders, and from 24 September he had to swallow his pride and await substantial German reinforcements, which, in the event, proved redundant.

Was Odessa a victory? On a political level Mussolini certainly thought so, and was reportedly furious that, as he had no comparable spoils, Antonescu was surpassing him in prestige. The Soviets, who had every reason to feel pleased with their defence, made Odessa a Hero City. As this distinction was shared only with Leningrad, Moscow and Stalingrad – names that reverberated round the world – it may be taken as a backhanded compliment to the determination of the Romanian assaults, which certainly impressed the Red Army, even if the primitive tactics employed did not.

Romanian attitudes to Odessa were mixed. In terms of purely Romanian material advantage, the only positive result of the Odessa campaign was the occupation, but not annexation, of the largely unwanted territory of Transnistria; a reward only a few ultra-nationalist fanatics thought worth the butcher's bill. However, there was also a certain pride in the eventual fall of Odessa, a city comparable in size to Bucharest, as it was the most significant conquest by any of the minor Axis powers in Europe, independent of substantial German support, throughout the war. That such a pyrrhic victory should hold this status also serves to illustrate just how isolated the Germans were. On 8 November Antonescu held a victory parade in Bucharest. Keitel, head of the office of the German OKW, attended. With a critical eye he noted the poor drill of the Romanian troops, but he also noted their evident pride as they passed before Antonescu. Less approvingly, he was struck by the slogan 'Now on to Budapest!' painted on a Romanian tank.

There is no doubt that the siege of Odessa had some beneficial repercussions for Romania's German co-belligerents. Certainly the Germans would have preferred the Romanians to have cleared their supply lines more rapidly and to have captured Odessa's garrison before it escaped to form part of the equally obdurate garrison of Sevastopol. On the other hand, at short notice they had undertaken an operation for which no provision had been made in German or Romanian planning for Operation Barbarossa, and had diverted four Soviet infantry divisions, a cavalry division, a fortified region and at least 39,820 other external reinforcements who could have been decisive in preventing the Germans breaking into the Crimea – itself a close-run thing. Including local manpower, the total Soviet commitment may have exceeded 120,000 men, on whom about 60,000 casualties were inflicted. It seems probable that the various Soviet returns of 16,578 or 12,565 dead and missing and 24,690 or 22,424 wounded are likely to be too light. The Romanians claimed over 16,000 prisoners alone and the commander of Independent Coastal Army had already declared 20,000 wounded by early September. Odessa may be counted a strategic, if not a tactical, victory, but its pyrrhic nature meant that it benefited Germany more indirectly than it benefited Romania directly.

It is also as well to note that the siege of Odessa was not the only action of its kind in 1941, for similar sieges elsewhere were causing Romania's allies similar embarrassment, if fewer casualties. The Finns had been blockading a single Soviet division in the naval base of Hanko on the Baltic since 22 June. It was only evacuated on 3 December. It took the Germans from mid-July to 27-28 August to mop up the isolated Baltic port of Tallinn's Soviet garrison of 20,000 men. In the Mediterranean, Tobruk frustrated the Germans and Italians from April to November 1941.

Sevastopol was to hold out for more than eight months in 1941–42, and the Oranienbaum beach head near Leningrad was never taken throughout the city's 1,000-day siege. Odessa was symptomatic of a general Axis inability to dominate the inland seas completely with their navies and air forces, even where their armies controlled the shores. Only at Tallinn did Kriegsmarine and Luftwaffe intervention secure an annihilatory success that the Ostheer had proved unable to clinch alone.

THE CHARACTER OF THE ROMANIAN ARMY

Odessa also served to highlight, for the first time, the way in which important internal political differences between Romania and the totalitarian Germans and Soviets affected the relative performances of their respective armies. Political opposition was not tolerated in Nazi Germany and the Communist USSR. However, since the suppression of the Iron Guard Antonescu had no organised party political base, and depended on a degree of nationalistic consensus amongst other political and military leaders. Some level of political debate had therefore to be tolerated among both civil politicians and the senior echelons of the army, and this naturally percolated downwards.

The civilians tended to respect Antonescu's patriotism but resent his usurpation of government. Consensus began to collapse from the moment the Romanian Army crossed the Dnestr from national territory in Basarabia into the Soviet Union proper, and major civilian leaders such as Maniu and Bratianu immediately began to demand its withdrawal on political grounds.

Many soldiers, particularly General Iacobici, also came to oppose further intervention in Russia because of the military weaknesses revealed at Odessa, and both military and civilians were appalled by the attendant casualties, not least because Hungarian losses were barely 20 per cent of their own. There was also a widespread suspicion, even in 1941, that Germany might not beat the Soviet Union; a defeatism which infuriated Antonescu. The Germans, filled with a sense of innate superiority born of propaganda and reinforced by repeated success, attributed Romanian fears to their 'terrific respect' for the Russians. This was certainly true, but in the long run Romanian respect was to prove a more accurate predictor than German overconfidence.

As elsewhere, Romania drew most of its officer corps from the middle classes. However, the emergence of a Romanian middle class had been a relatively recent phenomenon. For centuries Romania had been ruled by Turks, Austrians or Russians, who had largely displaced the native Romanian aristocracy who might otherwise have formed a military caste. The Russians, Turks and Austrians had used an assortment of Greeks, Jews, Armenians, Germans, Hungarians and others to administer and exploit their Romanian-populated provinces, and these minorities tended to dominate urban life, trade and commerce. Ethnic Romanians were overwhelmingly kept as illiterate, rural peasants.

With independence in the nineteenth century the urbanised Romanian middle class had made large advances, but by the First World War was still not sufficiently well consolidated to support an officer corps of the quality and numbers required for the effective administration and leadership of the large army then mobilised. By the

Second World War further expansion of the middle class had improved the civilian manpower reservoir available to the officer corps, but it remained relatively small and considerably burdened by a growth in wastage and corruption brought on by copious oil revenues and King Carol's dissolute example. Antonescu tackled both ills with vigour, if not with complete success.

Unlike the German Army, whose rapid recent expansion had projected large numbers of modern-minded, energetic young officers to General rank, the inheritance of the Romanian Army was an excessive number of stubbornly conservative, superannuated generals. Romanian generals had received extensive training abroad, especially in France, where they had a good academic reputation. However, their pride often made them resentful of subordination to dynamic younger German officers of much less seniority but greater practical campaign experience. Furthermore, after decades of close affiliation with the French Army, many senior officers also found it difficult to throw off their pro-French, and by extension pro-Western, sympathies and training. Initially, all of this combined to make them display a marked reluctance to assimilate modern German methods, which served to heighten the losses at Odessa. Throughout the war the German Military Mission found most resistance to their training from politicised desk-soldiers within Romania, and much of its most productive work was done with more receptive combat troops at the front.

Another major problem among senior officers was that decades of close involvement in civil government had given some of them a degree of political influence or immunity beyond their rank. For many of his contemporaries in the army, Antonescu remained only first amongst equals, notwithstanding the oath he extracted from them as Conducator. Despite Antonescu's best efforts to enforce respect for the military hierarchy and make promotions on merit, he was himself obliged to make political appointments and, in the face of considerable policy opposition within the officer corps, he was also obliged on occasion to replace professionally capable but dissident officers with more compliant but mediocre ones. Antonescu's efforts did produce a discernible improvement in the quality of leadership, but extended internal debate rather than swift obedience continued to plague the officer corps, and it was never reduced to unqualified obedience.

Often, only Antonescu's personal intervention could galvanise his senior commanders into action. In his absence, their own appreciation of the national interest sometimes led them to make operational decisions designed to conserve their formations – usually undelivered counterattacks or unauthorised withdrawals – rather than expend them for an Axis cause that was to them almost synonymous with German self-interest from late 1941. It was to arrest this tendency that the Germans twice more, in 1942 and 1944, gave serious consideration to appointing Antonescu as an army group commander, for he alone seemed convinced that a German victory was imperative for Romania. Another alternative they repeatedly tried was to integrate Romanian formations into their own at the lowest possible level.

Lower down in the hierarchy, the Romanian officer corps also differed markedly from its German and Soviet equivalents. By 1944 23 per cent of the Red Army, including most officers, were members of the Communist Party, and about 30 per cent of wartime German army officers were members of the Nazi Party, while most others shared many of its values. The Soviet officers were initially braced by Political Commissars, while the Germans began to appoint equivalent National Socialist Leadership Officers in 1943. This political penetration stifled diversity of opinion within their armed forces, and incessant ideological propaganda instilled a degree of single-minded fanaticism and consequent combat endurance rarely present in the Romanian Army. The fact that Soviet units at Odessa suffered even higher proportional losses than the Romanians, yet retained greater cohesion and higher morale whilst operating amongst a less than enthusiastic population, must in great part be attributed to the stiffening provided by an all-pervasive totalitarian state.

Although uniformly anti-Communist, the Romanian officer corps was primarily motivated by limited nationalist, not universal ideological, goals. These national goals extended only as far as Basarabia in the east and, ominously for the Germans, included Transylvania in the west. Once these limited goals were exceeded, a debate was automatically triggered which not only detracted from the determination of Romania's pursuit of campaigns deep in Russia in 1942–43, but similarly inhibited enthusiasm for the 1944–45 campaigns in Hungary and Slovakia. In its tolerance of a diversity of opinion, the character of the Romanian officer corps more closely resembled that of a western army than that of either of the main protagonists in the east, and outside its own borders it seldom matched their single-minded determination.

The training of the reservist officers who made up the bulk of the junior officer corps also left much to be desired. Modern professional and techical skills were lacking and few were confident enough to display personal initiative and tactical subtlety. As a result, uncomplicated mass frontal assaults were usually favoured. There was also a wide social gulf between officers and men which was exacerbated by an archaic and brutal disciplinary system and institutionalised corruption. For example, flogging, although rarely used, was still an official punishment, and food parcels seldom reached the officers and men at the front. However, although officers may have been lacking in modern man management technique, Romanian officer casualties indicate that they were not deficient in personal courage. Antonescu's influence, German training and the ruthless natural selection of battle ensured a discernible improvement in the quality of Romanian junior leadership during the war.

During the Second World War Romania was still overwhelmingly an agrarian country, and 75 per cent of conscripts were peasants, about half of whom were illiterate. French, British and German observers were unanimous that they were excellent raw material. German officers, who were often less than complimentary about Romanian officers, found their troops generally hardy, willing and uncomplaining. They had excellent marching powers and were able to subsist on lower scales of rations in worse conditions than most German troops. On the other hand, most lacked the education and industrial morale to conduct or face modern mechanised warfare without a great deal more battle inoculation than was available. In particular, it was difficult to prepare men against tank attack when many had had little prior contact with conventional motor vehicles, let alone armour. In this area the mass tractorisation programme of Soviet agriculture in the 1930s must have considerably benefited the Red Army in the Second World War. A similar tractorisa-

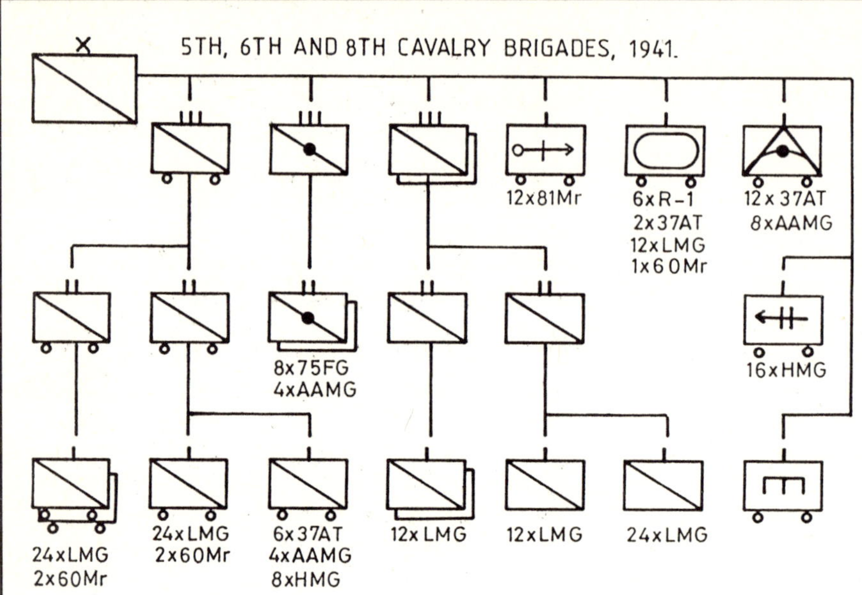
5TH, 6TH AND 8TH CAVALRY BRIGADES, 1941.
12x81Mr
6xR-1
2x37AT
12xLMG
1x60Mr
12x37AT
8xAAMG
8x75FG
4xAAMG
16xHMG
24xLMG
2x60Mr
24xLMG
2x60Mr
6x37AT
4xAAMG
8xHMG
12xLMG
12xLMG
24xLMG
NOTE: 1ST, 7TH AND 9TH CAVALRY DIVISIONS HAD THREE HORSED CAVALRY REGIMENTS AND FOUR R-1 LIGHT TANKS.

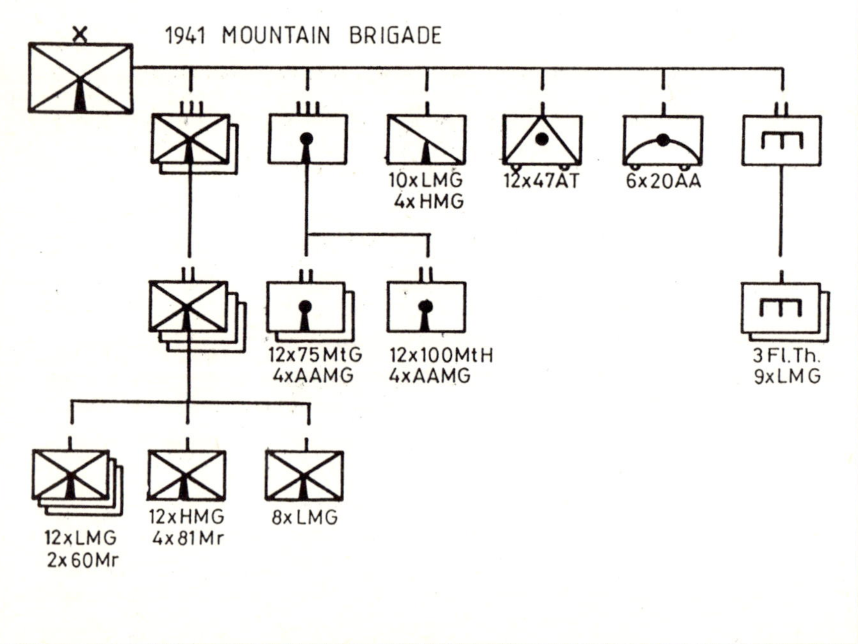
1941 MOUNTAIN BRIGADE
10xLMG
4xHMG
12x47AT
6x20AA
12x75MtG
4xAAMG
12x100MtH
4xAAMG
3Fl.Th.
9xLMG
12xLMG
2x60Mr
12xHMG
4x81Mr
8xLMG

tion programme only began in Romania during the war, in order to maintain food production when hundreds of thousands of peasants, horses and oxen were mobilised by the army.

The numerically weak corps of NCOs was drawn from the same manpower pool as the soldiers, and under German influence was expanded much more rapidly than the officer corps during the war. However, while they were competent within a restricted field of expertise, their limited education and training did not allow them to display the full range of initiative expected in a modern army.

In 1937–38 only 2.7 per cent of Romanian children were in secondary school, and only a small proportion of these received significant technical education. Although this highly selective education system produced a small number of excellent engineers, by and large the Romanians faced severe problems in finding sufficient numbers of technically qualified personnel to construct, maintain and operate advanced weaponry, except in the artillery, where inter-war training had been concentrated.

In conflict with other Balkan states none of this would have relatively disadvantaged the Romanian armed forces, but countering the large numbers of tanks, aircraft and ships fielded by the Soviet Union required a serviceability rate and qualitative advantage unattainable even by the far better resourced Germans. Bringing the crews of advanced weapons to the standards of those of the better-educated powers required a great deal more training within the Romanian armed forces, to compensate for the limitations of the nation's civil education and training system, and often needed more time than was available. As it was, little enough advanced weaponry was available to Romania, and the army in particular was doomed to conducting the Second World War with a force for the most part better equipped for the First World War. This largely shaped the course of the siege of Odessa.

3RD ARMY IN THE UKRAINE, JULY TO OCTOBER 1941.

Northern Bucovina was only lightly defended by the retreating Soviet 12th Army, and 3rd Army's 1st and 4th Mountain Brigades rapidly reoccupied its capital, Cernauţi, on 5 July, and had cleared the entire province by 9 July. During 17-19 July it crossed the Dnestr, captured 182 concrete emplacements in the Stalin Line in very heavy fighting, and completely breached it. On 19 July it and the German 11th Army came under the command of Army Group South. As the nearby Hungarians had committed a mechanised corps to the campaign, the continued commitment of 3rd Army was necessary in the competition for German favour, and it was ordered to pursue mobile operations across the southern Ukraine with the Cavalry Corps (5c, 6c, 8c), while the Mountain Corps (1m, 2m, 4m) force-marched in its rear. 3rd Army totalled 74,700 men. German requests to include 1st Armoured Division were frustrated by that unit's heavy early losses at Odessa.

The Romanian cavalry had extraordinary political influence. Five cavalrymen, including Antonescu, served as Prime Minister between 1918 and 1945. Romania had 25 cavalry regiments bearing the historical titles Roşiori (1-12) and Calaraşi (1-13). Seven provided a reconnaissance regiment for each standing infantry corps (I-VII), while the other eighteen formed six cavalry brigades.

Romania had hoped to mechanise one regiment in each brigade by 1941, but vehicle shortages meant that three brigades (1c, 7c, 9c) were still almost completely horsed, although each did have a mechanised reconnaissance squadron including two platoons of light tanks, each of two R-1s. These brigades were unable to conduct significant mechanised operations, and served with 4th Army at the siege of Odessa. The Romanian horsed cavalry regiments had been slow to adjust from the sabre-armed cavalry role to that of mounted infantry. As a result, their squadrons were initially very lightly equipped in 1941, having only a few LMGs as support weapons. Furthermore, the single artillery regiment had only sixteen old 75mm guns to support them.

Thus only the three more heavily armed, motorised regiments of the three cavalry brigades (5c, 6c, 8c) with 3rd Army had significant offensive potential and conducted extensive mechanised operations during the 1941 and 1942 campaigns. Each brigade, which had 285 motor vehicles in 1941, included a mechanised reconnaissance squadron (which contained two platoons of three R-1 light tanks each, a lorry-borne infantry platoon and a motorcycle platoon) and a four-squadron motorised cavalry regiment. Their other two cavalry regiments and the artillery regiment remained horsed.

The sixteen standing battalions (1-16) of the four mountain brigades contained the best infantry in the Romanian Army. In 1940 each brigade had been expanded from four to six battalions by the mobilisation of eight reserve battalions (17-24) which often fell below the standards of their seniors. Furthermore, 4th Mountain Brigade had been formed only in 1939, and never quite attained the effectiveness of the three older brigades. A brigade's six rifle battalions were paired into Groups, but

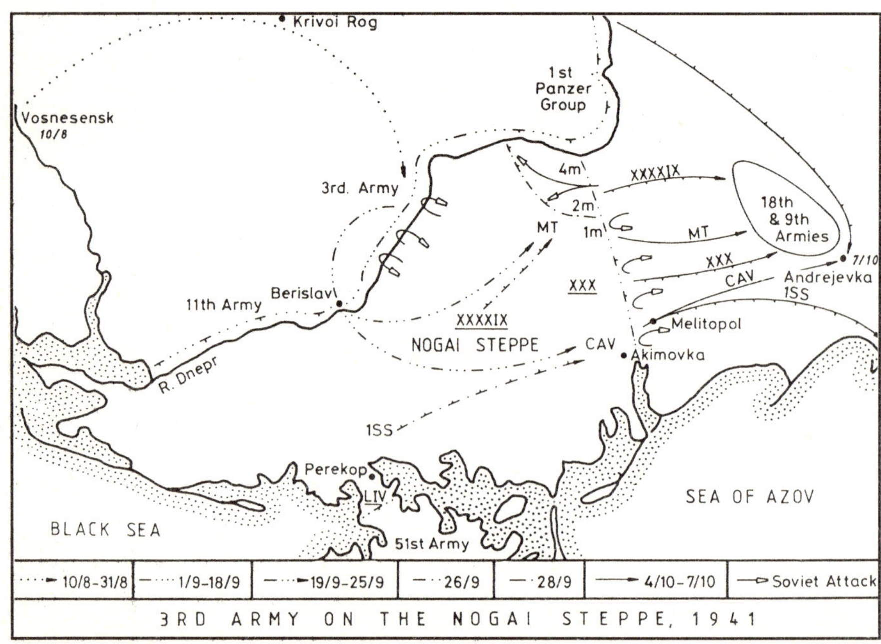

3RD ARMY ON THE NOGAI STEPPE, 1941

each was trained and equipped to act independently. This allowed command initiative and tactical flexibility to be displayed at a lower level than in the line infantry. Two other battalions (25, 26) were formed into an independent ski group. Each mountain brigade had two battalions of 75mm or 76.2mm mountain guns and one of 100mm mountain howitzers. However, in 1941 these were all worn First World War weapons of doubtful reliability and inferior performance.

Thus the cavalry and mountain corps were distinguished from the line infantry corps by their specialist skills, greater professionalism and the devolution of command initiative to the equivalent of battalion level, all of which gave them some offensive potential in mobile or mountain operations. However, their very weak artillery and light armament scales made them particularly vulnerable to attack on the open steppe.

On 17 July General Mihai Racoviţa's Cavalry Corps joined the German XI Corps in an assault crossing of the Dnestr north-west of Mogilev, and broke through the fortified Stalin Line on the 19th. Once the Stalin Line was crossed, the opportunity for mobile operations presented itself, and the Cavalry Corps formed the *ad hoc* Korne Mechanised Detachment to exploit the opportunity. It was a peculiarity of Romania's war that, in 1941–42, its mechanised cavalry gained more experience of mechanised operations than its armour once 1st Armoured Division was diverted to Odessa, and Colonel Radu Korne particularly distinguished himself, his activities even receiving favourable comment from Hitler. His detachment consisted of his own 6th Motorised Roşiori Regiment, 2nd, 3rd and 5th Mechanised squadrons (including 18 R-1 light tanks), a motorised pioneer platoon and a section of truck-borne 75mm mountain guns. In the absence of 1st Armoured Division, Korne operated with the German Lindemann armoured detachment.

3rd Army formed the link between the German 11th and 17th Armies, and played a role in clearing up the Uman pocket in late July and early August, during which the Soviet 12th Army was destroyed. It then pushed on to Vosnesensk on the River Bug by 10 August, where fighting almost broke out with the Hungarian Rapid Corps, and then on to Krivoi Rog. The Cavalry Corps took 12,783 prisoners, 450 motor vehicles and 70 tanks and armoured cars during these operations. On 17 August Antonescu agreed with Hitler to provide security troops between the Bug and Dnepr, and 3rd Army took up defensive positions on the River Dnepr north of Berislav from 1 September. There, protected by the river, it comfortably repulsed a series of diversionary attacks by the Soviet 18th Army, which failed in its intention of drawing German reserves away from 11th Army's crossing attempt downstream at Berislav.

A motorised bridging train which accompanied 3rd Army supplied 30 per cent of the Berislav bridge, the longest ever constructed under fire, which the German 11th Army built across the Dnepr on 2/3 September. In mid-month 11th Army's General von Schobert was killed, and on 19 September 3rd Army also crossed the Dnepr at Berislav at the personal request of his replacement, General von Manstein, who needed it to cover the rear of 11th Army's LIV and XXXXIX Mountain Corps as they tried to break into the Crimea. From 24/25 September, 3rd Army took up an exposed defensive alignment in the Nogai Steppe. The Mountain Corps' left flank rested on the Dnepr, while the Cavalry Corps' right flank was on the Sea of Azov. They were braced in the centre by two divisions of the German XXX Corps (72, 170).

On 26 September the Soviet 9th and 18th Armies attacked 3rd Army with twelve rifle divisions before it had time to dig in adequately. This was precisely the circumstance in which the two lightly-equipped Romanian corps were most vulnerable. According to von Manstein, the situation on the front of even the stronger German divisions in the centre became 'pretty tense'. They managed to seal off a breakthrough and hold out, but the situation of the Mountain Corps to their north was more serious. 4th Mountain Brigade's front and much of its artillery were overrun, and it was pushed back some 15km, causing 2nd Mountain Brigade to its south to pull back its left flank. 1st Mountain Brigade repulsed all attacks on its position. Because of their extended frontages, each brigade had only one of its six battalions in local reserve, and the corps had no reserve of its own capable of restoring the front. The breakthrough of 4th Mountain Brigade, although not properly exploited by the Red Army, threatened 11th Army's supply lines across the Dnepr, and von Manstein had to suspend his attack on the Perekop Isthmus and redirect XXXXIX Mountain Corps north to seal the breach on 29 September.

In the Cavalry Corps, each brigade had deployed its two horsed regiments forward on foot, keeping its motorised regiment in reserve. Between 26 September and 3 October they were attacked by at least four Soviet rifle divisions (including 30th, 99th, 176th and 218th) with strong tank, artillery and air support. Soviet tactics were primitive and they were usually repulsed with enormous losses. However, they did manage to overwhelm the front of 5th Cavalry Brigade at Akimovka by sheer weight of numbers on 26 September, inflicting nearly 50 per cent casualties on its two forward regiments, but Colonel Korne, with 2nd Mechanised Squadron and 6th Motorised Roşiori, counterattacked and sealed the breach. The situation remained serious until the arrival of the 1st SS Motorised Division in early October. The last Soviet assaults on 3rd Army were repulsed on 3 October, by which time the cavalry had lost 1,373 men, most from 5th Cavalry Brigade. On 1 October the Mountain

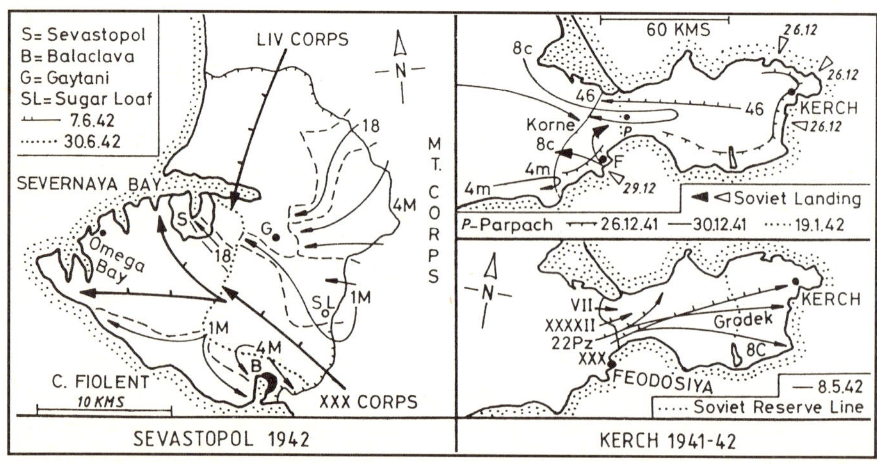

SEVASTOPOL 1942

KERCH 1941-42

Corps' strength was down to 63 per cent, and the Cavalry Corps to 68 per cent. Furthermore, all eighteen of the Cavalry Corps' R-1 tanks were out of commission.

In attacking 3rd Army, the Soviet 9th and 18th Armies had allowed themselves to be outflanked by the German 1st Panzer Group to their north-east. On 3 October 1st Panzer Group, 11th and 3rd Armies went over to the offensive. The Mountain Corps accompanied the German XXXXIX Mountain Corps in the centre, while the Cavalry Corps and the 1st SS Motorised Division advanced along the coast. 6th Roşiori and 2nd Mechanised Squadron again took a leading role in the Axis thrust which took Melitopol, and it was the Cavalry Corps which met 1st Panzer Group's 16th Panzer Division at Andrejevka on 7 October, thus closing the ring round 9th and 18th Armies. This at last destroyed the two Soviet armies which had put up a continuous resistance since the Romanian border. A total of 6,700 prisoners were taken by 3rd Army.

In mid-October 3rd Army reverted to Antonescu's control and was allocated to coastal protection on the Black Sea and Sea of Azov. Its losses from the beginning of the war to 1 November were 2,355 dead, 5,924 wounded and 1,913 missing, something under a third of the losses it had inflicted.

THE CRIMEAN CAMPAIGN, OCTOBER 1941 TO JULY 1942

Meanwhile, von Manstein's 11th Army had returned to its attempt to break into the Crimea. It initially consisted of only two corps with six German infantry divisions, and was too weak to occupy the Crimea fully. Manstein therefore directly approached Antonescu for the use of General Gheorghe Avramescu's Mountain Corps (1m, 4m, 8c) for coastal protection once he had broken into the peninsula. He had also lost the services of the 1st SS Leibstandarte Division, his only motorised division, so on 18 October, while 5th Cavalry Brigade's two horsed regiments were recovering from their earlier losses, 6th Motorised Roşiori and the 5th Mechanised Squadron of 8th Cavalry Brigade were combined into the Korne Motorised Detachment and subordinated to the *ad hoc* Ziegler Motorised Brigade formed from German divisional reconnaissance and motorised artillery units. It was the only Axis mechanised unit available in the Crimea.

From 18 October 11th Army fought its way along the Ishun Isthmus, finally breaking through the Soviet 51st Army and into the interior of the Crimea on the 28th. It was followed by the Mountain Corps. While 8th Cavalry Brigade deployed along the western shore of the Sea of Azov, 4th Mountain Brigade drew up on the southern Crimean coast. During the drive on Sevastopol most of the Independent Coastal Army, recently landed from Odessa, was defeated piecemeal and driven back into Sevastopol with heavy losses. Mopping up after this operation, 1st Mountain Brigade took 2,250 Soviet prisoners in the western Yaila Mountains. The Ziegler Motorised Brigade led the German pursuit of the Soviets into Sevastopol, but was too weak to break into the fortress. It subsequently formed the northern flank of the attempt by four German divisions to take the fortress off the march between 30 October and 21 November, and of the first full-scale assault, which began on 17 December. During the latter operation 1st Mountain Brigade captured a number of positions on the approach to Balaclava in the south, for which its commander, General Mihai Lascar, was awarded the *Ritterkreuz* on 18 January. Korne and Lascar lost 1,137 men between them.

The German 46th Infantry Division held the Kerch Peninsula between 8th Cavalry and 4th Mountain Brigades. On 26 December the Soviets made three landings against it around Kerch. The Korne Detachment, the only mechanised unit available, was rushed 200km across the Crimea from Sevastopol, and the bulk of 8th Cavalry and 4th Mountain Brigades were immediately force-marched to 46th Division's aid, some mountain units covering 120km through bitter cold in 48hr. Before they could arrive, however, a fourth landing in 46th Division's rear drove weak German security units out of Feodosiya on 29 December. The Romanian brigades were diverted to counterattack the Soviet 63rd and 157th Rifle Divisions at Feodosiya, but arrived piecemeal and were repulsed by the presence of tanks, against which they were poorly equipped.

In his memoirs, Manstein is critical of the Romanian failure to recapture Feodosiya, which he claims resulted in 11th Army having to suspend its attack on Sevastopol and 46th Infantry Division having to abandon the Kerch Peninsula precipitately, with the loss of much of its artillery. However, it is equally plausible to suggest that, without the intervention of 4th Mountain and 8th Cavalry Brigades, the 46th Division would have been cut off and destroyed. As it was, the three formations did succeed in sealing off the peninsula near its base. Romanian losses between 18 October and 31 December were 2,070 dead, 4,518 wounded and 399 missing.

By withdrawing troops from Sevastopol, three German divisions and 4th Mountain Brigade were able to retake Feodosiya on 15-18 January, but were too weak to exploit beyond the Parpach bottleneck. Simultaneously, a battalion of 4th Mountain Brigade had a share in destroying another landing at Sudak on 15 January, which cost the Red Army at least 1,650 casualties. As the German Eastern Front was everywhere in crisis, Manstein again had to request reinforcements from Antonescu, who immediately made available 18th Infantry Division. It was rushed forward to take over the northern Parpach position in late January 1942. During a major Soviet breakout attempt on 27 February, one of its regiments panicked under artillery fire and another failed to mount a counterattack to restore the line. The raw 18th Division was driven from its forward positions, but German intervention prevented a breakthrough.

In early April 1942 Antonescu toured his units in the Crimea. Manstein again approached him directly for yet more troops, and the Marshal obliged with VII Corps (10, 19). Furthermore, on 5 May the Korne Detachment was expanded by the addition of 11th Motorised Roşiori from 6th Cavalry Division, and formed the bulk of the German-commanded Grodek Motorised Brigade. The German elements were a motorised infantry company, part of the 22nd Panzer Division's reconnaissance group, some pioneers, and light artillery and nebelwerfer batteries.

On 8 May 11th Army attacked the Parpach position with five German infantry divisions and the newly formed 22nd Panzer Division. The role of VII Corps (10, 19) was to mount diversionary attacks to convince the Soviets that the main blow was to fall in the north. This it did successfully. The Grodek Brigade exploited a breakthrough of the Soviet defences further south by 22nd Panzer Division on 10 May. While the panzers swung north to the Sea of Azov to surround the Soviet defenders opposite VII Corps, the Grodek Brigade thrust directly on the tip of the Kerch Peninsula, piercing Soviet reserve positions before they could be occupied, disrupting communications and intercepting reinforcements. By 11 May the brigade had already taken more than 3,000 prisoners and overrun an airfield with 58 grounded aircraft. On 14 May Colonel Korne succeeded the mortally wounded Colonel Grodek, and the action was concluded under his leadership on 18 May. Numerous prisoners were taken and much materiel captured, and Manstein credited the brigade with frustrating every Soviet attempt to re-form a front further back. 8th Cavalry Division had also exploited the breakthrough of 22nd Panzer Division to occupy the southern coast of the Kerch Peninsula. Reportedly, 30,800 prisoners fell into Romanian hands for the loss of only 988 men.

During the diversion of most German divisions for the Kerch operation, the Mountain Corps (1m, 4m, 18) had held much of the Sevastopol perimeter and helped repulse breakout attempts by the garrison in March. When Manstein turned his attentions back to the fortress, the corps was tasked with mounting a secondary attack in the centre of his final assault of 7 June–4 July. 1st and 4th Mountain Divisions' First World War-vintage mountain artillery was too light and obsolete for the task, and in January they had each been given a field artillery regiment with two 75mm battalions and one 100mm battalion, which they were to retain until the Crimea was evacuated in May 1944. Three independent heavy artillery battalions were also brought up for the corps.

The terrain over which the Mountain Corps fought was extremely difficult. Opposite 18th Infantry and 4th Mountain Divisions in the north it consisted of steep mountain spurs of the Yaila Mountains, covered in thick undergrowth and defended by 25th Rifle Division (of Odessa notoriety) and 79th Marine Brigade from caverns largely invulnerable to artillery fire. Opposite 1st Mountain Division in the south was range of steep, dome-summitted hills converted into independent strongpoints held by 7th and 8th Marine Brigades. Although its initial aim was only to pin the Soviet defenders to its front and guard the flanks of the main German assaults, the Mountain Corps' task was formidable. Most of its frontal assaults were initially repulsed or made slow progress, but they were successful in that the Soviets were unable to withdraw troops from its front.

On 11 June 1st Mountain Division at last captured the Sugar Loaf Hill, securing the right wing of a decisive breakthrough by the German XXX Corps of the outer Soviet defences to its south. During the following week it was able to roll up the other positions opposing it from the flank and take 1,000 prisoners. 18th Division and 4th Mountain Division slowly advanced towards Gaytani in concert with the German LIV Corps to their right, taking Bastion II, the highest and most important Soviet observation post, on 25 June. By 26 June the outer defences of Sevastopol had been taken, and only the formidable Sapun heights stood before the city itself. 18th Division provided an important diversionary attack during LIV Corps' decisive assault crossing of Severnaya Bay in the rear of the Sapun position on 29 June.

As the German LIV Corps and XXX Corps converged, the Romanian divisions between them were slowly squeezed out of the line. Consequently, 4th Mountain Division was transferred south to clear the Soviet defences of Balaclava, which had already been outflanked by the German XXX Corps' advance. It took more than 10,000 prisoners, including most of the 109th Rifle Division, and earned its commander, General Gheorghe Manoiliu, the *Ritterkreuz.* 1st Mountain Division soon followed, and cleared the remains of the 388th Rifle Division from the batteries at Cape Fiolent. On 1 July 18th Division took part in the occupation of Sevastopol. The Mountain Corps lost 8,454 men during the final assault on Sevastopol. The Soviet Independent Coastal Army, which had caused 4th Army such problems at Odessa, was wiped out.

Manstein and his German divisions fought a brilliant campaign against great odds in the Crimea. However, without indirect and direct Romanian support, auxiliary though it usually was, it is doubtful whether he would have been able to break into the Crimea in late October 1941, rescue 46th Infantry Division in late December 1941, destroy the Kerch bridgehead in May 1942, or take Sevastopol in July 1942 solely with the German troops at his disposal. While at no time can the Romanian troops be said to have played a decisive part in offensive operations, they repeatedly released scarce German units for decisive attacks which they diligently supported with secondary assaults of their own.

Antonescu proved an impeccable ally to Manstein, releasing Romanian troops to the Germans as the situation demanded. Manstein in turn proved sensitive to the Romanians' limitations, and restricted their employment to tasks within their capacity, and Dumitrescu supported him loyally. Indeed, personal relations were so close that Manstein and his wife spent several weeks of leave in July and August as house guests of Antonescu and his wife in Romania. The Crimea was the high point of Romanian-German relations in the field, and operational results were mutually satisfactory to both. Even here, however, friction at a lower level was already apparent.

TAGANROG, IZIUM AND KHARKOV, JANUARY TO MAY 1942.

Nor was the Crimea the limit of Antonescu's services that winter. The Cavalry Corps (5c, 6c) had dug in on the north shore of the Sea of Azov, and repulsed several Soviet probes across the frozen Taganrog Gulf designed to turn the flank of the Germans defending the River Mius.

In January 1942 the Red Army broke through the German front at Izium, and at urgent German request Antonescu released 1st and 2nd Infantry Divisions and a ski detachment from 3rd Mountain Brigade from security duties behind the Dnepr and force-marched them 150–450km in temperatures down to -30°C to help seal off the penetration. Quite apart from the usual weapons deficiencies, the two infantry divisions (like 18th Division simultaneously on the way to the Crimea) were not equipped for winter operations in the field. As a result 30 per cent of the men went down with frostbite and 40 per cent of the artillery horses died en route. The survivors were fit to do little more than defend inhabited localities, which they generally did successfully but at a cost. The three Romanian formations were put under German corps commands, but, when ordered to mount a counterattack on Lozovaya on 20 February, 1st Infantry Division's commander refused because most of his divisional artillery had earlier been sent to beef up 1st and 4th Mountain Brigades in the Crimea.

In the spring, Antonescu sent General Dragalina's VI Corps HQ to take command of 1st and 2nd Infantry Divisions and added 4th and 20th Divisions to it. VI Corps reached a strength of 64,120 men. During May it was committed to oppose a Soviet offensive which broke through the German front south of Kharkov. During the early stages of this, the first Soviet attempt at a modern armoured offensive, there was considerable panic when it was found that none of the Romanian 47mm anti-tank guns had any effect against the new Soviet T-34 and KV1 tanks, and at least one divisional HQ had to decamp hurriedly to avoid being overrun. Fortunately the Germans cut off fuel supplies to the Soviet armoured spearhead, and in the subsequent Axis counterattack VI Corps took more than 26,432 Soviet prisoners for the loss of little more than 2,983 men. The corps' haul of new, fuel-starved T-60 light tanks was sufficient for the type to enter Romanian service as the TACAM T-60 the following year, and the first intact T-34 and KV1 were captured here.

Although not in operational command of any of the formations in the Crimea or Ukraine during the winter, Dumitrescu's 3rd Army was in charge of their communications, discipline and supply. It also garrisoned Transnistria and conducted security operations up to the Dnepr with a number of divisions (1C, 7C, 9C, 2M, 3M, 9) that it was simultaneously re-equipping to higher standards. Throughout the war, Romanian security operations in German-administered areas of the Soviet Union were governed by the ruthless German anti-partisan policies, mitigated only by their less efficient imposition. By contrast, the Romanian administration in Transnistria was more relaxed.

CONCLUSION

Every first-line Romanian division served at the front in the first year of the war, those not heavily engaged in 1941 being fielded during early 1942. Operations between 1 January and 30 June 1942 cost the Romanians 6,264 dead, 23,284 wounded and 1,002 missing, but this was more than justified by the results achieved, for the haul in Soviet prisoners alone was over twice the total Romanian losses. Romania was the only German ally to respond to the 1941/42 winter crisis facing the Wehrmacht on the Eastern Front, and had contributed usefully towards Army Group South gaining and holding a startline suitable for its subsequent invasion of the Caucasus.

In the first year of the war, 3rd Army had played a secondary role in five annihilatory battles (Uman, Nogai Steppe, Kerch, Sevastopol and Kharkov) in which nine Soviet armies were destroyed and 638,000 prisoners taken. Of the latter, at least 87,715 fell to 3rd Army. Both Dumitrescu and Dragalina were awarded the *Ritterkreuz* in recognition of their contributions. Even the long stalemate at Odessa had yielded 4th Army at least 16,000 prisoners.

The presumed unwillingness of the Romanians to show sufficient fight is a recurring theme of some German post-war memoirs. It is therefore sobering to note that each of 4th Army's three attacks on Odessa cost more casualties than the German 11th Army's final assault on Sevastopol – an action which the Germans regarded as an epic of sacrifice by their infantry, and in which Romanian troops also bore their fair share of losses.

During August and September 1941 the Romanian forces on the Eastern Front represented about 12 per cent of the German total, but suffered over 30 per cent of the casualties. Indeed, total Romanian casualties in 1941 were proportionally heavier than those which so shocked the Germans, and it took two years on the Eastern Front for such a prominent German formation as the Grossdeutschland Division to suffer similar percentage losses to those suffered by some Romanian divisions in just three months of 1941. It is not surprising, therefore, that by the end of 1941 most Romanians felt that they had already paid their blood dues to the Axis in full. Only when their 6th Army's offensive potential was broken on the rack of Stalingrad in August-October 1942 did the Germans undergo an experience similar to Odessa.

CHAPTER 3

THE SECOND CAMPAIGN July 1942 to January 1943

PREPARATIONS FOR THE 1942 SUMMER OFFENSIVE

Following the achievement of Romania's war aims in Basarabia and Northern Bucovina, and the added bonus of the fall of Odessa, extensive demobilisation had occurred. Of the 898,390 men under arms on 1 October 1941, only 464,961 remained by 1 January 1942, and of these only 54,357 were operational with 3rd Army.

Meanwhile, Romania's international situation had deteriorated. The ambiguity of the Romanian presence in Transnistria, even without formal annexation, had severe diplomatic repercussions, because it was widely interpreted as territorial aggrandisememt. The British had remained neutral during the reconquest of Basarabia and Northern Bucovina, the Soviet annexation of which had never been recognised by London, but once Transnistria was occupied they could no longer resist Stalin's pressure, and declared war on 6 December. Then, on 12 December, Antonescu declared war on the USA in solidarity with Germany and Japan. This drew the country into hostilities against major powers with whom it had no direct conflict of interests, but who later proved able to strike Romania from the air with great force.

On 29 December 1941 Hitler approached Antonescu for the use of more Romanian divisions beyond the Dnestr in 1942, and on 5 January 1942 Antonescu conditionally agreed, provided that Germany extensively re-equipped the formations concerned and the rival Hungarians became more heavily committed than they had in 1941. A formal agreement was signed on 17 January. However, in making this commitment Antonescu had to override the objections of General Iacobici, a native of Transylvania whose advocacy of early preparations against Hungary reflected the consensus in the officer corps. On 20 January 1942 he resigned in protest.

Antonescu was not insensitive to the Hungarian threat, and engaged in some intra-Axis diplomacy that led to a joint proclamation of friendship with Croatia and Slovakia in May 1942, aimed at countering further Hungarian expansion. Later in the war Slovak troops and Croatian naval and air units operated amicably from Romanian soil. In June the Hungarians responded with a particularly blatant cross-border raid at Turda, near Cluj; one of ten clashes that month. Matters had gone too far for Hitler, who brought pressure to bear on Antonescu and Hungary's Admiral Horthy to gain their public recognition that the Vienna Diktat was irrevocable. On 1 August 1942 an intransigent Antonescu grudgingly fudged the issue by announcing he would make no territorial claims until after the war, but in private he never ceased to press Hitler for the return of Northern Transylvania.

Mihai Antonescu pursued another policy inimical to German interests when he suggested to the Italians the formation of a 'Latin Axis' also including Vichy France,

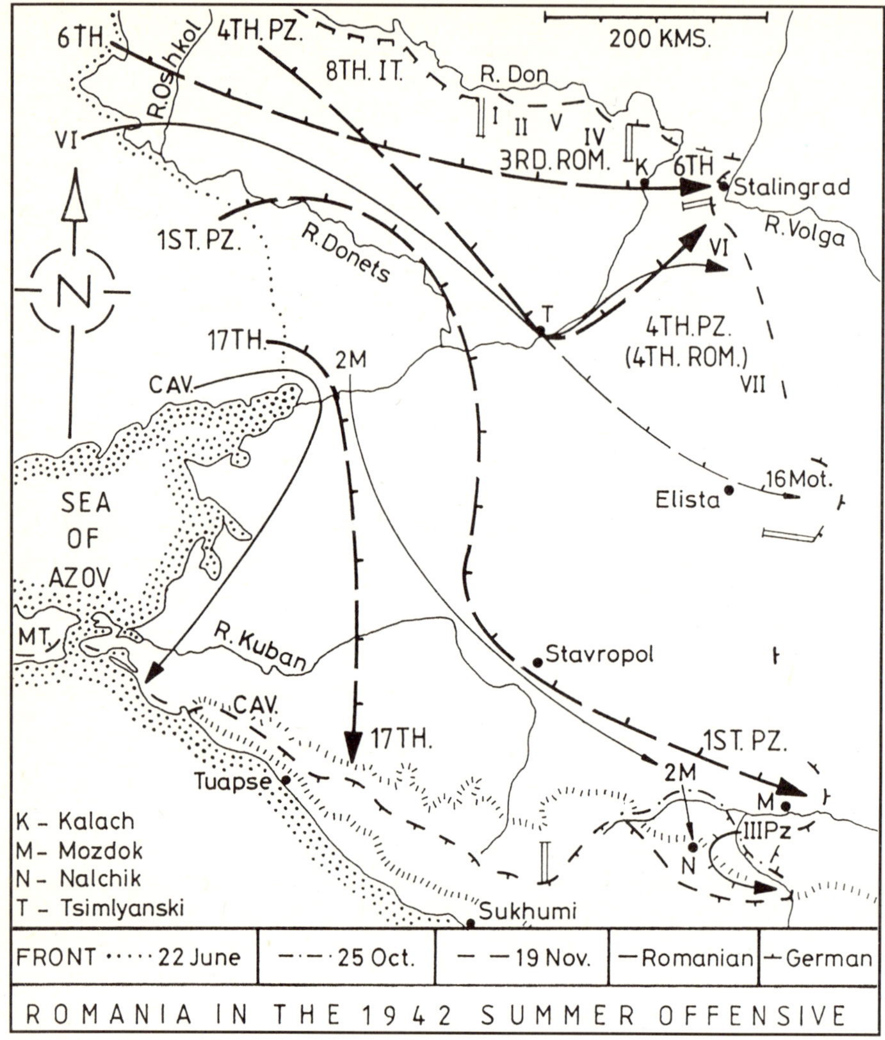

Spain and Portugal. As a consolidated bloc in a region of German weakness he hoped that they might become a significant counterweight to the Reich. However, he was unable to secure Italian support, and only succeeded in infuriating the Germans.

In late January Antonescu delegated the post of Defence Minister to General Constantin Pantazi, and General Ilie Şteflea was appointed Chief of the General Staff. Both had been conspicuous supporters of Antonescu during the Iron Guard coup. They had similar reservations to Iacobici, but accepted Antonescu's 'Russia First' policy and remained in these posts for the duration of his regime. General Constantin Constantinescu, who had commanded XI Corps at Odessa, took over 4th Army from Iacobici. However, all of Iacobici's sympathisers could not be dismissed, and many dissenting Romanian commanders, such as generals Mazarini and

Tataranu, entered the 1942 campaign with such little enthusiasm that it clearly weakened their operational steadfastness later in the year. All of this controversy was not without effect, because Romanian mobilisation had only reached 859,174 by 1 October 1942; somewhat lower than a year earlier, despite the recovery of Basarabian manpower.

On 10-11 February 1942 Antonescu and Hitler met for the fifth time, at Rastenburg, and thrashed out the details of the Romanian contribution to the 1942 summer campaign. Antonescu agreed to field half a million men, and during the second half of the year a peak of 490,190 were deployed. However, Şteflea later claimed that the total simultaneously on active operations reached only 382,000. Nevertheless, this was still nearly twice the Italian contribution, which was the next largest Axis contingent in the east. Indeed, during the key months of October/November 1942, when the decisive battles of El Alamein and Stalingrad were fought, the Romanian Army had more troops at the front than the Italian Army had in both Africa (54,000) and the USSR (229,000) combined. Furthermore, the Italian troops in the USSR were largely dependent on Romanian sources for fuel and food.

Despite its best efforts, Romanian industry was seriously short of materials and skilled artisans, and most of the major armaments plants were initially unable to maintain three- or even two-shift production, with a consequent failure to use existing machinery to its full potential.

Potential and Actual Monthly Armament Production, October 1942

		Potential Shifts			Actual Prod.
Plant	Weapon	1	2	3	
Astra	37mm AA gun	6	12	16	6
	75mm AA gun	3	6	8	5
Concordia	47mm AT gun	8	16	24	14
Regia Metalurgica	60mm mortar	26	52	100	26
Voina	81.4mm mortar	30	60	90	30
CMC	ZB30 7.92 LMG	250	333	500	250
	Oriţa 9mm SMG	666	833	1,080	666
Reşiţa	120mm mortar	27	55	80	80

However, two important new weapons entered production which filled significant gaps in the Romanian armoury. The Oriţa 9mm SMG was a joint Romanian-Czech design, but it suffered initial problems with its safety catch and only entered operational service in 1943. The M42 120mm mortar was a copy of the Soviet 120mm mortar, and may have been produced using plant captured in Transnistria. New two-wheeled horsedrawn carriers and ammunition wagons were put into production to support them. Bitter experience at Odessa led to locally-designed Costinescu 75mm anti-tank shells being issued to the field artillery in 1942, but the guns' low muzzle velocity meant that their performance was only marginally superior to that of the Schneider 47mm divisional AT gun, which was already known to be inadequate against Soviet medium and heavy tanks. Work also began on an anti-tank rifle.

A decline in weapons imports, already noticeable in 1941, became more marked in 1942 as most of the pre-war Czech contracts and those extracted from Germany during Romania's influential neutrality in 1939–40 were fulfilled, and the hard-pressed Germans showed reluctance to conclude new deals now that Romania was a captive ally. The Breda and Bohler 47mm AT gun and Gustloff 20mm AA gun orders were largely completed during the year. The first of 5,000 Italian Beretta M38 and 10,600 German MP40 9mm SMGs ordered the previous year were delivered during 1942, and 1,500 60mm and 360 81mm mortars were received from captured French stocks. Captured Soviet SMGs, anti-tank rifles and mortars had been informally pressed into service in the field since the outbreak of war, particularly by the Cavalry and Mountain Corps, and in 1942 the Soviet 45mm AT gun became a standard weapon in the cavalry.

On 25 June 1941 Romania had again attempted to order 287 Skoda T21 17-ton medium tanks armed with a 47mm gun for the armoured division and 160 CKD 7.5-ton light tanks armed with a 37mm gun (probably a derivative of the LT series) for the cavalry. However, in 1942 the Germans would only agree to deliver 26 old PzKpfw 35ts (Nos.201-226) as replacements for the 26 almost identical R-2s written off in 1941. The most important new vehicle deliveries during 1941–42 were of 700 Mercedes-Benz L3000S and 900 Opel Blitz 3-ton trucks. About 1,700 captured Soviet Ford 1.5-ton and Ziss 3-ton trucks were also taken on strength, but their performance and reliability was poor.

All of these trucks, and others mobilised from the civil sector, were 2WD vehicles whose use on the Eastern Front was limited for much of the year by the poor condition of Soviet roads. They were primarily of value for carrying supplies along the few main arterial roads, and were a particularly important factor in 1942, as that year's campaign saw the Romanian divisions fighting at their furthest from their depots. However, 2WD trucks did little to improve the Romanian Army's tactical possibilities, and the inability to acquire new AWD trucks halted the motorisation of the cavalry.

In the wake of Odessa the six reserve divisions were dissolved. Their equipment and training was totally inadequate, and only one (35R) had briefly campaigned in Basarabia, with conspicuous lack of success. Part of their manpower was used to make up the losses in the infantry divisions at Odessa, and the rest went to form 1st

Main Types of Romanian Army Motor Vehicles, Autumn, 1942

Cars		**Trucks 2WD**		**Trucks 4WD**	
Tatra Cdt 4WD	31	Ford 3t	1,563	Skoda 2t	142
Tatra Rec.4WD	171	Mercedes 3t	688	Skoda 4t 6/6	80
Horch 4WD	356	Opel Blitz	877	Skoda 4t 6/4	798
Stoewer 4WD	195	Ziss Soviet	544	Tatra 2t	590
Taunus 2WD	40	Ford Soviet	1,143	Praga 2t	373
Ordinary 2WD	1,748	Other	1,113	ADGR	48
				Ford Marmon	69
Totals	2,541		5,928		2,100
Ambulances		**Bowsers**		**Motorcycles**	
Tatra 4WD	25	Ford 2WD	109	Zundapp S/C	921
Other 4WD	5	Other 2WD	59	Other S/C	61
Ford 2WD	292	Tatra 4WD	30	BMW M/C	764
Other 2WD	57	Other 4WD	4	Other M/C	339
Totals	379		202		2,085

and 3rd Security Divisions to control the interior of Transnistria. 1st Fortress Brigade became the 1st Fortress Division garrisoning Odessa, and 2nd Fortress Brigade became 2nd Security Division, charged with the defence of the rest of the Transnistrian coast. They were grouped under III Corps.

In 1941 generals Ciuperca and Iacobici had both expressed a lack of confidence in 4th Army's combat capacity. Even the comparatively successful General Dumitrescu had offered such carping comments as, 'Attacks ought only to be undertaken with air and tank support or results will be small and losses heavy,' when he lacked both, and '75mm field guns are capable of breaking down neither physical nor moral resistance,' when they were virtually his 3rd Army's only artillery pieces. Antonescu therefore made strenuous efforts to improve the army. As a result, the Romanian divisions re-fielded in the summer of 1942 (1A, 1C, 7C, 9C, 2M, 3M, 5, 6, 7, 9, 11, 13, 14, 15) had undergone extensive retraining, reorganisation and re-equipment since Odessa, either at home or on occupation duties with 3rd Army. Collectively known as Echelon II, they were the first Romanian divisions to be fielded with their full weapons establishment.

For campaign purposes, all of the infantry divisions had now been reduced from nine to six infantry battalions per division, but the introduction of submachine guns and more mortars, LMGs, AT guns and AA guns had maintained their total firepower. A new seventh battalion was a Light Battalion for reconnaissance, earmarked for later motorisation that never materialised. Its organisational structure, which gave each rifle company its own support weapons, allowed for greater tactical flexi-

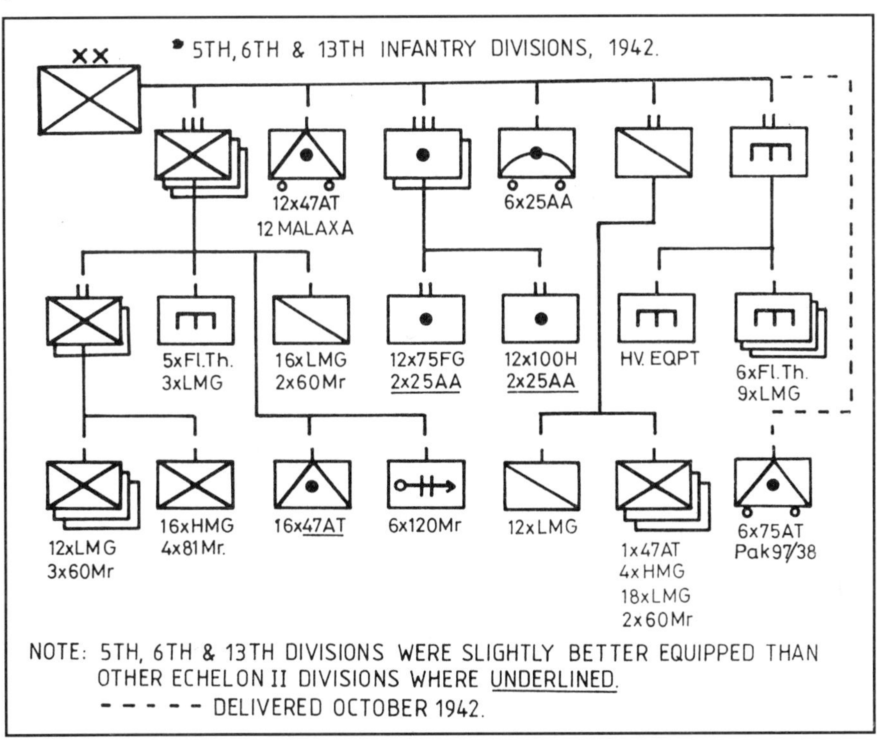

bility on the Mountain Rifles' model. The artillery had been reduced from five to four battalions, but the increased issue of 100mm howitzers had also increased overall firepower. The ratio of artillery to infantry had therefore grown significantly.

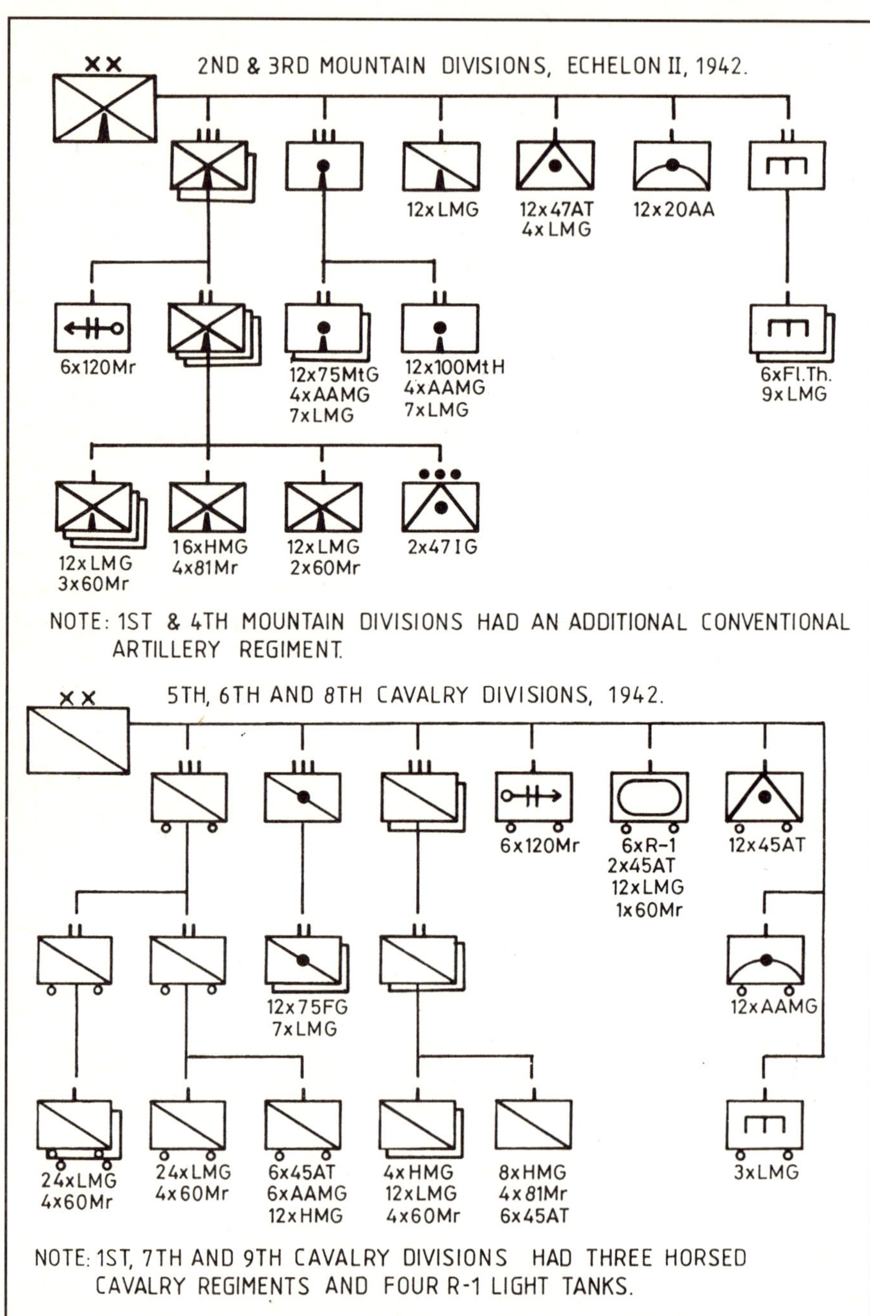

Furthermore, shooting skills, the provision of ammunition, and co-ordination of fire and movement in both infantry and artillery had improved greatly. Horse harnesses, wagons and workshops were standardised, but the huge horse-drawn divisional train could not be reduced significantly because of the lack of trucks. The ponderousness of their horsedrawn tail compromised the mobility and tactical flexibility of Romanian divisions, compared with the more mechanised German divisions and smaller Soviet divisions, throughout the war.

In view of the confidence-sapping casualties at Odessa, special attention had been given to building up morale in the Echelon II divisions by instilling 'Belief in the justice of the cause in the east, belief in the power of Romanian units, belief in the power of Germany, and belief in Victory'. The 5th, 6th and 13th Infantry Divisions, which had a slightly higher scale of AA and AT equipment than the other Echelon II divisions, were adjudged 'well instructed, well equipped and well led', and their subsequent conduct at Stalingrad was largely to justify this assessment.

However, the debilitated cavalry, mountain and infantry divisions which had already campaigned over the winter of 1941/42 (5C, 6C, 8C, 1M, 4M, 1, 2, 4, 10, 18, 19, 20), collectively known as Echelon I, were only partly reorganised, re-equipped or retrained in the field. To complete the process, it was planned that they should be withdrawn to the region of Rostov for a comprehensive overhaul during the winter of 1942/43.

The three infantry battalions and the 75mm artillery battalion cut from the field divisions remained at the divisional depots with the three regimental recruit battalions. Thus for each field division there now appeared an identically numbered training division with much of the manpower but little of the weaponry of the field divisions. That no new field divisions were formed during the war from these considerable manpower reserves was due to the heavy manpower losses of the existing field divisions and the inability to do more than replace losses of existing equipment.

On 25 March 1942 the Cavalry and Mountain Brigades were redesignated divisions. Manstein believed that this was done without changing their establishment, but this was not the case. By absorbing the eight reserve mountain rifle battalions at the outbreak of war, each mountain brigade had already grown to six battalions and had the manpower of a division. The cavalry brigades were already as large as Soviet cavalry divisions. Furthermore, their weapons establishments were substantially strengthened during 1942. The title change was probably spurred by the fear that the Romanian contribution would be undervalued by the Germans when compared with the Hungarians and Italians, whose binary divisions had only six battalions.

To be fully re-equipped, the mountain artillery required 116 Skoda M39 75mm mountain guns and 60 Skoda M39 100mm mountain howitzers, but deliveries in 1941/42 amounted to only 78 guns and 48 howitzers. During the winter of 1941/42, 2nd and 3rd Mountain Divisions were completely retrained and issued with the new artillery, but 1st and 4th Mountain Divisions, whose mountain artillery was obsolete, had two 75mm field gun battalions and a 100mm field howitzer battalion attached instead for their assault at Sevastopol, and kept them until May 1944. 1st Mountain Division received the new mountain artillery at the end of 1942, but 4th Mountain

Division never did so. Both the mountain troops and cavalry also benefited from the general increase in automatic weapons and mortars.

Cavalry squadrons received new packs to carry 60mm mortars and light, two-wheeled wagons for the ZB37 HMG, which brought their firepower up to infantry levels. The cavalry's divisional artillery was strengthened to 24 75mm light field guns, and captured Soviet 45mm AT guns were adopted as standard. However,

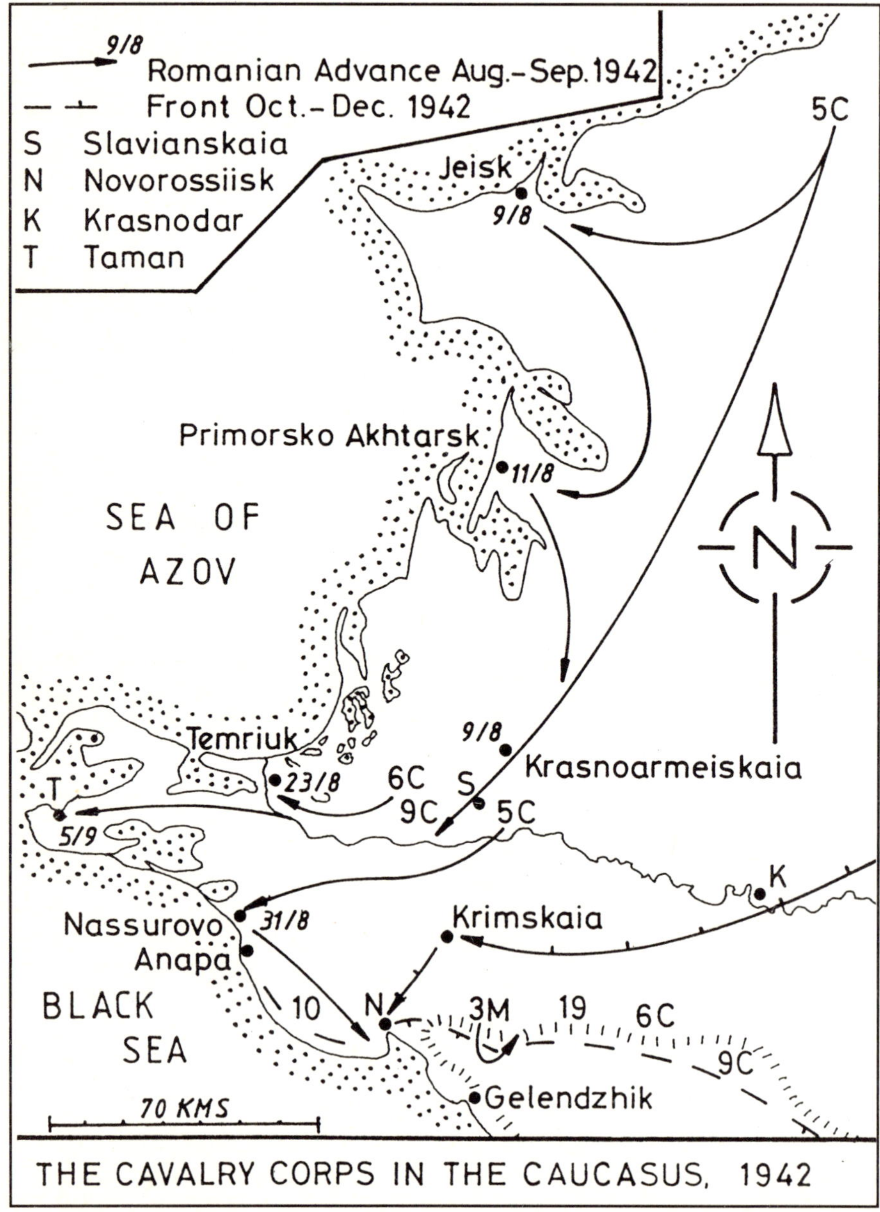

THE CAVALRY CORPS IN THE CAUCASUS, 1942

although 1st, 7th and 9th Cavalry Brigades were expanded to justify their new status as divisions and underwent extensive reorganisation and retraining, the full benefit could not be realised owing to the inability to acquire new AWD trucks to motorise one regiment of each as planned. Indeed, even cavalry horses were now in short supply, and 7th cavalry Division fought on foot at Stalingrad. Thus, unlike the mountain and line infantry, where the rested Echelon II divisions were the more powerful, in the cavalry it was the partly motorised Echelon I cavalry divisions (5C, 6C, 8C) that were more potent in 1942. Most of the R-1s disabled in 1941 were recoverable, and for the summer campaign of 1942 the cavalry divisions still fielded 29 (1C, 4; 5C, 5; 6C, 6; 7C, 6; 8C, 4; 9C, 4).

These preparations continued to excite both civilian and military opposition. From late 1941 Antonescu had been ill, and by mid-1942 many did not expect him to recover. As a result dissent became embarrassingly public. To reassert his authority, Antonescu had 23 generals and brigadiers retired between 12 June and 1 September, ostensibly on grounds of age, just before the Echelon II divisions were committed. However, when Hitler demanded that the equally outspoken Maniu be silenced, in September 1942, Antonescu robustly refused because 'Maniu is the only one who can talk authoritatively on Transylvania'. Maniu and Bratianu often disagreed with Antonescu on policy, but their impeccable patriotic credentials kept them out of prison throughout the war. On 22 September Antonescu invested himself with extraordinary powers in order to strengthen his increasingly beleaguered internal position.

Although rebuffed politically, the Germans did manage to gain more influence over operations. In 1941 they had only had liaison staffs down to corps level. In 1942 they extended this down to each Romanian division, and through their agency were increasingly able to circumvent higher Romanian command structures and thereby cut the most senior, but least politically sympathetic grades of Romanian generals out of operational decision-making at times of particular crisis. Romania normally only had liaison officers with the Germans at army group level.

THE ADVANCE INTO THE CAUCASUS, AUGUST TO OCTOBER 1942

Dumitrescu's 3rd Army commanded Romania's attack into the Caucasus, but only had General Racoviţa's Cavalry Corps (5C, 6C, 9C) under command. Şteflea and Dumitrescu struggled to bring all the Romanian forces in the Caucasus and Crimea under 3rd Army's operational control, but to no avail. Most remained dispersed under German command. The advance from Rostov on 5 August was led by 5th Cavalry Division. Its 8th Roşiori Regiment was detached to clear the ports of Jeisk (9 August) and Primorsko-Akhtarsk (11 August). Although well entrenched, the 4,000 Soviet marine defenders were evacuated by the Soviet Sea of Azov Flotilla to Temriuk because the deep advance of the rest of 5th Cavalry Division threatened their supply bases. By the time it returned to the division on 15 August, 8th Roşiori had ridden 800 kilometres.

The rest of the division was initially spearheaded by the Franc Mechanised Detachment, comprising 2nd Mechanised Squadron, a motorised battery of Schneider 105mm guns and a German assault pioneer battalion. In a rapid thrust, the detachment seized Krasnoarmeiskaia on 9 August. On the following day it was joined by Korne's 6th Motorised Roşiori from the Crimea. Up to this point the Soviet 47th Army had withdrawn before the Cavalry Corps, as it had been deeply outflanked by the German seizure of Stavropol far to the east, but it was now resolved to hold the line of the Kuban River. It therefore made a stand at Slavianskaia. However, the Korne and Franc Detachments stormed the town on 11 August, taking 600 prisoners in the process. 5th Cavalry Division had by then advanced 500km in seven days. Two days later a Soviet counterattack across the Kuban was repulsed, and the river was securely held from 15 August.

From 16-24 August 5th Cavalry Division patrolled the Kuban River, guarding the flank of the newly-arrived 6th and 9th Cavalry Divisions as they attacked westwards and captured the port of Temriuk. Its garrison of Soviet marines fell back into the Taman Peninsula. Temriuk was the key to direct communications with the Crimea, and soon more German and Romanian divisions began to land there.

On 27 August the Cavalry Corps attacked across the Kuban. The decisive advance was made by 5th Cavalry Division, which crossed the river near German-held Krimskaia and rolled up the Soviet defences from the east. Korne's Detachment (6th Motorised Roşiori, 2nd Mechanised Squadron and two batteries of the 2nd Horse Artillery Regiment) then played the key role in a rapid thrust which seized the heights of Nassurovo on the Black Sea coast on 31 August. There it captured two batteries of Soviet 152mm heavy artillery, which it turned on the port of Anapa, causing the rapid collapse of the defences the same day. 5th Cavalry Division's last operation in the Caucasus was to storm the south-west part of Novorossiisk on 11 September; an operation remarkably little delayed by the capture of six million bottles of local champagne.

The capture of Anapa had cut off two marine brigades of the Soviet 47th Army in the Taman Peninsula, and their 6,060 men had to be evacuated by the Black Sea Fleet under pressure from 6th Cavalry Division during 2-5 September, with consequent naval losses to Luftwaffe intervention. The 6th and 9th Cavalry Divisions' last offensive operation of the campaign was to attack southwards from the Krimskaia-Krasnodar railway line into the foothills of the Caucasus Mountains, where the front stabilised. The Cavalry Corps had made an important advance in seizing the Sea of Azov coast and a major stretch of the Black Sea coast, because it allowed four more German divisions and three Romanian divisions (10, 19, 3M) to land in the Caucasus from the Crimea. At least 1,000 prisoners had been taken, but the Cavalry Corps was continually frustrated by the ability of the Soviets to evacuate surrounded ports by sea. On 16 September 3rd Army HQ and 5th Cavalry Division were transferred to Stalingrad.

The Mountain Corps (1M, 4M), ill-equipped and recovering from its exertions at Sevastopol, passed the winter of 1942–43 on occupation duties in the Crimea, where it played a leading role in virtually annihilating the supply-starved local Soviet partisans. However, the two Echelon II mountain divisions (2M, 3M) had definite offensive potential and were used for attacks in the Caucasus Mountains. As the Soviet 47th Army's defences had hardened behind Novorossiisk, 3rd Mountain Division was committed to attack its right flank across the low western arm of the Caucasus Mountains in an attempt to capture the supply port of Gelendzhik in its rear. In fierce fighting during 19-22 September it drove a threatening wedge 6km through the defences of the Soviet 216th Rifle Division, but was dislodged by an equally fiercely contested counterattack by 77th Rifle Division and two marine brigades during 25-27 September.

The offensive potential of 3rd Mountain Division was exhausted. Through the winter, along with 19th Infantry Division and 6th and 9th Cavalry Divisions, it held a front on the northern slopes of the Caucasus Mountains between the German V Corps at Novorosiisk and XLIV Jaeger Corps at Krasnodar. Coastal protection between Novorosiisk and Taman was provided by 10th Infantry Division. The attack on Gelendzhik by 3rd Mountain Division was only one of three failed attempts by Axis mountain or rifle units to capture a Black Sea port across the Caucasus Mountains, for the XLIV Jaeger Corps was repulsed from Tuapse and the XLIX Mountain Corps was halted short of Sukhumi.

One other mountain formation, the Romanian 2nd Mountain Division, was also available. From early August it had advanced into the depths of the Caucasus through scorching summer heat in the wake of the mechanised formations of 1st Panzer Army, and it is doubtful whether any other Axis formation marched further with less organic motor transport during the 1942 offensive. From 21 September to the end of the month it became embroiled in heavy fighting along the River Baksan. Although its first attempt to force the river was driven back, its action was instrumental in diverting Soviet forces from a more important German thrust which took Mozdok at the end of August. By 19 October it had taken 1,858 prisoners.

On the Baksan the division faced a dangerous salient around Nalchik, on the northern slopes of the Caucasus Mountains. This threatened the communications of 1st Panzer Army as it struggled towards the Soviet oilfields beyond Mozdok. On 25 October 2nd Mountain Division went over to the offensive in concert with III Panzer Corps in order to eliminate the threat. While the German armour advanced up the valleys towards Nalchik, 2nd Mountain Division used its expertise to break through between 295th and 2nd Guards Rifle Divisions and advance against the grain of the country, crossing the Baksan, two other fast mountain rivers and steep intervening hills to capture Nalchik on 26 October. In the process it took 3,079 prisoners for the loss of 820 men, and trapped another 4,000 Soviets against the German armoured formations.

This was probably the only Romanian offensive afforded wholehearted Luftwaffe and Panzer support, and was crowned with a commendable success. General Dumitrache, 2nd Mountain Division's commander, was awarded the *Ritterkreuz* on 2 November. The capture of Nalchik was the last success of the Axis 1942 offensive. Indeed, it represented the furthest extension of Axis power throughout the war in Europe.

THE ADVANCE ON STALINGRAD

On 22 June, VI Corps made an assault crossing of the River Donets as part of 1st Panzer Army. During this operation it lost 906 dead and wounded, but captured 459 Russians. It then took up a defensive position on the River Oshkol until 7 July. From 8-27 July VI Corps (1, 2, 4, 20) took part in the German drive on the River Don as part of 4th Panzer Army. Conditions could not have been more different from those of its winter campaign. In blazing heat and short of water, the corps marched 450km across coverless steppe in twenty days, striving to keep up with the mechanised German troops ahead. Its advance was led by a two-squadron motorcycle reconnaissance group which captured the HQ of the Soviet 278th Division, 3,100 troops, fourteen guns and four tanks.

VI Corps then relieved 14th Panzer and 29th Motorised Divisions in the Tsimlyanski bridgehead across the Don, repulsing a Soviet counterattack in the process. This freed the Germans to press forward as the southern pincer of the advance on Stalingrad. They were followed by VI Corps, which formed the link between them and German troops still across the Don further west. However, on 8 August the Red Army counterattacked 14th Panzer and 29th Motorised Divisions and drove them from Abganerovo, throwing part of VI Corps back across the River Aksai at the same time.

During the final German approach to Stalingrad, in late August, VI Corps was switched east to guard 4th Panzer Army's exposed right flank, and in early September it dug in just beyond a line of lakes south of the city. The Germans were impressed by the stamina displayed by the corps' march of 800km in two months, which was unequalled by any of the German infantry divisions on the Stalingrad axis. Nor was this advance uncontested, for VI Corps had engaged the Russians in several frontal infantry assaults and river crossings, and repulsed a number of counterattacks which had cost it considerable losses.

On 20 August Hitler offered Antonescu command of Army Group Don (3rd and 4th Romanian Armies and the German 6th Army) once Stalingrad had fallen. General Friederich Paulus of 6th Army, who was married to a Romanian aristocrat, was to be his deputy, and General Hauffe was to be his Chief of Staff. Hauffe, and prominent German commanders such as Manstein, who were personally acquainted with Antonescu, knew he was both a capable soldier and the real motor behind Romania's war effort. They therefore anticipated that his appointment would give both competent leadership and powerful motivation to 3rd and 4th Armies, which were decidedly unenthusiastic about campaigning on the Don and Volga during winter. They also hoped that, as an allied head of state personally respected by Hitler, Antonescu would prove more influential in curbing the Fuehrer's wilder military fantasies than had German commanders constrained by their oath of loyalty to him. In October, Paulus, finding his own High Command resistant to strengthening the two Romanian armies on 6th Army's flanks with German troops from Stalingrad, took the irregular step of circumventing his own national chain of command by urging Dumitrescu to get Antonescu to use his influence to press Hitler for more German anti-tank guns and an armoured reserve. As his professional opinions usually coincided with theirs, Antonescu was regarded by several senior German generals as an influential intermediary with Hitler.

Always keen to be with his troops, Antonescu accepted Hitler's offer. However, he was too ill to take up early command, even had Stalingrad fallen. He was also concerned about the enormous strategic risks Hitler was taking at Stalingrad and in the Caucasus, where he was not only proposing to gamble with 20 per cent of the German Army, but with 80 per cent of the Romanian Army. As early as 28 August he pointed out to the Germans that the positions assigned to 3rd and 4th Armies over the winter were largely devoid of both provisions and shelter.

On 22/23 September he sent Mihai Antonescu to Hitler with a string of complaints and requests. All fourteen Echelon I divisions were subordinated to four different German armies (17, 1Pz, 4Pz, 6), and he was concerned at his resultant inability to exercise any co-ordinated control over their deployment. He therefore insisted on their withdrawal to Rostov for reinforcement, reorganisation, re-equipment and retraining to Echelon II standards over the winter, and their subsequent concentration in 4th Romanian Army. He also assailed Hitler with requests for armour, and complained at the delay in promised German weapons deliveries, bluntly contrasting this with prompt Romanian oil deliveries.

However, Hitler had earlier agreed to the withdrawal of the Echelon I divisions when he assumed that the Stalingrad and Caucasus campaigns would be victoriously concluded before winter and the length of front to be held much reduced. He declared that it was now too late to consolidate the Romanian divisions, but he did expedite limited deliveries of PzKpfw. III and IV tanks and 75mm anti-tank guns. Nevertheless, by Antonescu's estimate the Romanian infantry divisions would still remain only two-thirds as powerful as their German equivalents.

As Antonescu had troops in every German army engaged in the 1942 offensive, he was more aware of its weakness and failure than all but a handful of Germans. The plight of VI Corps particularly concerned him, as it had suffered heavy casualties and was seriously over-extended on open steppe without local provisions or shelter. 4th Division had to hold 60km of front, and on 29 September suffered heavy losses in a Soviet attack that penetrated to its command post. Throughout October the Red Army mounted a series of generally successful probing attacks on VI Corps which eliminated 1st and 4th Divisions' positions beyond the lake line and exposed their multiple weaknesses. The addition of VII Corps (5C, 8C) and 18th Infantry Division (all also worn Echelon I divisions) during 1-12 November was a mixed blessing, for although they reduced divisional frontages they further exacerbated the supply crisis. The situation was compounded by the Germans at Stalingrad, who dominated rail transport to such an extent that by 17 November VI and VII Corps had received no supply trains for ten days.

By 20 November the combat manpower of 1st, 2nd, 4th, 20th, 18th Infantry Divisions and 5th and 8th Cavalry Divisions stood at a miserable 25 per cent, 30 per cent, 34 per cent, 48 per cent, 78 per cent, 57 per cent and 64 per cent of establishment respectively, although their weapons status was rather better. Their casualties had not been made good because their replacements were being held back at Rostov in anticipation of their withdrawal for recuperation over the winter. By 19 November 4th Army's men were living half-starved and inadequately clothed in canvas-covered pits in temperatures of -20°C. The neighbouring Germans were only to experience these conditions some time after they were surrounded in Stalingrad. Morale was therefore extremely low.

During the summer the Red Army had been driven north of the River Don, but on 24 August it had successfully counterattacked over-extended German and Italian divisions and recaptured a large bridgehead at Serafimovitch and a smaller one at Kletskaya, both south of the Don. Thus, when 3rd Army's 171,256 men began to take over this front from 10 September, they found that almost all of their line was on exposed, open steppe. On 24 September General Dumitrescu requested German backing to mount an offensive with the still-uncommitted half of 3rd Army, to try to recapture the River Don line, which he badly needed as an anti-tank obstacle. However, the Germans did not want to divert any resources from their assault on Stalingrad, and refused, preferring to string 3rd Army ever more thinly along the existing Italian front despite Romanian objections.

The Red Army soon subjected 3rd Army to strong probing attacks to draw German forces away from Stalingrad and test the Romanians for weaknesses. However, the morale, training, equipment, frontage and strength of the fresh Echelon II divisions of 3rd Army were much better than those of the debilitated Echelon I divisions of VI Corps. 13th Division was very heavily assaulted on 14 October and 24-27 October in Soviet attempts to deepen their Kletskaya bridgehead. On its flank an independent regiment of 15th Division hung on to most of a prominent hill under fierce assault on 13-16 October. On 19-20 and 29 October 9th Division decisively repulsed Soviet attacks. Likewise, 11th Division repulsed an assault on 20 October with very heavy losses.

The Germans were encouraged by the Romanian performance in most of these predominantly infantry actions, and did not have to divert resources from Stalingrad. However, although these combats and numerous lesser raids were undoubtedly more costly for the Red Army than for 3rd Army, the Romanians nevertheless suffered 13,154 casualties (almost exactly the British 8th Army's losses at the simultaneous battle of El Alamein). Of these, 3,763 were from 13th Division, whose combat effectives were reduced to about 50 per cent, and another 2,261 were from 14th Division. Most seriously, prisoners and aerial reconnaissance revealed by late October that the Soviet attacks were only a preliminary to a full-scale offensive.

By the time Dumitrescu took full control of 3rd Army on 10 October, German policy had deprived it of the reserves needed for major offensive operations. Even when he requested permission to mount a local attack to improve his positions near Blinov on 16 October, the Germans vetoed the plan. With his army already under local attack, Dumitrescu then refused on 18 October to allow any more Romanian divisions to replace Italian divisions at the front unless Antonescu personally approved. But in late October he was obliged to do exactly that with 7th Infantry Division, the last infantry reserve on 3rd Army's left flank. By this time Dumitrescu had only five battalions of 15th Infantry Division, three dismounted regiments of 7th Cavalry Division and 1st Armoured Division left in reserve. As a result, most of the settlements in the army rear could not be put in an adequate state of defence.

Each division's front averaged 20km, nearly twice the recommended length. Consequently reserves were few at every level from company to army. All infantry battalions, light battalions and cavalry regiments in 9th, 14th and 13th Infantry Divisions and 1st Cavalry Division were in the line, instead of the recommended two being held in reserve. Even 7th, 11th, 5th and 6th Infantry Divisions each only had one battalion in reserve. 3rd Army only had adequate reserves of grenades and rounds for its 60mm mortars, Russian 45mm AT guns and Bohler 47mm AT guns. All other ammunition was short. The Germans delivered five or six of the promised Pak 97/38 75mm AT guns to each division in October. Unfortunately there was limited time to familiarise their crews in the weeks before the Soviet offensive. Furthermore, they were converted French field guns of only limited potential against Soviet medium and heavy tanks.

In view of the dangers facing Antonescu's prospective command, his supporters in Bucharest were anxious in case military defeat injured his standing at home, and thereby undermined his whole regime. In November, in an effort to have Hitler's offer rescinded, they used Colonel Ion Gheorghe, the Romanian Military Attaché in Berlin, to stress to the Germans that the Marshal was more important at home than in the field. Hitler wrote to Antonescu, emphasising that his appointment was only to follow the delayed fall of Stalingrad; a prestige prize he was reserving for himself.

Altogether, the advance into the Caucasus and on Stalingrad between 1 July and 31 October cost Romania 9,252 dead, 28,249 wounded and 1,588 missing. Although heavy, these losses were arguably commensurate with the positions gained and held, but Mihai Antonescu remained so concerned at the deteriorating situation that on 17 November he told von Killinger; 'The Russians are right now preparing a big action in exactly the region where our troops are situated. I am interested in assuring good living conditions and defensive works for our army because I don't want to lose it, for it is all we have.' By then, however, it was too late to redeem the situation.

1st Armoured Division and XLVIII Panzer Corps

The only significant mobile reserve of 3rd Army was 1st Armoured Division, which was now fully formed. On 5 July the German General von Knobelsdorff described it as 'weak in equipment but well trained and improving daily'. Its commander, General Radu Gherghe, was a political appointment by Antonescu. He did not impress the Germans, who felt that he was carried by his capable operations officer, Major Mavrici, and his experienced regimental commanders, who had proved themselves in 1941 and were to perform well again at Stalingrad. The division had detrained at Stalino on 29 August with 109 R-2s. From there it had driven to the vicinity of 3rd Romanian Army's HQ at Cernishevskaia by early October. Twelve R-2s broke down during the deployment and had to be withdrawn to Dnepropetrovsk for major repairs. Ten replacements arrived later from Romania.

During training with Army Group B, 1st Armoured Regiment witnessed test firings by an R-2 against a captured T-34. The T-34's armour was found to be invulnerable to its 37.2mm gun, and the bulk of 1st Armoured Regiment was to go into action the following month acutely aware of the hopeless inferiority of most of its tanks. However, this depressing demonstration did at least spur the Germans to expedite delivery of some more-modern equipment. On 17 October eleven PzKpfw IVGs and eleven PzKpfw IIINs were received, forming a medium tank company in each R-2 battalion of 1st Armoured Regiment. (One example of each was also delivered to 2nd Armoured Regiment in Romania for training.) During the campaign, nine 75mm Pak 40 and nine 50mm Pak 38 AT guns, nine SdKfz 10 1-ton half-tracks and nine SdKfz 11 3-ton half-tracks were accepted by the divisional AT com-

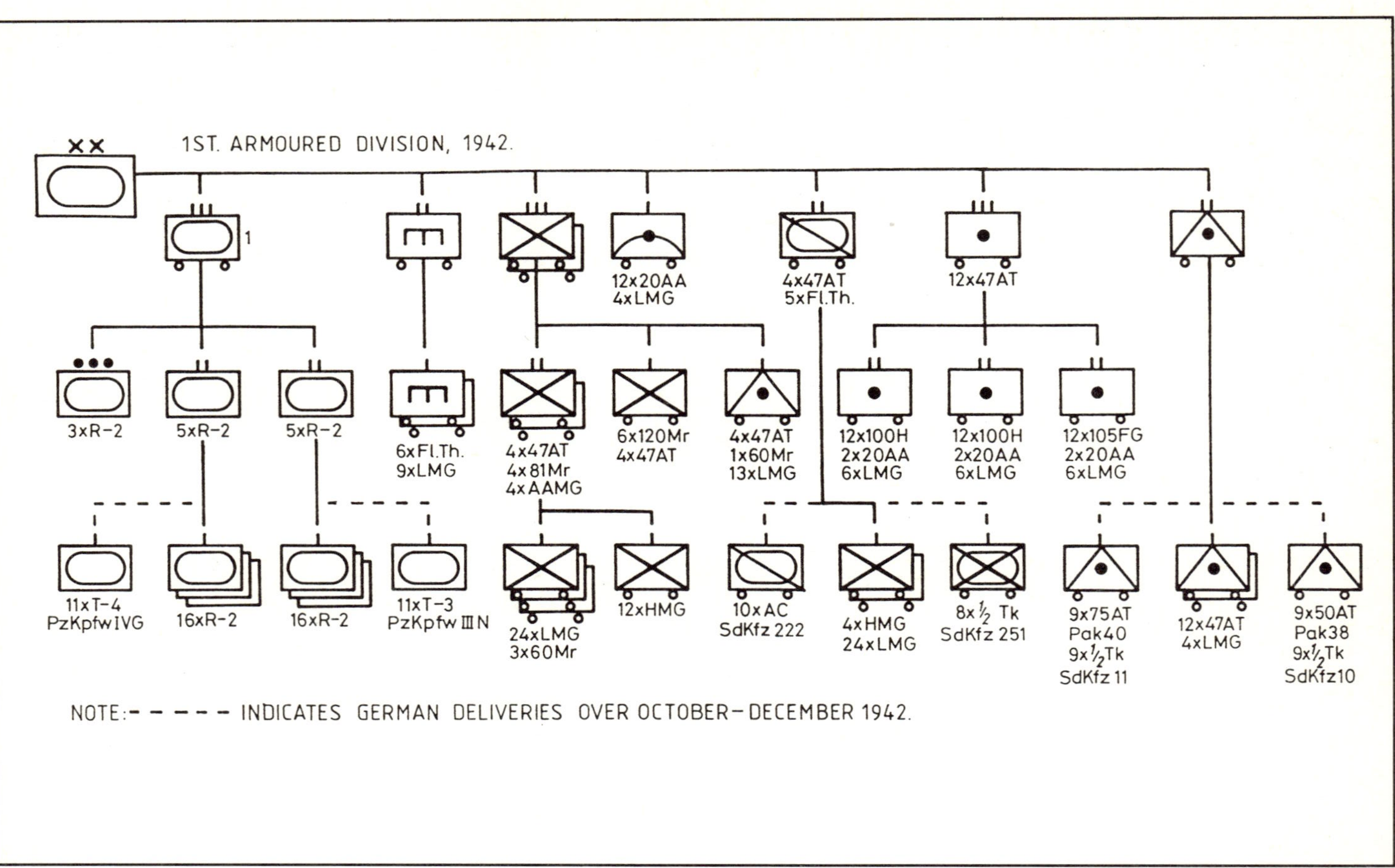
1ST. ARMOURED DIVISION, 1942.
1
12x20AA 4xLMG
4x47AT 5xFl.Th.
12x47AT
3xR-2
5xR-2
5xR-2
6xFl.Th. 9xLMG
4x47AT 4x81Mr 4xAAMG
6x120Mr 4x47AT
4x47AT 1x60Mr 13xLMG
12x100H 2x20AA 6xLMG
12x100H 2x20AA 6xLMG
12x105FG 2x20AA 6xLMG
11xT-4 PzKpfwIVG
16xR-2
16xR-2
11xT-3 PzKpfw III N
24xLMG 3x60Mr
12xHMG
10xAC SdKfz 222
4xHMG 24xLMG
8x½ Tk SdKfz 251
9x75AT Pak40 9x½Tk SdKfz 11
12x47AT 4xLMG
9x50AT Pak38 9x½Tk SdKfz10
NOTE:- - - - INDICATES GERMAN DELIVERIES OVER OCTOBER–DECEMBER 1942.

panies. However, its new PzKpfw. III and IV tanks only held their first battalion exercise on 16 November, and were thus not fully integrated into 1st Armoured Regiment by the time they were committed to action three days later. The new AT gun crews were also not yet fully familiar with their new weapons.

In late October, Romanian evidence regarding major Soviet offensive preparations against 3rd Army, obtained from aerial reconnaissance and prisoners, was initially discounted by the Germans, but recognition of 1st Armoured Division's weakness led them, belatedly, to promise 3rd Army the support of the full-strength 6th Panzer Division (141 tanks) and two infantry divisions from France on 4 November. They would arrive too late. In the interim they began the assembly of XLVIII Panzer Corps (22Pz, 14Pz, 1A) behind 3rd Army from 10 November. However, 14th Panzer Division (36 tanks) never arrived, and 22nd Panzer Division's combat capacity was famously reduced by mice gnawing through its tanks' electric wiring. 3rd Army was informed that its reconnaissance and infantry were at 68 per cent strength, but its Panzer regiment was down to two PzKpfw IIs, ten short-barrelled and eight long-barrelled PzKpfw IIIs, and one short-barrelled and nine long-barrelled PzKpfw IVs. There were also seven Panzerjaegers with 76.2mm guns and four with 47mm guns. 22nd Panzer Division was also short of fuel, and had to be given a third of 1st Armoured Division's reserves.

Soviet preparations for an offensive were well advanced by the third week of November, and XLVIII Panzer Corps was moved forward across the River Chir to the Perelazovski-Petrovka area. On 19 November 1st Armoured Division was 12,196 men strong, but it continued to suffer mechanical breakdowns and had only 84 R-2s, 19 PzKpfw IIIs and IVs, and two captured Soviet tanks (of 7 and 12 tons) serviceable. As many as 37 unserviceable R-2s and three panzers remained behind the Chir with the bulk of the division's services. Furthermore, one of its motorised Skoda 100mm howitzer battalions had been detached to support 1st Cavalry Division.

	XLVIII Pz. Corps					**Soviet SW Front**		
Tanks	1st Armd. Div +	22 Pz.Div +	14 Pz. Div =	Total	v	Total =	1st Line +	Reserve
Heavy	-	-	-	-	v	145	145	-
Medium	19	28	36	83	v	318	205	113
Light	84	13	-	97	v	267	217	50

THE SOVIET COUNTEROFFENSIVE ON 3RD ARMY, NOVEMBER 1942.

19 November

On 19 November 3rd Army's I Corps (7, 11), II Corps (9, 14), V Corps (5, 6), IV Corps (13, 1C, 15) and XLVIII Panzer Corps (22Pz, 1A, 7C) contained 155,492 Romanians and 11,211 Germans. Shortages of barbed wire and mines meant that only a small part of their front was adequately fortified, and reserves of artillery shells had yet to reach adequate levels. However, only 13th and 14th Infantry Divisions and 22nd Panzer Division were seriously below establishment, and the former was shortly due to be replaced in the line by 15th Infantry Division. Before this could be effected, the Soviet South Western Front attacked. Although it assaulted parts of most front-line Romanian divisions, its two designated break-

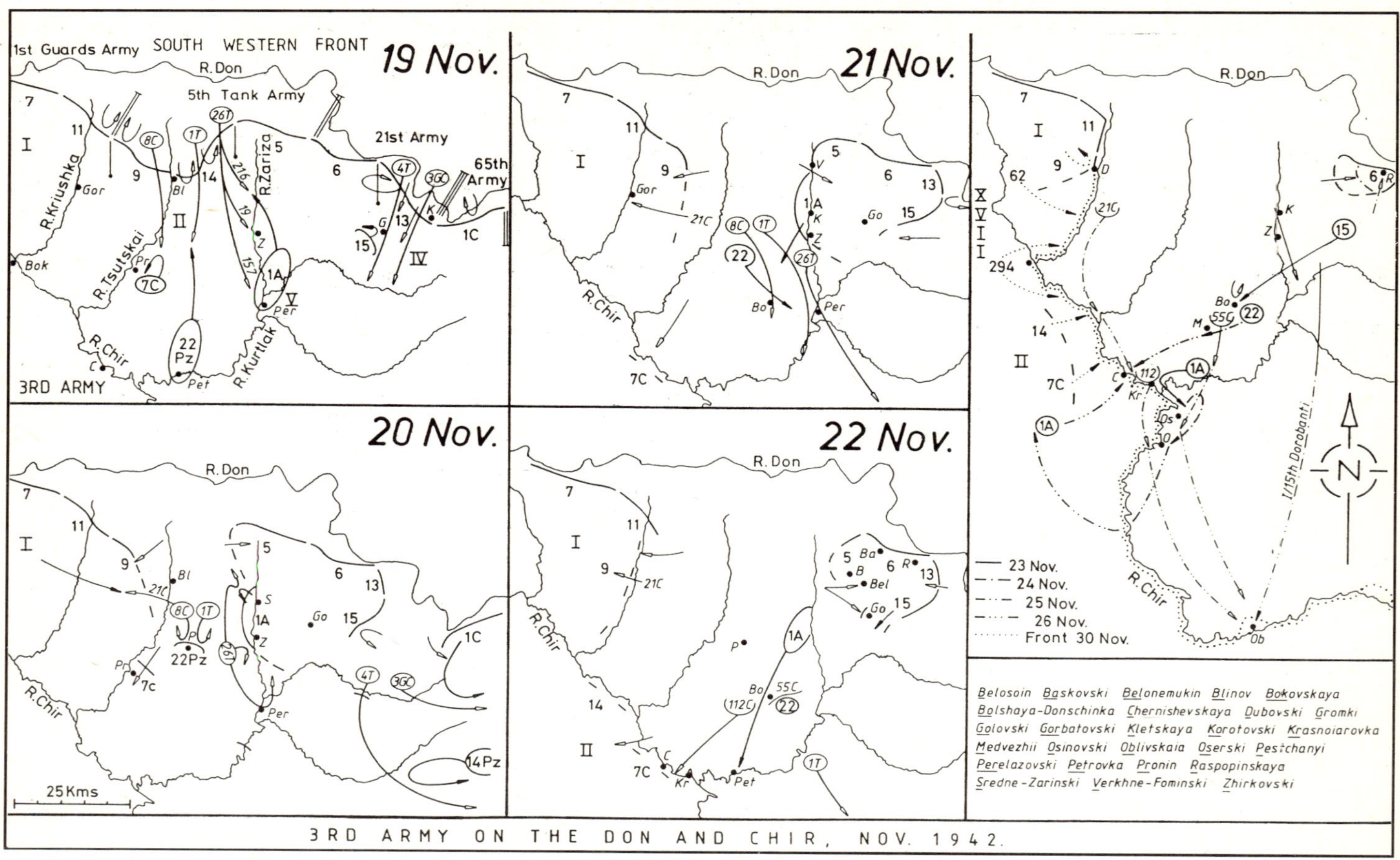
1st Guards Army SOUTH WESTERN FRONT
19 Nov.
R. Don
5th Tank Army
21st Army
65th Army
R.Kriushka
R.Tsutskai
R.Zariza
R.Kurtlak
R.Chir
3RD ARMY
21 Nov.
20 Nov.
22 Nov.
25 Kms
1/15th Dorobanti
23 Nov.
24 Nov.
25 Nov.
26 Nov.
Front 30 Nov.
Belosoin Baskovski Belonemukin Blinov Bokovskaya
Bolshaya-Donschinka Chernishevskaya Dubovski Gromki
Golovski Gorbatovski Kletskaya Korotovski Krasnoiarovka
Medvezhii Osinovski Oblivskaia Oserski Pestchanyi
Perelazovski Petrovka Pronin Raspopinskaya
Sredne-Zarinski Verkhne-Fominski Zhirkovski
3RD ARMY ON THE DON AND CHIR, NOV. 1942.

through sectors were on the fronts of the already weakened 13th and 14th Divisions.

South Western Front's 1st Guards, 5th Tank and 21st Armies were 338,631 strong. 1st Guards Army had four of its rifle divisions opposite the Italian 8th Army, but 21st Army was joined in its assault on the Romanians by four rifle divisions from Don Front's 65th Army. Thus the attacking force totalled eighteen rifle divisions, two cavalry corps, three tank corps and several independent tank units. A mechanised corps was in reserve. In raw manpower 3rd Army was outnumbered by only about two to one, but in materiel the Soviet advantage was much greater. Furthermore, the two designated breakthrough sectors totalled only 22km, equivalent to the front of a single Romanian division, and here all the Soviet armour and cavalry, and most of the infantry and artillery, were concentrated in overwhelming numbers. To support them, the heaviest artillery barrage of the war to date was opened at 0730. Having ranged-in over the previous month, the Soviet artillery was able to fire with considerable effect on the Romanian fixed defences, despite a thick mist. However, the Romanian artillery was less able to counter effectively because the same mist made it difficult to pinpoint the mobile Soviet attackers.

Although it was heavily attacked by several rifle divisions of the Soviet 65th Army on 19 November, 1st Cavalry Division lost only a couple of kilometres on its left wing, where it was outflanked by the Soviet 21st Army's breach of 13th Division near Kletskaya. After what the Soviets described as 'stubborn resistance', in which at least 25 Russian tanks were claimed knocked out, the debilitated 13th Division's right wing was broken decisively by three Soviet rifle divisions of 21st Army in the early afternoon. By 1400, armour of the Soviet 4th Tank Corps entered Gromki, putting the division's HQ to flight. 3rd Guards Cavalry Corps followed an hour later.

15th Division (less one regiment), in reserve behind 13th Division, attempted to counterattack but was driven back by tanks. Thereafter it put up an impressive defence along a line of small hills, where it was able to suppress the infantry supporting the Soviet tanks and knock out several of them. This unnerved the remainder, which then withdrew from their hitherto virtually invulnerable rampage through the Romanian positions. General Sion, 15th Division's commander, had been deputy comander of 1st Armoured Division in 1941, and his expertise may well account for its success against tank attack over the following days. Fifteen tanks exploiting the breakthrough of 13th Division also thrust westwards behind 6th Division's front, but eight were knocked out by evening and the rest withdrew. One 75mm field artillery battery had the unnerving experience of watching its supposedly armour-piercing shells bounce off one Soviet tank at only 5m range.

V Corps (5, 6) and the right wing of 14th Division had no difficulty in repulsing light infantry attacks by the 96th, 346th and 124th Rifle Divisions of 5th Tank Army. Even on the main axis of the Soviet 5th Tank Army's assault on the centre and left of 14th Division, the 47th Guards and 119th Rifle Divisions only managed to penetrate the Romanian defences during the morning, and failed to breach them as planned. This forced the premature commitment of 1st and 13th Tank Corps and 8th Cavalry Corps at 1300. Although this cost the unforeseen loss of a number of tanks, most of 14th Division, including its HQ, and the right wing of 9th Division were overwhelmed and put to flight during the afternoon. Operating on foot, 7th Cavalry Division put in an immediate counterattack to restore 9th Division's right wing, but ran straight into the Soviet 8th Cavalry Corps. It was driven back to Pronin with very heavy losses, including three of 4th Mechanised Squadron's six R-1s.

The left and centre of 9th Division successfully repulsed the 14th Guards Rifle Division. Unable to concentrate its 1st Mechanised Corps in time for the offensive, 1st Guard's Army tried to contribute with an assault towards Gorbatovski and Bokovskaia by its 302nd Rifle Division, supported by the entire available army artillery reserves. However, the attack was so bloodily suppressed by 11th Division that it was not resumed, and the Soviet plan to unhinge the entire left wing of 3rd Army failed. 7th Division was not attacked by 278th Rifle Division.

In judging the Romanian infantry's performance on this first day, it is worth noting that only on the front of two regiments of its most weakened formation, 13th Division, did Soviet rifle divisions, despite having a huge artillery barrage and infantry support tanks in attendance, manage to breach 3rd Army's front, and even here they were behind schedule. Elsewhere they either fell short of their objectives or were repulsed. Only when entire tank corps, followed by cavalry corps, fell on the Romanian infantry were there catastrophic collapses. On the whole the Echelon II divisions of 3rd Army had performed creditably in the face of the heaviest Soviet offensive of the war so far. It was now up to XLVIII Panzer Corps to handle the Soviet mechanised and cavalry corps that were beyond the capacity of the Romanian infantry divisions.

Army Group B immediately ordered 22nd Panzer Division to counterattack towards Blinov, and 1st Armoured Division and 14th Panzer Division to counterattack towards Kletskaya. However, 1st Armoured Division's orders were countermanded in mid-deployment, and it was redirected against Soviet forces east of Blinov. This dislocated XLVIII Panzer Corps' operations from the start, a situation that could not immediately be rectified because 1st Armoured Division's HQ at Zhirkovski was attacked by surprise during the night by leading elements of 26th Tank Corps. The Soviets were driven off, but only after the German liaison detachment's radio, through which XLVIII Panzer Corps passed its orders, was destroyed. It was a week before the corps' two divisions could be recombined.

20 November

14th Panzer Division was too distant and too weak to mount an effective counterattack on Kletskaya. Therefore, on 20 November 1st Cavalry Division had to abandon its front-line positions because the Soviet 4th Tank Corps and 3rd Guards Cavalry Corps were now operating in its rear. Elements of the division made a mounted counterattack south-westwards on the Soviet 5th Guards Cavalry Division in an endeavour to re-establish links with 3rd Army, but were repulsed. However, as General Paulus later testified, this did win time for XI Corps of the German 6th Army, to which 1st Cavalry Division was now subordinated, to draw back its left flank and avoid being attacked in the rear.

Thereafter, 1st Cavalry Division fell back in increasing confusion with XI Corps into Stalingrad. In the process, 1st Mechanised Squadron's four R-1s had to be set on fire for lack of fuel. A second Romanian group, Detachment Voicu, consisting of the remains of an independent regiment of 15th Division, fragments of 13th Division and the battalion of motorised 100mm howitzers detached from 1st Armoured Division, was similarly driven into Stalingrad with 14th Panzer Division.

Whereas only two divisional HQs (13 and 14) had been overrun or displaced on the first day, three corps HQs (V at Perelazovskii, IV at Kalmukov and II at Cistiakovo) had been put to flight or cut off from their troops by Soviet tanks within 24 hours. Only I Corps at Bokovskaia was still in full control of its divisions. The most decisive damage to 3rd Army thus occurred in its rear, where command structures, communications and supply lines were soon disrupted. Once the generally tenaciously held prepared positions at the front were pierced, fighting in the rear usually focused on such settlements as existed, for these alone offered the shelter on the freezing steppe which both sides required for survival in a bitterly hostile environment. Unfortunately, the previously noted lack of infantry reserves had meant that most settlements could not be put in an adequate state of defence.

Whereas German rear services were often well enough trained and equipped to have some combat value against Soviet breakthroughs, Romanian rear services, equipped with obsolete rifles and little else, were generally not, and a widespread panic invariably resulted. This often led to the abandonment of key settlements under only light pressure. It is notable that in the only place where a significant body of Romanian infantry (five battalions of 15th Division) were held in reserve, the Soviet assault came to a standstill for several days.

As they now lacked corps headquarters, 6th, 5th and 15th Divisions and adjacent regiments of 13th and 14th Divisions were formed into an *ad hoc* group under General Lascar, the *Ritterkreuz* winner from Sevastopol, who commanded 6th Division from Golovski. The Lascar Group was itself subordinated to XLVIII Panzer Corps, which was tasked with relieving it. However, they lacked direct communications, which had to be relayed via 3rd Army. 6th and 5th Divisions' fronts were not heavily attacked, and the latter was able to use its meagre reserves to support the counterattacks of 1st Armoured Division.

During the day, 15th Division repulsed an attack by 35–40 T-34s supported by two infantry battalions. The tanks again rampaged through its positions, destroying field telephone lines and crushing command bunkers and light anti-tank guns, but the Romanian infantry held fast and the supporting Soviet infantry were again mown down. The tanks eventually retired, leaving five of their number knocked out and 45 prisoners. The German-supplied 75mm AT guns proved ineffective in this action, which was decided by the infantry. The Soviets, probably a tank brigade of 4th Tank Corps, did not attack the division again, and it was able to swing its front to face south-eastwards, covering the rear of the Lascar Group. The repulse of this attack was decisive in securing the eastern flank of the Lascar Group for the next two days. Morale in 15th Division was extremely high after this. Its wounded were evacuated quickly and efficiently by 6th Division to Golovski, it was resupplied with ammunition, and surviving parts of 13th Division were subordinated to it. Although it was already short of food and fodder, it confidently awaited the arrival of XLVIII Panzer Corps.

However, the bulk of 14th Division and the right wing of 9th Division had ceased to exist, and XLVIII Panzer Corps was struggling ineffectually to seal the breach. 1st Armoured Division and the reserves of 5th Infantry Division were ordered to attack north-westwards and cut through the base of the Soviet break-through east of Blinov on 14th Infantry Division's old front. There they were to meet 22nd Panzer Division and 7th Cavalry Division, which were ordered to advance north and eastwards from Peschanyi and Pronin.

1st Armoured Division engaged in heavy fighting around Sredne-Zarinski and Zhirkovski against the Soviet 19th and 216th Tank Brigades, 119th and 124th Rifle Division, an independent 76.2mm AT artillery regiment and at least one flamethrower tank battalion. Although the division established a bridgehead 4km west of the River Zariza, it failed to regain contact with 22nd Panzer Division, which was itself pinned down the whole day at Peschanyi. 1st Armoured Division lost 25 tanks (five R-2s through mechanical failure and four panzers and at least fourteen R-2s knocked out), but it claimed 62 Soviet tanks and 61 motor vehicles destroyed and took 332 prisoners.

However, XLVIII Panzer Corps' stalled counterattack was not entirely without impact, as three of the six Soviet tank brigades committed to the offensive were bogged down engaging 22nd Panzer Division, and two were locked in combat with 1st Armoured Division for most of 20 November. The remaining tank brigade (157th) and other motorised troops had already burst through the gap between 22nd Panzer and 1st Armoured Divisions and captured Perelazovskii early on 20 November, overrunning V Corps HQ and some of 1st Armoured Division's rear echelons in the process, but they then also spent the day engaging 1st Armoured Division's tail. This was not at all according to the Soviet plan, which required them to bypass all resistance, leaving the following cavalry and rifle divisions to mop it up.

There was thus a fleeting prospect of the Soviet offensive stalling through loss of nerve on 20 November. In the words of a Soviet staff report of 1943; 'The 26th Tank Corps (19th, 157th, 216th Tank Brigades and 14th Motorised Rifle Brigade) spent the whole day clearing the enemy out of the region of Perelazovskii and carried on combat with units of 1st Romanian Armoured Division, despite the fact that, by utilising the delay in the movement of our forces, the Romanian divisions (of the Lascar Group) could have escaped from the blows of the 21st Army moving south'.

Just such a breakout was proposed by General Şteflea at Rostov, but Hitler ordered the Lascar Group to hold fast. Once the 1st and 26th Tank Corps had summoned up the nerve to leave the remains of XLVIII Panzer Corps to the cavalry and rifle divisions behind them and started to drive into the Axis rear towards Kalach on the night of 20/21 November, the opportunity to break out faded fast.

Now attached to I Corps, 9th Division held on to the left of its original front. In an attempt to regain the River Tsutskai line, I Corps committed its scanty reserves, but without success. However, it did delay Soviet attempts to roll up 9th Division, and forced the enemy to detach 21st Cavalry Division from 8th Cavalry Corps. The weakened 7th Cavalry Division tried to cover I Corps' exposed right flank, but was driven back from Pronin by 159th Rifle Division and supporting armour, which pursued its few survivors behind the Chir on the following day. The rest of I Corps (7, 11) had a quiet day.

The early success of the Soviet counteroffensive now made Antonescu's assumption of command impossible, because it was politically inconceivable that his name should become associated with a defeat already in the making. Field-Marshal von Manstein was therefore ordered to take over Army Group Don, but he would not arrive for another week.

21 November

Having failed to link up across the base of the Soviet offensive at Blinov, XLVIII Panzer Corps was now charged with reuniting further south at Peralazovskii on 21 November. Under continuous pressure from the Soviet 8th Cavalry Corps (55th and 112th Cavalry Divisions), 22nd Panzer Division withdrew south and tried to recapture Perelazovskii from the north-west, but was surrounded just south-east of Bolshaia Donschinka and dug in. Meanwhile, the bulk of 1st and 26th Tank Corps, containing the mass of Soviet tanks, had poured through the gap between it and 1st Armoured Division, and some elements of the latter corps were already 50km beyond Perelazovskii. However, this still left a cavalry corps, two independent tank brigades, two independent tank battalions, a motorcycle regiment and at least four rifle divisions between the Lascar Group and safety.

1st Armoured Division began the day defending the western flank of the Lascar Group between 5th Division's left wing at Verkhne Fominski and Korotovski. It was then ordered to attack south and link up with 22nd Panzer Division at Perelazovskii. By evening, however, its lead elements had been halted by fierce resistance from 8th Cavalry Corps 8km south-west of Zhirkovski, while its main body was still heavily engaged with 124th and 119th Rifle Divisions and 216th Tank Brigade 5km west of Korotovski. Twenty tanks were lost during the day, but 21 Soviet tanks were claimed and 315 prisoners taken.

The move south by 1st Armoured Division opened a gap between it and 5th Division, through which Soviet infantry and supporting tanks began to pour. As a result, 6th and 13th Divisions had much of their supply trains overrun. 5th Division's left wing had thus far repulsed heavy infantry and tank assaults, but was now outflanked and obliged to abandon Verkne Fomikinski and withdraw to high ground behind the River Zariza. There it repulsed its pursuers and fought on. The situation at Golovski, where the wounded, wagons and stragglers of much of the Lascar Group were being collected, now became critical. As 6th Division was still only lightly engaged, it sent a battalion of the 15th Dorobanţi and some Bofors guns to defend the town. The Lascar Group's eastern wing held firm when 15th and 13th Divisions repulsed a divisional-sized Soviet infantry assault in the afternoon and took more than 100 prisoners.

On 3rd Army's left flank the Soviet 21st Cavalry Division and some tanks broke through behind the right wing of 9th Division in heavy fighting, putting its HQ to flight. Also pressed by 14th Guards Rifle Division from the front, 9th Division fled westwards, some of it being surrounded and captured 11km east of Gorbatovski. As a consequence, 11th Division had to withdraw its right flank behind the River Kriushka.

During the day, 3rd Army had to move its HQ back from Chernishevskaia to Morozovskaia, as the former was now threatened by the leading Soviet units. Şteflea and Dumitrescu solicited Antonescu for the breakout of the Lascar Group, but he told them to follow the orders of Army Group B. However, this German command was shackled by Hitler's order to hold fast. At 2200 Şteflea and Dumitrescu took it on themselves and secretly ordered Lascar to make breakout preparations. Hauffe later suggested that this may have undermined the determination of the encircled divisions and precipitated their collapse, but it is unlikely to have altered their ultimate fate.

22 November

Early the following morning Hauffe made the German position over the Lascar Group clear to Şteflea, stating '... there are other, very grave issues – the fate of the Sixth Army, 4th Panzer Army and Stalingrad involved. The main point is not that an isolated military formation should be rescued, but that German and Romanian troops should stand and fight as they had been ordered.' The Lascar Group was to be sacrificed in an attempt to save larger German formations. From the wider Axis perspective such a trade-off was clearly necessary, but from a purely Romanian point of view it was extremely undesirable. In Romania, probably only Antonescu appreciated the wider Axis requirements. Romanian officers at the front, lacking the full strategic perspective, saw only that they were being sacrificed, and began to make their own arrangements for survival.

On the morning of 22 November 1st Armoured Division continued its drive to link up with 22nd Panzer Division and broke out westwards through 119th Rifle Division. However, in the afternoon it drove into the rear of the Soviet 8th Cavalry Corps attacking 22nd Panzer. Soviet reports of this action mistake the 1st Armoured Division for part of 22nd Panzer Division and, except for the time and location, vary greatly from the Romanian accounts. The Soviets claimed to have repulsed a tank attack with artillery, destroying 27 tanks and 60 trucks. The Romanians claimed to have repulsed an attack by tanks (possibly of 8th Independent Tank brigade), capturing 256 prisoners and destroying 65 tanks at the cost of ten Romanian tanks (at least two of which broke down), ten AT guns, 129 motor vehicles and 108 motorcycles. Losses in the Anti-Tank and Reconnaissance Battalions were severe, and fuel bowser losses were particularly serious.

Whatever the true details of the action, the core of 1st Armoured Division broke through the Soviet cavalry screen, but its drive to link up with 22nd Panzer Division was deflected towards Petrovka, which was reached that evening. The Soviet 112th Cavalry Division and corps troops were immediately ordered towards Krasnoiarovka to prevent its further escape across the River Chir.

At 0230 Red Army demands for the Lascar Group's surrender were firmly rejected by Generals Lascar and Mazarini of 6th and 5th Divisions, who responded 'We will continue to fight without thought of surrender'. In this they were firmly supported by General Sion, whose 15th Division was enjoying continued defensive success. Their reply was received with uncharacteristic emotion by their German liaison officers.

Right: Marshal Ion Antonescu with Hitler. The Fuehrer had a high personal regard for the Conducator, who was never intimidated at their meetings. Indeed, on purely military matters it was Hitler who often found himself on the defensive.

Right: Relations between the young King Mihai (centre) and Marshal Ion Antonescu (left) were abysmal. The King refused to endorse the war beyond the Dnestr, and Antonescu often threatened to abolish the monarchy. To the right of the King is Mihai Antonescu, the Marshal's distant cousin and deputy.

Left: Left to right: Generals von Manstein (11th Army), Avramescu (Mountain Corps) and Dumitrescu (3rd Army). Manstein was heavily reliant on Romanian support for his successes in the Crimea in 1941–42, which represented the high point of inter-Axis co-operation in the field. Dumitrescu and Avramescu commanded 3rd and 4th Armies respectively at the Battle of Iaşi-Chişinau in August 1944.

Below: Colonel Radu Korne (wounded) with German and Romanian staff after he took over command of the Grodek Motorised Brigade during the recapture of the Kerch Peninsula in May 1942. Korne, Romania's leading exponent of mechanised operations, rose to command 1st Armoured Division in 1944.

Right: The Romanian peasant soldier was generally hardy, willing and uncomplaining. He had excellent marching powers, and was able to subsist on lower scales of rations and in worse conditions than most German troops. On the other hand, he lacked the education and industrial morale to conduct or face modern mechanised warfare with confidence.

Below: Romanian cavalry en route to a railhead, late June 1941. Owing to its high proportion of regulars, the cavalry was of good quality. However, it was very lightly equipped in 1941, and only in 1942 did it receive weapons on a scale comparable to the infantry. By mid 1944 losses of specially schooled mounts had been so heavy that only one of the five surviving cavalry divisions remained fully horsed.

Above: Uncomfortable allies. German troops, made arrogant by success, had a low opinion of their allies, but failed to appreciate that in 1941–42 Romanian casualties had been proportionally heavier than their own. The issue of *Ritterkreuzen* told a different story. Romanians received twice as many as any other German allies.

Below: The last IAR 80Cs on the IAR-Braşov production line in late 1942. This single plant developed and/or produced all of the licence-built and Romanian-designed combat aircraft. However, difficulties in acquiring machine tools and materials in Axis Europe prevented its full production potential ever being realised. Despite some damage from US bombing in 1944, which the Romanians initially thought was from accidental overshoots from a raid on a nearby oil installation, production was never completely halted.

Above: A battery of Reşiţa/Vickers M.36 75mm AA guns ready for delivery by the Astra factory before the war. This was the heaviest gun produced in Romania, and 200 examples had been completed by 1944. Its performance as an AA gun was unexceptional, but it was found to have good armour-piercing potential and its rifling was adopted for the Reşiţa M.43 75mm AT gun.

Below: The launch of *Rechinul* at Galati naval yard on 5 May 1941. She and the related *Marsuinul* took so long to fit out that they did not enter operational service until 1944. During hostilities the Galaţi yard was heavily engaged in repairing damaged Axis vessels, and launched no major warships, although four German-designed minesweepers were nearing completion in August 1944.

Above: Romania's only significant vehicle factory was a Ford assembly plant. Before the war it turned out several thousand 4 x 2 trucks such as this for the forces, but, as it relied on imported parts, production stopped at the outbreak of war.

Below: Romania's only AFV production line at the Malaxa factory had to abandon the licenced production of the Renault UE chenillette and trailer in early 1941 owing to a lack of French components. The 126 Şenileta Malaxa Tipul UEs completed had negligible direct combat potential, and were only used as gun tractors for some divisional Schneider 47mm AT gun companies in 1941–42.

Above: General Pantazi, the Defence Minister, inspects a cavalry Mechanised Squadron equipped with R-1 light tanks on 8 August 1942. Thirty-six R-1s were acquired, but, lacking a radio, significant armour or armament, they had very little operational value. The turret insignia is of St. George, the patron saint of cavalry, slaying the dragon.

Below: Two R-35 infantry tanks tow a captured Soviet BT-2 in Basarabia, July 1941. Seventy-five R-35s formed 2nd Armoured Regiment in 1941. Although adequately armoured, they lacked the armament or mobility to conduct blitzkrieg operations. They were relegated to training and security duties from 1942.

Above: The rear of an R-2 light tank, 126 examples of which equipped 1st Armoured Regiment in 1941–42. This view illustrates the exterior differences between it and the PzKpfw.35(t), 26 of which were also received in 1942. The R-2 was still an adequate AFV against the mass of Soviet light tanks encountered in 1941, but the advent of large numbers of Soviet medium and heavy tanks in 1942 rendered it obsolete.

Left: Maintenance on a PzKpfw.38(t) in the Crimea in the spring of 1944. By the time 50 badly worn examples were received by 2nd Armoured Regiment in mid-1943, they were already obsolete. Their poor condition caused a major Romanian-German row.

Above: The TACAM T-60. Thirty-four were built in 1943 from captured T-60 and T-60A light tanks and M1936 76.2mm field guns, and served with 61st and 62nd TACAM Companies. The vehicle's AT potential was not spectacular, but it represented the best expedient then available to Romania from within its own resources. (10/5/43).

Below: The TACAM R-2, a local combination of the chassis of the R-2 or PzKpfw.35(t) tank and Soviet M1941 76.2mm L/46 field gun. Twenty-one were delivered to 63rd TACAM Company in early 1944. However, by then its gun was considered inadequate in the AT role, and further conversions were suspended pending an upgunning that never materialised.

Above: The Vanatorul de Care R-35, a local combination of the R-35 tank and a Soviet 45mm tank gun. Thirty were delivered to 2nd Armoured Regiment in 1943–44. A virtually useless tank-destroyer, it was only sent to the front in 1945 at Soviet insistence.

Below: The Vanatorul de Care Mareşal (M-05), the only indigenously-designed Romanian AFV. An inspiration for the German Hetzer, the Mareşal went through six prototypes in 1943–44. However, production of the first ten examples was halted by the Soviets in October 1944. It mounted the local Reşiţa 75mm AT gun and was considered to have excellent combat prospects.

Above: A mountain rifleman with the locally-produced Oriţa M41 submachine gun. The Romanian army began the war with no SMG, which was a great disadvantage in close-quarter fighting. During 1942 525 German and Italian SMGs were issued to each infantry division. Because of teething troubles, the Oriţa only entered service in 1943, but became the most common SMG during 1944, by which time there were 1,838 SMGs per division. There were still 1,488 SMGs in the smaller 1945 infantry division.

Below: A mountain rifleman with a ZB30 light machine-gun. Production of this useful weapon by CMC Cugir made Romania self-sufficient in LMGs throughout the war. The Mountain Rifles, trained to display initiative and tactical flexibility at the lowest level, were the best Romanian infantry. They often performed well in the Crimea and Caucasus.

Left: Mountain troops lay a Romanian copy of a Soviet 120mm mortar in Czechoslovakia in April 1945. Reşiţa built more than 500 120mm mortars, and smaller factories produced large numbers of Brandt 81mm and 60mm mortars. These smooth-bore weapons were much easier to produce on Romania's limited machine tools than rifled guns.

Below: Romanian pioneers (in Adrian helmets) prepare to ferry an ex-Polish Bofors 37mm AT gun. This was the most common regimental AT gun in 1941–42, but, like the Breda and Bohler 47mm AT guns and captured Soviet 45mm AT guns also in regimental service, it was totally useless against Soviet medium and heavy tanks.

Above: At the outbreak of the war, the bulk of divisional artillery consisted of inadequate, obsolete, horsedrawn 75mm field guns such as this Schneider M1897 field gun and similar old Putilov and Krupp pieces adapted to fire the same 75mm round.

Below: As the war progressed, an assortment of Skoda 100mm howitzers increasingly replaced the older 75mm field guns. The standard piece was the Skoda M34 100mm howitzer, seen here detraining from the front with the Guard Division in early November 1941. However, although they were an improvement, even 100mm howitzers were light by German divisional artillery standards.

Above and below: The motorised corps artillery alone was fully modern. Throughout the war it consisted of battalions of excellent motorised Schneider M36 105mm guns (above) and Skoda M34 howitzers (below) drawn by all-wheel-drive Skoda gun tractors.

Above: A Reşiţa M43 75mm AT gun of 9th Cavalry Division in Budapest in December 1944. This drew on design features from Russian, German and British guns to produce an AT weapon superior to its Soviet competitors. Its high angle of elevation also gave it value as a field gun, and a versatility unmatched by the German Pak 40.

Below: Romania's leading Bf 109 fighter aces of Grupuri 7 and 9 Vanatori in the summer of 1944. Left to right: Cantacuzino, Di Cesare, Greceanu, Şerbanescu and Milu. Between them they were credited with about 190 victories.

Above: Dan Vizante, commander of Grup 6 Vanatori, had 39 kills. Most were on the IAR 80, of which he was the leading ace. He is seen here commanding Group 1 Vanatori in Slovakia in 1945.

Below: A SET 7KB in wartime camouflage and markings. This was the first Romanian-designed combat aircraft to enter series production, sixty SET 7Ks being delivered between 1936 and 1938. During the war they were used as trainers or for communications. This example has the ICAR skis fitted to all fixed-undercarriage, Romanian-built types in snow.

During the night of 21/22 November the Soviet 124th Rifle Division, supported by tanks, drove behind 5th Division's left flank to Belonemukin, forcing it to fall back through Belosoin. Increasingly levered out of its fixed defences, the division began to disintegrate. Its remnants drew up a last defence line between Belonemukin and Baskovski. Soviet attacks on the right flank of 6th Division and the left of 15th Division also made some slight progress for the first time in several days.

Notwithstanding its bravado in rejecting Soviet surrender demands, the Lascar Group's situation was now desperate, and they communicated this to 3rd Army in no uncertain terms early on the morning of 22 November. Artillery ammunition was down to 40 rounds per gun, mortar ammunition was also short, many men had not eaten for three days, the wounded could no longer be adequately tended and even the recently supplied German 75mm AT guns had proved of limited effect. The Germans later suggested that the shortage of ammunition and food, and the lack of medical evacuation, were the result of faulty Romanian administration, but the Romanians attributed it to the German domination of the railways and their own lack of motor transport. In view of the increasing gravity of their situation, Lascar requested permission to break out towards Chernishevskaia on the night of 22/23 November, but Army Group B reiterated Hitler's hold-fast order. A second Soviet surrender demand was rejected at 1000.

At 0900 a Romanian Fieseler Storch landed at Golovski and established the landing strip's viability. Two hours later ten German Heinkel He 111s dropped supplies there, and at 1300 five Romanian Junkers Ju 52s landed food, fuel and ammunition and evacuated 60 wounded officers. This level of support could do little to improve the Lascar Group's situation, however. At 1600 Generals Lascar, Mazarini and Sion met at Golovski again. General Mazarini, whose 5th Division was collapsing, had opposed the 1942 campaign from the start, and now abdicated responsibility entirely to Lascar and Sion. They decided to break out simultaneously at 2200 that night; 6th Division towards Peschanyi and 15th Division towards Bolshaia Donschinka. A battalion of 6th Division's 15th Dorobanţi and various divisional troops were ordered to replace the departed 1st Armoured Division in Zhirkovski, there to act as flank guard for the breakout.

However, in the late afternoon Soviet infantry attacked Golovski from the west. Initially driven off by a counterattack, they returned later with tanks and ejected the HQ of 6th Division from the town at 2100. This cut the last radio link with 3rd Army. The survivors fled either north towards the bulk of 6th Division or south towards 15th Division, the last two organised formations in the pocket.

The fall of Golovski effectively closed 6th Division's escape route. General Lascar was apparently captured during the night near the settlement, and never learned that Hitler had recognised his stand with the first award of the *Ritterkreuz* with Oak Leaves to a non-German. During the day Antonescu had at last solicited Hitler's permission for the Lascar Group to break out, but by the time Hitler acceded on the morning of 23 November its fate was already sealed. Lascar's second-in-command at 6th Division, General Stanescu, continued to resist throughout that day and into the evening of 24 November from the prepared defences on the division's original front around Raspopinskaia. The fact that this last resistance on 3rd Army's initial line took place at virtually the only point where its defences were on the River Don is an indicator of how valuable the river line might have been if fully in 3rd Army's hands. Even at this late stage, 30 artillerymen managed to walk out carrying their battery's rangefinders. Romanian aerial reconnaissance still detected isolated pockets of resistance on 25 November, but none the next day. About 27,000 men were captured in the pocket.

On 3rd Army's left flank the demoralisation of the remains of 9th Infantry Division, fleeing behind the River Kriushka, and II Corps, reassembling the survivors of 14th Infantry and 7th Cavalry Divisions behind the River Chir, was almost complete. They were driven from both river lines by comparatively weak Soviet spearheads. Fortunately the belated arrival the German XVII Corps (62, 294) of General Hollidt over the following days prevented the Soviets exploiting these opportunities and surrounding I Corps against the Don. Hollidt was given command of the Romanian I and II Corps and the German XLVIII Panzer Corps and XVII Corps on the upper Chir-Kriushka-Don line, and ordered to hold those rivers at all costs. Dumitrescu's 3rd Army retained command of the remains of IV and V Corps and took over such German forces as could be scraped together on the lower Chir.

23 November

For 15th Division's breakout, General Sion organised an advance guard of an anti-tank battalion, two artillery batteries and a mounted reconnaissance platoon. Behind it followed his two surviving infantry regiments and an artillery regiment. Because of the length of its original front, 15th Division's column stretched over 12km, and when the huge horde of stragglers descended on it from Golovski it might have reached back 30km. 15th Division cleanly broke contact with the Soviets that night, and by first light its spearhead had managed to cross the River Zariza. However, the ice broke as the first heavy equipment began to follow across. At that moment the Soviet 119th Rifle Division and some tanks, which had taken Korotovski and Zhirkovski during the night, fell on the stranded rear of the column. It fled south, but was forced to surrender on the evening of 23 November. Some 3,160 stragglers of IV and V Corps escaped south across the Chir over the next few days.

Sion's advance guard (which the Soviets flatteringly claimed contained 30 tanks!) pressed on westwards, ambushing six Dodge trucks full of Soviet infantry en route. The three still-serviceable vehicles captured were loaded with Romanian wounded. Late that morning Sion broke through to Bolshaia Donschinka and made contact with 22nd Panzer Division; 3,680 men, 18 trucks, 1,045 horses and two guns had escaped. The Germans ordered Sion to assume the defence of Bolshaia Donschinka, supported by some German anti-tank guns. In taking up these positions, 200 Soviets were flushed out of the houses and taken prisoner. Soviet attacks were repulsed during the afternoon and evening, the German gunners knocking out five tanks and the Romanian infantry mowing down their supporting infantry.

By 23 November, 1st Armoured Division was down to 50 per cent of its combat strength and very low on fuel. This forced it to attack due westwards by the shortest route towards its depots behind Cernishevskaia. However, the Soviet 112th Cavalry

Division, 179th AT Artillery Regiment and 511th Tank Flamethrower Regiment had been redeployed around Krasnoiarovka precisely to foil such an attempt, and 1st Armoured Division was repulsed. Seven R-2s were lost to mechanical failure, and nineteen without fuel had to be set on fire and abandoned. Only one tank appears to have been lost to enemy fire, and only two Soviet tanks were claimed. However, the Soviets had also suffered some losses, including 61 taken prisoner, and did little to interfere with 1st Armoured Division as it withdrew south of the Kurtlak River and regrouped north of Oserski.

The division now had only eleven PzKpfw IIIs and IVs and nineteen R-2s, many of the latter under tow by the former owing to mechanical failure or fuel shortage. Fortunately it was spotted by an IAR.39 returning from a failed attempt to contact the Lascar Group, and communication was re-established with 3rd Army, which was using Romanian staff officers and German liaison officers to scrape together a defence behind the nearby River Chir.

24 November

During the night of 23/24 November the German anti-tank guns were withdrawn from Bolshaia Donschinka without General Sion's knowledge. As a result, attacks by elements of 346th Rifle Division and 8th Guards Tank Brigade the next morning caused heavy losses among the Romanian infantry, which was now short of even small-arms ammunition. The Soviet tanks only withdrew once their supporting infantry had been shot down in a counterattack by 15th Division's HQ staff and German liaison staff. Urgent support was requested from 22nd Panzer Division, but it did not arrive and Sion set out personally for 22nd Panzer Division's HQ. However, Bolshaia Donschinka was now surrounded, and he is presumed to have been killed during the 3.5km journey.

At 1100 a German reconnaissance company at last reached Bolshaia Donschinka and the 800 shattered survivors of the Romanian garrison fled into 22nd Panzer Division's perimeter. During the breakout of 22nd Panzer Division, which began on the night of 24/25 November, they were mounted on 35 stray trucks of 1st Armoured Division, which had also reached the German perimeter. The escape of 22nd Panzer Division was much assisted by the fact that 1st Armoured Division had drawn most of 8th Cavalry Corps on itself.

During the night of 23/24 November a fuel column got through to 1st Armoured Division from 3rd Army, and the following morning more fuel was air-landed. The partly resupplied division was then ordered to attack north towards Medvezhii to help release 22nd Panzer Division from encirclement. However, the Soviet 8th Cavalry Corps (55th and 112th Cavalry Divisions) and a strong column of tanks attacked it from the north, and it was forced to retreat further south towards Osinovski, where FARR and Stuka support enabled it to halt the Soviets. Its own losses were almost 400 men, two panzers, six AT guns and 59 motor vehicles. Soviet sources attest to their own heavy losses on this day, which reportedly exceeded 2,100 men, 52 motor vehicles and 20 artillery pieces, most to air attack. On the night of 24/25 November 1st Armoured Division was able to break contact with 8th Cavalry Corps cleanly and cross the River Chir.

25-26 November

8th Cavalry Corps was now ordered south to take the German airfield at Oblivskaia, but between 26 November and 3 December it was frustrated by a single battalion of 6th Division's 15th Dorobanţi Regiment, backed by intense Luftwaffe support. This was the only formed unit of the Lascar Group to break out southwards, and its commander, Major Rasconescu, became the most junior non-German recipient of the *Ritterkreuz*.

Meanwhile, across the Chir, 3rd Army hurriedly resupplied 1st Armoured Division before rushing it north to mount another counterattack, this time engaging the 21st Cavalry and 47th Guards Rifle Divisions, which had established bridgeheads across the Chir around Chernishevskaia. It at last met 22nd Panzer Division and the remains of Sion's 15th Division there on 26 November. The much-reduced XLVIII Panzer Corps and II Corps (7C, 14) now set about re-establishing a front on the River Chir.

1st Armoured Regiment now had only nine PzKpfw IIIs and IVs and nineteen R-2s serviceable. 1st Motorised Artillery Regiment's two battalions had lost little manpower, and had preserved eleven of their twelve 100mm Skoda howitzers and eight of their twelve Schneider 105mm guns. The Reconnaissance Group and Pioneer Battalion had virtually no serviceable equipment, the AT Battalion had only two 75mm and two 47mm AT guns remaining, and the AA Company had only two 20mm guns. 3rd and 4th Motorised Rifle Regiments were down to one very weak battalion each. The division had lost 70 per cent of its combat strength.

1st Armoured Division lost a further 26 dead, 208 wounded and 250 frostbite cases between 27 November and 1 December while it and 22nd Panzer Division destroyed several small Soviet bridgeheads across the Chir established earlier by 8th Cavalry Corps. Fourteen anti-tank guns and over 50 prisoners were captured, and 690 Soviet dead were claimed on the battlefield. As a result, II Corps (7C, 14) was able to return to the river line. The newly-arrived German XVII Corps (62, 294) re-established the line on the River Kriushka between 25 and 28 November. I Corps' 11th and 7th Divisions counterattacked Dubovski seven times in late November and early December, but were repeatedly repulsed. Their 1,500 casualties were bearable, but the confidence gained by earlier defensive successes was undermined.

By 2 December, 1st Armoured Division was reduced to only three serviceable tanks, its combatant manpower being only 944 officers and men. Nearly 5,000 men had been lost, but its support elements, which had remained safely behind the Chir, were still 6,335 strong. Its irrecoverable vehicle losses since 19 November were 77 R-2s, five T-3s, seven T–4s, the two captured Russian tanks, 457 all-wheel-drive trucks and 335 motorcycles. On 4 December its surviving combat elements on the Chir were formed into a detachment under Colonel Nistor, the experienced commander of 3rd Motorised Rifle Regiment, while General Gherghe, the division's commander, took over II Corps. Four repaired tanks were returned that day, and they were reinforced in early December by one R-2 and 700 men from the Armoured Division's depots in Romania. On 6 December the 993rd Independent Infantry Battalion, a security unit, was also subordinated to the Nistor Detachment.

By 8 December, 3rd Army, exclusive of its troops encircled in Stalingrad, had been reduced to 83,000 men, of whom only 36,000 were combat troops. The Soviets announced the capture of 37,000 others. Although only 5 per cent of their combat troops escaped, about half of the rear services personnel of IV (13, 1C, 15) and V Corps (5, 6) and much of their meagre motor transport had got away, not only indicating a collapse in rear echelon morale, but suggesting that an early breakout by the Lascar Group had had considerable prospect of success.

THE SOVIET COUNTEROFFENSIVE ON 4TH ARMY, NOVEMBER 1942

20 November

On 20 November the Romanian presence south of Stalingrad consisted of five infantry and two cavalry divisions. They now had only 75,380 of the 101,875 men with which they had begun the campaign, and although they were part of 4th Panzer Army they had no Germans in immediate reserve. General Constantin Constantinescu's 4th Army HQ was due to take over command of VI Corps (1, 2, 18, 4) and VII Corps (5C, 8C) from 4th Panzer Army on 21 November, but it lacked a mobile reserve beyond the recently-arrived 6th Motorised Roşiori (1,074 men and 120 vehicles) at Plodovitoye. On 9 November, therefore, Antonescu ordered 8th Cavalry Division to be formed into a motorised division under the newly-promoted General Radu Korne by exchanging its two horsed regiments for the motorised regiments of 5th and 6th Cavalry Divisions.

However, these transfers had yet to be effected when the southern arm of the Soviet Stalingrad counteroffensive struck the weakest divisions of VI Corps on 20 November. Stalingrad Front had managed to assemble nine rifle divisions, a fortified region, a cavalry corps and two mechanised corps with 397 tanks against the seven Romanian divisions. The designated breakthrough sectors were on the 30km and 18km fronts of 1st and 2nd Infantry Divisions, where all the armour and cavalry were concentrated. Casualties had forced these two divisions to amalgamate their infantry battalions, so they had only five and four respectively, all at the front. Consequently they only had the density of an outpost line.

Three rifle divisions, followed by 4th Mechanised Corps and 4th Cavalry Corps, crashed through the left wing of 1st Division and the right wing of 18th Division at dawn on 20 November and reached Plodovitoye in the early afternoon. To oppose them there remained only 6th Roşiori, 2nd Mechanised Squadron and a motorised Schneider 105mm artillery battery from VI Corps. These put in a hopeless counterattack, during which part of 6th Roşiori was surrounded and annihilated. Fortunately Soviet intelligence appears to have duplicated this collection of trucks and handful of R-1s into two separate mixed tank/infantry regiments. When 4th Mechanised Corps' three tank brigades ran into a rare Romanian minefield and lost 50 tanks on the first day, these two factors combined to impose a degree of caution on its command, and it lost momentum. Firm orders from the Soviet command were needed to hurry it north on 21 November.

Further north, two-and-a-half rifle divisions broke into the positions of 2nd Division towards Tinguta Station during the morning, and 13th Mechanised Corps

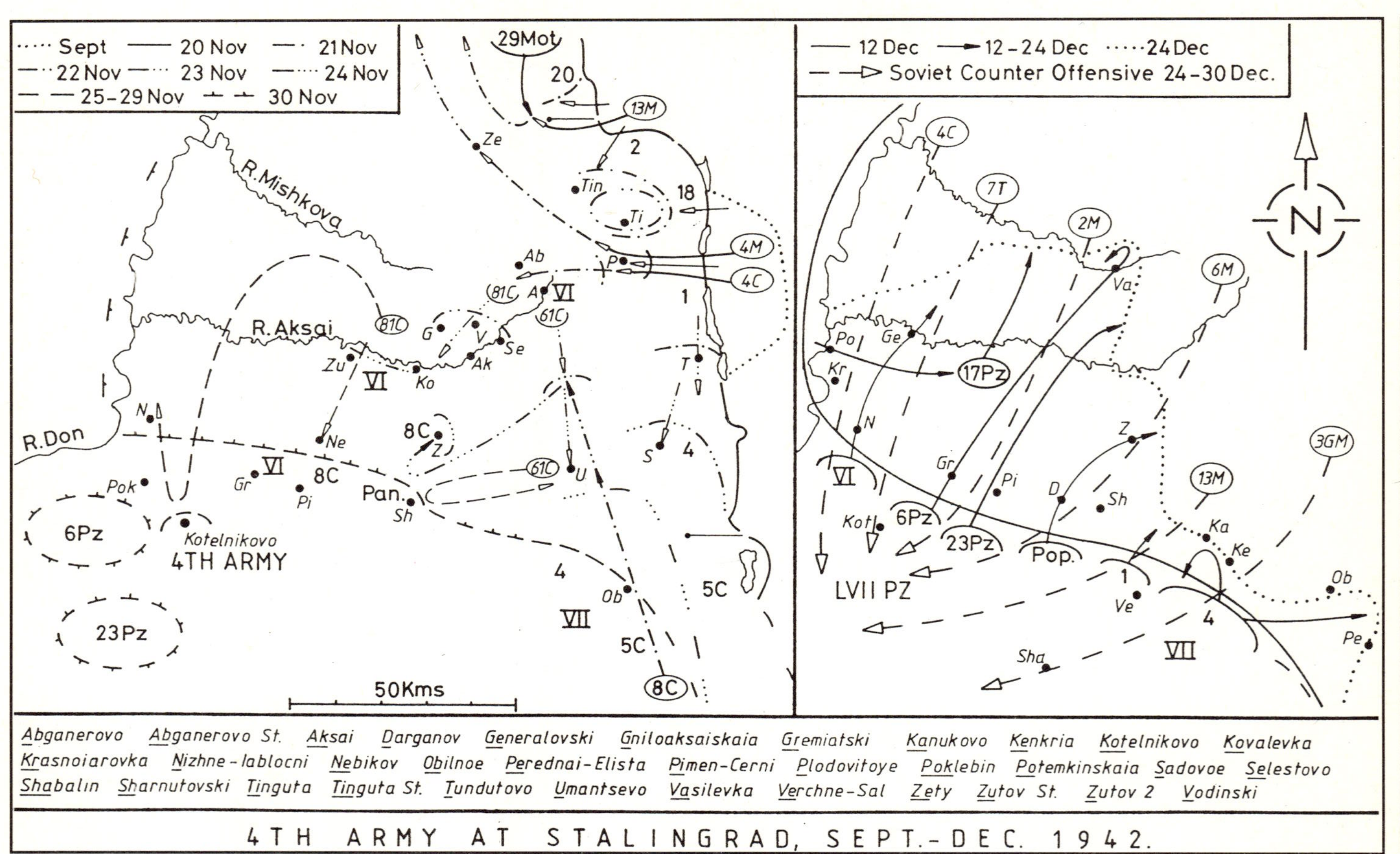

4TH ARMY AT STALINGRAD, SEPT.-DEC. 1942.

was released into the breach during the afternoon. This formation outflanked 20th Division to its north and overran its right wing. During the late afternoon the German 29th Motorised Division counterattacked with 55 medium tanks and inflicted considerable losses on 13th Mechanised Corps, rescuing the right wing of 20th Division in the process. However, it was then ordered by Paulus to defend the southern flank of 6th Army, leaving 13th and 4th Mechanised Corps to continue the encirclement of 6th Army largely unopposed and 4th Army completely unsupported.

General Korne and most of 8th Cavalry Division (4th Roşiori, 3rd Motorised Calaraşi, a battalion of 2nd Horse Artillery Regt and four motorised 105mm guns) were rushed north towards Aksai to provide a mobile reserve for VI Corps. From 20 November to late December this left only 2nd Calaraşi Regiment to cover over 80km of front between 5th Cavalry Division (to which it was subordinated on 27 November) and the German 16th Motorised Division at Elista. It performed this lonely task so successfully that its commander, Colonel Hristea, received the *Ritterkreuz*.

21 November

The situation of VI and VII Corps was already so catastrophic that General Constantinescu's 4th Army HQ was never able to take over operational control of them from 4th Panzer Army. The earlier supply difficulties had led almost immediately to a shortage of munitions and fuel. During the day the Soviet 13th Mechanised Corps swung north towards Kalach, and following rifle divisions gradually forced 20th Division into the Stalingrad perimeter. 4th Mechanised Corps also swung north to Zety, surrounding the bulk of 18th and 2nd Divisions between Tinguta and Tinguta Station. They were largely destroyed by following rifle divisions during the next day.

Meanwhile 4th Cavalry Corps (81C, 61C), three rifle divisions (126, 302, 91), 76th Fortified Region and an independent tank brigade exploited south and westwards. Early on 21 November, 4th Cavalry Corps drove VI Corps' HQ from Abganerovo, taking 600 prisoners, and dug in there until joined by 126th Rifle Division the following day. This gave time for VI Corps HQ to assemble the remains of 6th Rosiori Regiment, 1st, 2nd and 18th Infantry Divisions to defend Gniloaksaiskaia, Vodinski and Seletsovo south-west of Abganerovo, and to be joined by a small group of tanks and assault guns purloined by 4th Army's German liaison officers from 4th Panzer Army's rear workshops.

The only still-intact elements of VI Corps outside the developing encirclement were now the southernmost regiment of 1st Division around Tundutovo, which swung its front round to face north and repulsed local attacks, and 4th Division, which was not attacked. Both were taken under command by VII Corps, which reinforced Tundutovo with its meagre corps reserves. 5th Cavalry Division and 2nd Calaraşi Regiment remained only lightly attacked.

22 November

Between Tundutovo and Vodinski there now yawned a large gap, through which the Soviet 61st Cavalry Division began to drive south on the morning of 22 November. 8th Cavalry Division made contact with it in the early afternoon. Although the presence of a small amount of Soviet armour inflicted heavy early losses on 4th Roşiori, no decisive advantage was gained by either side over the next 24hr. However, further east Tundutovo was captured from 1st Division in the early afternoon by 91st Rifle Division after a morning of heavy fighting.

On the night of 22/23 November the Soviet 81st Cavalry Division and 126th Rifle Divisions captured Gniloaksaiskaia, Vodinski, Seletsovo and Aksai against stubborn but brief resistance, and the remnants of VI Corps were withdrawn south of the River Aksai to a more tenable line between Zutov Station and Kovalevka.

23 November

On 23 November, 4th Division was attacked energetically by 91st Rifle Division and 76th Fortified Region for the first time. Outflanked by the loss of Tundutovo the previous day, it began to fall back, offering stiff resistance around Sadovoe. 8th Cavalry Division continued to resist 61st Cavalry Division, but by late in the day it was outflanked to both east and west by the earlier Soviet successes at Tundutovo and Aksai. It hurriedly fell back south-west to Zutov 2, losing some of its artillery in the process. 1st, 2nd and 18th Divisions received an induction of inexperienced troops from their march battalions on the Aksai River line, but were not heavily pressed.

General Constantinescu was inclined to withdraw all Romanian units into a close perimeter around Kotelnikovo to avoid the continued infiltration of their overextended front by Soviet cavalry, but 4th Panzer Army ordered them to hold on to the most advanced positions possible, because it was from this direction that Manstein proposed to mount his drive to relieve 6th Army in Stalingrad.

24 November

The retreat of 8th Cavalry Division left the way clear for the Soviet 61st Cavalry and 91st Rifle Divisions to capture Umantsevo from the left wing of 4th Infantry Division on 24 November, causing it to fall back further. Another opportunist Soviet thrust threatened the link between 4th Infantry and 5th Cavalry Divisions, causing the latter to fall back in conformity.

25-30 November

The Soviet 51st Army now planned to take Kotelnikovo in a pincer movement which entailed 126th and 302nd Rifle Divisions frontally attacking VI Corps across the River Aksai while 81st Cavalry Division outflanked it from the west and 61st Cavalry Division outflanked 8th Cavalry Division from the east. 91st Rifle Division and 76th Fortified Region were to maintain pressure on VII Corps.

However, at Sharnutovski on 26 November the Soviet 61st Cavalry Division ran headlong into the approaching German Pannwitz Detachment (a mixed battalion of German motorised and tank troops and a motorised Romanian heavy artillery battery). In a combined counterattack with the Pannwitz Detachment, 8th Cavalry Division took more than 500 prisoners, ten anti-tank guns and a field artillery battery, and drove 61st Cavalry Division back into Umantsevo. With its flank thus secured, 4th Infantry Division was able to dig in around Obilnoe. On 27 November Korne's 8th Cavalry Division took over the remains of his old 6th Roşiori Regiment, which had suffered 65 per cent casualties, from VI Corps, and thus at last became largely motorised.

On the western flank, 81st Cavalry Division reached Kotelnikovo early on 27 November but was emphatically repulsed by the German-Romanian garrison. The Germans withdrew motorised troops from supporting VI Corps in an effort to surround 81st Cavalry Division near Poklebin on 28 November, but it escaped to Nizhne-Iablocni. Thus weakened, VI Corps lost the Aksai river line to 126th and 302nd Rifle Divisions, which reached Nebikov on the 29th. This outflanked 8th Cavalry Division, which fell back from Zutov 2 to Pimen Cerni, where it held 126th Rifle Division. VI Corps dug in at Gremiaski Station, facing 302nd Rifle Division. Thanks largely to the intervention of the leading elements of 6th Panzer Division, the front now began to stabilise.

THE DESTRUCTION OF 3RD ARMY, DECEMBER 1942

In December 1942 and January 1943 the Italian 8th Army and Hungarian 2nd Army were to suffer similar defeats to those endured by 3rd and 4th Romanian Armies in November 1942, and were immediately withdrawn from operations. However, during December 1942 the remains of 3rd and 4th Romanian Armies, with a strength equivalent to about six or seven divisions, still held long sections of front, tying down the equivalent of about seven or eight Soviet divisions, and would require the deployment of further Soviet forces before they could be dislodged. That they still had a valuable operational role to play was a testament to Antonescu's stronger political commitment to the war in the east. However, it was to expose his troops to a second and conclusive disaster.

26th Tank Corps from the north and 4th Mechanised Corps from the south had completed the encirclement of the German 6th Army at Kalach on 22 November. Hitler ordered 6th Army to hold fast, and General von Manstein was ordered to effect its relief with Army Group Don, comprising a heavily reinforced 4th Panzer Army, Army Detachment Hollidt and the remains of 3rd and 4th Romanian Armies. He inherited the embryonic staff prepared for Antonescu, and took effective command on 27/28 November. 3rd Army HQ was given command of the lower Chir, but this was largely notional. Almost all of its troops were German, and General Dumitrescu had only theoretical operational control, being primarily engaged in organising *ad hoc* formations from Romanian stragglers and the army's rear echelons. These, the remains of IV and V Corps, retained barely 5 per cent of their combat value. Amongst Dumitrescu's German subordinates was a certain Colonel Stahel of the Luftwaffe, who was to be tasked by Hitler with the capture of Bucharest 21 months later.

I, II and the German XVII Corps were subordinated to the German-commanded Army Detachment Hollidt on the Don-Kriushka-Upper Chir line. Of its Romanian formations, only I Corps' 7th and 11th Infantry Divisions were largely intact. I Corps' 9th Infantry Division, which had lost a third of its manpower and over two-thirds of its heavy weapons, had to be braced by a German regiment from 62nd Division. II Corps' 7th Cavalry had retained less than 30 per cent of its combat strength, and 14th Infantry Division little more than 5 per cent, but they were supported by the remains of 22nd Panzer Division and 1st Armoured Division, which still exhibited some offensive potential. By 8 December the Nistor Detach-

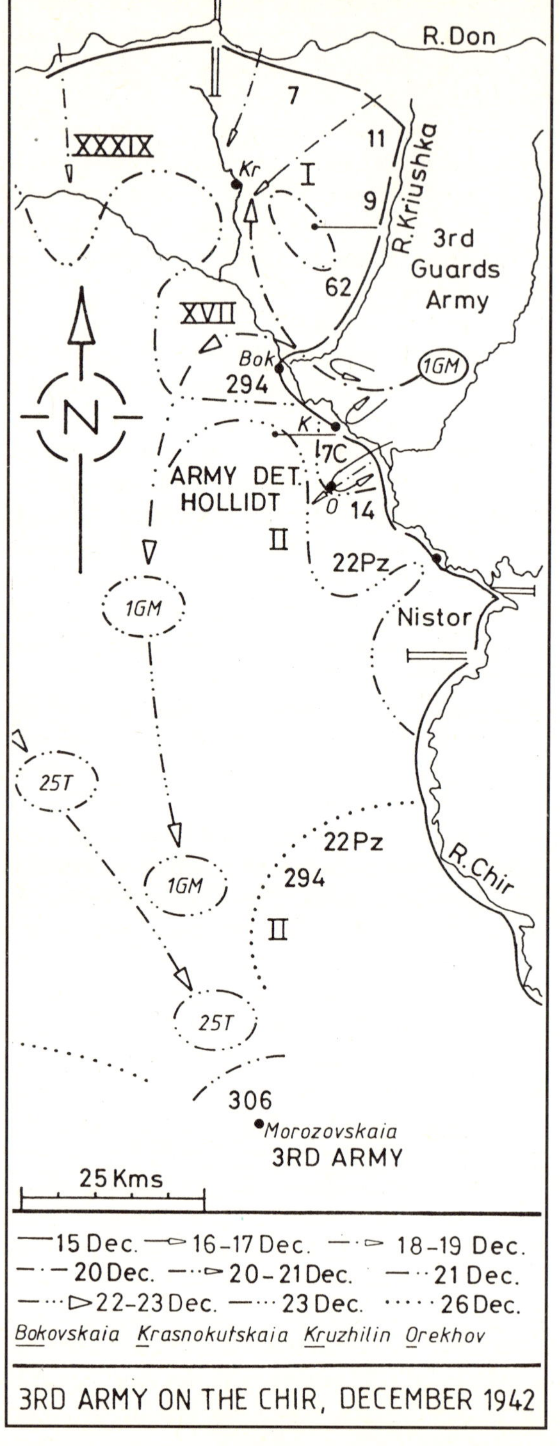

3RD ARMY ON THE CHIR, DECEMBER 1942

ment again had eight serviceable and twelve disabled tanks. On 12 December ten unspecified armoured vehicles (probably SdKfz 222 armoured cars) were belatedly received by its reconnaissance group, and on 19 December eight half-tracks were also delivered, probably SdKfz 251s.

The newly-introduced 3rd Guards Army, whose front coincided almost exactly with that of Army Detachment Hollidt's, began its offensive across the Chir on 16 December. It contained eight rifle divisions, a mechanised corps and several independent tank units, totalling 110,000 men and 234 tanks. Its main weight fell on the German XVII Corps at Bokovskaia and Krasnokutskaia, but it was repulsed virtually everywhere. Romanian units of II Corps joined 22nd Panzer Division in counterattacks at Krasnokutskaia. 50th Guards Rifle Division managed to cross the Chir on II Corps' sector, but was immediately pinned down. Throughout the following day 3rd Guards Army continued to make little progress on its main axis. 50th Guards Rifle Division managed to take Orekhov on 17 December, but was driven out by a II Corps counterattack. The Nistor Detachment's front-line strength gradually rose to 1,587 men on 17 December, despite the loss of ten dead and 46 wounded in repulsing 50th Guards Rifle Division's probes across the Chir and 341 men from frostbite.

Army Detachment Hollidt's position was finally undermined on 18 December, when the Italian XXIX Corps on I Corps' left, which had the Soviet 25th Tank Corps operating deep in its rear, began to fall back. Simultaneously, the Germans lost Bokovskaia to 1st Guards Mechanised Corps. Hollidt ordered I Corps to hold fast but, mindful of the fate of the Lascar Group under similar circumstances, it began to withdraw. 7th Division was promptly attacked by 278th Rifle Division and a tank brigade. The 197th Rifle Division also immediately set off in close pursuit of 11th Division.

The speed of Soviet mechanised operations in its rear outpaced I Corps' flight, and 1st Guards Mechanised Corps met 197th Rifle Division near Kruzhilin on 19 December, surrounding the bulk of 11th and 9th Divisions and the neighbouring German 62nd Division, most of which were effectively annihilated over the next couple of days. 7th Division's rearguard was overwhelmed in Kruzhilin on 20 November. One regiment of 7th Division, which managed to retreat 80km westwards to Alekseevo with its full weaponry, was obliged to surrender on 21 December after a determined effort to break through 35th Guards Rifle Division. Of I Corps, only elements of 7th Division escaped south in significant numbers.

To support the breakthrough at Bokovskaia, the Soviet 50th Guards Rifle Division continued to attack II Corps' front, advancing slightly to take Fomin on 19 December. General Gherghe's inclination was to withdraw II Corps before it too was surrounded, but on being inaccurately informed that Soviet armour was already in his rear he followed Hollidt's orders to hang on on the Chir, even mounting a successful local counterattack on 19 December. The Nistor Detachment killed or captured over 400 Soviets during this period, with little loss to itself. II Corps' stand did much to prevent the hard-pressed German 294th Infantry Division to its north being surrounded.

On 22 December the Chir line had to be abandoned because 1st Guards Mechanised Corps and 5th Tank Corps were deep in the Axis rear, and the remains of Army Detachment Hollidt began to retreat hurriedly southwards towards Morozovskaia, where 3rd Army was still in nominal command of German forces on the lower Chir. Fortunately both Soviet corps were now at the limits of their endurance and had lost momentum when they ran into the newly-arrived German 306th Infantry Division. This allowed II Corps and the German 22nd Panzer and 294th Infantry Divisions time to escape. Nevertheless, the remains of 7th Cavalry and 14th Infantry Divisions lost their residual cohesion.

Only the Nistor Detachment retained significant fighting value. During the retreat it lost five field guns, three AT guns and 42 motor vehicles on 23 December and three tanks on the following day, but still had a sting in its tail. On 26 December it turned on the 1st Guards Mechanised Corps' 22nd Guards Motorised Rifle Brigade, and inflicted on it the loss of two tanks, two armoured cars, ten anti-tank guns, 27 motor vehicles, 480 dead and 187 taken prisoner at a cost of two tanks and 206 dead, wounded and missing. This was the last significant combat by the remains of 3rd Army at Stalingrad, and it was withdrawn from the front in late December as more German units arrived to stabilise the front before Morozovskaia.

The Nistor Detachment had to abandon four more tanks with mechanical failure as it broke contact over 28-31 December. On 1 January, 1st Armoured Division crossed the Donets at Novoshakhtiuk and passed out of the operational zone. At this time it still had 6,646 officers and men (the vast majority from its non-combatant tail), 40 tanks (mostly unserviceable R-2s held in rear workshops), six armoured cars and half-tracks, 33 field guns and howitzers, 27 mostly light AT guns and 797 motor vehicles. 1st Armoured Regiment had lost 81 R-2s (30 from lack of fuel, 24 from mechanical failure and 27 knocked out by the enemy), ten PzKpfw IVs and ten PzKpfw IIIs. By 31 March 1943 all of 1st Armoured Division was back in its depots in Romania. Total R-1 losses of the four cavalry divisions at Stalingrad were fourteen, while the infantry divisions had lost 42 Malaxa chenillettes.

By Stalingrad, the bulk of 1st Armoured Division's tanks and anti-tank guns were obsolete, and there was no time for the various PzKpfw III and IV tanks, SdKfz 222 armoured cars, SdKfz 251 armoured half-tracks, and Pak 40 75mm and Pak 38 50mm anti-tank guns delivered to be properly integrated. Despite this, the division inflicted considerable (though doubtless somewhat exaggerated) damage on several Soviet armoured, infantry and cavalry formations, prevented the encirclement of the Lascar Group for three days in temperatures averaging below -20°C, and might have been able to rescue parts of it but for Hitler's stand fast order.

Many of 1st Armoured Division's 60 per cent losses among its combat elements between 20 and 25 November were subsequently attributed to the inability of the infantry's and specialists' unarmoured and trackless 4WD trucks to follow the tanks closely when under fire or in the difficult terrain conditions experienced. This frequently forced both to fight unsupported. Despite its losses, 1st Armoured Division remained a cohesive force when it broke out across the River Chir, and was able to perform a role in holding the river line over the following month. Even when forced to abandon the Chir line, the division still had sufficient strength and morale to mount a very effective local counterattack on 26 December.

1st Armoured Division was let down primarily by its obsolete equipment, aggravated by the tardiness of German deliveries of modern weaponry and inadequate

German operational support. However, the debilitated condition of 22nd Panzer Division, which did what it could to support 1st Armoured Division, is illustrative of the severe armour shortages that prevented the Germans from releasing new equipment to their allies in 1942, even if the political will had existed. The best appreciation of XLVIII Panzer Corps' achievement was offered by the Soviets, who conceded that its resistance had turned the annihilation of the Lascar group from a planned three-day operation into a five-day battle. Unfortunately the German high command was quite unable to take advantage of the 48hr grace its sacrifice earned.

THE DESTRUCTION OF 4TH ARMY, DECEMBER 1942

From early December, 4th Army's mission was to cover the assembly of the German LVII Panzer Corps (6Pz, 23Pz). Opposing it were three rifle divisions (302, 126, 91), 61st Cavalry Division and 76th Fortified Region of the Soviet 51st Army. In VI Corps' 1st, 2nd and 18th Divisions only 20 per cent of the personnel had survived, of whom only a third were combat troops. Only VII Corps' 4th Infantry and 5th and 8th Cavalry Divisions were still capable of active operations. 4th Division retained about 30 per cent of its combat strength. 5th Cavalry Division had lost only about 5 per cent of its strength on 19 November, including all of 2nd Mechanised Squadron's five R-1s. 8th Cavalry Division had lost some 15 per cent. The army's front was far from continuous, and much of it had to be covered by unsupported artillery batteries with nothing between them and the Soviet lines.

On 3 December the Soviet 51st Army tried to capture Kotelnikovo by repeating its earlier pincer operation, in the hope of disrupting the assembly of LVII Panzer Corps. 8th Cavalry Division and VI Corps were assaulted by 126th and 302nd Rifle Divisions and driven back from Pimen-Cerni and Gremiatski Station in heavy fighting, but the front was stabilised just to the south with the support of the Pannwitz Detachment on 5 December. 4th Division lost Obilnoe to 91st Rifle Division and 61st Cavalry Division at the same time, but they advanced no further. On 8 December 4th Army retained about 39,000 men, of whom barely 12,000 were combat troops.

Operation Wintergewitter, the attempt of LVII Panzer Corps to relieve 6th Army in Stalingrad, began on 12 December. For the task it had 230 tanks and self-propelled guns. That LVII Panzer Corps at least partly caught the Soviets by surprise must in some measure be attributed to the presence, if not always the performance, of the screen of Romanian covering units which had obscured the state of German preparations. Although LVII Panzer Corps burst through 302nd Rifle Division and reached the River Aksai within a day, it took another six days of heavy fighting and the loss of 173 tanks to reach the River Mishkova on 19 December.

Of 4th Army, only 18th Infantry Division, which had been covering the assembly of 6th Panzer Division, took a light offensive role on 12 December, participating in the capture of Gremiatski Station. Under the cover of Wintergewitter, 4th Army had its first chance to rest and reorganise its troops, and the remains of 18th, 1st and 2nd Divisions were taken out of the line to regroup around Kotelnikovo. VI Corps was given the task of covering the left flank of LVII Panzer Corps up to the River

Don. On 15 December its corps troops relieved elements of 6th Panzer Division which had taken Nizhne Iablocni. On the next day 18th Division arrived and occupied Krasnoiarovka, followed by Potemkinskaia and its bridge over the Don on 17 December. This allowed 17th Panzer Division to cross the Don and join LVII Panzer Corps with 44 more tanks.

On 19 December VI Corps reached Generalovski on the River Aksai, and by the time 2nd Division was added to its strength on 22 December it had established a bridgehead across the river. Despite its title, VI Corps was still little stronger than a brigade, and its advance was only possible because the Soviet 81st Cavalry Division opposite it had been outflanked by LVII Panzer Corps and fell back, offering only light resistance.

To provide a Romanian mobile formation to support the Germans, two regiments of 5th Cavalry Division were shifted from the eastern flank to join 8th Cavalry Division and the Pannwitz Detachment. Under 5th Division's General Popescu, who was senior to Korne, they were combined into the Popescu Cavalry Group. After a couple of days reorganising, the group took Darganov on 14 December and pushed on to take Zutov 2 from 126th Rifle Division and 61st Cavalry Division on the 18th, capturing two tanks in the process. On that day Radu Korne received a well-deserved *Ritterkreuz*.

On 15 December VII Corps (4th Infantry Division and a right flank guard of one regiment of 5th Cavalry Division) began its attack, capturing a number of small localities from 91st Rifle Division north of Verchne-Sal in what the Soviets described as especially violent fighting. On 20-22 December it launched heavy assaults on both Kenkria and Kanukovo, but without success. On the latter day the returning 1st Infantry Division took over positions on VII Corps' left flank, allowing VII Corps to shift its attack further east, and on 24 December the Soviet 76th Fortified Region was complaining that its strongpoints between Obilnoe and Perednaia-Elista had been surrounded in a hard battle. Insignificant though it was, this small Romanian success was the last offensive move by the Axis forces towards Stalingrad.

On 22 December LVII Panzer Corps had made a final effort and crossed the River Mishkova at Vasilevka, but on 23 December its attack had to be abandoned owing to its own losses and the Soviet breakthrough of the Italian 8th Army and Army Detachment Hollidt, which threatened the Stalingrad relief forces' left flank. On the following day the Red Army began a counteroffensive against LVII Panzer Corps and 4th Army with 149,000 men and 635 tanks, the bulk of which were directed at the vulnerable Romanian flank guards. On 24 December the Popescu Cavalry Group was driven from Zutov 2 by 6th Mechanised Corps, and after two days of resistance was virtually destroyed at Sharnutovski. On 25 December VI Corps' right wing was overrun by tanks of 7th Tank Corps, and the following day the rest of the corps began to disintegrate as it fell back before 4th Cavalry Corps.

The Germans ordered 4th Army to hold on to buy time for their own withdrawal, but in an attempt to save its remnants Constantinescu ordered all Romanian units to retreat on the night of 26/27 December, apparently without reference to the Germans. In the face of overwhelming Soviet mechanised forces it was a hopeless gesture, and on the 27th it was the turn of VII Corps to suffer. The remains of 1st Division were scattered by tanks of 13th Mechanised Corps, and 3rd Guards Mechanised Corps crashed through 4th Division, overwhelming its last determined resistance at Shabalin the following day. On 29 December the retreating LVII Panzer Corps lost Kotelnikovo to 7th Tank Corps.

Functionally, 4th Army was destroyed. Von Manstein's later claim that the withdrawal of LVII Panzer Corps was made inevitable by failures in morale and leadership in 4th Army is disingenuous. To expect the remains of 4th Army to hold five Soviet mechanised, tank and cavalry corps which his three panzer divisions had not only failed to defeat, but even to pin down on their front, was unrealistic, even given Romanian morale and leadership of heroic proportions. Soviet post-battle references to violent battles and hard fighting on the fronts of the Popescu Cavalry Group and VII Corps indicate that they at least had made some impact, however limited, on the defending Soviet 51st Army, though the preoccupied Germans were unaware of their activities.

The fact is that neither LVII Panzer Corps nor 4th Army were adequate to the tasks set them. When the Germans allowed them to be withdrawn from combat at the end of December, VI Corps (2, 18) consisted of a weak battalion of infantry and another of artillery, VII Corps (1, 4) had about one battalion of infantry and two of artillery, and the Popescu Cavalry Group (5C, 8C) had two weak squadrons and two horse artillery batteries.

INSIDE STALINGRAD

The agony of 1st Cavalry's and 20th Infantry Division's 12,607 men in Stalingrad endured to the end of January 1943. Believing that 20th Division represented a weak link in the southern perimeter, the Soviets had attacked its 82nd Regiment on 31 November but were firmly repulsed, leaving ten tanks knocked out in the Romanian positions. Further attacks on 3 and 10 December also failed. The Germans awarded more than 50 Iron Crosses for these actions, and the division's commander, General Tataranu, was awarded the *Ritterkreuz* on 17 December.

Fortunately the Romanian infantry and cavalry used the same 7.92mm round as the Germans, and could be kept supplied with small-arms ammunition. However, although the two divisions had reached Stalingrad with half their artillery and anti-tank guns intact, they soon ran out of shells and the Germans, who did not use compatible rounds, had thereafter to be relied on for artillery support. 20th Division's infantry regiments were therefore distributed around the German IV Corps. 1st Cavalry Division's horses were eaten by 6th Army during December, and its personnel were then distributed in combat teams to a variety of German divisions in XIV Panzer Corps.

Regular external contact with 20th Infantry and 1st Cavalry Divisions was lost on 13 January when General Tataranu, an influential former Deputy Chief of the Army Staff and supporter of General Iacobici, flew out of the pocket without authority, to complain to Antonescu that Romanian commanders were being deprived of control of their troops. Antonescu was furious that he had deserted his division, and would have put him before a court martial had Hitler not intervened at the request of General Jaenecke, his German corps commander inside the pocket. The remnant of 20th Division appears to have been kept in the line until 26 January, when it finally collapsed, the day after 6th Army could no longer supply its rations.

Only between two and three thousand Romanians survived to go into captivity. Field Marshal Paulus, the commander of 6th Army, said of them:

> In the circumstances the fighting spirit and leadership displayed by the Romanian units in the army under my command deserve special commendation. With the assistance of heavy weapons of the normal German type issued to them, and thanks to determined leadership by their officers, these troops fought gallantly and showed great steadfastness in the face of all the hardships to which they were subjected.

AFTERMATH

The value of the Romanian armies in late 1942 was that they occupied hundreds of kilometres of front, and so released the German forces needed for the assault on Stalingrad (a fixation of Hitler's which had no military merit) and the drive on the Caucasus oilfields (a more meritorious but equally risky economic goal). In doing so, they also tied down an equivalent number of Soviet divisions away from the decisive struggles waged by the Germans. Had the German attack on Stalingrad succeeded, or even been so threatening as to draw in all Soviet reserves, then 3rd and 4th Armies might never have been seriously threatened, and 6th Army would not have been lost. However, the Germans had badly overreached themselves and seriously underestimated Soviet strength. As a result, the Red Army was able to assemble overwhelming force against both 3rd and 4th Armies.

By contrast, between August and November 1942 the Romanians had correctly perceived both the strategic and tactical dangers of their situation, had fully informed the Germans of their fears in good time and had even proposed practical solutions. However, the Germans believed that the Romanians were congenitally alarmist and responded with too little support too late. Antonescu then found that he had surrendered too much control of his army to the Germans and was consequently powerless to take independent action to redeem the situation.

The actions that ensued between the Red Army and Romanian Army in October, November and December showed generally consistent results. The fresh Romanian Echelon II infantry divisions of 3rd Army were usually capable of holding Soviet infantry assaults, even when these were accompanied by support tanks, but the exhausted and overextended Echelon I infantry divisions of 4th Army were usually no longer able to do so. Romanian cavalry divisions performed similarly to Echelon II infantry divisions when used in a static role.

However, neither the infantry nor the cavalry divisions were constitutionally capable of holding the decisive medium and heavy tank assaults of Soviet mechanised and tank corps. Only 1st Armoured Division could do so, but it was itself constitutionally incapable of counterattacking them effectively. 22nd Panzer Division proved equally limited. Nevertheless, most Soviet armoured corps commanders were highly nervous of their flanks. On 20 November this lack of confidence almost paralysed the outer arms of both their northern and southern attacks, and 1st and 26th Tank Corps and 4th Mechanised Corps all had to be leaned on heavily by their army and front commanders before they would complete the decisive penetrations that surrounded 6th Army. The mere action of driving 200km through the Romanian defences imposed such heavy attrition in breakdowns, quite apart from battle losses, on Soviet armoured formations that they were often reduced to only a third of their initial tank strength. This factor forced the Red Army to take any armoured offensive against the Romanian forces seriously, and might have proved a fatal flaw had the Germans retained a significant armoured reserve near Stalingrad. Unfortunately, neither 14th Panzer Division nor 29th Motorised Division proved capable of dealing effectively with the inner arms of the Soviet offensive.

Only against Soviet cavalry, an arm in rapid decline, could more have been reasonably expected of Romanian troops. That the lightly-armed Soviet cavalry corps proved effective in the exploitation phase, when they used their mobility to lever Romanian HQ staffs and rear echelons out of settlements which could have been held with more determination, was largely due to the early collapse of Romanian rear morale, provoked by the tank and mechanised corps. This was compounded by the fact that the fast-moving Soviet cavalry had no facility to hold prisoners and tended to massacre them. Soviet cavalry usually drove back Romanian cavalry because numbers, the availability of some armour, and the strategic initiative were in their favour, but failed to defeat them conclusively. Moreover, Soviet cavalry suffered disproportionately heavy losses on the occasions they ran up against a solid defence, and never played such a prominent role in the war again.

There was a clear weakening of German control over Romanian forces between November and December. In November Romanian commanders had usually grudgingly accepted German demands that they hold on to the most advanced positions possible – with the consequent loss of the Lascar Group, but the relief of I Corps. However, by late December they were increasingly ignoring similar instructions, and all of the major surviving Romanian formations undertook, or attempted to undertake, unauthorised withdrawals in order to avoid a similar fate; not that this did I, VI and VII Corps much good. This seems to have reflected a shift in the collective attitude of the senior officer corps at the front, rather than a formal policy change by Antonescu.

4th Army's operational deployment finished on 3 January. Manstein was unhappy with the lack of determination displayed by the unfortunate General Constantinescu, who had inherited the debilitated 4th Army from 4th Panzer Army in the midst of disaster. He was not re-employed. On 7 January General Dumitrescu's 3rd Army HQ was tasked with organising the return of the remains of both 3rd and 4th Armies to Romania. German reports testify that Dumitrescu had striven throughout to hold his army together, and his continued employment indicates that he was not held responsible for its destruction. Some Germans accused both Romanian army headquarters of abandoning their positions at Chernishevskaia and Kotelnikovo prematurely. In this context it should be noted that their own 6th Army's HQ sensibly fled the initial Soviet encirclement, and Paulus had to be ordered to fly back into Stalingrad to rejoin his troops.

As usual, Antonescu had behaved as an impeccable ally – so much so that his refusal to overrule Hitler's hold-fast order and allow an early breakout by the Lascar Group had been a major contributory factor to its loss. In post-war memoirs, both Şteflea and Dumitrescu, who had advocated such an early breakout to him and who otherwise served him loyally, were highly critical of Antonescu for this fatal delay. However, at the time Şteflea had to placate the Germans, and let Hauffe know his intention to court-martial the survivors of 15th Division for pre-empting orders to break out. In fact no such action was seriously considered, and was easily avoided because the two men responsible, Generals Sion and Lascar, had otherwise fought courageously, according to their German liaison officers, and were both thought to have died.

Some confusion exists regarding Romanian losses at Stalingrad. On 7 January, 3rd and 4th Armies between them could account for only 73,062 men, almost all of them from the non-combatant tail. On the basis of these figures, Antonescu told Hitler that Romanian losses totalled 158,854 dead, wounded and missing during the entire Stalingrad campaign. However, on 7 January thousands of men were still serving with *ad hoc* German-Romanian units or were simply adrift. The current best estimate of Romanian losses on the Stalingrad axis is about 140,000; some 110,000 of them since 19 November. 3rd and 4th Armies lost combat personnel and weaponry equivalent to at least sixteen of their eighteen divisions. This represented over half of Romania's 31 active field divisions. By contrast, Germany lost only some 10 per cent of its active divisions. Bad as Stalingrad was for the Ostheer, it was many times worse for the Armata Romana, and only during the second half of 1943 were German proportional losses on the Eastern Front to exceed those of the Romanians finally and conclusively.

Bitter exchanges occurred at all levels between the Romanians and Germans, ranging from Antonescu and Hitler, down through Şteflea and Hauffe, to troops in the trenches. The Romanian commanders accused the Germans of ignoring their warnings and of strategic blunders; charges the German High Command found embarrassingly difficult to dismiss. The Germans responded by accusing the Romanians of fighting poorly and without enthusiasm, an over-generalisation which the Romanians were able partly to counter with numerous specific instances of courage on the part of their troops (which the liberal issue of Iron Crosses tended to confirm), and partly to justify by citing the materiel deficiencies which the Germans had promised to redress, but had only partly resolved.

German troops in the line, unaware that Romanian losses in the East were thus far proportionally higher than their own, came to believe that all the Romanians had simply fled, and they treated them with increasing physical abuse and contempt. Some of this may be attributed to their own stress in defeat and desperate efforts to make demoralised Romanian troops restore the front, but much of it was gratuitous and probably had its roots in the racial arrogance instilled by a decade of Nazi propaganda. Among the Romanians there were numerous stories of retreating German motorised units deserting their allies and smashing the knuckles of Romanian footsloggers with their rifle butts as they tried to board their trucks – a tale that matches contemporary Italian complaints from El Alamein.

Romanian-German relations, already strained by diverging war aims in 1942, never recovered. The liaison officers of the German Military Mission, who had their own radio net, had frequently been used by Army Group Don to circumvent Romanian command structures, and the tension between Steflea and Hauffe was now so great that the latter had to be returned to German service in January 1943. He was killed in action in July 1944. Most disillusioned were the prisoners, and General Lascar, like Field Marshal Paulus, later joined a Soviet-sponsored organisation opposed to the Axis.

In March 1943 24th Infantry Division began to be formed on the Nogai Steppe from survivors of 7th and 11th Infantry Divisions, admixed with conscripted criminals. It was no more than a weak security division of two, two-battalion infantry regiments with a two-battalion artillery regiment attached. It represented the last active remnant of the two armies lost at Stalingrad.

RELATIVE AXIS PERFORMANCES

At Odessa, attacking Romanian troops were prepared to endure casualties matching anything experienced by the Germans on the offensive, but Stalingrad now called into question their defensive endurance. However, Stalingrad was not the first the time the Axis front had been breached in the East. The German front had already been broken within hours at Moscow and Kharkov, where their average divisional frontages were denser than those of the Romanians at Stalingrad and the Soviets were less well equipped and less experienced. Yet some German commentators have treated the Romanian defeat at Stalingrad as an unprecedented occurrence largely attributable to Romanian national characteristics. It is therefore worth pointing out that the ultimately ineffective Romanian performance at Stalingrad had close parallels within the Ostheer.

The average German division, of whatever type, was undoubtedly superior in experience, training, armament and leadership to the equivalent divisions of either its opponents or allies on the main Eastern Front. However, German divisions were not of a uniformly high standard. Even the much-vaunted armoured formations were not always rock solid when first committed. Entire battalions of 18th Panzer Division had fled from the front in panic, led by their officers, as early as 26 June 1941. The first engagement of 22nd Panzer Division in March 1942 miscarried, and the first action of 25th Panzer Division in November 1943 was also marred by panics.

German infantry divisions failed the test of combat on many occasions, especially the more junior formations created later in the war with scales of equipment and a level of experience sometimes little better than those of Romanian divisions. Guderian records 112th Infantry Division as the first of his formations to panic, on 17 November 1941, owing to high frostbite losses, its machine-guns freezing and the ineffectiveness of its 37mm AT guns against the T-34. At Stalingrad on 24 November 1942, 94th Infantry Division was withdrawn from its winter bunkers against orders and was caught by Soviet rifle divisions while on the move and cut to ribbons. It was disbanded.

At Kharkov in early August 1943 the newly-arrived 282nd Infantry Division was ordered to disengage from well-built positions and wheel back. During the manoeuvre one regiment was caught in the open by Soviet armour, suffered heavy casualties, panicked and fled. The panic proved contagious, and the entire division broke down in confusion, allowing a breakthrough that threatened the entire front. The deficiencies cited for the division's failure were that some of its officers and men lacked experience on the Eastern Front, it still had horsedrawn transport and the old MG34 machine-gun, and its infantry regiments only had 37mm AT guns. The circumstances and experience of all of these German infantry divisions closely matched those of Romanian divisions at Stalingrad.

The eight SS panzer divisions and three Western European SS divisions often disappointed the German Army when first committed at the front. However, army support, their high motivation and preferential weapon allocations almost always redeemed them and they became formidable formations. Other SS formations were less impressive. The senior SS divisions had got over their panics in the campaigns of 1939–40, but new formations underwent theirs in the east. On 2 July 1941 the 6th SS Mountain Division decamped from the Finnish front in panic. Another six German or Germanic SS divisions were primarily anti-partisan formations with limited front-line value. Mere race was no guarantee of combat excellence.

On 15 February 1943 the SS Panzer Corps abandoned Kharkov, the second largest Soviet city to have fallen into German hands, to avoid being surrounded. This was despite Hitler's direct instructions to hold on to it. The consensus is that this was done for eminently sensible military reasons and was therefore justified. However, if the recently rested 1st and 2nd SS Panzer Divisions, the best-equipped and reportedly most highly motivated of German formations, could abandon the second most prestigious prize gained on the Eastern Front against their Fuehrer's specific orders, it may well be wondered why so much scorn was poured on often exhausted and always comparatively poorly equipped Romanian, Italian or Hungarian divisions when they sometimes abandoned inherently worthless expanses of anonymous steppe under very similar circumstances.

The Luftwaffe field divisions, despite a very high educational standard of recruit and a good complement of motor vehicles, were notoriously inexperienced and poorly led, and were eventually all disbanded. Basing his decision on little more than racial arrogance, Hitler sent 7th and 8th Luftwaffe Field Divisions to provide stiffening for 3rd Romanian Army at Stalingrad, and 5th Luftwaffe Field Division to the Caucasus to stiffen the Cavalry Corps. All of them broke down within days of commitment and proved as big a burden on the German Army as did its allies. One of their claimed deficiencies was that they were initially issued with obsolete ex-French AT and field artillery. The same models were standard issue in Romania. Similarly, the standard Romanian LMG and HMG were also standard issue with the numerous German security and occupation divisions that were never even hazarded at the front.

The above examples are taken from the first three years of the Eastern campaign. Even at this early stage they were not unique. By 1944, as the quality of German troops fell, collapses were increasingly common and catastrophic, some on army-wide scales comparable to Romanian, Italian and Hungarian experience at Stalingrad. By 1945 even sub-units of élite formations such as the Grossdeutschland Division were sometimes abandoning their posts.

However, the failure of weak and inexperienced German divisions was less likely to prove decisive (and has therefore gone little noticed) because they were usually flanked and supported by more-seasoned and better-equipped German formations able to restore the situation. For example, 94th Division's collapse was sealed off by 24th Panzer Division, and 282nd Division was saved by 6th Panzer Division to fight again another day. Such experienced and well-equipped support was never available within the Romanian Army and too seldom available from its German allies. Essentially, a German army was a relatively strong chain with the occasional weak link, whereas a Romanian/Italian/Hungarian army tended to be a constitutionally weak chain with the occasional strong link. Thus inexperienced Romanian infantry divisions seldom survived their first major Soviet offensive to build up an accumulation of combat experience comparable with that of most German divisions.

That an inability to deal with a major Soviet offensive was not exclusively or inherently a Romanian (or Hungarian, or Italian) national characteristic, as is implied by some German sources, is illustrated by the above comparisons to German formations of similar experience, equipment and circumstance. Before accepting contemporary German comments on their allies at face value, it is as well to remember that, although their authors were often highly qualified to pass military judgements, they were also highly influenced by the prevailing prejudices of the times. There is thus often an unconscious racial subtext to their opinions. Furthermore, many were anxious to find not only reasons, but excuses for their own defeats.

Yet, for all their criticism, the Germans recognised the Romanians as the best of their allies, both qualitatively and quantitatively. Apart from them, only the Hungarians and Italians fielded complete armies on the main Eastern Front where the war was ultimately decided, but their materiel deficiencies were as great as Romania's, their motivation was less and their presence only intermittent. Owing to restrictions placed on it after the First World War, the bulk of the Hungarian army was poorly trained and equipped for the campaigns of 1941–42 and, having no territorial claim on the USSR, the country was poorly motivated. The Italian leadership had a strong ideological hostility to the USSR, but the country at large did not. Furthermore, its armed forces had been the first to complete a rearmament cycle in the late 1930s, and their equipment was obsolescent by the early 1940s. They were also impeded by Italy's remoteness from what was to them a secondary theatre of war.

Therefore, in 1941 the Italians and Hungarians committed only a small mechanised corps each against the Soviet Union; select formations with superior equipment which flattered the poor capabilities of the bulk of their armies. This was exposed in 1942 when they fielded a complete army each, both of which were rapidly annihilated in the wake of Stalingrad. Italy never returned to the Eastern Front, but the Hungarians were dragooned back into action by the Germans in mid-1944 and sometimes fought with determination in defence of their homeland in 1944–45. Slovakia also fielded a motorised division in 1941, but after 1942 it and the country's infantry divisions were never fit for more than anti-partisan operations.

The experienced Finns, who campaigned largely independently, were excellent infantry, but their performance in 1941–44 was aided by advantages of geography and climate. The passivity of their secondary front in 1942–43 gave the Finns little influence on the course of decisive operations, and they were contained by only half their number of Soviet troops during these years. However, they used the time to build a series of fortified lines from which they fought most effectively in 1944. A similar opportunity to use the FNB Line fortifications was denied to the Romanians by Hitler in the same year.

The performance of the Spanish Blue Division is not directly comparable with that of the other minor Axis powers, as it was composed of volunteers who were closely integrated into the German Army, with all the advantages in motivation, equipment, logistics and operational support that this implied. Of the six non-Germanic SS divisions fully formed in 1943–45, only one Estonian and one Latvian division proved to have enduring front-line combat value and fought well in defence of their homelands. However, they too were closely bound into the German front.

Only the Romanians managed to maintain an army of never less than six divisions, and on occasion up to 30 divisions, continuously on operations from 1941–44, usually supported by their air force, navy and armoured units, and they alone were considered by the Germans to have even limited offensive potential. In many ways Romania is more aptly bracketed in the Axis line-up with Italy than with the minor satellites. Indeed, because most of the Italian Army was engaged on occupation duties whilst every Romanian division saw front-line service, it is even arguable that Romanian divisions spent more months at the front with more effect than Italian divisions, and that, by this measure, Romania's army, if not its navy and air force, was second only to Germany's in its active contribution to the Axis cause in Europe.

Anglo-American histories tend to dismiss the efforts of the minor Axis satellites on the Eastern Front as relatively insignificant and certainly not worthy of comparison to their own. In terms of operational effectiveness this is certainly the case, but in terms of human sacrifice it is definitely not. It is therefore very sobering to note that the two-month siege of Odessa in 1941, the month after the Soviet counteroffensive at Stalingrad on 19 November 1942, and the week after the opening of the Battle of Iaşi-Chişinau on 20 August 1944 each cost Romania more dead, wounded and missing than the four times more populous British Isles lost in nearly four years of war against Japan. Hungarian and Italian losses in the wake of Stalingrad were equally large. War on the Eastern Front, even for unenthusiastic minor participants, was an enormously grimmer proposition than anything experienced in the west.

CHAPTER 4

THE BLACK SEA CAMPAIGN January 1943 to May 1944

DIPLOMATIC DEVELOPMENTS AND PEACE FEELERS, 1943

Horia Sima deeply resented Hitler's betrayal in January 1941 and his subsequent impotent detainment in Germany, so on 24 December 1942 he slipped across the Reich border into Italy on a false passport. He hoped that Mussolini would be more inclined to support a Latin fellow-Fascist and allow him to set up an Iron Guard bureau in Rome. However, Mussolini, who was dependent on Romanian oil, could ill afford to cross Antonescu, let alone Hitler, over so trivial an issue, and when Himmler demanded Sima's extradition he immediately complied. Thereafter Sima and his cronies were kept in closer custody at Dachau, while Antonescu rounded up sympathisers in Romania.

On 10-11 January 1943 Antonescu and Hitler met for the sixth time, at Rastenburg, for a tense Stalingrad post mortem. Antonescu's misgivings of the previous autumn had proved all too justified and, when Hitler tried to blame his unfortunate Romanian and Italian allies for the defeat at Stalingrad, the Marshal delivered a stinging rebuke on German attitudes and policy towards Romania, and gave a detailed and spirited defence of his armies' performances at Stalingrad and elsewhere. With his usual bluntness he pointed out that the German 1942 summer offensive had failed completely, and suggested that only a separate, compromise peace with the Western Allies would now allow a decisive concentration of Axis power in the east. Hitler rejected the idea outright, and countered by suggesting that, as Germany now guaranteed Romania's borders, Antonescu should send his other ten (actually five) divisions to the front.

However, it was no time to undermine their already weak position further by a public dispute, so they agreed a joint protocol pledging a continuation of the common struggle and the first German commitment to make major new armaments deliveries to Romania since 1940. Nevertheless, Antonescu came away profoundly troubled by the condition of Germany. He confided to his intimates on the return train journey, 'Germany has lost the wider war. We must make every effort to ensure that we don't lose our own war.' (One source attributes much of the above conversation to a supposed meeting between Antonescu and Hitler in October, but convincing corroboration of such an encounter appears not to exist.)

With Romania's compromise peace suggestions rebuffed by Germany, Mihai Antonescu suggested to the Italians and Bulgarians that the Axis ought soon to come to a settlement with the Western Allies if Europe was not to be overrun by the Red Army. However, Mussolini's position was the reverse of Antonescu's. On the previous 18 December, with his 8th Army in Russia in the process of losing 114,520 of its 221,875 men, he had already had Ciano suggest to Hitler a compromise peace with the USSR so that Axis forces could be concentrated against the Western Allies. He therefore rejected the opposite Romanian proposal on 21 January and, according to Ciano, decided to march with Germany to the end. On 5 February Mussolini dismissed his entire cabinet for advocating peace negotiations. Without Italy, which alone had a contiguous front with the Western Allies, the other minor Axis powers were too weak, remote and divided to attempt a co-ordinated escape into the western camp. Their later efforts to jump ship became competitive rather than co-operative, and the Germans and/or Russians were able to pick them off one by one.

Mussolini's tough stance was in part provoked by President Roosevelt's public advocacy of a policy of Axis unconditional surrender at the Casablanca Conference in mid-January. Thereafter, Hitler was able to use the intransigence of this demand to demonstrate the futility of both Romanian and Italian compromise peace proposals. Nevertheless, Mihai Antonescu now pressed ahead with independent peace feelers in Ankara and Madrid. However, on 12-13 April Hitler summoned Ion Antonescu to a seventh meeting, at Klessheim, and there showed him documentary evidence of these contacts. The Marshal swore to his deputy's loyalty, claiming that his efforts were in the interests of the whole Axis, and categorically refused to dismiss his closest confidant. Hitler told Antonescu coldly that when he considered the Axis had lost the war he would be the first to tell him. Antonescu wisely suspended peace contacts, but thereafter the cloud of suspicion that had long hung over Mihai Antonescu gradually began to attach itself to the Marshal. Tensions between the Marshal and Mihai Antonescu over the urgency of peace negotiations also began to surface.

Stalingrad also began to undermine Antonescu's dominance of the army. Şteflea quietly began to display a mind of his own, some staff officers in the capital began to establish contacts with the court and political opposition, and the most outspoken general, Nicolae Radescu, wrote such a scathing letter to von Killinger over German interference in Romanian internal affairs that Antonescu had to detain him for sixteen months. However, until mid-1944 their activities remained insignificant.

In early July Antonescu assisted German diversion plans before their attack on Kursk. On 1 July Manstein flew to Bucharest to award Antonescu a unique Gold Crimea Shield. He then secretly flew on to take command of the Kursk attack which opened on 4 July. To cover his departure the Romanian media were used to publicise a series of fictitious official engagements by Manstein in the country. Unfortunately, the ruse was wasted because the Soviets had a spy at Hitler's headquarters.

The loss of two armies at Stalingrad had rendered Romania's military situation so weak relative to Hungary that, in early January 1943, Mihai Antonescu even began to canvass the possibility of reconciliation with Budapest. However, in mid-month the Red Army destroyed the Hungarian 2nd Army, which lost 147,971 of its 205,000 men, and he was spared this distasteful expedient. Of particular concern to Romania was the fact that Hungary was making large advances in its armament industry, which had become more closely integrated with that of the Reich than Romania's, and benefited accordingly during the war.

The licence for the Czech T-22 tank that the Hungarians had acquired from Germany in 1940 allowed them to build 300 Turan I and 322 Turan II medium tanks and 40 Zrinyi assault guns between 1942 and 1944. These were equivalent to the obsolescent German PzKpfw III and Stug III. By 1943 Hungary had two armoured divisions and part of its cavalry division forming on this equipment which, if of limited value against the Red Army, was a serious threat to Romania. Hungary also managed to produce a few 105mm howitzers. A joint German-Hungarian armament programme agreed in June 1941 also set up assembly plants for the Ju 52, Me 210 and Bf 109, the products of which were to be divided 2:1 in Germany's favour. This gave Hungary less independence than Romania in armament production, but by late 1943 it was producing larger numbers of more advanced weapons and was drawing ahead in the local intra-Axis armaments race.

With both national armies largely at home throughout 1943, tension on the border mounted. In July Antonescu ordered two new Graniceri regiments (9th and 10th) and five more territorial battalions raised. They were fielded in October. In the meantime a new crescendo of 21 border incidents had been reached in August-September. The situation grew so serious that in August Antonescu had Hypothesis 'U' prepared – a plan to hold any Hungarian attack and then drive them from Northern Transylvania. Until March 1944 this was the main operational contingency for which the divisions rebuilding at home were on standby.

Rising Romanian-Hungarian hostility was only one sign of Axis internal decay. On 25 July Mussolini paid the price for his obstinacy and was deposed. The non-Fascist Badoglio government that succeeded him immediately began secret negotiations to withdraw Italy from the war. On 28 August the pro-German King Boris of Bulgaria died in suspicious circumstances and popular anti-German feelings in the country surfaced openly. On 2-3 September Hitler invited Antonescu, now the second man in the European Axis, to an unscheduled eighth meeting at Rastenburg to strengthen his resolve, and was himself relieved both by Antonescu's confidence in the strength of his own internal position and his continued professions of loyalty to the Axis. They had barely parted when Italy signed an armistice with the Allies which was announced on 8 September, promoting Romania to the unenviable status of second Axis power on the continent. After Mussolini's rescue on 12 September, Romania became the first country after Germany to recognise his new Republic of Salo, much against Mihai Antonescu's advice. However, Antonescu prudently also kept pro-Badoglio Italians secure from the Germans.

Hitler's other satellites were led by non-soldiers who lacked the expertise and nerve to contest the optimistic briefings he invariably gave them, but Antonescu's military training and blunt character gave the Fuehrer little scope to dissemble, although this never stopped him trying. Antonescu could also be devious when it suited him. He arrived at each meeting armed with reams of statistics carefully prepared by Şteflea to prove that Romania was both weaker than it actually was and fighting harder than was really the case. His aim was to gain more weapons and recognition than might otherwise have been merited. After this ritual initial fencing was over, their meetings often became remarkably candid.

The impression of their interpreter, Paul Schmidt, was that Antonescu became one of Hitler's closest intimates in later years. Undoubtedly their similar circumstances ensured that there remained a measure of rapport between the two men.

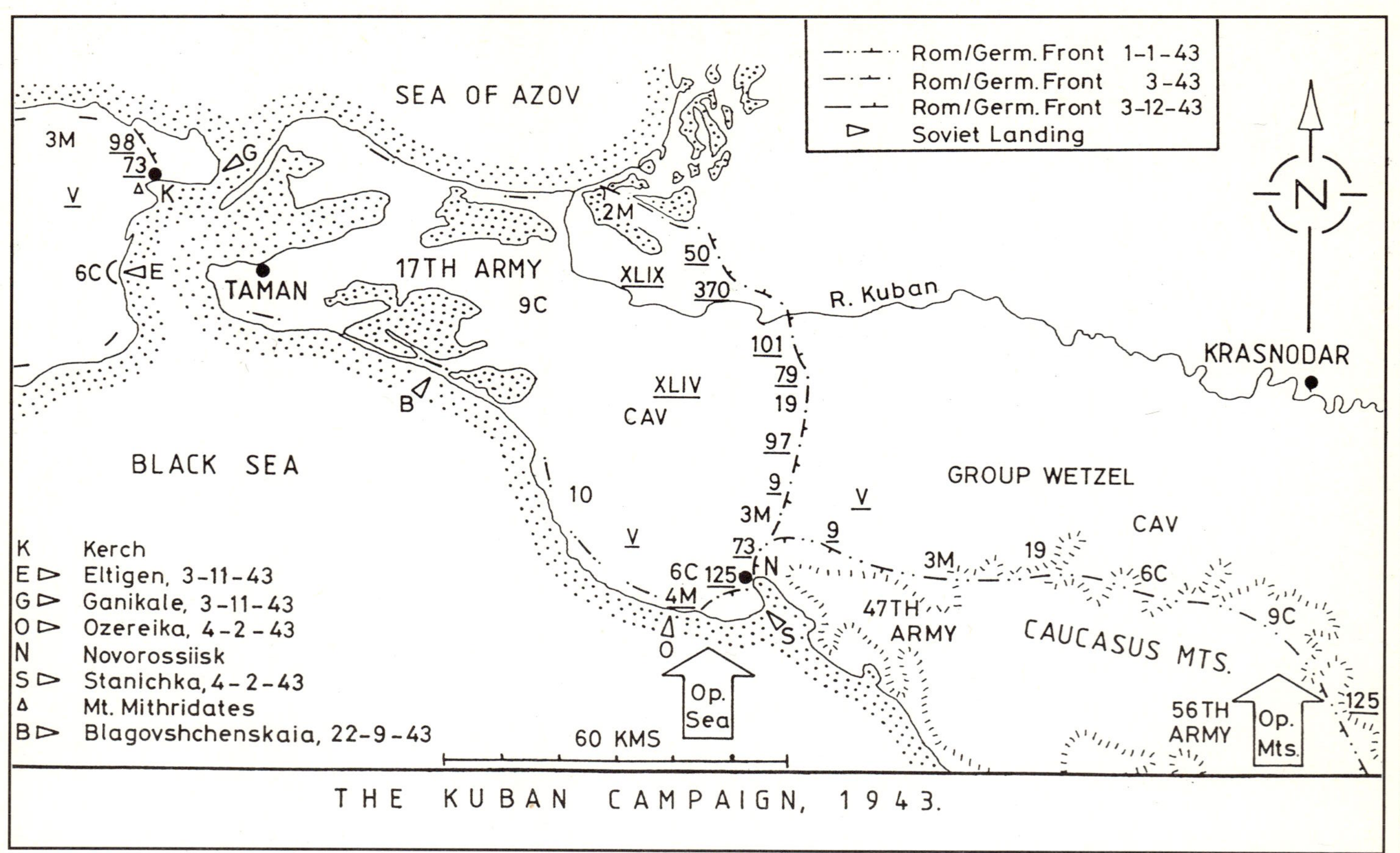

THE KUBAN CAMPAIGN, 1943.

Both were imbued with a strong sense of their personal and national destinies, both had therefore led their countries into a disastrous war, both were now jointly faced with looming catastrophe and both were isolated from their compatriots by the loneliness of power. Both were also in poor health, and Hitler even employed his personal cook on the Marshal's recommendation. King Mihai's observation of Antonescu as 'Once erect and brisk – now bent and round shouldered with care,' closely reflected the parallel deterioration in Hitler.

However, although Antonescu continued to offer Hitler sensible military advice to the very end, he was necessarily moving away from the Fuehrer politically. Hitler's September pep talk could not negate the cumulative damage done by the Soviet victory at Kursk in July, the USAAF bombing of Ploieşti in August, the turmoil in Bulgaria, the running skirmishes with Hungary and the defection of Italy on 8 September. On 15 September, in response to a hint from the American Embassy in Ankara, the Marshal authorised Mihai Antonescu to resume contacts with the Western Allies.

Mihai Antonescu appointed Alexandru Cretzianu, a known supporter of Maniu, Ambassador to Turkey in order to act as main intermediary with the Western Allies. Maniu had remained in touch with the British by radio and courier throughout the war, and Antonescu's negotiations were therefore undertaken with the full knowledge and tacit support of the traditional political parties and the Court, and in parallel with their own contacts. So when a secret British mission to Maniu, Operation Autonomous, was captured on 22 December 1943, Antonescu took care to shield its members from too close a German interrogation in order to protect the negotiations. Mihai Antonescu even used his legal expertise to ensure that the agents' statements gave the Germans no excuse to demand their extradition!

It has been suggested that Operation Autonomous was actually part of Operation Bodyguard, the D-Day deception plan, and not a serious mission to Romania at all. Certainly discussions with the Western Allies did not progress well, because they would not consider a separate peace and kept the Soviet Union fully informed. Indeed, barely had contacts begun in September than the Allied position was hardened by the formal extension of the unconditional surrender demand to Axis satellites at the Moscow Conference of October 1943.

THE EVACUATION OF THE KUBAN BRIDGEHEAD

While Romania's diplomatic campaign began to gain momentum, its army remained heavily committed on the Eastern Front. After the transfer of Dumitrescu's 3rd Army HQ to Stalingrad in September 1942, the troops in the Caucasus had passed from even notional Romanian operational control. The Mountain Corps (1M, 4M) remained in the Crimea on anti-partisan operations under the German Crimea Command. The Cavalry Corps retained command of three divisions (6C, 9C, 19), but was subordinated to the German Group Wetzel. Group Wetzel also had 10th Infantry Division and 3rd Mountain Division under direct command as well as two German divisions (*73*, *9*). Both German higher formations were in fact corps (V, XLII) with their titles elevated so that they could take the two larger Romanian corps under command.

All thought of offensive operations died with the full onset of winter in mid-November, and Group Wetzel was tasked with holding the western extremity of Army Group A from the Taman Peninsula to the foothills of the Caucasus Mountains south of Krasnodar. The remaining mobility of the Romanian units was lost because the horses of the five mounted regiments of the two cavalry divisions had to be withdrawn from the mountains to milder winter pastures 180km north of their front. The partly motorised 6th Cavalry Division still had 301 vehicles, but their condition had deteriorated badly and its motorised regiment (10th Roşiori) was partly immobilised. By the spring 9th and 6th Cavalry Divisions had only two serviceable R-1 light tanks left in their mechanised squadrons, and these were withdrawn to Romania shortly afterwards as obsolete.

At their January crisis meeting Hitler announced his intention to hold the Kuban Bridgehead in the Caucasus as a springboard for further offensives, and asked Antonescu to keep the surviving Romanian divisions there. Antonescu pointed out to Hitler that, since the outbreak of war, his army had lost or worn out sufficient weaponry to equip 24 divisions, and that keeping the remaining Romanian divisions at the front, given the proven inadequacy of their existing scale of weaponry, was pointless.

The bulk of the Romanian divisions in the Caucasus were Echelon I divisions, and were under-equipped by even Romanian standards. The only two Echelon II divisions were the especially hard-hit 2nd and 3rd Mountain Divisions, which were 4,500 and 6,000 men below establishment. Furthermore, the Mountain and Cavalry Corps lacked the full scale of corps troops available to the seven infantry corps. Before Antonescu agreed to keep troops in the Kuban and Crimea, Hitler had to promise the large-scale re-equipment of not only the Mountain Corps and Cavalry Corps (1M, 2M, 3M, 4M, 6C, 9C, 10 and 19), but of a total of eighteen Romanian divisions.

The Kuban and Crimea divisions were promised 50 PzKpfw 38(t) tanks, 20 Skoda 150mm howitzers and Hanomag half-tracks, 84 Pak 75/38 anti-tank guns and 100 RSO tractors, 120 Pak 38 50mm anti-tank guns and 108 Lanz Bulldog agricultural tractors, and 64 Skoda M14/19 100mm howitzers. In addition, the infantry were to receive 4,000 MP41 SMGs, 440 MG42 LMGs, 50 ZB37 HMGs, plus 185 60mm and 50 81mm mortars. This influx of German equipment later made the establishment of the Crimea and Kuban divisions distinctive and superior to those re-forming in Romania, but it was not until the summer that the bulk of it could be delivered.

Antonescu was as keen as Hitler to keep the Soviets as far from Romania as possible, but it was nevertheless an act of very considerable political courage to commit 60 per cent of Romania's few surviving field divisions to so dubious a military enterprise as the Kuban 'Springboard'. To offset the risk he therefore prudently allowed their strength to run down by not sending replacements. As a result, six of the divisions (6C, 9C, 2M, 3M, 10 and 19) were a total of 21,600 men below establishment by June 1943.

The disaster at Stalingrad unexpectedly turned the Cavalry Corps' passive backwater into a vital hinge for the retreat of Army Group A from the depths of the Caucasus into the Kuban Bridgehead, via its main depot at Krasnodar. The most advanced troops of 1st Panzer Army, including 2nd Mountain Division, lay some 600km to the Cavalry Corps' east, and began their withdrawal on 1 January 1943. To cut off the retreating German troops, the Soviets planned two offensives: Operation Mountains and Operation Sea. Operation Mountains was to thrust north and capture Krasnodar, then swing north-east to meet a second pincer advancing from the east, thus surrounding 1st Panzer Army and part of 17th Army. Operation Sea was to capture Novorossiisk and the Taman Peninsula, driving the remainder of 17th Army into the sea. In both cases, much would depend on the steadiness of the Romanian Cavalry Corps, the collapse of which would make the success of either Soviet operation very possible. In early January 1943, before Antonescu's agreement to hold fast became known, senior Romanian commanders in the Caucasus had suggested that their divisions be evacuated to the Crimea. Group Wetzel distributed some of its German battalions in support of the Cavalry Corps lest this occurred.

The main weight of Operation Mountains, mounted by the Soviet 56th Army, fell on the German XLIV Jaeger Corps to the Cavalry Corps' east on 11 January. It met limited success, so the Soviet offensive was extended to include 9th Cavalry Division from 16 January. At that date 1st Panzer Army was still 250-300km east of Krasnodar, which lay less than 40km north of 9th Cavalry Division. On this and subsequent days the division repulsed attacks by two Soviet rifle divisions (20 and 83) and an independent brigade. However, the build-up against it continued, and on 21-22 January elements of two more rifle divisions (55 and 61) were identified. By now 9th Cavalry Division had suffered considerable casualties and was beginning to lose ground under the pressure, but the timely arrival of part of the German 97th Jaeger Division stabilised the situation. On 27 January 9th Cavalry Division was even able to join a counterattack on the 55th and 61st Rifle Divisions.

On 26 January the Soviet 47th Army attacked 3rd Mountain and 19th Infantry Divisions, whose fronts lay some 100km west of Krasnodar at a time when much of Army Group A still lay 150km east of the city. The Soviets were at the end of extremely extended lines of communications, had only a 30 per cent advantage in numbers and limited armoured support, and were hindered by appalling weather conditions. Their assumption in mounting this otherwise unpromising assault was that the Romanian units would collapse. They did not, and by 31 January the attack had come to a bloody standstill with only local gains.

Operation Mountains had failed, and the faster mechanised elements of 1st Panzer Army escaped through Rostov. 17th Army was cut off from Rostov and was ordered by Hitler to fall back within the Kuban Bridgehead, where it was to dig in. 2nd Mountain Division had abandoned Nalchik on 4 January and, having less organic transport than the Germans, it arrived in the Kuban Bridgehead in a state of absolute exhaustion after forced marches of up to 80km a day in mid-winter.

Although none of their fronts had broken, there was an increasing collapse of morale in several Romanian units in the Kuban as the scale of Romanian losses at Stalingrad and their own predicament became apparent. Disgruntled officers again openly began to express a preference for campaigning in Transylvania. On 2 February Hitler asked Antonescu to take urgent steps to prevent physical disintegration.

Antonescu responded as usual by emphasising the materiel weaknesses of his divisions, and accused German troops of maltreating his own. There had been a sharp rise in hostile incidents between troops of the two armies in the wake of Stalingrad, for which the average German soldier held the Romanians responsible, rather than his own higher leadership. Antonescu immediately dispatched his Defence Minister, General Pantazi, to the Caucasus, and gave divisional commanders authority to pass summary death sentences on their men. A subsequent Romanian-German Commission found that Romanian morale, although shaken, was not as poor as alleged.

On 4 February the Soviet 47th Army launched Operation Sea. This consisted of a direct assault on Novorossiisk against Group Wetzel, combined with a major seaborne landing in its rear at Ozereika and a diversionary landing at Stanichka, just south of Novorossiisk. The land assault was again repulsed, but the two seaborne landings fell on the thin coastal defences of 10th Division. After a naval bombardment by two cruisers and three destroyers, the first wave of 1,427 marines and ten tanks was landed at Ozereika against determined resistance from 38th Infantry Regiment, and at considerable cost a small bridgehead was established. However, a breakdown in communications led to a loss of nerve by the Soviet command, and no further assault waves were landed. As a result, 10th Division and German reinforcements were able to wipe out the landing over the next three days. Of 32 tanks lost, 21 Stuart light tanks had never got off their landing barges and a number were captured intact. They were briefly used by the Cavalry Corps' two mechanised squadrons on coastal protection until they broke down through lack of spares.

Unfortunately, the diversionary landing at Stanichka had gained a firm foothold. German coastal artillery had failed to spot the approaching assault force, and a sudden artillery barrage from massed Soviet guns across Novorossiisk Bay panicked the 10th Division defenders. Axis counterattacks threatened to destroy the weak landing on 6 February, but on that day the Soviet command reinforced it with the bulk of the force that had failed to land at Ozereika. Within a few days 17,000 Soviets were ashore. Despite costly German and Romanian counterattacks over a period of months, including a major offensive during 17-25 March, the Stanichka beach head could never be reduced because it received a steady stream of reinforcements and artillery support across Novorossiisk Bay.

Romanian morale remained shaky. Shortly after 19th Infantry Division's commander was wounded in action, an entire battalion refused to return to the line on 23 February. 17th Army was not reassured, and increasingly dispersed Romanian regiments at the front amongst German divisions. 3rd Mountain and 19th Infantry Divisions were distributed round XLIV Jaeger Corps in the front line, parts of 6th Cavalry and 10th Infantry Divisions were subordinated to V Corps opposite Novorosiisk and Stanichka, and the rest of 10th Infantry and 6th Cavalry Divisions and the whole of 9th Cavalry Division were subordinated to the Cavalry Corps and tasked with guarding the south coast of the bridgehead. 2nd Mountain Division held the Sea of Azov flank of XLIX Corps, which was also now threatened with Soviet landings.

In 1941–42 Antonescu was the most tolerant of Germany's allies in allowing the subordination of his major formations to German operational control when military logic demanded it. However, it was deeply embarrassing even to the pragmatic Antonescu to have to accept the further dispersal of even individual regiments or battalions among German units. Yet in early 1943 he had little alternative, because only firm German direction and the support of their heavy weapons could give many of his units the necessary steadiness. The Germans had to accept the risks involved in employing demoralised Romanian troops at the front owing to lack of their own troops, over 100,000 of whom were gradually transferred from the Kuban to the main front in the Ukraine. The continued Romanian presence made much of this possible.

On 10 March General Dumitrescu's proven 3rd Army HQ, having organised the repatriation of the Stalingrad survivors, took over the administration and discipline of all Romanian troops east of the Bug. Their numbers had stabilised at 110,191 by 1 April, some two-thirds of them in the Kuban. Dumitrescu had reinforced disciplinary powers but no operational responsibilities beyond rear area security, and under his familiar direction morale began to improve. Throughout March and the first half of April, 3rd Mountain and 19th Infantry Divisions were frequently attacked during Soviet attempts to seize Krimskaia from the Germans. 19th Division's performance improved and Major Ioan Palaghita, a battalion commander in 94th Infantry Regiment, was awarded the *Ritterkreuz* on 7 April for leading a counterattack on his own initiative that restored the German 101st Jaeger Division's front. In July both divisions were taken out of the line; 19th Division rotating with 10th Division to coastal protection.

During the invasion of the Caucasus, 2nd and 3rd Mountain Divisions had suffered heavy cumulative casualties, so they were withdrawn to the Crimea for rest and recuperation during March and July respectively. They were replaced by 1st and 4th Mountain Divisions, which were subordinated to V Corps in June and August respectively. On 23 July the Soviets overran 1st Mountain Division's 23rd Vanatori de Munte in a local attack, inflicting 454 casualties. A counterattack by 24th Vanatori de Munte was repulsed, and the Germans intemperately accused the Romanians of fighting poorly. These two battalions were the most junior in the Mountain Corps and probably not up to the standard of the rest of the division, but the Romanians protested, pointing out that 24th Vanatori de Munte had been force-marched 15km at night through pouring rain and had at least sealed off the penetration. Probably for political reasons, the Germans climbed down somewhat, qualifying their charges as they had in February by explaining that the Romanian troops were well enough disposed but their officers lacked energy.

During July the promised armour arrived in the Kuban. The Romanians had been anxious to rebuild their armoured strength after Stalingrad, but the Germans were not willing to deliver modern tanks immediately as they were themselves seriously short of armour. However, they were anxious to keep the maximum Romanian commitment at the front, and in January agreed to supply 50 refurbished PzKpfw 38(t) Ausf.A, B and C light tanks. The Romanians wanted to use them to form tank battalions in the 5th and 8th Motorised Cavalry Divisions, then rebuilding in Romania, but the Germans made the sale conditional on their direct delivery to the operational zone. The 38(t) was only marginally superior to the R-2 in mobility and armour and identical in gun power, but the Romanians were not in a position to quibble, and the vehicles, known as T-38s in Romanian service, were handed over to crews of 2nd Armoured Regiment in the Crimea between 15 May and 24 June 1943.

The crews underwent conversion training by 23rd Panzer Division at Staryi Krim. On 5 July the T-38 battalion was organised into 51st, 52nd and 53rd Companies of fifteen T-38s each. Five were kept in reserve with battalion HQ for training. However, the Romanians found that only seventeen of the 50 were serviceable on delivery, and this figure fell to only eight by 5 July. It transpired that the Germans had sold 102 of the best remaining PzKpfw 38(t)s to the Hungarians the previous year, leaving the Romanians with the dregs. This caused a considerable scandal, and as a result the Romanians insisted that all future German tank deliveries had to be made to Romania, where the vehicles could be inspected before acceptance. The Germans thereafter complied.

On 28 July, 51st and 52nd Companies were ferried across to the Kuban bridgehead and subordinated to the Cavalry Corps, which had to provide them with the necessary supporting motor transport. They formed a mobile reserve with the reconnaissance group of 19th Division. On 10 September the Soviets began a final offensive to clear the Kuban Bridgehead, capturing Novorossiisk on 16 September. The Germans began a phased withdrawal to the Crimea, during which a threatening Soviet seaborne landing was made at Blagoveshchenskaia in the sector of 19th Division on 22 September. Its object was to cut off the retreat of the erstwhile defenders of Novorossiisk. In their first substantial action, 51st and 52nd Tank Companies played a leading role in the annihilation of the landing, but once again Soviet anti-tank rifles and 45mm AT guns played havoc with the lightly-armoured tanks, and seven T-38s were knocked out and others damaged. On 27 September 51st and 52nd Companies were withdrawn to the Crimea.

All six Romanian divisions (10, 19, 6C, 9C, 1M, 4M), totalling 50,139 men, were successfully evacuated to the Crimea by 2 October, and the last Germans escaped on 8 October. Romanians had provided up to 40 per cent of the Axis manpower in the Kuban. Their losses between 8 February and 31 September 1943 were a sustainable 1,598 dead, 7,264 wounded and 806 missing, which still left 106,578 Romanian troops east of the Bug on 1 October. In the depressing wake of Stalingrad some Romanian units in the Kuban had fought poorly, and morale in others was so low that they could not be hazarded for long at the front. However, with the single exception of the Stanichka 'Little Mainland' landing this had not caused the Germans insuperable difficulties, and the low proportion of missing indicates that no mass surrenders occurred.

In their favour, it should be noted that Romanian units in the Kuban had played leading roles in frustrating two Soviet landings and were the last allies of the Germans still employable on the main Eastern Front, the Italians and Hungarians having withdrawn totally. The Germans had particular cause to be thankful that the Romanians had not also decamped at the time of Operations Mountains and Sea. This was largely due to Antonescu's determined higher direction of Romania's war effort. Whether the Kuban Bridgehead should have been held at all is much to be doubted, because it reduced three German and two Romanian corps to impotence at the end of an unnecessarily tenuous and strained supply line at a time when the fate of the entire Eastern Campaign was being irrevocably sealed at Kursk.

THE CRIMEA

One formation withdrawn from the Kuban, 4th Mountain Division, was so poor that it was transferred out of the Crimea in September and amalgamated with 24th Infantry Division. As 4/24th Division it was intended for security duties on the Nogai Steppe, but in mid-October the German 6th Army fell back and the division became involved in front-line fighting around Melitopol on 21 October. On 28 October the Soviets broke through 6th Army and bundled it across the lower Dnepr, thus cutting off the Crimea. The disintegrating 4/24th Division was for a while surrounded with the German XLIV Corps on the Nogai Steppe, but escaped with it across the Dnepr at Berislav in early November. It had lost two-thirds of its combat strength.

A single Romanian infantry battalion and a 75mm artillery battery were still deployed on the isolated Kimburn Peninsula opposite Ochakov to protect the southern approaches to the Dnepr estuary. However, by 23 November it had been overwhelmed, and Soviet artillery thereafter halted Axis coastal traffic to Nikolaiev and the Red Army threatened to land behind the German front on the Dnepr. 4/24th Division, an *ad hoc* collection of demoralised survivors of Stalingrad, penal conscripts and rejects from the Crimea, was the poorest Romanian division fielded, and it had almost no front-line potential. It was withdrawn to Transnistria.

To Antonescu's horror, Hitler had initially hoped to garrison the as yet inviolate Crimea with the dangerously diluted force of only one German and seven Romanian divisions. However, Soviet landings near Kerch and the peninsula's isolation in early November meant that six (later reduced to five) German and seven Romanian divisions became tied down holding two fronts in the Crimea. Initially, 75,000 Romanians were trapped in the peninsula, and Antonescu immediately drew up plans for evacuation.

Antonescu was justifiably dubious about the military practicability of holding the isolated Crimea for long in the face of growing Soviet air and naval advantage. German commanders felt the same, and hoped that he would demand the early withdrawal of his Romanian divisions from Hitler, thus ensuring the simultaneous withdrawal of the German divisions, which were too weak to hold the peninsula alone. On 29 November, however, Hitler wrote to Antonescu contending that the Red Army and Navy lacked the resources to mount a successful conquest of the Crimea, and stating that in any case evacuation was practicable at any time. He vowed to defend the Crimea with all means at his disposal, and promised to launch an early counteroffensive across the Dnepr to re-establish land links with the peninsula. In anticipation, Antonescu ordered his troops to remain in the peninsula.

Of the seven Romanian divisions left in the Crimea, the Germans considered four (6C, 3M, 10, 19) capable of defensive front-line duty, while three others (9C, 1M, 2M) were better suited to coastal defence and anti-partisan operations. The main defence of the Perekop isthmus fell upon German divisions, but the Romanian 10th Division became involved in defending its eastern flank, where the Soviet 10th Rifle Corps established a 13km-deep bridgehead across the Sivash during 1-6

November. The Romanians were supported by the twelve T-38s of 53rd Tank Company, which the Mountain Corps had supplied with supporting motor transport. Two T-38s were lost in counterattacks near Karanki on 4 November, and four more on subsequent days in actions near the Kriatskoe and Aigulskoe Lakes. The front was held and local counterattacks were launched to consolidate the line. During one of these, on 26 November, a detached battalion of 2nd Mountain Division captured its objective while flanking German units were repulsed. German radio reports omitted the Romanian role and claimed it as a German success, and the Romanians, starved of good news from the front, protested indignantly.

The Mountain Corps (1M, 2M) was tasked with defending the southern and south-western coasts of the Crimea and with anti-partisan operations in the Yaila Mountains, where 24 guerrilla bands operated. The danger of a major naval landing by the Black Sea Fleet so deep in the rear receded after German Stukas sank three Soviet destroyers raiding the coast on 6 October. However, the Yaila Mountains comprised some of the best guerrilla country on the Eastern Front. Furthermore, they were now within easy flying distance of the Caucasus, and the local partisans were able to establish landing strips on which ample supplies and numerous reinforcements were landed in the winter of 1943/44. Their activities reached a crescendo during Soviet assaults on Perekop or Kerch.

From 2 November 1943 to 21 January 1944 the Mountain Corps was supported by the *ad hoc* 54th Tank Company, formed from the T-38 battalion's five HQ reserve tanks and three from the 53rd Company. The Mountain Corps was experienced and well-adapted to anti-guerrilla operations in this environment, and despite their growing strength the Yaila Partisans never closed the tenuous Axis lines of communications for any length of time. On the other hand, the Mountain Corps was unable to eradicate them and became tied down away from the front.

3rd Mountain Division defended the north coast of the Kerch Peninsula and repulsed several, probably diversionary, landing attempts between 1 and 10 November. 6th Cavalry Division held the south coast of the Kerch Peninsula. They were initially supported by 51st and 52nd Tank Companies, but on 30 November 51st Company with fifteen T-38s was evacuated to Romania and another five tanks were withdrawn from 52nd Company on 12 December.

Although the heavy units of the Black Sea Fleet no longer dared approach the Crimea, its numerous coastal craft were still a threat to the Kerch Peninsula. On 1 November Romanian forces sank a Soviet landing vessel off Eltigen with AT fire. Then, on 3 November, the Independent Coastal Army made two surprise landings against German forces at the peninsula's tip. The northern landing at Ganikale was within range of massed Soviet artillery positions in the Taman Peninsula, and all of V Corps' German troops and part of 3rd Mountain Division became bogged down in a fruitless struggle to eliminate it. German light naval vessels were unable to cut the Soviets' supply line because they had intensively mined the short stretch of water to the Taman Peninsula.

However, the southern landing at Eltigen, which quickly drove the few Romanian defenders off the beaches, was out of normal artillery range from the Taman Peninsula and its longer sea approach could not be adequately mined. Consequently the German naval forces began a close blockade of the landing force there. By December they considered it a 'ripe plum ready for the picking'. The elimination of the Eltigen beach head was allocated to General Corneliu Teodorini's 6th Cavalry Division HQ, which formed a battle group of squadrons drawn from its three cavalry regiments, two full battalions from 3rd Mountain Division and two batteries of German assault guns.

While the cavalry squadrons mounted holding attacks to the south, the mountain battalions and assault guns made the principal assault from the west on 4 December. Soviet resistance was bitter and cost the Romanians 886 casualties, but the bridgehead was eliminated on 7 December. Half of the 1,570 prisoners taken were wounded, and 1,200 dead were found. German estimates of Soviet losses over the preceding month were even higher at 10,000 dead and 2,827 prisoners. In addition, 38 tanks and 25 AT guns fell into Romanian hands. These formed the bulk of the 41 captured tanks (4 x T-34, 4 x T-38, 1 x KVI, 4 x Lee, 5 x Stuart, 4 x Valentine Mk.III, and 19 unspecified Vickers tanks) evacuated to Romania in March 1944 and subsequently used for AT training.

Success at Eltigen was marred by the northward breakout of 820 Soviets in an effort to get through to the Ganikale beachhead. In the attempt they overran vital German artillery positions on Mount Mithridates which supported the German lines facing the Ganikale beachhead. As V Corps had no German reserves on hand, it was General Mociulschi of 3rd Mountain Division who restored the situation with a counterattack mounted by 6th Vanatori de Munte and elements of 9th Roşiori. Mount Mithridates was recaptured on 10/11 December and its exhausted Soviet defenders killed, captured or dispersed at little cost. Mociulschi's action may well have saved the V Corps' already strained front at Ganikale from being breached, and he was awarded the *Ritterkreuz* on 18 December. According to Romanian sources, Teodorini also received the *Ritterkreuz*.

An important aspect of the Eltigen and Mount Mithridates actions was the successful use on both occasions of mixed cavalry/mountain rifle battle groups, indicating that 6th Cavalry and 3rd Mountain Divisions were now sufficiently confident and flexible to operate efficiently outside their formal divisional structures. This capacity was widely admired in the Germans but more rarely achieved in other armies.

On 1 October 1943 Romania still had 106,578 men east of the Bug, and the defensive battles for the Crimea and Nogai Steppe cost the Romanians 1,309 dead, 3,817 wounded and 1,360 missing between then and 31 December 1943. By the latter date only 63,413 men remained in the Crimea. Despite their most unpromising predicament in the Crimea, Romanian divisions had performed useful service at Perekop and Eltigen and in the Yaila Mountains, and there was a discernible improvement in determination and morale, probably attributable to a combination of General Dumitrescu's influence and the arrival of competitive German weaponry.

THE FALL OF THE CRIMEA

On 26 January 1944, Hitler, increasingly suspicious of all of his allies, had had a contingency plan, Operation Margarethe-II, prepared for the occupation of Romania. Exactly a month later Antonescu met him for the ninth time, at Klessheim. Hitler's

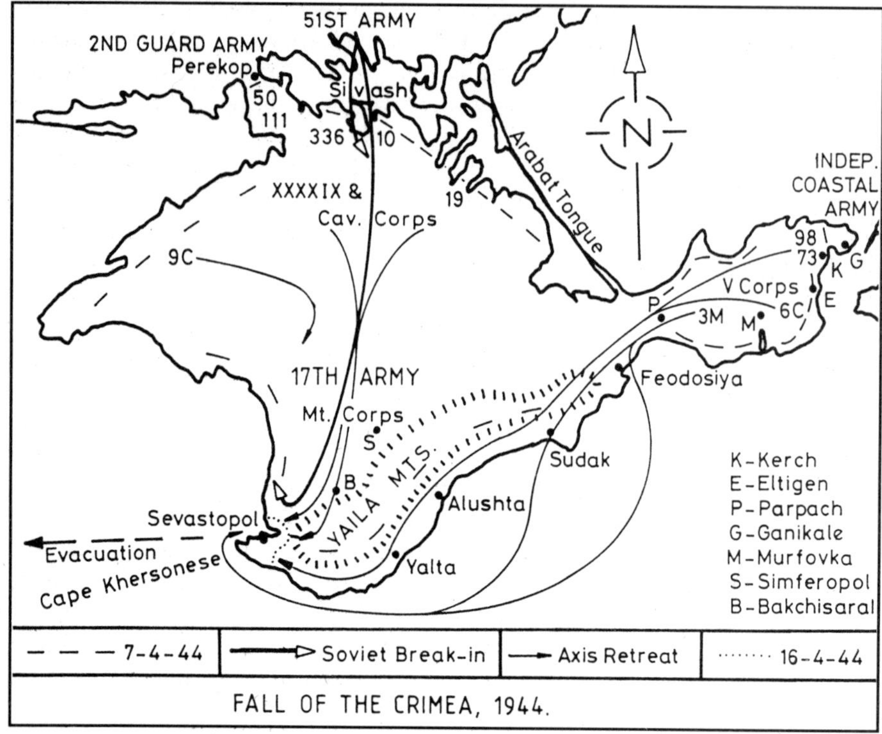

FALL OF THE CRIMEA, 1944.

failure to launch the promised attack across the Dnepr to relieve the Crimea had steeled Antonescu to demand the Crimea's immediate evacuation, and German commanders, including von Kleist of Army Group A, were hopeful he would secure the Fuehrer's approval.

According to the interpreter who was present, Dr Paul Schmidt, Antonescu began to lay bare the weaknesses and errors of Hitler's military strategy in ruthless and determined style. Recognising the futility of arguing with him on narrow military grounds, Hitler instead reiterated to Antonescu certain compelling strategic and geopolitical arguments in favour of its defence. Holding the Crimea would prevent the Allies bombing Romania from airfields there; a Soviet naval invasion of Romania was unlikely until Axis air bases in the Crimea were in their hands; and a declaration of war by Turkey, which supplied all Axis chrome, might result from its abandonment.

Having laid his wider Axis considerations before the Marshal, Hitler adopted the unprecedented device of meekly asking Antonescu's advice as to whether he should evacuate or hold the Crimea. Antonescu took the Fuehrer's unwonted humility in his stride, but cautiously declined to commit himself until Hitler revealed whether he had finally given up the Ukraine for lost. Hitler immediately leapt at the opening and announced his intention to recapture the Ukraine in June 1944, and Antonescu found himself manoeuvred into advising him to hold on to the Crimea in the meantime.

Such steadfast support from Antonescu, although given against his better judgement, reassured Hitler. To clinch Antonescu's conversion he made another unprecedented concession by suggesting that plans be prepared both to hold and evacuate the Crimea. This temporarily satisfied Antonescu's conflicting desires to keep the Soviets at a distance while not unduly risking Romanian troops in the process, and he condescendingly agreed. As a result, Hitler rotated another division through the peninsula and Romanian strength there in March was actually marginally higher than it had been in December. Operation Margarethe-II was suspended for the first time.

However, by their next meeting, on 23-24 March, the Crimea's main supply port of Odessa was under immediate threat (it fell on 10 April), and Antonescu more firmly advocated a withdrawal from the Crimea. As a result some non-essential Romanian personnel began to be evacuated in early April. On 1 April 1944 there were 32,561 men under the administration of the Mountain Corps (1M, 2M, 3M) and 32,151 under the Cavalry Corps (6C, 9C, 10, 19) in the Crimea; a total of 64,712. For operational purposes, however, most divisions were integrated with German corps. Early in 1944 the Cavalry Corps, which was subordinate to the German XLIX Mountain Corps on the Perekop Isthmus, was given command of 10th and 19th Divisions guarding the Sivash, a shallow inland sea, and the Arabat Tongue, an extended spit covering the Crimea's north-eastern flank. The German 336th and Romanian 10th Divisions had to contain the Sivash bridgehead which the Soviet 51st Army had built up to seven or eight rifle divisions and 150 tanks by 6 April 1944. 10th Division's own armoured support consisted of only 53rd Tank Company with ten T-38s (it had absorbed 54th Tank Company on 21 January) and seven German assault guns.

On 7 April the Soviet 2nd Guards Army mounted a secondary attack on the German 50th Division on the Perekop Isthmus, while 51st Army made the main assault from the Sivash bridgehead with its 1st Guards and 63rd Rifle Corps on the Romanian 10th Division. During the winter 10th Division had dug in effectively, and it largely held its front throughout the day; 1st Guards Rifle Corps was everywhere repulsed, and 36th Rifle Corps had only penetrated the Romanian forward lines. Their losses were enormous for little gain and Tolbukhin, the anxious front commander, turned up at 51st Army HQ to put pressure on its leaders.

However, a battalion-strength Soviet landing across Lake Aigulskoe, behind 10th Division's left flank, had gained a lodgement in its rear. Part of 53rd Tank Company and a handful of German assault guns made an immediate counterattack, but lost two T-38s knocked out and two rendered impotent owing to gun failures, and were repulsed. It was the overnight reinforcement of this landing with tanks which, on the following day, began to unhinge 10th Division's left flank and forced it to retreat from its forward defences. On 9 April the Soviets were able to penetrate the division's last line at Tomashevka, and by 11 April they had released 19th Tank Corps into its gun lines. Although the 20th Field Artillery Regiment knocked out four tanks, it was overrun.

The Soviets had now broken into the Crimea, and there were no Axis reserves capable of ejecting them. As a result, all of the horsedrawn Axis divisions began a precipitate retreat to the Sevastopol perimeter in desperate competition with the Soviet 19th Tank Corps. 10th Division and 19th Division, which had successfully repulsed several Soviet diversionary landing attempts across the Sivash and on the Arabat Tongue, poured back with the German XLIX Mountain Corps from the north.

On the night of 10/11 April, V Corps (*73*, *98*, 6C, 3M) in the Kerch Peninsula began its westward retirement on Sevastopol. 3rd Mountain Division, already in the rear, was ordered to Feodosiya for evacuation by sea to Sevastopol. An intermediate position had been prepared at the Parpach bottleneck for the rest of the Corps, but before this could be reached 6th Cavalry Division was overrun on open steppe at Murfovka by Soviet tanks and motorised infantry on the afternoon of 11 April. Its two mounted regiments were broken up, and only the motorised regiment reached the Parpach position intact on 12 April. For the rest of the retreat along the coast road to Sevastopol it fought with the German 73rd Division.

The Mountain Corps was the only Axis formation not in headlong retreat. On 10 April it was charged with occupying the northern defences of Sevastopol with three mountain battalions and all the corps' artillery, holding the north-south Yaila passes against Soviet attempts to interfere with the retreat of V Corps from the direction of Simferopol, preventing the Yaila partisans from blocking the vulnerable coast road in its rear and setting demolition charges to impede the Soviet pursuit. These tasks it generally carried out successfully.

Unfortunately V Corps did not have transport to carry the various Romanian mountain rifle battalions that it encountered on its retreat. Those of 3rd Mountain Division who were caught up with at Feodosiya and Sudak were evacuated by sea on 13/14 April, but this was not immediately possible for 23rd and 7th Vanatori de Munte, who had been holding the pass to Simferopol and had fallen back on the port of Alushta. To keep them in the line as a rearguard while it continued its retreat, V Corps tried to arrange German artillery support and evacuation by German landing craft, but although they repulsed the first Soviet probes, the bulk of both battalions were lost on the night of 15/16 April. The Romanians considered them to have been deserted, and the incident led to serious recriminations. However, at Yalta V Corps managed to find room for a mountain battalion which had been holding the pass to Bakchisarai and reached Sevastopol on 16/17 April.

As they became available, the Mountain Corps rushed more of its battalions into the old Soviet fortifications on the northern perimeter of Sevastopol over 12-14 April. These had been badly damaged during the siege of 1941–42, but were still formidable. The following day the leading Soviet tanks tried to break into Sevastopol off the march, but were repulsed, leaving twelve hulks in 2nd Mountain Division's positions and eleven in front of 1st Mountain Division. The Mountain Corps' steadiness on this day was particularly important because the retreating Germans had yet to consolidate their positions. The combined losses of the seven Romanian divisions over the preceding week totalled 17,652 men. This was proportionally far higher than German losses, and yet again reflected the comparative lack of mobility of Romanian divisions. Of the five forward divisions, only 9th Cavalry, which had been guarding the quiet north-western seaboard of the Crimea, made its way into Sevastopol without catastrophic losses.

Dozens of local tank and infantry attacks were made on the Mountain Corps until the end of the month, 2nd Mountain Division bearing a particularly heavy burden, but with German artillery support its line held firm. About 35 per cent of the Sevastopol perimeter was held by Romanian troops. The northern part was commanded by the German XLIX Mountain Corps, but the majority of its front was held by the two comparatively intact mountain divisions of the Romanian Mountain Corps (1M, 2M, 10), as its two German divisions (336, 50) were down to only 22 per cent of establishment. The southern sector was held by the German V Corps (73, 111, 98) and the subordinate Romanian Cavalry Corps (3M, 19, 6C, 9C). Of the latter, only the remains of 3rd Mountain Division were fit to be in the line. Its General Mociulschi was actually made acting commander of V Corps from 20-24 April, during which period a Soviet attack was repulsed.

By now Antonescu absolutely insisted on evacuation, and Hitler agreed to uplift the non-combatant tail of the German and Romanian divisions, followed by the Cavalry Corps. Between 14 and 27 April 27,140 Romanians were shipped out to Constanta. On 28 April the shattered Cavalry Corps (6C, 9C, 10, 19) had only 3,894 combat troops still ashore guarding the coast, and the three mountain divisions had 9,436 men in the line. At this point Hitler suspended the evacuation.

From 1 May 2nd Mountain Division came under daily softening-up attacks, and on 5 May the Soviets began their final assault with a very heavy diversionary attack on 2nd Mountain Division by five rifle divisions of 2nd Guards Army, designed to draw in German reserves. 2nd Mountain Division repulsed them, some units fighting on from encirclement. This earned warm congratulations from the German 50th and 336th Divisions. Soviet attacks on 1st Mountain Division on 6 May were also repulsed with great loss after only local penetrations, and it was possible to withdraw virtually all German support from the Romanian Mountain Corps when the main Soviet offensive opened against V Corps on 7 May. However, V Corps' situation grew immediately desperate when the German 50th and 98th Divisions were forced to retreat. As a result the Romanian Mountain Corps had to be withdrawn from its positions north of Severnaya Bay on the night of 7/8 May, lest it be cut off. This was skilfully managed without arousing the Soviets.

On 8 May Hitler at last permitted a final withdrawal from Sevastopol, and 2nd Mountain Division's HQ was evacuated and its remaining troops consolidated under 1st Mountain Division. This was put into reserve, charged with manning a final defence line for the Germans across the neck of the Khersonese Peninsula while the remnants of 6th and 9th Cavalry Divisions guarded its coast. On 9 May 2nd and 24th Vanatori de Munte suffered heavy losses counterattacking in support of the German 98th and 73rd Divisions. Over the next two days the cavalry slaughtered their remaining horses and they, the HQs of 3rd Mountain Division and the Mountain Corps were evacuated. Meanwhile, 1st Mountain Division repulsed Soviet breakthroughs of the German line which reached the Khersonese position, claiming six tanks on 11 May. On the night of 11/12 May 1st Mountain Division's HQ was evacuated, leaving a last rearguard of 2,756 men of 1st, 3rd, 4th, 9th and 10th Vanatori de Munte with 1st Division's 75mm AT and 120mm mortar companies ashore. Almost all were lost at Omega Bay the following day.

All together, 22,522 of the 64,712 Romanians in the Crimea were lost, the vast majority from combat elements during the initial Soviet break-in. Of those that escaped, 39,134 were evacuated by sea and 3,056 by air from Sevastopol. Only 35,877 of the 42,190 evacuees were still fit. Romanian dead, wounded and missing therefore totalled about 28,835. Only 9th Cavalry Division managed to reassemble about half of its establishment strength in depot. All the other divisions, already well below strength on 7 April, were down to nearly a third of establishment when they returned to depot, and had lost all of their heavy equipment.

The Romanian contribution was vital in the Crimea. The available German divisions alone could never have held the isolated peninsula for six months, and would therefore not have tied down more than 30 Soviet divisions and a tank corps away from the main front. The same Axis forces would not have had equal impact on the main front, because only the unique geography of the Crimea afforded them the necessary defensive advantages to hold down such a large enemy force. The German situation was so precarious that Romanian forces, for all their limitations, may several times have made the difference between survival and disaster – notably at Eltigen and Mount Mithridates in December 1943, and in holding the Yaila passes and the northern perimeter of Sevastopol in mid-April 1944. Even in defeat at the Sivash and Sevastopol, Romanian units had shown unexpected determination, given the earlier morale problems in the Kuban and their precarious situation. However, nothing could compensate for the serious damage done to Romania's most experienced surviving divisions.

THE OCCUPATION OF TRANSNISTRIA

Concurrently with the Crimea campaign, Transnistria was being overrun by the Red Army. The name 'Transnistria' had its origins in the title of a 1930s refugee group, 'Associatia Romanilor Refugiaţi Transnistrieni' – the Association of Romanian Refugees from across the Dnestr. On 14 August 1941 Hitler suggested that Romania take over the administration of the whole territory between the Dnestr and Dnepr, but three days later Antonescu declined the area beyond the Bug, although he did offer to supply security troops once Odessa had fallen. Therefore, on 19 August the Romanians and Germans signed an agreement at Tiraspol, formally creating Transnistria in the more restricted area between the Dnestr and the Bug. It was followed by the Tighina Accord of 30 August between General Hauffe and General Tataranu, then Romanian Army Chief of Staff, which gave the Germans control of the trunk rail lines and the port facilities of Odessa vital to the supply of their armies to the east, but left almost everything else to the Romanians.

Hitler tried repeatedly to get Antonescu to annex Transnistria formally, but the Romanian cannily declined to do so until the war was over and a plebiscite had been held. In this he was consistent with the established Romanian policy, already exhibited over Ruthenia and the Banat, of not accepting territory from the Germans that did not have a large Romanian element in the population to justify the claim. In Transnistria, Romanians, known locally as Moldavians, amounted to only 11 per cent of the population. Antonescu's primary interest in Transnistria was as a bargaining counter for the return of Northern Transylvania. He wanted Germany to

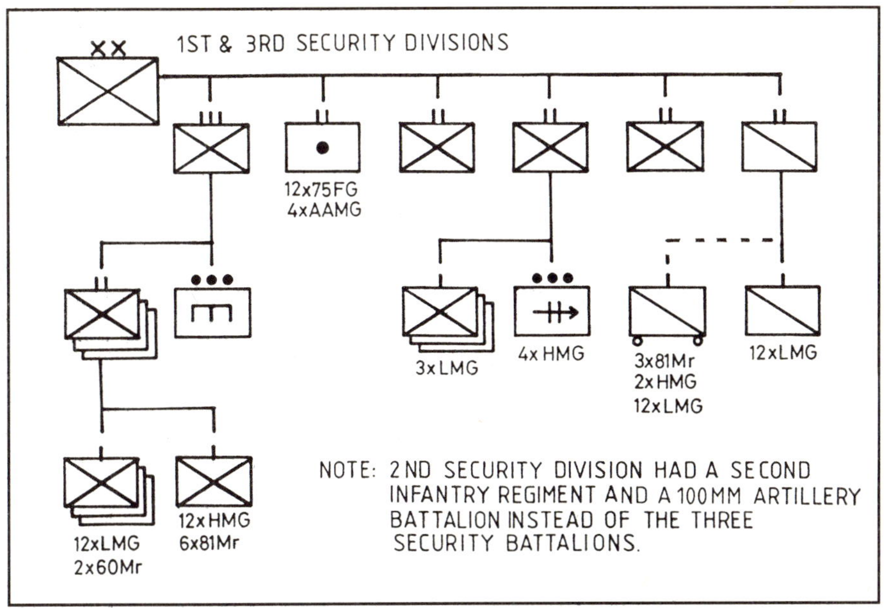

take over Transnistria, Northern Transylvania to be returned to Romania, and Hungary to receive Galicia as compensation. However, the Germans rejected the idea.

The suppression of the Iron Guard had muted the ultra-nationalist fringe which might have used the small Moldavian minority as an excuse for extending the concept of Romania Mare to include Transnistria, and Romanian political opposition to the occupation, let alone annexation, was otherwise universal. Romanian basic law never superseded Soviet basic law in Transnistria, there was no freedom of movement between that territory and Romania, German occupation marks remained the official currency, and not even the Moldavian minority had military obligations. Antonescu restricted himself to exploiting Transnistria's largely agricultural resources to make up for the decline in Romania's own production caused by widespread mobilisation of peasants for the army. This was not in accord with German plans, which had envisioned Transnistria's agricultural surplus going directly to the Reich.

Before the war, Transnistria had a population of 3.4 million, but extensive Soviet evacuation reduced this to 2.25 million by October 1941. Of this, approximately 80 per cent were Ukrainian, 11 per cent Romanian (Moldavian), 5 per cent Russian and 4 per cent German. The initial tone of the Romanian occupation was harsh. In the rural areas this was because 4th Army had to live partly off the land, and treated the hinterland as a war zone which it pillaged without legal restraint. On 22 October 1941 a massive bomb, set by the retreating Soviet garrison the previous week, demolished the new Romanian HQ in Odessa, killing the commander of 10th Infantry Division, General Glogojanu, and 51 other troops. In retaliation there were mass executions which largely fell on the remaining Jewish population.

By December, however, the initial terror had subsided, most of the army had been withdrawn and the more professional and discriminating Serviciul Special de

Informaţii (army secret police) had been installed. A civil administration under Professor Gheorghe Alexianu then assumed control. Alexianu was a close friend of Mihai Antonescu, and his brief was to restore normal economic life, repair the transport infrastructure, establish a locally raised police force under the Romanian gendarmerie, and reopen schools and churches.

The civil administration was headed by Romanians but largely composed of locals, a disproportionate number of whom were Moldavians. The Transnistrian Moldavians, who numbered approximately 250,000 and had exhibited little previous Romanian national consciousness, became a privileged minority under Alexianu's policy of 'Romanisation', and acquiesced to his plans for their elevation. Under the new administration they received widespread state support, educational advantages and job preferment. The Germans reported a further 23,000 Moldavian families living in areas under their control east of the Bug, but an October 1942 plan to consolidate them in Transnistria in exchange for the local Germans was halted by the outcome of the battle of Stalingrad the following month.

Alexianu, who displayed megalomanic tendencies, was jealous of his autonomy, and not only placed severe restrictions on German attempts to recruit forced labour, but even got them to release some Transnistrian prisoners. In the autumn of 1942 he raised his own labour force and lent 40,000 of them to the Germans in the Ukraine for the duration of the harvest. In October 1942 he put this on a permanent basis by creating his own Work Army (Armata Muncii), based on the Todt Organisation.

Transnistria had lost 70-80 per cent of its horses, cattle and sheep in the enforced collectivisation of the early 1930s, and agriculture had remained depressed owing to high Soviet state appropriations. Although the Romanians did not fully abolish the collectives because of the likely disruption of production, they greatly reduced their size. Romanian state appropriations fell in 1942, only returning to Soviet prewar levels in 1943, and a free market was allowed for the surplus. All of this increased incentives and productivity in the countryside, despite the removal of 1,876 tractors to Basarabia and Northern Bucovina in 1942, where local agriculture had been badly damaged by the Soviet occupation of 1940–41. It also ensured that there were few food shortages in Odessa. This contrasted with the lack of incentive for peasants in German-held areas, which resulted in a decline in rural productivity, and therefore food shortages in the cities that led to a migration to the countryside.

The Soviets had largely evacuated heavy industry from Odessa, but by October 1942 the Romanian administration calculated that it had 997 of Transnistria's 1,421 enterprises back in production. This again contrasted with the Germans, who sent both captured plant and labour back to the mother country. The most striking phenomenon of the Romanian occupation was the growth in private commercial activity, hitherto suppressed by the Soviet Union. The Romanians licensed private businesses and provided policy direction, but left further development to the free market. The result was a major boom in services, especially in Odessa, which became a remarkably vibrant commercial centre.

Some effort was also made in social provision. Schools were reopened and instruction was allowed in the language of choice, largely Ukrainian. Odessa University became the only institution of higher education restored in the whole of the east, but here Romanian was the language of instruction. Alexianu reopened the churches, monasteries and seminaries, and religious instruction was made compulsory in schools. Largely owing to the availability of food, Transnistria had a very good health record compared with the rest of the occupied USSR, and epidemics were eliminated by late 1942. Odessa's health facilities were so good that they even attracted German patients from Nikolaiev. A cultural revival through the media of film, theatre, ballet and opera was also fostered. In 1942 7,000 Transnistrian-born POWs were released, and in 1943 all sanctions against ex-communists were lifted and the local population was allowed to supply food directly to other POWs held in Transnistria. Almost none of these 'hearts and minds' exercises were adopted by the Germans.

This economic and administrative stability in 1942–43, combined with a relatively lax security policy, made even less implacable by widespread corruption, tended to moderate the attitude of most Transnistrians towards the Romanian occupation after December 1941, even though political freedoms remained suppressed through Romanian fear of Ukrainian nationalism. This is not to say that the Romanians were liked or respected; only that, by comparison with the previous Soviet regime and the relentless harshness and appalling conditions in German-occupied areas, their administration of Transnistria appeared relatively benign. The result was to undermine Soviet attempts to raise a significant partisan movement in Transnistria.

Shortly before evacuating Odessa in 1941, the Soviets organised stay-behind parties in the city and in the 200km of catacombs beneath it, one of which may have been responsible for detonating the 22 October bomb blast. The Serviciul Special de Informaţii had some early success against the Soviet surface networks in January 1942, and, thanks to documents captured at Sevastopol, rounded up three squads from the catacombs and killed 50 more from surface bands in July. However, the catacombs proved too extensive to clear, so the Romanians sealed 160 known exits. Some partisans died of malnutrition as a result. Romanian agents infiltrated another surface group and arrested sixteen members in February 1943, and in March a substantial number of the underground group were arrested. The remainder kept a low profile until liberation. Soviet propaganda subsequently made much of the catacomb partisans, but in reality they amounted to significantly fewer than 100 men for most of the war, and achieved virtually nothing beyond providing an example of tremendous endurance.

In rural areas, where the open terrain was not conducive to guerrilla operations, there was also little support for partisans. At Dubosari some railway workers organised minor sabotage, and in the Savransk-Gorovanesk area a group organised by the Pervomaisk party organisation proved a total operational failure. It never amounted to more than 60 men until it was reinforced by air in the winter of 1943/44. The same was true of another group at Il'ichevski. The only other significant group was at Krimy, west of Pervomaisk. This consisted of youths engaged in little more than vandalism and distributing leaflets. When they tried to mine the railway near Pervomaisk in February 1943 they were ambushed by the Romanians. Ninety people were arrested and 30 of them were executed.

By late 1943 it was obvious that Romania could not hold Transnistria, and the attitudes of both the administration and the local population began to change. Alexianu was dismissed in February 1944 amidst rumours of monumental corruption, and was replaced by General Potopianu, a military engineer and former Economy Minister. He switched from a self-sustaining exploitation of the territory to an outright pillaging of its resources more reminiscent of German policy. Alexianu had already begun sending entire factories to Romania, and Potopianu accelerated it. Even Odessa's trams were taken. At the same time the Transnistrians began to exhibit increasing signs of lawlessness, most of which still fell well short of organised resistance. Despite growing support from the main Soviet front, the Transnistrian partisans were still not a major threat when the territory was abandoned in April 1944. The final days under German Army occupation were marked by a scorched-earth policy.

The successful economic liberalisation, supported by Romanian-sponsored educational, religious and cultural revivals, offset the unfavourable local reactions to the initial severity and later corruption of the Romanian administration, and did much to prevent the growth of active political opposition to Romanian rule amongst the Transnistrian population. This lack of political opposition in turn undermined Soviet attempts to set up an effective partisan campaign in the territory, and saved the Romanian Army from having to engage in the protracted guerrilla war that the far more powerful German Army was unable to suppress elsewhere. For years after its liberation Odessa was little restored by the Soviet authorities, and its food rations and living conditions remained more severe than those of most liberated cities. The impression was that the city was being punished for its relatively easy time under Transnistria.

ROMANIA AND THE FINAL SOLUTION

Throughout central Europe there was almost universal suspicion of the international commercial connections and professional and material success of some within the various Jewish minorities. This was exacerbated by the heightened chauvinism of the newly resurrected, but insecure, nation states, and resulted in a rash of anti-semitic legislation throughout the region in the 1930s. In Romania the growing electoral success of the Iron Guard in December 1937 led Carol II's government to steal some of its policies by eventually withdrawing citizenship from about 300,000 Jews in the territories regained after the First World War. This created a legal difference between the largely alien Jews of Basarabia, Northern Bucovina and Transylvania and the predominantly citizen Jews of the core of the country. Carol later imposed restrictive legislation on the Jewish population's professional and commercial activities.

The brief period of the Iron Guard's tenure of power (September 1940 to January 1941) was marked by widespread extra-legal expropriations of Jewish property, and its coup in January was accompanied by a pogrom in Bucharest that left about 120 Jews dead. Antonescu's suppression of the Iron Guard in January 1941 resulted in a more pragmatic and legalistic regime under which the more brutal excesses within Romania were halted.

Antonescu's exclusive Romanian nationalism made him functionally anti-semitic, but his chauvinism was not directed solely at Jews. On 3 May 1941 he created the National Centre of Romanisation. 'Romanisation' was not exclusively anti-semitic, although Jews were undoubtedly hardest hit. The National Centre of Romanisation also kept comprehensive statistics on the employment of other ethnic groups, and its responsibilities included keeping Hungarians out of sensitive strategic industries and élite armed forces units. It even controlled the proportion of Volksdeutsche employed in these areas.

Antonescu kept in direct communication with internal Jewish leaders throughout the war, even to the point of trying to justify his policies in writing. Virtually all of the ±342,000 Jews in the core of the Romanian state he inherited in 1940 survived – the largest Jewish community in continental Europe to escape the Final Solution almost intact. Expropriations and ghettoisation were never completed, and according to Radu Lecca, the Commissioner for Jewish Questions, the Romanians abandoned preliminary preparations and definitively refused to deport their Jews to Germany as early as August 1942, a stage at which the German summer offensive was progressing well. Ironically, this appears to have been at least in part due to Antonescu's nationalism, for he considered German pressure for the surrender of Jews with Romanian citizenship to be unwarranted interference in Romanian internal affairs.

Antonescu's preferred alternative was to authorise the Jewish community to purchase passages to Palestine by giving the government two 2 billion Lei 'loans'; a profitable expedient that began in a small way in 1941 and which provided an escape route for perhaps 14,000 people by 1944. Antonescu asked the Western Allies to take 70,000, but they refused. That he could successfully operate what some Germans considered a policy of obstruction was largely thanks to his earlier suppression of the Iron Guard, which would undoubtedly have collaborated in the Final Solution. Its Hungarian equivalent, the Arrow Cross, collaborated enthusiastically, handing over 149,000 Northern Transylvanian Jews to the Germans in May-July 1944.

However, events in Basarabia and Bucovina were influenced by specific local factors and followed a very different course. There, Romanian-Jewish ethnic tensions were particularly strong. Much of the local Jewish population had arrived in the previous century as part of Tsarist Russia's frontier colonisation programme. This was resented by the local Romanian majority. In 1918 both provinces joined Romania Mare, and the anti-Semitic Iron Guard in particular prospered there between the wars. Its founder, Codreanu, was a native of nearby Iaşi, and he introduced a more violent edge to intercommunal tensions. King Carol's withdrawal of citizenship formalised the legal alienation of most Basarabian and Bucovinan Jews.

When the USSR occupied Basarabia and Northern Bucovina in June 1940, considerable numbers of both the local Romanian and Jewish populations were sent into internal exile in the USSR. However, some disaffected Jews were more inclined to collaborate with the Soviets than with the Romanians, and in the year up to the outbreak of war lurid tales of Jewish treachery and atrocity therefore gained currency in Romania. These were amplified by the Iron Guard to inflame prejudices even further, and succeeded in undermining rational discussion of the issue. The withdrawing Romanian Army, already deeply humiliated by the bloodless surrender of the two provinces, had had to contend with the further insult of occasional sniper attacks by armed civilians, which were indiscriminately attributed to Communists or Jews.

Some units took reprisals against the more easily identified Jews, and one officer, Major Valeriu Carp, was cashiered as a result.

However, it was the reprisals rather than the disciplinings which set the tone for operations in 1941. Indeed, before the Romanian Army had even crossed the border there was a pogrom at Iaşi, inside Romania, in late June, in which at least 3,600 Jews are estimated to have died, and both 3rd and 4th Armies were to be involved in the killing of Jews during the reconquest of Northern Bucovina and Basarabia. Later in the year, 3rd Army was amongst those Axis formations tasked with carrying out von Manstein's overtly anti-semitic, counterpartisan order of 20 November 1941 in the Crimea.

More than 100,000 of the approximately 285,000 Jews in Northern Bucovina and Basarabia had been sent into internal exile by the Soviets or had fled with the Red Army at the outbreak of war. In the case of Cernauţi, only about 10,000 of its 43,000-strong Jewish population were found in or near the city when it fell on 17 July. About 13,000 Jews are estimated to have been killed during the reconquest of Basarabia in July, most in Chişinau, and some 3,000 during the reconquest of Northern Bucovina. Approximately 6,000 of these deaths were attributable to the German Einsatzgruppe D.

On 8 July Antonescu decided that the moment was favourable for the expulsion of the remaining Jews from the two provinces, and the Romanian Army was instructed to wash its hands of the problem by driving them across the River Dnestr into German military jurisdiction. This occurred on 7 August. However, although Einsatzgruppe D killed many, it could not yet handle such numbers, and the Germans promptly drove most of them back across the river, where they had to be placed in makeshift camps. About 17,000 Jews are estimated to have died on the march or of starvation in the camps between August and October. At this time the Romanian 4th Army was suffering huge losses at Odessa, and Romanian propaganda was placing greatly exaggerated emphasis on the Jewish contribution to the defence. There is no doubt that this heightened the general hostility to the suspect Jews in its rear, who often fell into the custody of anti-semitic fanatics.

On 19 August the Tiraspol Agreement established Transnistria, and on 30 August Hauffe and Tataranu agreed as part of the Tighina Accord that Basarabian and Bucovinan Jews could now cross into the territory. Some 119,000 Jews were driven into ill-serviced concentration camps across the Dnestr in late 1941, where they were joined by about 5,000 more in 1942. In February 1942 the Romanians again tried to push them further east across the River Bug into German administration, but they were once more sent back to the Transnistrian concentration camps. A combination of forced marches, cold, little food, lack of hygiene and heavy labour led to the deaths of most of the inmates in 1942, the majority through typhus. Some executions also occurred, but most fatalities were due to the malign neglect which followed the repeated failure to pass the problem on to the Germans. In late 1942 Antonescu belatedly eased the conditions in the concentration camps. However, it was too late to reverse Romania's most discreditable act in the Second World War, and only about 52,000 survived to be repatriated to Romania in late 1943, indicating a further 67,000 deaths.

The specific trigger for Romanian action against Transnistrian Jews was the 22 October bomb blast in Odessa, after which Antonescu, already frustrated by the long and bloody siege, certainly ordered a specific reprisal ratio of 200 communists per dead Romanian officer, and 100 per other rank, without specifying their racial origins. In the case of the bomb blast this authorised the deaths of 7,800 people in Odessa. He also ordered the remaining communists and one member of each Jewish family to be held hostage against further partisan action. However, on the ground in Odessa the distinction between those to be executed and the hostages was not observed, especially by Einsatzgruppe D, and there is little doubt that total deaths far exceeded Antonescu's official quota, reaching an estimated 19,000. The remaining Transnistrian Jews were put into concentration camps over the following winter and suffered the same fate as the Basarabian Jews, most dying from malign neglect.

Jewish deaths in Romanian hands are poorly documented compared with deaths in German hands, and far higher figures than those quoted above have been postulated. One source states that 200,000 Basarabian Jews, 124,632 Bucovinan Jews, 105,000 Northern Transylvanian Jews and 40,000 Jews from the core of Romania died during the war; a total of 469,632. However, the 324,632 deaths of Basarabian and Bucovinan Jews seems to be based on a population estimate, and on the assumptions that all of the prewar Jewish population remained in the provinces when the Romanians recaptured them and that there were no survivors. A similar problem exists in estimating the Transnistrian Jewish population and its losses, because the Soviets claimed to have evacuated virtually all of them. A maximum figure of 92,852 has been estimated. The deaths of all 105,000 Northern Transylvanian Jews were attributable to German/Hungarian action, and the Germans were also responsible for the deaths of a proportion of those from Basarabia, Bucovina and Transnistria as well. It thus seems that Romanians were responsible for a minimum of about 110,000 Jewish deaths, and quite possibly over twice as many.

Antonescu does not appear to have specifically ordered the extermination of Jews, preferring to expel them. However, when this failed in Basarabia, Bucovina and Transnistria, a very large number died in Romanian custody without the culprits being appropriately punished for it, even after Antonescu admitted learning of their fate two years later. A few officers were prosecuted. One committed suicide, but the others took the option of going to the front rather than face imprisonment.

Although the precise total of Jewish deaths was impossible to establish with exactitude, the overall order of magnitude was inescapable, and was a major reason why Ion Antonescu, Mihai Antonescu and Gheorghe Alexianu were executed as war criminals in 1946. These events seriously undermined Romania's otherwise plausible case that it was simply one of the war's victims, and were to deprive Antonescu of an honourable postwar reputation to match that of Marshal Mannerheim of Finland. Yet, although Antonescu was held ultimately responsible for over 100,000 Jewish deaths, the fact that he had managed to exclude the Iron Guard, Himmler's chosen tool, from power undoubtedly inadvertently saved hundreds of thousands of others.

Anything between about 10,000 and 36,000 Gypsies are also estimated to have died in Romanian hands. Yet, as Romania had the largest Gypsy population in

Europe, Gypsy losses in Romania were proportionally among the lowest suffered on the continent.

ROMANIAN VOLKSDEUTSCHE

A point of irritation to the Romanians was the considerable autonomy the Germans managed to extract for the Volksdeutsche minority in Transylvania, and later for Transnistria's 125,000 Volksdeutsche. In 1939 Romania's German population was estimated at 782,000, but the territorial losses of 1940 reduced this to about 542,000, most of the remainder going to Hungary with Northern Transylvania. In 1940 Himmler's SD raised a 40,000-strong paramilitary organisation and dominated the Volksdeutsche community so totally that its loyalties, hitherto the least suspect of all minorities, became divided. Andreas Schmidt, the man appointed by Himmler to head the Romanian Volksdeutsche, was the son-in-law of the head of Waffen-SS recruitment. In early 1941 he enlisted Artur Phleps, formerly a general in the Romanian Mountain Corps, who began to use his contacts to poach Volksdeutsche from the Romanian Army. By 1942 he had sufficient to form a high proportion of the 7th SS Mountain Division, which gained a particularly brutal reputation in Yugoslavia, and later much of 8th SS Cavalry Division. By March 1943 more than 10,000 Romanian Volksdeutsche were also serving with the German Army.

Initially the Romanians forbade German recruitment of Volksdeutsche because it infringed their national sovereignty and because Volksdeutsche were disproportionally prominent in the already weak technical branches of the Romanian Army. A compromise was reached on 13 April 1943, by which Romania was able to veto the transfer of key personnel from its army and the Germans gained the right to conscript 17-year-old Volksdeutsche into the Waffen-SS. Eventually, 60,000 Romanian-born Germans served in the SS. Not everyone with a trace of Volksdeutsch ancestry went over to the Reich. At least two Romanian corps commanders, Hugo Schwab and Carol Schmidt, were of German stock but remained loyal. Contrary to some reports, Radu Korne was not of German stock. His family retained an ancient spelling of the Romanian surname Cornea.

Partly to avoid upsetting Romanian sensibilities, no specifically Romanian Volksdeutsche SS divisions were formed. Transylvanian Volksdeutsche suffered discrimination within the SS because they were thought to have been tainted by their centuries of residence among Romanians and Hungarians. As a result they were widely used to flesh out the lower ranks of under-recruiting Germanic Waffen-SS formations raised elsewhere in Europe, notably 17th and 18th SS Panzer Divisions. Another 15,000 served in the German Army and Todt Organisation.

CHAPTER 5

THE 1944 CAMPAIGN
March to August 1944

ARMY REORGANISATION, 1943–1944

In the year and a half following Stalingrad, Hitler's main aim was to keep as many Romanian units at the front as possible, which essentially meant those in the Kuban and Crimea, while Antonescu sought to rearm and mechanise his army before returning the bulk of it to battle. The combined effects of Odessa, Stalingrad and the Crimea evacuation were the complete loss of the combat capacity of every Romanian field division, either by virtue of prohibitive infantry losses (G, F, 3, 8, 21 at Odessa), total equipment losses (6C, 9C, 1M, 2M, 3M, 10, 19 in the Crimea) or both (1A, 1C, 5C, 7C, 8C, 1, 2, 4, 5, 6, 7, 9, 11, 13, 14, 15, 18, 20 at Stalingrad). Even 4/24th Division had suffered heavily on the Nogai Steppe. Thus the Romanian Army of June 1941 had had to be completely rebuilt by August 1944. In the shadow of Stalingrad, mobilisation fell again to only 594,119 on 15 April 1943, but thereafter the increasing threat of invasion led to a rise that reached a peak of 1,163,347 on 15 August 1944.

On 1 September 1943 Antonescu told his ambassador to Turkey that he had rebuilt all the divisions lost at Stalingrad except the mechanised formations (1A, 5C, 8C). Superficially, almost all of the Romanian infantry divisions had, indeed, already been re-formed, but Antonescu was being disingenuous for diplomatic effect in implying that they were combat worthy, for they were in no condition to return to the fast-moving armoured duel in the Ukraine, which remained the crucible of the entire world war. The only three divisions which might have survived there were precisely the mechanised formations admittedly yet to be rebuilt.

At the time of the Stalingrad disaster in November 1942, the Guard, Frontier, 3rd, 8th and 21st Divisions, which had remained in depot after Odessa, were at peacetime establishment. They had all the necessary manpower reserves but were not equipped to Echelon II standards. However, full mobilisation and the hurried issue of German 75mm and 50mm AT guns had brought them to operational status by March 1943.

The manpower of the divisions lost at Stalingrad was relatively quickly replaced. The Frontier Division was dissolved and its infantry divided between 4th Infantry Division, which again became operational in June 1943, and 18th Division, which became operational as a mountain division in August. 1st, 2nd and 3rd Security Divisions and 1st Fortress Division in Transnistria were redesignated 5th, 15th, 9th and 6th Infantry Divisions respectively, because too little of these formations had escaped Stalingrad to provide a base for their reconstruction. By adding manpower from the divisional depots in Romania they were largely up to strength by June. During July and August the 1st, 2nd, 11th, 14th and 20th Divisions were also brought up to strength from their own depots.

This was all made possible because the reduction of regimental field strengths from three to two battalions in late 1941 had left every division with three trained infantry battalions and three of recruits with its training division. Only 7th Division, which had given up its Stalingrad survivors to 24th Division, and the completely annihilated 13th Division had to await the induction of new recruits in September before they topped-up their manpower. As the defence of the country was now at stake, all of the field divisions were rebuilt with three battalions per regiment for the 1944 campaign, but the training divisions remained at six battalions each.

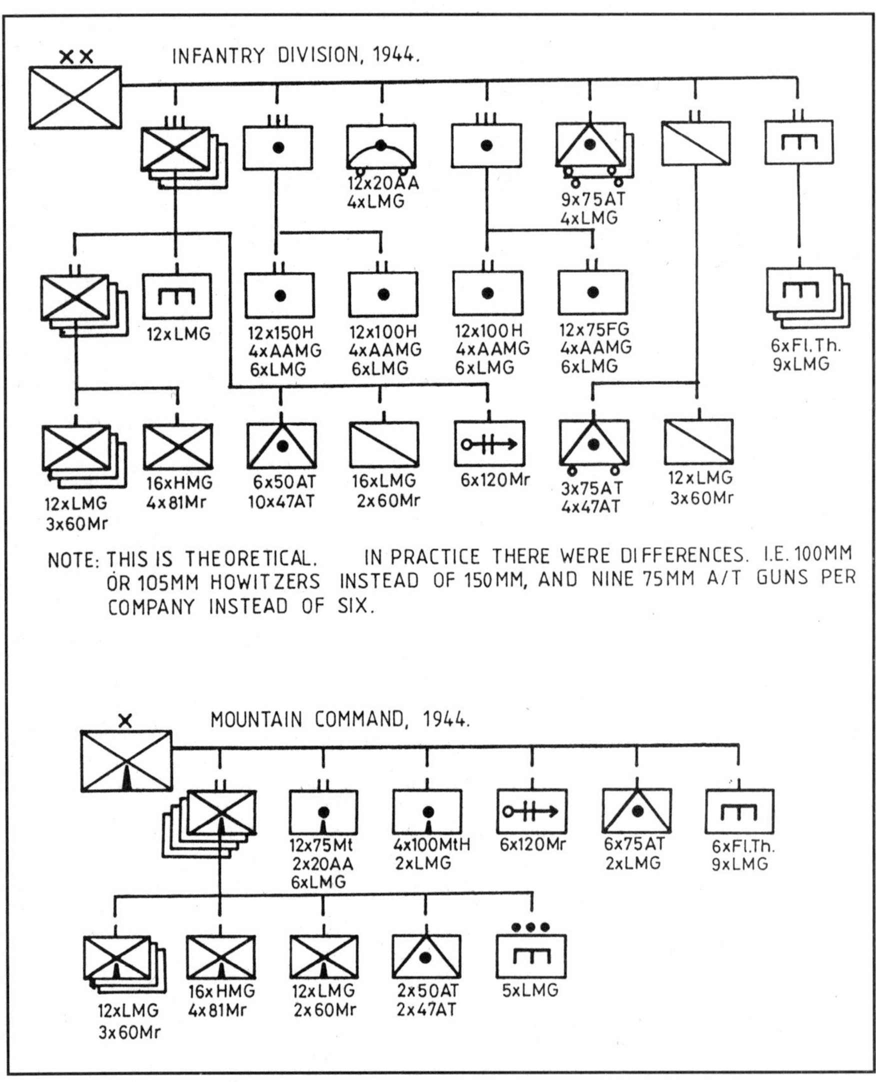

The mountain troops were more easily replaced than the line infantry because their losses in the Crimea were less catastrophic and they never lost their experienced cadre. The cavalry was more difficult to rebuild because it included a high proportion of regulars whose specialist equestrian skills were difficult to replace, and because remounts had to be specially selected and schooled, a task made all the more difficult because by mid-1943 Romania had lost several hundred thousand horses. In 1943 7th Cavalry Division was disbanded and its regiments were used to bring 1st, 5th and 8th Cavalry Divisions up to four regiments each. Of these, only 1st Cavalry Division kept its regiments mounted in 1944. In the Crimea, 6th and 9th Cavalry Divisions remained at three regiments apiece, the latter having one motorised, until they lost all their horses and vehicles in the evacuation. They were never fully remounted.

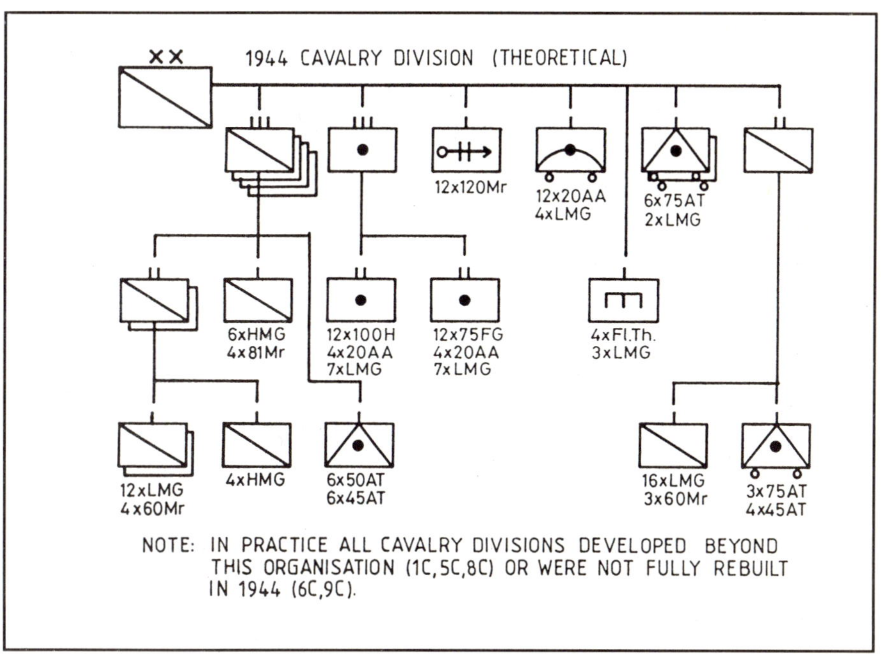

Romanian Armament Losses, 22/6/41 to 1/6/43			
	Issued	**Losses**	**Remaining**
ZB 24 Rifles	445,640	178,685	266,955
Old Rifles	213,777	41,592	172,185
SMGs	9,786	4,038	5,748
ZB 30 LMGs	17,981	7,667	10,314
ZB 37 HMGs	5,539	2,640	2,899
Old HMGs	1,063	197	866
60mm Mortars	2,740	1,184	1,556
81mm Mortars	1,004	420	584
120mm Mortars	437	153	284
37–47mm A/T Guns	2,100	990	1,110
75mm Field Guns	1,187	634	553
100mm Howitzers	625	307	318

Most problematical was the replacement of weapons and equipment. On 20 February 1943 General Şteflea noted privately that most of the necessary equipment and manpower for rebuilding the lost divisions was available, but that he was pretending that this was not the case in order to extract the maximum deliveries of modern matériel from the Germans. However, much of the surviving weaponry was unserviceable and the men were untrained.

The stated Romanian rearmament requirements in August 1943 included 191,898 SMGs; 290,104 ZB24 rifles; 1,124 HMGs; 7,900 AT rifles; 519 FH18/40 105mm and 451 FH18 150mm German howitzers; 70 Skoda M39 75mm and 45 Skoda M39 105mm mountain guns and howitzers; 3,756 Pak 40 AT guns; 1,034 37mm Flak 43, 284 88mm Flak 37 and 62 105mm Flak 39 AA guns; 855 10/12-ton, 520 16/20-ton and 150 22-ton tanks; 1,982 AWD field cars; 1,564 buses; 8,944 3-ton 2WD, 5,697 2-ton 4WD and 2,981 4-ton 4WD trucks; 1,900 tracked AT gun tractors and 1,580 Praga T6 tracked artillery tractors; 1,318 ambulances; 2,920 motorcycles and 6,707 sidecar combinations. These may well have been what the army required to hold its own on the Eastern Front, but, in terms of practicable deliveries within the timescale needed to refield the army, these figures were wholly unrealistic because of the incapacity of German industry to fulfil them.

During 1943 the Germans actually supplied 27,000 Kar98k rifles (almost identical to the ZB24); 5,800 MP41 SMGs; 2,360 LMGs; 1,390 ZB37 HMGs; 800 60mm and 600 81.4mm French mortars and 80 German 81.4mm mortars; 250 Pak 38 50mm, 184 Pak 97/38 75mm, and 45 Pak 40 75mm AT guns; and 252 ex-Czech, Polish and Yugoslav Skoda M14/19 100mm howitzers (obsolete forerunners of the standard Skoda M34). In late February 1944 Clodius agreed to deliver a further 60,000 rifles, 3,700 LMGs, 900 HMGs, 88 Skoda M14/19 100mm howitzers, 60 FH18/40 105mm howitzers, and 375 4WD trucks. Other deliveries in 1943–44 included most or all of orders for 100 Bohler 47mm AT guns, 500 Ford 4 x 2 trucks, 220 tracked Praga T6 heavy artillery tractors and 400 Lanz Bulldog tractors. Replacement Schneider M.1936 105mm guns and 222 new Hotchkiss 25mm AA guns were ordered in France, but delivery of most of these is doubtful.

Not only did these actual German deliveries fall far short of Romanian requirements, but it was immediately obvious that much of the equipment could take up to a year to arrive. The Romanians therefore immediately began to press the most common captured Soviet equipment into service. On 15 April 1943 they had (with numbers repaired in 1943 in brackets): 709 (486) 45mm AT guns; 693 (405) assorted 76.2mm infantry, field or mountain guns; 477 (209) 122mm howitzers and guns; and 148 (±60) 152mm howitzers and guns. Also repairable for the infantry were 116,000 rifles, 7,817 LMGs, 3,650 HMGs, 1,236 AT rifles and 1,555 50mm, 801 82mm and 136 120mm mortars.

Although a small proportion of this weaponry was delivered by Germany in 1943, the vast majority represented the Romanian share of the spoils of the joint victories in the Ukraine and Crimea in 1941–42. In quantity it was roughly comparable with Romanian losses up to and including Stalingrad (see above), and it implies that until then the Romanian Army had captured heavy matériel sufficient to equip at least twenty Soviet rifle divisions. In 1943 Romanian factories put 45mm, 122mm and 152mm ammunition into production to supply the captured artillery. The 76.2mm guns were converted to take 75mm rounds.

The last source of weaponry was Romania's own armament industry. Production of Schneider 47mm AT guns, Vickers 75mm and Rheinmetall 37mm AA guns, 60mm, 81mm and 120mm mortars, ZB30 LMGs, Oriţa SMGs, 75mm barrel liners and Bungescu AA fire directors continued. Skoda M14/19 100mm howitzers were modified to M34 standard, Skoda 100mm and 150mm barrels were built and 88mm barrel liners produced. Attempts were also made to increase the muzzle velocity of the old 75mm field guns to improve their AT potential, but without viable success.

In addition, a series of major new AT programmes were launched to meet the August 1943 rearmament requirements for AT rifles, AT guns and tractors, and light tanks, which the Germans clearly could not meet. A prototype 15.2mm anti-tank rifle based on the Soviet 14.5mm PTRD–41 was completed in 1943, but the weapon never reached production because the tungsten-cored ammunition could not be manufactured; a factor which also restricted the issue of captured AT rifles. In any case, the weapon was obsolescent and was superseded by the issue of numbers of Panzerfausts and 3,000 German rifle grenade launchers in 1944.

In December 1943 1,100 of Romania's own Reşiţa M43 75mm AT guns were ordered from the Resita, Astra and Concordia plants, and the first 30 entered service in February 1944. By 7 August 1944 Resita alone had produced 132, and by 1 December 1944 total production had reached 372 (Resita 210, Astra 120, Concordia 42). It was intended for Ford Romana to produce over 1,000 fully tracked gun tractors, designated the T-1, for the Reşiţa gun during 1944–45. The T-1 was based on the Soviet STZ agricultural tractor, but only five prototypes were completed because priority had to be given to the Maresal tank destroyer programme.

A thousand Mareşal tank destroyers, mounting the Reşiţa 75mm gun, were ordered for 1944–45, but only six prototypes had been built by August 1944. A programme to mount Vickers 75mm AA guns on Bofors-style twin-axle carriages and provide them with a gun shield, to give them a dual AA and AT role, was also advanced. These programmes provoked a major improvement in the organisational, technical and productive capacities of the Romanian armament industry in 1943–44. However, the increasingly acute Axis supply difficulties in 1944 meant that all of the programmes were delayed and, apart from the Reşiţa 75mm gun, were to be halted after Romania's defection in August 1944.

By December 1943 100 per cent of rifles, LMGs and HMGs had been replaced. Mortars and light infantry guns stood at over 80 per cent of establishment, and the deficit could soon be made up from local production and captured weapons. However, because their establishment had been doubled, divisional SMG holdings varied between only 10 per cent and 30 per cent. In 1942 45,000 of Romania's own Oriţa 9mm SMGs had been ordered, and by October 1943 CMC Cugir had produced 6,000. It became the most common SMG by mid-1944. The first German-trained divisions (5, 6, 13) were those most comprehensively annihilated with the Lascar Group at Stalingrad, and over the winter of 1943–44 even their infantry weapons were Soviet captures. However, because of this their infantry, and those of the four mountain commands (101-104), were the first to be largely re-equipped with German weapons in mid-1944.

More artillerymen than infantry had escaped Stalingrad. Furthermore, the reorganisation of late 1941 had reduced the number of 75mm field artillery battalions on campaign from three to two, so a fifth of each division's trained artillerymen and guns were also available in depot. When added to the 75mm pieces held by the nine divisions still in Romania or Transnistria (G, Ft, 3, 8, 21, 1F, 1S, 2S, 3S) and captured Soviet 76.2mm pieces, this was sufficient to provide each infantry division with two battalions of light field artillery almost immediately.

The situation with Skoda 100mm howitzers was much worse, as initially there were only 142 serviceable pieces in country. However, the German Skoda M14/19 100mm howitzer deliveries allowed each division to refield both howitzer battalions by August 1943, and by August 1944 it appears that more Skoda M14/19 100mm howitzers allowed the formation of a third battalion. In July 1944 5th, 6th and 20th Infantry divisions (and possibly others) even received a battalion of German M18 105mm howitzers. Plans to introduce 150mm divisional artillery were stillborn.

Because of its mobility and 4WD traction, losses in the motorised corps artillery had not been so severe, and were more easily compensated by imports of ex-French 105mm or ex-Czech 150mm guns, or by transferring the guns and tractors of the army-level independent motorised artillery battalions. These last were supplemented in the army artillery by captured Soviet 122mm and 152mm artillery and old Debange 120mm guns, which formed at least fourteen independent heavy artillery battalions in 1944. Light AA guns, whose primary responsibility was defence of the divisional artillery, were at 80 per cent of establishment by December 1943, and in such good supply by August 1944 that even the training divisions had a number.

The most serious deficit was still in AT artillery. By December 1943 the divisions in Transnistria and on the coast of Romania had only 50 per cent of their 50mm and 75mm AT guns, while those in the interior had only 10 to 30 per cent. However, this disguised a 150 per cent increase in their official establishment, from six to fifteen. The assorted inadequate Bohler, Breda and Bofors guns remaining were relegated to use as infantry guns, and the AT niche was temporarily filled by Romanian-built Schneider 47mm and captured Soviet 45mm AT guns, which were only effective against light tanks. The regimental 50mm Pak 38s received in 1943 had some marginal potential against Soviet medium tanks, but most of the heavy AT guns delivered that year were still worn examples of the barely adequate 75mm Pak 97/38, which had been superseded in German service. As much as 40 per cent of all German production of this gun eventually found its way into Romanian service.

Only when the 75mm Pak 40 and Reşiţa M43 arrived in numbers during 1944 did the Romanian Army acquire significant anti-tank guns, and even these were stretched by the new JS series of Soviet heavy tanks. By August 1944 many divisions actually had in excess of their official establishment of fifteen 75mm AT guns, and the Frontier Division's two field artillery regiments were converting into motorised army anti-tank regiments, each with 36 Reşiţa 75mm guns. An important by-product of the artillery programme was a major expansion in the Romanian Optical Industry (IOR), which allowed increased local production of gun sights and the introduction of the Septilici field periscope, which entered service with the infantry in 1943/44.

Motor vehicle losses at Stalingrad had been proportionally far lighter than manpower and armament losses, but were nevertheless serious:

Romanian Vehicle Holdings and Losses at Stalingrad

	Holdings			Losses		
	3rd + 4th Armies	Armd. Div.	Total	3rd + 4th Armies	Armd. Div.	Total
4WD Trucks	760	635	1,395	228	292	520
2WD Trucks	3,265	521	3,786	751	146	897
AWD Field Cars	219	120	339	46	48	94
2WD Cars	716	15	731	215	6	221
Motorcycles	675	558	1,233	270	335	605

However, the situation was rather worse than it appears, because the majority of the surviving vehicles were badly worn, especially the tactically vital AWD types. A further 1,000 vehicles were lost in the Crimea in 1944. Romanian vehicle strength never fully recovered:

Romanian Army Vehicle Holdings, 1941–1945

<table>
<tr><th></th><th>22/6/41</th><th>Aut.1942</th><th>1/6/43</th><th>23/8/44</th></tr>
<tr><td>Cars 2WD</td><td rowspan="2">1,932</td><td>1,788</td><td>1,125</td><td>2,238</td></tr>
<tr><td>Cars AWD</td><td>753</td><td>503</td><td>443</td></tr>
<tr><td>Trucks 2WD</td><td>1,263</td><td>5,928</td><td>3,975</td><td>5,025</td></tr>
<tr><td>Trucks 4WD</td><td>2,296</td><td>2,100</td><td>1,828</td><td>1,369</td></tr>
<tr><td>Bowsers</td><td>145</td><td>202</td><td>97</td><td>172</td></tr>
<tr><td>Ambulances</td><td>374</td><td>379</td><td>253</td><td>335</td></tr>
<tr><td>Buses</td><td>89</td><td>?</td><td>73</td><td>181</td></tr>
<tr><td>Motorcycles</td><td rowspan="2">2,063</td><td>1,103</td><td>516</td><td>678</td></tr>
<tr><td>Sidecar Teams</td><td>982</td><td>898</td><td>1,146</td></tr>
</table>

During 1943 the Romanians decided to re-equip 1st Armoured Division, fully motorise 5th and 8th Cavalry Divisions and later convert them to armoured divisions. To oversee this activity they created the Mechanised Troops Command on 1 November, and planned a Mechanised Corps HQ to command them in the field. This at last concentrated the motorised cavalry and armoured units under a unified command. However, their wastage of motor vehicles at Stalingrad had been severe, and the three divisions began their reconstruction at a very low ebb. On 15 July 1943 1st Armoured Division, which should have had 2,767 vehicles, and the two cavalry divisions, had the vast majority under repair:

	1st Armoured Div		5th Cav.Div.		8th Cav. Div.	
	Holding	Repair	Holding	Repair	Holding	Repair
Trucks 4WD	356	305	52	50	30	27
Trucks2WD	424	336	43	41	86	81
Cars 4WD	92	75	11	11	12	9
Cars 2WD	48	28	16	14	33	21
M/C & S/C	254	226	29	29	28	25

The full motorisation of 8th Motorised Cavalry Division was delayed until the summer of 1944, and could only be achieved by taking AWD vehicles from 5th Cavalry Division because German delivery of new trucks was so slow. The motorisation of 5th Cavalry Division therefore never even began, and it later fought on foot.

The pace of armoured re-equipment was almost entirely dependent on German deliveries, which did not begin in quantity to 1st Armoured Division until December 1943. During the first months after its return to Romania, 1st Armoured Division's main concern was the repair of the matériel saved from Stalingrad. On 1 April 1943 it still possessed 59 R-2s, including some hulks destroyed in 1941, but only 16 were serviceable. A single T-3 and T–4 had also been saved from Stalingrad. 2nd Armoured Regiment still had 52 R-35s, a T-3 and a T–4 on 4 February 1943, and a further 8 R-35s were distributed to training centres. It also had 62 FT-17s. Fourteen R-1s were also retrieved from the front by the Cavalry Training Centre. Thus, on 15 April Romania still had 207 tanks, but 203 were obsolete and even the two T-3s had ceased to be classed by the Germans as main battle tanks. Only the two T–4s were first-line material.

There was thus no chance of 1st Armoured Division returning to the front, so during the summer of 1943 its serviceable tanks were used to train the rebuilding infantry divisions in anti-tank tactics. With the exception of the 50 T-38s of 51st, 52nd and 53rd Tank Companies delivered to the Crimea, the only major increases of armoured strength in 1943 were Romania's own completion of 34 TACAM T-60s for 61st and 62nd TACAM Companies and the repair of 30 Komsomolyets armoured artillery tractors for the AT artillery. Only in August were the armoured division's specialist services reassembled in embryo form as the Rapid Detachment, with a signals company (one armoured car), a mixed AT and AA company, a TACAM T-60 company (12 x T-60), a motorised artillery battalion and some services. The two motorised rifle regiments, which had suffered most heavily at Stalingrad, were still rebuilding, and on 30 August the remaining tanks were distributed as follows:

	1st Armd. Regt.		2nd Armd. Regt.		Cavalry & Training	
Type	In Service	Under Repair	In Service	Under Repair	In Service	Under Repair
R-1	-	-	-	-	5	8
R-2	25	30	-	-	-	4(?)
R-35	-	-	46	6	5	3(?)
FT-17	-	-	54	8	13	-
T-3	1	-	1	-	-	-
T-4	1	-	1	-	-	-

On 23 September 1943 the Germans agreed the Olivenbaum I tank and assault gun delivery programme, and the Olivenbaum II and III programmes were subsequently added to it. The last delivery programme, Quittenbaum I, is unclear, but may have included assault guns only.

In addition, 3 T–4 command tanks, 40 SdKfz 222 armoured cars, 8 Italian armoured cars and 27 armoured half-tracks were promised. The Germans kept reasonably closely to the delivery programmes, but many of the AFVs were worn vehicles handed over by panzer divisions redeploying out of the theatre, and their serviceability was often poor. Most of the tanks were PzKpfw IVHs, but there were

Planned and Actual German Deliveries of Tanks and Assault Guns, 1943–44

		1943			1944										
		O	**N**	**D**	**J**	**F**	**M**	**A**	**M**	**J**	**J**	**A**	**S**	**Totals**	
Olivenbaum I	T-4	2	2	2	2	2	2	2	2	2	2	2	2	24	} 115
Olivenbaum II & III	T-4	-	-	13	13	13	13	13	13	13	-	-	-	91	
Quittenbaum I	T-4	-	-	-	-	-	-	-	-	-	13 ?	13?	?	??	
Actual	T-4	-	4	27	19	2	15	15	17	15	15 ?	?	-	129?	
Olivenbaum I	TAs	2	2	2	2	2	2	2	2	2	2	2	2	24	} 80
Olivenbaum II & III	TAs	-	-	8	8	8	8	8	8	8	-	-	-	56	
Quittenbaum I	TAs	-	-	-	-	-	-	-	-	-	20 ?	20?	?	??	
Actual	TAs	-	4	-	2	12	10	10	20	20	20	10 -	-	108	

numbers of F2s and Js among them. Meanwhile, Romanian industry was striving to fit larger guns to older tanks. Thirty up-gunned R-35/45s were returned to 2nd Armoured Regiment, and 21 TACAM R-2s were delivered to 63rd TACAM Company by mid-1944.

Tank Holdings in Romania, 1943-44

Type	**30/8/1943**	**25/03/1944**	**19/07/1944**
FT-17	62	62	62
R-1	13	14	14
R-35	60	47	30
R-35/45	-	13	30
R-2 & 35(t)	59	63	44
T-38	-	20	19
T-3	2	2	2
T-4	2	50	81
TACAM T-60/A	34	34	34
TACAM R-2	-	1	20
TAs	-	10+	60
STZ	30	30	34

During 1943–44 Antonescu expanded his Bodyguard Regiment to three battalions, with the obvious intention of further expanding it to divisional size. The first battalion remained motorised rifles, the second battalion formed specialist AT, AA and assault pioneer companies and a six-tank FT-17 platoon, while the third battalion contained three officer cadet companies and three recruit companies who would form a cadre for further expansion.

From the outbreak of war Antonescu had preferred to weed out officers from the overmanned rear echelons and send them to the front, rather than commit new officer graduates from the years 1941, 1942 and 1943. These younger officers had yet to acquire the defects of their seniors, and were more receptive to intensive training in German methods. The 80 per cent losses among regular regimental officers and NCOs by early 1943 ensured that this new generation of Romanian officers formed by Antonescu dominated junior leadership posts when the army returned to the front in 1944. However, owing to the length of training required to instil the necessary professional expertise into new regular graduates and reservists, divisional officer strengths had recovered to only about 75 per cent of establishment by mid-1944. The troops, although also reasonably trained and fully up to strength, were similarly inexperienced, and where experience did exist it was almost invariably of the unpleasant variety gained at Odessa and Stalingrad. Morale was therefore fragile.

Although it still fell far short of German standards, the Romanian Army was generally better equipped in 1944 than it had been in 1941 or even 1942. However, this did not necessarily mean that it was fit to take the field with confidence, as the Red Army had achieved a far greater accretion of strength over the same period.

THE FAILURE OF PEACE NEGOTIATIONS, 1944

On 16 January 1944 the British informed the Romanians that from then on the Russians would have the leading role in establishing armistice conditions. This followed closely on an independent approach from the Soviet Union in Sweden on 26 December 1943. For the Russians, dealing directly with the authoritarian Antonescu was preferable to dealing via the Western Allies with the King, Bratianu or Maniu, who were all avowedly pro-western, constitutional monarchists. Antonescu also brought to the negotiations two indispensable attributes not possessed by the pro-western Romanians. He controlled the army and had the confidence of the Germans, both of which were vital to the success of an early capitulation attempt and the quick passage of the Red Army across Romania. However, Antonescu's anti-Bolshevism was non-negotiable, and he continued to prefer contacts with the Western Allies. In March he helped Maniu send Prince Barbu Ştirbei to Cairo to try again to enlist western support. Ştirbei was a close confidant of the Royal Family, who had played a prominent role in negotiations with the Allies in the First World War.

In late March the Red Army burst through the Germans and into Northern Bucovina. The same Soviet advance prompted Hungary to attempt to leave the war, but this was foiled by the German Operation Margarethe-I, which occupied the country on 17 March 1944. In its wake a suspicious Hitler, who had learned of Stirbei's negotiations with the Western Allies in Cairo from the British press, again gave serious consideration to occupying Romania pre-emptively in Operation Margarethe-II. However, Germany no longer had the resources to administer the country, let alone fight a protracted guerrilla war there, and was as nervous of provoking a second Yugoslav-style partisan war around the oilfields as Romania was of suffering a Yugoslav-style occupation.

Instead, Hitler invited Antonescu to an emergency tenth meeting on 23-24 March, at Klessheim. There he assured him that sufficient German panzer divisions would remain in Basarabia to defend the province against the Red Army. This had a dual purpose, as the presence of this amount of armour also left so much German power in the theatre that any Romanian defection attempt was unlikely to succeed. Hitler also told the Marshal confidentially that he no longer considered Hungary's occupation of Northern Transylvania under the Vienna Diktat valid, and said he would reverse it, although he could not specify when for fear of the Hungarian Army collapsing.

The terms thus far offered by the Allies in Cairo gave Antonescu very little positive incentive to surrender. They demanded not simply that Romania capitulate, but that it immediately turn its weapons on Germany; something he found totally dishonourable. Realpolitik had already induced the British and Americans to reverse their earlier policy and recognise the Soviet possession of Basarabia and Northern Bucovina, and the Allies offered no cast-iron guarantees about the full return of Northern Transylvania, which was also a tool in their attempts to detach Hungary from the Axis. Although in theory the Soviets were not demanding the right to occupy Romania, their insistence that the Red Army be allowed complete freedom of movement inside the country in order to secure its lines of communication was tantamount to the same thing. This rendered Soviet assurances that they had no intention of changing the existing social order in Romania highly suspect. The Western Allies refused to land paratroops in Bucharest to provide a counterweight to the Red Army, and promised only air support. Ruinous reparations were also demanded. Both Antonescu and the opposition were deeply dissatisfied.

In these circumstances, Hitler's combination of assurances, implied threats and confidential offers, reinforced by the stabilisation of the Basarabian front as promised, appears to have been decisive in inducing Antonescu to suspend peace negotiations with the Allies after a harsh set of demands from Molotov on 12 April 1944. The result was an uneasy stalemate throughout the summer, under which German occupation plans were suspended indefinitely and Romanian official peace feelers were downgraded. Antonescu still hoped to come to a more favourable arrangement with the Allies because there remained certain minor differences between the Western and Soviet positions which, if they could be exploited, might secure better terms. The German occupation of Hungary had removed the threat of attack from this source in March, and allowed him to concentrate on building up his army in Basarabia to strengthen his future negotiating hand with the Soviet Union.

In early June Antonescu's tactics were rewarded when the Soviets in Stockholm softened their conditions to meet some of his counter-demands without consulting their Western Allies. They agreed to relax the reparation terms slightly, leave a sovereign area free of Russian troops from which the Romanian government could rule, and allow the Romanians to give the Germans fifteen days to evacuate the country peacefully. If they did so, Romania could remain neutral. If they fought, Romania would join the Allies. Nevertheless, Antonescu failed to take up these terms because he still hoped to secure western intervention. Unbeknown to him, however, the Western Allies had conceded the Soviet Union primacy in Romania in June, in return for Soviet recognition of their primacy in Greece, and the always slim prospect of securing a counterbalancing western presence on the ground had evaporated.

THE RETURN OF 3RD AND 4TH ARMIES TO THE BASARABIAN FRONT, SPRING 1944

In 1941 Antonescu had willingly pursued the campaign in the east, but at heavy cost. In 1942 he was still prepared to risk his forces, but the results were catastrophic. By 1944 even Antonescu no longer had the political will to do more than defend Romania's eastern frontier. Romania's strongest natural defence line ran along the Carpathians and the lower Danube. However, between these two formidable natural features there was an 80km gap along the lower Siret between Focşani-Namaloasa-Braila. Here Antonescu had prudently doubled the density of the prewar FNB Fortified Line with an additional 1,500 concrete emplacements since 1942. Sixty kilometres of anti-tank ditches were concentrated at the most vulnerable crossing points on the Siret. The FNB Line was permanently manned by the 106th, 115th and 121st Fortress Detachments raised from the depots of the local 6th, 15th and 21st Infantry Divisions.

The effectiveness of mobile operations in the Second World War has tended to obscure the importance of fixed fortifications, and the Romanian emphasis on them in 1943–44 had considerable merit, as the Finns proved in the summer of 1944. Interwar French influence had made the Romanians capable military engineers and, lacking the ability to mechanise, they were left with no choice but to rely on fixed fortifications to avoid being forced into mobile operations in which they would be at a hopeless disadvantage. Thus, unlike Hitler's largely fictitious Eastern Wall on the Dnepr, the FNB Line had real substance and, when combined with the natural strength of the Carpathians and lower Danube, presented the most powerful defensive line available to the Axis on the Eastern Front.

Dumitrescu's 3rd Army HQ had returned to active operations on the Eastern Front in December 1943, taking over security behind the German front on the lower Dnepr. For this purpose it commanded III Corps (4M/24, 15, 8) and assorted German and Slovak security units. No complete armoured formations were available, so the *ad hoc* Cantemir Mixed Tank Group was formed from elements of 1st Armoured Division on 24 February in threatened northern Transnistria, some 55km south of Vinnitsa. It consisted of two tank companies with 30 T–4s and 2 T-3s, a TAs battery of 10 pieces, an R-2 company, an R-35 company and 14 TACAM T-60s in two batteries.

On 8 March the Red Army achieved a major breakthrough of the German front in the northern Ukraine and overran Northern Bucovina, capturing its capital, Cernauţi, on 29 March. On 15 March 4th Army was reactivated under General Racoviţa, commander of the Cavalry Corps in 1941–43, but the Soviet tanks advanced with such speed and force that the locally-raised IV Corps (5C, 4mt, 7, 8) found its proposed defensive line already in enemy hands, and could do no more than evacuate the province's administration and about half a million refugees. The latter flooded across the rest of the country to join the existing quarter of a million Transylvanian refugees, and were soon joined by tens of thousands made homeless by Anglo-American bombing. This exodus, plus declining food stocks in the cities and rising inflation, made the country's precarious situation apparent to the population, and the Siguranţa was flooded by reports of discontent.

The next clash for the Romanians loomed in Transnistria, where the German Army had taken over effective control in February and official control on 1 April 1944. Virtually no Romanians seriously considered Transnistria an integral part of Romania, even fewer considered it worth defending, and nobody thought it practicable to do so. Thus, in early April 1944, when the Red Army broke through the Germans and into the north of the territory, outflanked the one viable defensive line on the lower Bug and began to descend on Odessa, III Corps was hurriedly withdrawn over the Dnestr or by sea. The outmatched Germans were similarly keen to fall back behind the natural obstacle of the Dnestr, and therefore Odessa fell on 10 April without any serious resistance being offered. Unfortunately for Axis hopes,

Soviet momentum allowed them to seize several bridgeheads across the Dnestr before they were brought to a standstill. This partly negated its defensive value. After recrossing the Dnestr, 4/24th Division was retitled 4th Mountain Division on 7 May.

If Northern Bucovina was lost and Transnistria was expendable, Basarabia was neither. Antonescu was keen to try to hold the province, as its recovery was the main reason he had brought Romania into the war. Moreover, by showing a strong front he hoped to improve his bargaining position with the Allies. The passive evacuation of the province in 1940 still rankled and, despite the war obviously being a lost cause, the army was similarly inclined to put up at least a token defence of Basarabia, if only to affirm by this action Romania's claim for future generations. 4th Army dug in just forward of the hastily constructed Traian fortified line between the foothills of the Carpathians on the River Siret and the River Dnestr. This covered the exposed northern approach to Basarabia, which had no major river line to act as a natural defence. Behind the eastern Traian Line the much weaker and less complete Ştefan Line was also begun, largely for the benefit of the German 6th Army; 3rd Army dug in along the lower Dnestr.

Most retreating Germans were unfamiliar with the restraint necessary when operating on allied soil, and many initially treated the local Romanian population with the harshness they had become accustomed to displaying in the Soviet Union. There, forced labour and scorched-earth policies were in force, and plunder and rape had long since ceased to be treated as serious military crimes. After furious Romanian protests, German discipline was tightened up, but not before relations had been further soured.

Despite subsequent Soviet assertions that the Basarabian population supported the return of the Red Army, there is no evidence of serious partisan activity in the province except for a weak movement among the non-Romanian minority of the far south. There was even less active opposition in the interior of Romania, where there were only a handful of very recently organised Communist partisan bands assembling in the Carpathians. Thus Army Group South Ukraine no longer had the added complication of a major guerrilla war across its rear communications.

However, this did not mean that all was well in Romania. In the first year of the war Antonescu had been able to tell Hitler that 22,000 German trains had crossed Romania without a single act of sabotage. Romania's own railways were fully mobilised for the war and known by the propaganda title of '2nd Army'. Although derided by the Germans for their inefficiency, they were vital to the supply of Army Group South Ukraine. However, during the summer of 1944 Army Group South Ukraine began to notice a growth in agitation and a decline in co-operation, both in the oilfields and railways, where it appears that the Communists were taking advantage of the destruction wrought by Anglo-American air raids to stir up the workforces, and the management was increasingly obstructive. There were even isolated acts of sabotage.

On 16 March Antonescu told the Germans that he wished to form 3rd and 4th Armies into a Romanian army group under Romanian command. The Germans were against this, but as they were now on Romanian soil they had to compromise. They conceded the creation of two new mixed groups of armies, one German-commanded and one Romanian-commanded. Group Wohler, created on 26 March 1944 as the Red Army first entered Northern Bucovina, comprised the German General Wohler's 8th Army and Racoviţa's newly refielded Romanian 4th Army. Group Dumitrescu consisted of Dumitrescu's own 3rd Army and the German 6th Army. All four armies contained divisions of both nationalities and had integrated command structures.

In reality, Dumitrescu had less than full operational control over the much larger German 6th Army, while 4th Army was firmly sandwiched between the two wings of Wohler's smaller German 8th Army. The structure was capped by the German Army Group South Ukraine, conveniently situated at Slanic, where it could keep a close eye on 4th Army HQ only 40km away at Bacau. This integrated command was to lead to considerable confusion on both sides at the time of Romania's defection. The whole of eastern Romania, from a line running barely 40km east of Bucharest, passed into Army Group South Ukraine's operational area, and nine locally raised Romanian training divisions (5ct, 8ct, 4mt, 6t, 7t, 8t, 14t, 15t, 21t) were transferred westwards into the interior to avoid overburdening the supply system.

On 25 March, the day after Antonescu left Hitler, von Manstein attended what was to prove his last meeting with his Fuehrer, where he suggested that Antonescu be made head of an army group comprising the four armies defending Romania, but with a German chief of staff. Hitler rejected the suggestion, and it died when von Manstein was dismissed five days later. Antonescu's position in the command structure was thereafter ambiguous. For matters of administration, supply and discipline he had direct authority over his two armies in the field, but on operational matters he was obliged to defer to Army Group South Ukraine. However, his position as an allied head of government, on whose national territory its forces stood, meant that Army Group South Ukraine had necessarily to secure his approval before taking major operational decisions.

Despite this, Antonescu, a hard-headed soldier, caused Army Group South Ukraine rather less operational problems than Hitler, who was motivated by wider political and diplomatic considerations. In April, soon after General Schorner replaced Manstein, Antonescu suggested that Army Group South Ukraine be given freedom to fall back to the Carpathian-FNB-Danube line if necessary. This was consistent with all Romanian interwar planning against an attack by the Soviet Union, but Hitler, to whom the concession of captured territory was treasonous and surrender of national territory inconceivable, was immediately suspicious of Antonescu's motives. He repeated that sufficient German panzer divisions would remain in Basarabia to defend the exposed province. Such an offer involved an enormous personal and political sacrifice for Antonescu, but unlike Hitler he was less inclined to allow political considerations to cloud his military judgement. Indeed, it could be argued that he suffered from the reverse problem, in that he sometimes allowed narrow military considerations to cloud his wider political judgement.

While Group Dumitrescu's position on the Dnestr quickly solidified during May, that of Group Wohler in northern Basarabia remained threatened into June. Consequently, most of the newly refielded Romanian divisions of 4th Army were deployed there. Owing to their inexperience, they were initially introduced to naturally strong positions in the Carpathian Mountains and their foothills, but as the front quietened they gradually took over the line in the lowlands to the east. The first Romanian troops of Army Group Wohler to re-enter combat were frontier guard regiments and ski-trained mountain troops holding the northern Carpathian passes with the German XVII Corps in April. On 23-24 April 26th Ski Battalion particularly distinguished itself by annihilating a Soviet battalion which had penetrated the mountains. The same month, 4th Army began to return to the front with the deployment of I Corps in the Carpathian foothills west of the River Siret.

By mid-May VII Corps had moved into the Carpathians to I Corps' west and V Corps across the Siret to its east, and by the following month VI Corps and IV Corps (the latter under the German 8th Army) had extended the Romanian line east to the River Prut. In late May and early June the Soviets feigned a build-up opposite Groups Wohler and Dumitrescu which successfully pinned down German armoured reserves in Romania far from their imminent attack on Army Group Centre. To add substance to this diversion they mounted a heavy local attack on Tirgu Frumos which was only repulsed with great difficulty by a counterattack from the Grossdeutschland and 24th Panzer Divisions, supported on 2–4 June by the infantry of the Romanian 18th Mountain Division. On 3 and 7 July respectively, General Radulescu of 11th Division and General Racoviţa became the last Romanian *Ritterkreuz* winners for their roles in holding this attack. The front at last stabilised just north of the Traian Line.

The evacuation of the Crimea in April-May 1944 returned to Romania the much-reduced personnel of another seven, largely disarmed divisions (6C, 9C, 1M, 2M, 3M, 10, 19). Most of their trained reserves (and those of 4th Mountain Division) were sent to the front as the 101st, 102nd, 103rd and 104th Mountain Commands and 110th Infantry Brigade while the Crimea survivors were rested and began re-equipping at divisional depots. As the 6th and 9th Cavalry Divisions could not be remounted quickly, they remained wholly in depot, where they absorbed their reserves. 19th Infantry Brigade remained near its depots opposite the Yugoslav frontier where Tito's partisans had begun to use Romanian territory as a refuge from German counterinsurgency operations. Because of their total equipment losses in the Crimea, these divisions began to re-equip with mostly German infantry weapons.

It is probable that failure to secure early Romanian collaboration was a factor in the Soviet decision, taken in late April, to shift the main focus of operations away from Army Group South Ukraine and on to Army Group Centre for the first time in two years. The summer months were therefore quiet in Romania, although active raiding, particularly by the Soviets, kept the troops alert and cost the Romanians a sustainable 3,849 casualties in June, 4,344 in July and 2,591 up to 19 August. 3rd Infantry Division suffered particularly heavily and, the lessons of Stalingrad having been learnt, it was pulled back in good time to reorganise in the Traian line in July. It was replaced by the small 5th Motorised Cavalry Division. This had yet to receive any vehicles, and plans for it to receive its first eight tanks and twenty assault guns were pre-empted by the Soviet offensive of 20 August. It therefore fought entirely on foot.

The quiet summer of 1944 benefited the Romanians considerably, as they were able to blood their raw infantry without undue risk. However, defeatism was rife and morale remained shaky. Army Group South Ukraine also used the respite to bring its German infantry divisions up to strength for the first time in a year. This increased their numbers, but at the cost of diluting the quality of German manpower in Romania. Worse, the desperate need to restore their collapsing fronts in France and Byelorussia in July led the Germans to reduce their armoured presence on the passive Basarabian front from nine panzer and panzer grenadier divisions on 22 June to three by early August, one of which (20Pz) was unfit to take the field. The other two (13Pz, 10PzG) were badly under strength. Force of circumstance had rendered worthless Hitler's assurances about keeping sufficient armour to guarantee the security of the exposed Basarabian front, and on 22 July 4th Army warned; 'If the withdrawal of German armour continues to weaken the front the Romanian Army will have to reconsider its position'.

Unfortunately, the flow of Soviet armour was soon in the opposite direction, because after the destruction of Army Group Centre in July the Red Army returned its attention to Romania. From 31 July 4th Army noted Soviet artillery ranging on its positions, the construction of forward shelters for Soviet assault troops, heavy motor traffic, increased propaganda and the dropping of saboteurs in its rear. On 1 August Racovita went on leave. In the interim his place was taken by the commander of VI Corps, General Gheorghe Avramescu, who had commanded the Mountain Corps in 1941–43. Avramescu was in turn replaced at VI Corps by the German General Abraham of 76th Infantry Division.

On 20 July Hitler had narrowly escaped assassination at the hands of his own army in the Bomb Plot. Determined to test Antonescu's loyalty, he summoned him to their eleventh and final interview, at the Wolfschanze. Worried by the withdrawal of indispensable German armoured support, Antonescu attended promptly on 5-6 August. However, he took the precaution of putting some of his forces in the interior on the alert in case the Germans attempted a coup in his absence, as they had done to Pierre Laval of Vichy France in November 1942, and to Admiral Horthy of Hungary in March 1944. He also reportedly nominated Pantazi his successor as Conducator, and instructed him to combine with the opposition in agreeing an immediate armistice in the event of his arrest in Germany. Mihai Antonescu, well aware of the depth of German dislike of him, thought that he was probably going to his doom. His relations with the Marshal had also deteriorated in 1944, as he tried to force the pace of peace negotiations faster than Ion Antonescu would tolerate, but despite a series of quarrels his resignation was twice rejected.

The tone of the conference was immediately menacing, Hitler emphasising the awful retribution meted out to the German bomb plotters and the Warsaw Uprising, and by implication hanging over Romania as well. He then asked Antonescu directly whether Romania would continue to stand by Germany. Antonescu disarmed the question by stating that Romania could not go to total destruction with Germany, but that, provided the Germans could reassure him about their ability to hold the Basarabian front, Romania's loyalty was not yet at breaking point. Hitler immediately gave such an assurance.

Antonescu tactlessly pointed out that similar assurances about the Crimea and Ukraine over the last year had proved ill-founded. This Hitler promptly blamed on the dismissed Field Marshals Manstein and Kleist, and Antonescu found himself in the peculiar position of defending them against their own commander in chief. He suggested that investigation would place responsibility elsewhere. Hitler, at whom this remark was implicitly directed, became more candid, and Antonescu extracted the frank confessions that Germany could neither absolutely guarantee to hold the Basarabian front against the Red Army, nor provide adequate air defence against the Western Allies. In view of these admissions, Hitler's reiterated promise of Northern Transylvania ceased to have any significance, and his references to secret weapons remained pure fantasy. Hitler then attacked Romania over its lack of economic co-operation. This was increasingly true, but Antonescu, who had taken enormous risks for his German allies, took it as a personal slight and reacted furiously. After Hitler had warned Antonescu that the Soviets would never allow a British landing in the Balkans, the meeting broke up in mutual exhaustion.

The meeting between Hitler and Ion Antonescu, and a subsidiary meeting between Mihai Antonescu and Ribbentrop, had been brutally confrontational. Afterwards, Antonescu described the Germans to his entourage as 'gangsters', and Hitler as a 'raving lunatic'. Nevertheless, he had extracted from Hitler admissions which effectively conceded that Germany's 1940 guarantee of Romania's territorial integrity no longer had practical value, and he now had the necessary reasons to withdraw from the alliance on grounds that satisfied his honour. Both sides clearly knew that Romania's surrender was now only a matter of time, but for both a little mileage remained in the alliance. Antonescu dared not make the break immediately, and Hitler dared not precipitate the break prematurely.

During a later briefing by Guderian, who was very much impressed by him, Antonescu showed a pragmatic grasp of the crises facing the Germans in both East and West, and grudgingly accepted that no German armour was immediately available. However, he insisted that a Russian offensive was in preparation against Romania, and that the early return of the panzer divisions was imperative. Failing this, he again proposed that Basarabia be evacuated to the Carpathian-FNB-Danube line if the common interests of the Axis should make this desirable. As this line could be held by as few as ten divisions without substantial armoured support, such a withdrawal might have released further German divisions for deployment elsewhere. However, a suspicious Hitler was more forcibly struck by the proposed reduction of German strength on Romanian soil than by the operational advantages to be gained, and again rejected the offer.

However, when General Friessner pointed out a few days later that, by taking up Antonescu's option, German divisions would be able to hold the proposed front without necessarily having to depend on unreliable Romanian divisions, Hitler reluctantly agreed to the withdrawal in principle. However, he made it conditional on hard evidence being obtained of a Soviet offensive, an event he was predisposed to consider unlikely as he did not believe that the Soviets had sufficient resources to mount another major assault so soon after their destruction of Army Group Centre.

Hitler was wrong. By 10 August 4th Army had detected the arrival of four Soviet corps from Poland, and underestimated that 600 tanks were opposite it. Avramescu predicted that a Soviet offensive was probable any time after 15 August. This was highly disturbing, but Hitler and most of his commanders considered the Romanians to be congenitally alarmist and continued to discount their reports. However, this Romanian intelligence was generally accurate. By the time the gravity of the situation was acknowledged, it was too late to make strategic redeployments of German armour to the theatre. Indeed, there was not even any redeployment of German infantry divisions within the theatre. On 16 August 4th Army's operations diary recorded; 'The situation is critically weak on the Basarabian Front. Only the presence of a mass of German armour justified holding this front, which is naturally vulnerable. The consequences [of the withdrawal of German armour] could be disastrous.'

Rebuilding the Mechanised Troops

As a partial replacement for their departing armour, the Germans made much of the fact that not only would 1st Armoured Division shortly be fully re-equipped, but 8th Motorised Cavalry Division would soon follow as a second armoured division. The embryos of the two divisions had been rushed into reserve behind the front during April, even though they were still far from complete. On 7 April Detachment Cojocaru was hurriedly formed from available parts of 8th Motorised Cavalry Division and deployed in support of the front at Huşi. It consisted of 12th Motorised Roşiori Regiment, 3 TACAM T-60s from 62nd Battery, 3rd Motorised Artillery Regiment, and 670th, 760th and 750th independent infantry battalions. It remained at the front until 30 June, when it was withdrawn to complete the rebuilding of 8th Motorised Cavalry Division, command of which was given to General Teodorini.

On 28 March the obsolete R-35s and R-2s with the Cantemir Group had been withdrawn, and it was transferred from Transnistria to Roman in northern Basarabia. There it was absorbed into the new Rapid Armoured Detachment. This comprised a four-company reconnaissance group, an anti-tank battalion with one battery of six Pak 97/38 75mm AT guns (shortly replaced by the first Reşiţa 75mm AT guns) and a battery of seven TACAM T-60s, the first battalion of 1st Armoured Regiment with two 16-tank T–4 companies and a battery of 12 TAs, a battalion from 3rd Motorised Rifle Regiment, a battalion from 1st Motorised Artillery Regiment, a 20mm AA company and assorted services. It was the embryo of 1st Armoured Division.

On 7 April Romania's leading exponent of mechanised warfare, General Radu Korne, was at last appointed commander of 1st Armoured Division, and on 22 April 1944 the divisional HQ took over the Rapid Armoured Detachment near Roman. On 26 April the division was named the 'Romania Mare' (Great Romania) Division in emulation of the German élite Grossdeutschland Division, then playing a conspicuous role in defending the nearby front. The political concept of Romania Mare included Northern Bucovina and Basarabia, taken by the USSR in 1940, and through which the front currently ran. The division's title therefore implied a continued Romanian determination to fight for them.

Throughout the summer the division gradually built itself up with new German equipment. It initially trained intensively with 23rd Panzer Division, from which it is thought to have received at least 32 worn T–4s in April and May. On 5 July the division had 48 T–4s and 20 TAs, but it was to receive little more. 23rd Panzer Division was replaced from 30 July by the remains of 20th Panzer Division, which had been virtually annihilated at Bobruisk in late June and was charged with rebuilding itself at the same time as training 1st Armoured Division.

Its lack of AFVs led the German division to cast covetous eyes at the tanks and assault guns arriving for the Romanians. At the end of July their mutual HQ, the German LVII Corps, tried to persuade the Romanians to allow experienced German instructors from 20th Panzer Division to man their tanks in the event of a Soviet assault. The Romanians, who had watched Hitler withdraw six panzer and panzergrenadier divisions from their front in the previous month, indignantly refused. With a Russian offensive imminent, an unseemly squabble on the subject broke out in early August. The Romanians tried to get 20th Panzer Division to release the remaining tanks and assault guns of the 2nd Battalion of 1st Armoured Regiment to 1st Armoured Division, and to send their German instructors to begin training 2nd Armoured Division. The Germans wanted 20th Panzer Division to retain the vehicles in the custody of its instructors until re-equipped itself, and insisted that the Romanian crews were not yet trained.

In the event, 1st Armoured Division was ordered forward on 11 August, and it had to leave 16 TAs in 20th Panzer Division's assembly area and 23 T–4s and 7 TAs in the charge of German instructors with the newly forming 2nd Armoured Division. It appears that 1st Armoured Regiment had to make up its tank deficit in part with assault guns originally intended to form an independent battalion at the disposal of 4th Army. Furthermore, both 4th Motorised Rifle and 1st Motorised Artillery Regiments were still short of a battalion. 1st Armoured Division was thus still incomplete on 20 August, and subsequent German reports often describe it not as a panzer division, but as a panzergrenadier division. (See diagram overleaf.)

In mid-August, 8th Motorised Cavalry Division was in the process of conversion into 2nd Armoured Division at its depots, and was widely dispersed. Its armoured regiment was to be 4th Roşiori, which was to be re-equipped with two companies of 28 T–4s each and 6 TAs. Shortly before the Soviet attack of 20 August, its 2nd Armoured Detachment was ordered to Tecuci, a strategically vital point in the Focşani Gap between the naturally strong Carpathian and lower Danube positions, and the rest of the division was ordered to form on it. 2nd Armoured Detachment consisted of 4th Armoured Roşiori Regiment with 23 T–4s and 7 TAs, 12th Motorised Roşiori Regiment, and 3rd Motorised Artillery Regiment with 36 Soviet 76.2mm field guns pending the delivery of new Reşiţa 75mm guns. It had 2,492 men, 27 all-terrain vehicles, 191 trucks, 115 motorcycles and three SPWs. 4th Armoured Roşiori's armour was actually the disputed 2nd Battalion of 1st Armoured Regiment with German instructors. Only seven additional T–4s and 14 TAs of its own were to reach 4th Roşiori at Tecuci.

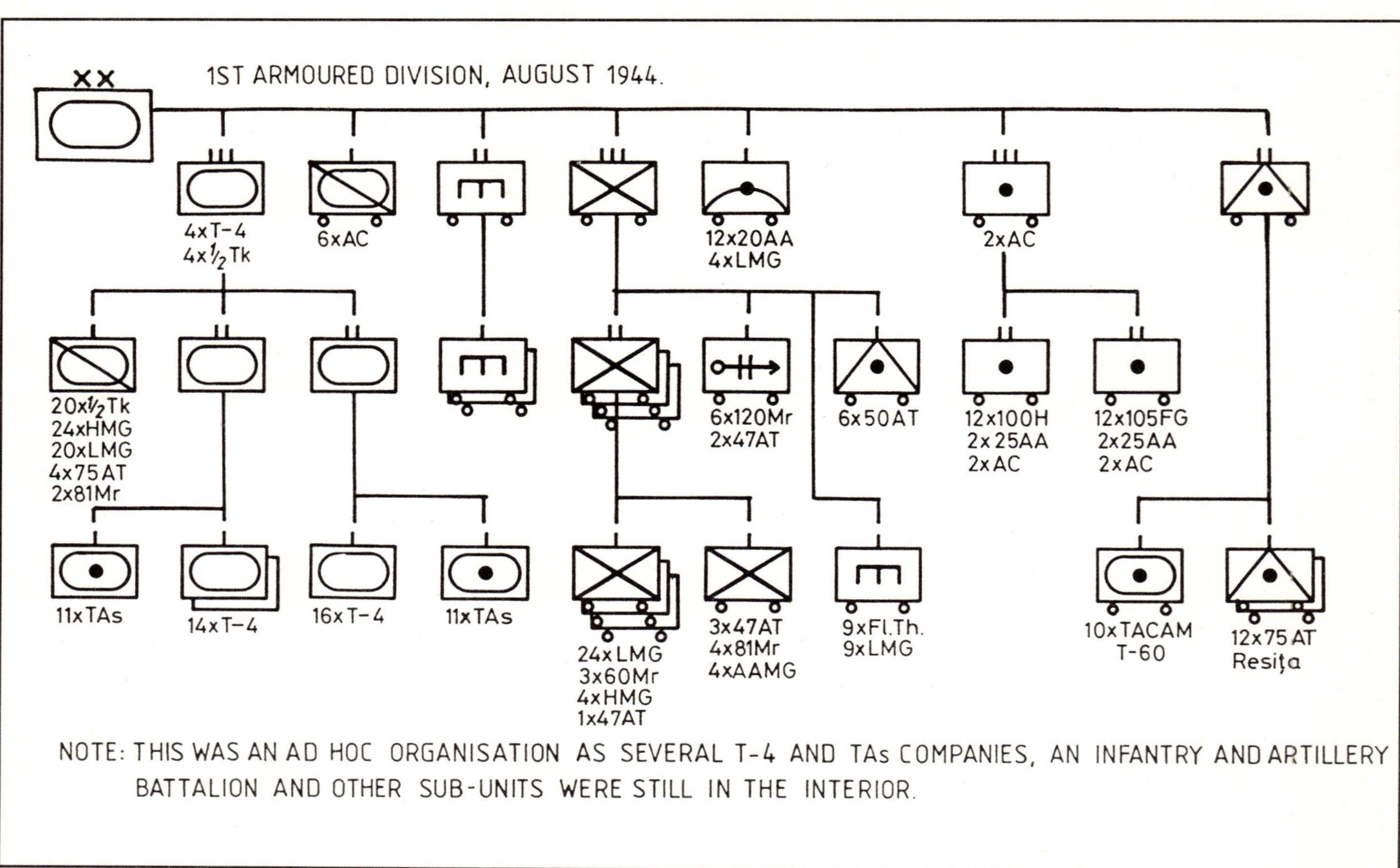

1ST ARMOURED DIVISION, AUGUST 1944.

NOTE: THIS WAS AN AD HOC ORGANISATION AS SEVERAL T-4 AND TAs COMPANIES, AN INFANTRY AND ARTILLERY BATTALION AND OTHER SUB-UNITS WERE STILL IN THE INTERIOR.

THE BATTLE OF IAŞI-CHIŞINAU, 20-23 AUGUST 1944

The Soviet military directive for their offensive of 20 August envisioned an advance of 200km, which would breach the Carpathians-FNB-Danube line and reach Bucharest and Ploieşti, but any further exploitation was expected to be contingent on securing Romania's capitulation.

By 20 August, 4th Army had VII Corps (103m, 104m), I Corps (20, 6), V Corps (4, G), the German LVII Corps (1, *46*, 13) and VI Corps (*76*, 5, 101m). 8th

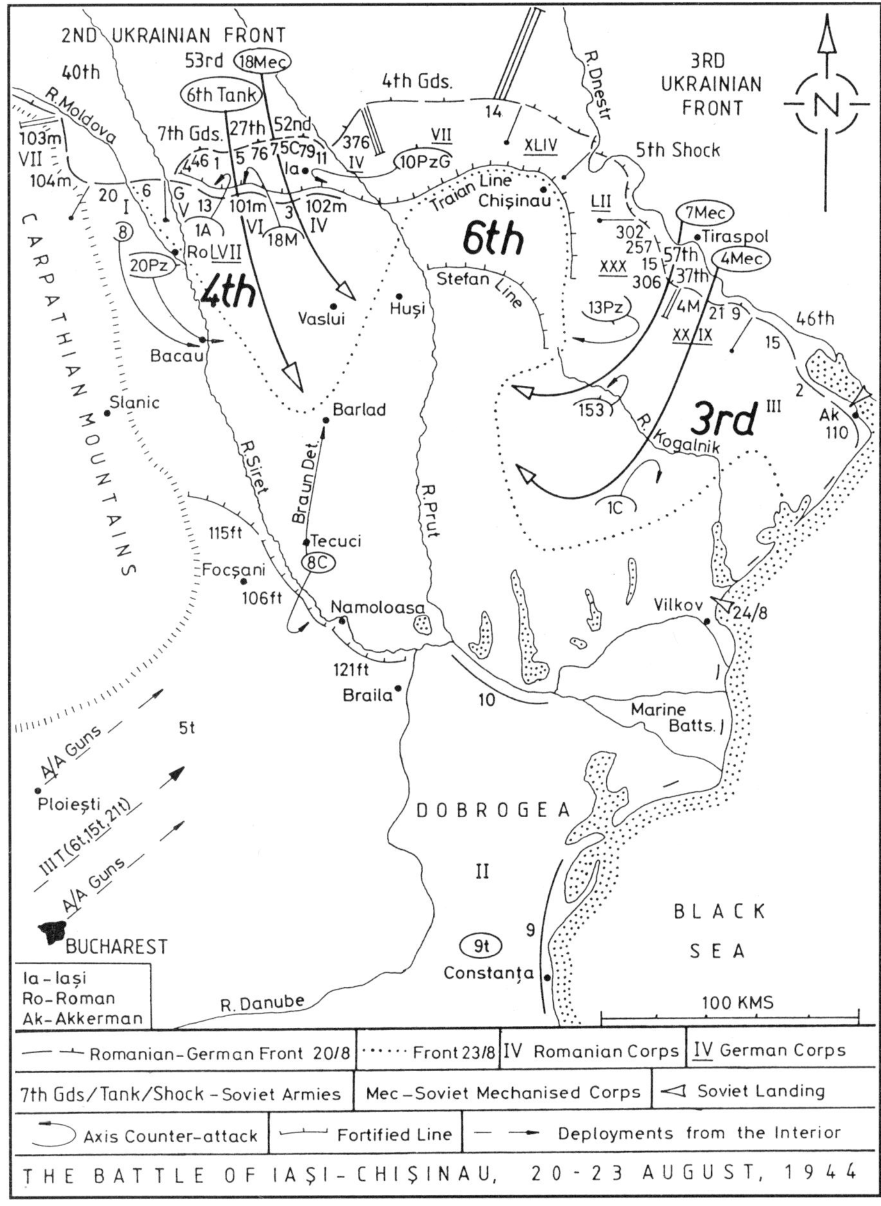

Army had the two-division German XVII Mountain Corps and the Romanian 3rd and 6th Frontier Guard regiments in the Carpathians on 4th Army's left, and the Romanian IV Corps (5C, 7, 3, 102m) and German IV Corps (*376*, 11, *79*) on its right. The bulk of the Guard Division, and the whole of 13th Infantry Division, 101st and 102nd Mountain Commands were to the rear, holding the Traian line between the Rivers Siret and Prut. Army Group Wohler's reserves were 1st Armoured Division, 18th Mountain Division, 8th Infantry Division and 20th Panzer Division.

Against Group Wohler, 2nd Ukrainian Front had concentrated 771,200 men in eight armies, four independent tank and mechanised corps, 55 rifle and cavalry divisions, 11,000 guns and mortars, and 1,283 tanks and SP guns, almost all of them against 4th Army. More specifically, 50 per cent of its rifle divisions and artillery, 80 per cent of its tanks and all of its aircraft were concentrated on the 16km designated as primary breakthrough sectors on the fronts of the Romanian 5th and 7th Infantry Divisions.

Within its order of battle, 2nd Ukrainian Front had the Romanian Tudor Vladimirescu Volunteer Division, organised as a Soviet rifle division. This had been assembled over the winter of 1943–44 from ex-POW 'volunteers' whose main incentive to enlist was to escape probable death in Soviet captivity. It was led by Colonel Nicolae Cambrea, a former staff officer in 6th Division, but real power lay with the Russian officers found at every level and a small number of exiled Communists who politicised the unit. A condition of its employment was that it should not be used against fellow Romanians.

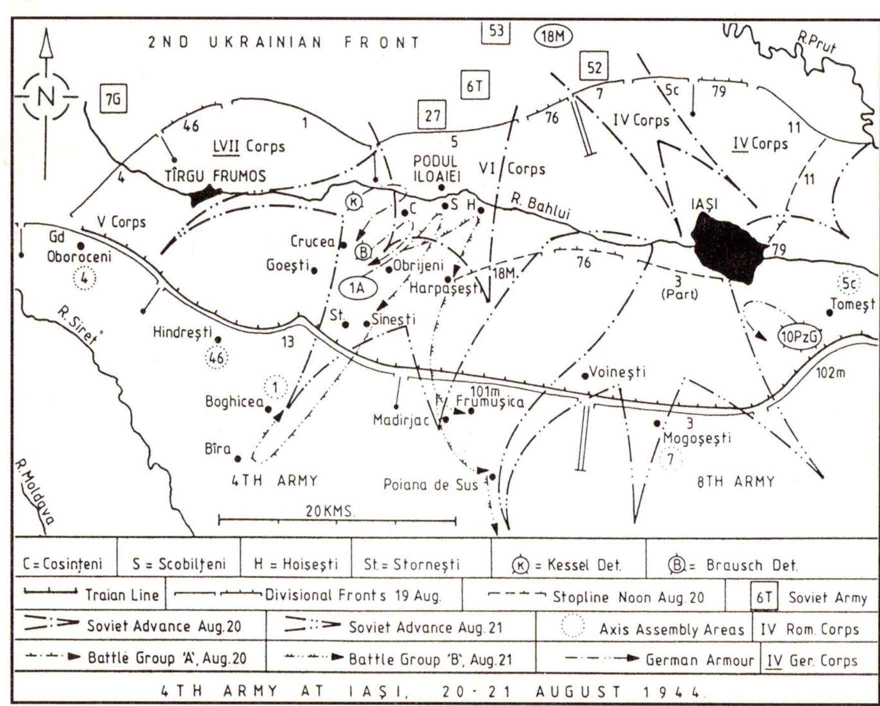

4TH ARMY AT IAŞI, 20-21 AUGUST 1944

On 17 August 4th Army noted; 'The forces facing the Germans are weak. Those facing the Romanians are strong.' The aims of the anticipated Soviet offensive were thus starkly obvious to the Romanians. A rerun of Stalingrad was in prospect, with the Romanian 3rd and 4th Armies being overrun and the German 6th Army surrounded. Given the scarcity of Axis armour, the only practical way to avoid this would have been to take up Antonescu's earlier suggestion and withdraw pre-emptively to the Carpathians-FNB-Danube line. However, the German assessments were far more complacent than the Romanian. For example, on 19 August the best prediction 6th Army could make was, 'The possibility exists that something is brewing on our right flank'. Furthermore, General Friessner no longer had the strength of character to withdraw on his own initiative. He had received his previous appointment at Army Group North because his predecessor had been dismissed by Hitler for requesting freedom of action to retreat, and he had himself then been shuffled sideways to Romania in late July because he had had the temerity to make the same request. Thus did Hitler undermine the initiative of otherwise capable commanders.

On 19 August Antonescu had a heated discussion with Clodius, in which he told him that if at least one German panzer division was not immediately returned to face the imminent Soviet offensive he would consider himself to have recovered full liberty of action. 'Full liberty of action' was code for the freedom to conclude a separate armistice, as Germany was patently unable to fulfil its 1940 guarantee of Romania's reduced borders.

4TH ARMY AT IAŞI

20 August

On the night of 19/20 August, LVII Corps moved 1st Armoured Division, now divided into Battle Groups 'A' and 'B', further forward to the villages of Goeşti, Crucea and Sineşti, 10-14km south-east of Podul Iloaiei, in support of 1st and 5th Infantry Divisions. Two small German assault gun units, the Kessel and Brausch Detachments, were subordinated to it. The centre of gravity of the Soviet blow and its approximate timing had been established, and it was ordered to prepare a counterattack to the north or north-east.

On the army's left wing, VII Corps was not attacked on 20 August. However, the whole fronts of I Corps, V Corps and the German-led LVII Corps were subjected to holding attacks of varying intensity. 20th Division held its line comfortably, but there were local penetrations of 6th Division, the Guard Division and 4th Division. However, local counterattacks largely restored all but the 6th Division's lines during the day. The German 46th Division and Romanian 1st Division held their front against considerable secondary Soviet assaults by 7th Guards Army, but by evening the latter's right had been deeply outflanked by the main Soviet assault, which fell on VI Corps and IV Corps.

From 0740 on 20 August a particularly massive $1^1/2$-hour artillery barrage 'pulverised' 5th Infantry Division's forward defences, which were in five lines, 4-6km deep. When attacked by the Soviet 27th Army, which had 155 tanks and assault guns in its first echelon alone, it was rapidly annihilated. By 1230 27th Army had taken

Podul Iloaiei against only weak, residual opposition and forced a crossing of the River Bahlui. Further east, the Soviet 52nd Army had similarly overwhelmed the 7th Infantry Division by 1300, and had entered north-western Iaşi by evening. 5th Division had ceased to exist, but the remnants of 7th Division were collected in the rear at Mogoşeşti. The front of the German 76th Division between them was also broken, and it was quickly forced to retire to avoid encirclement.

5th Motorised Cavalry Division's left flank regiment, 7th Roşiori, was outflanked by the Soviet breakthrough of 7th Division and surrounded. The remains of the small division fell back precipitately to Tomeşti. On the extreme right flank the German IV Corps' Romanian 11th Division fought well against local attacks and held its front until exposed by the forced withdrawal of the outflanked German 79th Division to its west.

4th Army promptly tried to form a stop line on the heights behind the Bahlui, where two trench lines had previously been prepared. It threw 18th Mountain Division forward south-east of Podul Iloaiei, and part of 3rd Infantry Division supported by German assault guns into the south-western suburbs of Iaşi. The gap between them was to be bridged by the retreating German 76th Division. 18th Mountain Division ran headlong into the powerful 6th Tank Army (±450 tanks), recently released into 27th Army's breach at Podul Iloaiei. Such an early commitment of exploitation armour, before the front had been fully breached (the Traian Line still lay ahead), was an innovation, and caught the defenders by surprise. Elsewhere, the exploitation force was released only on the second day.

While 18th Mountain Division put up a stubborn resistance in the wooded hills behind the Bahlui, 1st Armoured Division was committed to a counterattack on its left flank at 1400 to wipe out 6th Tank Army's massive armoured penetration south of the Bahlui. General Korne ordered the Kessel Detachment to retake Podul Iloaiei from the west and the Brausch Detachment to recapture Cosinţeni and Scobilteni from the south. They were to cover 1st Armoured Division's left flank as it delivered the main blow at Hoisesti.

However, Soviet armour was present in overwhelming strength. The Kessel Detachment was repulsed well short of Podul Iloaiei, and the Brausch Detachment only managed to reach Cosinţeni. 1st Armoured Division had to divert its Battle Group 'A' to support the Brausch Detachment in attacking Scobilteni. Meanwhile, Battle Group 'B', which included 1st Armoured Regiment, attacked north-east from Harpaşeşti and retook the heights at Hoişeşti. There its advanced elements briefly overlooked the Bahlui. However, the counterattack was at best a partial and temporary success, and caused no more than a brief hiccup in the smooth development of Soviet operations. At 1915 the masses of Soviet armour and infantry began to overwhelm 18th Mountain Division and seep round the positions of the Axis armour. The Brausch Detachment's flank was turned and the rear echelons of Battle Group 'A' were put to flight. The Brausch Detachment fell back on Obrijeni, and Battle Group 'A' to Sinesti. The Kessel Detachment was also forced to fall back south-westwards. This left Battle Group 'B' out on a limb, and it retreated to Harpaşeşti .

At noon, Şteflea, who was already on site, had asked Antonescu to come to 4th Army's HQ immediately. At 1850 the Marshal arrived and went into immediate conference with Wohler, Şteflea, Avramescu and Colonel Dragomir (4th Army Chief of Staff). Antonescu, Wohler and Şteflea advocated standing on the Bahlui and launching immediate counterattacks, and overrode Avramescu and Dragomir, who favoured a retreat to the south. The latter's attitude reflected the demoralised confusion reigning in 4th Army's staff. Although General Tataranu had arrived to take over VI Corps, Antonescu instructed that the German General Abraham, who was familiar with the situation, should retain command.

21 August

On the night of 20/21 August, with his division split, General Korne amalgamated Battle Group 'A' (4th Motorised Rifle Regiment, 1st Motorised Artillery Regiment, 101st Anti-Tank Battalion, the SPW company, the Reconnaissance Group and the TACAM Battery), the ten surviving assault guns of the Brausch Detachment and the Kessel Detachment into the Colonel Constantinescu Detachment. Battle Group 'B', which still included about twenty T–4s and ten TAs and 3rd Motorised Rifle Regiment, became the Colonel Nistor Detachment. Korne signalled 20th Panzer Division urgently to send up the tanks and assault guns left in its custody. They were not forthcoming, as 20th Panzer Division had already purloined 16 Romanian assault guns in its own assembly area, and was later to seize the vehicles of the 2nd Battalion of 1st Tank Regiment training with 2nd Armoured Division.

Army Group Wohler's counter-stroke on 21 August envisaged 1st Armoured Division, supported by 20th Panzer Division, recapturing Hoişeşti from the south-west while 10th Panzer Grenadier Division was to attack Iaşi from the south-east. The front was to be consolidated on the Bahlui. However, the hopelessly inadequate 20th Panzer Division did not even appear, and 10th Panzer Grenadier Division, with only about twenty tanks, made no significant impression on the fresh 18th Mechanised Corps exploiting 52nd Army's breakthrough at Iaşi with a mass of some 300 tanks. 1st Armoured Division was already so heavily engaged in merely trying to hold its ground against the 600 Soviet tanks on its front that it was unable to mount its part of the attack.

Early on 21 August, 18th Mountain Division was completely overrun and the Nistor Detachment, which was nearest the centre of gravity of the Soviet advance, was forced southwards to Madirjac, Frumuşica and Poiana de Sus, where it joined 101st Mountain Command in temporarily holding the Soviets on the porous Traian Fortified Line, a series of separate strongpoints. Tataranu was now belatedly ordered to take over the remains of VI Corps (5, 18M, 101m) and hold this line. However, the advance of 18th Mechanised Corps further east through Iasi, having repulsed the counterattack of 10th Panzer Grenadier Division, overwhelmed the forward units of 3rd Infantry Division south of the city, and by midday was already threatening to break through its rear units and the remains of 7th Infantry Division on the Traian Line. About 150 Soviets tanks were reported opposite Mogoşeşti and another 50 at Voineşti, and their further advance would destroy the last link between VI and IV Corps and definitively breach the front at the junction between 4th Romanian Army and 8th German Army's two right flank corps (IV, *IV*).

Antonescu's arrival had invigorated the atmosphere at 4th Army and restored firm direction. With the Bahlui line clearly irrecoverable, he now ordered the western Traian Line between Strunga and Dealul Mare to be held as the new main line of defence at all costs. To meet the looming crisis in the centre, the Nistor Detachment was ordered to counterattack eastwards on Voineşti, while 102nd Mountain Command was to reinforce Mogoşeşti from the west. General Staff Officers and members of Antonescu's personal military cabinet were dispatched to the front to give his orders maximum weight. Antonescu then flew on to Slanic, where he told General Friessner at Army Group South Ukraine of the action he had taken. In a very frank 'soldier to soldier' discussion, Friessner tackled Antonescu about reported unrest within Romania. Antonescu told him bluntly that, given the German-sponsored dismemberment of the country in 1940, this was not surprising and that, furthermore, there was a limit to what he, as an individual without formal political support, could now achieve. Antonescu then returned to 4th Army.

VII and I Corps had a relatively quiet day. However, LVII Corps' 1st Infantry Division had had its right flank turned by the Soviet 23rd Tank Corps, and on 21 August its remains and the neighbouring German 46th Infantry Division and Romanian 4th Infantry Division fell back in accordance with Antonescu's orders through Tirgu Frumos to behind the Traian Line at Boghicea, Hindreşti and Oboroceni respectively. Covering their exposed right flank, the Constantinescu Detachment held on to Sineşti and Storneşti for as long as possible before being forced back in heavy fighting behind 13th Infantry Division's position in the Traian Line. 7th Guards Army followed up closely.

However, in the centre Antonescu's orders were already redundant. Before the Nistor Detachment's counterattack could be launched, the Soviet spearhead from Voineşti broke through the Traian Line and descended on 3rd Motorised Regiment as it assembled in Poiana de Sus, driving it south during the night of 21/22 August. The front was irrevocably broken. At midnight Hitler at last accepted the incontrovertible evidence of the Soviet offensive and belatedly approved Army Group South Ukraine's withdrawal to the Carpathian-FNB-Danube line. In fact Friessner, who had already lost confidence in his Romanian subordinates, had ordered 6th Army to fall back as early as 1430.

22 August

In the face of imminent catastrophe, Antonescu seems finally to have accepted that he might have to settle with the Soviets on the terms they had offered in June. Mihai Antonescu in Bucharest accordingly sent off a flurry of telegrams to Sweden, Turkey and Switzerland during 22 August. However, in order for Romania to retain some influence over events, it was vital that the army survive as intact as possible.

Accordingly, Antonescu personally arranged the phased withdrawal of 4th Army to the FNB Line with General Wohler of the German 8th Army at 1100. VII Corps and 20th Infantry Division were to hold their positions covering the Carpathian passes, but the rest of 4th Army was to move south to the FNB Line as quickly as possible. The intervening stretch of the Carpathians was to be left to any available German forces and the Hungarians, whose 1940 Transylvanian frontier ran close to their eastern foothills. On the night of 22/23 August the line was to fall back behind the Siret, while 1st Armoured and 1st Infantry Divisions were expected to hold a bridgehead east of the Siret at Roman to receive any Axis units breaking out across the Soviet breakthrough.

During the afternoon Antonescu flew on to Slanic to meet General Friessner at 1500. Increasingly, Romanian staffs had been freezing their German liaison officers out of the command process and referring operational decisions to Antonescu rather than Army Group South Ukraine; a sure indication that they no longer considered German and Romanian interests to be necessarily the same. Conversely, the Germans had begun to cut Romanian staffs out of the joint command structure, and Friessner was issuing direct orders to the German 6th Army and LVII Corps over the heads of Dumitrescu and Avramescu. Friessner was most concerned about rescuing 6th Army, but Antonescu had to explain to him that, if the Red Army reached the FNB Line first, Romania was completely lost, and securing this position had to be his own main priority. Friessner reluctantly agreed not only to the planned withdrawal of 4th Army to the FNB Line, but to the withdrawal of 3rd Army to the lower Danube as well. Until this was achieved his 6th Army was effectively on its own.

On 22 August the Soviets tried to provoke a collapse in VII and I Corps, both now well aware of the developing disaster to their east, by attacking them robustly with the largely infantry holding forces on their fronts. 103rd Mountain Command and 6th Division bloodily repulsed them. The 4th and Guard Divisions successfully held the Traian Line throughout the day, but most pressure fell on 13th Division.

General Korne and his divisional headquarters took personal command of the remains of the Nistor Detachment. This largely consisted of 1st Armoured Regiment, which appears to have been cut off at Madirjac when 3rd Motorised Rifle Regiment was driven from Poiana de Sus. It was successfully withdrawn westwards and reunited with the Constantinescu Detachment. 1st Armoured Division reorganised itself under constant air attack around Boghicea and Bira, and then counterattacked the first Soviet penetrations of 13th Division's front. They held the Soviet advance until midnight, at which point the defences of 4th Motorised Rifle Regiment were breached and the retreat resumed. 1st Armoured Division continued a fighting withdrawal, mounting a successful counterattack that temporarily drove the leading Soviet troops out of Boghicea. This covered the planned retirement of the remains of the Guard, 4th, 13th and 1st Divisions and 46th German Infantry Division across the River Siret north of Roman in the early hours of 23 August.

3rd Motorised Rifle Regiment held up the Soviet drive south from Poiana de Sus for several hours during the early morning of 22 August, but with daylight the build-up of Soviet armour on this main line of its advance became overwhelming, and the regiment was forced again to retreat southwards. Tataranu reported that VI Corps (5, 18M, 101m) no longer existed, and was ordered to reassemble its remains behind the FNB Line. The remnants of IV Corps' 3rd and 7th Infantry Divisions were driven far south of the Traian Line during the night, and from noon on 22 August they and parts of the 76th German Division began to break out across the rear of the Soviet spearheads, towards the Siret. At 2045 the always unenthusiastic Avramescu resigned in protest because the German-led LVII Corps was refusing to fall back in accordance with Antonescu's timetable and was being supported by Wohler. Şteflea took over 4th Army from him early the next morning.

Antonescu was noticeably downcast when he returned to Bucharest that evening. At meetings with representatives of Maniu and Bratianu he agreed for the first time to discuss possible joint armistice negotiations with the opposition the following day. Even at this late stage his residual authority in the army was a valuable commodity to the opposition. He then saw Carl Clodius, and during commercial negotiations made it clear to him that Romanian military resources were nearly exhausted, and that Romania was doomed if the FNB Line was breached.

Antonescu, who prided himself on his honour, apparently wanted to convey through Friessner and Clodius to Hitler that he had remained loyal to the alliance to the last practical moment, but that owing to the Reich's inability to fulfil its obligations to Romania he could do no more for the common cause without irrevocably damaging the interests of Romania. He wanted Hitler to release him from his alliance, and thereby avoid fighting the Germans. However, Friessner had his own problems and Clodius was apparently unaware of how serious the collapse of the front actually was. Thus, fortunately for the success of Romania's *volte face*, Hitler was not properly briefed on Antonescu's state of mind until 24 August.

23 August

On 23 August the withdrawal continued. As was so often the case with Romanian infantry divisions forced into rapid mobile operations, 1st and 13th Divisions of LVII Corps had largely disintegrated by the time they crossed the Siret, and 1st Armoured Division was ordered to co-operate with V Corps' still combatworthy Guard and 4th Divisions in covering a further withdrawal from the River Siret to the River Moldova. 4th Army's last uncommitted division, 8th Infantry, which had been held in reserve behind I Corps, was ordered south to hold a bridgehead east of the Siret at Bacau with 20th Panzer Division. Their objective was to cover the southerly withdrawal of 4th Army and receive 6th Army's westward breakout attempt across the Prut via Vaslui.

The previous day, Army Group South Ukraine had also ordered the German instructors from 20th Panzer Division to seize all the T-4s and TAs of 2nd Armoured Division at Tecuci. These were formed into the Braun Detachment and ordered north to Barlad and Vaslui to secure 6th Army's line of retreat. With the loss of its armour, 2nd Armoured Division reverted to its old title: 8th Motorised Cavalry Division. It was then ordered by Antonescu to assemble in reserve behind the FNB Line. The separation and deployment of these two units in opposite directions was symptomatic of Friessner and Antonescu's differing priorities. Antonescu also began to redeploy the locally raised 6th, 15th and 21st Training Divisions, then training in the Danube valley south-west of Bucharest, to join 106th, 115th and 121st Fortress Detachments in the FNB fortifications, and ordered the redeployment of all mobile 88mm and 75mm AA guns at Bucharest and Ploiesti to support them in the AT role.

On I Corps' front a counterattack by 6th Division virtually restored the remaining part of its line lost on 20 August, and as late as 2040 that day it repulsed another Soviet attack. Behind 6th Division's front the withdrawal to the River Moldova continued, elements of 1st Armoured Division crossing it by midnight. Only at 0030 on 24 August were the Romanian divisions of 4th Army formally told of the cease-fire with the Soviets.

1st Armoured Division had reportedly lost 34 AFVs, but claimed 60 Soviet tanks on 20 August alone. For the division the battle of Iaşi had uncanny echoes of Stalingrad. Once again it had been married to an operationally inadequate German panzer division which had to raid 1st Amoured Division's resources (fuel at Stalingrad, armour at Iaşi) to retain some offensive potential. On both occasions, and despite the best efforts of its debilitated German sister units, a combination of German weakness and wider strategic misjudgements had left an under-equipped 1st Armoured Division little supported in counterattacking a major Red Army armoured offensive. On both occasions the division had had some local, but expensive, success before being washed away in an avalanche of Soviet tanks.

Yet on both occasions it had retained cohesion and emerged from the debacle much reduced but intact. From the German point of view the military logic of seizing Romanian armour and replacing its raw crews with their experienced German instructors was inescapable, but for the Romanians this unilateral action by their ally represented a major diminution in their already limited armoured strength at a moment of the gravest national crisis. Indeed, during the battle of Iasi they appear to have lost as much armour to the depredations of their allies as to the fire of their enemies.

3RD ARMY ON THE DNESTR

By 20 August, 3rd Army included II Corps (9, 10, 9t) on coastal protection in the Dobrogea, a group of Marine and Frontier Guard battalions in the Danube Delta, III Corps (110b, 2, 15) on the Basarabian coast and in the line on the lower Dnestr, and the German XXIX Corps (*9*, 21, 4M) opposite a Soviet bridgehead south of Tiraspol. The neighbouring German 6th Army included 14th Infantry Division amongst its thirteen German infantry divisions. Army Group Dumitrescu held 1st Cavalry Division, two companies of R-35 tanks, 13th Panzer Division and 153rd German Infantry Division in reserve.

3rd Ukrainian Front had 523,000 men in five armies, two independent mechanised corps and 37 rifle divisions. It had packed about 600 tanks into its bridgeheads across the Dnestr, and had 8,000 guns and mortars in support. It concentrated 70 per cent of its rifle divisions and artillery, and virtually all of its tanks and aircraft, on a primary breakthrough sector of only 18km on the front of its 37th Army, mostly opposite the German 15th and 306th Divisions. Secondary assaults were mounted by 57th Army on two more German divisions, and by 46th Army on the Romanian 4th Mountain Division.

3rd Ukrainian front began its attack on Group Dumitrescu at 0820 on 20 August with a 1hr 45min bombardment. The main weight of the subsequent assault fell on the right flank of the German XXX Corps (*306*, *15*, *257*, *302*) and the left flank of the mixed XXIX Corps (*9*, 21, 4M). The German 15th Division suffered 20 per cent infantry losses in the initial bombardment and lost its forward positions.

Their 306th Division lost a third of its strength in the initial bombardment, and much of its infantry fled. By 1000 Soviet tanks had reached its command post, and only the most tenuous line remained. The Romanian 4th Mountain Division also bore a heavy attack, and either fled or was evicted from its forward defences in what the Soviet 46th Army described as 'fierce fighting'. The division disintegrated during the day, and the Soviets advanced up to 12km. The lightly attacked 21st Infantry Division to its south was badly shaken by this penetration on its northern flank, and began to withdraw in conformity. The 13th Panzer Division, with only 35 tanks, counterattacked the Soviet breakthrough from the north but was repulsed with the loss of 15 of them.

21 August

Further counterattacks by 13th Panzer Division and 153rd Division were similarly repulsed on 21 August. The remains of the Romanian 4th Mountain Division were effectively destroyed by morning and the German 306th Division by noon, at which points the Soviet 4th and 7th Mechanised Corps were then released into the respective breaches. 21st Infantry Division collapsed, exposing the left flank of the German 9th Division, which then had to fall back south.

22 August

During 22 August the two Soviet mechanised corps penetrated 80km into the rear of Group Dumitrescu and destroyed 13th Panzer Division's last tanks. Dumitrescu's final reserve, 1st Cavalry Division, tried to hold the River Kogalnik but was driven off by the weight of Soviet armour, losing 20 per cent of its strength. The right wing of 3rd Army had continued to hold its front on the lower Dnestr, but on 22 August the Soviet 46th Army made a large amphibious assault across the Dnestr estuary against the overextended 110th Infantry Brigade. The Soviets landed 8,000 troops, 200 guns and eight tanks, and were easily able to repulse a counterattack by a single regiment. They then overcame 'desperate resistance' to take Akkerman by late evening. This threatened 3rd Army's III Corps with encirclement from both left and right. 6th Army was in a similar predicament, and Group Dumitrescu began to retreat to the west on 22 August in accordance with the new orders Army Group South Ukraine had agreed with Antonescu. 6th Army was to break out west across the River Prut towards the Carpathians. 3rd Army's 1st Cavalry Division, III Corps and XXIX Corps were ordered behind the FNB Line, while the hitherto unengaged II Corps in the Dobrogea was assigned the defence of the Danube between Galaţi and the sea.

23–24 August

3rd Army was not physically surrounded on 23 August, because the Red Army concentrated on wheeling north in order to surround the German 6th Army. However, neither could it reach the Danube on foot along the coast in a single day, and it was still far behind the Soviet flank. Apparently, large elements did not lay down their arms after receiving ceasefire orders at 0030 on 24 August, for the following day, the Soviets report, 'The Romanians tried hard to break out of encirclement and fought desperately to push to the towns of Jibrieni and Vilkov. To seal its escape route the Soviets landed marines by sea at Jibrieni late on 24 August, and this finally induced most of 3rd Army's capitulation.

THE COUP: THE OVERTHROW OF ANTONESCU AND DEFECTION FROM THE AXIS

The German Foreign Ministry had heard hints of Mihai Antonescu's renewed negotiations with the Allies, but in the first half of the year its suspicions were outweighed by reports from von Killinger, Hansen and Gerstenberg that, despite his declining influence, Antonescu was still loyal and the Romanian opposition lacked the nerve to act against him. Antonescu tactlessly told Guderian on 6 August that a generals' conspiracy of the sort that only three weeks before had attempted to take the Fuehrer's life in the Bomb Plot was inconceivable in Romania. By mid-1944 this was no longer true, for while none proposed to assassinate him, some Romanian generals were beginning to connive with the opposition. There is evidence that during July Antonescu had, in fact, been made highly nervous by well founded rumours of internal conspiracies against him and less convincing suspicions of a possible Soviet commando raid against him. However, confiding this to the Germans would have invited immediate occupation.

Killinger and Hansen also spoke to Guderian in August and revealed their growing disenchantment with Antonescu, but were so out of touch with reality that they apparently advocated switching support to a puppet government under King Mihai, who was actually the focus of efforts to defect from the Axis! Gerstenberg was so smug that he boasted he could capture Bucharest with a single Luftwaffe flak battery. Only Friessner exhibited the degree of anxiety the situation merited, but he was new to Romania and his opinion on its internal politics was less valued. In the end Antonescu's apparent self-confidence seems to have been decisive. It convinced Hitler and became the key factor contributing to German inertia in Romania. Not only had Operation Margarethe-II been indefinitely postponed after their meeting in March, but a proposal by Ribbentrop to move the 4th SS Motorised Division to Bucharest from Yugoslavia was vetoed after their meeting in August.

If paralysis at the front was partly the result of the confused German-Romanian command structure, German paralysis within Romania was partly the result of their own self-inflicted command confusion. Friessner's Army Group South Ukraine was subordinated to OKH, and it had command of only the German and Romanian army formations east of the Carpathians and Danube. German Army units in the rest of Romania were under General Hansen of OKW, Gerstenberg's Luftwaffe units around Ploieşti were under OKL and Admiral Brinkmann's naval units around Constanta were under OKM. The Romanian 1st Army, which commanded all Romanian units in the interior, was entirely outside German jurisdiction. On top of this, the withdrawal of German armour from Basarabia in July 1944 made it technically feasible for Soviet forces to penetrate Romania faster than the Germans could for the first time in the war. This fundamentally altered the internal political balance of the country, making Antonescu's collaboration less than vital to any defection, and a coup against him practicable.

Into the vacuum left by German jurisdictional confusion and Antonescu's failure to agree terms in June stepped the National Democratic Bloc, which was formed that month. This was a coalition of the King and royalist army officers under General Sanatescu (Head of the King's Military Household), Bratianu of the Liberal Party and Maniu of the National Peasants' Party, who began to plot their own independent way out of the war. To them was added Titel Petrescu of the Social Democratic Party, the moderate branch of the Romanian socialist movement. Finally, the minute but suddenly influential Communist Party under Lucreţiu Patraşcanu had to be included, because no accommodation could be reached with the Soviet Union without it. Their agreed aims were the overthrow of Antonescu, an unconditional armistice, the restoration of national sovereignty and the institution of a democratic constitutional regime.

However, the Communist Party's concept of national sovereignty and a democratic constitutional regime were to prove markedly different from those of the other conspirators. Many of its exiled leaders were not ethnic Romanians, and had a distinctly more internationalist view than Patraşcanu. The Romanian Communist Party of 1944, with a minuscule prewar membership, was essentially the Soviet Union's creature, and expected to come to power through its agency.

The objective of the other, largely pro-western conspirators, who between them could claim the prewar electoral allegiance of most Romanians except the virtually defunct Iron Guard, was to try to retain a genuine independence from the Soviet Union. For this they required an interval between the overthrow of Antonescu and the arrival of the Red Army in order to establish their regime. They still hoped that Western paratroopers might support them and the Red Army subsequently bypass areas already under their control – particularly Bucharest. The conspirators were not to know that the Western Allies had conceded the Soviet Union primacy in Romania in June 1944, and that, thereafter, all their machinations to enlist western support were as foredoomed to failure as were Antonescu's.

All of the National Democratic Bloc parties lacked significant armed support. Even if the Communists' claim to have 160 'Patriotic Combat Formations' in Bucharest was true, it was of little value because they lacked weapons. In these circumstances the role of the King and Sanatescu in securing army co-operation, with or without Antonescu, was vital. In June they prevailed upon Şteflea and some of his GHQ staff secretly to undertake Operation Cosma, an analysis of German deployments within Romania. This was, in fact, no more than a compilation of intelligence reports always prepared for Antonescu. However, when such front-line soldiers as Racoviţa, his chief-of-staff Colonel Dragomir, and General Niculescu of V Corps were approached for support, they sensibly balked at supporting a July coup because too much German armour was in the theatre.

As a result a July coup was ruled out, and the mechanics of what became the August coup were apparently planned by a small group of rear area officers, of whom the most significant were General Sanatescu at the Court, General Teodorescu and Colonel Damaceanu (commander and chief-of-staff of the Comandamentul Militar al Capitalei – CMC – the corps-status military command of the capital), and General Vasiliu-Raşcanu (commander of 5th Territorial Corps around

Ploieşti), whose commands coincided with the main German concentrations in the country.

The military conspirators knew from Operation Cosma that there were considerably more German personnel in Bucharest than combat-ready Romanian troops. The capital was almost undefended because Antonescu had sent the locally-raised Guard and 4th Divisions to the front, and their training divisions were deployed along the Danube facing Bulgaria. Only the King's Guard Calaraşi Regiment and a mixed R-35, T-38 and FT-17 battalion of 2nd Armoured Regiment were of any significance. On 30 July the CMC acquired two recruit battalions from the Guard and 4th Training Divisions, but this still left more uniformed Germans than trained Romanian troops in the capital. Thus the units firmly under the CMC conspirators' command at the coup's initiation were remarkably few. They were therefore forced to rely on the commanders of the field army honouring their higher oath to the King if Antonescu had to be arrested. The fact that their June approach to Şteflea, Racoviţa and Niculescu was not betrayed made this a realistic hope, but not a foregone conclusion. These generals had been approached precisely because they were believed to be receptive. Many more, such as Pantazi, Dumitrescu, Korne and Teodorini, were not approached because their reaction was at best unpredictable and quite possibly hostile. Even some of the military conspirators saw the coup more as an action against the Germans than against Antonescu.

Although the conspirators had approached the Soviets in Stockholm on 8 August about possible military collaboration, no reply had been received. Thus the exact timing of the Soviet offensive of 20 August caught them by surprise. At hurriedly arranged meetings called by the King on 21 August, the National Democratic Bloc set the date for a coup against the Germans, and Antonescu if necessary, for 26 August and all of its civilian leaders went into hiding. However, the following day the rapid Red Army advance upset their timetable, because the Soviets threatened to reach Bucharest before an independent, pro-western government could be securely installed. Furthermore, Antonescu was spending most of his time with the army at the front, where he retained many adherents, and might be absent from Bucharest on 26 August.

Thus, when he learnt that Antonescu had returned to Bucharest late on 22 August, the King unilaterally resolved to confront Antonescu on 23 August before he could return to the front, even though it was too late to forewarn any of his civilian and all but his most intimate military co-conspirators at court. Fortuitously, this greatly reduced the possibility of a leak. The King's decision also unknowingly preempted possible German action resulting from the disconcerting interviews Friessner and Clodius had had with Antonescu on 21 and 22 August.

At 1030 on 23 August Antonescu agreed verbally with representatives of Maniu and Bratianu to conclude a joint armistice subject to a written guarantee of their support. However, at his last cabinet meeting that morning he still hedged his bets by also making provision for a defence of the Carpathian-FNB-Danube Line and, failing this, the evacuation of the government from Bucharest to Haţeg in the west of the country, where it could form a national redoubt with German support. This was not as irrational as it might appear, as within Antonescu's own experience Romania had formed a similar redoubt in the east of the country with Russian help in the First World War, and had held out for a year. At 1300 Antonescu learnt of a further deterioration at the front, and resolved to return to 4th Army HQ that evening. However, Mihai Antonescu, who had been persuaded to adopt a common peace policy with the opposition, but was not a party to the coup preparations, convinced him to pay a courtesy visit to the King before doing so.

This was no easy task, as Antonescu had long dismissed the young King as an irrelevant, immature youth. The King was strongly anglophile, and Antonescu had prudently never asked him to declare war, a responsibility he took entirely on himself as Conducator. Nevertheless, the King had accompanied Antonescu to the front in Basarabia in 1941. However, the Germans had turned a later royal visit to Romanian troops in the Crimea in 1942 into a propaganda exercise, and thereafter he had consistently signalled his disapproval for continuing the war by refusing to visit the front when it lay deep in Russia. For most of the war the King was impotent before Antonescu, who, when exasperated by lack of Court co-operation, often threatened to abolish the monarchy. He therefore had to content himself in public with a petty campaign to prevent Antonescu usurping court precedence. However, he had always kept in contact with the opposition, and in August 1943 had actively joined them. By August 1944 rivalries amongst the National Democratic Bloc's leaders and the allegiance of army officers had given him more than symbolic prominence. On 5 August Hitler had warned Antonescu against venturing into the palace, but the Marshal's self-confidence and low opinion of the King made him unwary.

Despite his distaste for the Court, Antonescu arrived at 1600 and met the King, Mihai Antonescu and General Sanatescu. The King he regarded as little more than a child, Mihai Antonescu was his kinsman, and Sanatescu was an old cavalry colleague, so he was not suspicious and entered unarmed and without his escort. It seems probable that, as the youthful King's long-standing misgivings about the war were proving correct, the proud Marshal was in no mood to admit that he was being forced into diplomatic compromises long urged on him by the Crown, let alone surrender any authority to him.

The King began by asking Antonescu his intentions. Bratianu's and Maniu's written support for joint armistice negotiations had not yet been forthcoming, as both were in hiding outside Bucharest, and no firm reply had yet come to Mihai Antonescu's recent telegrams to the Allies in neutral capitals. This apparently left a disillusioned Antonescu in a political limbo, and he seems to have expounded only on his alternative plan to try to hold the FNB Line until he received either Hitler's release from his alliance or guarantees from the Western Allies that the country would not be overrun by the Soviets. Neither was a realistic possibility, as even Mihai Antonescu now indicated. When Antonescu remained unbending, the King asked him whether he would stand down and allow someone else to treat with the Allies. The Marshal replied 'Never!'.

Antonescu often seemed to think that no human or material sacrifice was too high a price to pay to uphold Romania's honour. To his credit this included his own life. This attitude of 'Death before Dishonour' ran as a consistent thread through his career. The young King therefore had good reason to take him at his word now. In the face of such apparently total intransigence, he ushered members of his palace guard into the room to arrest the Marshal. At 1700 a stunned and furious Ion Antonescu was shut in a large wall safe with Mihai Antonescu, and during the next hour the Defence Minister, General Pantazi, and the Under-Secretary of the Interior, General Vasiliu, were summoned in Antonescu's name and arrested. The King promptly reasserted the 1923 Constitution usurped by his father in 1938 and ignored by Antonescu since 1940. Under it he appointed General Sanatescu interim Prime Minister and the absent Maniu, Bratianu, Petrescu and Patraşcanu Ministers without Portfolio.

Although both the political and military conspirators were caught by surprise by the King's early action, coup plans in the capital were sufficiently flexible to be put into action from 1830. The German headquarters in Bucharest began to be isolated, and their telephones were cut off. Eugen Cristescu, the head of the Serviciul Special de Informaţii, was too canny to obey a summons to the palace, and at 1930 told the Germans of his suspicions. By 2000 Hitler knew of the coup and von Killinger had rushed to the palace to try and browbeat the young King, but he and Sanatescu ordered the evacuation of all German forces from the country and promised that they would not be attacked if this was begun immediately. At 2230 the King broadcast to the nation the news of his coup, his new government and his terms to the Germans. Hansen and Gerstenberg, who had already been ordered by Hitler to suppress the coup, then arrived at 0200 to be faced by the same evacuation demand from Sanatescu. Gerstenberg offered to go immediately to Ploieşti to begin the evacuation, but when he was allowed to do so by a naive Sanatescu he promptly took command of the attack on Bucharest being assembled at Otopeni.

As far as the Romanian Army was concerned, the conspirators' calculations were right, and the Germans ruefully noted that every single Romanian general remained loyal to the King. These included Steflea, Dumitrescu and Korne, who, when contacted by Friessner late on 23 August, expressed surprise at the coup but remained firm in their loyalty to Bucharest. King Mihai's role in taking personal responsibility for arresting Antonescu in the absence of the politicians, and the binding nature of the officer corps' oath of allegiance to the Crown, made him indispensable to the success of the coup and ensured that Romania's break with Germany was unanimous and total.

Nevertheless, the ceasefire terms eventually agreed with the Soviets by the National Democratic Bloc were essentially those negotiated by Antonescu. Given his ambiguous preparations on 23 August, it remains debatable whether or not Antonescu would finally have brought himself to break with Germany had he not been arrested. The opportunity was certainly there, and if he had done so it seems probable that the country would have followed his lead as unanimously as it did that of the King, for the army had also taken an oath to him as Conducator. However, it is entirely possible that his further prevarication would have provoked a German coup, and the King's action had the undeniable merit of a decisiveness that Antonescu was not displaying.

The change in national leadership did not immediately result in a change of Romanian movements at the front, because Antonescu's German-approved instruction for 3rd and 4th Armies to retreat to the FNB line, to pre-empt the Soviets militarily, conformed with the initial stages of the Bucharest coup leaders' subsequent order to retreat even further to secure the capital in order to pre-empt them politically.

OBSERVATIONS ON THE BATTLE OF IAŞI-CHIŞINAU AND THE COUP

In some German accounts of the battle of Iaşi-Chişinau there is a strong presumption that the Romanian Army put up no fight and defected to the Red Army *en masse* by prearrangement, thus causing the loss of their 6th Army and much of 8th Army. However, while there is clear evidence of Romanian Army contingency planning against the Germans in Bucharest, and a knowledge of this by some officers at the front, there is no convincing evidence of operational collusion with the Red Army before 24 August. If there had been, the postwar Communist government would have been only too pleased to publicise the fact. Nor do Soviet reports mention it.

The Germans accurately noted a suspiciously high rate of leave among 4th Army's senior officers in the traditional holiday month of August, and an early abdication of responsibility by some of those who remained after 20 August, but both fell far short of active collaboration with the Red Army. Other German reports cited as evidence for collaboration are improbable, such as one claiming that Romanian troops contacted the Soviets by the highly unclandestine use of flares. Others are misinterpreted, such as the replacement of Racoviţa by Avramescu, which if anything disrupted rather than strengthened the potential influence of the conspirators over the field army. Avramescu had strong family connections with the Iron Guard, and was later arrested by the Soviets in March 1945 for alleged contacts with the Germans.

Still other reports are confused, demonstrably backdating incidents occurring on 24 August, such as attacks by Romanian frontier guards on the German XVII Mountain Corps. It is significant that neither Racoviţa nor Niculescu, the most influential front-line Romanian officers connected with the conspirators, played an operational role in the Soviet breakthrough. Racoviţa was absent, while Niculescu's V Corps successfully held its front against local Soviet attacks on 20 August. Neither Racoviţa nor Niculescu were subsequently re-employed in the field as allies of the Soviets. The main Soviet breakthrough actually came on the front of VI Corps, which was then under the temporary command of the German General Abraham.

However, this does not mean that the Romanians remained compliant allies to the Germans before 24 August, for there were not simply German or Soviet interests in play at Iaşi-Chişinau; there remained a quite distinct Romanian national interest which was incompatible with both. Even Antonescu's own deployments from 22 August illustrate this. His final negotiations with the Soviets in Sweden on 22-23 August had insisted that, 'The Romanian Government shall allow the German Army a fifteen-day period to evacuate the country. Only in the event of a refusal will the Romanian Army fight side-by-side with the Red Army to drive the Germans out of Romania.' This was also the formula accepted by Sanatescu's government after Antonescu's arrest. Given Hitler's inevitably violent reaction, such a passive German withdrawal was highly improbable, but Antonescu's honour had been satisfied. As neither Antonescu nor the conspirators against him were in active collaboration with the Red Army, this was not a significant factor on the battlefield before 24 August.

The generally pro-western Romanian officer corps had never forgotten the Vienna Dictat of 1940, and it was deeply disillusioned with the course of the war. It had become an increasingly sullen and unco-operative ally to the Germans during the summer of 1944, and this had not gone unnoticed by Friessner. On the whole, Romanian officers were therefore predisposed to co-operate with subsequent action against the Germans, but it is very doubtful whether a significant number were fore-warned. The security risks alone precluded this. V Corps' Niculescu and several staff officers around Colonel Dragomir, who Avramescu inherited from Racoviţa at 4th Army, were undoubtedly aware of coup preparations, and, even though they had rejected acting in July, their foreknowledge of a possible *volte face* can only have put them on their guard against the Germans and undermined their later determination to fight the Soviets to the bitter end. However, they and the vast majority of Romanian officers were still overwhelmingly anti-Bolshevik, and most therefore remained reluctantly prepared to resist the Red Army as long it appeared to be in the national interest, albeit without prospect of success and therefore with limited enthusiasm and effect. Active hostility to the Germans was contained until 24 August.

The resistance of only three Romanian divisions (5, 7, 4M) demonstrably collapsed completely under direct attack during the first 24 hours, after all had suffered heavy casualties. 5th and 7th Infantry Division were in the direct path of a mass of Soviet armour. Yet even here 2nd Ukrainian Front's 6th Tank Army recorded a maximum advance rate of only one kilometre an hour with tanks capable of 50km/hr unopposed road speed, and 52nd Army rather less. 3rd Ukrainian Front's 46th Army only managed an average of 500m/hr against 4th Mountain Division. These would have been excellent rates of progress against a determined defence, but fell far short of what might have been expected with Romanian collaboration, and imply that the Red Army was facing something between the two; an ineffective Romanian defence.

Reports from the German 306th and 15th Divisions, which faced the main weight of 3rd Ukrainian Front's attack, indicate that the initial Soviet artillery barrage alone killed or wounded a third and a fifth of their respective front-line infantry and caused the flight of others. By the end of the day the former had been driven back 10km, almost as far as the neighbouring Romanian 4th Mountain Division, which was the third main focus of 3rd Ukrainian Front. The casualties of the unseasoned Romanian 5th and 7th Divisions facing the spearhead of the more powerful 2nd Ukrainian Front were probably even worse, but their resilience was less. The fact that 2nd Ukrainian Front claimed only 3,000 prisoners on the first day indicates that there were no mass Romanian surrenders. There was undoubtedly mass flight in many places, but had it been universal the tally of walking Romanian prisoners would have been much higher if pursued by so much unhindered Soviet armour.

The action of 4th Army in throwing forward its two available reserve divisions, 1st Armoured and 18th Mountain, in an immediate counterattack into the path of the Soviet offensive contradicts any suggestion of collaboration with the Red Army on their part. If they were collaborating, these divisions' heavy casualties imply that the Red Army was certainly not collaborating with them! In fact, Soviet reports relating to these two divisions refer to some strong resistance on 20 August. It is probably significant that the one Romanian division to escape from the direct path of the Soviet armour with significant combat capacity intact was 1st Armoured Division, the only one with significant mobility or anti-tank potential.

Another group of divisions, those which soon retreated when their flanks were unhinged by Soviet breakthroughs (21, 1, 4, 5C, 13), must also include a number of German divisions (i.e. *76*, *79*, *46*). These divisions subsequently began to disintegrate, but this is reasonably attributed to their usual lack of mobility, which rendered them often unable to retain cohesion in the face of rapidly developing Soviet mechanised operations.

Yet another group of divisions were on relatively passive fronts. VII and I Corps on 4th Army's left flank had ample opportunity to collapse under the cover of local Soviet infantry attacks, but did not. This not only indicates that they had no prearranged collusion with the Red Army, but that Romanian infantry still had the morale to rebuff Soviet infantry, provided it was not supported by an uncontainable mass of armour. German reports confirm that 11th Division on the right flank of the Soviet breakthrough initially fought determinedly, and its commander, a *Ritterkreuz* holder, even apologised to his German neighbour for the retreat of other Romanian units. However, even he could not stop its later disintegration in retreat.

Perhaps of particular significance is the fact that the King's own Guard Division put up a considerable resistance at the front; a strong indicator that the conspiracy against Antonescu was not co-ordinated with the Red Army. Likewise, the German 62nd Division reported; 'The Romanian 14th Division (integrated with the German 6th Army) fought as bravely ... as the German divisions'. In 14th Division's case this could be explained by the fact that it was raised around Chişinau and was therefore in immediate defence of its own homes. It only disintegrated on 24 August, after the ceasefire, when the Germans ordered it to retreat from its native province. German reports also indicate that 1st Cavalry Division fought well. In general there is little that is inexplicable in the combat performance of 3rd or 4th Armies to suggest that a single division collaborated with the Red Army before 24 August.

The conspirators in Bucharest had no warning of the Soviet offensive, and only agreed their coup date late on 21 August, by which time the front of 4th Army and VI Corps had already been breached. They tried to get Soviet clearance for General Aldea to establish direct contact with Red Army field commanders, but it was only forthcoming after 23 August.

The outcome of the battle of Iaşi-Chişinau was largely predestined by the decision to continue to hold Basarabia forward of the Carpathian-FNB-Danube line once the German armour needed to support such an exposed position had been withdrawn. In view of the fact that Antonescu twice offered to make such a militarily sensible sacrifice of territory, the responsibility for this must lie primarily with Hitler.

Local errors were also made. In particular, Army Group South Ukraine's decision to allocate most of its German divisions to 6th Army in the apparently more-threatened bulge around Chişinau proved mistaken. However, although its better trained, better equipped and more experienced German divisions would almost inevitably have put up a stronger resistance than the raw Romanians, the recent example of the failure of the veteran infantry divisions of Army Group Centre in the face of Soviet armour in June held out little prospect of a dramatically different end result at Iaşi-Chişinau. Indeed, the effective resistance of several German divisions there lasted little longer than that of neighbouring Romanian formations, and all were annihilated in little over a week. The unprecedented speed of 6th Army's destruction owed much to the inability of its retreating, largely horse-drawn infantry divisions, which were virtually devoid of tank support, to retain cohesion in the face of fast-moving Soviet mechanised operations – something with which the Romanians were only too familiar.

In the final analysis, credit must go to the Red Army, which created the strategic circumstances of fatal Axis weakness in Basarabia and then proceeded to exploit them impeccably. Romanian collaboration was not considered a vital prerequisite to launching their offensive, and they did not forewarn the Romanians of its timing. However, brittle Romanian morale was certainly a key factor in their planning. On 27 August, with the Romanian 3rd and 4th Armies scattered, Romania's defection secured, the FNB Line crossed and the German 6th Army surrounded, the Soviet High Command superseded its original operational directive with another ordering unrestricted exploitation across Romania and Bulgaria. 2nd Ukranian Front had lost 7,316 dead and 32,669 wounded, and 3rd Ukranian Front 5,820 dead and 21,126 wounded between 20 and 28 August, in what was arguably the most economical Soviet victory of the European war. German losses were claimed as 150,000 dead and 106,000 captured.

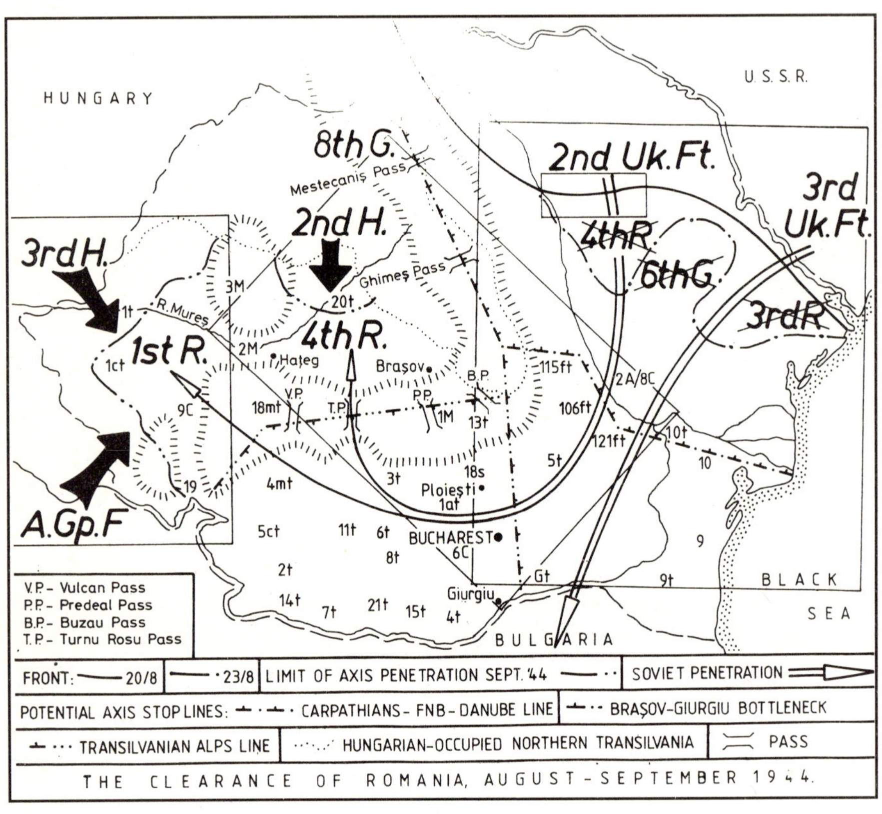

THE CLEARANCE OF ROMANIA, AUGUST-SEPTEMBER 1944.

CHAPTER 6

THE WESTERN CAMPAIGN August 1944 to May 1945

THE LIBERATION OF ROMANIA

Romanian losses at Iaşi-Chişinau were catastrophic. Although 8,305 dead and 24,989 wounded were recovered, a further 153,883 were missing from the 431,800 men of 3rd and 4th Armies. Some of the missing were unrecorded dead on the lost battlefields, and others had been captured before Romania's defection, but the overwhelming majority were taken by the Soviets after 23 August. A few were made prisoner as late as 12 September, the day on which armistice terms were finally agreed. Many of the remaining 244,623 men, assuming the war was over, simply went home, and took months to reassemble.

On 25 August Dumitrescu's 3rd Army reported that, of its units previously engaged at the front, only 1st Cavalry Division retained 80 per cent of its combat capacity. III Corps had only service elements of 2nd and 15th Divisions and 110th Brigade left. 21st and 4th Mountain Divisions had no current combat value, but thought they could assemble a small combat group in four or five days. The fate of the two R-35/45 companies apparently attached to 3rd Army is unclear. However, II Corps (9, 10), which had been guarding the coast south of the Danube, was intact.

Şteflea's 4th Army was even worse hit, almost all of its divisions being functionally dispersed. The cases of 1st Armoured Division and the Guard, 4th, 6th, 8th and 20th Infantry Divisions are particularly telling, as they were largely intact at the time of the ceasefire. Something less than half of the men of 4th Army had straggled back to the region of Bucharest by the end of August, but they were mostly rear-echelon, non-combatant elements and largely devoid of equipment. Only parts of 18th Mountain Division picked up by the Soviet 6th Motorised Infantry Brigade appear to have returned in condition for combat.

Early on 24 August 1st Armoured Division crossed the Moldova River, and during that night was ordered to head for Bucharest with all speed, avoiding contact with both Russians and Germans. General Korne intended to follow the route Roznov-Oneşti-Adjud-Maraşeşti-Bucharest. However, to avoid the inevitable complication of running into retreating German troops, including 20th Panzer Division, crowding into Oneşti (yesterday's allies but not officially enemies until tomorrow), the bulk of the division lost time diverting its march via Casin. As a result it ran into the Red Army on 25 August and, notwithstanding Romania's declaration of war on Germany, was largely taken prisoner by the Soviets. Only 1,000 men and 120 vehicles reached Bucharest via Focşani. Most were probably remnants of 3rd Motorised Rifle Regiment.

A few other units of 4th Army managed to come to local arrangements with neighbouring Soviet corps. These seem to have been those that obviously offered immediate advantages to the Soviets in their attempts to force the Carpathians. Thus the 3rd and 6th Frontier Guard Regiments guided the Soviet 50th Corps through the Mestecanis Pass in the northern Carpathians at Cimpulung. One major detachment of 1st Armoured Division under Lieutenant Colonel Matei was delayed in Roznov by the crowded roads, and came to a local understanding with the Soviet 7th Guards Army's 24th Corps on 25 August, subsequently helping it to force the Ghimes Pass. The *ad hoc* 103rd Mountain Division was hastily flung together from parts of 103rd and 104th Mountain Commands and 8th Frontier Guard Regiment supported by 6th Infantry Division's artillery, and used to eliminate German pockets behind Onesti in 24th Guards Corps' rear.

With most of 4th Army and 3rd Army lost or cut off, the Romanian army command only had immediately available the residue of 3rd Army and the resources of General Nicolae Macici's 1st Army left within the country. In terms of raw manpower these amounted to a considerable 382,524 men organised in thirty divisions and assorted fortress brigades, military schools etc. However, this concealed the reality that only one division, 9th Infantry at Constanţa, was at full strength. Two others, 1st Cavalry and 8th Motorised Cavalry, were adequately equipped for operations, but the former's combat strength now stood at only 80 per cent, while the latter's components were still widely dispersed and had never conducted a full divisional exercise.

The other regular divisions in the country (6C, 9C, 1M, 2M, 3M, 10, 19) were those rebuilding after the Crimea. Four (1M, 2M, 3M, 10) had since lost their best remaining equipment and most of their trained reserves with their offshoot mountain and infantry brigades in 4th and 3rd Armies. 10th and 19th Infantry Divisions had 7,304 and 11,507 men respectively, and a full battalion of twelve 75mm field guns and about three 100mm howitzers each. 6th and 9th Cavalry Divisions had a little over 3,000 men and an understrength, mixed battalion of 75mm and 100mm guns each. 1st, 2nd and 3rd Mountain Divisions had 7,473, 6,431 and 10,746 men respectively, each supported by a half-battalion of old 75mm or 76.2mm mountain guns and a single 100mm mountain gun. Each of the ex-Crimea divisions had a handful of 20mm AA guns but no anti-tank artillery above 47mm. They were re-equipping with German automatic weapons, but these were also short.

However, even these units were well equipped compared with the eighteen training divisions of the lost field divisions (Gt, 1t, 2t, 3t, 4t, 5t, 6t, 7t, 8t, 9t, 11t, 13t, 14t, 15t, 18Mt, 19t, 20t, 21t). These had an average of 6,491 men organised in six battalions and supported by only a half-battalion of about four 75mm and two 100mm guns. The two training cavalry divisions (1Ct, 5Ct) had only 3,574 and 2,612 men respectively and only a single, mixed battery of two 75mm and two 100mm guns each. The one training mountain division (4mt) had only four 75mm mountain guns and one 100m mountain gun supporting six rifle battalions. Most training divisions had between two and four 20mm AA guns, but none had any anti-tank guns above 47mm, and they had precious few of these. Automatic weapons for the infantry were also desperately short.

On 6 September, in terms of matériel, these 30 divisions between them had only enough artillery to equip four infantry divisions, two and a half cavalry divisions and a single mountain division. Of the artillery pieces, 61 per cent were pre-1914 75mm guns. Moreover, there were only enough 75mm AT guns for four divisions, enough 50mm AT guns for two, and sufficient 20mm AA guns for seven.

In the week before the Red Army could reach Bucharest, these seriously flawed units had to disarm 70,832 Germans known to be in the interior and an unknown proportion of the 128,666 Germans belonging to the rear echelons of Army Group South. There were also thousands of men in Nazi paramilitary groups among Romania's own German population. They then had to hold the national frontiers against probable intervention from Hungary and the Germans in Yugoslavia (and possibly from Bulgaria as well) for a further two to four weeks before the Red Army could draw up in strength on Romania's western border. For reasons of diplomatic leverage it was vital not only that the Germans be eliminated, but that this be done before the Red Army arrived, for by liberating itself the new Romanian government hoped to prove itself capable of action as a free and independent ally, and thus, like Italy, worthy of cobelligerent status.

SECURING THE INTERIOR, 23–30 AUGUST 1944

Special Forces Fiasco

Hitler's first instinct was to mount special-forces operations against the coup. The Brandenburg Division's recently formed parachute battalion, Otto Skorzeny's SS Parachute Battalion 500 and Artur Phleps, by now the commander of V SS Mountain Corps, were all put on standby in nearby Yugoslavia.

On 24 August a pair of Ju 52s landed at Boteni airfield, and two more at Tandarei airfield, disgorging a platoon of Brandenburgers at each. Their objective was to immobilise the German-supplied aircraft of Corpul 1 Aerian, but they were wiped out or captured by Romanian paratroopers and FARR security companies without achieving any success. The bulk of the Brandenburg parachute battalion was therefore ordered to the already secured Otopeni airfield north of Bucharest on 25-26 August to spearhead General Gerstenberg's stalled attack on the city. However, their unarmed Ju 52s and Me 323s proved vulnerable to both Romanian AA fire and fighters, and the survivors who reached the airfield were forced to surrender with Gerstenberg a couple of days later. It was probably the quickest and most comprehensive defeat suffered by German special forces in the war.

Skorzeny was ordered to mount an operation similar to those which kept some of the Italian and many of the Hungarian forces in the German camp by rescuing Mussolini in September 1943 and kidnapping Admiral Horthy's son in October 1944. In his command Skorzeny already had a Romanian officer, believed to be the same Major Valeriu Carp cashiered for taking reprisals against Jews in June 1940, and it was proposed to mount a rescue of Antonescu from Bulgaria. However, Antonescu's whereabouts could not be discovered because the coup leaders in Bucharest, fearful that he might be freed by loyal officers, had handed the Marshal over to the Communists early on 24 August. They kept his whereabouts secret even from the government until 30 August, when they handed him over to the Red Army. The Soviets immediately whisked him off to Moscow with his closest collaborators. Himmler subsequently released Horia Sima and his cronies and set them up as a puppet government-in-exile in Vienna.

On 25 August Artur Phleps was ordered to take command of the Nazi paramilitary organisations of the Volksdeutsche population of southern Transylvania. However, with their best manpower already dispersed around Europe in the Waffen-SS, few offered any significant resistance to the Romanians. Before the war Romania's German minority was regarded as the least threatening and most productive in the country. However, about 200,000 had been resettled in Poland, and the extent to which the remainder identified with the Reich during the war led to thousands being arrested by the Soviets in January 1945 and sent to the USSR. This provoked the terminal decline of the community through postwar emigration to West Germany.

Struggle for the Interior

The Germans had three hopes of halting the Soviet advance within Romania: on the FNB Line, which was fortified; on the Brasov-Ploiesti-Bucharest-Giurgiu line, where they had had an estimated 44,925 Luftwaffe and rear-echelon troops on 15 June; or in the Transylvanian Alps, where the terrain was favourable. The FNB Line quickly proved untenable as the Romanians dismantled it on 25 August and withdrew, allowing the Red Army to vault it before the retreating German 6th Army

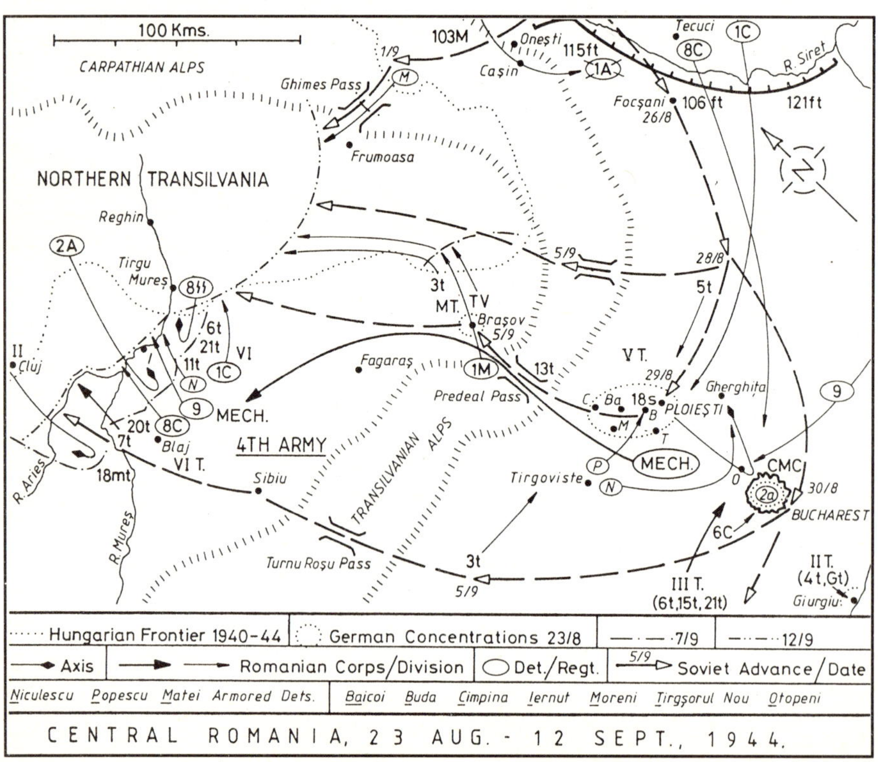

could reach it. The Germans initially had threatening troop concentrations in four vital central areas of Romania – Giurgiu (±4,203 men), Bucharest (±11,031 men), Ploieşti (±24,887 men) and Braşov (±4,804 men). Although these were largely rear-echelon or Luftwaffe troops, they posed a considerable threat if they were allowed to consolidate and await reinforcement.

Fortunately, the experienced Romanian Mountain Corps had 1st Mountain Division refitting near Braşov in the Predeal Pass, and by 25 August that city had been cleared and 4,641 prisoners taken. The Romanian occupation of the Predeal Pass, which 13th Training Division was left to hold, cut off the obvious reinforcement or escape route for the German forces in Ploieşti, Bucharest and Giurgiu. The Germans tried to reinforce their AA units in Giurgiu across the Danube from Bulgaria, but the town and river line were securely in the hands of 2nd Territorial Corps (Gt, 4t) by 26 August. Around Giurgiu the corps eventually captured 9,000 Germans trying to escape from the capital or up the river.

With a speed of reaction so typical of many German commanders in the war, General Gerstenberg had already ordered a motorised column of 2,000 men with 16 88mm and 42 20mm AA guns from Ploiesti to Bucharest on the evening of 23 August, even before he and Hansen saw Sanatescu. After deceiving Sanatescu into allowing him out of Bucharest, Gerstenberg took personal command of this force, which had secured the German nightfighter airfield of Otopeni, north of the capital. Gerstenberg's earlier boast that if there was a coup in Bucharest he could 'quell it with a Luftwaffe flak battery' was now put to the test and found wanting.

In Bucharest the CMC initially had only 7,000 Romanian troops, only half of whom were of high quality. The rest were recruits. The units in normal residence were the Guard Calaraşi Regiment (the King's personal bodyguard) and a mixed battalion of 2nd Armoured Regiment (a company of nine R-35 tanks, two three-tank platoons of T-38s and ten FT-17s). On the airfields around the capital there was the FARR's 4th Parachute Battalion. Fortuitously in transit to Tecuci through Bucharest were 8th Motorised Cavalry Division's assault pioneer squadron, 2nd Reconnaissance Calarasi Regiment and the heavy weapons squadron of 4th Rosiori. Of less value were a battalion from each of the Guard and 4th Training Divisions. The balance of forces in the capital was not obviously in Romanian favour, and these units were soon fully engaged in establishing a defensive perimeter against Gerstenberg and rounding up German HQ, administrative and other rear-echelon personnel in the city.

The Romanian High Command therefore summoned 1st Armoured Division from 4th Army, 1st Cavalry Division from 3rd Army, the rest of 8th Motorised Division from the FNB Line, 1st Training Armoured Division from Tirgoviste, and 6th Cavalry Division from nearby Bolintin to make for Bucharest by road with all speed to form a strategic reserve. Antonescu's bodyguard regiment at his residence at Snagov was hastily redesignated 115th Motorised Infantry Regiment and also ordered to Bucharest. Finally, most of 9th Infantry Division was to entrain at Constanţa for the capital. In Bucharest these 40,000 men were to form the new Mechanised Corps of which General Korne was initially designated commander. Also redirected to Bucharest was 3rd Training Corps (6t, 15t, 21t), then en route piecemeal to the FNB Line in accordance with Antonescu's orders.

Twelve kilometres north of Bucharest, some trucks of 115th Motorised Infantry Regiment on their way into the capital were ambushed in the early hours of 24 August by Gerstenberg's column. This marked the start of open hostilities by Germany. Gestenberg pressed on into the northern outskirts of the city, but was halted at the Baneasa bridge early on 24 August by a squadron of the Royal Guard Calaraşi Regiment supported by a T-38 platoon. Attempts to find other routes into the city were also foiled, so Gerstenberg asked for the Luftwaffe to soften-up the capital. At 1035 it obliged. Bucharest was sporadically bombed over the next three days and nights, but its AA defences were considerable while Luftwaffe resources were weak, and the bombing had minimal influence on the ground fighting. Nor was civilian morale affected, because the population had already received its battle inoculation at the hands of the far more formidable USAAF.

On the afternoon of 24 August reinforcements from the Mechanised Training Centre at Tirgoviste, organised as the Niculescu Armoured Detachment, brushed aside weak German positions at Crevedia, Buftea, Mogoşoaia and Straule̦şti and secured the western flank of Bucharest's defenders. It captured a battery of 88mm AA guns, which it added to its strength. The Niculescu Detachment was essentially the remaining elements of 1st Armoured Division and its training cadre. It consisted of a reconnaissance group (one platoon of armoured cars and one of amphibious VW field cars), an armoured battalion (one company of ten T–4s and one of ten TAs), a battalion of twenty TACAM R-2s, a battalion from 4th Motorised Rifle Regiment, a company of twelve Reşiţa 75mm AT guns and signals and supply elements.

With Gerstenberg stalled, 2nd Calaraşi Regiment, supported by 2nd Armoured Regiment's FT17s, were free to help storm both the German Army and Luftwaffe Mission Headquarters in the city during 24 August. By the following day, German resistance within the capital had been much reduced and a secure front established along the northern outskirts of the city against Gerstenberg's force. This was strengthened by the arrival of elements of III Training Corps. The Niculescu Detachment began to assemble to Gerstenberg's west, and the newly detrained 9th Infantry Division began to close in from the east.

On 26 August the last Germans in the city surrendered and the Niculescu Armoured Detachment and 9th Infantry Division began to compress Gerstenberg's force, the command of which was taken over by General Stahel, a specialist in counterinsurgency who had helped secure Rome after Italy's defection. He was flown in from the Warsaw Uprising. The immediate obstacle was the Baneasa Forest, held by some 4,000 Germans, and the Romanians requested a USAAF bombing raid to soften it up. Unfortunately, co-ordination was inadequate and half a company of the 4th Parachute Battalion was wiped out by American bombs. This exercise in inter-Allied co-operation, the only western contribution to Romania's liberation, was not repeated.

On 27 August the leading elements of the Niculescu Detachment and 9th Division closed the ring around the Baneasa Forest and the Germans therein shortly surrendered. Stahel and Gerstenberg were north of the encirclement at Otopeni airfield, organising the bombing of Bucharest and trying to secure an airhead through which to land more troops. They managed to escape towards Ploieşti with 1,900 men, including the surviving Brandenburgers, in about 200 vehicles. However, on 28 August they ran into retreating elements of VI Corps' corps troops at Gherghita. With units of the Niculescu Detachment in close pursuit, Stahel and Gerstenberg surrendered.

Approximately 7,000 Germans, including seven generals, were captured around Bucharest. Among them were Hansen, who was found in hiding by armed civilians on 30 August, and Admiral Tillesen. Carl Clodius was captured at the German Legation, but von Killinger committed suicide there on 2 September rather than surrender to the Russians. Romanian losses totalled 1,400. The Niculescu Detachment lost three T–4s and a TAs during the Bucharest operation, but captured 3,000 prisoners, 322 trucks, two tanks (probably PzKpfw IIs from Ploieşti), three 88mm guns, nineteen 20mm AA guns and a number of aircraft. It had shot down four aircraft, including two Me 323 Gigants. Of the other divisions detailed to defend Bucharest, 1st Armoured Division had been largely disarmed by the Red Army and the horsed 1st Cavalry Division was too slow to reach Bucharest in time. Most of 8th Motorised Cavalry Division also arrived too late to influence events. Nevertheless, Romanian provisions had proved adequate.

In fact, the Germans in Bucharest were not especially strong, but their potential could not be underestimated because, on similar occasions in Italy and Hungary, small German forces had nevertheless achieved complete success by paralysing opponents with their resolution and speed of action. On this occasion, much to the Germans' surprise, the Romanians displayed similar characteristics in the vulnerable early stages of their *volte face*, and within two days had concentrated sufficient force to extinguish the threat. Unfortunately, although the military objective had been achieved, no diplomatic advantage was gained, because when the Red Army and the Tudor Vladimirescu Division entered Bucharest on 30-31 August they simply ignored the embarrassing fact of its prior liberation and promptly 'liberated' it again. In terms of great power politics it was this second 'liberation' that carried weight, and Romania failed to achieve independent cobelligerent status by *fait accompli*.

The last major pocket of German resistance was in the Ploiesti oilfields, in the jurisdiction of the Romanian 5th Territorial Corps (18s, 5t, 13t). The Romanians totalled about 23,000 men and were intermingled with a similar number of Germans from 5th Flak Division and its attached security troops. In Ploieşti itself was the bulk of 18th Security Detachment. This division-sized unit included six reserve battalions drawn from various infantry divisions, and an FT-17 platoon. It was supported by 4th AA Brigade. These Romanian formations held the city and its inner AA defences, but were effectively surrounded by an outer ring of German heavy AA positions. However, there were also Romanian concentrations, including 18th Security Detachment's HQ, in an arc north and west of these Germans, blocking their escape routes towards the Predeal Pass, but these had further German AA positions to their west and north-west at Moreni and south-east of Cimpina. Beyond these, 13th Training Division held the Predeal Pass. 5th Training Division was based east of Ploiesti.

The situation was essentially a stalemate, and it required external intervention to break it. Because Bucharest was of overriding political importance, Ploiesti's relief force was far weaker. The most potent element was the Popescu Armoured Detachment. This was organised on 24 August from the residual elements of 1st Training Armoured Division not sent to Bucharest. It consisted of an R-2 company, a T-38 platoon, an R-35 platoon, training elements of 3rd Motorised Rifle Regiment and some non-divisional units under Major Victor Popescu. A second group without armour consisted of training elements of 4th Motorised Rifle Regiment and the divisional AT and AA training group. As the 5th Flak Division included some 167 88mm, 105mm and 128mm AA guns, the Popescu detachment had to operate its armour with caution. The Germans also had a handful of obsolete PzKpfw II light tanks on security duties.

The first objective was to prevent a German breakout to the north. On 25-26 August the Popescu Detachment and 18th Security Detachment overwhelmed the German positions at Moreni, and 4th Training Motorised Rifle Regiment helped elements of 6th Cavalry Division clear Cimpina. On 27 August the Popescu Detachment was joined by two batteries of self-propelled guns (probably TACAM R-2s) and pressed on to take the main German airfield at Tirgsorul Nou, which was being used to bomb Bucharest and supply 5th Flak Division. The Germans made several attempts to break into Ploiesti but were repulsed.

By 28 August the Romanian forces around Ploiesti had grown to 40,000 men drawn from the 6th Cavalry Division and 1st Armoured, 1st Guard, 5th, 6th and 13th Training Divisions placed under the command of 5th Territorial Corps. These annihilated the last German positions south-east of Cimpina on 29 August, leaving the remaining Germans restricted to the area immediately around Ploiesti. On the same afternoon the leading units of the Soviet 6th Motorised Infantry Brigade, carrying elements of the Romanian 18th Mountain Division, relieved the garrison of Ploieşti from the east. This was the only place within Romania where Soviet troops arrived before Romanian troops had completed the elimination of organised German resistance.

On 30 August 5th Territorial Corps launched a general offensive on the trapped Germans, supported by the arrival of Romanian units from Bucharest in the south and the mixed Romanian and Soviet troops now in Ploieşti. During this offensive the Popescu Detachment knocked out an armoured train at Buda Station, capturing SS General Hofmayer and 335 prisoners. By the end of the day the Germans were reduced to a single constricted pocket around Paulesti, 10km north of Ploieşti. On 31 August two motorised columns, headed by a couple of PzKpfw II light tanks, tried to break out northwards but were repulsed and forced to surrender, as did those Germans still at Paulesti. For the loss of about 800 Romanians, 1,500 Germans had been killed and 2,300 wounded. Four generals and 9,072 other prisoners were taken. About 2,000 Germans straggled across the mountains into Hungarian lines and the remainder fell into Soviet hands.

German resistance in other parts of the country was less well organised and armed. Supported by Romanian naval personnel, II Corps (10, 9t) rounded up 12,000 Germans in and around Constanţa for the loss of only 230 men. There were fewer Germans in the east of the country, where 1st Army's 1st Territorial Corps (2t, 3t, 11t, 5ct, 4mt), 4th Territorial Corps (7t, 8t, 14t), 6th Corps (2M, 18mt, 20t) and

7th Territorial Corps (9C, 3M, 19, 1ct, 1t, 19t) rounded up a further 9,900 prisoners. Small detachments of 2nd Armoured Regiment on internal security duties in the area played a useful role in Fagaraş (a platoon of R-35s) and at Sibiu and Reşiţa (FT-17 platoons). These important industrial centres were all cleared of Germans by 26 August.

Another 7,000 Germans were arrested by police or civilians across the country. The credit for these was subsequently taken by the Communist Party, which claimed to have 2,000 partisans, but in fact there is little evidence that its scanty 'Patriotic Combat Formations' had any significant influence on operations. By 31 August all German positions in Romania had been taken. During 23-31 August 56,455 Germans were captured by the Romanians. All had to be handed over to the Red Army. Another 5,048 had been killed. Romanian casualties totalled 8,586 killed and wounded.

Throughout much of the war the most consistent German criticism of the Romanian officer corps had been that it lacked energy. The rapid clearance of German forces from Romania in August 1944 revealed that lack of motivation had done rather more to inhibit their performance on the Eastern Front than lack of energy.

HOLDING THE TRANSYLVANIAN FRONTIER

With the interior secure, the task of securing the frontiers remained. The basis of planning was the staff work already prepared for Antonescu's Hypothesis 'U'. Having led the remnants of 3rd and 4th Armies back into the interior, General's Dumitrescu and Şteflea, long-time Antonescu loyalists, had been dismissed on 29 and 31 August respectively, and 3rd Army was not resuscitated as a field formation. As General Macici's 1st Army could not adequately control impending operations along nearly 1,000km of frontier with Hungary and Yugoslavia, it relinquished the central Transylvanian front to the newly reappointed General Avramescu's 4th Army HQ on 31 August.

4th Army inherited 6th Territorial Corps and the Mountain Corps, but they initially had only 20th Training Division, 1st Mountain Division and a few frontier guard battalions covering 300km of frontier. Therefore reinforcements were rushed, largely by train and foot, from south of the Transylvanian Alps, where German resistance had now collapsed. War was declared on Hungary on 30 August and, having secured Braşov, the Mountain Corps wasted no time before probing across the border north of Sfintu Gheorghe with 1st Mountain Division; 3rd Training Division was sent to its support. 6th Territorial Corps brought up 18th Training Mountain Division and 7th Training Division via the Vulcan Pass and Turnu Rosu Pass respectively. Between these two corps, General Tartaranu's VI Corps was re-formed from 6th, 11th and 21st Training Divisions which were brought up through the Predeal Pass.

However, all of these training divisions were little more than poorly-equipped infantry brigades, and the Mechanised Corps was therefore allocated as 4th Army's reserve as soon as the Bucharest/Ploieşti fighting finished. By 28 August it had become apparent that 1st Armoured Division had not escaped the Red Army. General Rozin was then appointed to command the corps, because, although General

Korne managed to reach Bucharest, his record against the Soviets disqualified him from further field employment.

The Mechanised Corps, Romania's last strategic reserve, incorporated the Niculescu Armoured Detachment (1,970 men) from Tirgovişte, the 8th Motorised Cavalry Division (6,922 men) from Tecuci, the horsed 1st Cavalry Division (3,359) from 3rd Army, and the 9th Infantry Division (14,025) brought by train from Constanţa. The Niculescu Detachment, incorporating the Popescu Detachment, was reinforced to a reconnaissance company (five SdKfz 222 armoured cars, one SPW, a group of amphibious VW and Horch field cars), an armoured battalion (one company of twelve T–4s, one company of twelve TAs and one company of twelve TACAM R-2s), a battalion of 4th Motorised Rifle Regiment, 101st AT company (twelve Reşiţa 75mm AT guns), 52nd Motorised Heavy Artillery Battalion (eight Skoda 150mm guns), 115th Motorised Infantry Regiment (formerly Antonescu's bodyguard), 1st and 3rd Motorised Heavy Artillery Regiments and a motorised supply company.

By temporarily commandeering any available Romanian and captured German transport and sending other elements by rail, the mechanised Corps (less 1st Cavalry Division, lagging six days behind with horse transport) was rushed 250km north-westwards to Blaj by 4 September, some five days ahead of the Soviet spearheads. It was just in time. On 5 September Army Group South Ukraine's Hungarian 2nd Army attacked south towards the Turnu Rosu and Vulcan Passes, which the Soviet spearheads had not yet reached.

Elements of the Hungarian II Corps (7, 9, 25, 26) struck south-east from Cluj, 8th SS Cavalry Division (including about a dozen tanks) thrust south-west from Tirgu Mureş, and between them 2nd Hungarian Armoured Division (which included 50-60 tanks) thrust due south. The Romanian frontier guards evacuated the 30–40km of exposed land beyond the River Mureş and fell back behind it. There, 6th Territorial Corps (7t, 18mt, 20t) and VI Corps (6t, 11t, 21t) were digging-in their training divisions as they arrived piecemeal. The left flank of 6th Territorial Corps halted the Hungarian II Corps on the Mureş, but 2nd Hungarian Armoured Division broke through the over-extended 21st Training Division at Ludus on 6 September. 11th Training Division on the left flank of VI Corps was outflanked by this, and withdrew before 8th SS Cavalry Division to the River Tirnava Mica.

On 6 and 7 September the lead elements of the Mechanised Corps were committed to the breach, and 8th Motorised Cavalry Division and 9th Infantry Division supported by the Niculescu Detachment halted 2nd Hungarian Armoured Division. In doing so they saved a large part of Romania's armament industry, as sections of the SET and ICAR aircraft factories and the CMC small-arms factory were only a few kilometres behind the front.

The Romanians asked to form a national army group of their own to liberate Northern Transylvania, but, like the Germans in March, the Soviets agreed to only two mixed army groups. On 7 September both Romanian field armies were brought under the command of 2nd Ukrainian Front for the first time; 4th Army being subordinated to General Trofimenko's 27th Army and 1st Army to General Managarov's 53rd Army. On 8 September the Mechanised Corps began a counteroffensive which drove the 2nd Hungarian Armoured Division and 8th SS Division back across the Mureş by 12 September. The first Soviet formation, 5th Mechanised Corps, was only committed in support of 6th Territorial Corps on 9 October. Between them they drove the Hungarian II Corps back across the River Aries by 13 September. On 16/17 September 9th Infantry Division seized a bridgehead across the River Mureş near Iernut, where it engaged in an inconclusive struggle with the 8th SS Cavalry Division until the end of the month. 4th Army had fielded 113,759 men during 1-20 September and suffered 10,535 casualties. The Mechanised Corps' field HQ was disbanded at Soviet behest on 30 September.

FORCING THE CARPATHIANS

On 4th Army's right flank, the Mountain Corps (1M, 3t, 6t) advanced steadily through the tip of Hungarian-occupied Transylvania, recapturing the four Hungarian-populated counties which had formed the core of Hungary's claim in 1940. On 28 September it stormed the city of Tirgu Mureş, thus drawing itself into line with 4th Army on the Mureş. During the early part of the month it had been supported by the Tudor Vladimirescu Division, but this was soon transferred to the north-western border.

From 2 to 11 September the 1,058-man Matei Detachment, the remnants of 1st Armoured Division, led the Soviet 7th Guards Army across the Ghimes-Palanca Pass through the Carpathian Alps to Frumoasa. It consisted of an armoured battalion (one company of nine T–4s, one company of seven TAs), a battalion of 4th Motorised Rifle Regiment, a pioneer company, a 25mm AA company, 101st AT company (twelve Reşiţa 75mm AT guns), a services company and 133 vehicles. The Carpathians were the strongest natural defensive feature ever available to the Germans on the Eastern Front, but were not yet strongly manned. During the operation the Matei Detachment knocked out two tanks and captured three. It then pushed on to 12km south of Tirgu Mureş by 16 September, where it annihilated an enemy penetration between the Soviet 6th Guards Rifle Division and the Romanian 103rd Mountain Division. Finally, it drove north with the Soviet XXIV Guards Corps and forced a crossing of the River Mureş just south of Reghin on 28 September.

At the end of September, having successfully forced the eastern Carpathians, the Soviets dismissed the Romanian units which had aided their passage; 3rd and 6th Frontier Guard Regiments, the Matei Detachment and 103rd Mountain Division. Their operations, and those of the Tudor Vladimirescu Division had cost 1,136 casualties out of 21,068 men. The Matei Detachment had suffered 245 casualties and lost five T–4s, two TAs, eight trucks and three Reşiţa 75mm guns, but had taken 1,800 prisoners and captured or destroyed six PzKpfw IVs, two Tigers which had run out of fuel, three Stug. IIIs, sixteen other vehicles and six AT guns.

HOLDING THE WESTERN FRONTIER

The last chance the Germans had of holding a strong line on Romanian soil was to seize the western end of the Carpathians before the Red Army arrived. To oppose this, Romania had its sedentary 1st Army, which had been subordinated on 7 September to the Soviet General Managarov's 53rd Army, whose own troops were still hundreds of kilometres distant. Fortunately it took another week for the Germans and Hungarians to assemble an offensive force.

On 13 September 1st Army's front opposite Yugoslavia up to Deta was held by 19th Infantry Division (with 19th Training Division under command). 7th Territorial Corps (9C, 1Ct) covered from Deta to Macea on the Hungarian border, and Grup Crişuri (3M, 1t) from there to Topa in occupied Transylvania. In the mountainous country from there to the boundary with 4th Army at Gilau there was only Grup Bihor with parts of 2nd Mountain Division covered by three territorial battalions. Divisional sub-units were frequently mixed, and between them they had sufficient artillery and AA guns for only a single division and no AT guns above 47mm on 6 September.

The German force on the Yugoslav border was under Army Group F. It had rushed several motorised regiments from the 4th SS and Brandenburg Divisions, elements of the 7th SS Mountain Division and assorted other Banat Volksdeutsch SS Security Regiments to the border. Behind the Hungarian frontier 3rd Hungarian Army was assembled. Its most potent formations were IV Corps opposite Arad with the Hungarian 1st Armoured and 6th Reserve Divisions, and VII Corps further north with 10th and 12th Reserve Divisions. These all began a general offensive on 13 September.

1st Army's forward position along the border was for the most part in the exposed lowlands and too extended for it to form a continuous line. The grain of the rivers in western Romania was also unfavourable to the defence. Given this, the absence of armour or air cover, and its inferiority in artillery and general mobility, 1st

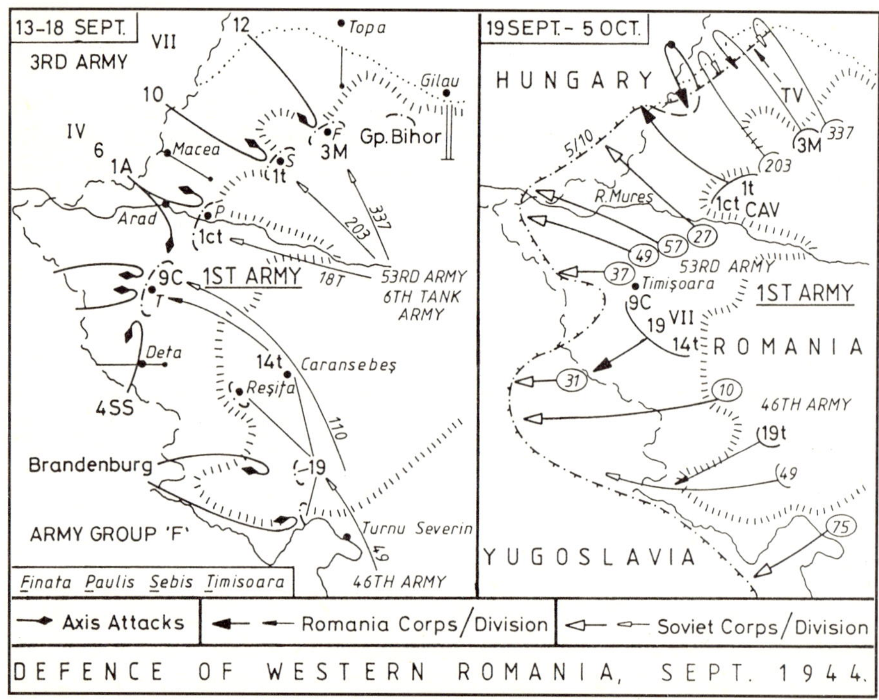

DEFENCE OF WESTERN ROMANIA, SEPT. 1944.

Army was obliged to withdraw its forward screen of lightly armed Graniceri battalions immediately they were attacked.

Motorised elements of the Brandenburg Division quickly managed to penetrate 20-30km into Romania, but failed to reach either of the important centres of Reşiţa or Turnu Severin in 19 Division's sector before the Soviet 49th Rifle Division arrived on 16 September. Similarly, 4th SS Motorised Division and other German units advanced to the outskirts of Timişoara, then probably the second largest city in Romania, but failed to take it in a concentric attack on 9th Cavalry Division. The city was made secure by the arrival of elements of 19th Division and 14th Training Division from Caransebes, followed by the Soviet 110th Rifle Division on 17 September.

On the Hungarian border, 1st Cavalry Training Division was too weak to hold Arad against the 1st Hungarian Armoured Division and the city was quickly abandoned on 13 September. The cavalry withdrew south of the River Mureş, and 1st Army created a detachment at Pauliş to hold four villages blocking the mouth of the Mureş defile north of the river. The position was already covered by an anti-tank ditch because the Mureş valley presented the easiest route into the heart of the mountains. The backbone of Detachment Pauliş comprised a training battalion of senior reserve NCOs with four anti-tank guns, supported by two batteries of captured Soviet 122mm guns and a stray training battalion of 19th Division.

The terrain obliged the Hungarian 1st Armoured and 6th Reserve Divisions to attack Detachment Pauliş in the Mureş defile frontally, and they were repulsed on 14 and 15 September. However, the two northernmost villages were stormed by Hungarian infantry and tanks on 16 September, and the battalion of 19th Division was driven off. On 17 September the Hungarians tried to penetrate behind Paulis but were repulsed, and during the afternoon the arrival of a Soviet motorised rifle battalion and the return of the battalion from 19th Division drove this last Hungarian thrust back. By 20 September all four villages were back in Romanian hands; 387 Hungarians were captured, more than 900 other casualties inflicted and 23 Toldi and Turan tanks damaged or destroyed. Romanian casualties were 377.

The successful defences of Pauliş and Timisoara blunted the most potent Axis thrusts before they even reached the mountains and provided the Red Army with a springboard for further operations. However, further north, 3rd Mountain Division and 1st Training Infantry Division were too extended to form a continuous front in the lowlands and fell back before the Hungarian VII Corps, which had some armour in support, into the Carpathian foothills at Sebis and Finaţa respectively. There they were reinforced by the Soviet 203rd and 337th Rifle Divisions on 18 September and the whole front stabilised. 1st Army had engaged 73,844 men and suffered 4,483 casualties by 20 September.

With the centre of its front taken over by the Soviet 53rd Army, 1st Army hastily concentrated its divisions under two experienced corps staffs – VII Corps (9C, 19, 14t) and the Cavalry Corps (1Ct, 1t). As part of a general Soviet offensive, VII Corps drove the Germans back over the Yugoslav frontier south of Timişoara on 26 September. The Cavalry Corps, 3rd Mountain Division and weaker Soviet forces that included the Tudor Vladimirescu Division from 27 September, chased the Hungarian VII Corps back into Hungary at Ujvaros by 28 September. However, their enthusiasm carried them too far, and they were themselves thrown back across the border by a counterattack involving elements of 3rd Hungarian Army's 1st Hungarian Armoured Division and 22nd SS Cavalry Division, and the German 6th Army's 23rd Panzer and 76th Infantry Divisions and the Hungarian 4th and 6th Infantry Divisions.

THE IMPORTANCE OF ROMANIA'S DEFECTION

On 24 August the only remaining Romanian forces with significant mobility and offensive potential were the embryonic Mechanised Corps and lesser armoured detachments. In the greater scheme of the Red Army's campaign in August-September 1944, their scattered armoured operations were not of primary importance, but they were initially disproportionally useful auxiliary forces operating well in advance of the Soviet battlefront, and were largely responsible for depriving the Germans of two possible stop-lines several days ahead of the Red Army's arrival. Still several days in advance of the Red Army, the Mechanised Corps was rushed 300km north-west to repulse the German/Hungarian counterattack to re-establish the Axis front in the Turnu Rosu and Vulcan Passes. The neutralisation of the Germans in Bucharest, Ploieşti and the Transylvanian Alps gave the Red Army a clear run to the Yugoslav/Hungarian frontier.

The fighting on the frontiers had been exceedingly scrappy, most of the German and Hungarian units committed being either reserve or anti-partisan divisions and the Romanians fielding predominantly training units or divisions recuperating from their losses in the Crimea. Neither side was immediately prepared for front-line combat. The experienced Soviet units arrived piecemeal after an exhausting two- or three-week advance that left them understrength, short of supplies and deprived of much of their vigour.

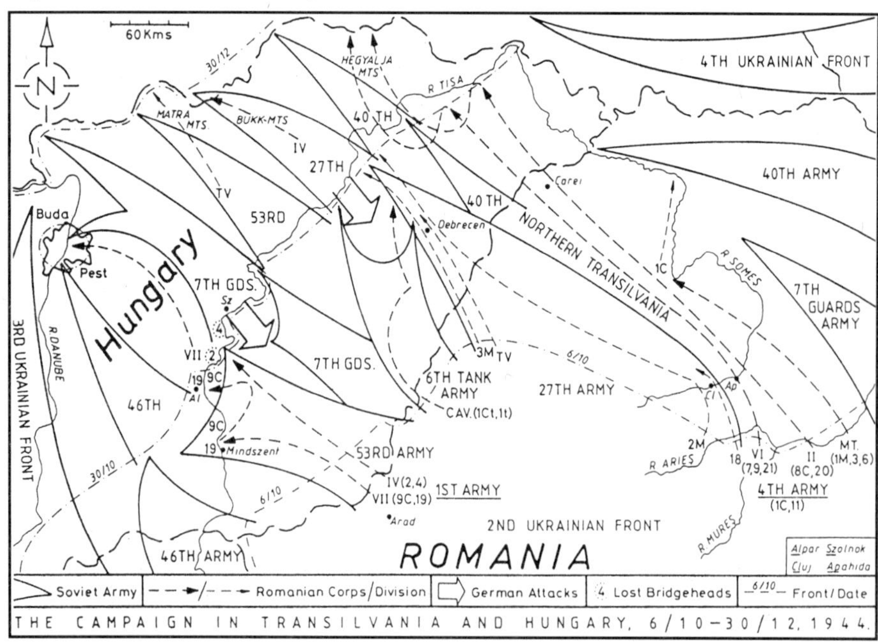

In these circumstances of general debility, the weak Romanian forces were able to play a significant strategic role with almost complete success. 4th Army had halted the Axis offensive of 5-8 September towards the Turnu Roşu and Vulcan Passes, and was solely responsible for restoring the Mureş river line. 1st Army had played the leading role in holding the Axis offensive of 13-18 September short of the mountains, and played a part in retaking the frontier line by the end of the month. Given their multiple handicaps, little more could have been expected of either Romanian army. Their total losses during 1-20 September were 16,275 men out of 274,919 eventually deployed.

The Romanians had learnt well from the fiascos of earlier Vichy French, Italian and Hungarian attempts to escape German domination, which had only resulted in formal occupation, and were active agents of their own liberation. The military consequence of the Romanian action was to extend the results of the Soviet Iaşi-Chişinau operation far beyond its original ambitions. General Friessner commented; 'The (Axis) failure to win the southern Carpathian passes proved fatal because the mountains were our best allies. The enemy could have been stopped here with only a few specialist troops.' Greece, Albania and southern Yugoslavia had to be abandoned as a result.

On the diplomatic front, Romania's initiative began to unravel the Axis in a way that Italy's earlier capitulation had not. It created favourable strategic circumstances for the approaching Red Army to pressurise Bulgaria into declaring an end of its state of war with the Western Allies on 4 September and declaring war on Germany on 8 September, and it set the climate in which Finland concluded a ceasefire on 5 September and an armistice on 19 September. Less successful were an uprising in Slovakia in late August, which was crushed by the Germans; an internal conspiracy to unseat the leader of Croatia on 18 September, which led to the plotters' arrests; and the abortive conclusion of an armistice by Hungary on 15 October, which led the Germans to install a fascist puppet regime in place of Admiral Horthy.

On the economic front, Albert Speer, the Reich Armaments Minister, regarded Romania's defection as one of the decisive events of the war, as it not only deprived him of Romanian oil but also irrevocably cut off access to vital supplies of Turkish chrome. All of this had been achieved at the cost of minimal damage to the infrastructure of Romania, as the core of the country never became a battlefield.

This was the last time Romanian actions had any significant influence on the wider course of the war, for although 1st and 4th Armies campaigned to its conclusion in May 1945, they were treated by the Soviet command as particularly expendable infantry armies to be employed in expensive secondary actions.

THE LIBERATION OF TRANSYLVANIA AND THE DEBRECEN OPERATION, 9–25 OCTOBER 1944

There remained one more operation into which the Romanian Army entered with enthusiasm – the final clearance of Northern Transylvania. Transylvania was also a major reason why the Hungarian Army continued to fight on with the doomed Germans. While Hungarian units were reluctant to engage the Red Army, their historical enmity with Romania over Transylvania made them a much stiffer proposition for 4th and 1st Armies. Both countries had been preparing for this bitter war-within-a-war since the early 1930s, and it was fiercely fought. For both armies the Eastern Front had represented a massive and unwanted diversion, but owing to their much lighter commitment and consequently lower losses the Hungarian Army had not suffered as heavily as the Romanian. As a result, by late 1944 the Romanians had lost a clear qualitative advantage they had held in 1941–43.

The second half of September and first week of October were used to reorganise 4th Army's training divisions according to new, smaller field establishments. Unlike 1st Army in Hungary, 4th Army was in full operational control of its Mountain Corps (1M, 3, 6), II Corps (8C, 20) and VI Corps (7, 9, 21) at the front, and held 1st Cavalry Division, 11th Infantry Division and its Armoured Group in reserve. The Axis opposition included the 8th SS Division, and the Hungarian 2nd Armoured, 3rd, 9th, 16th, 25th and 26th Infantry Divisions. 4th Army had only approximate parity in infantry and artillery with its opponents, and a clear inferiority in armour, so its planning focused on achieving a decisive local superiority on the front of VI Corps.

On 29 September the Niculescu and Matei Detachments had been amalgamated into an *ad hoc* Armoured Group at the disposal of 4th Army. It consisted of a reconnaissance company (five SdKfz 222 armoured cars, one SPW, a section of amphibious VWs and Horch field cars), an armoured battalion (one company of ten T-4s, one company of eight TAs and one company of sixteen TACAM R-2s), a motorised rifle battalion, a motorised AT company (twelve Reşiţa 75mm guns), a motorised heavy artillery battalion (eight guns?), a pioneer company, a 25mm AA company, a signals platoon and a services company.

On 9 October the Armoured Group led the breakout of VI Corps' 7th, 9th and 21st Infantry Divisions across the River Aries against the Hungarian 25th and 26th Divisions and rapidly pressed on some 40km, occasionally clashing with 2nd Hungarian Armoured Division, to capture Apahida, east of Cluj, on 11 October. A detached rifle corps of the Soviet 27th Army, with the Romanian 2nd Mountain and 18th Infantry Divisions attached, took Cluj, the largest city in Northern Transylvania, on the same day. II Corps and the Mountain Corps forced the River Mureş line and advanced in echelon behind VI Corps. The Armoured Group was then used to support VI Corps in establishing a bridgehead across the River Someş and resisting counterattacks by newly committed elements of 23rd Panzer Division. Its losses in battle and breakdowns were considerable, and on 14 October it was withdrawn for a week's recuperation.

Whereas the reconquest of Northern Transylvania was an end in itself for the Romanians, it was viewed by 2nd Ukrainian Front only as a necessary preliminary designed to draw Axis attention and reserves away from the assault of its 6th Tank Army and 27th Army on Debrecen in Hungary, which opened on 14 October. This was intended to surround the 8th German and 1st and 2nd Hungarian Armies defending Northern Transylvania. The Romanian Cavalry Corps (1Ct, 1t) played only a minor role in the decisive flanking operation by 6th Tank Army. However, 2nd and 3rd Mountain Divisions and the Tudor Vladimirescu Division had been subordinated to the Soviet 27th Army, and it was primarily the latter divisions which stormed

Debrecen, Hungary's second city, on 19/20 October. A Soviet-sponsored Hungarian Government was later set up in the city. In recognition, the Soviet High Command awarded the Tudor Vladimirescu Division the honorific suffix '-Debretin' to its title.

The fall of Debrecen and the further advance of the Soviet 6th Tank Army towards the River Tisa, combined with another failed Hungarian defection attempt, made the Axis position in Transylvania extremely precarious, and it began a hasty withdrawal from the province. While it was in progress, the Germans reported that several Hungarian divisions, including the 2nd Armoured Division, effectively disintegrated. 4th Army pressed on after them, picking up stragglers as it went, but its lack of mobility rendered it unable to disrupt their retreat significantly. However, it outpaced the Soviet 7th Guards Army to its east, and on 14–19 October was able to send 1st Cavalry Division in a thrust down the western bank of the River Somes to meet the Soviet 40th Army. This narrowing of the front led to the Romanian Mountain Corps and the Soviet 7th Guards Army being squeezed out of the line in mid-October, leaving only 4th Army's VI and II Corps and the Soviet 40th Army to clear the rest of Transylvania. From 20 October the remains of the Armoured Group was committed to action again, supporting the infantry of VI Corps in driving the last Axis forces from Romanian soil around Carei on 25 October.

Between 21 September and 25 October 4th Army appears to have suffered 24,630 casualties out of 120,861 men engaged. It had taken the central role in liberating Northern Transylvania, but ultimately the Axis withdrawal was dictated by events north of Debrecen in Hungary, where the Germans had to mount a considerable counterattack on the Soviet 6th Guards Army south of the River Tisa to buy time for the defenders of Northern Transylvania to escape encirclement.

HUNGARY I: FORCING THE RIVER TISA

1st Army's VII and IV Corps were concentrated at Arad for the invasion of Hungary in early October. However, in terms of re-equipment and armoured and air support, 1st Army was 4th Army's poor relation, because the latter was engaged in the more important task of recovering national territory in Transylvania. In particular, the two training divisions of its IV Corps (2, 4) were redesignated field divisions without receiving the full scale of equipment, especially anti-tank weaponry, that this implied. Two other divisions available on 5 October (5t, 15t) could not be committed at all owing to lack of equipment. Only VII Corps (9C, 19), which contained two experienced divisions that had fought in the Crimea, could be considered combatworthy.

1st Army remained in the second echelon of the overextended Soviet 53rd Army's initial invasion of Hungary, until on 11 October VII Corps was rushed to the rescue of the Soviet 243rd Rifle Division, which was struggling to hold a bridgehead across the Tisa at Mindszent against the Hungarian 1st Armoured and 23rd Infantry Divisions.

However, when IV Corps' 4th and 2nd Divisions took over two other bridgeheads across the Tisa below Szolnok, the former was violently attacked on 19 October by the Hungarian 1st Infantry and 1st Cavalry Divisions. These frontal attacks were initially held, but simultaneously a major armoured assault by 24th Panzer Division, 4th SS Panzer Grenadier Division and a battalion of Tiger tanks broke out across the River Tisa behind 4th Division's right wing at its junction with the Soviet XXVII Corps, and surrounded all three of its infantry regiments in their bridgehead on the west bank. After thirty hours of resistance most were captured on 20 October. For a while only the motorised corps artillery and a motorised battery of Vickers AA guns were left to oppose the German armour by fire and movement. They claimed four tanks for the loss of two guns and slowed its advance perceptibly.

To seal the breach, VII Corps was pulled back across the Tisa and rushed north, but the Soviet 7th Guards Army retook the lost ground without its assistance during the following week. 19th Division therefore again crossed the Tisa at Alpar. Encouraged by the German success against 4th Division, elements of the Hungarian 1st Cavalry and 1st and 20th Infantry Divisions attacked the raw 2nd Infantry Division's bridgehead on 25 October. With the fate of 4th Division in similar circumstances fresh in its memory, 2nd Division was panicked by the presence of a few tanks, and allowed itself to be rapidly driven back across the river. However, when the Hungarians mounted concentric attacks on the more experienced 19th Divisions' bridgehead at Alpar on 26-29 October, with elements of their 3rd and 8th Infantry Divisions and armour from their 1st Armoured Division, they were repulsed with loss.

The destruction of 4th Division on the Tisa remained the most serious setback suffered by the Romanian Army in 1944–45. It was the third time the division had been effectively destroyed in less than two years, and the second time in as many months. VII Corps took over 2nd Division on 30 October, and IV Corps HQ was sent to take command of 2nd and 3rd Mountain Divisions. As a result, 1st Army's HQ only really had administrative and disciplinary control of VII and IV Corps during the campaign in Hungary. Their operational deployment was largely dictated by affiliated Soviet Armies. 1st Army's losses between 21 September and 25 October appear to have been 8,720 out of a strength of 67,347.

Between 1 September and 25 October Romanian casualties totalled 49,744. Although 19,820 prisoners had been taken, only 1,614 Axis dead were found on the battlefield. Undoubtedly most Axis dead were recovered by their own side, and there is no reliable estimate of their wounded. However, it is apparent that Romanian battle casualties were much higher than those of their opponents. This can largely be explained by their chronic equipment shortages and the inexperience of the training divisions, which led to a tactical crudity in attack not displayed since Odessa. The casualties were further compounded by a general determination to press on with the liberation of national territory in Northern Transylvania regardless of these constraints and the resultant human cost.

MILITARY REORGANISATION

As the Western Allies had conceded the Soviet Union primacy in Romania in June 1944, they refused all Romanian requests for military assistance once their POWs had been repatriated in late August. Both the British and Americans favoured granting Romania cobelligerent status, a fact which kept Romanian hopes alive. However, they did not consider it an issue of such vital interest that they were prepared to confront the Soviet Union over it. The latter was therefore able to exercise a largely free hand in Romania.

The armistice terms of 12 September had committed Romania to field at least twelve divisions against the Axis, and this total had been comfortably exceeded by 1st and 4th Armies, which had employed nineteen divisions during early October. However, the armistice had not enforced the disbanding of the other divisions, whose fate was under negotiation. Their remains had been subordinated to 3rd Army HQ in the interior, where the Soviets perceived them as an obstacle to their Romanian Communist protégés' efforts to agitate their way to power.

Therefore, on 26 October 1944, the day after the last Axis forces were driven from Romanian soil, the Allied Control Commission (Soviet) cut short negotiations and imposed an additional military protocol to the original Romanian armistice terms. It called for a reduction of the Romanian Army to nine infantry, one mountain and two cavalry divisions. The Romanians protested, and received Soviet dispensation to maintain more divisions provided they were kept at the front. As a result sixteen divisions (if one includes the Guard and Tudor Vladimirescu Divisions) served in Czechoslovakia in 1945. Nevertheless, even with this Soviet dispensation, the army was still halved, and all of the specialist corps commands were disbanded.

The headquarters of 3rd Army and the Cavalry, Mountain, Mechanised, I, III and V Corps were abolished. 1st, 4th, 5th, 7th, 8th, 13th, 14th, 15th and 20th Infantry Divisions were absorbed into 19th, 10th, 9th, 6th, 11th, 3rd, 2nd, 21st and 18th Infantry Divisions respectively. 6th Cavalry Division went to 8th Motorised Division, and 5th Cavalry Division became an anonymous manpower pool for the Inspectorate of Cavalry to supply replacements to 1st and 9th Cavalry Divisions. 1st and 4th Mountain Divisions were absorbed into 2nd and 3rd Mountain Divisions. The demise of 8th and 14th Infantry Divisions was inevitable, as they were raised in Northern Bucovina and Basarabia, where the Red Army wasted no time in pressing local Romanians into service – a little-known and unquantifiable Romanian contribution to the Allied cause.

In the operations to liberate Northern Transylvania, the depleted Armoured Group, increasingly debilitated by mechanical failure, battle damage and a lack of spares, had played an ever diminishing infantry support role, to the point of imminent operational extinction on the Romanian border. It was withdrawn from the front in early November, shortly after taking part in the capture of the Hungarian border town of Nyirbator. Having squeezed the remnants of 1st Armoured Division dry, the Soviets then disbanded it. What was left of 1st Armoured Regiment was taken into 2nd Armoured Regiment, while the remains of much of the armoured division's rifle and artillery regiments were absorbed into the Guard Division and mountain rifles. The Red Army had taken great pains to round up this politically hostile formation after the battle of Iaşi in August. Consequently it had little seasoned manpower to call on when rebuilt, and the influx from 1st Armoured Division was therefore most welcome. As a result the Guard Division returned to the front in April 1945 with considerably more motor vehicles than other Romanian infantry divisions, but it was nevertheless far from motorised.

The Soviet Union operated an unofficial arms embargo against Romania in 1944–45 as part of its campaign to curtail its political independence. This embargo contrasted notably with the extensive issue of Soviet equipment to the Bulgarians and Yugoslavs in 1944–45; countries in which the Western Allies and Soviet Union were meant to share equal interest but which had historic, ethnic and/or ideological affinities to the Russians. The Soviet-raised Polish People's Army and Czech Corps on the Eastern Front were already entirely Soviet equipped and led by Communists. Only in Romania was there an allied army not inclined towards the Soviet Union on either ideological or ethnic grounds. There, the Red Army repossessed all captured Soviet matériel and confiscated more besides. Between 24 August 1944 and 12 May

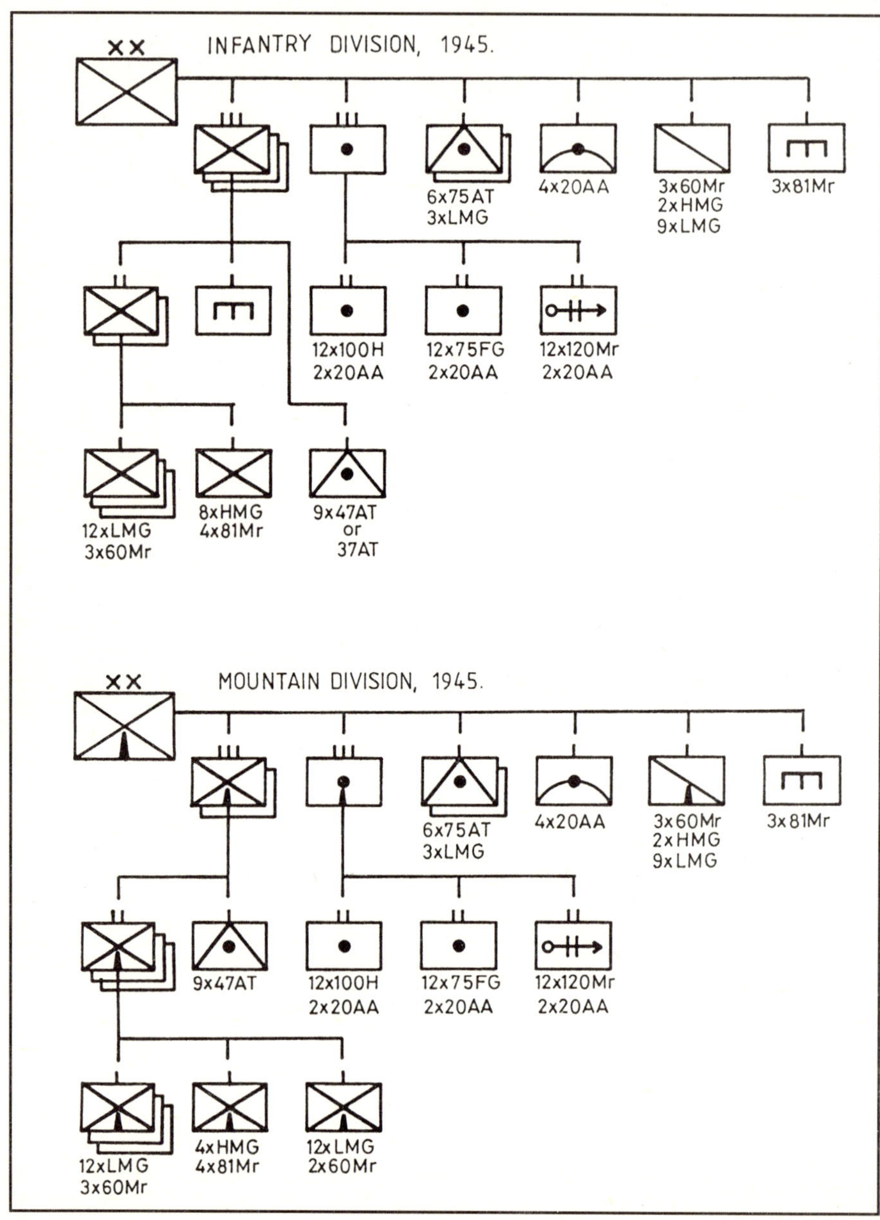

1945 the Red Army relieved the Romanian Army of 10 to 60 per cent of its various classes of weaponry, 10 to 35 per cent of its different types of motor transport and 30 per cent of its engineering equipment. Furthermore, although Soviet advisers were appointed to every Romanian unit down to battalion level, no Romanian liaison officers were allowed at affiliated Soviet armies, whereas, for instance, Bulgarian officers were.

By the end of September the Romanian GHQ was forced to make reductions in official corps and division establishments to conform with existing equipment shortages. Corps motorised artillery was contracted by a third to a regiment of eight 150mm and eight 105mm guns. The two divisional artillery regiments were amalgamated to form a single regiment with only one battalion of twelve 100mm howitzers and one of twelve 75mm field guns. To strengthen it further, all heavy mortars were withdrawn from the infantry regiments to form a third artillery battalion of twelve 120mm mortars. The divisional anti-tank artillery was temporarily reduced to a single battery of six 75mm guns.

Romania's own armament industry now necessarily came closer to supplying the full needs of the army than ever before. Indeed, the unofficial arms embargo on Romania meant that among the Allies probably only the USA was as self-reliant in 1945. The British and other western Europeans received numerous American tanks and aircraft, the other eastern Europeans were equipped by the USSR, and even the latter was largely reliant on the Americans for trucks. The Romanian Army received virtually nothing beyond what it captured. In these straitened circumstances the enforced halving of the army's strength proved beneficial, as it became easier to standardise and sustain the equipment levels of the remaining field divisions.

Romania could still build replacement 150mm and 100mm barrels. The dual-purpose Reşiţa 75mm gun remained in full production and filled gaps appearing in the light field gun and divisional anti-tank gun inventories most effectively. Indeed, it was soon possible to re-form a second, six-gun, divisional anti-tank battery and field two 36-gun independent army anti-tank regiments. Thus out of a divisional establishment of 48 100mm, 75mm and 120mm guns or mortars, 36 could be fully supplied from local sources and the remainder could be re-barrelled. Mountain guns could not be replaced, so the mountain divisions received standard artillery pieces. An incidental result of the halving of the number of divisions and the decrease in the remainder's artillery establishments was that the Romanian armament industry was for the first time able to produce more than sufficient shells for sustained campaigning, and built up large stockpiles.

In September infantry regiments were again reduced from three to two battalions each, a move which conformed to the existing structure of the former training divisions. Continued deliveries of the Orita SMG, ZB30 LMG and 60mm and 81mm mortars to the infantry were sufficient to replace wastage in these classes of infantry weapons. Rifle and HMG supplies were finite but adequate, but personal anti-tank weapons were restricted to captured Panzerfausts.

Owing to force of circumstance, the Romanian infantry and mountain divisions came to resemble each other closely in structure, armament and size in 1945. Soviet pressure to make them both conform even more closely to the Soviet rifle division was fiercely resisted, and in practice they were reorganised around such weaponry as was available, not as was desirable to either Romanians or Russians. For all the achievements in self-sufficiency there was no escaping the fact that the new divisions' firepower was necessarily less than that of their Soviet equivalents, the corps artillery was much weaker, and supporting army artillery was immeasurably inferior. This being said, 1st or 4th Armies' results were not to be demonstrably inferior to those of neighbouring Soviet infantry armies.

The capture of the entire equipment of the German 5th Flak Division in August 1944, and the virtually non-existent German air threat to Romania thereafter, allowed the creation of 1st Anti-Aircraft Division on 1 January 1945. Its 73 batteries served throughout the Czechoslovak campaign and gave the army the heaviest AA protection it ever enjoyed.

POLITICAL AND ECONOMIC DEVELOPMENTS

The Soviet Union treated Romania as a defeated rather than an allied country, even depriving the Romanian government of civil control in Moldova for some months. 'Occupation' is a much more accurate description of the Soviet, rather than the German, presence in Romania. The army was the only Romanian institution possibly capable of resisting a Communist takeover, so between 23 August 1944 and late February 1945 the King appointed three successive military-led governments. The first two were under General Sanatescu. However, while he pursued the war energetically, Sanatescu took the Soviet assurance that they had no intention of changing the existing social order in Romania too literally. He failed to enact convincing war crimes legislation as demanded by the armistice, and arrested only a handful of Antonescu's appointees, most of them at direct Soviet prompting. In particular, the Interior Ministry, which had been one of the main pillars of Antonescu's regime, had been left largely intact.

On 19 September Sanatescu was obliged to appoint Patraşcanu Minister of Justice. This effectively made the Communist Party immune to legal sanction, and it took to the streets in Soviet-sponsored protests against his government in October. This forced him to form a new government on 4 November, which introduced Communists as Minister of Communications and Under Secretary of the Interior as well. Yet they and their Soviet backers remained dissatisfied, and they forced the formation of a third government under General Nicolae Radescu on 4 December 1944.

The anti-German Radescu had shared his imprisonment under Antonescu with Communists. The Soviets therefore initially assumed him to be well disposed towards them, and it was at their request that Sanatescu appointed him army Chief-of-Staff on 13 October. However, he was pro-western, and bitterly protested the dissolution of half of the army. As Prime Minister, Radescu prudently kept the Interior Ministry to himself, but was saddled with his communist deputy, under whom party members penetrated the police and provincial administration, and the Siguranta began its evolution into the Securitate. Radescu introduced the demanded war crimes legislation, but proved so resistant to other Soviet demands that the Communists orchestrated the usual street protests against his government. They also brought in three rifle divisions from Poland to increase the pressure.

However, Radescu's resistance was rendered futile when Churchill conceded Stalin a 90 per cent interest in Romania at the Yalta Conference of 4 February 1945. On 8 February the Soviets ordered 2nd Armoured Regiment from Bucharest to the front and thereafter disarmed the rest of the city's garrison. Then, on 27 February, Soviet Foreign Minister Andrei Vyshinski personally flew to Bucharest to secure Radescu's dismissal. He accused Radescu of being incapable of maintaining public order on the Soviet lines of communication, of preparing a coup against the Red Army and of appointing several generals whom the Russians wanted as war criminals, including General Macici of 1st Army, who had been involved in the killings at Odessa in late October 1941. Radescu resigned on 28 February and sought asylum with the British Legation shortly afterwards.

In Radescu's place Vyshinski insisted on the selection of the Soviet-leaning Petru Groza of the left wing Ploughman's Front as Prime Minister on 6 March and, amongst other appointments, the selection of a Communist as Interior Minister and the increasingly pro-Communist General Vasiliu-Raşcanu as Defence Minister. To defuse nationalist opposition, Stalin returned Northern Transylvania from Red Army to Romanian administration on 13 March. Groza, who took the credit for this, continued as the Communists' front man until they took power in their own name in 1948.

To buttress Groza's unpopular administration, all of the armed political militias that had unofficially sprung up during the insurrection against the Germans were disbanded, except for those affiliated to the Communists, which continued to recruit energetically and claimed to be 70,000-strong by March. In an act of remarkable cynicism even ex-Legionaries were actively recruited. However, when the first communist political officers were sent to the field armies in April, both 1st and 4th Armies' commanders rejected them.

The internal political struggle in Romania was reflected in the careers of the communist Tudor Vladimirescu and royalist Guard divisions. Soviet plans to take over the Romanian Army gave the Tudor Vladimirescu Division a central role, and it was essential that its core of indoctrinated cadres be conserved and not wasted on short-term military objectives. Although its periods of combat were intense, they were interspersed with extended periods of recuperation not allowed to other Romanian divisions. Safe in 2nd Ukrainian Front's reserve from 19 March, it took no part in the final campaign of the war. In April Vasiliu-Rascanu absorbed it into the Romanian Army and ordered it back to Bucharest, where its prestige was built up further by the award of the Soviet Order of the Red Banner on 3 May. Simultaneously, he ordered the royalist Guard Division, which had been rebuilt over the winter, from Bucharest to the front. However, it arrived too late to see significant action.

Now that Romania and the Soviet Union were allied, recruitment among Romanian POWs became easier, and a second communist division, the 'Horia, Cloşca si Crişan', was raised by General Lascar in April and became operational in July. By the time the field armies returned home they found the capital fully occupied by Romanian communist troops and militia backed by the 80,000 Red Army troops in the country.

As the political grip of the Soviet Union progressively tightened on the country, a series of purges of the Romanian officer corps ensued. Almost all of the experienced corps and divisional commanders of 3rd and 4th Armies were quickly replaced in September because of their participation in the war against the Soviet Union – another indication that collaboration with the Soviets before 23 August 1944 was not widespread, or at least not rewarded. An exception was 3rd Mountain Division's General Mociulschi, who proved himself so useful in the field that, despite having won the *Ritterkreuz*, he retained his command until April 1945.

A rolling purge of the officer corps continued until the end of the war and beyond. The command of 4th Army had proved insecure enough employment for Generals Ciuperca, Iacobici, Constantinescu, Racovita and Avramescu when allied to the Germans, but it became a veritable merry-go-round when allied to the Soviets. 4th Army had three commanders between 23 August 1944 and May 1945, Generals Şteflea, Avramescu and Dascalescu, the latter two both being appointed twice. Lower down, VI Corps had seven commanders, 6th Infantry Division no fewer than nine, and 18th Infantry Division eight, an average of nearly one a month to the end of the war. This lack of continuity of command could only be damaging to the effectiveness of most Romanian formations in 1944–45. Indeed, the ideologically motivated agitation and general inefficiency of the administratively inexperienced Communist Party across the whole range of military, political and economic activity often seriously disrupted Romania's war effort.

The depth of resentment towards the Soviets is illustrated by the fact that, whereas they had been unable to engineer any defections by Romanian generals in August, the Germans were able to enlist 4th Division's commander, General Platon Chirnoaga, as Horia Sima's Defence Minister shortly after his capture during the crossing of the Tisa in October. Under the aegis of the SS they tried to organise two infantry regiments from 6,000 Romanians who had been training or labouring in Germany at the time of Romania's defection, or had recently been captured on the Tisa. However, these regiments proved totally unreliable when briefly committed to combat in February 1945, and languished as labour units for the rest of the war. As late as March 1945 General Avramescu was arrested by the Soviets for allegedly contacting the Iron Guard across his 4th Army's lines.

The armistice terms had also made Romania largely responsible for the supply of food, fuel and construction materials to most of 2nd and 3rd Ukrainian Fronts for the rest of the war. Most of the national economy had survived virtually intact owing to the successful defection. Only the oil industry, which had been devastated by Anglo-American bombing in mid 1944, had to be rebuilt. This was done with such speed and effect that between September 1944 and June 1945 2,300,000 tons of oil were delivered to the Russians. This nearly matched the peak deliveries to Germany in 1941, when the industry was unencumbered by bomb damage, and hints at the extent to which Romanian obstructionism must have retarded oil deliveries to the Reich in the intervening years. It also shows that Romania had less power of dissension under Stalin than under Hitler.

As the Russian railway gauge was different from the Romanian, the Soviets had to make huge transport requisitions in Romania in order to maintain their momentum, and 11,400 motor vehicles, 96,360 horses, 517 locomotives, 47,460 railway wagons (including virtually all fuel tankers), and 125 barges were commandeered to support the Red Army. The Romanian 1st and 4th Armies were left with barely 3,000 motor vehicles and 50,000 horses at the front. The national railways retained only 12,222 serviceable wagons, and the river fleet 49 barges with which to sustain the national transport infrastructure. These appropriations more than mirrored the support Germany had earlier demanded for Army Group South.

HUNGARY II: BUDAPEST

Following the defeat of 4th Division, the Soviets recognised VII Corps' (9C, 2, 19) lack of anti-tank weapons, and placed their 114th AT Regiment under its command. During November and December VII Corps advanced with 7th Guards Army in the direction of Budapest, and when 2nd Ukrainian Front decided to storm Pest on the east bank of the Danube it was the central of three corps charged with the assault.

From 1-15 January 1945 VII Corps ground its way forward for over 6km in vicious street fighting comparable in intensity only with the last apocalyptic days in Berlin that same year. Totally unprepared for urban fighting, VII Corps paid a heavy price for its gains. The most heavily defended position in Pest was the racecourse, which the garrison was using as an emergency airstrip for Ju 52s to land ammunition and evacuate wounded. This fell to 9th Cavalry Division in the second week of January. Then, on 15-16 January, the Soviets pulled VII Corps out of the line and sent it north to rejoin IV Corps on the Czechoslovak frontier. This deprived it of its share of the tens of thousands of Germans and Hungarians who surrendered when Pest fell two days later. Of VII Corps' 36,348 men, nearly 11,000 had become casualties since early November, but it had taken 6,522 prisoners.

2nd and 3rd Mountain Divisions and 4th Army continued to advance with the Red Army through north-eastern Hungary. On 1 November they reached the upper Tisa, across which they established bridgeheads over the succeeding weeks. 2nd and 3rd Mountain Divisions remained under the command of separate rifle corps in the Soviet 27th Army until IV Corps HQ took them over on 22 November.

In north-eastern Hungary a series of small mountain ranges – the Matra, Bukk and Hegyalja – offered the last natural defences before the Czechoslovak border. Romanian units were given the central role in taking all of them in increasingly bitter winter weather. 4th Army captured the Hegyalja Mountains between 20 November and 18 December, while the Soviet 27th Army took advantage of IV Corps' (2M, 3M) mountain training to use it as its spearhead through the Bukk Mountains and across the Czechoslovak border between 23 November and 31 December. The Tudor Vladimirescu Division was kept in reserve by the Soviets between 2 November and 19 December, but was then sent through the very centre of the Matra Mountains by the Soviet 53rd Army and entered Czechoslovakia by the end of the month.

More than a third of 2nd Ukrainian Front's infantry divisions in Hungary were Romanian. In addition to 4th Romanian Army, four of 2nd Ukrainian Front's six Soviet armies had included at least two Romanian divisions during their conquest of eastern Hungary, a dispersal outside national control analogous to that experienced under the Germans in the Caucasus in 1942. The Romanians deployed 210,006 men in Hungary between 6 October and 15 January and suffered 42,700 casualties. A total of 21,045 prisoners were taken and 9,744 dead were found by 4th Army alone on the battlefield, so it is probable that more losses were inflicted than sustained. This improvement probably reflected higher levels of organisation, equipment and experience among the former training divisions, and a decline in Hungarian and German morale.

However, a menacing pattern began to reveal itself in the Soviet use of the Romanian forces. It was probably no coincidence that they were committed to attack the centre of the two largest cities in Hungary and three mountain massifs, all of which were strong defensive features likely to cause high casualty rates.

CZECHOSLOVAKIA

Although the Czechoslovak frontier had been crossed, the remaining Hungarian divisions did not immediately leave the line because they were still standing on Hungarian-populated parts of Slovakia annexed in 1939. Indeed, with German support they tried to recross the frontier on 23-27 December, but were repulsed by 4th Army.

The Soviet plan for 1945 was to advance on Germany along two main axes. The first was through Hungary and Austria. The purpose of this advance was to draw German reserves away from the second, decisive thrust from Poland on to Berlin. Between the two lay Czechoslovakia. In this secondary theatre Stalin proposed to keep up continuous pressure with infantry armies. Amongst them were 1st and 4th Romanian Armies, whose allocated line of advance along the declining spine of Slovakia's mountains was among the most physically demanding of all, especially in mid-winter.

The first phase was the conquest of the Ore Mountains, which 4th Army's VI Corps (6, 18, 21) and II Corps (9, 11) undertook from 12 January to 20 March. The Axis defence initially consisted of the German XVII Corps and Hungarian V Corps. The Hungarians were broken before the mountains were reached and most of their

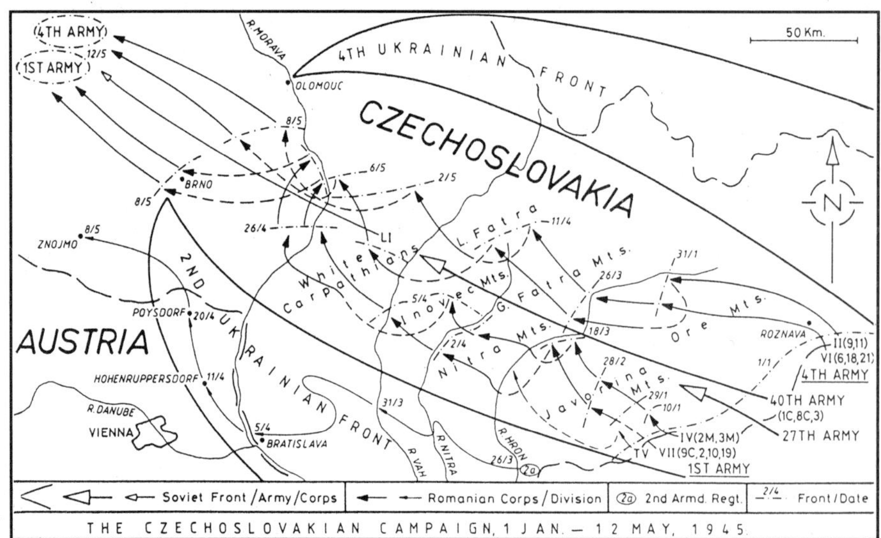

THE CZECHOSLOVAKIAN CAMPAIGN, 1 JAN. — 12 MAY, 1945

units disintegrated, 9th Infantry Division capturing 1,700 prisoners in Roznava on 22/23 January alone and effectively destroying their 1st Mountain Brigade. As a consequence, the half of the Ore Mountains covered by the Hungarians were seized rapidly and the upper reaches of the River Hron were reached by the end of the month. However, the Soviet 40th Army was having more problems taking the rest of the range from the Germans, and the bulk of 4th Army was switched south to its front. It took another six weeks of campaigning in appalling winter conditions to clear the Ore Mountains and draw up along the length of the Hron.

Meanwhile, 1st Army had consolidated the various Romanian divisions previously scattered around 2nd Ukrainian Front, and took over the front of the Soviet 27th Army. Its IV Corps (2M, 3M) and VII Corps (9C, 2, 19, 21) were mostly pitched against the German 8th Jaeger and 76th Infantry Divisions well entrenched in the Javorina Mountains. There it took until 16 March to reach the River Hron. During the campaign, on 13 February, General Macici lost his post as army commander to General Vasilie Anastasiu as a result of the advent of the Groza government. 1st Army suffered 15,825 casualties, nearly a quarter of its strength, in seven weeks of fighting a well-ensconced enemy over heavily-wooded mountainsides, impeded by violent blizzards and deep snows in sub-zero temperatures. The Tudor Vladimirescu Division fought under similar conditions with the Soviet 49th Corps of 53rd Army in the western Javorina range from 1 January to 19 March. It was then put into reserve by 2nd Ukrainian Front and was later sent to Bucharest.

If anything, 2nd Ukrainian Front's neighbouring Soviet 40th and 53rd Armies made even slower progress than the Romanians, and the commander of 4th Ukrainian Front on 4th Army's right flank was dismissed by Stalin in late March because of the slowness of his advance. Stalin then overrode requests from both front commanders that the offensive in Czechoslovakia be delayed, and furiously ordered that it was to be pressed ahead rapidly, regardless of ammunition shortages, and therefore presumably without regard to casualties. If the Soviet supply situation was poor, the Romanian supply situation can only have been worse, and heavy losses were inevitable.

The new Soviet intention was to encircle the bulk of Army Group Centre in its mountainous salient in Slovakia before it could fall back towards Prague. This was to be achieved by 4th Ukrainian Front seizing Olomouc from the north while the left flank of 2nd Ukrainian Front captured Brno from the south. The role of the Romanian armies and the Soviet 40th Army in the centre was to keep the Germans tied to their front by continuous pressure. The Hron was forced by both 1st and 4th Armies on 25 March, and they proceeded to fight their way through the Nitra and Great Fatra Mountains respectively. Although weather conditions were still bad, they had begun to moderate, but the melting snows now added the new obstacle of flooded rivers. On 2 April the River Nitra was crossed by 1st Army, which penetrated the Inovec Range and reached the River Vah two days later.

4th Army crossed the River Turjec on 7 April, and the Hungarian 24th Infantry Division, composed of Slovakian Hungarians and the last non-German formation in the theatre, surrendered to it *en masse*. However, it then became bogged down against the Germans on the crest of the Lesser Fatra range. As a result, II Corps was switched westwards through the Soviet 40th Army's bridgehead across the River Vah in mid-April. The bulk of 40th Army, which usually included several Romanian divisions, was now squeezed out of the line by the convergence of the two Romanian armies, and only the Soviet 5th Rifle Corps separated them for the rest of the war – even then, two of its four divisions were Romanian. The final mountain obstacle was the White Carpathians, which 1st Army crossed to reach the River Morava on 18 April.

On 15 April the Soviet thrusts on Olomouc and Brno began, but they were delayed by fierce German resistance, which bought sufficient time to evacuate the White Carpathians before the pincers closed. The Romanian armies followed up, 1st Army clearing the west bank of the Morava while 4th Army cleared the east bank and its part of the White Carpathians. During the last week of the campaign up to 12 May both Romanian armies advanced virtually side-by-side, following the German withdrawal towards Prague.

One other Romanian unit, 2nd Armoured Regiment, campaigned in 1945. In early February 1945 it could assemble the following working or repairable AFVs:

No.	Type	No.	Type	No.	Type
8	T-4	13	TAs	12	TACAM R-2
8	T-38	5	R-2	26	R-35 & R-35/45
40	FT-17	8	Sdkfz 222	5	SPW

On 8 February the Soviets ordered the 2nd Armoured Regiment to the front and all unserviceable vehicles to be handed over to the Soviet depot at Mizil. Rather than hand even obsolete vehicles over to the Soviets, 2nd Armoured Regiment detrained at Sahy in Slovakia on 26 February 1944 with anything that moved and much that did not. The Romanians tried repeatedly to bring the regiment under command of their 1st or 4th Army, where its resources could be husbanded, or at least expended in supporting their own troops, but the Soviets subordinated it to 27th Guards Tank Brigade of 7th Guards Tank Army for the rest of the war.

The Soviets sent all of the FT-17s, most of the R-2s and TACAM R-2s and some other unrepairable vehicles to one of their captured weapons depots, but did give a handful of captured PzKpfw IVs and Stug. IIIs in exchange. They were subsequently joined by eleven R-1s which, having been subordinate to the cavalry, appear to have escaped earlier Soviet inspections. On beginning operations on 26 March the 1,027-strong regiment had the structure shown in the diagram.

On 26 March 2nd Tank Regiment was sent into the assault supporting the 141st Rifle Division as it broke out from a bridgehead across the River Hron. The regiment breached the front and advanced 9km the following day, but lost two T–4s, one TAs and eight R-35s destroyed and two R-35s damaged in the process. In driving on the River Vah the regiment lost a number of tanks to mechanical failure and consequent confiscation by the Soviets, and by 30 March had only 25 left serviceable. The next day it reached the Vah but had lost three more T-38s and one R-35. The serviceable matériel still included five T–4s, six TAs, two R-2s and two TACAM R-2s. On 2 April it assaulted across the Vah with 141st Rifle Division and entered Bratislava on 4 April. On 5-6 April the regiment supported the 409th Rifle Division in clearing the eastern bank of the Morava, losing another TAs in the process, and provided fire support for the Soviet assault across that river near its confluence with the Danube.

On 9 April 2nd Armoured Regiment was sent across the Danube into Austria. There it co-operated with the Soviet 4th Rifle Division in the capture of Hohenruppersdorf, north-east of Vienna, on 11 April. However, on the following day elements of 3rd Panzer and 25th and 26th SS Divisions (both Hungarian units of only regimental strength) counterattacked in an effort to ensure the retreat of the garrison of Vienna. The 2nd Armoured Regiment found itself virtually cut off in the town, but in the heaviest fighting of its campaign it repulsed the Germans in close-range combat in the streets, claiming two Tigers, two PzKpfw IVs and seven 75mm guns. Two more German tanks were claimed during counterattacks over the following days, but the regiment only avoided annihilation at the cost of twelve more of its own tanks.

On 19-20 April the remaining tanks, now concentrated in a single mixed company, took part in the resumed drive northwards back into Czechoslovakia through Poysdorf, losing three TAs to mechanical failure. On 24 April the armoured company still possessed four T–4s, two TAs, two TACAM R-2s, three R-35s and an R-1. However, two T–4s, the two TAs, a TACAM R-2 and an R-35 were lost in the capture of the Pasohlavki area between 26 and 30 April. On 7-9 May the company, now consisting of two T–4s, one TACAM R-2, two armoured cars and three SPWs, mopped up German resistance some 50km south-west of Brno, losing the TACAM R-2 and two armoured cars in the process. Only on 14 May, after the final German surrender, were the remains of 2nd Armoured Regiment returned to the Romanian 1st Army. It arrived with only a single T–4 and three SPWs, the Soviets having sent all of its damaged vehicles to their own depots of captured weapons.

Given its small size, obsolete equipment, its use in exclusively infantry support actions, the caution and risks entailed in using Axis equipment when operating with

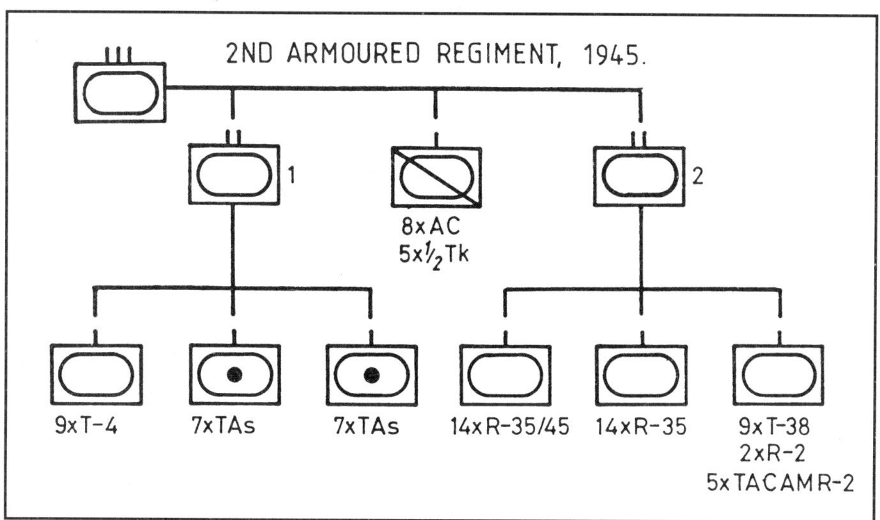

the Red Army, and the clear Soviet determination to run the unit into the ground, it is not surprising that no dramatic operational results are directly attributable to 2nd Armoured Regiment. Nevertheless, it was credited by the Soviets with 4,000 Axis prisoners and the capture or destruction of nine PzKpfw IVs, six Panthers, three Tigers and 49 assorted guns. Its own casualties were 102 men, but its loss of AFVs in combat or to Soviet depots after damage or mechanical breakdown was almost total. Soviet confiscations had once again ensured that Romania's armoured losses to its allies were as heavy as those to its enemies – only the roles of the Germans and Soviets had reversed.

The 1945 campaign was both expensive and unrewarding for Romania, except insofar as it could claim a major role in the liberation of Slovakia. From a combination of its own weakness and the necessity to press its claim for cobelligerent status, the Romanian government was obliged to acquiesce to Soviet plans for 1st and 4th Armies. The Red Army gradually reduced its presence in central Slovakia from two armies to only two divisions, leaving the most difficult terrain to the Romanians. The Soviets displayed little regard for the sufferings of their own infantry, and displayed even less for those of their allies. 1st and 4th Armies' 248,430 men suffered 66,495 casualties in the process, many of them victims of the winter weather. Although 20,478 prisoners were taken, only 2,325 enemy dead were found by 4th Army on the battlefield. It is thus probable that Romanian battle casualties were several times as heavy as those of their German opponents owing to the unfavourable terrain.

A remarkably high proportion of missing for this late stage of the war indicated numerous desertions, many taken prisoner, or a failure to recover the casualties of repulsed attacks, all of which are indicative of low morale. The responsibility for this ultimately lay with Stalin's determination to press the assault along the eminently unsuitable spine of Slovakia. Far from pinning significant German forces down, it served only to tie down several Soviet and two Romanian Armies against the small number of well-ensconced infantry divisions of the German 8th Army. These were often obliged to withdraw because of wider Soviet strategic envelopments on their flanks, and not necessarily as a result of Romanian-Soviet frontal assaults.

Romania had fielded 538,536 men with the Allied forces between August 1944 and May 1945. In terms of raw manpower this put Romania's contribution against the European Axis fourth, behind only the USSR, the USA and Great Britain. However, the fact that the smaller French and Polish Armies were fully equipped by the Allies probably put their combat power ahead of the self-resourced Romanians. In terms of losses over the same period, the Romanian losses of 167,525 were heavier than those of the British in north-west Europe – yet another graphic illustration of the enormously greater human toll exacted by combat in the east, even on secondary fronts. A total of 117,798 Axis prisoners had been taken and, discounting 1st Army, which made no returns, 18,731 Axis dead had been found on the battlefield. The totals of Axis dead and wounded are unknown, but probably pushed total Axis losses above the Romanian figure.

Notwithstanding these efforts, Romania never gained cobelligerent status like Italy, which fielded only a single corps. This was largely because the Western Allies had already surrendered their influence over its fate to the USSR, which had no intention of allowing any of Eastern Europe genuine political autonomy. It was little consolation that King Mihai became one of only five foreigners awarded the highest Soviet decoration, the Order of Victory, on 6 July 1945, or that the others were Eisenhower, Montgomery, Tito and the leader of the Soviet-sponsored Polish People's Army, all representing long-standing Allied nations. Such prestige by association was worthless without the political recognition that accompanied cobelligerent status.

POST-WAR

According to American intelligence estimates, far from declining at the end of the war, the Red Army presence in Romania shot up from about 80, 000 men in May 1945 to a peak of some 615,000 in March 1946, and still stood at some 240,000 at the time of the November 1946 elections which consolidated Communist control. In retrospect, it became clear even to the Western Allies that the Soviet Union's capture of much of 3rd and 4th Armies after the ceasefire with Romania, its halving of the remaining Romanian Army on 26 October 1944 and the dissolution of all of its specialist field commands, the confiscation of captured and other weapons, and the continuous dismissal of field commanders were only the first steps of the Soviet plan to undermine the Romanian Army's independence from the Communist Party. The remaining half of the army was deliberately run into the ground in Northern Transylvania, Hungary and Czechoslovakia, where it lost nearly 100 per cent of its frontline infantry strength and 2nd Armoured Regiment was reduced to the point of extinction.

Soviet-induced demobilisation rapidly reduced the Romanian Army to 100,000 men. With this strict ceiling imposed on it and confirmed by the Peace Treaty of 1947, the army could only maintain one mountain and four infantry divisions in addition to the two Communist formations. In early 1946 Groza's government drafted a law retiring 6,000 largely royalist officers. This was only ratified, in modified form, by the King in mid-year after he received a Soviet ultimatum. After falsifying general election results on 19 November 1946, the Communists secured several more key ministries, including Defence, which went to General Lascar. Over the following year the Tudor Vladimirescu Division was re-equipped as an armoured division with the 40 light, 70 medium and 21 heavy tanks (mostly Panthers), 31 TAs and 13 armoured cars recovered after the war. The Horia, Cloşca si Crişan Division also became motorised. By late 1947 the two Communist divisions, backed by occupying Soviet troops, had a monopoly of armour and mobility.

On 30 December 1947, with his palace surrounded by tanks of the Tudor Vladimirescu Division, King Mihai was forced to abdicate. Romania's isolation from an unsupportive West made any physical resistance futile. By then, successive purges had suppressed open opposition in the officer corps, which was now dominated by communists. Thus the army as an institution did not oppose the Communist takeover in 1948. As the Western Allies failed to challenge the rigged November 1946 election results with any vigour, the Communists were able to arrest, try and sentence Bratianu, Maniu and Petrescu in 1947 with impunity. The first two died in captivity in 1950 and 1953 respectively, while Petrescu was only released in 1965, when he was known to be terminally ill. This broke the leadership continuity of the traditional political parties. Even the communist Patrascanu was purged in 1948 and later executed for nationalistic tendencies.

During the early 1950s the army underwent several consecutive internal reorganisations which effectively broke the historic lineages of all the old Romanian regiments. A small number of royalist officers and other anti-communists took to the mountains as partisans and maintained a hopeless struggle before finally succumbing in the late 1950s. Horia Sima escaped to Spain and died in 1993. At the time of writing King Mihai lives in exile in Switzerland.

Ion Antonescu and the leading figures of his regime – Professor Mihai Antonescu (Foreign Minister), General Mihai Pantazi (Defence Minister), General Piki Vasiliu (Under Secretary at the Interior Ministry), Eugen Cristescu (Head of the Serviciul Special de Informatii), Radu Lecca (Commissioner for Jewish Questions) and Professor Gheorghe Alexianu (Governor of Transnistria) – were held in the Lubianka prison in Moscow until they were returned to Romania after the war and tried as war criminals.

Antonescu behaved with dignity at his trial, and accepted full responsibility for the conduct in Romania's war, though not for all of its consequences. For the minor charges, which largely related to accusations that he had delivered Romania up to German exploitation and occupation, he received life imprisonment. In defence he contended that his relationship with Germany was one of equality, not vassalage. He insisted that the permanent German Army presence was never more than a training mission, and that given Ploieşti's vital importance to the Axis it was perfectly reasonable for the Luftwaffe later to provide half of its AA defences. He rebutted the

Romanian Army: Fielded Strengths and Losses 1941–45

Period	Fielded[1]	Dead	Wounded	Missing	Total	Main Campaign
26/06/41–17/10/41	585,930	27,051	89,632	14,624	131,307	Basarabia, Odessa, S. Ukraine
18/10/41–31/01/42	259,031	2,070	4,518	399	6,987	Crimea
01/02/42–07/05/42	248,497	2,371	10,798	717	13,886	Kerch, Sevastopol
08/05/42–30/06/42	260,547	3,893	12,506	285	16,684	Kharkov, Sevastopol
01/07/42–31/10/42	472,269	9,252	28,249	1,588	39,089	Caucasus, Stalingrad advance
01/11/42–31/12/42	490,150	7,236	31,751	70,355	109,342	Stalingrad
01/01/43–31/10/43	393,470	5,840	20,372	13,636	39,848[3]	Stalingrad, Kuban Bridgehead
01/11/43–31/12/43	225,775	1,309	3,817	1,360	6,486	Crimea, Eltigen Bridgehead
01/01/44–31/03/44	209,885	1,275	3,749	1,403	6,427	Crimea, Transnistria
01/04/44–31/05/44	100,290	1,603	4,169	18,400	24,172	Crimea, Basarabia
01/06/44–23/08/44	466,766	10,376	32,864	154,721	197,961	Basarabia, Iasi-Chisinau
Identified later		15	-	5,834	5,849	
Total V. USSR		72,291[2]	242,425	283,322[2]	598,038	
24/08/44–12/05/45	v. Axis	21,035	90,344	58,443	169,822	Romania, Hungary, Czech
Grand Total 1941–45		93,326	332,769	341,765	767,860	

1. Includes the garrison of Transnistria between October 1941 and March 1944. 2. Only about 80,000 Romanians survived Soviet captivity; some 20,000 of them by volunteering for Soviet sponsored units in 1943/4/5. Thus the total of military dead was actually in the region of 275,000–300,000 against the Soviet Union. 3. Approximately 30,000 were probably belated registrations from Stalingrad.

See also the next table. These two sets of statistics are drawn from different sources and do not conform exactly. Nevertheless they are close enough to confirm their general level of accuracy.

Romanian Losses by Armed Service, 1941–45

Service	Dead	Wounded	Missing	Total
Army	91,061	332,094	365,450	788,605
Air Force	1,328	1,538	1,306	4,172
Navy	231	334	1,220	1,785
Total	92,620	333,966	367,976	794,562
1941–1944	71,585 [2]	243,622	309,533 [2]	624,740
1944–1945	21,035	90,344	58,443	169,822

See notes for previous table.

economic charge by pointing out that in the midst of war he had nevertheless run a balanced budget and more than doubled Romania's gold reserves in the process.

The major charges, for which he received the death sentence, were of waging a war of aggression against the Soviet Union and the Allies, breaking the international rules of war conduct, mistreating POWs and hostages, ordering massacres of civilians in occupied territories, ordering mass racial and political repression, and employing deportation and forced labour. In defence, Antonescu contended that the recovery of Basarabia and Northern Bucovina was entirely legitimate. He admitted ordering the deportation of Basarabia's Jews in 1941, but claimed that it was consistent with the normal expulsion of suspect alien civilians from a militarily sensitive area, and he denied authorising their extermination. He also admitted ordering specific reprisals, but not an indiscriminate massacre, in the wake of the bomb blast at Odessa on 22 October 1941, and argued that this was justified by the Soviet mobilisation of all civilians to the city's defence and their subsequent resorting to partisan activity outside the laws of war.

Antonescu and his co-defendants were all sentenced to death. All except the Marshal appealed to King Mihai for this to be commuted to life imprisonment, but the latter's powers were now so constricted that Groza and Patrascanu only allowed him to reprieve Pantazi, Cristescu and Lecca. The others were executed on 1 June

Allied Prisoners of War in Romanian Hands, 1941–44

Nationality	Taken	Died	Escaped	Released	23/08/44
Soviet	82,090[1]	5,221[2]	3,331[3]	13,682[4]	59,856
American[5]	1,123	-	-	-	1,123
British[5]	39	-	-	-	39
Italian[6]	496	2	-	-	494
Total	83,748	5,223	3,331	13,682	61,512

1. Where Romanian divisions were subordinate to German higher formations their prisoners were often passed back to the Germans. The figure of 82,090 is therefore a considerable understatement of the total actually captured. Based on individual unit returns a figure in excess of 120,000 is probable.
2. This death rate, although demonstrably worse than that of Western POWs in Romanian hands, was a great deal better than that of Romanians or Germans in Soviet hands or Soviets in German hands, the majority of whom died.
3. Many Transnistrian-born POWs were held in the territory and found it relatively easy to escape into the local population.
4. In 1943 the Romanians released most remaining Transnistrian born POWs, an indication of how passive the territory was under them.
5. Aircrew
6. Mostly naval personnel

1946. There was reportedly great difficulty in selecting a willing firing squad, even from the Tudor Vladimirescu Division, and those eventually assembled were Gardieni Publici; ill-trained, common security guards from public buildings. Determined to be in command to the end, Antonescu raised his hat in his left hand and delivered his formal last words to the firing squad; 'Gentlemen, we are ready. Aim true. Long Live Romania! Fire!' At the last word he dropped his arm. However, the volley was ragged and only Alexianu might have been killed outright. Antonescu slumped to his knees. Perhaps apocryphally, his reported final words were a more characteristically irascible; 'You can't even shoot straight. Aim better! Finish it now!' In a gruesome massacre Antonescu, Mihai Antonescu and Vasiliu each had to be shot at least three times before they were deemed dead.

CHAPTER 7

ROMANIAN ARMOUR

In the first years of the war, Romania's attempts to produce R-1, R-35 and T-21 tanks under licence were repeatedly frustrated, and German deliveries were meagre, so from December 1942 force of circumstance led first to the refurbishment and upgrading of existing and captured vehicles, and then to an attempt to develop armoured vehicles capable of production by local industry.

Holdings and Deliveries of Fully Tracked Armoured Vehicles, 1941–44

Romanian Designation	At 22/6/41	In 1942	In 1943	To 23/8/44	Original Designation
Malaxa UE	126	-	-	-	Renault UE
FT-17	75	-	-	-	Renault FT-17
R-1	35	-	-	-	CKD AH-IV
R-35	75	-	-	-	Renault R-35
R-2	126	26	-	-	Skoda S-II-a & PzKpfw 35(t)
T-3	-	12	-	-	PzKpfw III
T-4	-	12	31	83	PzKpfw IV
TACAM T-60 & T-60A	-	-	34	-	Converted Soviet T-60 & T-60A
Şenileta Ford Rusesc	-	-	34	-	STZ Komsomolets
T-38	-	-	50	-	PzKpfw 38 (t)
TACAM R-2	-	-	1*	20*	Converted R-2 or PzKpfw 35(t)
TAs	-	-	4	104	Stug. III
Mareşal	-	-	3	3	Prototypes
R-35/45	-	-	-	30*	Converted Renault R-35
Imported	311	50	85	187	
Romanian	126	-	72	53	Production, conversions and prototypes

* Conversions of existing chassis

CAPTURED TANKS

In the first three months of the war Romania captured 59 Soviet tanks. Some were put straight into service at the front in 1941–42 by the cavalry mechanised squadrons, and at least four light Soviet tanks were used in combat at Stalingrad by them and the armoured division. However, their operational lives were limited owing to lack of spares, and they were normally sent back to Romania when they broke down. As a result of the 1941 and 1942 campaigns the Romanians had the recoverable Soviet tanks in country on 1 November 1942 shown overleaf.

This was enough to have equipped a Soviet tank corps, but only the T-60s and STZs could be put back into service, as they had Ford-type engines familiar to the Romanians and for which spares were available. The Romanians could not produce

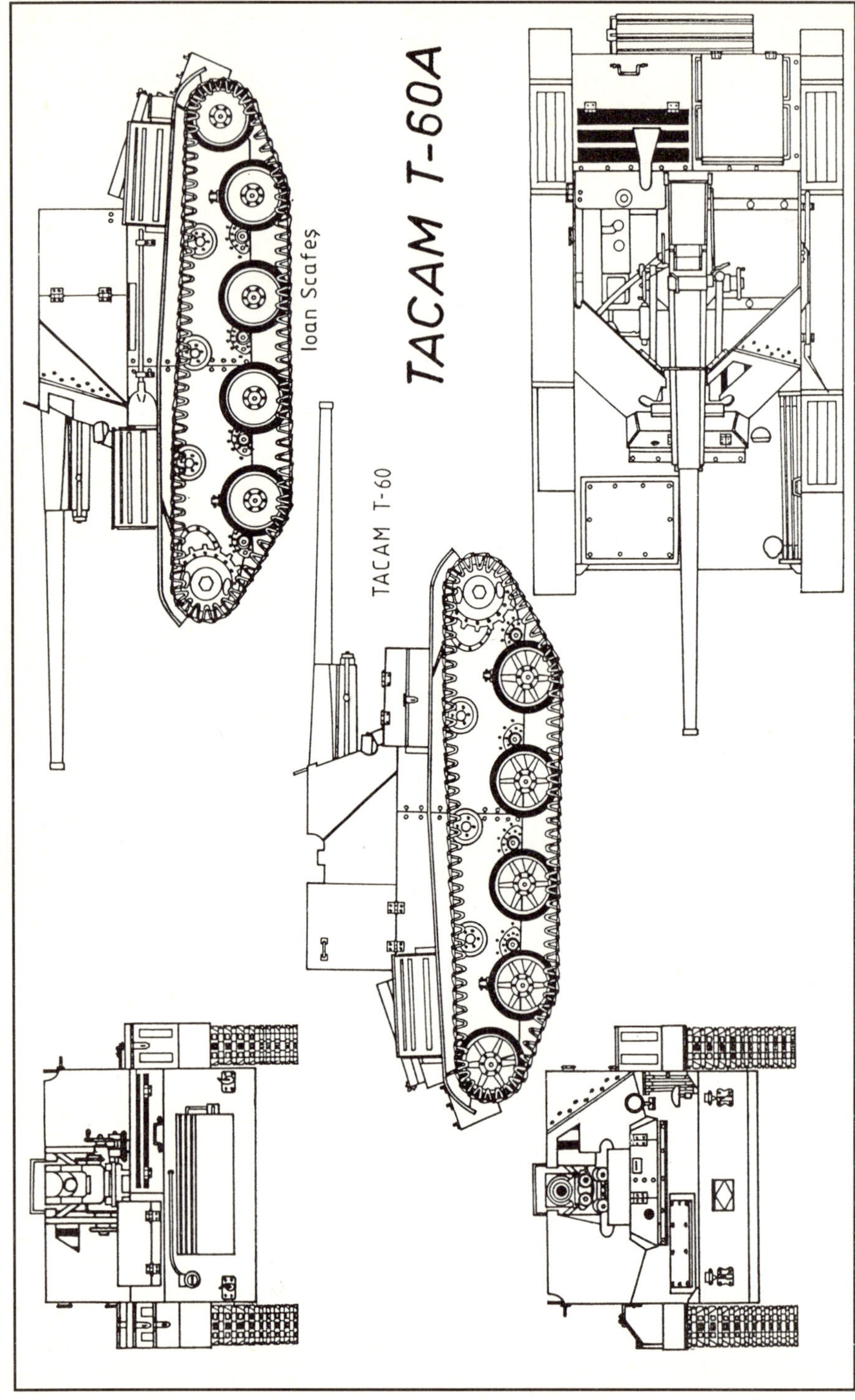
TACAM T-60A
Ioan Scafeş
TACAM T-60

Recoverable Soviet Tanks in Romania, 1 November 1942

No.	Type	No.	Type	No.	Type	No.	Type
1	KV1A	2	T-34	2	T-28 M-2	32	BT-7
33	T-26	1	T-40	30	T-60	19	T-37
3	T-38	2	T-27A	36	Komsomolyets	14	STZ Odessa

high-grade armour plate, so others, such as the BT-7s, had their armour cut away and applied to the fighting compartments of the TACAM T-60 and TACAM R-2. During the defensive fighting in the Kuban and Crimea a considerable number of Anglo-American-supplied tanks were captured, many from failed landing attempts. In March 1944, 41 captured tanks were repatriated from the Crimea (four T-34s, four T-38s, one KVI, four Lees, five Stuarts, four Valentine Mk.IIIs, and nineteen unspecified Vickers tanks) and used for AT training. During counterattacks on the Romanian border between 28 May and 7 June 1944, six broken-down or damaged but recoverable Soviet tanks were taken. These included a new IS-2 heavy tank and an ISU-152 heavy tank destroyer which were displayed in Bucharest; an exhibition which must have been profoundly depressing to anyone familiar with Romania's own AFVs.

All captured Allied tanks had to be returned to the Soviets after Romania's defection to the Allies. During the campaign against the Axis, two fuel-less Tigers were taken on 31 August 1944 but were immediately confiscated by the Soviets. A number of unserviceable Hungarian Toldi and Turan tanks were taken in September, and two Hetzers and a Hungarian Zrinyi assault gun were captured intact in Transylvania during September/October and were used for a while by Romanian troops. However, as a general rule all captured Axis equipment had to be immediately surrendered to the Red Army.

ŞENILETA FORD RUSESC DE CAPTURA

In the spring and summer of 1943 the Romanians undertook the relatively simple task of refurbishing 34 captured Soviet STZ Komsomolyets armoured artillery tractors to replace some of the lost Malaxas. As these vehicles were based on an agricultural tractor of which very large numbers had been captured in Transnistria, they were easily maintained. In early 1944 they had hooks fitted, enabling them to tow German Pak 38 50mm AT guns, and twelve each were issued to 5th and 14th Infantry Divisions and six to 2nd Armoured Regiment. The other four were sent to 5th Cavalry Division in August 1944. All seem to have been lost at the battles of Iaşi-Chişinau or confiscated by the Soviets shortly afterwards.

TACAM T-60

From the moment the Romanians first encountered Soviet T-34s and KV1s in late 1941, it was obvious that there was not a single tank or gun in the Romanian inventory capable of tackling them on reasonable terms and, furthermore, that the Germans were not prepared to supply such weapons as long as their own forces were short. Antonescu initially wanted to produce a copy of the T-34, but this soon proved far beyond the resources of Romanian industry. By late 1942 the only new weapons immediately available were the 175 captured Soviet tanks and 154 76.2mm

TACAM T-60 Specifications.
Vehicle Type: Tank destroyer. **Chassis:** Soviet T-60. **Conversion:** Leonida, Bucharest. **Designation:** Tun Anti Car cu Afet Mobil T-60. **Introduction:** 1943. **No. produced:** 34. **Crew:** 3.
Weight: 9 tons (fully loaded). **Chassis length:** 4.24m. **Length with gun:** 5.51m. **Width:** 2.35m. **Height:** 1.75m. **Ground clearance:** 0.33m. **Hull Armour:** 15mm to 35mm. **Shield armour:** 15mm.
Armament: Soviet 76.2mm, L/51, M1936 Field Gun. **Elevation:** -5° to +8°. Traverse: 32°. **Ammunition:** 44 x Costinescu 6.6kg. A.P. rounds. **Muzzle velocity:** 751m/s. **Secondary:** One ZB53 7.92mm HMG; one SMG.
Engine: Fargo F.H.2., 6 cylinders, water cooled. **Horse power:** 80hp; 3,500rpm. **Fuel/Capacity:** Petrol / 2 x 140 litres. **Maximum speed:** 40kph with rubber rimmed wheels, 32kph with all metal wheels. **Average road speed:** 40kph. **Average cross country speed:** 15-20kph. **Vertical obstacle clearance:** 0.5m. **Trench clearance:** 1.3m. **Gradient:** 32°. **Fording depth:** 0.6m. **Road range:** ±200km. **Cross country range:** ±150km.

field and anti-tank guns of various types. Locotenent Colonel Constantin Ghiulai was ordered to develop a project for an anti-tank gun on a mobile carriage using this material.

Ghiulai chose the T-60 light tank and its T-60A variant (with thicker frontal armour and disc road wheels), 23 of which could immediately be made serviceable. He favoured the T-60 because it was a modern tank which had only entered production in November 1941, it was highly manoeuvrable and it was of unsophisticated construction appropriate to Romania's limited industrial capacity. Furthermore, it was powered by the GAZ 202 engine, which was actually the American Dodge-Derotto-Fargo F.H.2 engine built under licence in the Soviet Union, and for which spares were available in both Romania and Germany.

For the carriage on which the artillery piece was to be mounted, Ghiulai suggested the Soviet M1936 semi-automatic 76.2mm field gun, of which there were 38 immediately usable pieces in depot at Tirgovişte. The combined weapons system was designated the Tun Anticar cu Afet Mobil T-60 (self-propelled gun with mobile carriage), known in its abbreviated form as the TACAM T-60 or TACAM T-60A.

Ghiulai's suggestions were approved, and the 23 T-60s were sent to the Leonida factory for repair. It was there that the prototype TACAM T-60 was built under his supervision between November 1942 and 19 January 1943. Also in January another eleven T-60s were sent to the Leonida factory for conversion. The modifications made to the T-60 by the Romanians were as follows:

- The turret was removed and replaced by a three-sided fighting compartment with an open back. This shield was constructed from 15mm armour plate from captured Soviet BT-7s.
- The original engine cover was replaced by one of Romanian construction, and a system of gratings was fitted so that the driver could cool the engine. The air vent from the radiator was modified to allow the stowage of more ammunition close to the gun. The driver's seat was modified, and new padding fitted for the driver's and gunner's heads. Engine parts, the instrument panel and other accessories were imported from Germany.
- The suspension was adjusted to suit the new centre of gravity, heavier weight (approximately 9 tons) and greater recoil of the 76.2mm gun. The stronger torsion bars this required, and new rubber-rimmed wheels, were based on the original Soviet designs. These, and a more durable all-metal wheel, the Ghiulai model, were cast and finished to the higher specifications by the Industria Sirmei (Wire Industry) in

Turda, IAR at Braşov and Concordia at Ploieşti. A brake to lock the wheels during firing was added.

● The gun's carriage was replaced by a special base plate designed and cast at the Concordia works in Ploieşti and finished at the Astra works in Braşov and Lemaitre works in Bucharest. The gun was then mounted at the Army Arsenal in Bucharest. The gun-laying mechanism was modified to conform with the positions of the sight, the gunner's seat and the firing pedal, and a recoil guard was fitted to protect the gunner.

By mid-June 1943 seventeen TACAM T-60s had been completed and assigned to the Mechanisation Training Centre and 1st Armoured Regiment for training. The remaining seventeen pieces were ready by the end of 1943. The 34 TACAM T-60s were then assigned to the re-forming 1st Armoured Division; sixteen to 1st Armoured Regiment and eighteen to 2nd Armoured Regiment. There they formed 61st and 62nd Tacam Companies.

The TACAM T-60 saw service with 1st Armoured Division and 8th Motorised Cavalry Division in 1944, and most of those that survived combat had to be returned to the Red Army after October 1944. It is interesting to note that Soviet attempts in 1942 to mount the same 76.2mm gun on a T-60 were abandoned owing to the inadequate size of the chassis.

TACAM R-2

The disaster at Stalingrad in November 1942 highlighted the total inadequacy of the 37.2mm guns of the surviving R-2 tanks. However, as the Germans were initially only able to deliver 50 similarly-armed T-38s as replacements, it was clear that the R-2s would have to continue in operational service. It was therefore decided to convert them into TACAMs.

In December 1942 the project was entrusted to Ghiulai, because of his experience with the TACAM T-60. The actual conversion was again to be done by the Leonida factory, and the prototype was built between July and September 1943. The artillery piece chosen was the captured Soviet 76.2mm L/51 M1936 field gun. It was mounted within a three-sided, partly roofed fighting compartment built from armoured plate recovered from captured BT-7 and T-26 tanks.

The preliminary trials showed that the gun's recoil was well tolerated by the chassis, which showed good stability and just a little rearing during firing. Although the original Soviet ammunition was replaced with Romanian Costinescu-model HE and AP rounds, the gun preserved its original ballistic qualities. The original sights were replaced by the Romanian Septilici anti-tank sights made by the Romanian Optical Industry (IOR) and German panoramic sights.

Although test firings against a captured Soviet T-34 showed that the gun's effective range was only 500-600m, the piece proved an efficient field gun able to achieve a good grouping at 3km. The technical performance of the TACAM was essentially the same as that of the original R-2. However, its height of 2.32m gave it an unavoidably high profile, and the great length of the barrel overhang made the crossing of wider trenches awkward.

After comparative tests at the Sudiţi proving ground in late 1943, the Mechanised Troops Command gave clearance for further conversions. However, General

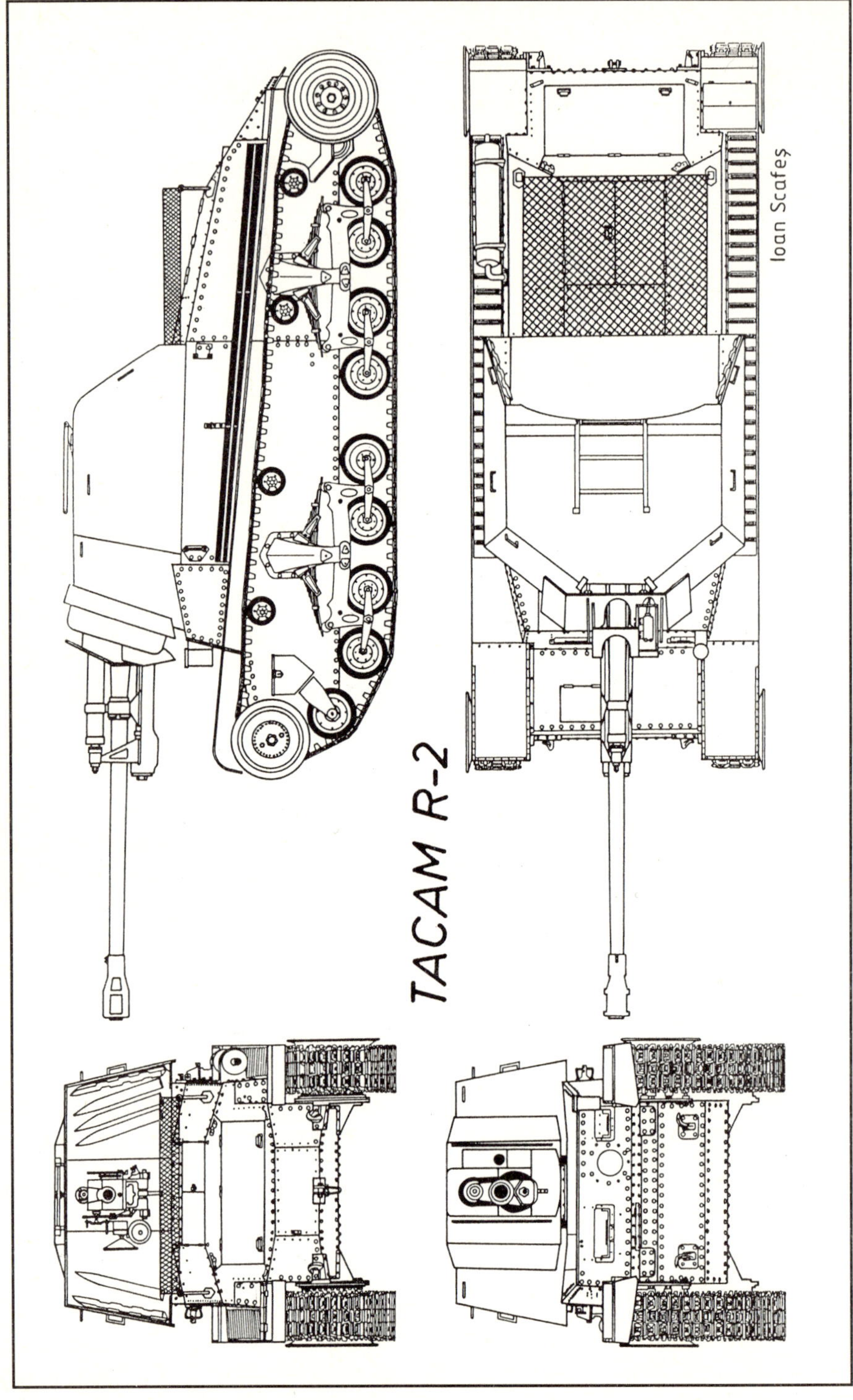
TACAM R-2
Ioan Scafeș

Above: The IAR 38 had a 700hp German motor as a stop-gap, because a reliable Romanian engine was not available. Seventy-five were built in 1939. Three escadrile saw operational service in 1941, but the aircraft were underpowered and were disarmed and reduced to training from 1942.

Below: The IAR 37's maiden flight was delayed until after that of the IAR 38 by problems with its 870hp IAR 14K II C32 engine. Fifty were completed in 1939, and the type served intermittently as a light bomber between 1941 and 1944. Probably its most important work was preparing aircrew for more modern bombers.

Above and below: Two SET-produced IAR 39. The first of 255 IAR 39s were built by IAR-Braşov in 1940. However, pressure of fighter and bomber production at Braşov led to IAR 39 production being transferred to SET in 1941. The IAR 39 was the main army co-operation type throughout the war. The last dozen were completed as glider tugs.

Right: IAR engineers in front of the IAR 47 prototype, built in 1942. Using components from the IAR 80, this aircraft was designed to replace the IAR 39. However, although it displayed pleasing flight characteristics, it did not enter production.

Right: One of 95 PZL 11Fs licence-built by IAR in 1937–38. This was the first fighter built in Romania in series, and was the lineal forebear of the indigenous IAR 80. However, it was already obsolete as a fighter by the time it entered combat in 1941, and was fitted with ight bombs or grenade aunchers for ground attack. t served as a trainer from 1942.

Right: IAR built 25 PZL 24Es under licence in 1939–40. The aircraft was a ransitional type between the PZL 11F and IAR 80. In 1941 they, too, were fitted with grenade launchers and were used extensively for ground attack. From 1942 hey were relegated to raining.

Above: An IAR 81C of Grup 6 Vanatori refuels at Popeşti-Leordeni in the summer of 1944. The IAR 80 was a very competitive design when the prototype first flew in 1939. The IAR 80A, powered by the 1,025hp IAR 14K 1000A engine, was still a match for Soviet fighters in 1941, but, although the armament was regularly upgraded, it proved impossible to up-engine the type.

Below: A cut-away drawing of the IAR 81C. Only the superior standard of Romanian aircrew allowed the IAR 81C to continue facing the Soviets in 1944. However, it had to be withdrawn from confronting the more lethal USAAF in mid-1944.

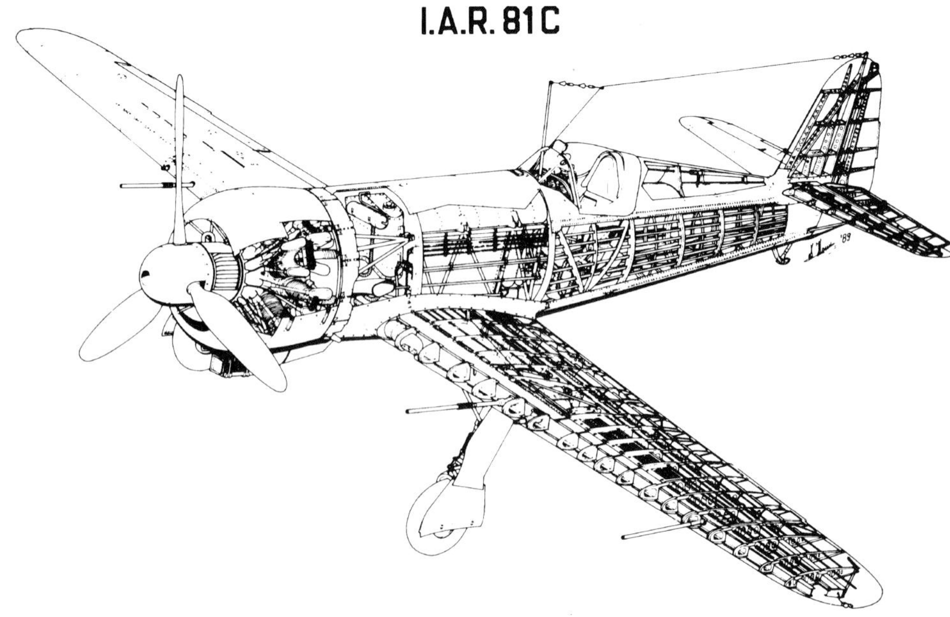

Above: In an effort to rectify the IAR 80's lack of engine power, an attempt was made in 1942 to fit a 1,200hp Jumo 211Da, as used on the JRS 79B, to an IAR 80A airframe. However, the engine shook loose from its mount on its maiden flight and the project had to be abandoned.

Below: An IAR 81 fully armed with a 225kg bomb. Only 60 fighter-bombers were built. The sub-type was not a success because the aircraft's performance was seriously compromised by the ventral bomb cradle. It was therefore very little used as a bomber during the 1942 campaign, the only year it saw significant operational service.

Above: The first IAR-built Bf 109G completed after the war, in June 1945. Six had been built while Romania was still with the Axis, and eleven while it was with the Allies. After the last of 75 Bf 109Gs had been delivered in November 1947 the Soviets turned IAR into a tractor factory.

Below: SM 79Bs of Escadrila 72. The original Italian trimotor was modified to be powered by two Romanian 870hp IAR 14K II C32 engines. However, the resulting aircraft was underpowered and suffered considerable attrition in 1941. It therefore became an advanced trainer for the JRS 79B from 1942.

Above: A JRS 79B of Escadrila 75. At Romanian request, the Italians modified the SM 79B to have two 1,200hp Jumo 211Da engines. IAR produced 36 in 1941–42 as the JRS 79B and they first served in the Odessa campaign. However, they were still found to be underpowered, underarmed and underprotected.

Below: A JRS 79B1 of Escadrila 82 in 1945. The JRS 79B1 incorporated 101 modifications designed to address the weaknesses of the JRS 79B. The new engine was the more powerful 1,350hp Jumo 211F, and armour plate and a variety of stronger armaments were fitted. Thirty-one were built in 1943–44, and served in the 1944–45 campaigns. The order for the remaining five was completed in 1946.

Above: The first Fleet 10G built by IAR in 1936, seen during the war years at Braşov in 1943. It sports the dark olive green paint applied to all Romanian military types. Combat types had additional broad dark-earth stripes applied to break up their outline. IAR, SET and ICAR built 380 Fleet 10Gs between 1936 and 1943, and it became the basic trainer and light communications aircraft.

Below: A pair of IAR 27s. Eighty IAR 27s were built by SET during 1939–42. The design utilised much of the fuselage of the Fleet 10G, and the type was used for advanced training.

Above: One of 124 Nardi FN 305s licence-built by SET between 1939 and 1946. The Nardi was the most advanced Romanian-built trainer. In 1944 they were ordered to be fitted with grenade launchers for ground attack, and this may account for the two-colour combat camouflage.

Below: A civilian registered Fi 156C-3 Storch built in Romania immediately after the war. Production began at ICAR in late 1943, and by the time it finished in 1946 80 Storch had been delivered.

Above: An I-16 in Romanian livery in 1941. A comprehensive selection of captured Soviet aircraft were tested by IAR early in the war.

Below: The first refurbished B-24 Liberator in Romanian livery at Braşov in 1944. The pilot who flew it there was awarded a medal for taking the not inconsiderable risk of flying across the Ploieşti AA defences. It is believed that four Liberators were airworthy by August 1944.

Opposite page, top: The destroyer *Regina Maria* in 1944. Romanian destroyers were distinguished by the symbols of each playing card suit on the bows and stern. *Regina Maria* had Spades. Her sister, *Regele Ferdinand*, was considered the fleet's lucky ship after a number of narrow escapes from mines, torpedoes and bombs. The 'R' Class destroyers were the most powerful Axis ships in the Black Sea.

Opposite page, bottom: The destroyer *Maraşeşti*. Her sister, *Maraşti*, was the lame duck of the fleet. She had a cracked shaft which prevented her from exceeding 22–24kt, and was therefore rarely hazarded far from the coast. Unlike the 'R' Class, the 'M' Class was never re-equipped with modern German submarine location devices.

Top: The three gunboats *Stihi*, *Ghiculescu* and *Dumitrescu* were reliable vessels with good seakeeping qualities. They were initially armed with a 37mm AA gun fore and aft, but the latter was replaced by a German submarine-type 88mm gun later in the war.

Above: The torpedo boats *Sborul* (seen pre-war), *Smeul* and *Naluca* were weak, elderly vessels nearing the end of their lives. They were kept on coastal escort duties.

Opposite page, top: The elderly and mechanically unreliable submarine *Delfinul* before the war. As the only Axis submarine in the Black Sea in 1941, she was valued more as a ship-in-being than for what she might sink. She therefore had extremely constricting operational orders, and sank only one vessel.

Opposite page, bottom: The depot ship *Constanţa*, the submarine *Rechinul* and the surviving Vosper MTB *Viscolul*. The best naval cadets usually volunteered for MTBs but were sent to submarines. However, neither arm had great operational success, as they effectively had no operational vessels for most of 1942–43 and saw little service in 1944.

Left: The minelayer *Amiral Murgescu* was the first significant warship built in Romania. Whilst it is difficult to apportion specific credit for vessels sunk by mines, the fact that the *Murgescu* laid a disproportionate share of them probably means that she was responsible for the loss of several Soviet submarines. Her 105mm guns were also extremely effective AA pieces. This all combined to make her probably the most popular vessel in the fleet.

Left: Most of the Romanian merchant fleet was lost during the war, but ironically the greatest loss of life occurred on one of the few vessels to survive. On 18 April 1944 the *Alba Julia* was bombed and damaged whilst evacuating troops from the Crimea. In the panic, about a thousand men jumped overboard, half of whom were drowned. The *Alba Julia*, seen here from a rescue vessel, was saved.

Above: A *Kogalniceanu* Class river monitor under highly effective vegetal camouflage. Romania's considerable river monitor fleet had a quiet war until it was ordered to strip off its vegetal camouflage and sail to meet its new Soviet allies on 24 August 1944. The Red Air Force promptly sank the *Kogalniceanu* and *Catargiu*.

Below: Odessa docks on 16 October 1941. Soviet histories have presented the evacuation of Odessa as an immaculate operation. However, while it was undoubtedly a considerable success, a large quantity of repairable equipment was abandoned and 7,000 prisoners were rounded up by the Romanians.

Above: The Soviet-raised Tudor Vladimirescu Volunteer Division parades through Bucharest on 30 August 1944. The Soviet 'liberation' of the capital came some four days after it had already fallen completely into Romanian Army hands on 26 August. Equally illusory was the 'volunteer' status of the men in the Tudor Vladimirescu Division. Most were POWs whose alternative to service was probable death in Soviet captivity. The division eventually became the instrument used by the Communists to overthrow the Monarchy in 1947.

Below: This contemporary Romanian cartoon, which displays a healthy sense of humour at their own expense, hides an underlying truth. The war Romania really wanted to fight was with Hungary. Here, aircrew study a map of Arad, a major town briefly occupied by the Hungarians in September 1944, while a map of Budapest adorns the wall.

Racoviţa, then chief of the MTC, delayed the project because it would have meant depriving 1st Armoured Division of its only tanks before their replacements, purchased in Germany, had arrived. As a result the projected conversion of 40 R-2s into TACAMs by Leonida did not begin until late February 1944. In the intervening period a further modification was made. The prototype's M1936 76.2mm L/51 field gun was replaced by the more modern M1941 76.2mm L/46 field gun.

By the end of June 1944 twenty production TACAM R-2s had been built. It was then decided to halt the project because the gun was deemed inadequate in the face of the latest JS series of Soviet heavy tanks. It was proposed either to up-gun the remaining chassis with the Romanian Reşiţa M1943 75mm AT gun or the German Krupp 88mm gun, or to convert them to flamethrower tanks. However, no further work was done on these proposals after Romania defected to the Allies on 23 August 1944.

The TACAM R-2s, organised as 63rd Tacam Company, appear to have entered service with the 1st Training Armoured Division in late July 1944. They were used during the liberation of Bucharest, Ploieşti and Northern Transylvania up to 26 October 1944, during which ten were lost. In November 1944 the remainder were issued to the 2nd Armoured Regiment, which used them during its campaign in Moravia and Austria in 1945. All were knocked out, but at least one has survived to become an exhibit in the Muzeul Militar National in Bucharest.

TACAM R-2 Specifications.
Vehicle Type: Self propelled gun / Tank destroyer. **Chassis:** R-2 (Skoda S-II-a). **Conversion:** Leonida, Bucharest. **Designation:** Tun Anti Car cu Afet Mobil R-2. **Introduction:** 1944. **No. produced:** 21. Crew: 3. **Weight:** 12 tons (fully loaded). **Chassis length:** 5.0m. **Width:** 2.064m. **Height:** 2.32m. **Ground clearance:** 0.35m. **Hull Armour:** 12mm to 25mm. **Shield armour:** 10mm to 17mm.
Armament: Soviet 76.2mm, L/42, M1941 Field Gun. **Elevation:** -5° to +15°. **Traverse:** 30°. **Ammunition:** 21 x Costinescu H.E. rounds, 9 x Costinescu A.P. rounds. **Muzzle velocity:** 680m/s. **Secondary:** 1 x ZB53 7.92mm HMG. **Engine:** Skoda, 6 cylinders, water cooled. **Horse power:** 125hp; 1,800rpm. **Fuel / capacity:** Petrol / 153 litres. **Average road speed:** 25-30kph. **Average cross-country speed:** 8-15kph. **Vertical obstacle clearance:** 0.5m. **Trench clearance:** 2.0m. **Gradient:** 45°. **Fording depth:** 0.8m. **Road range:** ±160km. **Cross country range:** ±130 km.

TACAM ORGANISATION

In 1944 TACAMs were organised into batteries of ten. Battery HQ had an armoured car for reconnaissance, a command car and one TACAM. Subordinate to it were a train of fourteen supply trucks and three platoons of three TACAMS each. This organisation was very similar to that of a contemporary German Sturmgeschutz III battery.

VANATORUL DE CARE R-35

At the end of the siege of Odessa, in October 1941, 2nd Armoured Regiment's R-35 tanks were withdrawn for repairs, which relied largely on parts made by various Romanian factories. Drive sprockets were produced by the Reşiţa factory; track links and metal-rimmed wheels, designed by Ghiulai to be ten times as durable as the rubber-rimmed originals, were made at the Concordia Works; and cylinder heads and drive shafts were cast at Basarab Metallurgical Works in Bucharest and finished by

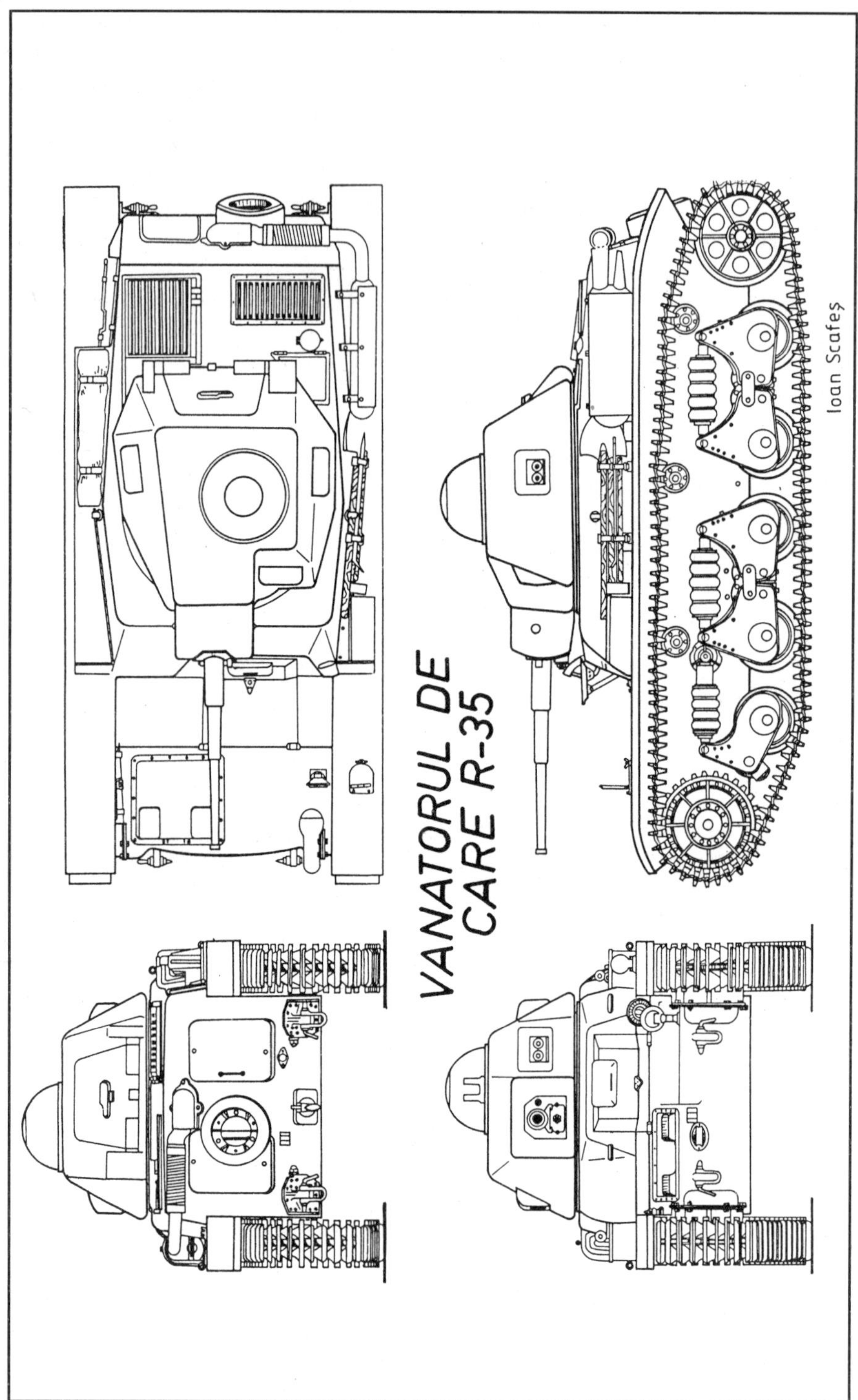
VANATORUL DE
CARE R-35
Ioan Scafeş

IAR at Braşov. The repair of the last R-35s coincided with the battle of Stalingrad, from where the operational reports of 1st Armoured Regiment emphasised the urgent need to modernise the tanks in service by improving both armour and armament if they were to fight the latest generation of Soviet tanks effectively.

The command of 2nd Armoured Regiment put forward some suggestions, even developing a prototype of an R-35 with its turret and gun replaced by those of a Soviet T-26 in its own workshops. An extension of this was a proposal to fit the T-26 turret with the Romanian-produced Schneider 47mm AT gun and ZB53 HMG, while another alternative considered was to replace the R-35's M1916 37mm Puteaux gun with a Soviet 45mm AT gun or the 47mm Schneider AT gun. This stream of suggestions aroused the interest of the Ministry of Supply. In late December 1942 its technical department advised that studies should be concentrated on fitting the R-35 with Soviet 45mm tank guns from BT-7 and T-26 tanks which had been captured in more than sufficient numbers to up-gun all the remaining R-35s.

The project was entrusted to the ubiquitous Colonel Ghiulai and a Captain Dumitru Hogea on 15 December 1942. In early January 1943 they reported that the best solution was to mount the Soviet 45mm tank gun in the R-35 turret in a similar manner to that employed in the BT-7 and T-26; in a forward extension of the turret designed to contain the recoil mechanism. However, they rejected the idea of mounting a co-axial ZB53 machine-gun, as this would have further constricted the already cramped turret.

The prototype, fitted with a Septilici telescopic sight, was ready by the end of February 1943. A major shortcoming was immediately apparent in that the 45mm rounds were three times as large as the 37mm rounds, and far fewer could be carried. However, after trials in the summer of 1943 the overall improvement was deemed sufficiently marked for the Mechanised Troops Command to order the conversion of 30 R-35s. The 45mm guns were reconditioned at the Tirgovişte branch of the army arsenal, while their mounts were cast and finished at the Concordia factory in Ploieşti. The mounting itself was carried out at the Leonida factory under Ghiulai's supervision.

By June 1944 all 30 pieces, now officially designated the 'Vanatorul de Care R-35 (Transformat)', were completed and assigned to the 2nd Armoured Regiment. Confusingly, they were still usually referred to as R-35s, and it is often only possible to differentiate them from unconverted R-35s by 45mm ammunition deliveries. In July the Mechanised Troops Command decided that further R-35s should be converted, but although work began immediately at the Leonida factory, it was halted by Romania's defection to the Allies and never resumed.

VANATORUL DE CARE R-35 (TRANSFORMAT) Specification.
Vehicle Type: Tank destroyer. **Chassis and turret:** Renault R-35. **Conversion:** Leonida, Bucharest. **Designation:** Vanatorul de Care R-35 (Transformat). **Introduction:** 1944. **No. produced:** 30. **Crew:** 2. **Weight:** 11.7 tons. **Chassis length:** 4.02m. **Width:** 1.85m. **Height:** 2.05m. **Ground clearance:** 0.35m. **Hull Armour:** 14mm to 40mm. **Armament:** Soviet 45mm, L/44, M1932 A/T Gun. **Elevation:** -8° to +25°. **Traverse:** 360°. **Ammunition:** 35 armour piercing rounds. **Engine:** Renault, 4 cylinder, watercooled. **Horse power:** 82hp; 2,200rpm. **Fuel:** Petrol. **Average road speed:** 20kph. **Average cross country speed:** 15kph. **Vertical obstacle clearance:** 0.5m. **Trench clearance:** 1.6m. **Gradient:** 38°. **Fording depth:** 0.6m. **Road range:** 120km. **Cross country range:** 100km.

It is probable that two R-35 squadrons which were reportedly serving with 3rd Army in August 1944 were equipped with this 45mm tank destroyer variant. In February 1945 two companies of R-35 tank destroyers and the remaining R-35s formed part of the 2nd Armoured Regiment during its campaign in Czechoslovakia and Austria. By the end of the war not a single R-35 tank destroyer remained serviceable.

While it could hardly be considered a competitive tank by 1943, the R-35 tank destroyer was at least better armed and armoured than the R-1, R-2 or T-38, although its actual combat effectiveness was doubtless compromised by its one-man turret and slow speed.

TACAM R-1

On 22 November 1943 the General Staff decided to rearm the fourteen surviving R-1s with captured Soviet 45mm AT guns as self-propelled guns for security duties. The conversion was provisionally dubbed the TACAM R-1, but was quickly recognised as a virtually useless expenditure of scarce productive capacity and was cancelled.

TACAM T-38

In 1943 40 captured Soviet 76.2mm field guns were reserved for future fitting to the T-38 chassis. This vehicle would presumably have resembled the German SdKfz 139 Panzerjaeger, but as the TACAM R-2 programme was never completed, conversion of TACAM T-38s never began.

VANATORUL DE CARE MAREŞAL (MAREŞAL TANK DESTROYER)

In parallel with the conversion of older or captured tanks, the military cabinet of Marshal Antonescu initiated research into the creation of an indigenous light tank destroyer in December 1942. Antonescu believed that the deficiencies in the equipment of 1st Armoured Division, and the AT capability of Romanian troops in general, could only be made up by the development of a light and mobile tank destroyer with strong firepower that Romanian industry could produce itself. The research panel, Maior Nicolae Anghel and Capitan Engineer Gheorghe Samboţin, faced the task of creating from scratch a completely new vehicle with no equivalent then in service anywhere in the world. For this reason they decided to forgo theoretical preliminary plans and mate an artillery piece with an existing tank chassis immediately in order to study the practical problems. By continuous testing and modification within the capacity of local industry, they planned to develop a truly local design.

With the assistance of Ghiulai and engineer Radu Veres, director of the Rogifer (formerly Malaxa) factory, they fitted a captured Soviet 121.9mm L/12 Putilov-Obuhov howitzer M1904/1930 and a co-axial 7.92mm ZB53 HMG to the chassis of a captured Soviet T-60 tank which had its turret and upperworks replaced by tortoise-shaped armour. Christened the 'Mareşal' (Romanian for Marshal), after Marshal Antonescu, this first prototype was designated M-00. It was tested at the Sudiţi proving ground, east of the town of Slobozia, on 30 July 1943. There was some controversy beforehand, some specialists maintaining that the vehicle could not withstand a test firing and might even turn over. They were wrong, but the trials did reveal a number of deficiencies, such as the failure of the bolts securing the gun mounting, track slippage and a rather weak engine. However, the tests were deemed sufficiently promising to encourage further development.

'M' Staff, a special committee directly responsible to Antonescu's cabinet, was entrusted with the project's supervision from August 1943 because production would require the involvement of an increasing variety of military and industrial agencies. The construction team was allocated a workshop at Rogifer, and by mid-October 1943 they had constructed three improved models, M-01, M-02 and M-03, which, from the point of view of the armour, retained the external characteristics of the original M-00.

The M-03 chassis was 34.2cm longer and 13.4cm wider than that of the T-60, and the armoured plates were welded. The internal structure of the vehicle was reinforced with caissons to make it more robust. The two-man crew sat either side of the gun. The driver, who also aimed and fired the gun, sat at the right/front, while the loader sat in the left centre. The howitzer used a specially developed cumulative-charge shell of the Hohllandung type.

On 23 October 1943 the three new prototypes were tested at Suditi in the presence of Marshal Antonescu. That same day Antonescu had attended a demonstration firing of the new Reşiţa M1943 75mm AT gun which revealed exceptional qualities in its class. When one of the tank destroyer's constructors, Locotenent Colonel Paul Draghiescu, proposed replacing the howitzer with the new Reşiţa gun, Antonescu immediately approved. This modification was to be incorporated into the next prototype, M-04.

FINAL PROTOTYPES AND PRODUCTION

Before further tests and serial production were undertaken, the head of 'M' Staff, Maior Nicolae Anghel, and the directors of Rogifer, who would have to supervise serial production, were sent to tour several German factories to acquaint themselves with the latest developments in the field. They concluded that their design solution was correct, and that they were actually further advanced than the Germans. In November-December 1943 preparations began for serial production. A commission was sent to France to order 1,000 Hotchkiss engines, and a Romanian representative was despatched to the German OKH to purchase those other components that could not be made in Romania. This drew German attention to the vehicle.

On 7 December 1943 Hitler belatedly approved the development of the Jagdpanzer 38(t) Hetzer from the PzKpfw 38(t) light tank. Also in December Antonescu commended the Mareşal project to Hitler, who saw plans of the M-04 on 6 January 1944. There is little doubt that the Mareşal M-04 plans strongly influenced Hetzer development, for the armament, armour configuration and the broadening of the chassis were very similar. In May 1944 Lieutenant Colonel Ventz, the delegate of the Waffen Amt, admitted that the 38(t) tank destroyer had followed the Romanian design solution. Owing to the ready availability of PzKpfw 38(t) components and the massively greater capacity of the Reich's industry, the Hetzer was able to enter production in April 1944 and go into service by July 1944, well before the Mareşal.

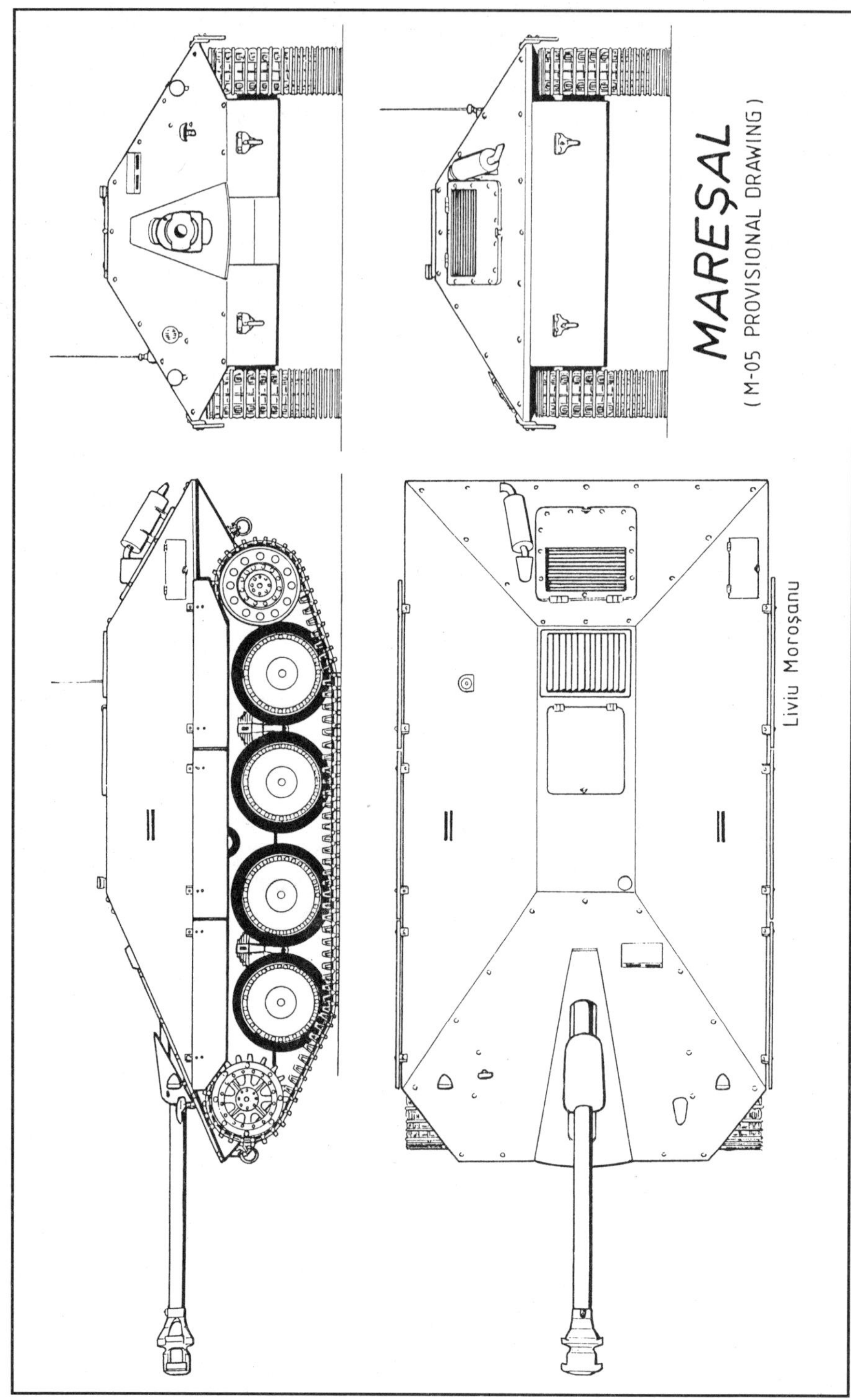
MAREŞAL
(M-05 PROVISIONAL DRAWING)
Liviu Moroşanu

Work on the Mareşal M-04 was carried out from November 1943 to January 1944. The vehicle was fitted with a 120hp Hotchkiss H-39 tank engine and armed with a 75mm D.T.-UDR No.26 Romanian AT gun, later designated the 75mm Reşiţa M1943. In early February 1944 the M-04 was tested at Sudiţi. Before the test

MAREŞAL T60/122MM PROTOTYPES

Model	M-00	M-01	M-02	M-03
Crew	2	2	2	2
Armament	Soviet 121.9mm, Putilov M1904/30 howitzer------			
Optics	IOR Septilici A/T sight------			
Armour shape	Turtle------			
Armour	200mm-300mm steel plate------			10mm steel
Chassis	T-60	Enlarged, reinforced T-60	Rogifer-built enlarged reinforced, T-60 type	Rogifer design
Weight	±6.7 tons	±6.7 tons	±6.4 tons	±6.6 tons
Engine	Ford V8 85hp	Buick 120hp------		
Cooling	Ford modified by Rogifer------			
Gear box	Ford V8	Opel Blitz 75hp------		
Controls	T-60, manual steering	Improved T-60	Rogifer. Pedal steering, manual clutch and accelerator	As M-02
Transmission	T-60------			
Suspension	T-60	Reinforced T-60------		
Wheels	T-60------			
Tracks	Widened T-60------			Lengthened, widened T-60
Electrics	T-60	Rogifer------		
Interior com-	Rogifer------			
munications	Nil	Radio------		

MARESAL ROGIFER/75MM PROTOTYPE SPECIFICATIONS

Model	M-04	M-05	M-06
Crew	2	2	3
Armament	75mm, DT-UDR, M1943, Reşiţa A/T gun------		
Optics	IOR Septilici A/T sight and IOR panoramic telescope------		
Armour shape	Half a hexagon------		
Armour	10-20mm Reşiţa armour plate	10-20mm Bohler armour plate	10-20mm Reşiţa under Bohler licence
Chassis	Rogifer------		
Weight	?	10 tons	10 tons
Engine	Hotchkis H-39 120hp------		
Cooling	Improved Hotchkiss made by Rogifer------		
Gear box	Hotchkiss------		
Controls	Rogifer. Pedal steering, manual clutch and accelerator------		
Transmission	Hotchkiss	Rogifer------	
Suspension	Rogifer------		
Wheels	Rogifer------		
Tracks	T-60 widened to 26cm	CKD LT 38------	
Electrics	Rogifer------		
Interior	Rogifer------		
communications	Radio	Telefunken U.K.W.E.e 10W radio------	

it was again feared by some that the recoil would be more than the vehicle could withstand. There was universal relief when the recoil proved to be a tolerable 0.3m. These field tests were attended by Lieutenant Colonel Ventz and Lieutenant Colonel Hayman, the OKH representative, who were very impressed by the mobility of the Mareşal and the viability of the novel design solution. They asked if the builders of the M-04 had previously designed armoured vehicles. Upon receiving a negative reply, Ventz commented that this accounted for the novelty of the solution.

From the start, Hitler was enthusiastic about the Mareşal and agreed to support the project, despite the misgivings of German planners, who were worried that the diversion of materials for the Mareşal would disrupt the Reich's own AFV production. In fact, seven Mareşals used the same amount of armour plate as a single PzKpfw IV tank, and had been designed to avoid dependency on other German components as far as possible. To this end the Romanians had concluded a series of agreements with firms in France, Bohemia, Austria, Switzerland and Sweden for the supply of materials, components and machine tools to set up the Romanian end of the production process. Noting that the production of the Mareşal might relieve German industry of the obligation to provide the Romanian Army with armoured vehicles, Hitler decided to assist the initiation of serial production with specialists, components, spares, armour plate, etc. It was planned that Romanian enterprises would gradually assimilate the licences for all imported items, so that the Romanian economy could subsequently take over the whole production process.

By March 1944 the Romanian design team, now including Wohlrath of the Alket company of Berlin and Locotenent Colonel Valerian Nestorescu, one of the designers of the Reşiţa 75mm AT gun, were working on M-05 and M-06, intended to be the final prototypes on the basis of which production would begin. Unlike previous prototypes, which had utilised many components of the T-60, M-05 was largely Romanian-built. The main remaining foreign components were the Hotchkiss engine and gearbox, tracks from CKD and a German radio and part of the sights. It was completed in May 1944, preliminary tests taking place late that month.

In June 1944 Mareşal M-05 was presented to Antonescu in competition with a Sturmgeschutz III and a Reşiţa 75mm AT gun. Over a range of tests for speed, handling, slope management, obstacle clearance and firing the Mareşal performed best, and was much praised by attending German officers. From 24 July to 21 August the M-05 underwent further confirmatory tests which were then interrupted by a failure in the gun mounting.

On 10 May 1944 the Mechanised Troops Command took over responsibility for the programme, which now included not only the design team and preparation for serial production, but the organisation of the units to operate the Mareşal. 2nd Armoured Regiment set up 'M' Battalion and began to prepare Mareşal crews. Initially, 1,000 Mareşals were ordered. They were to form 32 AT battalions, each of 30 Mareşals. The proposed battalion organisation resembled that of a German Sturmgeschutz-Brigade. Battalion HQ had three Mareşals, and subordinated to it were three batteries, each of three sections of three Mareşals. The first seven battalions were allocated as follows: one for tests and training ('M' Battalion), two for 1st Armoured Division, two for 2nd Armoured Division (8th Motorised Cavalry Division), and two for 5th Motorised Cavalry Division. For the first time in Romanian armour the technical specifications included the use of anti-magnetic concrete and a multicoloured camouflage scheme.

As early as 3 March 1944 Rogifer had begun producing components for Series 0, comprising ten Mareşals, and on 4 May it began Series I and Series II of 40 and 50 pieces respectively. The production rate was intended to reach four per day. Series 0 was originally expected in June, with monthly production rising to 100 by September. However, the Anglo-American aerial bombardment, which began in April 1944, began to disrupt the Mareşal programme, not only inflicting a little direct damage, but also causing time to be lost in dispersing sections of the Rogifer factory around Brasov, Sibiu and Fagaras, and interrupting the flow of imports by the progressive degradation of Axis rail communications. As a result the Series 0 delivery date was set back to 1 November 1944, and Series I and II were rescheduled for January 1945. It was decided that the first 200 Mareşals would follow the design of the M-05 prototype, while the remaining 800 would progressively incorporate lessons learnt from a final prototype, M-06, and Series 0.

As the Mareşal had met with approval from German specialists and effective support from Hitler for its serial production, a preliminary convention was signed on 8 June 1944 between the Romanian Ministry of Defence and the German OKH for co-operation in expediting mass production. By the time the convention was finalised, the Germans were interested in ordering several dozen Mareşal chassis to mount Rheinmetall 37mm AA guns, and not only offered Romania full licence manufacture of the Hetzer's 160hp Praga engine for the Mareşal (the Western Allies had overrun the French Hotchkiss plant), but also, because the two vehicles would then have a high commonality of parts (engine, radio, tracks and sights), offered a licence for the entire vehicle.

Preliminary talks on the proposed joint production Hetzer/Mareşal established that the Germans would supply an uprated 220hp diesel engine, the armour, the tracks and part of the sights, while the Romanians would build the same parts they were already producing for the Mareşal – the chassis, suspension, wheels, controls, part of the sights and the Reşiţa 75mm gun. Deliveries were to be divided equally between Romania and Germany. To familiarise the Romanians with the Hetzer, Hitler decided to give them fifteen, with a delivery date of 25 August. However, both this delivery and the entire project were halted by Romania's defection on 23 August.

By 23 August 1944 M-05 had completed its proving programme with the single exception of its endurance trial. Owing to the passage of Soviet troops across the country, the Romanian General staff suspended production on 29 August. On 31 August they were told that production of Series 0 was at an advanced stage and that final assembly was in preparation. It was decided to finish the tests on M-05 and to complete series 0, but to suspend production of the later series, presumably because sufficient parts for only the first ten vehicles had been received from the Axis before Romania's defection.

On 21 September 1944 test firings and endurance trials on M-05 were resumed with good results. Series 0 was nearing completion when, on 26 October, the Soviet

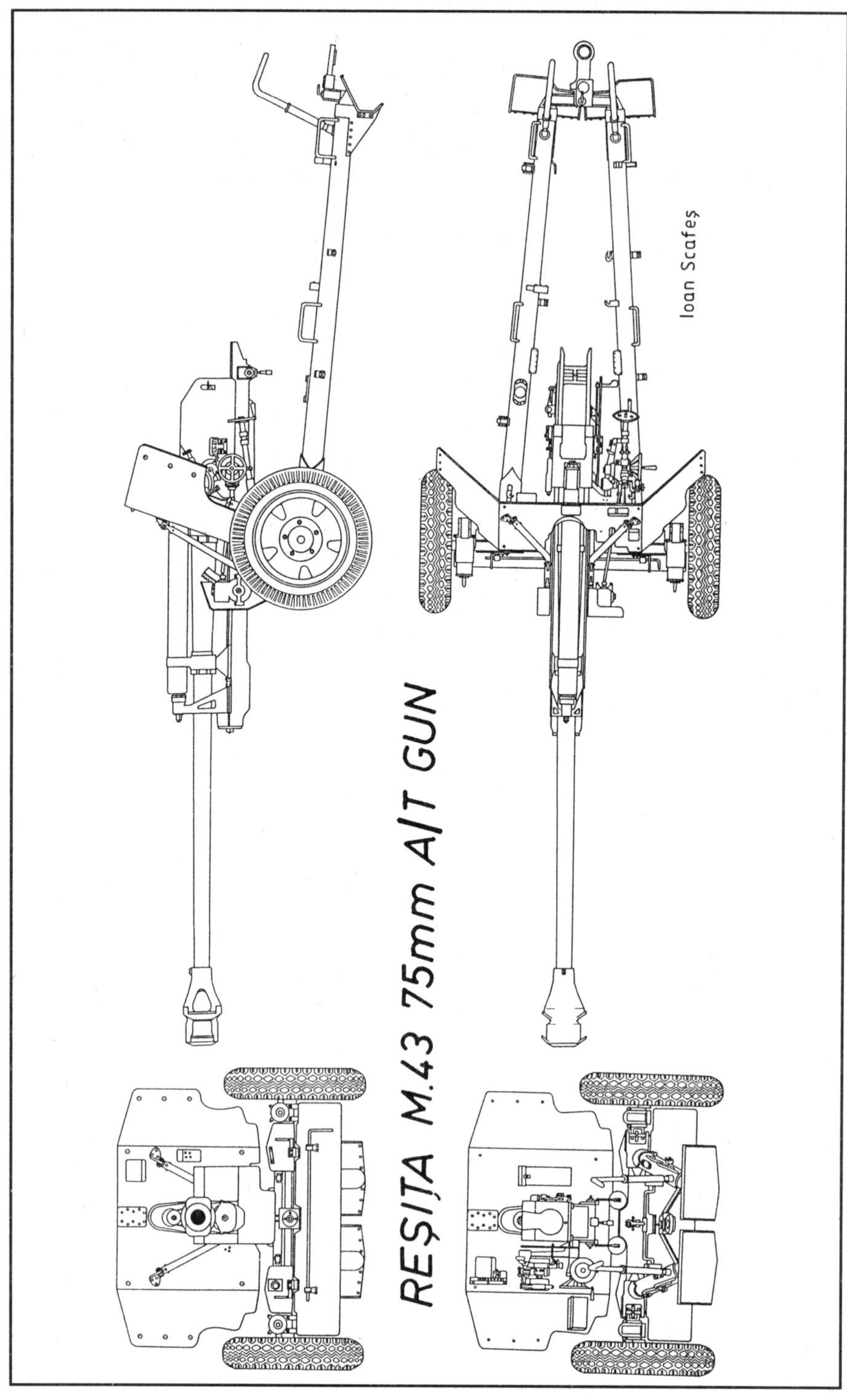
REŞIŢA M.43 75mm A/T GUN
Ioan Scafeş

Armistice Commission imposed a secret additional protocol to the original Armistice which included the dissolution of the Mechanised Troops Command. Thus, on the very verge of fruition, the Mareşal project was finally brought to an end. The Soviets either confiscated or destroyed most available plans and photographs and all completed examples of the Mareşal.

The Mareşal's design embodied an imaginative use of limited resources. Its trials gave every indication that it was destined for a successful service life, and its performance certainly impressed the Germans. Unfortunately a combination of Romanian and wider Axis industrial weakness retarded its production and it was destined never to see action.

75MM REŞIŢA ANTI-TANK GUN, M1943

In mid-1942 Romania began to experiment with the AT potential of its larger guns, and it became immediately apparent that only the high-velocity Reşiţa/Vickers M1936 75mm AA gun had the potential to penetrate Soviet medium and heavy tanks. An order for 30,000 armour-piercing shells was immediately placed with Costinescu. On at least two occasions during the battle of Stalingrad – on 22-23 November, when Soviet armour overran the airfield at Karpovka, and in late December, when they overran the airfield at Tazinskaia – Reşiţa/Vickers 75mm AA guns engaged Soviet armour with some success, claiming five Soviet medium tanks on the latter occasion. The gun also engaged German tanks at Szolnok in October 1944.

However, the Reşiţa/Vickers gun was not destined to become the Romanian army's 'pocket 88' because it was heavy at 2,500kg, could not fire from its carriage, was slow to deploy, and had a very high profile and no gun shield. Thus, although experiments with a twin-axle Bofors carriage and gun shield in 1944/45 solved some of these problems, it remained an air force AA weapon, and its production run was cut short at 200 pieces as plant was converted to produce a true AT gun, the Reşiţa 75mm M1943, which adopted the Reşiţa/Vickers' rifling.

Two of the Romanian army's major deficiencies were its lack of a powerful AT gun and the obsolescence of its light field guns, all of which dated from the turn of

REŞIŢA M1943 75MM ANTI-TANK GUN

	Reşiţa M1943	**Pak 40**	**Zis 3**
Calibre	75mm	75mm	76.2mm
Length of piece	3,635mm	3,700mm	3,246mm
Length of rifling	2,501mm	2,461mm	2,588mm
Traverse	70°	65°	54°
Elevation	-7° to +35°	-5° to +22°	-5° to +37°
Weight complete	1,430 Kg	1,500 Kg	1,120 Kg
MV	1,030 m/s	933 m/s	680 m/s
Shell weight	6.6 Kg (Costinescu A.P.)	6.8 Kg	6.7 Kg
Armour penetration	Over 100mm at 500m (30°)	106mm at 500m (30°)	?
Components	680 pieces	1,200 pieces	610 pieces
Max. Range	12,000m	-	13,290m
Crew	Commander + 6 gunners		
Length	5.45m		
Width	1.82m		
Height	1.55m		

the century. The idea of building a dual-purpose anti-tank and field gun was first raised on 2 June 1942, at a conference between the Ministry of Supply and the General Staff. Colonel Valerian Nestorescu, known for the expertise he had acquired during the calibre unification of Russian, French and German field guns in the 1930s and the assimilation of licences for the Vickers/Reşiţa 75mm M1936 AA gun and 120mm mortar, was charged with preparing a report. Taking into account the performance of the latest German and Soviet anti-tank pieces and the limited technical capacity of the Romanian armament industry, Nestorescu suggested that the proposed Romanian anti-tank gun should not be of original design, because testing would take too long, but should combine the best features of those proven guns already in service in Romania or captured from the Soviets.

Nestorescu's suggestion was accepted, and development was entrusted to the technical division of the Ministry of Supply. Prototype production was delegated to a team headed by Nestorescu, and the Reşiţa factory was selected for its previous experience developing the Vickers/Reşiţa 75mm AA gun. The Romanian artillery provided Nestorescu's team with examples of all appropriate Romanian, German and Soviet guns available, and three prototypes were produced from pieces adapted from the Soviet 76.2mm M1936 and M1942 field guns, the Vickers/Reşiţa 75mm M1936 AA gun and the German 75mm Pak 40 AT gun.

The third prototype was a 75mm piece which used the muzzle brake, recoil and firing mechanism and carriage from the Soviet Zis M1942 field gun; the barrel, rifling and cartridge chamber from the Vickers/Reşiţa M1936 AA gun, and the projectile chamber from the German Pak 40. The gun had 680 components, more than the 610 pieces of the Soviet gun, but a great deal fewer than the 1,200 pieces of the more complex Pak 40. The initial velocity was 1,030m/s, compared with the 745m/s of the Soviet gun and 990m/s of the Pak 40. It thus combined the virtues of both, approaching the simplicity and range of one and exceeding the penetrative power of the other.

The split-trail carriage gave an increase in the firing arc and was extremely stable, allowing three rounds to be fired in six seconds before requiring adjustment. A firing rate of up to twenty rounds a minute could be achieved, compared with up to fifteen rounds from the Soviet gun. The shield comprised two 6mm plates set 2cm apart. The shells combined features of those for the German Pak 40 and Vickers M1936 75mm AA guns, and were made by Costinescu. The prototype was tested and refined throughout the summer of 1943, and the barrel life was found to be 500 rounds of AP.

In September 1943 comparative tests were held of the three prototypes, their German and Soviet AT gun competitors (Zis 3 76.2mm M1942 and Pak 40), a Reşiţa-built copy of the Zis 3 and the M1902/36 75mm Putilov. The DT-UDR Nr.26, Md.1943 proved to have the greatest armour-piercing capacity. In October tests were held before Mareşal Antonescu, taking place on the same day as a demonstration of the Mareşal tank destroyer. The promising possibility of marrying the two weapons was immediately realised, and a joint development was team set up.

The 'DT-UDR Nr.26, Md.1943', renamed the 'Tac-75-Nr.26' but popularly referred to as the '75mm Reşiţa, 1943 Md.', was quickly put into production by the

Ministry of Supply, and on 10 December 1943 an initial order for 1,100 pieces was placed with Reşiţa, Astra in Braşov and Concordia in Ploieşti. The last two factories were supplied with the necessary blueprints, technicians and machine tools by Reşiţa, and production continued to the end of the war. The first 24 were issued to 1st Armoured Division in the spring of 1944, and later to two newly created 36-gun army anti-tank regiments formed from the disbanded Frontier Division's artillery regiments. During the summer of 1944 the first guns began to reach the cavalry and infantry divisions. By the end of 1944 342 pieces are thought to have been produced, and, despite heavy losses in August 1944, most divisions at the front had six, and in some cases twelve Reşiţa 75mm AT guns by February 1944. Their tractor before August 1944 was the RSO/1, but most were horsedrawn thereafter. Although in 1944 the Romanians had under development a Romanian-built derivative of the Soviet Stalinetz tractor, known as the T-1, which was specifically designed for the Reşiţa 75mm AT gun, only five prototypes were produced and it did not reach the troops.

The combat record of the gun against Soviet armour at the battle of Iaşi-Chişinau is lost, but on one occasion during the subsequent campaign against the Germans and Hungarians a Reşiţa AT gun knocked out three PzKpfw IVs in rapid succession. Comparisons show the Reşiţa M1943 75mm gun to have been arguably the most versatile gun of its class in the Second World War, outperforming its German, Soviet and Western equivalents. For a country with such limited experience and industrial base this was a very creditable achievement. However, it suffered from the usual Romanian problems – it was introduced later than its competitors and could only be produced in small numbers.

CHAPTER 8

THE ROMANIAN AIRCRAFT INDUSTRY

THE EVOLUTION OF THE ROMANIAN AIRCRAFT INDUSTRY

The Royal Romanian Air Force (Forţele Aeriene Regale ale Romaniei, or FARR) was founded in 1913. As Romania only entered the First World War in mid-1916, the FARR immediately found itself outclassed by better-equipped and more experienced opponents and reliant on distant foreign suppliers. Consequently the government subsidised the creation of an indigenous aircraft industry between the wars. The SET factory was founded at Bucharest in 1923, the IAR factory, including the country's only aero-engine assembly plant, at Braşov in 1925, and the ICAR company at Bucharest in 1932. IAR's orders between 1925 and 1933 were exclusively for French types, and between 1928 and 1933 it only built 184 Potez XXVs in series.

In 1935 Romania decided to become self-sufficient in warplane production, and IAR was nationalised in September 1938. The government raised capital through a special air fund and expanded IAR Braşov to twin assembly lines and a larger engine plant. SET and ICAR also grew considerably to meet government contracts. However, the government's provision of finance initially outpaced the managerial, organisational and technical ability of the small aviation industry to absorb it usefully, and the late 1930s were marked by a great deal of inefficiency, waste and corruption; aircraft consistently being delivered late and with faults. This provoked a major internal inquiry, and from 1939 the situation improved greatly.

However, the crises of 1940 caused a fall in production and forced Romania to cut back its planned expansion of production for 1942 from sixteen IAR 80s, ten IAR 39s and five JRS 79s per month to ten, six and three respectively. But even these levels were seldom consistently attained owing to persistent bottlenecks caused by difficulties in obtaining a regular supply of the necessary French and Italian materials and components in German-dominated Europe. Thus in some months there were no deliveries at all, whereas in May-June 1942 139 aircraft were

Romanian Aircraft Production, January 1939–May 1945

	Army Co-operation		Fighters			Bombers	Trainers			
Year	IAR/37/38/39	Fi 156	PZL 24	IAR 80	Bf 109G	JRS 79B	Fleet	IAR 27	FN 305	Total
1939	125	-	25	-	-	-	50	9	-	209
1940	70	-	-	-	-	-	45	21	40	176
1941	25	-	-	119	-	13	36	-	30	223
1942	50	-	-	151	-	23	±40	50	-	±314
1943	50	3	-	130	-	24	±39	-	4	±250
1944	60	7	-	50	6	7	-	-	-	130
1945	-	6	-	-	11	-	-	-	14	31
Total	380	16	25	450	17	67	210	80	88	1,333

delivered (35 IAR 80A, 24 IAR 80B, 20 IAR 39A, 10 JRS 79B, 47 IAR 27 and 3 ICAR civil types).

The USAAF raids on the IAR factory on 16 April and 6 May 1944 reportedly damaged or destroyed at least two IAR 81C, three JRS 79B and four Bf 109G airframes, and the IAR 47 prototype. However, although production was disrupted, it was never completely halted, and continued at a reduced level to the end of the war.

IAR, SET and ICAR were largely responsible for major repairs or modifications to their own products, and this sometimes disrupted production. In addition, a repair organisation, ASAM, was set up in 1939 with workshops on six airfields strategically distributed around the country, each specialising in different types of imported aircraft. In 1944 the largest ASAM repair workshop, at Pipera, near Bucharest, which was now so developed that it had production potential, was relocated to Ghimbav to avoid US bombing. Between 1940 and 1944 3,312 aircraft underwent major repairs at these nine centres; 249 in 1940, 624 in 1941, 565 in 1942, 1,076 in 1943 and 798 up to August 1944. A further 473 were repaired between August 1944 and May 1945. In addition, IAR repaired at least 66 Soviet aircraft and 239 aero-engines in 1944–45.

IAR ENGINE DEVELOPMENT

The French Lorraine-Dietrich aero-engine company had been a founding shareholder in IAR, and continued as the dominant influence until another French company, Gnome-Rhône, secured a contract in 1933 to supply its 500hp 9Krsd engine for the PZL 11B. On 21 January 1936 Gnome-Rhône achieved a monopoly when its G-R 7Kfs, G-R 9Krsd and G-R 14K engines were selected for development and production at IAR. Almost all Romanian-built combat aircraft were thereafter powered by IAR derivatives of Gnome-Rhône engines.

In 1936 Romania planned the construction of a new generation of fighters, bombers and army co-operation aircraft and, owing to the country's limited manufacturing resources, a requirement was developed for a single engine to power them all. Gnome-Rhône was now so well established that it was able to persuade the relevant officials to accept its GR 14K motor without due regard to the practicality of improving it locally.

This became increasingly apparent during its troubled further development, which took Romania's small aircraft industry years longer than expected, and consequently set back all of its combat aircraft programmes seriously. A pre-production batch of 20 Gnome-Rhône 14Ks was ordered on 21 January 1936. They were due in May-August 1936, but were only delivered in August-November 1937. Nevertheless, the needs of rearmament were so pressing that on 19 November 1936 173 production IAR 14K II C32s were ordered for delivery in May 1937-June 1938 for the IAR 37 and SM 79B, and 40 IAR 14K III 36s for the PZL 24. However, they were only delivered between September 1938 and April 1940. After the introduction of the IAR 14K IV C32 and IAR 14K 1000A in early 1941, production settled down to a more predictable rhythm.

Unfortunately, the IAR 14K 1000A reached the peak of the G-R 14K's development possibilities in 1941. At that point the IAR 14K 1000A's performance was adequate up to 4,000m, but fell some 10 per cent below that of its competitors above that altitude. All of the Romanian types powered by it were thereafter to experience a relative decline in their operational effectiveness as their Soviet opponents introduced more powerful engines. Furthermore, it was found that the IAR 14K 1000A was extremely sensitive and not sufficiently robust to absorb much battle damage. As the better-resourced Germans never solved similar problems with the related Gnome-Rhône 14M, this did not necessarily reflect badly on Romanian engineers.

Aero-Engines Used in Aircraft Production, 1935–1945

Engine (*Import)	**HP**	**Aircraft** (P-Prototype)
IAR 4 GI	130hp	ICAR Universal, Fleet 10G
IAR 6 GI	200hp	IAR 27, Nardi FN 305 I
* Argus As10C	240hp	Fi 156, Nardi A-FN 305, SET 14 (P)
* G-R 7KFs	400hp	SET 7K
IAR K7	420hp	SET 7Kb, SET 7Kd
* G-R 9Krsd	500hp	PZL 11B, SET XV (P)
* G-R 9Krse	600hp	IAR 15
IAR K9	640hp	PZL 11F
* G-R 14K	660hp	IAR 37 (P)
IAR 14K I C32	690hp	Modified G-R 14K prototype
* BMW 132A	700hp	IAR 38
IAR 14K I C36	780hp	Modified G-R 14K prototype
IAR 14K II C32	870hp	SM79B, IAR 37 & 39, PZL 24, IAR 80 (P)
IAR 14K III C36	930hp	PZL 24, IAR 80
IAR 14K IV C32	960hp	SM 79B, IAR 39A, IAR 80, IAR 47 (P)
IAR 14K 1000A	1,025hp	IAR 80A, B, C, IAR 81, IAR 81A, B, C
* Jumo 211Da	1,200hp	JRS 79B
* Jumo 211F	1,350hp	JRS 79B1
* DB 605	1,475hp	Bf 109G, IAR 471 (P)

The Romanians were well aware of the IAR 14K 1000A's limitations, and applied for a licence to build the Fw 190's BMW 801 radial engine in 1941. The Germans refused, but did sell a licence for the DB 605 engine for licence-built Bf 109Gs in November 1942. DB 605 assembly was due to start in July 1944, but was delayed by US bombing and eventually abandoned. The Bf 109Gs built after Romania's defection were powered by the large stock of new German engines captured in August 1944.

Romania also produced the de Havilland Gipsy Major engine as the IAR 4 GI and the Gipsy Six as the IAR 6 GI for its trainer and light communications aircraft. In 1944/45 they were due to be superseded in production by the more powerful German Argus As 10C-3. However, it appears that production was never begun, and that the Fieseler Fi 156s built after August 1944 were powered by captured engines.

ARMY CO-OPERATION AIRCRAFT

The SET 7 Series

The SET factory had designed and produced a series of closely related training aircraft from 1925. The most significant of these were ten SET 3s in 1929-30, twenty SET 31s in 1930-31 and twenty SET 4s in 1931-32, all powered by 230hp Salmson

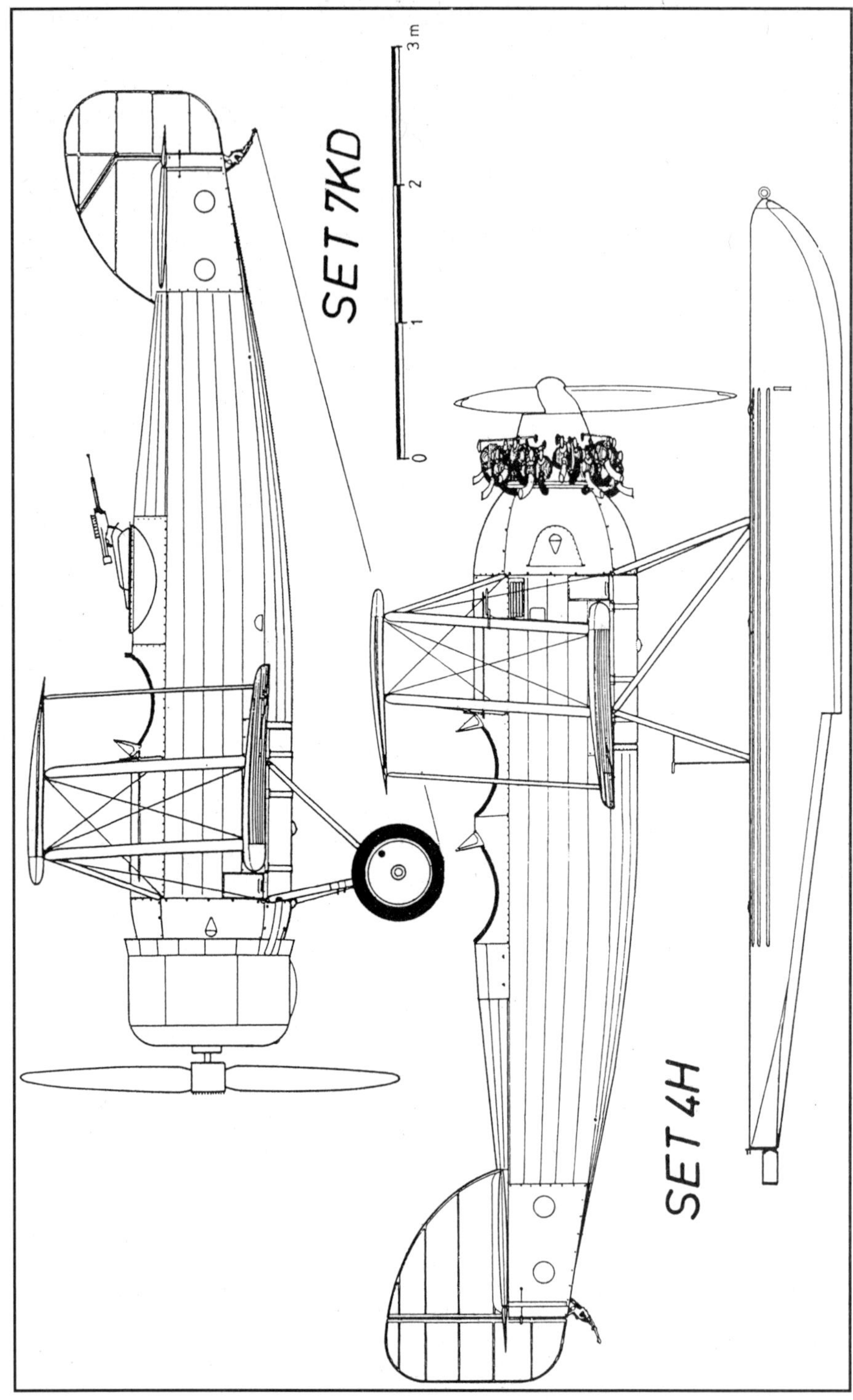
SET 7KD
SET 4H
0
1
2
3 m

9AB engines. These were then followed by 50 SET 7 trainers powered by the 360hp Jaguar 3 engine (Nos.1-50) in 1932-34.

On 26 January 1934 SET won its first contract for a combat aircraft with an order for twenty SET 7Ks (Nos.101-120), which combined observation, communication and training roles. They were delivered by August 1936. The SET 7K carried a camera and the observer was armed with twin Lewis machine-guns. The 'K' denoted that the aircraft was powered by the 400hp French Gnome-Rhône K7fs. This engine shortly went into licensed production at IAR as the slightly uprated 420hp IAR K7. Thus, when another order was won for twenty SET 7KB reconnaissance and observation aircraft (Nos.121-140) on 22 June 1936, they were powered by the new IAR K7. In addition to the SET 7K's armament, the SET 7KBs had a synchronised Vickers machine-gun firing through the propeller arc and could carry six bombs. They were delivered by September 1937.

The imminent delivery of the more advanced IAR 37 brought the SET 7's combat development to a halt, and the final order, placed on 20 August 1937, was for twenty communications aircraft (Nos.141-160), designated SET 7KD. Delivered between October and December 1938, these were basically SET 7KBs stripped of their cameras and armament, apart from a single Lewis gun for the observer. The SET 7K played an important role in preparing crews for the IAR 37, 38 and 39, but never saw operational squadron service itself. However, during the war one was usually attached to each observation squadron, and to many bomber and fighter squadrons, as a unit run-about.

IAR 37, IAR 38 and IAR 39

To supersede the SET 7K, IAR designed the IAR 37 observation and light bombing aircraft in 1936. This aircraft inherited the sesquiplane wing form of the Potez XXV, of which it may be considered a remote development. Its powerplant was intended to be the new IAR 14K, but as this engine's development programme had barely begun, the prototype IAR 37 (No.1) was tested successfully with the Gnome-Rhône 14K. The aircraft's performance promised to be even better with the more powerful IAR 14K, and on 19 November 1936 50 IAR 37s were ordered for delivery between July and October 1937.

The 50 IAR 37 airframes were soon built, but the IAR 14K proved to have numerous teething problems, and the first reliable variant, the 870hp IAR 14K II C32, did not appear until 1938, and even then the first examples were allocated to the SM 79B. As a consequence the Air Ministry, which planned to equip twelve squadrons with the IAR 37, had to find an alternative, interim powerplant.

As a stop-gap it was decided to fit the reliable 700hp BMW 132A motor, which the Germans, anxious to gain political leverage in Romania, delivered promptly. No

SET 7KB & KD Specification

Type: Two-seat Observation and Communications Aircraft. **Power Plant:** One IAR K7-120, 420hp. **Armament** (SET 7KB): One forward-firing Vickers MG, one Lewis MG on flexible mounting in rear cockpit, six 12kg bombs. **Performance:** Maximum speed 255kph. at 1,500m. Climb to 2,000m 5'40", to 3,000m 9'05", to 4,000m 13'31". Ceiling, 7,000 metres. Max. range 580km. **Weights:** Empty 1,010kg, Bomber 1,650kg. **Dimensions:** Span 9.8m, Length 7.15m, Height 3.15m, Total Wing Area 26.6m^2.

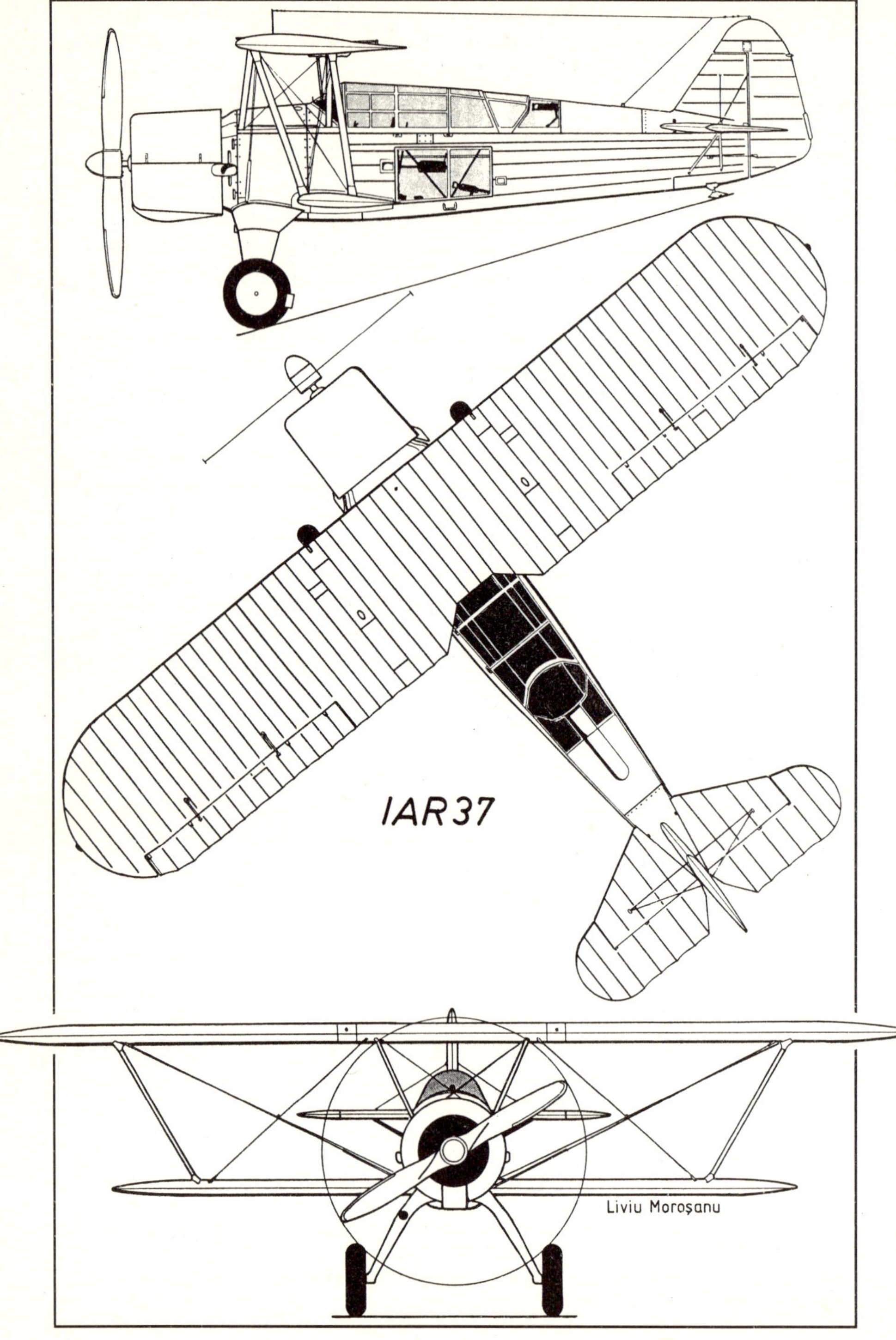
IAR 37
Liviu Moroşanu

prototype was necessary, as minimal modifications were required to fit the BMW 132A to the IAR 37 airframe, and the new combination was designated IAR 38. At the same time, but in an unrelated development, the opportunity was taken to modify the tail. The first IAR 38 (No.1) made its maiden flight on 12 January 1939, and such was the urgency that deliveries began in April, even before the contract for 75 aircraft (Nos.1-75) was formally signed on 22 May 1939. The ready availability of the engine allowed the order to be completed on 25 October, more than a month ahead of schedule. The IAR 38 could carry 24 12kg bombs, but it was primarily devoted to tactical reconnaissance and artillery spotting, being underpowered with the BMW engine.

Meanwhile, an IAR 14K II C32 engine had been fitted to IAR 37 No.1, which first flew with the new engine on 20 January 1939, eight days after the debut of the IAR 38, and the remaining 49 aircraft were at last delivered with this engine between March and September 1939. However, the delay had led to some deterioration in the stored airframes, and substantial refits were necessary in 1940/41. The IAR 37 carried twelve 50kg bombs and was primarily considered a light bomber.

On the same day that the first contract for the IAR 38 was signed, a follow-on order for a further 50 of the type was placed. However, when it became apparent that the IAR 14K II C32 was at last performing satisfactorily in the IAR 37, these airframes were ordered to be completed with this engine. The new airframe/engine combination was designated IAR 39. The engine conversion delayed production by four months, and the prototype first flew on 13 March 1940. The first 50 IAR 39s (Nos.1-50) were delivered between April and September 1940. The IAR 39 could carry 24 12kg bombs or 144 anti-personnel grenades, and was not only used to attack ground targets but was even hazarded in deeper-penetration reconnaissance missions in 1941, though at considerable risk.

Even before the IAR 39's maiden flight, a follow-up order for an additional 45 aircraft (Nos.51-95) was placed on 30 January 1940. The first twenty (Nos.51-70) were delivered between October and December 1940. At this point a new engine, the 960hp IAR 14K IV C32, was introduced, and the remaining 25 aircraft (Nos.71-95) were completed with it between January and March 1941. They were redesignated IAR 39A, although the new 'A' suffix was rarely used.

By the latter half of 1940 IAR Braşov was fully engaged in producing the first IAR 80s and JRS 79Bs, so airframe production and final assembly of the IAR 39 was transferred to the SET factory in Bucharest. This received its first order, for 50 IAR 39s, on 17 August 1940. The first 25 (Nos.96/s-120/s) were completed as IAR 39s between December 1941 and May 1942, and the last 25 (Nos.121/s-145/s) as IAR 39As between May and August 1942. The first SET-produced IAR 39s received the suffix 's' to their constructor's numbers.

IAR 37 Specification

Type: Three-seat Tactical Reconnaissance, Light Bomber and Army Co-operation Aircraft. **Power Plant:** One IAR 14K II C32, 870hp. **Armament:** Two fixed forward-firing Browning 7.92 MGs in wings, one Browning 7.92 MG on flexible mounting in rear cockpit, one Browning 7.92 MG on flexible mount in ventral hatch. Twelve 50kg bombs under wings. **Performance:** Maximum speed 335kph at 3,200 metres. Ceiling 8,000 metres. Max. range 650km. Endurance 2'30". **Weights:** Recce 3,189kg, Bomber 3,459kg. **Dimensions:** Span (upper wing) 12.2m, Length 9.5m, Height 3.97m, Total Wing Area 35.7m^2.

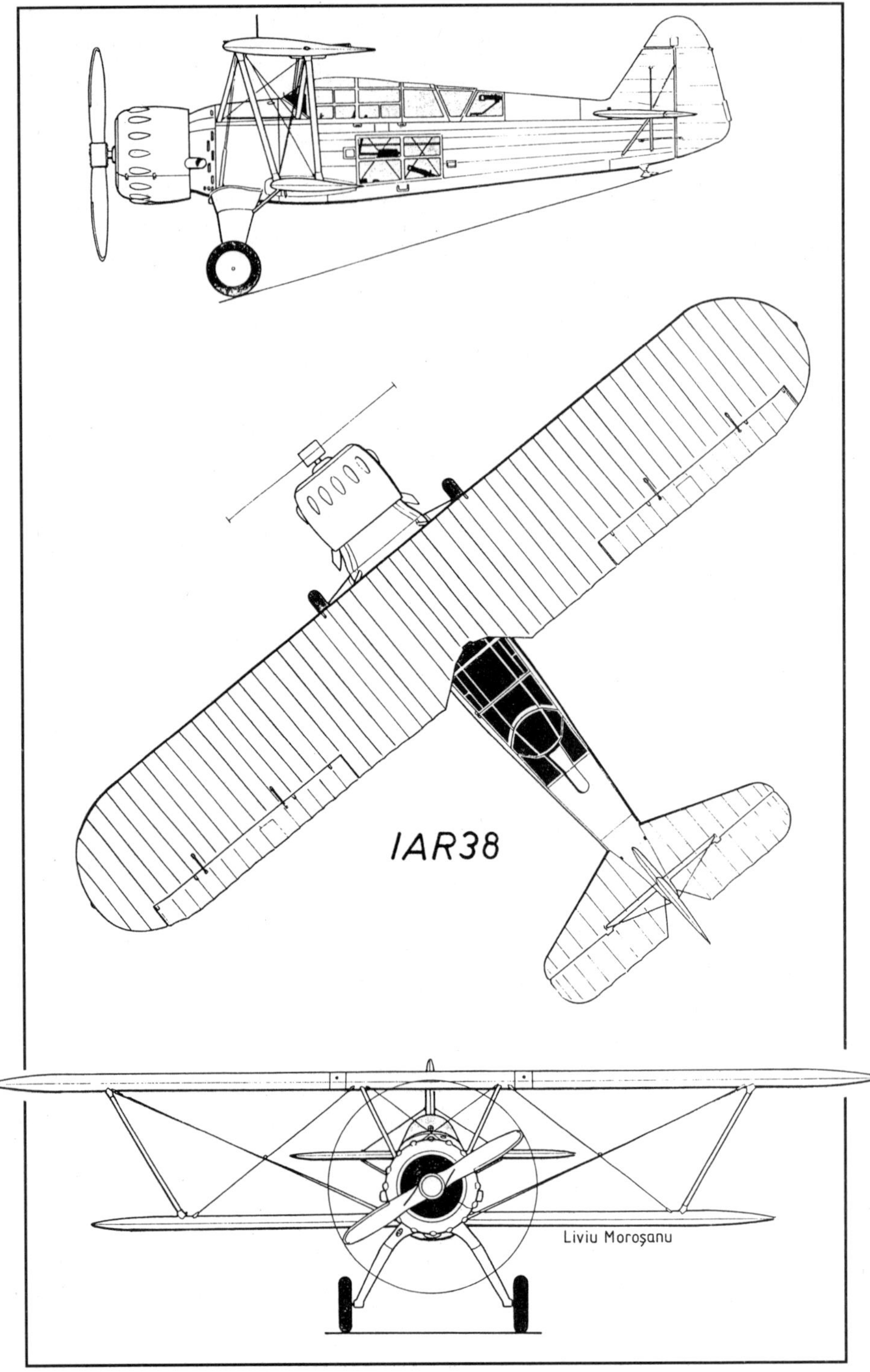
IAR38
Liviu Moroşanu

SET received a further order for 50 IAR 39As (Nos.146-195) on 15 December 1941, and these were delivered in June and July 1943. A final order for 60 IAR 39As (Nos.196-255) was received on 6 September 1943. Forty-eight were delivered between March and August 1944, and the final twelve in September and October 1944 after Romania's defection from the Axis. These last aircraft were completed as tugs for the DFS 230 glider.

From mid-1940 to late 1944 reserves and production of the IAR 37, 38 and 39 were sufficient to maintain at least twelve army co-operation squadrons (Escadrile 11-22). When at the front, each of the nine army corps and the armoured division normally had an integral IAR 37, 38 or 39 squadron to provide them with tactical photographic reconnaissance, and each squadron's ground services included a mobile photographic laboratory to provide on-the-spot analysis to associated army units. Other tasks included artillery fire control, light bombing, ground strafing and deep reconnaissance, but these increased the vulnerability of the relatively slow aircraft as it was required respectively to maintain a steady position which made it vulnerable to AA fire, fly at a low altitude where it was vulnerable to massed small-arms fire, or engage in deep penetration, when it became prey to opposing fighters.

By 1944 the operation of IAR 39s over Soviet lines was extremely risky, and they were usually restricted to artillery spotting and reconnaissance from behind their own front, night nuisance raids or anti-partisan operations. For the latter missions some were fitted to carry 120mm mortar bombs from June 1944. For winter operations the IAR 37, 38 and 39 were provided with skis manufactured by ICAR, as were the SET 7K, PZL 11 and PZL 24.

In March 1941 two IAR 37 and three IAR 38 squadrons had their aircraft replaced by IAR 39s. The IAR 37s and IAR 38s had to be temporarily disarmed, as their three Browning machine-guns were needed to equip the first IAR 80As and IAR 81s (Nos.51-100). From April to July 1942 all remaining IAR 37s, 38s and 39s had to give up their Brownings for the same purpose, and were rearmed with Rheinmetall 7.92mm machine-guns. The Romanians tried to obtain a Browning production licence from the Germans in 1942, but were refused. All subsequent IAR 39As produced were therefore fitted with Rheinmetall machine-guns.

In September 1941 it was decided not to refit the underpowered IAR 38s with IAR 14K IV C32 engines, and they were all relegated to communications and training. Thus in 1942–43 all twelve army co-operation squadrons flew the IAR 39 or IAR 39A. The rearmed IAR 37s were used to equip four new light bomber squadrons in 1942–43 (Escadrilas 81-84), but only Escadrila 81 saw brief service in

IAR 38 Specification

Type: Three-seat Tactical Reconnaissance and Army Co-operation Aircraft. **Power Plant:** One BMW132A, 700hp. **Armament:** One fixed forward-firing Browning 7.92 MG with 300 rounds in left wing, one Browning 7.92mm MG with 400 rounds on flexible mounting in rear cockpit, one Browning 7.92mm MG with 200 rounds on flexible mount in ventral hatch. (Belgian Brownings replaced by Polish Brownings in 1941). Twenty-four 12kg bombs or 144 anti-personnel grenades. **Performance:** Maximum speed 252kph at 1,000 metres, 251kph at 2,000 metres, 247kph at 3,000 metres, 241kph at 4,000m. Climb to 1,000 metres 3'17", to 2,000 metres 7'28", to 3,000 metres 14'21", to 4,000 metres 23'29". Ceiling, 7,000 metres. Max. range 680km. Endurance 3 hours. **Weights:** Recce 2,592kg, Bomber 2,660kg. **Dimensions:** Span (upper wing) 13.2m, (lower wing) 10.0m, Length 9.56m, Height 3.8m, Wing Area (upper wing) 28.10m^2, (lower wing) 12.2m^2.

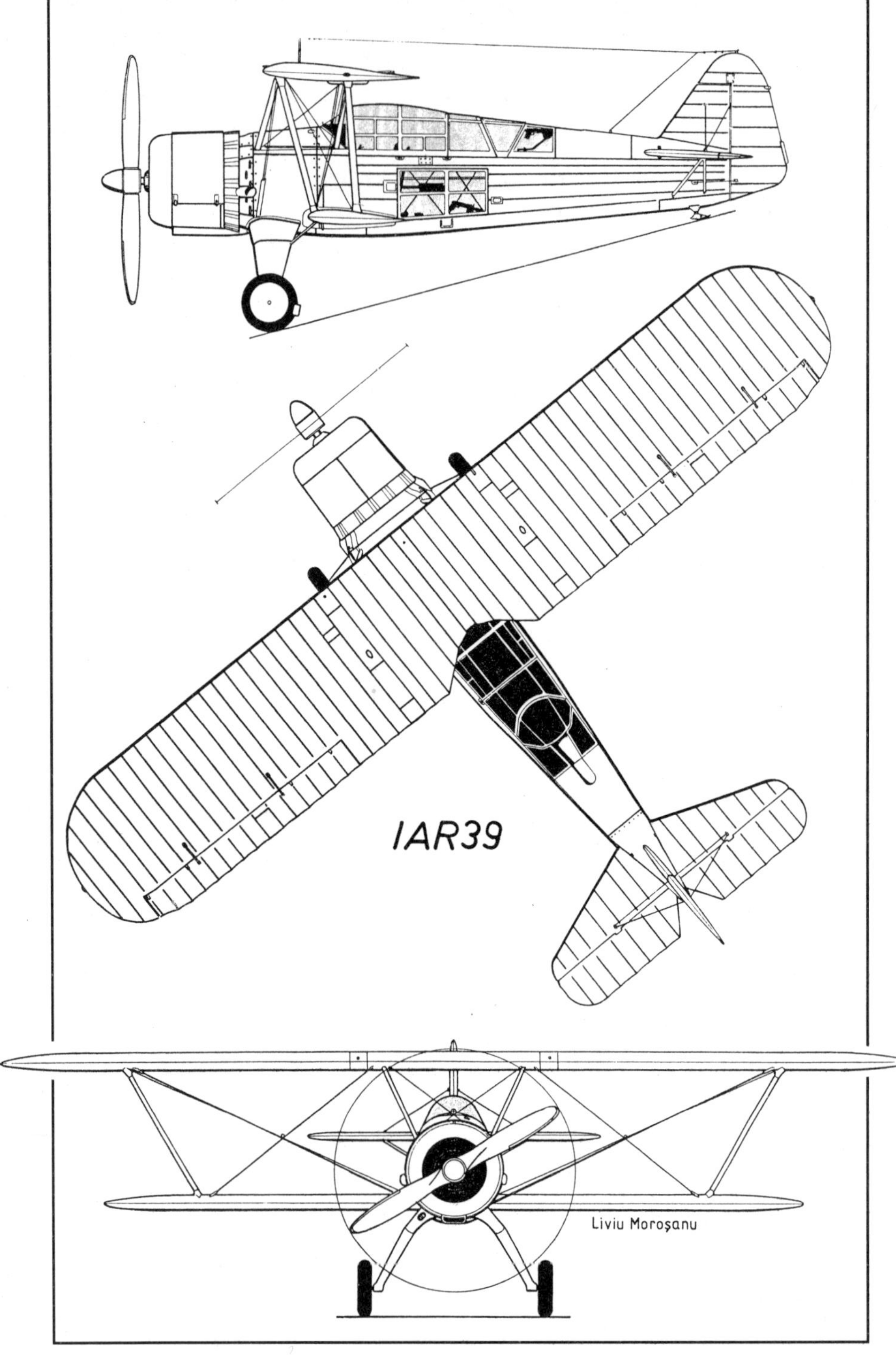
IAR39
Liviu Moroşanu

this role at Stalingrad. Unsurprisingly, it had little operational impact and was soon withdrawn. Two of these squadrons were re-equipped with JRS 79B1s in 1943, and many of their crews were passed on to the newly equipping Stuka squadrons. In 1944 the remaining IAR 37s were reissued as light bombers to Escadrilas 17 and 18, where they proved well suited to the night nuisance raids also performed by obsolescent Soviet and German aircraft.

Among the IAR 39's missions during 1942–1944 was coastal reconnaissance and convoy escort on the Constanţa-Odessa-Sevastopol route. However, the IAR 39's anti-shipping potential was limited because its bombs were light and had to be dropped in horizontal flight, thus lessening their accuracy. Nevertheless, in late 1941 the development of 30 IAR 39A floatplanes was ordered when the Germans failed to deliver promised He 114C floatplanes. The fitting of floats weighing 420kg put the aircraft's weight up to 3,404kg in the reconnaissance role and 3,464kg in the bombing role, and required major structural modifications. The aircraft was accordingly redesigned as a parasol monoplane with a wing area of 32m². However, wind tunnel tests gave poor results, and the SET designers suggested that if the project was to succeed they would need to submit a completely new design. In the event the Germans belatedly began delivery of the He 114C in early 1942, and the project was abandoned on 30 March.

On 19 November 1943 Escadrila 109 was formed with German DFS 230 transport gliders and a dozen converted IAR 39A glider tugs. It was then decided to convert IAR 38s to this role, and in April 1944 five were fitted with towing gear. However, it was found that the drag of the glider brought the underpowered IAR 38 perilously close to its stalling speed, so the last twelve production IAR 39As (Nos.244-255) were completed as glider tugs instead. A second squadron (Esc.110) was projected but never formed owing to attrition among the gliders. Although Escadrila 109 was also trained to land heavy equipment for the Parachute Regiment, it was only used operationally for transport purposes in 1944/45.

Fi 156

The Romanians were so impressed with their first Fieseler Fi 156C-1s that they asked for a licence to build the type in July 1940. This was granted in March 1942, and 80 Fi 156C-3s were ordered from ICAR to replace the Fleet 10G in Escadrile 111-116. The first appeared in October 1943, but only ten (Nos.51-60) were completed by May 1944, when the ICAR factory was forced to relocate by US bombing. Production only resumed late in 1944, after Romania's defection to the Allies, and a

IAR 39 (IAR 39A) Specification

Type: Three-seat Tactical Reconnaissance and Army Co-operation Aircraft. **Power Plant:** One IAR 14K II C32, 870hp. (One IAR 14 IVK C32, 960hp) **Armament:** One fixed forward-firing Browning PWU 7.92mm MG with 300 rounds in left wing, one Browning 7.92mm MG (Rheinmetall 7.92mm MG) with 400 rounds on flexible mounting in rear cockpit, one Browning 7.92mm MG (Rheinmetall 7.92mm MG) with 200 rounds on flexible mount in ventral hatch. Twenty-four 12kg bombs or 144 anti-personnel grenades. **Performance:** Maximum speed 330kph at 3,600 metres (336kph at 3,500 metres). Cruising speed 295kph, Climb to 4,000 metres 7'50", to 5,000 metres 10'30", to 6,000 metres 13'46" (to 3,000 metres 5'32", to 6,000 metres 12'30"). Ceiling 8,000 metres. **Weights:** Empty 2,177kg, Recce 2960kg (3,007kg), Bombed 3,020kg (3,085kg). **Dimensions:** Span 13.1m, Length 9.6m, Height 3.99m, Wing Area 40.3m².

further six were completed by February, when pressure of repair work halted production. These and the 64 aircraft completed after the war used captured Argus engines. The 30 imported and 16 licence-built Fi 156Cs were insufficient to replace the Fleet 10G in Escadrile 111-116 and only supplemented them from 1940. In 1943 further orders were placed with ICAR for 24 casualty evacuation Fi 156D-1s to replace the RWD 13s of Escadrila 108 and 70 more Fi 156C-3s for liaison, but these were cancelled after the war.

Romanian Army Co-Operation Aircraft production, 1934–45

Ordered	No.	Type	Delivered	Engine	Serials (Note)
26/01/34	20	SET 7K	08/36	Gnome-Rhône K7fs 400hp	101-120 (SET)
22/06/36	20	SET 7Kb	09/37	IAR K7 420hp	121-140 (SET)
20/08/37	20	SET 7Kd	10/38-12/38	IAR K7 420hp	141-160 (SET)
19/11/36	50	IAR 37	01/39-10/39	IAR K14 CII 32 870hp	1-50 (Delayed by lack of engine)
22/05/39	75	IAR 38	04/39-10/39	BMW 132/A 700hp	1-75
22/05/39	50	IAR 39	04/40-09/40	IAR K14 CII 32 870hp	1-50 (Originally an IAR 38 order)
30/01/40	45	IAR 39	10/40-12/40	IAR K14 CII 32 870hp	51-70
		IAR 39A	01/41-03/41	IAR K14 CIV 32 960hp	71-95
17/08/40	50	IAR 39	12/41-05/42	IAR K14 CII 32 870hp	96-120 (SET)
		IAR 39A	05/42-08/42	IAR K14 CIV 32 960hp	121-145 (SET)
15/12/41	50	IAR 39A	06/43-07/43	IAR K14 CIV 32 960hp	146-195 (SET)
06/09/43	60	IAR 39A	03/44-08/44	IAR K14 CIV 32 960hp	196-244 (SET)
		IAR 39A	09/44-10/44	IAR K14 CIV 32 960hp	245-260 (SET - glider tugs)
25/04/42	80	Fi 156C-3	10/43-05/44	Argus As10 C-3 240hp	51-60 (ICAR, versus Allies)
		Fi 156C-3	12/44-02/45	Argus As10 C-3 240hp	61, 62, 64, 66–68 (ICAR, versus Axis)
		Fi 156C-3	06/45-??/46	Argus As10 C-3 240hp	63, 65, 69-130 (ICAR - postwar)
??/??/43	24	Fi 156D-1	Cancelled	Argus As10 C-3 240hp	
??/??/43	70	Fi 156C-3	Cancelled	Argus As10 C-3 240hp	

FIGHTERS

IAR 11CV, IAR 12, IAR 13

The first stirrings of Hungarian rearmament prompted Romania to search for a locally produced fighter. In 1930 and 1931 IAR adventurously developed a succession of mixed-construction, low-wing, fixed-undercarriage monoplane fighter prototypes; the IAR 11CV, IAR 12 and IAR 13.

PZL 11B

However, a Polish PZL 11 prototype tested in Romania in December 1931 proved superior to the IAR prototypes, and 50 PZL 11Bs were ordered from Poland in February 1933. The engine selected for the PZL 11B was the Gnome-Rhône 9Krsd. As this represented an expensive and unnecessary change from the Bristol Mercury engine selected for Poland's own PZL 11s, it was strongly suspected that corruption had secured Gnome-Rhône the contract. By the time of Romania's entry into the Second World War the PZL 11B had been withdrawn from operational service, and was subsequently only used as a trainer. However, the PZL 11B was of great significance, because its adoption led to a line of related fighters developed for or by the Romanians in parallel with their development of a succession of Gnome-Rhône-derived aero engines which remained jointly in production until mid-1944.

IAR 14

To develop IAR's productive capacity, an interim order for 20 IAR 14 single-seat advanced fighter trainers was placed in June 1934, but the number actually completed is unclear. Certainly none remained on strength by the Second World War.

IAR 15, IAR 16 and SET XV

In the competition to succeed the PZL 11B in operational service and the IAR 14 on the production line, IAR and SET produced three prototypes with performances superior to that of the PZL 11B during 1934; the IAR 15 and IAR 16 low-wing monoplane fighters and the SET XV biplane fighter, all with fixed undercarriages.

No.	Type	Year	Engine	Serials
1	IAR CV11	1930	Hispano-Suiza 12 Mc 500hp	Prototype
1	IAR 12	1931	Lorraine 12 Eb 450hp	Prototype
1	IAR 13	1931	Hispano-suiza 12 Mc 500hp	Prototype
20	IAR 14	1934	Lorraine 12 Eb 450hp	Trainer
1	SET XV	1934	Gnome-Rhône 9Krsd 500hp	Prototype
1	IAR 15	1934	Gnome-Rhône 9Krse 600hp	Prototype
1	IAR 16	1934	Bristol Mercury 560hp	Prototype

PZL 11F

However, on 21 January 1936 IAR was awarded a contract to licence-build 95 superior PZL 11Fs, a development of the PZL 11B powered by the more powerful Romanian-built 640hp IAR K9 engine. On 10 July 1940 PZL 11Fs still equipped Escadrila 41, 42, 43, 44, 45 and 46 but were obsolete as fighters, so from May 1941 40 per cent began to be fitted with IAR 39-type light bomb racks and 60 per cent with grenade launchers for ground attack. However, although they were used for strafing at Odessa they saw little action with these weapons in 1941. In mid-1941 the Romanians concluded that two IAR 80As were worth more than three PZL 11Fs, and began to disarm the latter to provide Browning machine-guns for the former. From 1942 they were replaced in squadron service by IAR 80As and were relegated to training.

PZL 24E

In 1936 IAR pressed ahead with the design of a low-wing monoplane fighter, introducing a retractable undercarriage into its specification, but later that year the air ministry selected the PZL 24E to succeed the PZL 11F. Five PZL 24Es were ordered as pattern aircraft in Poland, and they and 25 PZL 24Es built under licence in Romania were delivered in 1939. The PZL 24E was essentially an interim design based on the PZL 11F but incorporating new features later included in the IAR 80, such as the IAR K14 III C36 engine (except for the first six, which were initially fit-

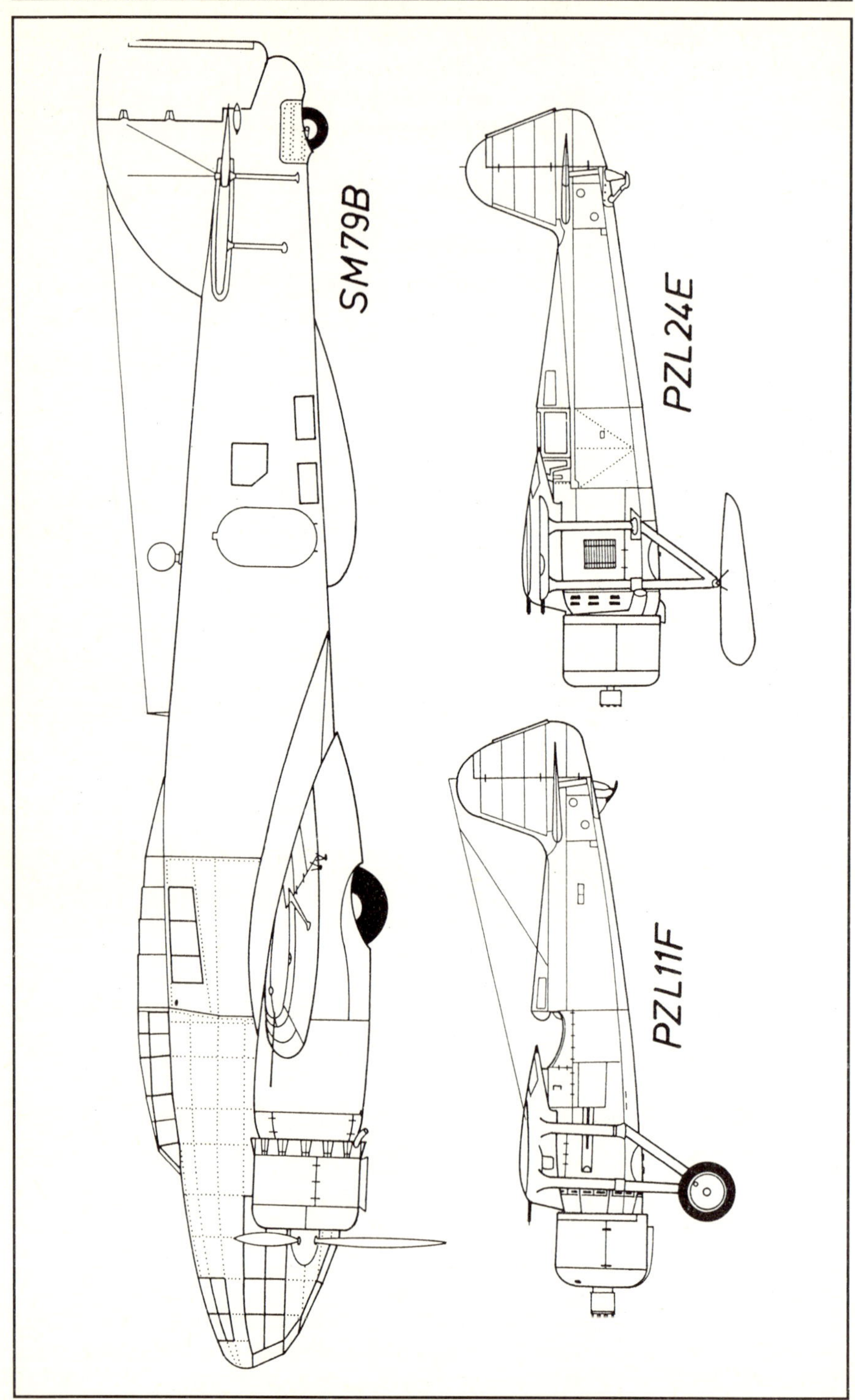
SM79B
PZL24E
PZL11F

ted with the IAR K14 II C32) and the entire tail section. Initially they were to have been issued in three ten-aircraft squadrons (Esc.61, 62, 63) to Grup 6 Vanatori, but in the event two twelve-aircraft squadrons (Esc.61, 62) plus six reserve aircraft were found to be more practical. In mid-1941 they were fitted with grenade launchers and were largely used in the ground-attack role later in that year's campaign. The PZL 24E was replaced by the IAR 81, and from 1942 it was relegated to training.

IAR 24

In 1935 IAR flew a single IAR 24, a low-wing monoplane touring aircraft powered by a 350hp Gnome-Rhône 7Kd engine. It drew on experience gained with the earlier IAR 11CV-IAR 16 series, and it was from this aircraft that the wing form of the later IAR 80 prototype was apparently largely derived.

IAR 80 Prototype

Despite the continuous rebuffs received from their own air ministry, IAR engineers were rightly convinced that their designs for a low-wing monoplane fighter with retractable undercarriage were superior to the gull-wing, fixed-undercarriage Polish fighters repeatedly accepted into service. In October 1937 Professor Ion Grosu and the IAR design team pushed ahead with their plans in secret, using many PZL 24E components, including the entire tail assembly and the 870hp IAR 14K II C32 engine. The wing structure was based on Savoia-Marchetti practice. The resulting aircraft, dubbed the IAR 80, was completed with a token armament of two FN Browning 7.92mm machine-guns. It first flew in April 1939. The IAR 80 prototype (No.0) proved to have a performance approaching that of the best fighters then in service anywhere in the world, and on 18 December 1939 the government placed an

SM 79B SPECIFICATIONS

Type: Four—seat Medium Bomber and Reconnaissance Aircraft. **Power Plant:** Two IAR 14K II C32, 870hp (or IAR 14K IV C32, 960hp). **Performance:** Maximum Speed 326kph (330kph) at sea level, 402kph (394kph) at 3,750m, 398kph (397kph) at 3,950m, 360kph (381kph) at 5,000m. Cruising speed 350kph. Time to 1,000m 3'36" (3'58"), to 2,000m 7'23" (7'56"), to 3,000m 11'15" (11'54"), 4,000m 15'54" (15'35"), to 5,000m 22'22" (20'14"), (to 6,000m 34'30"). Maximum Range w/o bombs 3,000km (1,980km), with 950kg bombs 1890kms (1,000kg bombs 1,170kms/350kph), 1,500kg bombs 1,150kms/350kph. (1,575kg bombs 755kms/350kph). Practical ceiling 7,000m. **Weights:** 10,100kg w/o bombs. **Dimensions:** Span 21.2m, Length 16.2m, Height 4.1m. **Bombs:** Standard bomb load 9x100kg bombs internally and 2x300kg bombs externally.

SM 79B/JIS 79B/JRS 79B/JRS 79B1 ARMAMENT.

	Nose	Dorsal	Ventral	Lateral	Belly	Right Engine
SM 79B 1-24	Br 13.2mm	Br 13.2mm	Br 13.2mm	Vi 7.92mm	-	-
JRS 79B 101-111	Br 13.2mm	Br 13.2mm	Vi 7.92mm	Vi 7.92mm	-	-
JRS 79B 112-129	PWU 7.92mm	Br 13.2mm	Vi 7.92mm	2 x 7.92mm	-	-
JRS 79B 130-136	Rh 7.92mm	Rh 7.92mm	Rh 7.92mm	2 x Rh 7.92mm	-	-
JIS 79B 149-156	Br 13.2mm	Br 13.2mm	Vi 7.92mm	Vi 7.92mm	-	-
JRS 79B1	Rh 7.92mm	Rh 7.92mm	Rh 7.92mm	2 x Rh 7.92mm	IK 20mm	-
JRS 79B1	Rh 7.92mm	2x Ma 7.92mm	Rh 7.92mm	2 x Rh 7.92mm	IK 20mm	-
JRS 79B1	Rh 7.92mm	2x Ma 7.92mm	Rh 7.92mm	2 x Rh 7.92mm	IK 20mm	PWU 7.92mm
11/08/44	Ma 13.2mm	Ma 13.2mm	Ma 13.2mm	2 x Ma 13.2mm	IK 20mm	Ma 13.2mm

Br: Browning. Vi: Vickers. PWU: Polish Browning. Rh; Rheinmetall. Ma: Mauser. IK: Ikaria order for 100 IAR 80s (Nos.1-100). A second order for a further 100 (Nos.101-200) followed on 22 August 1940.

However, Romania's own toolmaking capacity was minimal, and with the whole of Europe rearming frantically the international situation in early 1940 was not conducive to the quick import of machine tools to prepare IAR for early series production. German conquests in mid-1940 then cut Romania off from many imported components. Licence manufacture of the French Messier undercarriage was deferred, aluminium supplies temporarily dried up, and an order for 600 Browning 7.92mm machine-guns placed with FN in Belgium was lost. The Germans would not begin to supply substitutes until Romania joined the Axis in November 1940, by which time the IAR 80's essential design was well established, but from early 1941 increasing numbers of German internal components were adopted, including instrument panels, oxygen systems and gunsights.

As a result of the machine-gun shortage, Romania had to strip its IAR 37s, IAR 38s, IAR 39s, PZL 11Fs and PZL 24Es of their 7.92mm FN Browning machine-guns in late 1941 and early 1942 in order to equip the new IAR 80As and IAR 81s. The

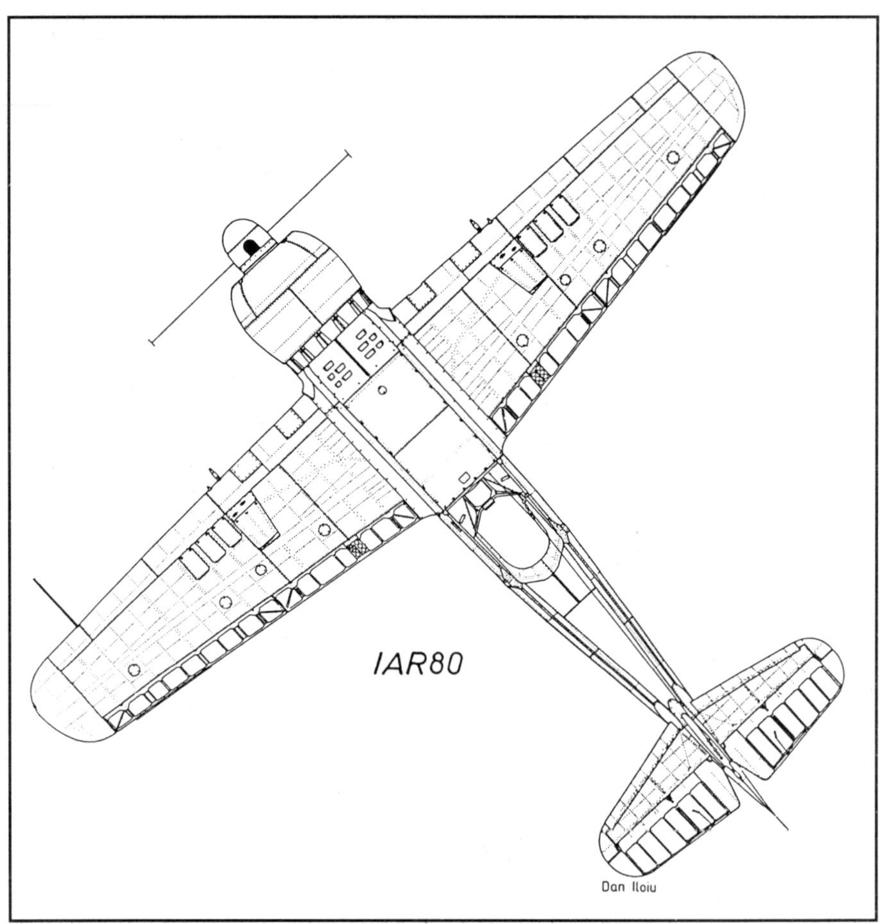

Germans refused a Romanian application to licence-build the 7.92mm FN Browning in early 1942, but appear to have resumed delivery of the weapon later in the year.

IAR 80

The first twenty production IAR 80s (Nos.1-20), substantially modified from the original prototype, began to appear in February 1941. They were fitted with the 930hp IAR 14K III C36 engine, the cockpit was equipped with a radio and oxygen beneath a fully-enclosed canopy, and armament was increased to four FN Browning 7.92mm machine-guns. Nos.21-50 were given the more powerful 960hp IAR 14K IV C32. The IAR 80 largely equipped Grup 8 Vanatori (Esc.41, 59, 60) at the opening of the Russian Campaign in June 1941. Its pilots considered the IAR 80 generally competitive but underarmed and underpowered.

IAR 80A

The IAR design team had already reached the same conclusion, and from May the IAR 80A, powered by the uprated 1,025hp IAR 14K 1000A engine and armed with

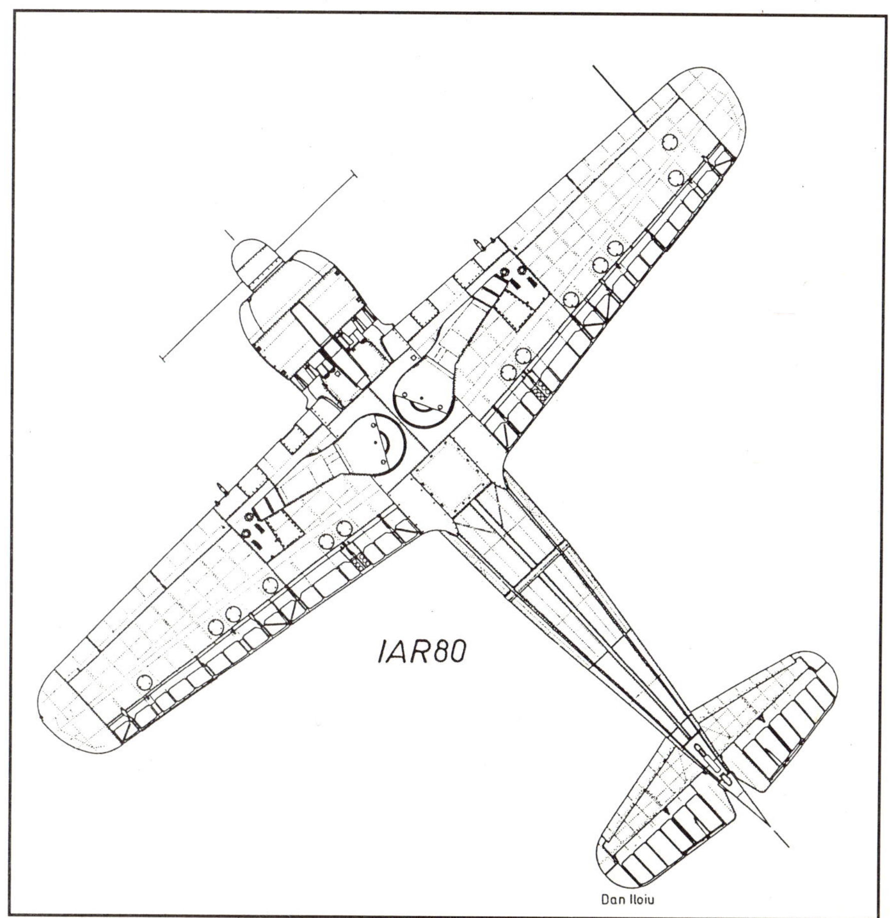

IAR 80 AND IAR 81 SPECIFICATIONS

MODEL	**80**	**80**	**80A**	**81**	**80A**	**81**	**80A**	**80B**	**80B**	**80B**	**81**	**80C**	**81A**	**81C**
Serials	0	1-50	51-90	91-105	106-150	151-175	176-180	181-200	201-211	212-230	231-240	241-290	291-300	301-450
Role	Prot.	Ftr.	Ftr.	F/B	Ftr.	F/B	Ftr.	Ftr.	Ftr.	Ftr.	F/B	Ftr.	F/B	Ftr.
Armament														
FN 7.92mm	x2	x4	x6	x6	x6	x6	x6	x4	x4	x4	x4	x4	x4	x2
FN 13.2mm	-	-	-	-	-	-	-	x2	x2	x2	x2	-	x2	-
Ikaria 20mm	-	-	-	-	-	-	-	-	-	-	-	x2	-	-
Mauser 20mm	-	-	-	-	-	-	-	-	-	-	-	-	-	x2
Dimensions														
Length (m)	8.16	8.90	8.97	8.97	8.97	8.97	8.97	8.97	8.97	8.97	8.97	8.97	8.97	8.97
Height (m)	3.60	3.60	3.60	3.60	3.52	3.52	3.52	3.52	3.52	3.52	3.52	3.52	3.52	3.52
Span (m)	10.00	10.52	10.52	10.52	10.52	10.52	10.52	10.52	11.00	11.00	11.00	11.00	11.00	11.00
Wing (m^2)	15.50	16.00	16.00	16.00	16.00	16.00	16.00	16.00	16.50	16,50	16.50	16.50	16.50	16.50
Weights (kg)														
Empty	1780	2080	2125	2125	2125	2155	2125	2135	2135	2190	2130	2200	2190	2200
Loaded	2270	2685	2720	2750	2750	2780	2750	2810	2810	2870	2800	2880	2870	2900
+325kg bombs	-	-		3075	-	3105	-	-	-	-	3125	-	3195	-
+Drop tanks	-	-	-	-	-	-	-	-	2960	3020	2950	3030	3020	3060
Ceiling (m)	11,000	10,500	10,500	10,000	10,500	10,000	10,500	10,000	10,000	10,000	10,000	10,000	9,500	10,000
Climb to 5,000 metres														
(Minutes)	6'00"	6'15"	5'50"	6'30"	5'50"	6'30"	5'50"	6'30"	6'30"	6'35"	6'30"	6'35"	6'30"	6'30"
+325kg bombs	-	-	-	7'30"	-	7'30"	-	-	-	-	7'30"	-	7'30"	-
Max speed at 4,500 metres (kph)														
Maximum	510	514	500	500	500	500	500	500	500	500	500	500	500	500
+325kg bombs	-	-	-	470	-	470	-	-	-	-	470	-	470	-
+Drop tanks	-	-	-	470	-	470	-	-	470	470	470	470	470	480
Minimum	?	200	205	205	205	205	205	205	205	205	205	205	215	210
Landing	?	170	175	175	175	175	175	175	175	175	175	175	180	175
Distances (m)														
Take off	?	260	300	300	300	300	300	350	350	350	350	350	350	350
+325kg bombs	-	-	-	400	-	500	-	-	-	-	500	-	500	-
Landing	?	430	350	350	350	350	350	400	400	400	400	400	400	400
Range (km)	?	760	730	730	730	730	730	730	730	730	730	730	730	730
+325kg bombs	-	-	-	695	-	695	-	-	-	-	695	-	690	-
+Drop tanks	-	-	-	1030	-	1030	-	1030	1030	1030	1030	1030	1030	1030

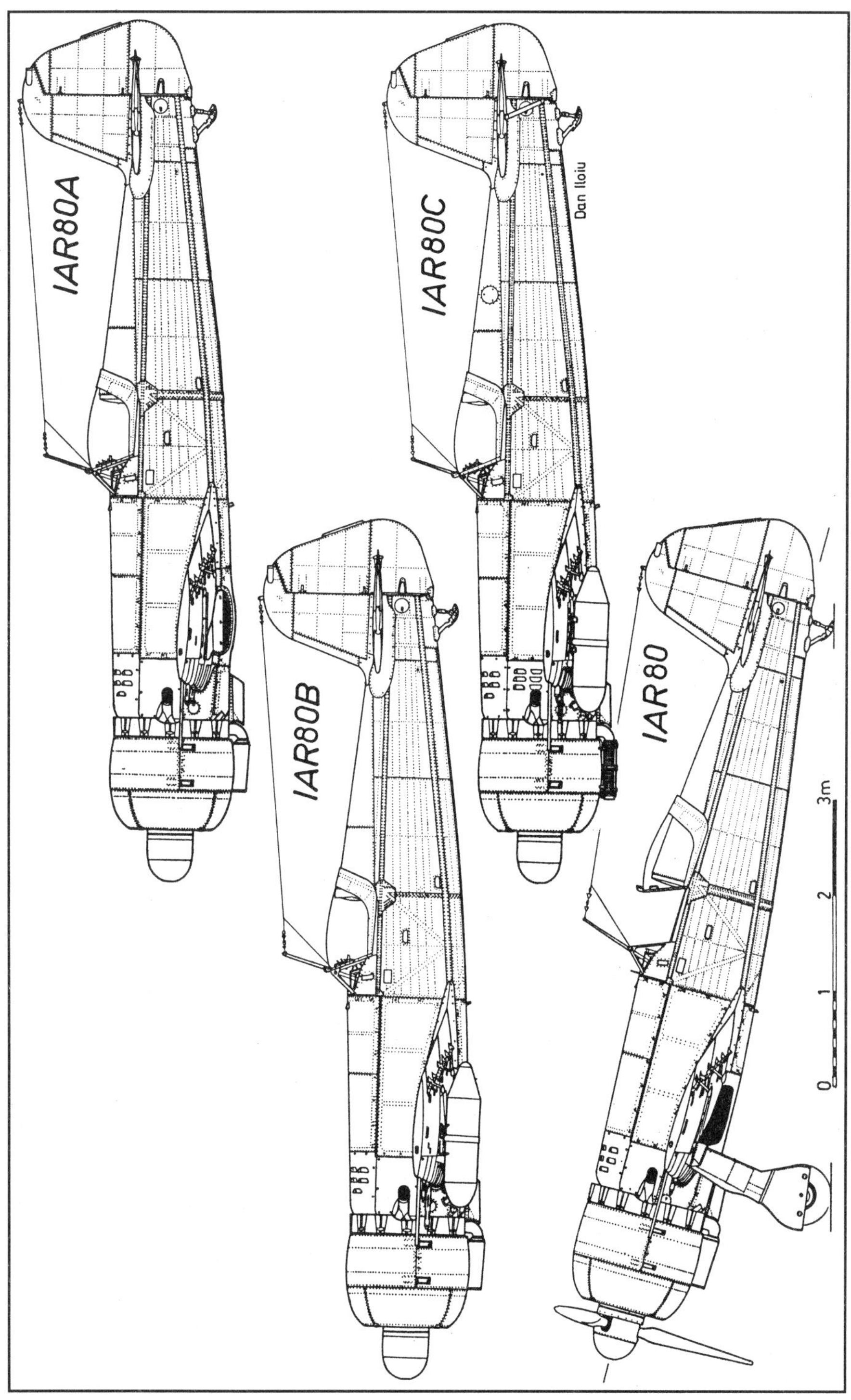
IAR80A
IAR80C
Dan Iloiu
IAR80B
IAR80
0
1
2
3m

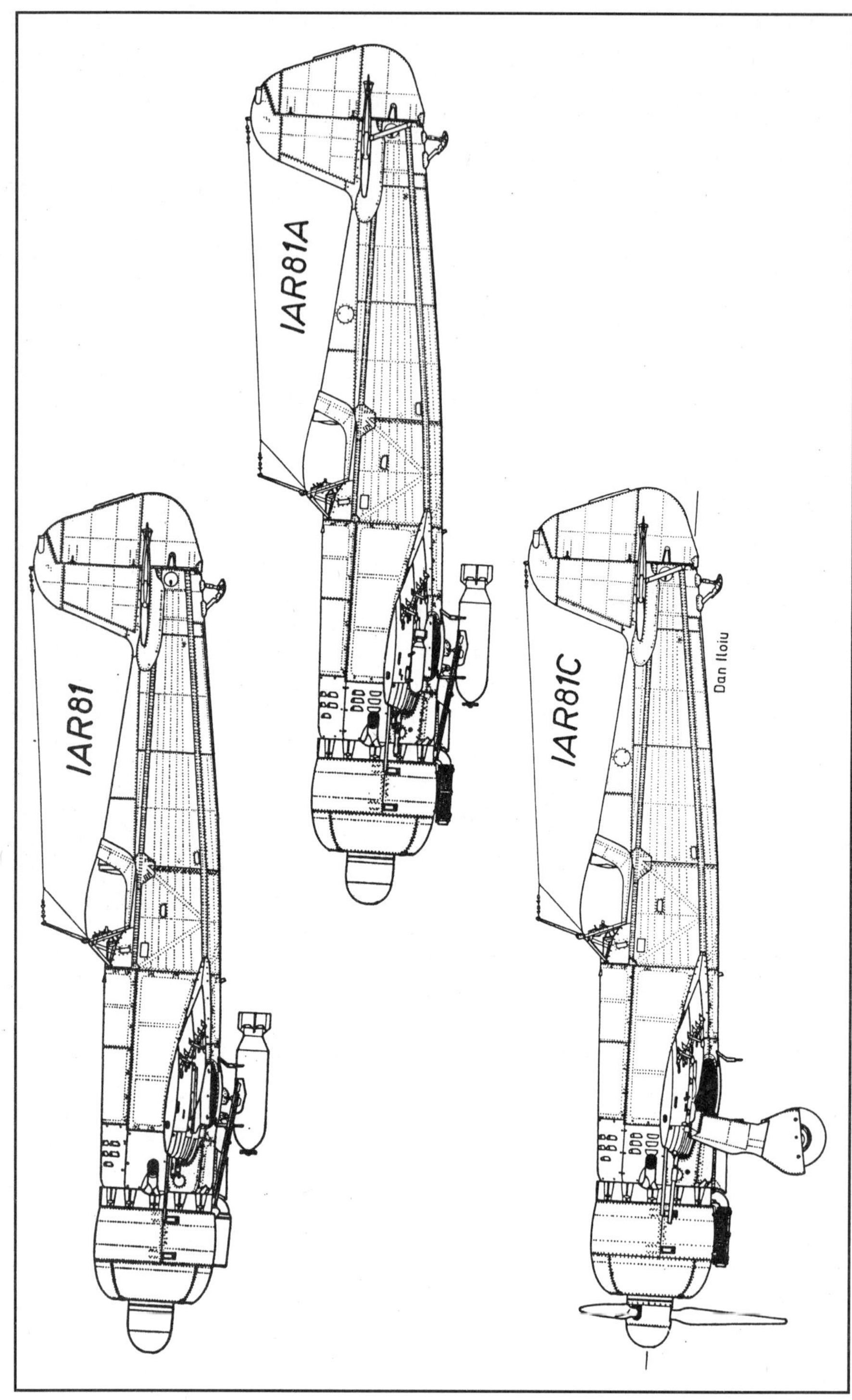
IAR81A
IAR81
IAR81C
Dan Iloiu

six FN Browning 7.92mm machine-guns, entered production. An armoured windscreen and seat back were added, and the Goerz gunsight, which could also be used for dive bombing, was adopted. Eight IAR 80As had been completed by the outbreak of war, and the type gradually superseded the IAR 80 in Grup 8 Vanatori (Esc.41, 59, 60) during the 1941 campaign.

Several pilots became 'aces' on the IAR 80A in 1941, and photographic evidence indicates that one claimed thirteen victories. Attrition was considerable, however, and the IAR 80 and IAR 80A suffered a monthly loss rate of 13.75 per cent, a serious damage rate of 20 per cent, requiring withdrawal from operations, and a further

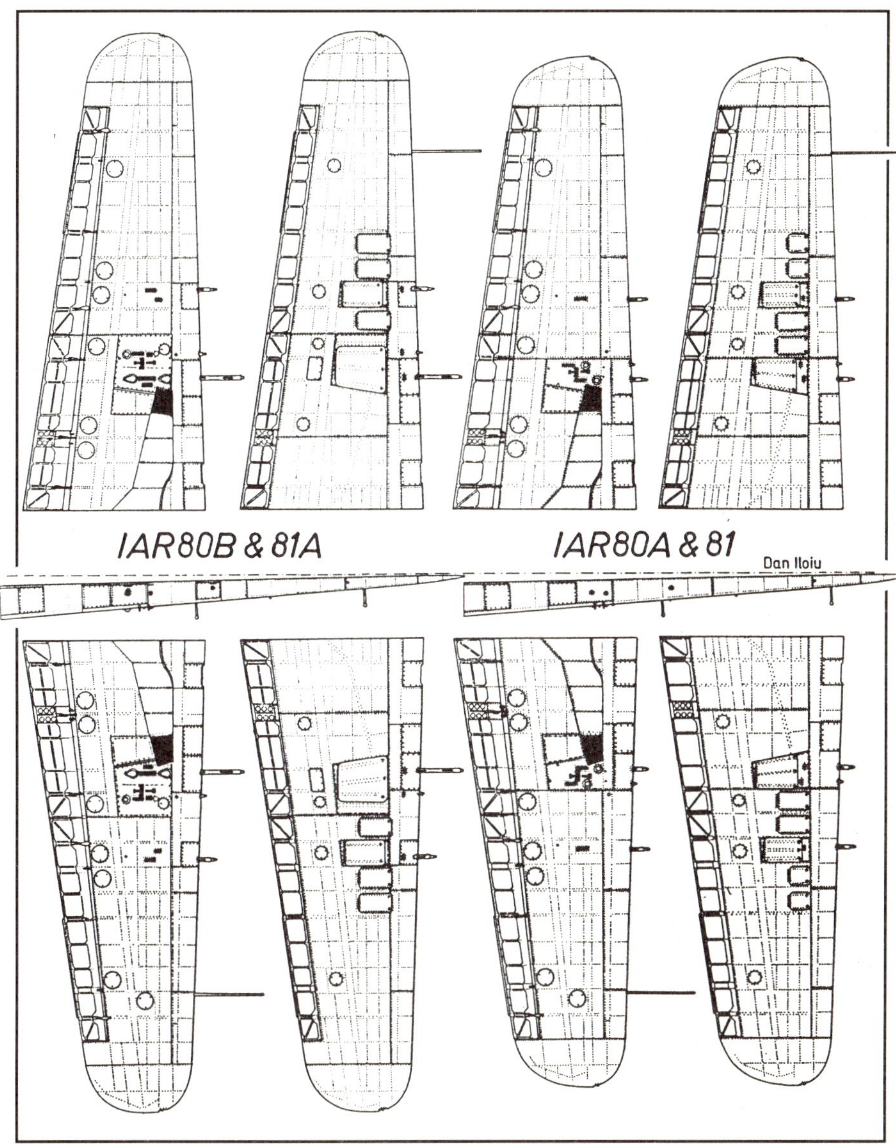

16.8 per cent repairable within the unit. This was slightly higher than production and repair rates, and a further 50 IAR 80s (Nos.201-250) were ordered on 5 September 1941, and 50 more (Nos.251-300) on 13 April 1942.

Grup 8 Vanatori (Esc.41, 42, 60) continued to use the IAR 80A at Stalingrad in 1942, but converted to the Hs 129B in the summer of 1943. Grup 9 Vanatori (Esc. 47, 48, 52) and Grup 3 Vanatori (Esc.43, 44, 50) converted from the PZL 11F to the IAR 80A in 1942. After a year on coastal protection the latter group was relegated to advanced fighter training in 1943–44. The IAR 80A first supplemented and then replaced the He 112 in Escadrila 52 and the Hurri-

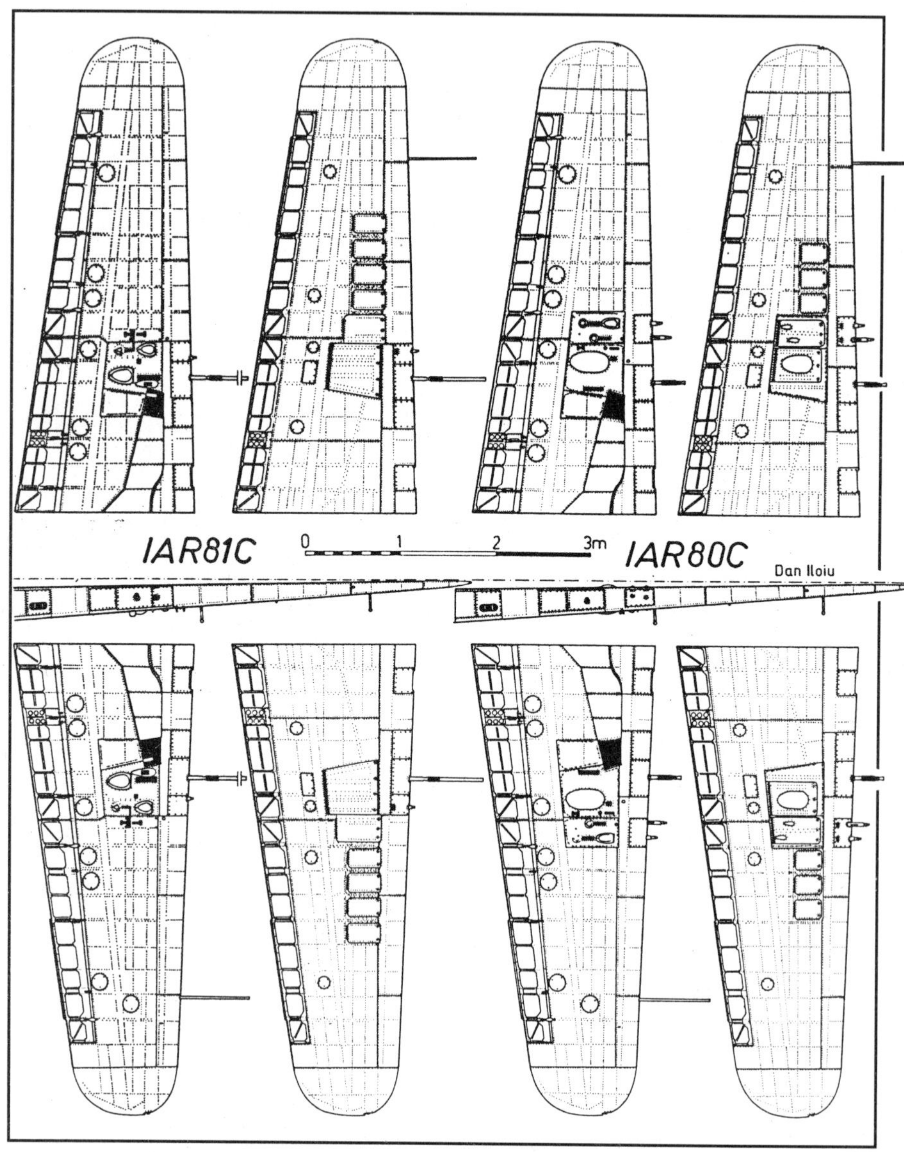

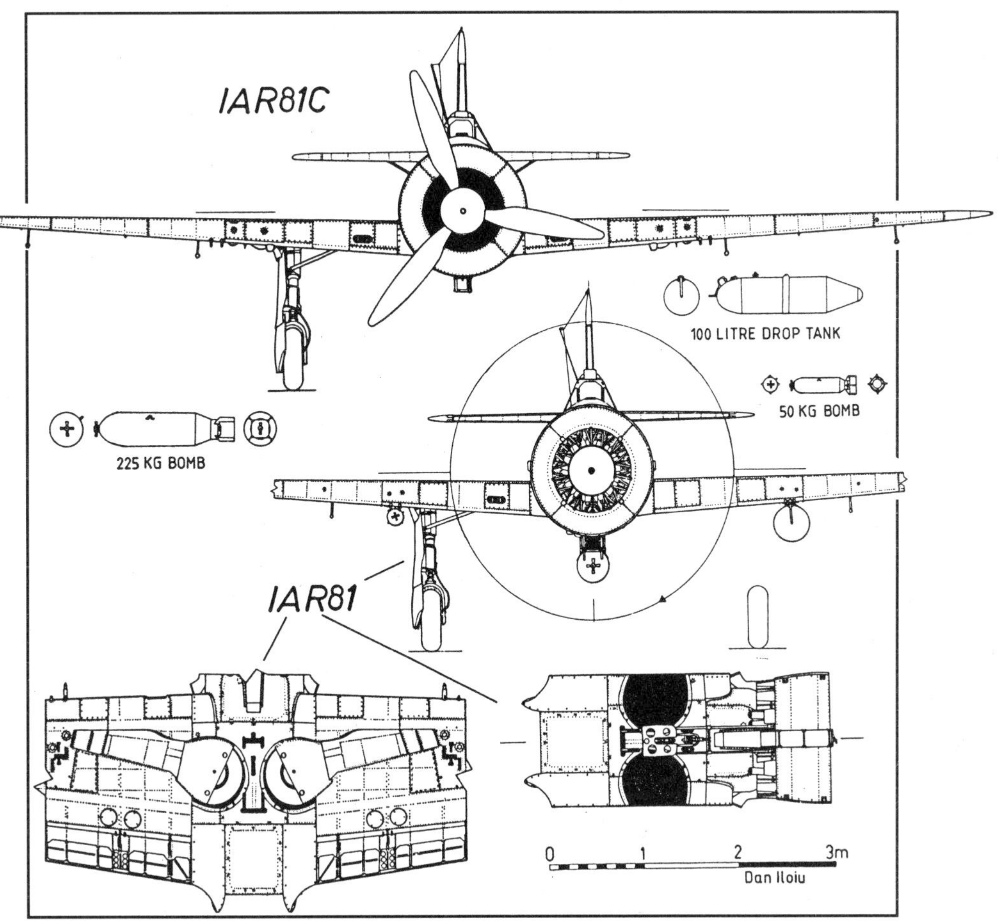

cane in Escadrila 53 as their serviceability dropped. Both squadrons converted to the Bf 109E-7 and G in 1943–44.

IAR 81

The German refusal to deliver 50 Ju 87Bs requested on 23 August 1939, and the failure of the IAR 37 dive-bomber project of July 1940, forced the Romanians to adapt the IAR 80A for dive bombing. In May/June 1941 IAR 80A No.54 was tested with a belly cradle carrying a 225kg bomb and flaps modified to act as airbrakes. The technique developed was to dive from 2,500/3,500m and release the bombs at 1,000m at a speed of 460–480kph. The results were adjudged sufficiently successful for deliveries of the new aircraft, designated IAR 81, to begin in October 1941, just too late to join in that year's campaign. A total of 50 IAR 81s were delivered between then and September 1942, and it replaced the PZL 24E in Grup 6 Vanatori (Esc.61, 62). The last ten IAR 81s (Nos.231-240) also had provision to carry a 50kg bomb under each wing. The formation of a third squadron was prevented because the erratic tempo of IAR 81 production barely outpaced normal wastage.

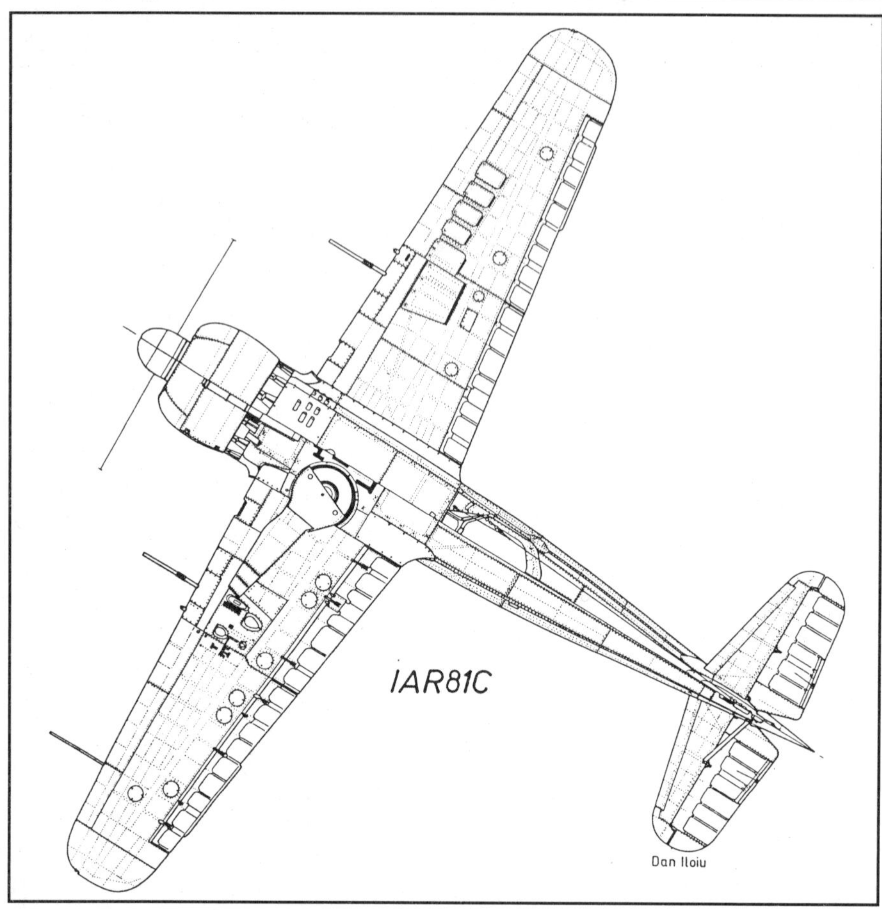

During the 1942 campaign Grup 6 Bopi served at Stalingrad. However, the IAR 81 was not popular with its pilots as the drag of the unusually large ventral bomb cradle, which was necessary to lower the 225kg bomb clear of the propeller arc, severely compromised its already relatively declining performance as a fighter. On only two particularly desperate days, 12 and 13 December, were its operations recorded by Corpul 1 Aerian as bomber missions, and it may well have otherwise been used as a ground-attack fighter. In 1943 the experienced Escadrile 61 and 62 were converted to the IAR 80B, and Escadrile 45 and 50 inherited their aircraft.

Attempts to Improve the Performance of the IAR 80

By the close of their 1941 campaign the Romanians had already noted that the performance of the IAR 80A was more suited to combat in the Balkans, for which it was designed, than to fighting the major powers. Earlier, in March 1941, a German test pilot, Major Handrick, had flown the first IAR 80 modified to IAR 80A standard. In his opinion the aircraft was a truly modern design, but he found its performance inferior to that of the Bf 109 when it was fully armed and fuelled and fitted with the new armoured glass windscreen and armour plate for the pilot's seat. However, he felt that with a more powerful engine than the IAR 14K 1000A its performance might be comparable with that of the Bf 109E.

The Romanians calculated that if the IAR 80 was mated to the Fw 190's compatible BMW 801 radial engine, it would have a potential speed of 600kph. In late 1941 they tried to obtain a production licence for this engine, but the Germans refused because they had seen their own front-line strength decline seriously during the 1941 eastern campaign, and could not spare either the necessary machine tools or completed engines.

As a last resort, in early 1942, the Romanians experimentally fitted IAR 80A No.111 with one of the numerous Junkers Jumo 211Da engines they had earlier ordered for the JRS 79B. Unfortunately the stresses imposed by the original radial engine were very different to those of the new in-line engine, and on the aircraft's only flight the engine mounting worked loose and the pilot had to make an emergency dead-stick landing. Work was discontinued.

Although further refinements to armament and endurance continued to be made, and kept the IAR 80 and IAR 81 abreast of Soviet developments in these areas, no further drastic uprating or replacement of the engine to bring them up to contemporary fighter performance was possible. Consequently, from 1942 the IAR 80 and IAR 81 began to fall behind the performance of newer Soviet fighter designs. Thus the main factor which rescued contemopary Italian design – the provision of more powerful German engines – was denied to Romania

IAR 80B

As a result of continuing demands from pilots for greater firepower, IAR decided to replace the pair of 7.92mm FN Browning machine-guns with a heavier weapon. The supply situation was so difficult in 1942 that this could only be done by stripping 13.2mm FN Browning heavy machine-guns from SM 79B, JIS 79B and JRS 79B bombers. The use of this larger weapon required the fitting of a new, larger wing, which caused some delay in production. The new combination was designated IAR 80B, and 50 (Nos.181-230) were built between June and September 1942. Nos. 201-211 introduced provision for a 50kg bomb or 100lit drop-tank under each wing. The similarly equipped Nos.212-230 had reinforced fuselages, as they were originally intended to be IAR 81A dive-bombers. The IAR 80B entered service with Grup 6 Vanatori (Esc.61, 62) in 1943.

IAR 80C (IAR 81B)

The supply of cannibalised 13.2mm Brownings was limited, and fighter production in late 1942 was again delayed by the search for a 20mm cannon capable of bringing down the US heavy bombers which had made their first appearance over Romania in June 1942. The Germans could not immediately supply them, so imported Swiss 20mm Ikaria cannon replaced the 13.2mm Brownings, more wing modifications causing further delay. Airframes Nos.241-290 were originally intended to be dive bombers and were provisionally designated IAR 81B, but after the IAR 81's unimpressive performance at Stalingrad they were completed as Ikaria-armed IAR 80C fighters between December 1942 and April 1943 and used by Grup 4 Bopi (Esc.45, 46, 49) with some success as convoy escorts over the Black Sea in 1943/44. They retained the capacity to carry two underwing 100lit drop tanks or two 50kg bombs as an anti-submarine measure, but no ventral bomb cradle was fitted.

IAR 81A

The original IAR 81As (Nos.212-230) had been converted into IAR 80B fighters on the production line. However, by early 1943 the Germans had still not agreed to deliver the Ju 87, so the Romanians felt obliged to press ahead with the production of a new batch of IAR 81A dive bombers, and ten (Nos.291-300) were produced in April-May 1943. Dive-bomber production was then halted and never resumed, as the Germans at last began to lend Ju 87D-3s. The ten IAR 81As were stripped of their ventral bomb cradles and delivered as fighters to IAR 80B squadrons.

IAR 81C

An order for 100 additional IAR 80s (Nos.301–400) was placed on 28 May 1942. All were to become IAR 81Cs. The IAR 81C was also originally intended to have the capacity to carry two underwing 50kg bombs and a 225kg underfuselage bomb – hence its '81' designation. In the event the requirement for a dive bomber had passed, and the bomb slips were only fitted with drop tanks. It thus became a pure fighter. In place of the IAR 80C's two 20mm Ikaria cannon and four 7.92mm FN Brownings it carried two German Mauser MG 151 20mm cannon and two 7.92mm FN Brownings. Two supplementary orders for 35 and 15 IAR 81Cs were placed in February 1943 and January 1944 to allow for natural wastage and to keep IAR fully occupied pending the production of the Bf 109G. A total of 150 IAR 81Cs (Nos.301–450) were therefore built between June 1943 and July 1944. Holdings of IAR 80/81s peaked at just over 300 in early 1944, of which over 200 were serviceable.

The first IAR 81Cs re-equipped Grup 9 Vanatori (Esc.43, 47, 48), which served in Transnistria from mid-1943. When Grup 9 took over Grup 7 Vanatori's Bf 109G-6s its IAR 81Cs served with Grup 7 in Romania until that unit received Bf 109G-2s in March 1944. Grup 6 Vanatori (Esc.61, 62) also converted to the IAR 81C in late 1943 until it, too, began to re-equip with Bf 109Gs in mid-1944. The IAR 81C also equipped the new Grup 1 Vanatori (Esc.63, 64) and Grup 2 Vanatori (Esc.65, 66, 67), which were deployed on home defence against the USAAF during the winter of 1943/44.

When the IAR 81C was first introduced, its armament gave it considerable potential to oppose unescorted USAAF bombers, against which its lack of engine power was not an insuperable disadvantage. It contributed considerably to American losses during the low-level Tidal Wave raid on Ploieşti on 1 August 1943. However, when high-flying USAAF bombers returned with fighter escorts in April 1944, the IAR 81C was totally outclassed by the much superior Mustang, although it performed creditably against Lightnings at low altitude. The IAR 81Cs had great difficulty in breaking through to the US bombers and, despite some victories, their losses were considerable. Consequently most were redeployed to oppose the less formidable

Soviets in late May. In an effort to further enhance the aircraft's potential against bombers, one IAR 81C was experimentally fitted with the German Werfer-Granate 210mm mortar in 1944, but the weapon was not installed in series.

IAR 80M, IAR 81M and IAR 80DC

The surviving IAR 80s and early IAR 80As (Nos.1-90) were obsolete by 1944, and were relegated to advanced fighter training with Escadrila 44 at Ghimbav. However, in 1944 plans were made to bring the later IAR 80As and all IAR 81s (Nos.91-180 and 231-240) up to IAR 81C standard by installing the same armament. The conversions were designated IAR 80M and IAR 81M respectively. Conversion was certainly begun by mid-1944, but it is not clear how many were completed. The unrealised 1944/45 programme called for all IAR 80s and IAR 81s to be superseded by the Bf 109G in operational service and to be relegated to advanced training. A dual-control trainer, the IAR 80DC, was designed, but conversions from old airframes only occurred well after the war.

No fewer than 21 squadrons flew the IAR 80 or IAR 81 at one time or another. In 1939 the prototype IAR 80 had been highly competitive by international stan-

IAR Fighter production, 1934–1945

Ordered	No.	Type	Delivered	Engine	Serials (Note)
21/01/36	95	PZL 11F	02/37-11/38	IAR K9 640hp	51-145 (Polish licence)
19/11/36	25	PZL 24E	11/39-02/40	IAR K14 CIII 36 930hp	6-30 (Polish licence)
??/??/37	1	IAR 80	04/39	IAR K14 CII 32 870hp	0 Prototype
18/12/39	100	IAR 80	02/41-0?/41	IAR K14 CIII 36 930hp	1-20
		IAR 80	0?/41-05/41	IAR K14 CIV 32 960hp	21-49
		IAR 80A	05/41-09/41	IAR K14 1000A 1,025hp	50-90
		IAR 81	10/41	IAR K14 1000A 1,025hp	91-100
22/08/40	100	IAR 81	10/41	IAR K14 1000A 1,025hp	101-105
		IAR 80A	10/41-05/42	IAR K14 1000A 1,025hp	106-150
		IAR 81	07/42	IAR K14 1000A 1,025hp	151-175
		IAR 80A	05/42	IAR K14 1000A 1,025hp	176-180
		IAR 80B	06/42	IAR K14 1000A 1,025hp	181-200
05/09/41	50	IAR 80B	06/42	IAR K14 1000A 1,025hp	201-211
		IAR 80B	07/42-09/42	IAR K14 1000A 1,025hp	212-230
		IAR 81	09/42	IAR K14 1000A 1,025hp	231-240
		IAR 80C	12/42	IAR K14 1000A 1,025hp	241-250
13/04/42	50	IAR 80C	12/42-04/43	IAR K14 1000A 1,025hp	251-290
		IAR 81A	04/43-05/43	IAR K14 1000A 1,025hp	291-300
28/05/42	100	IAR 81C	06/43-12/43	IAR K14 1000A 1,025hp	301-400
12/02/43	35	IAR 81C	01/44-03/44	IAR K14 1000A 1,025hp	401-435
20/01/44	15	IAR 81C	04/44-07/44	IAR K14 1000A 1,025hp	436-448 (449, 450 lost in US raid?)
26/11/42	15	Bf 109G-4	05/44-08/44	DB 605 1,475hp	301, 304, 305, 307, 311, 312 (v. Allies)
11/08/43	60	Bf 109G-4	11/44-05/45	DB 605 1,475hp	302, 303, 306, 308-310, 313-315, 318, 319
			06/45-11/47	DB 605 1,475hp	316, 317, 320-375 (built after war)
24/09/43	175	Bf 109-G	Cancelled	DB 605 1,475hp	

dards, and the IAR 80A was a match for its Soviet contemporaries, the Lagg-1, Lagg-3, Yak-1 and MiG-1, in 1941. However, later models of IAR 80 and 81 fell increasingly behind later marks of Lagg, MiG and Yak, all of which were substantially re-engined. Yet despite this, and the fact that the best Romanian pilots were sent to the Bf 109 squadrons, the IAR 80/81 squadrons always retained some combat value on secondary sectors of the Eastern Front owing to the generally poor quality of Soviet aircrew. Perhaps most importantly, the IAR 80/81 allowed Romania to build up a considerable reserve of qualified fighter pilots, and guaranteed a continuity in fighter deliveries, which the Germans could not.

Bf 109G-4

The Romanians had sought a licence to build the Bf 109 since 1939, but it was only forthcoming in the immediate wake of the Stalingrad disaster, when the Germans badly needed to restore their credibility with their allies. It was initially planned to assemble 75 aircraft from German components. Deliveries began in May 1944, but owing to US bombing of the IAR factory at Braşov only six were completed and delivered to Grup 6 Vanatori before Romania left the Axis in August. Another eleven were completed while Romania served with the Allies. The final 58 were completed after the war. Local production was planned at 530 engines and 465 fuselages in 1944/45, and was to have been dispersed around the country: engine manufacture at Ucea, Cugir, Satul Lung and Colibaşi, propeller manufacture at Campulung, and fuselage construction at Caransebes, Barlova and Herculane. SET and ICAR were to supply other components from Copşa-Mica-Cugir and Blaj. Final assembly was to be carried out at Caransebeş. However, the inability to secure early delivery of the necessary Swedish machine tools prevented local production.

BOMBERS

SM 79B

On 25 May 1937 Romania began to diversify its sources of supply by ordering 24 SM 79B twin-engined bombers (Nos.1-24) from Italy. The Romanians were attracted by both the earlier SM 79 trimotor's performance in the Spanish Civil War and by the twin-engined prototype's use of Gnome-Rhône 14Kfs engines, and had the Italians modify the latter to mount their first production IAR 14K II C32 engines. This allowed the fitting of a machine-gun for the bomb aimer in the glass-panelled nose. Twenty-four were delivered between February and June 1938.

The SM 79B was found to be underpowered and inferior in performance to the Italian trimotor original. In early 1941, therefore, SM 79B No.7 was tested with the new IAR 14K IV C32. At the cost of greatly increased fuel consumption this engine gave the bomber slightly more power at altitude, though still less than the trimotor model, and eight more SM 79Bs were converted by the outbreak of war on 22 June. The SM 79Bs formed Grup 1 Bombardament (Esc.71, 72) and served in the 1941 campaign, but suffered a high attrition rate and were reduced to advanced trainers for the new JRS 79Bs from 1942. The FN Browning 13.2mm cannon with which the SM 79B was primarily equipped were removed and used to arm the IAR 80B in mid-1942.

JRS 79B and JIS 79B

The SM 79B, then one of the world's more advanced bombers, was immediately popular with the FARR, and on 27 May 1938 an order for 36 licence-built SM 79Bs (Nos.101-136) was placed with IAR. Initially it was intended to cure its lack of power by reverting to the original trimotor format and fitting a third IAR K14 II C32 engine in the nose. However, tooling-up for production took a very long time, and when in late 1939 the Germans delivered 32 He 111H-3s powered by the Junkers Jumo 211Da it was decided to fit this more powerful and streamlined engine to the 36 SM 79 airframes to be constructed at IAR. The new variant was designated JRS 79B (J=Jumo, R=Romania, S=Savoia). After the Germans refused IAR a production licence, 210 Jumo 211s were ordered direct from Germany on 30 October 1939, and an additional 36 JRS 79Bs were ordered from IAR on 30 January 1940.

Such a drastic redesign of the SM 79B was still beyond Romanian resources alone, so on 28 February 1940 the design contract and an order for the first eight JRS 79Bs (Nos.149-156) was placed in Italy. They were known as the JIS 79B (I=Italia) in Romania and as the SM 79JR in Italy. In addition to the new Jumo 211Da engines, the JIS 79B also featured a redesigned tail section and a deeper fuselage, allowing it to carry its standard 1,575kg bomb load internally, with consequent advantages in streamlining over the SM 79B. The first flight took place in Italy in December 1940. The aircraft proved to be 8 per cent faster than the SM 79B, and the altitude at which it achieved its maximum speed was 1,650m higher.

However, delivery of the eight Italian aircraft, set for May-October 1940, was delayed by Italy's own entry into the war and did not occur until August 1941-February 1942, after acceptance of the first Romanian-built JRS 79Bs. The JIS 79B replaced the SM 79B in Escadrila 71 and served in 1942 at Stalingrad as part of Grup 1 Bombardament. In 1943–44 the remaining JIS 79Bs were increasingly mixed with the more numerous JRS 79Bs of Grup 1 Bombardament (Esc.71, 72), and the occasional survivor was still in operational service with Escadrila 72 in 1945.

By May 1940 the air ministry had laid out an ambitious production plan for IAR to build 84 JRS 79Bs between September 1940 and July 1942. Unfortunately, priority had to be given to the IAR 80 on the production line, and component deliveries were disrupted by the entry into the war of Italy, which had insufficient spares for its own fleet of SM 79s. The first Romanian-built JRS 79B (No.101) was not tested until May 1941, and it was only in 1944, after the upgrading of the later aircraft to B1 standard and the cancellation of twelve others, that IAR was in a position to complete the order. Even then, US bombing delayed the final deliveries to 1946.

Deliveries of the JRS 79B began in July 1941, and the type replaced the Potez 63 in Escadrila 75 during the latter part of the 1941 campaign, and the SM 79B in Escadrila 72 in early 1942. Escadrila 72 served at Stalingrad in 1942 and in Romania in 1944 as part of Grup 1 Bombardament. Escadrila 71 also became predominantly a JRS 79B unit in 1943–44 as attrition depleted the JIS 79Bs. It was originally intended to form Grup 1 Bombardament of three eight-aircraft squadrons (Esc.71, 72, 75) but attrition was such that Escadrila 75 never returned to operations after 1941.

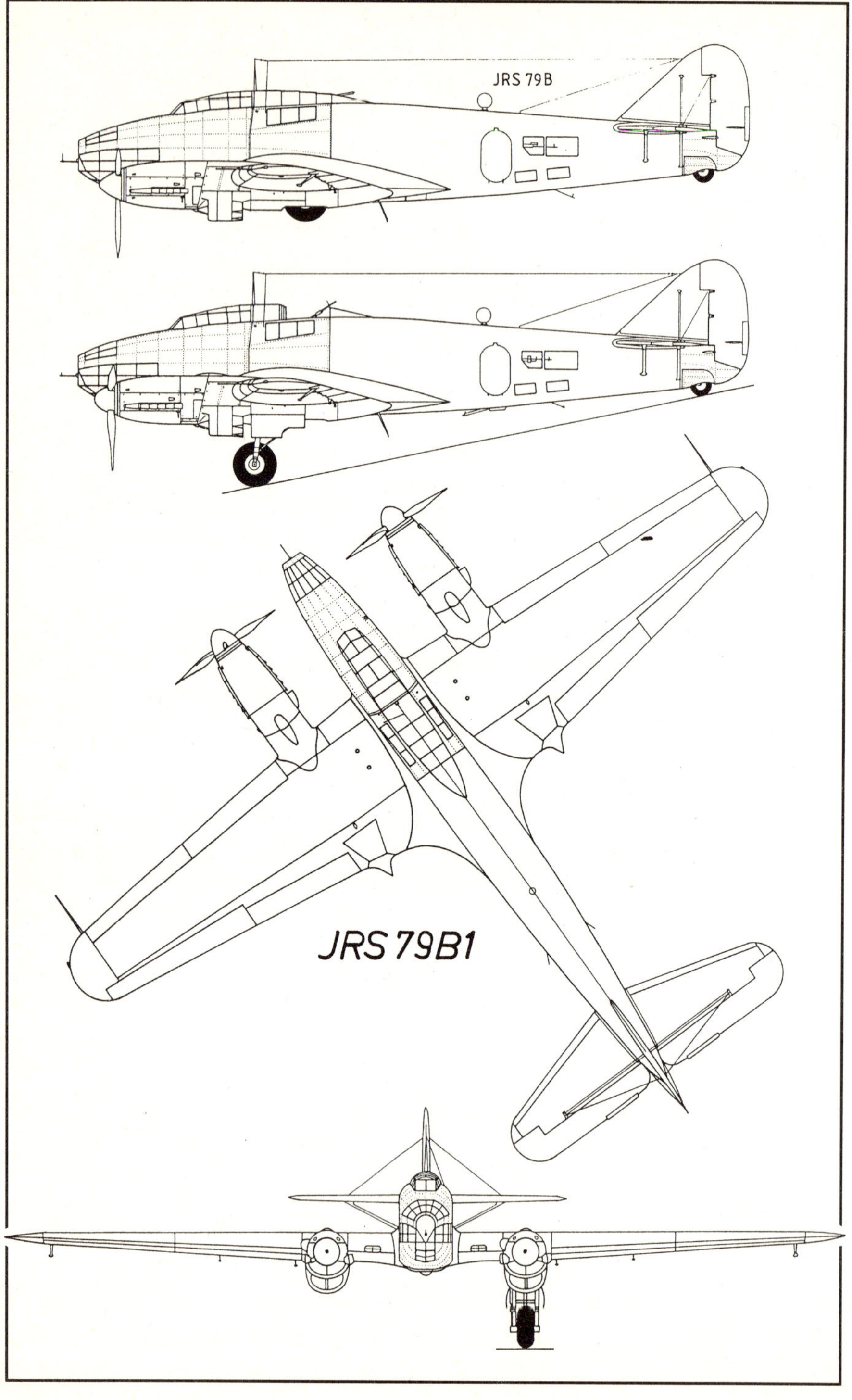
JRS 79B
JRS 79B1

The 13.2mm FN Brownings fitted to the JIS 79Bs and the first JRS 79Bs were removed to arm more IAR 80Bs and the IAR 81As, and they and the PWU and Vickers 7.92mm machine-guns were apparently replaced by a unified armament of Rheinmetall 7.92mm machine-guns in all JIS 79Bs and JRS 79Bs in mid-1942. Thereafter it appears that the JIS 79B's and JRS 79B's defensive armament was periodically modified in keeping with the latest practice in the JRS 79B1 (see below).

JRS 79B1

The 36th and last JRS 79B (No.136) was delivered in June 1942. There then followed a production lag of six months, during which airframe No.137 was fitted with the more powerful Jumo 211F engine. The new engine gave the aircraft a 5kph faster maximum speed at 400m greater altitude. In addition, 101 other modifications were made, including the armouring of the crew positions, which was retrospectively also carried out in the JRS 79B and JIS 79B. Airframe No.137 was renumbered No.201, and the new engine/airframe combination was designated JRS 79B1.

Delivery resumed in February 1943, and Grup 2 Bombardament (Esc.82, 83) was formed with Nos.201-224 that year, serving at the front during the summer of 1944. The final twelve aircraft (225-236) were intended to equip Grup 2 Bombardament's third squadron, Escadrila 84, but, after the airframes of Nos.232-234 were damaged by the US bombing of the IAR factory in 1944, Nos. 225-231 were used to replace attrition in Escadrile 82 and 83. The last five aircraft (232-236) were completed in 1946 utilising many parts from stricken aircraft.

In a desperate attempt to improve the FARR's limited ground-attack and anti-shipping potential, the JRS 79B1 had a fifth crew member added to man a forward-firing Ikaria 20mm cannon positioned in a ventral hatch just aft of the wings, to engage surface targets at between 600 and 1,000m – a tactic that resulted in high losses when briefly used in the spring of 1944. To compensate for the extra weight, the standard bomb load was reduced to 1,400kg. It is not thought that the Ikaria was retrofitted to the JIS 79B and JRS 79B. The continuing improvement in Soviet fighters prompted further additions to the defensive armament, including twin 7.92mm Mausers in the dorsal position and the fitting of a PWU 7.92mm machine-gun in the starboard engine cowling. At the time of Romania's defection to the Allies in August 1944, consideration was being given to replacing all 7.92mm machine-guns with 13.2mm Mausers, but it is unlikely that this last upgunning actually occurred.

JRS79B (JRS79B1) SPECIFICATIONS

Type: Four (Five) seat Medium Bomber. **Power Plant:** Two 1,200hp Junkers Jumo 211Da (1,350hp Junkers Jumo 211F). **Performance:** Maximum speed 371kph (357kph) at sea level, 376kph (369kph) at 1,000m, 380kph (382kph) at 2,000m, 383kph (384kph) at 3,000m, 391kph (386kph) at 4,000m, 411kph (408kph) at 5,000m, 431kph at 5,600m, (436kph at 6,000m). Cruising speed 385kph at 5,000m. Time to 1,000m 2'11" (1'42"), to 2,000m 4'56" (3'24"), to 3,000m 8'16" (5'34), to 4,000m 12'16" (8'42"), to 5,000m 15'27" (11'54"), to 6,000m 20'02" (15'22"). Maximum range w/o bombs 1,850km (1,750km), with 950kg bombs 1,625km (1,500km), with 1,575kg bombs 1,250km (1,150km). Ceiling: reconnaissance 9,500m, bomber 8,800m. **Weights:** Reconnaissance 10,335kg (10,770kg), Bomber + 1,575kg bombs 11,525kg (11,785Kg), (Bomber +1,575kg bombs + Ikaria cannon 11,996kg). **Dimensions:** Span 21.2m, Length 16.2m, Height 4.1m. **Bombs:** Standard bomb load 1,575kg carried internally (1,400kg with Ikaria cannon).

On 23 August 1944 there were still 27 operational JRS 79Bs and B1s with Groups 1 and 2 Bombardament, but their serviceability was low. Grup 2 Bombardament was absorbed into Grup 1, which returned to the front in late 1944 with Escadrile 72 and 82. The group served operationally to the end of the war, at which point it still had seventeen aircraft on strength.

Between 1938 and 1943 the Romanians displayed an interest in the SM 83 transport version of the SM 79, but none were purchased. By late in the war the JRS 79B1 was increasingly obsolete as a bomber, and serious consideration was given to replacing it on the IAR production line with an IAR 14K IV C32-powered version of the SM 83 trimotor. This would have extended the useful life of both the IAR 14K engine and the JRS 79B airframe production facilities, which otherwise faced run-down when IAR 81C, IAR 39A and JRS 79B1 production was due to cease in mid/late 1944. However, the war ended before the project could be taken up.

When Romania first opted to buy the SM 79B in 1937 it was arguably the best medium bomber then in service. However, it was rapidly overtaken by developments elsewhere, and by the time the FARR first used the type in action, in 1941, it was already a vulnerable aircraft. Thereafter, the best Romanian efforts to armour, re-engine and up-gun the type could do little to alleviate its fundamental weaknesses, and by 1944 it was being committed to operations only when Romania was directly threatened by Red Army offensives, and then more in hope than in expectation. Lack of effective Axis fighter opposition even extended its useful life into 1945. However, production was never sufficient to sustain continuous operations in significant strength, and in the end the JRS 79B proved a waste of scarce productive capacity.

IAR Bomber production, 1934–1945

Ordered	**No.**	**Type**	**Delivered**	**Engine**	**Serials** (Note)
27/5/38	36	JRS 79B	07/41-06/42	Jumo 211Da 1,200hp	101-136
30/01/40	36	JRS 79B1	02/43-12/43	Jumo 211F 1,380hp	201-224
		JRS 79B1	01/44-10/44	Jumo 211F 1,380hp	225-231
		JRS 79B1	1946	Jumo 211F 1,380hp	232-234 (Damaged by US bombing. Finished 1946)
		JRS 79B1	1946	Jumo 211F 1,380hp	235-236 (Built in 1946)

PROTOTYPES

IAR 47

The need for an effective reconnaissance aircraft of superior speed, range, armament and survivability to the IAR 39 was emphasised in 1941, probably as a direct result of the failure to detect the Soviet withdrawal from Odessa. There, the IAR 39 was too vulnerable to operate over the heavily defended port, and the IAR 80s and Bf 109Es used in its place lacked cameras.

IAR's solution, designated IAR 47, was a cross between the IAR 39A and IAR 80, and it shared their IAR 14K IV C32 engine. Its wood and metal fuselage was loosely based on that of the IAR 39A. The observer's side windows were eliminated, the crew being reduced to the pilot and a rear gunner armed with a Rheinmetall 7.92mm machine-gun. The IAR 47 was a low-wing monoplane like the IAR 80, and

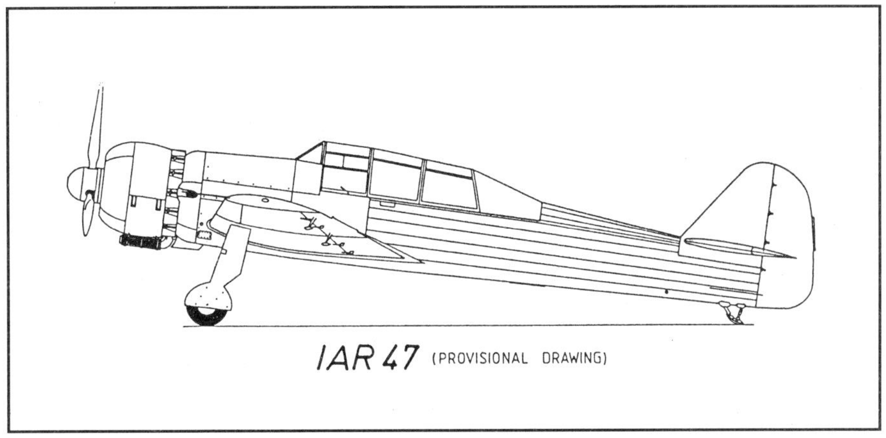
IAR 47 (PROVISIONAL DRAWING)

IAR 47 Specification
Type: Two-seat Reconnaissance and Light Bomber Aircraft. **Power Plant:** One IAR 14K IV C32, 960hp. **Performance w/o armament:** Maximum speed 396kph at sea level, 406kph at 1,000m, 419kph at 2,000m, 435kph at 3,000m, 456kph at 4,000m, 464kph at 4,300m, 460kph at 5,000m. Climb to 4,000m 7'16", to 5,000m 12'25". Normal range 850km. **Weights:** Recce 3,550kg. **Dimensions:** Span 12.5m, Length 11.0m, Height 3.2m, Wing Area 23.8m^2. **Armament:** Two wing mounted, forward-firing 7.92mm MGs, one rear-facing, Rheinmetall 7.92mm on flexible mounting in rear cockpit. Six 50kg bombs.

had a reinforced version of the same Messier retractable undercarriage. It mounted a Rheinmetall 7.92mm machine-gun in either wing, and could carry six 50kg bombs in a bomb bay between the pilot and gunner. However, its primary role was reconnaissance, and for deep-penetration missions the bomb bay was fitted with an extra fuel tank which increased the fuel load from 580lit to 950lit and the normal range of 850km in proportion. Three cameras were fitted beneath the fuselage – one vertical and two at 45°.

The prototype was tested without armament in the autumn of 1942, and revealed good handling characteristics. However, the improvement in Soviet fighters, its relatively low-powered engine and weak armament had already rendered its design obsolescent, and Bf 109 production was due to take up all production capacity. As a result development of the IAR 47 was stopped in January 1943. The prototype was destroyed by US bombing in 1944.

IAR 471

The IAR 81 had not proved a great success as an improvised dive bomber, and experience with the IAR 47 showed that the IAR 14K engine would not be up to the demands of powering a full-sized dive bomber. Thus by early 1943 the Romanians still lacked an effective ground-support aircraft. In November 1942 IAR had at last secured a licence for the manufacture of the German DB 605 engine, and planning now centred on this powerplant. On 16 January 1943 a new dive-bomber project, the IAR 471, powered by the DB 605, was commissioned. Although the Germans lent Romania numerous Stukas from mid-1943, they would not sell any. The design of the IAR 471 was therefore persevered with for reasons of self-sufficiency.

Despite its designation, the IAR 471 bore little resemblance to the smaller IAR 47, and was essentially a different aircraft. It was designed to have a superior performance to the Stuka, much helped by a retractable undercarriage, but a lighter bomb load, and on 7 May 1944 the Stuka's two underwing 37mm cannon were ordered to be included in its specification. It was planned to order 100 IAR 471s and 136 engines from IAR in 1944/45, but IAR was in the throes of both dispersing its factories and beginning production of the Bf 109G, and declared itself currently incapable of simultaneously producing the IAR 471. This halted the project even before Romania's defection to the Allies in August. No prototype flew.

IAR471 Estimated Specifications
Type: Two-seat Dive Bomber. **Power Plant:** One Daimler Benz DB605, 1,475hp. **Performance:** Speed (+500kg bombs) 395kph (380kph) at sea level, 445kph (430kph) at 3,000m, 490kph (475kph) at 7,000m. Time to 1,000m 1'35" (2'10"), to 3,000m 4'40" (6'25"), to 7,000m 12'50" (20'00"). Ceiling 9,500m (8,000m). Weights: 4,300kg w/o bombs. **Dimensions:** Span 14m, Length ?, Height ?, Wing area 29m^2. **Armament:** One 20mm MG151 cannon firing through airscrew spinner, two wing mounted 7.92mm MGs, two 7.92mm MGs on flexible twin mount in rear cockpit. One 500kg bomb or one 250kg and two 100kg bombs.

SEAPLANES

From the mid-1920s to 1942 Romania relied on Italy for seaplanes. However, in 1936 Romania dabbled briefly in the field to make up losses amongst the Italian types, when five reconnaissance SM 62bis airframes were ordered from IAR and ICAR. Their engines were taken from stricken aircraft or reserves. The same year, eight SET 4H seaplane trainers (Nos.51-58) powered by 360hp Jaguar 3 engines were ordered. All were delivered by 1938.

TRAINING AND COMMUNICATIONS AIRCRAFT

In tandem with their fighter, bomber and army co-operation aircraft programmes, the Romanians had primary, intermediate and advanced trainer programmes which made them largely self-sufficient in single-engined trainers throughout the war. Although SET designed the SET 20 twin-engined trainer, and plans were made and then cancelled to produce the Fw 58 under licence from February 1944, no twin-engined trainer was produced locally. Instead, 32 Fw 58s were imported.

Fleet 10G

In 1934 Romania bought twenty US-built Fleet 10G two-seat biplane primary trainers (Nos.1-20) and acquired a manufacturing licence for both the Fleet 10G and its 130hp Gipsy Major engine, which was subsequently manufactured as the IAR 4 G.I. Forty (Nos.51-90) were built by IAR in 1936 and 80 (Nos.21-50 and 91-140) by SET between 1936 and 1938. In the latter year production was moved to ICAR, which built 210 Fleet 10Gs (Nos.141-350) between April 1939 and March 1943. A final order for another 50 was delayed owing to lack of materials and cancelled with the introduction of the Fi 156 on the ICAR production line. The Fleet 10G was not only the most widely-used Romanian training aircraft, but also served operationally throughout the war as the backbone of the six light communications squadrons (Escadrile 111-116). In addition, a Fleet 10G was issued to every FARR squadron for its own communications.

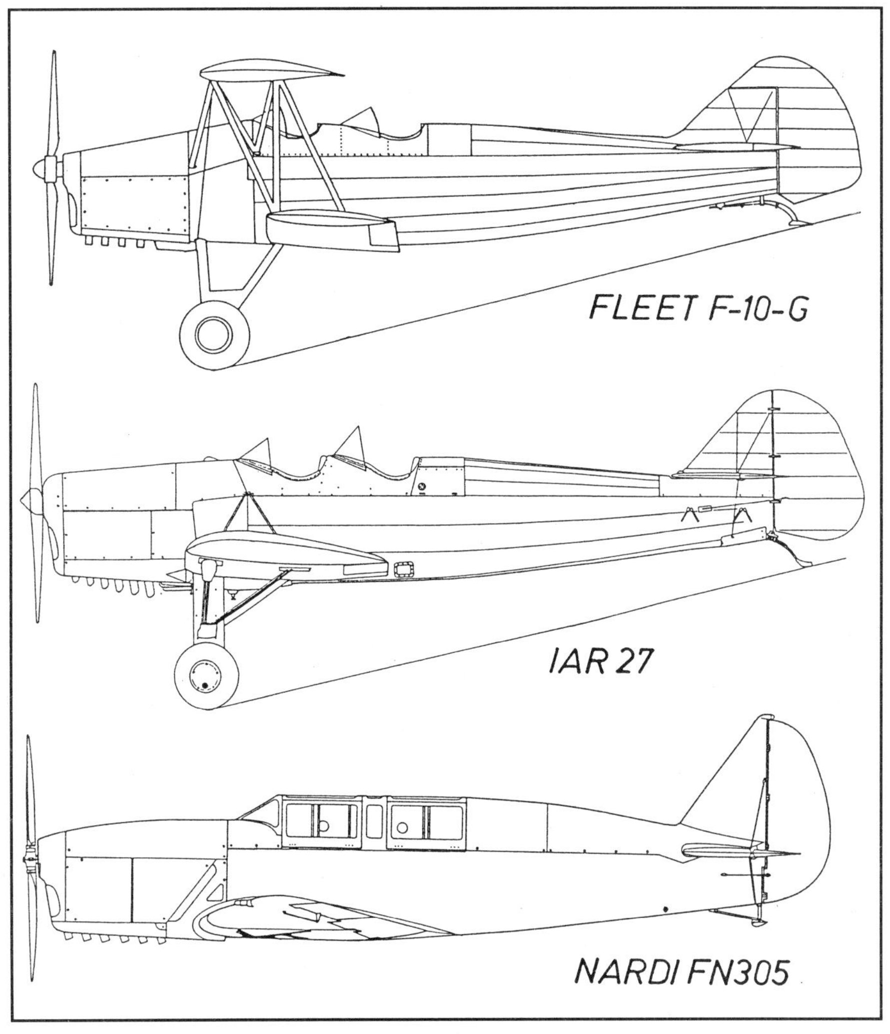

IAR 27

On 19 November 1936 the government ordered the prototype of an intermediate monoplane trainer, designated IAR 27, from IAR. IAR had just built 40 Fleet 10Gs, and modelled the IAR 27's fuselage very closely on that type. However, its engine was the more powerful 185/200hp Gipsy Six, which was produced under licence by IAR from May 1939 for both the IAR 27 and Nardi FN 305. The wings were an IAR design. As IAR was heavily engaged in producing combat aircraft, the production contract for 80 IAR 27s (Nos.1-80) was awarded to SET on 23 May 1939. However, as SET was also engaged in producing the more important IAR 39 and Nardi FN 305, it received a low priority, only 30 being produced between December 1939 and July 1941. Production resumed a year later, the remaining 50 being delivered in June-August 1942.

SET 14

SET believed that it could produce a better intermediate trainer than the IAR 27, and on 9 July 1940 it received an order for a prototype, designated SET 14. SET then had the Nardi A-FN 305 in production, and the SET 14 utilised both its 240hp Argus As 10C-3 engine and retractable undercarriage. During tests in 1941 its performance was found to be superior to that of the IAR 27, but the type was rejected because visibility from the cockpit was restricted and judged to be too dangerous for trainee pilots. Had it been accepted it would have replaced the last 50 IAR 27s on the SET production line.

Nardi FN 305

For its advanced fighter trainer the FARR selected the Italian Nardi FN 305 IV and ordered 30 (Nos.1-30) on 21 January 1938. They were powered by the 195hp Alfa Romeo 115/1, an Italian version of the Gipsy Six, and were delivered between February and August 1938. They were judged a success, and a production licence was bought by SET, which received an order for 40 Nardi FN 305 Is (Nos.31-70) powered by the Romanian-built Gipsy Six on 23 May 1939. These were all delivered by November 1940.

On 17 August 1940 a further 34 were ordered (Nos.71-100 and 122-125), this time powered by imported German 240hp Argus As 10C-3 engines and designated Nardi A-FN 305. Thirty were delivered between July and September 1941, and the remainder in May 1943. A final batch of a further 21 Italian-built FN 305 IVs (Nos.101-121) arrived from Italy in September 1941. On 6 September 1943 another 50 Nardi FN 305 Is (Nos.126-175) were ordered from SET, but delivery only started in March 1945. Only Nos.126-139 were completed during the war, the rest arriving between July 1945 and June 1946. As the Argus As 10C-3 was due to enter production in Romania for the Fi 156, a final order for 100 Nardi A-FN 305s (Nos.176-275) was placed on 18 April 1944, but this was cancelled in 1945.

Romanian Trainer Production, 1934–45

Ordered	No.	Type	Delivered	Engine	Serials (Note)
27/03/34	10	ICAR Universal	03/35-04/35	Gipsy Major 130hp	1-10 (ICAR)
1935–1939	215	Fleet 10G	09/36-04/40	Gipsy Major 130hp	20-235 (40xIAR, 80xSET & 95xICAR)
17/08/40	65	Fleet 10G	??/41-??/42	Gipsy Major 130hp	236-300 (ICAR)
07/07/41	50	Fleet 10G	07/42-03/43	Gipsy Major 130hp	301-350 (ICAR)
??/??/42	50	Fleet 10G	Cancelled	Gipsy Major 130hp	351-400 (ICAR)
19/11/36	1	IAR 27	??/??	IAR 6G1 185hp	Prototype (IAR)
23/05/39	80	IAR 27	12/39-07/41	IAR 6G1 185hp	1-30 (SET)
		IAR 27	06/42-08/42	IAR 6G1 185hp	31-80 (SET)
09/07/40	1	SET 14	1941	Argus As 10C-3 240hp	Prototype (SET)
23/05/39	40	Nardi FN 305 I	??/39-11/40	IAR 6G1 185hp	31-70 (SET)
17/08/40	34	Nardi A-FN 305	07/41-09/41	Argus As 10-C3 240hp	71-100 (SET)
		Nardi A-FN 305	05/43	Argus As 10-C3 240hp	122-125 (SET)
06/09/43	50	Nardi FN 305 I	03/45-04/45	IAR 6G1 185hp	126-139 (SET)
		Nardi FN 305 I	07/45-06/46	IAR 6G1 185hp	140-175 (SET, built post-war)
18/04/44	100	Nardi A-FN 305	Cancelled	Argus As 10C-3 240hp	176-275 (SET)

PWS

In 1941–42 SET assembled 36 Polish PWS trainers from parts delivered by Heinkel. The components had been taken from Polish factories by the Germans.

Arming the Trainers

The Italians originally offered the Nardi FN 305 IV with two Browning 7.92 machine-guns, but the FARR took them unarmed. However, with the Red Army approaching Romania's borders in late 1943 desperate measures were necessary, and 70 IAR 27s, 80 Nardis and 50 PWSs were fitted with IAR 39-type grenade launchers. It is very possible that, immediately following Romania's defection to the Allies on 23 August 1944, all three types were used to harass German columns retreating through Romania.

PRE-WAR FOREIGN DELIVERIES

In the late 1930s Allied and Axis powers competed for influence in Romania, and the Romanians were able to play them off against each other and acquire numbers of modern aircraft from both sides. In addition, the bulk of the surviving Polish Air Force fled to Romania in late 1939. The period was marked by a trend away from initial reliance on fellow Latin countries, France and Italy, and towards more powerful northern European suppliers, such as Britain and Germany. The fall of France in 1940 also undermined British influence and finally pitched Romania irrevocably into the German camp. Although in terms of numbers and modernity the FARR's Allied aircraft were a considerable accretion of strength, the fact that few spares were available during the war seriously reduced the numbers that could be kept serviceable and greatly limited their operational careers.

French Aircraft Deliveries

France's Potez and Gnome-Rhône companies began the period with a virtual monopoly of the supply of twin-engined aircraft and aero-engines to Romania. Apart from ten Bloch 210 bombers (Nos.1-10) delivered to Escadrila 82 in 1937 and demoted to transports after the 1941 campaign, all French aircraft imported in the years before the war were from Romania's traditional supplier, Potez. Sensibly, all French deliveries were powered by variants of the familiar Gnome-Rhône 14K engine, for which many spares could be manufactured in Romania. The Potez 543, Potez 651, Potez 561 and Potez 566TB were all transports, and were mostly allocated to the state airline, LARES.

In March 1938 twenty Potez 63B2 bombers (Nos.1-20) were ordered to balance the SM 79s already contracted in Italy. They were delivered in April-August 1939 to Escadrile 74 and 75, and another twenty were ordered on 27 August. In the event the fall of France halted delivery, and the Romanians had to negotiate with the Franco-German armistice commission to complete the order. In November-December 1941 the Germans allowed Vichy to deliver ten Potez 63C2s to replace losses in the 1941 campaign, and these served with Ecadrila 74 at Stalingrad. Ten Potez 63.11A3s were due to complete the order in August 1942, and were allocated to Escadrila 3 to replace their Blenheims, but it is not certain that they were actually delivered.

French Aircraft Deliveries, 1934–1942

Ordered	No.	Type	Delivered	Engine	Serials (Note)
??/??/??	10	Bloch 210 BN5	??/??/??	Gnome-Rhône K14N 10/11 870hp	1-12
??/??/??	6?	Potez 651	05/36-07/36	Gnome-Rhône K14N 10/11 870hp	
24/10/35	1	Potez 541	1936	Gnome-Rhône K14 Kirs 870hp	
	10	Potez 543	09/35-05/36	Gnome-Rhône K14 Kirs 870hp	1-10
11/03/38	1	Potez 63C3	05/39	Gnome-Rhône K14 Mars 6/7 700hp	1
	20	Potez 63B2	04/39-08/39	Gnome-Rhône K14 Mars 6/7 700hp	1-20
27/08/39	10	Potez 63C2	11/41-12/41	Gnome-Rhône K14 Mars 4/5 700hp	Kept French serials
	10	Potez 63.11A3	08/42?	Gnome-Rhône K14 Mars 4/5 700hp	Delivery uncertain
24/06/37	2	Potez 566TB	??/??/??		

Italian Aircraft Deliveries

Italy supplied its first twelve SM 59 reconnaissance seaplanes to Romania in 1926. In 1932-36 Romania ordered fourteen SM 62bis reconnaissance seaplanes, seven SM 55 torpedo bombers and six SM 56 trainers for the Flotila de Hidroaviaţie (Esc.101, 102, 103). In May 1939 twelve Cant Z501 seaplanes were ordered, and these were delivered to Escadrila 101 during April-August 1941. Serviceability was so low among the older Italian seaplanes that they were all concentrated in Escadrila 102. The Cant Z501s bore the brunt of operations, but the other Italian seaplane types were also operated fitfully over the Black Sea until replaced by He 114s in 1942–43 and relegated to training.

The real Italian breakthrough came in 1937, with the already noted sale of 24 SM 79Bs to the FARR and a production licence for the JRS 79B to IAR in 1938. This was followed in 1939 by the sale of 30 Nardi FN 305 IVs to the FARR and a production licence for the Nardi FN 305 I and A-FN 305 to SET. Although small follow-up orders for eight JIS 79Bs and 21 more Nardi FN 305 IVs came in 1940 and 1941, the Italians found themselves completely eclipsed by the Germans, and made no more sales to Romania during the war. The Romanians expressed an interest in a Gnome-Rhône 14K-powered variant of the SM 83 transport between 1938 and 1943, even placing one or two small orders, but firm evidence of delivery is lacking.

Italian Aircraft Deliveries, 1932–1942

Ordered	No.	Type	Delivered	Engine	Serials (Note)
25/05/37	24	SM 79B	02/38-06/38	IAR K14 II C32	1-24
28/02/40	8	SM 79JR	08/41-02/42?	Jumo 211Da 1,200hp	149-156 (JIS 79B)
21/01/38	30	Nardi FN 305 IV	02/38-08/38	Alfa Romeo 115/1 195hp	1-30 (Piaggio)
09/04/41	21	Nardi FN 305 IV	09/41	Alfa Romeo 115/1 195hp	101-121 (Piaggio)
01/04/31	12	SM 62bis	04/32-??/??	Issotta-Fraschini Asso 750hp	I-XII
01/04/31	6	SM 55	08/33-09/33	Issotta-Fraschini Asso 500hp	I-VI?
	1?	SM 55	06/36	Issotta-Fraschini Asso 500hp	VII?
01/04/31	6	SM 56	05/32-09/33	Walter Major 120hp	1-6?
20/05/39	12	Cant Z501	04/40-08/40	I.F. Asso 11K2 C15 860hp	1-12
??/??/??	3	SM 83	08/38-09/38		(Delivery doubtful)
09/04/41	4	SM 83	??/??/??		(Delivery unlikely)

British Aircraft Deliveries

In 1939 Britain began to support the overstretched French in supplying aircraft to Romania. Between June 1939 and January 1940 40 Bristol Blenheims (Nos.1–40) were sent, forming long-range reconnaissance Escadrile 1, 2, 3 and 4. The Romanians also requested 50 Hurricanes to form Escadrile 53, 54 and 55. In the event the British could supply only twelve (Nos.1-12) for Escadrila 53, which were delivered in March 1940. The fall of France threw the British on to the defensive, and the other 38 Hurricanes anticipated from July 1940 were held back for the Battle of Britain after Romania renounced the redundant Anglo-French guarantee of its security. Maintenance of the British types was a major problem, especially after Romania joined the Axis in November 1940. The Germans sold Romania three ex-Yugoslav Blenheims, three ex-Yugoslav Hurricanes and assorted spares in September 1941, but nevertheless the Hurricanes had to be withdrawn from operations in 1942 and the Blenheim squadrons dwindled from four in 1941 to only Escadrila 1 by 1944.

British Aircraft Deliveries, 1939–42

No.	Type	Delivered	Engine	Serials (Note)
40	Blenheim	06/39-01/40	Mercury VIII 730hp	1-40
3	Blenheim	09/41	Mercury VIII 730hp	41-43 (ex-Yugoslav)
12	Hurricane	03/40	Merlin III 900hp	1-12
3	Hurricane	09/41	Merlin III 900hp	13-15 (ex-Yugoslav)

Polish Aircraft

The 50 PZL 11Bs ordered from Poland in 1933 only served as trainers in the Second World War. When Poland fell in 1939 more than 200 Polish aircraft were flown to Romania, and Heinkel delivered 114 aero engines in 1940–41 to keep them flying. Thus the FARR was able to equip two fighter squadrons (Esc.49, 50) with the PZL 11C, two medium bomber squadrons (Esc.76, 77) with the PZL 37A and B, one light bomber squadron (Esc.73) with the PZL 23 and the casualty evacuation squadron (Esc.108) with the RWD 13. The Romanians only used the Lublin and

Deliveries of Polish Combat Aircraft, 1934–1939

Ordered	No.	Type	Delivered	Engine	Serials (Note)
?//??/33	50	PZL 11B	04/34-12/34	Gnome-Rhône 9Krsd 500hp	1-50
19/11/36	5	PZL 24E	07/39-10/39	IAR K14 CIII 36 930hp	1-5
Interned	13	PZL 7	09/39	Jupiter F VII 450hp	Polish serials
Interned	10	PZL 11A	09/39	Mercury VS2 550hp	326, 327, 329. Others Polish serials
Interned	33+	PZL 11C	09/39	Mercury IVS2 510hp	Romanian serials 301-325, 328. Others Polish serials
Interned	21	PZL 23	09/39	Pegasus VIII 670hp	1-21?
Interned	4+	PZL 37A	09/39	Pegasus XII???	201-222
	15+	PZL 37B	09/39	Pegasus XX 900hp	
Interned	17+	RWD 13	09/39	Gipsy Major 130hp	1-17+
Interned	16	Czalpa	09/39	Mars II 430hp	
Interned	22	Lublin	09/39	Mars I 340hp	
Interned	37?	PWS	09/39	Wright 220hp	

Czalpa for training, as they had sufficient superior IAR 37s and 39s for their army co-operation requirements.

The PZL 11C was too obsolete to be given a significant operational role in 1941, and was replaced by the IAR 80 in early 1942. In June 1944 the surviving PZL 11Cs were fitted with IAR 39-pattern grenade launchers, but there is no record of their use. The PZL 37 and PZL 23 had only four months of spares in June 1941, and these were largely used up by the end of the year. Escadrila 73 served briefly at Stalingrad in 1942, and Escadrila 76 briefly in Basarabia in the summer of 1944, but lack of spares led to their withdrawal from combat within weeks. Only the RWD 13s, which were powered by the locally produced Gipsy Major, remained operational throughout the war. Several private Romanian RWD 13s were also taken over by the FARR.

German Aircraft Deliveries

German aircraft deliveries fluctuated with Germany's political requirements, which the Romanians were initially able to exploit to their own advantage. In 1939–40 the Germans needed to keep Romania out of the Allied camp and retain access to its vital oil supplies. They first insinuated themselves into Romania fairly innocuously by selling 22 Fw 58 twin-engined trainers, 15 Go 145A trainers and 85 BMW 132A engines for the IAR 38 in early 1939. However, the real breakthrough came later in the year, with Heinkel's sale of 13 He 112B-0s and 17 He 112B-1s (Nos.1-30), a type rejected by the Luftwaffe in favour of the superior Bf 109E, to equip Escadrile 51 and 52 in a move to neutralise Romania only weeks before the invasion of Poland. Romania also requested the Ju 87B-2 and Do 215 only days before the attack on Poland. The Germans subsequently declined the orders in 1940, but only well after Poland had been subjugated. During the Phoney War Germany countered the Allied deliveries of Potez 63B2s, Blenheims and Hurricanes by accepting considerable contracts for 32 He 111H-3s, ±30 Bf 109E-3s, ±20 Bf 109E–4s, 5 Fi 156C-1s, 10 Fi 156 C-2s, and 10 Bf 108s, all state-of-the-art types. In addition, 210 Jumo 211 engines were ordered for the JRS 79B.

However, with the fall of France, Romania's leverage over Germany disappeared. A 4,869-strong Luftwaffe Mission arrived in October, and Romania joined the Axis on German terms in November 1940. The Luftwaffe's mission was threefold; firstly to organise Romanian oil production, drilling, pumping, refining, storage and transport; secondly to prepare a Luftwaffe ground organisation to support the impending invasion of Russia; and only thirdly to reorganise, re-equip and retrain the FARR in the latest German combat techniques. By the outbreak of war with the USSR the Luftwaffe reportedly had 50,000 personnel in the country, but, as it was their lowest priority, only a small proportion were attached to the FARR. Some of these were helping Grup 7 Vanatori (Esc.56, 57, 58) and Grup 5 Bombardament (Esc.78, 79, 80) to familiarise themselves with the Bf 109E-3/E–4 and He 111H-3, but more attention was paid to the formation of the Romanian 4th AA Brigade to defend the vital oilfields around Ploieşti.

With Romania in their power, the Germans thereafter did little more between early 1941 and mid-1944 than sell replacements at inflated prices to make up for attrition among the types already delivered. The prices demanded in real terms for the Bf 109, He 111 and Fi 156 increased by 150 to 200 per cent between 1939 and 1942. This led the Romanians to request several production licences, as local production costs were only a third to a half of the German prices, but these were either rejected or granted too late to make a significant contribution to the FARR's strength. Furthermore, not only were almost all of the Bf 109E-7s, He 111H-6s, Do 17Ms and Hs 129Bs delivered in 1942–44 secondhand Luftwaffe aircraft, but they were also approaching obsolescence, having already in most cases been superseded in Luftwaffe combat service. Another acquisition, the He 114, had initially been rejected by the Luftwaffe before the war. The only significant new aircraft received were the Fi 156 Storch and Ju 52 transports, which Romania was able to demand in 1941–42 as a necessity if its forces were to campaign deep inside the Soviet Union in the Crimea, at Stalingrad and in the Caucasus. Neither was a true combat type.

Provisional List of German Aircraft Deliveries, 1937–1944

					23/08/44		
First Ordered	**No.**	**Type**	**Delivered**	**Serials**	**Captures**	**Cp.1 Aer.**	**Total**
36/37	32	Fw 58		1-32	3?	-	±35
22/05/39	15	Go 145A		1-15	5	-	20
18/08/39	13	He 112B-0		1-13	-	-	13
18/08/39	17	He 112B-1		14-30	-	-	17
30/10/39	32	He 111H-3		1-32	1	-	33
02/12/39	50	Bf 109E-3/4		1-50	-	-	50
02/12/39	10	Bf 108		1-10	5	-	15
16/01/40	5	Fi 156C-1	04/40-04/42	1-5	}	-	}
16/01/40	10	Fi 156/C-2	04/40-04/42	6-15	} 9	-	} 38
19/09/41	14	Fi 156C-3	04/42	16-28, 30	}	-	}
30/10/41	12	He 111H-6	01/42-03/42	49-60	1	-	13
14/11/41	19	Bf 109E-7	05/42-06/42	51-69	-	-	19
22/11/41	30	Ju 52		1-30	11	-	41
22/04/42	10	Do 17M	04/42-05/42	1-10	-	-	10
24/07/42	27	DFS 230	??/43-??/44	1-27	-	-	27
20/08/42	1	Fi 156D-1	07/42?	29	-	-	1
27/02/43	29	He 114	06/43-08/43	1-29	-	-	29
17/07/43	9	Bf 110F-4		1-9	4	-	13
17/07/43	48	Bf 109G-2	Su/43-08/44	201-248	5	-	±53
15/10/43	3	He 42		1-3	-	-	3
28/01/44	±15	Hs 129B	06/44-08/44	??	14	32	±61
09/02/44	10	He 111E-3		71-80	-	-	10
05/05/44	10	Ju W-34	05/44	51-60	8	-	18
05/05/44	12	Ju 86E	05/44	1-12	-	-	12
??/??/??	±50	Bf 109G-6	07/44-08/44	???	76	18	144
Captured		Fw 189	08/44	1-2	1	-	3
Captured		Bf 109G-4	08/44		7	-	7
Captured		Bf 109F	08/44		2	-	2
Captured		Ju 87D-3/5	08/44		2	52	54
Captured		Ju 88A-4	08/44		3	16	19
Captured		Fw 44	08/44		5	-	5
Captured		Fw 190	08/44		22	-	22
Captured		He 111H-20	08/44	1001	1	-	1
Captured		Ju 88D-1	08/44			4	4

In 1941–42 German aircraft production was low and they were themselves short of aircraft. They therefore tried partly to satisfy Romania with captured aircraft. In 1940–42 they delivered 114 Polish aero-engines and 36 PWS trainers, allowed Vichy to deliver ten or twenty Potez 63s ordered in 1939, and sold three Hurricanes and three Blenheims from captured Yugoslav stocks in order to keep existing foreign types operational. However, these were no substitute for modern German types.

By early 1943 the Germans were increasingly short of trained aircrew but were producing larger numbers of new aircraft, whereas the Romanians had increasing numbers of trained aircrew but few modern aircraft. It therefore became advantageous for the Germans to supply Romanian aircrew with new aircraft. However, the Germans suspected that the Romanians, mindful of the Hungarian threat, would be reluctant to commit them all to the front, and did not wish to lose control of their deployment, so the 703 assorted Bf 109G-6s, Ju 88A-4s and D-1s, Ju 87D-3s and D-5s and Hs 129B-2s used by Corpul 1 Aerian during 1943–44 were only loaned by the Luftwaffe and did not belong to the FARR. All were delivered directly to Romanian units at the front, where they formed part of Luftflotte 4, which was responsible for major repairs and replacements.

Only in the summer of 1944, when they had to transfer the bulk of Luftflotte 4's aircraft from Romania to France and Byelorussia, did the Germans sell a number of Bf 109G-2s and G-6s to the FARR to replace them, but by then not only were these aircraft decidedly inferior to the US Mustangs they were expected to confront, but it was too late to convert any IAR 80 groups fully before Romania's defection to the Allies, and they subsequently saw more service in Allied than Axis ranks. During its defection Romania acquired 122 of Corpul 1 Aerian's loaned aircraft and captured dozens of repairable combat aircraft from Luftflotte 4 which helped keep existing German types in service to the end of the war. It therefore appears that at least 782 German aircraft were purchased or fell into Romanian hands during the war, and a further 582 passed through Corpul 1 Aerian in 1943–44.

LARES

During 1941–44 LARES, the Romanian state airline, continued to operate scheduled flights on civil routes (Bucharest-Vienna-Berlin, Bucharest-Zagreb-Venice-Milan, Bucharest-Sofia-Athens, Bucharest-Odessa, Bucharest-Istanbul). In 1939 the bulk of the Polish civil air fleet, including many Lockheed 10s, fled to Romania and was absorbed by LARES. In 1941 LARES camouflaged its aircraft and provided the FARR with a mixed transport squadron drawn from its fleet of twelve Lockheed 10As, eight Potez 561s, five Lockheed 14s, four Potez 560s, two DC-3s and a Ju 52. From 1942 considerable numbers of Ju 52s began to be delivered directly to the FARR, which formed its Escadrila 105 with them in that year, and Escadrila 107 in 1943. The crews for these two squadrons were largely drawn from LARES, and the aircraft were maintained by the company workshops. It is probable that the orig inal LARES aircraft formed a notional Escadrila 106. Romania's leading ace, 'Buzu' Cantacuzino, was a LARES employee.

TRANSNISTRIA

The Transnistrian administration had its own budgetary autonomy. It maintained a small air section initially comprising one Fw 58 and three SET 7Ks, and later five RWD 13s. In 1943 it was able to buy two Ju 52s direct from Germany which, after the loss of the territory in early 1944, were absorbed into the FARR and given the serial numbers 31 and 32.

CAPTURED AIRCRAFT

Particularly in 1941 and 1942, a considerable number of Soviet aircraft were captured, many of them intact. However, at this stage none were significantly superior to Romania's own aircraft and no attempt was made to put them into operational service. Instead they, and the occasional later capture, were tested in Romanian colours against the IAR 80 and Bf 109 by IAR to study their construction and performance and to develop tactics to oppose them.

The USAAF's Ploieşti raid of 1 August 1943 delivered one B-24 Liberator in almost immediately airworthy condition, and this was flight-tested in Romanian colours during the winter. The next raid on 5 April 1944 provided two more recoverable Liberators, and others followed throughout the summer in sufficient numbers for the FARR to consider the formation of a squadron of Liberators in July. Spares were initially available from the scores of wrecked Liberators around the country, but as a precaution the Germans were approached for replacement engines from Liberators brought down over the Reich, and consideration was even given to fitting new German engines. It is believed that three B-24Ds and one B-24J were made airworthy before Romania's defection to the Allies killed the project. The defeat of the USAAF low-level Lightning raid of 10 June left four recoverable Lightnings in Romanian hands, but they appear not to have been flown.

TAIL NUMBERS

Each Romanian aircraft had a national serial number on its tail. Only a very few insignificant exceptions retained foreign serial numbers (i.e. Potez 63C2, PZL 7 and some PZL 11s). In the case of Romanian-built types, aircraft were numbered consecutively from 1 in order of production. Those types bought from Poland, France, Britain, Italy and Germany were numbered consecutively from 1 in order of delivery. Where Romania both built and imported the same or very similar types, they could have a combined numerical sequence (i.e. PZL 11, PZL 24, Nardi FN 305 and JIS 79B). Where a substantially different model of an existing type was introduced, a new sequence could be begun from 101, 201, 301, etc. (i.e. JRS 79B or Bf 109). Occasionally the cancellation of orders caused breaks in the logical sequence of numbering (i.e. between the He 111H-3 and He 111H-6 or the JRS 79B and JIS 79B). Polish bomber types interned in 1939 appear to have received serials from 201, fighters from 301 and other types from 1.

The most complex numbering system was that for the Bf 109. The Bf 109E-3s, E-4s and E-7s sold to Romania in 1940–43 were numbered 1-69. The Bf 109G-6s variously lent, sold or captured in 1943–44 were theoretically numbered from 101 upwards, but in fact adopted their own numbering system (see below). The Bf

109G-2s delivered in 1944 under the Antonescu-Clodius Protocol were numbered from 201 upwards. The Bf 109G–4s built by IAR in 1944–47 were numbered from 301 upwards.

The German types lent to Corpul 1 Aerian in 1943–44 received squadron serials, but the system varied from group to group. Escadrila 2's Ju 88D-1s were numbered 1-12. Grup 5 Bombardament's Ju 88A–4s were numbered 101-137 (Esc.77 1-12, Esc.79 13-24, Esc.80 25-36). Grup 8 Asalt's Hs 129Bs were numbered approximately 112-132 (Esc.41), 214-236 (Esc.42) and 313-334 (Esc.60). Grup 3 Bopi's Ju87D-3s and D-5s were initially numbered 1–45 to include their nine reserve aircraft, but later used only 1-36 (Esc.73 1-12, Esc.81 13-24, Esc.85 25-36). When Grup 6 Bopi's Ju 87Ds joined Corpul 1 Aerian in 1944 they took the serials 178-204 and 862-872 (Esc.87 178-192, Esc.74 193-204, Esc.86 860-872). Each Bf 109G-6 squadron in Grup 7 and 9 Vanatori had its aircraft numbered from 1 to 15 in large figures on the fuselage. Their individual squadrons were distinguished by the colours of the numbers; red (Esc.48, 57), yellow (Esc.56), blue (Esc.58) or white (Esc.53, 57). Throughout Corpul 1 Aerian replacement aircraft took the number of the machine they supplanted and successively added the suffix 'a', 'b', 'c' etc.

Squadron Numbering

Mission	Squadron	Mission	Squadron
Reconnaissance	1-4	Seaplane	101-103
Army Co-operation	11-22	Transport	105-109
Fighter (and Ground Attack)	41-68	Communications	111-116
Bomber	71-87		

CAMOUFLAGE

All Romanian-built aircraft were finished in dark olive green with light blue undersides. Combat types additionally had broad dark earth stripes applied, resulting in a camouflage very similar to Anglo-French schemes. Anglo-French types therefore retained their original camouflage in Romanian service, whereas new German types sold to the FARR were delivered in the dark olive green, while Polish types retained their original lighter olive green. Secondhand German aircraft sold to Romania used their existing German camouflage. Romanian-built Bf 109s were also finished in a German camouflage scheme. In 1941–42 most FARR combat and communications aircraft had a yellow band applied around the rear fuselage, yellow engine cowlings, and sometimes yellow wingtips, these being the intra-Axis recognition features on the Eastern Front. In addition, the prewar red/yellow/blue roundel was replaced by the similarly coloured Mihai Cross, which was more in keeping with Axis insignia. The roundel was restored after August 1944. German types lent to Corpul 1 Aerian kept their German camouflage but adopted the Mihai Cross.

CHAPTER 9

FARR OPERATIONS 1941–1945

THE OUTBREAK OF THE AIR WAR

The Romanian army's ground offensive into Basarabia and Northern Bucovina could only begin on the night of 2/3 July. However, the air offensive had to take advantage of surprise, and went in simultaneously with the German attack of 22 June. Thus, right from the beginning, there was an enforced dislocation between Romanian ground and air operations.

The main offensive component of the Romanian air effort in June 1941 was the Grup Aerian de Lupta (GAL), based between Focşani and Buzau, which initially contained the most modern bombers and fighters. 3rd and 4th Armies had their own integral air units of reconnaissance and army co-operation aircraft, and 1st Armoured Division also had its own army co-operation squadron. In the interior, the 2nd and 3rd Air Regions each had squadrons of obsolete fighters for home defence. Air Force headquarters kept the heavy transport and casualty evacuation squadrons under direct command. The area around the port of Constanţa included two seaplane squadrons for reconnaissance over the Black Sea. The neighbouring

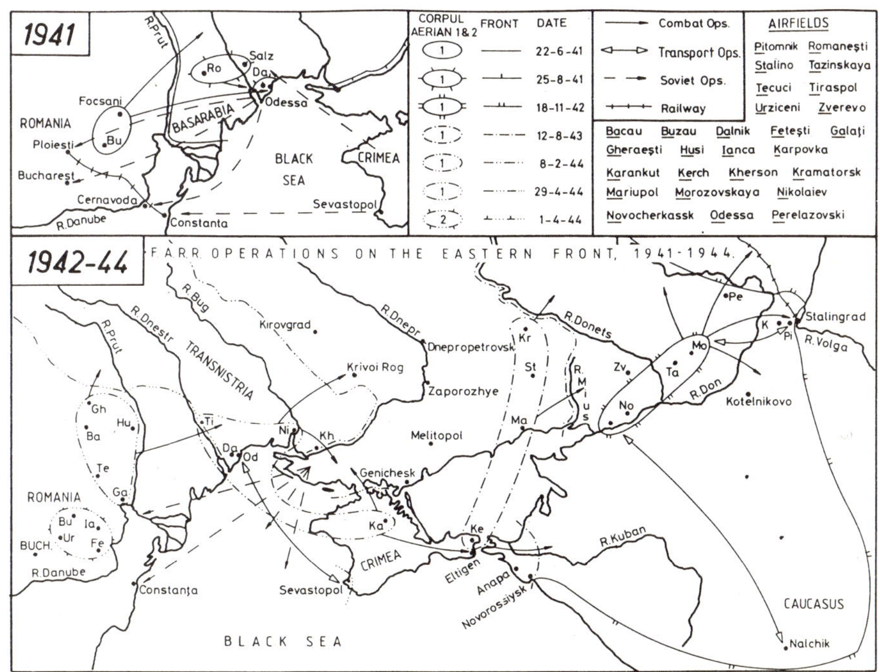

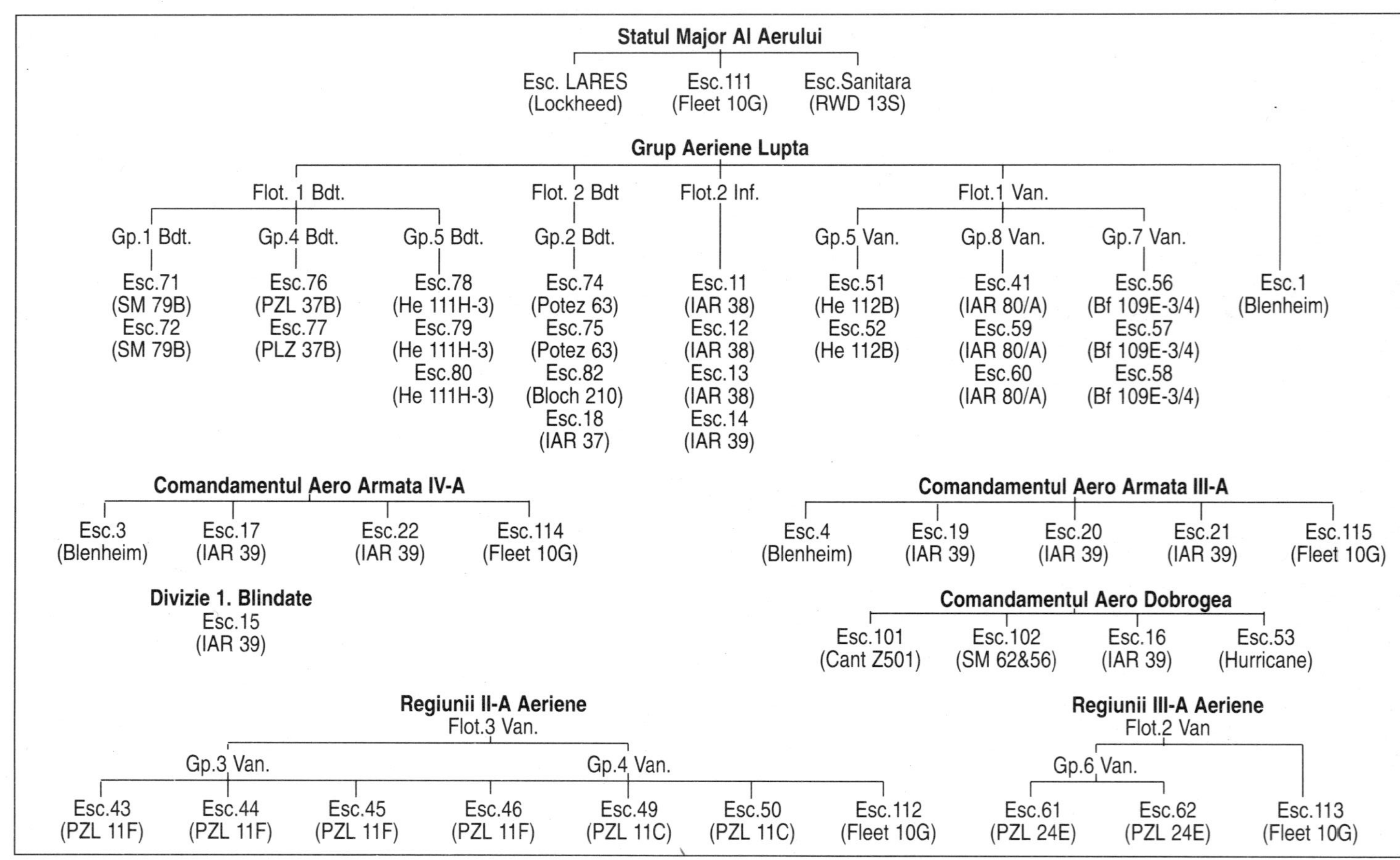
Statul Major Al Aerului
Esc. LARES
(Lockheed)
Esc.111
(Fleet 10G)
Esc.Sanitara
(RWD 13S)
Grup Aeriene Lupta
Flot. 1 Bdt.
Flot. 2 Bdt
Flot.2 Inf.
Flot.1 Van.
Gp.1 Bdt.
Gp.4 Bdt.
Gp.5 Bdt.
Gp.2 Bdt.
Gp.5 Van.
Gp.8 Van.
Gp.7 Van.
Esc.71
(SM 79B)
Esc.72
(SM 79B)
Esc.76
(PZL 37B)
Esc.77
(PLZ 37B)
Esc.78
(He 111H-3)
Esc.79
(He 111H-3)
Esc.80
(He 111H-3)
Esc.74
(Potez 63)
Esc.75
(Potez 63)
Esc.82
(Bloch 210)
Esc.18
(IAR 37)
Esc.11
(IAR 38)
Esc.12
(IAR 38)
Esc.13
(IAR 38)
Esc.14
(IAR 39)
Esc.51
(He 112B)
Esc.52
(He 112B)
Esc.41
(IAR 80/A)
Esc.59
(IAR 80/A)
Esc.60
(IAR 80/A)
Esc.56
(Bf 109E-3/4)
Esc.57
(Bf 109E-3/4)
Esc.58
(Bf 109E-3/4)
Esc.1
(Blenheim)
Comandamentul Aero Armata IV-A
Esc.3
(Blenheim)
Esc.17
(IAR 39)
Esc.22
(IAR 39)
Esc.114
(Fleet 10G)
Comandamentul Aero Armata III-A
Esc.4
(Blenheim)
Esc.19
(IAR 39)
Esc.20
(IAR 39)
Esc.21
(IAR 39)
Esc.115
(Fleet 10G)
Divizie 1. Blindate
Esc.15
(IAR 39)
Comandamentul Aero Dobrogea
Esc.101
(Cant Z501)
Esc.102
(SM 62&56)
Esc.16
(IAR 39)
Esc.53
(Hurricane)
Regiunii II-A Aeriene
Flot.3 Van.
Gp.3 Van.
Gp.4 Van.
Esc.43
(PZL 11F)
Esc.44
(PZL 11F)
Esc.45
(PZL 11F)
Esc.46
(PZL 11F)
Esc.49
(PZL 11C)
Esc.50
(PZL 11C)
Esc.112
(Fleet 10G)
Regiunii III-A Aeriene
Flot.2 Van
Gp.6 Van.
Esc.61
(PZL 24E)
Esc.62
(PZL 24E)
Esc.113
(Fleet 10G)

German Luftflotte 4 included twelve bomber groups and seven fighter groups.

Until 3 July the FARR concentrated primarily on counter-air attacks on the Red Air Force. The Romanians claimed eight Soviet aircraft destroyed in the air, 37 on the ground and three by AA fire on the first day, but lost four Blenheims, two PZL 37s, two SM 79Bs, a Potez 63, an IAR 37 and an IAR 39 in what was to be their second-heaviest day of losses throughout the war. This rate of attrition was unsustainable, and FARR operations were much reduced on subsequent days. This, and the long delay between the start of air and ground operations, meant that the Soviets had ample time to recover, and the Romanian army was unable to gain significant advantage from the surprise achieved by the original air strike. From 3 July the air force switched to ground-support operations in Basarabia.

THE USSR'S ONLY STRATEGIC BOMBER OFFENSIVE: ROMANIA 1941

From the initial quantity, quality and disposition of the 1,270 Soviet aircraft on the Romanian border, there is strong evidence that they had already prepared offensive operations against Romania. Immediately war broke out they were able to initiate their only serious strategic bombing campaign of the war against the vital oilfields around Ploieşti, the capital, Bucharest, and the port of Constanţa. (Contemporary raids on Berlin were only a propaganda exercise.) The aircraft used were predominantly unescorted DB-3 medium bombers.

The German effort in preparing the Romanian AA artillery around Ploieşti was rewarded. They were able to report that; 'The success achieved by the Romanians in terms of Russian aircraft shot down was highly satisfactory'. Only on 13 July was minor damage inflicted on Ploieşti's oil facilities. The Soviets then switched to attacking rail targets, with the intention of stopping the movement of oil. Their most threatening attacks were three raids on the vital Cernavoda rail bridge over the Danube on 10 August, but again without success. The day bombing of Bucharest also quickly proved too costly, and the Red Air Force switched to night raids. However, the Romanians cleverly drained a major lake north of Bucharest which was the Soviets' main nocturnal navigational aid, and by means of decoy fires and dummy installations led many of their raids astray.

The port of Constanţa, Romania's main naval base and the terminal for oil shipments to Italy, was particularly heavily raided. However, it had strong AA and fighter defences, and only a single tug was sunk on 1 July. In 1941 Romanian fighters claimed 51 victories over Constanţa, the AA defences 25 and German fighters 69. In one memorable incident on 23 June, the lone Romanian pilot Horia Agarici scrambled in a Hurricane under repair and minus its engine cowling, and succeeded in shooting down three Soviet bombers from a formation of nine in successive passes over the heads of the Romanian fleet. Agarici had the twin misfortunes to have a name that rhymed with the Romanian for 'Bolshevik' and a brother-in-law who was a poet. He thus became the subject of a popular ditty commemorating his feat, with the belated result that after the war the Communists came down more heavily on him than was merited by his lowly position in the list of Romanian fighter aces.

As a consequence of the Soviet raids, many of Romania's more modern fighters had to be temporarily diverted from the front in July to support the old PZL 11s in home defence. The Soviet raids of 1941 were conducted by slow, obsolescent and unescorted bombers, largely DB-3s, most of which were shot down, and they soon began to avoid Romanian and German fighters. Nevertheless, Soviet nuisance raids on Romania continued almost daily until the Germans attacked the Crimea in October, and the threat remained until Sevastopol fell in July 1942.

THE LIBERATION OF BASARABIA, JULY 1941

As Basarabia was national territory, the FARR put intensive effort into ground support for the army during its liberation and suffered considerable attrition. The defensive success gained by diverting several modern fighter squadrons to oppose the Russian strategic bomber offensive on Romania proved to be at the expense of weaker escorts for Romania's own vulnerable medium bombers, which suffered accordingly, without, however, having any profound influence on the ground fighting.

During the air defence of Romania and the liberation of Basarabia and Northern Bucovina up to the end of July, the Romanian Air Force flew 754 observation and reconnaissance, 1,032 bomber, 2,162 fighter and 1,160 communications sorties; a total of 5,108 sorties. Although 1,100 tons of bombs were dropped, 58 Romanian aircraft were lost. However, 88 Soviet aircraft were claimed in aerial combat, 108 on the ground and 59 by AA fire.

AUGUST TO OCTOBER 1941: THE SIEGE OF ODESSA

Among the Soviet reasons for holding the port and communications hub of Odessa was the fact that the bombers which raided Ploieşti refuelled there. The Soviet air defences initially consisted of about 48 I-16 fighters and a small MBR-2 seaplane unit for patrolling the Odessa end of the city's vital Black Sea supply lines. On 12 August, 30 Pe-2 bombers were flown in from the Crimea, and at the end of August a naval I-16 squadron and several miscellaneous aircraft, including two Il-2s, joined them. Other Soviet bombers were also able to operate over Odessa from the Crimea. As Odessa was a major naval base, its AA defences were particularly strong, though they later had to economise on ammunition.

Although Odessa was bombed from the first day of the war, the FARR's main role was to provide ground support for 4th Army's assaults on Odessa, which began in earnest on 18 August. However, as early as 19 August the FARR had to report that, since 22 June, its available strength had fallen from twelve observation squadrons to nine, from eighteen fighter squadrons to fourteen, and from four reconnaissance squadrons to two as repair and production facilities were quite unable to cope with the loss rate, and spares for Polish, French and British types began to run out. Only the bomber force maintained its availability at eight squadrons, thanks to the formation of Escadrila 73 with PZL 23s and Escadrila 75 with JRS 79Bs. Worse still, attrition projections suggested that the FARR's availability would fall to 60 per cent of its 22 June strength by 1 September, and to 20 per cent by 1 October. The FARR's operational potential was thus already in serious decline before 4th Army's first unsuccessful assaults on Odessa between 18 August and 5 September, during which period a further 22 aircraft were lost.

Aircraft Available to Operational Squadrons, 22 June – 18 August 1941

	← 22/6/41 →			← Losses and deliveries →			← 18/8/41 →			10/12/41
Type	Available	Damaged	Total	Accident	Combat	Deliveries	Available	Damaged	Total	Total
IAR 37*	14	1	15	-	2	-	9	4	13	32
IAR 38*	46	6	52	3	8	-	26	15	41	56
IAR 39	77	13	90	4	10	-	48	28	76	66
IAR 80	55	3	58	6	5	25	46	26	72	75
Bf 109E	35	13	48	3	2	-	15	28	43	39
He 112B	24	3	27	2	3	-	10	12	22	22?
Hurricane	10	3	13	-	-	-	4	9	13	11
PZL 11C	23	5	28	-	2	-	12	14	26	26
PZL 11F	56	12	68	2	8	-	24	34	58	52
PZL 24	23	5	28	1	-	-	21	6	27	26
He 111	26	2	28	-	4	-	13	11	24	23
JRS 79B	-	-	-	-	-	8	7	1	8	8
SM 79B	18	4	22	2	2	-	12	6	18	16
PZL 37	13	3	16	1	2	-	3	10	13	10
PZL 23	10	-	10	1	-	-	8	1	9	?
Potez 63	15	3	18	1	4	-	9	4	13	12
Blenheim	28	3	31	1	5	-	14	11	25	20
S 55	5	-	5	-	-	-	5	-	5	5
S 62bis	5	-	5	-	-	-	5	-	5	5
Cant Z501	10	-	10	2	-	-	8	-	8	6

* Most IAR 37s and many IAR 38s had been disarmed in early 1941 and were used for communications and training during the 1941 campaign.

At this early stage in the war the FARR was far less adept than the seasoned Luftwaffe at rapidly setting up forward airstrips to maintain air support on an advancing front, and during the siege of Odessa had largely to rely on airfields around Romaneşti in Basarabia, some distance from Odessa. Only Flotila I Vanatori was based forward, at Salz, south of Tiraspol. Thus the Soviets were often able to offset Romanian numerical superiority by maintaining a higher sortie rate owing to their closer proximity to the front, higher aircraft availability owing to the easier maintenance task presented by their small variety of indigenous types, and the availability of bomber support directly from the Crimea. The successful Romanian infantry assault of 11-15 September, and most other Romanian attacks, were carried out under conditions of local Soviet air superiority. This led General Courbiere, the commander of the German support units with 4th Army, to observe on 19 September; 'The enemy ... has a very active air force, superior to that of the Romanians'.

The Romanian ground advance of 11-15 September brought the existing Soviet airfields near Dalnik, which the FARR had been unable to eliminate, within artillery range, and the surviving Soviet aircraft had to be transferred to a new airstrip in a built-up area at Chubayevka which remained undetected by the FARR to the end of the siege. By the end of September only 23 Soviet I-16s and the two Il-2s remained serviceable. Chubayevka could not operate Soviet bombers, so Odessa could no longer support raids on Romania.

Day and night medium bomber raids were conducted on the city and port without decisive result owing to the heavy Soviet AA defences. The aerial mining of the harbour and effective anti-shipping strikes, which might have had a decisive impact but were beyond the FARR's resources because it lacked dive-bombers, torpedo bombers or air-dropped mines, had to be left to the overstretched Fliegerkorps IV which, despite a string of early sinkings, was unable to make a decisive impact on the fleet of 20-25 Soviet merchant vessels supplying Odessa from the Crimea and Caucasus. The arrival in the theatre of some German Ju 87s on 21 September was too late to disrupt the Soviet naval landing and counterattack on 22 September which led to the suspension of the Romanian ground offensive on the 23rd. Between 11 and 22 September the FARR lost a further sixteen aircraft from its dwindling serviceable reserves and had largely exhausted itself. By contrast, the Red Air Force claims to have flown 1,500 sorties over Odessa between 22 and 24 September alone, most from the Crimea.

Despite its best efforts, Romania's medium and light bomber force had proved of little value in providing the close ground support the army badly needed. During the latter stages of the siege of Odessa, Grup 3 Vanatori and Grup 6 Vanatori made their debuts with grenade- and bomb-equipped PZL 11Fs and PZL 24Es in the ground-attack role, but the lack of a dive bomber continued to be badly felt. Romania's own IAR 81 fighter-bomber was to fly its first combat mission over Odessa with Escadrila 59 on 15 October, too late to have any influence on the outcome of the siege.

Once the Romanian ground assaults on Odessa were suspended on 23 September, air operations became desultory and only another seven aircraft were lost up to 16 October. Romanian reconnaissance over the city was reduced to an average of only two high-altitude IAR 80 or Bf 109E flights a day during the first two weeks of October. As a result the FARR failed to detect the gradual Soviet evacuation of their 86,000 troops from Odessa between 2 and 16 October. The overstretched Luftwaffe units covering the sea lanes also failed to detect the reversal of Soviet sea movements between Sevastopol and Odessa until the 15th, by which time it was too late to intervene decisively.

The Romanians flew 1,962 observation and reconnaissance, 2,223 bomber, 6,352 fighter and 1,723 communications sorties between 1 August and 16 October; a total of 12,260 sorties, and a daily average of 157. A small proportion of these were in other theatres than Odessa. In opposition, the Red Air Force flew more than 8,000 sorties from Odessa between 10 August and 16 October; a daily average of 117 sorties. However, as this does not count the contribution of aircraft based in the Crimea, total Soviet sorties may have exceeded those of the FARR.

The FARR dropped 1,749 tons of bombs and claimed 248 Soviet aircraft shot down in combat, 42 destroyed on the ground and 56 by AA fire during the siege. As the Soviets probably committed 150 aircraft at most to Odessa itself, and at least 23 of these were evacuated, it seems that Romanian claims were perhaps three times the actual Soviet losses. The Romanians quickly realised this, and the evidence required to confirm a victory was tightened up enormously for subsequent campaigns, to the point that Romanian fighter pilots were complaining in 1942/43 that their criteria for confirming a victory were stiffer than those of German units with whom they were sharing airfields.

The Soviets at Odessa made even wilder overestimates. Their best claim was for nine Romanian Bf 109s in a single action on 9 August. Romania lost no aircraft that day. On 22 September they claimed twenty Romanian aircraft on the ground in a single air strike, whereas the Romanians lost only five aircraft on a day of exceptionally intensive air activity. Actual Romanian combat losses during the period from 1 August to 16 October totalled 56 aircraft, AA fire being the most common cause of loss.

By December the only Romanian air units still on operations were Escadrila 19, 21 and 111, which accompanied 3rd Army's Mountain and Cavalry Corps into the Nogai Steppe and the Crimea. The rest of the air force was returned to Romanian or Transnistrian bases for reorganisation.

THE 1941 CAMPAIGN: CONCLUSION

For a number of reasons, Romanian offensive air operations in 1941 did not meet with great success. By contrast to the Germans, and to a lesser extent the Russians, the Romanians were handicapped by a complete lack of combat experience, further exacerbated, according to the Germans, by the initial reluctance of the FARR command to learn from Luftwaffe experience. Their largely obsolescent, multinational collection of aircraft was plagued by lack of spares and low serviceability, and many older types were inferior to their Soviet equivalents. The attainment of air superiority was largely dependent on the three Bf 109E and three IAR 80/A squadrons, which were themselves initially handicapped by inexperience and later by airfields distant from the front. This left all of the medium bombers potentially vulnerable to Soviet fighters. However, the greatest weakness was the lack of a dedicated ground-support aircraft.

Furthermore, the speed of the German panzer advance, which quickly overran forward Soviet airfields on the northern and central sectors of the Eastern Front, could not be duplicated by the later, slower, largely horse-drawn Romanian-German offensive in Basarabia. There the Soviets could not be surprised and were able to conduct a comparatively orderly ground retirement, behind which they managed to preserve a core of experienced fighter pilots later able to contest air superiority with both the FARR over Odessa and the adjacent German IV Fliegerkorps over the Crimea.

On the positive side, the value of Romania's own fledgling air industry had been proved. The Germans had not delivered a single aircraft to replace losses, and most other foreign types had shown a catastrophic decline in serviceability. Only among Romanian-built types had production or reserves made it possible to maintain operational strengths, and they came to play a proportionally greater role as the campaign advanced. However, Odessa had proved that the FARR was not capable of effective, sustained, independent operations, and thereafter it was obliged to co-operate more closely with the Luftwaffe.

REORGANISATION, 1941–1942

Romania's 1942–43 aviation plan, which formed the basis of planning for most of the war, envisaged 69 squadrons with a front-line total of 734 aircraft plus a 40 per cent reserve:

24 Fighter squadrons of	12 aircraft each	288 aircraft
12 Bomber squadrons of	8 aircraft each	96 aircraft
12 Observation squadrons of	10 aircraft each	120 aircraft
3 Reconnaissance squadrons of	10 aircraft each	30 aircraft
6 Dive-bomber squadrons of	12 aircraft each	72 aircraft
2 Seaplane squadrons of	10 aircraft each	20 aircraft
6 Communication squadrons of	12 aircraft each	72 aircraft
2 Transport squadrons of	12 aircraft each	24 aircraft
2 Casevac squadrons of	6 aircraft each	12 aircraft

The availability of imported Allied aircraft types declined greatly by early 1942. Escadrila 53's Hurricanes were relegated to operational training owing to maintenance problems, despite the delivery of three ex-Yugoslav aircraft (Nos.13-15). The remaining Blenheims were concentrated in Escadrile 1 and 3. By early 1942 only thirteen were serviceable, despite the delivery of three ex-Yugoslav Blenheims (Nos.41–43). All PZL 11 and PZL 24 fighters were withdrawn as obsolete, but single squadrons of the PZL 37 (Esc.76) and PZL 23 (Esc.73) were kept tenuously operational by cannibalisation. Only Escadrila 108's RWD 13s could comfortably be kept in service, because engine spares were already made in Romania.

Romania had an order for twenty Potez 63B2s still outstanding with the French government, and the Franco-German Armistice Commission eventually gave clearance for delivery of ten Potez 63C2s to Escadrila 74 in November/December 1941, keeping this unit operational throughout 1942. The order was to have been completed in August 1942 with the delivery of ten reconnaissance Potez 63A3s to Escadrila 3, but it is not certain whether this occurred. The Bloch 210 was relegated to the transport role.

Even some older Axis types had to be withdrawn. The SM 79B was relegated to advanced training for the JRS 79B, while the remaining examples of the He 112, scarce and long out of production, were concentrated in Escadrila 51, which became an operational training unit at Constanţa. Germany's own attrition in late 1941 had been so severe that it was not able to replace Romanian wastage fully, even with secondhand Luftwaffe aircraft. Thus, although three squadrons of He 111H-3s had been fielded in 1941, the twelve replacement aircraft (Nos.49-60) received between January and March 1942 were only sufficient to make two squadrons available for the 1942 campaign. Fifteen Bf 109E-7s (Nos.51-65) were delivered in May/June 1942 to Escadrila 56, but by mid-1942 the Bf 109E had been out of production for nearly a year, so even this most advanced of FARR aircraft was no longer state-of-the-art.

Escadrila 2 was converted to the Do 17M, ten of which (Nos.1-10) were delivered in April/May 1942, but they, too, were old Luftwaffe aircraft and were to prove difficult to maintain. The only new aircraft received were non-combatant. The new Escadrila 105 received eighteen Ju 52s, which were necessary if the Romanian army was to operate in the depths of Russia during 1942 as the Germans wanted. Although Fi 156s continued to be delivered, their numbers were too small to supersede the Fleet 10G in any squadron. Attempts to acquire the Ju 87 remained unsuccessful.

The main source of new equipment was Romania's own aircraft industry. New IAR 80As re-equipped Grup 9 Vanatori (Esc. 47, 48, 52), Grup 3 Vanatori (Esc.43, 44, 50), Escadrile 52 and 53, and Grup 8 Vanatori (Esc.41, 42, 60). The latter's old IAR 80s were relegated to training Grup 4 (Esc.45, 46, 49). The IAR 81 re-equipped Grup 6 Bopi (Esc.61, 62). Although three IAR 80A and two IAR 81 squadrons were sent to the front in mid-1942, the majority were still forming in Romania and were to be deployed in Transnistria, in defence of Constanţa, Bucharest and Ploieşti or escorting coastal convoys. Grup 1 Bombardament (Esc.71, 72) re-equipped with the JRS 79B and JIS 79B, while the IAR 39A re-equipped Escadrile 11, 12, 13 and 18. The old IAR 37s temporarily equipped a new light-bomber group (Esc.81, 82, 83, 84), while the IAR 38s were used for training and communications.

Unfortunately, the Romanian aircraft industry's achievement of this considerable level of self-sufficiency in 1942 coincided with the beginning of its relative decline, as the full development potential of all of its locally produced engines had now been reached. By 1942 the only way that the performance of existing Romanian types could be significantly augmented was by the fitting of more powerful German engines, but this only happened with the JRS 79B1. Thereafter Romania became locked into the production of increasingly obsolescent types.

JULY 1942 TO JANUARY 1943: STALINGRAD

In early 1942 FARR activity was low. Between 16 October 1941 and 1 August 1942 Romanian aircraft flew 1,380 observation and reconnaissance, 1,021 fighter and 1,038 communications sorties. There were no missions flown by bombers. The observation and reconnaissance missions were mostly either in support of 3rd Army in the Crimea or over the Black Sea coast, and only 116 tons of bombs were dropped. The fighter sorties were mostly over the Black Sea. Only seven Soviet aircraft were claimed in the air and three on the ground during this period, but 111 were claimed by AA guns. However, Romanian transport aircraft continued to be fully occupied servicing 3rd Army in the Crimea, and by 1 August 1942 6,458 Romanian and 174 German wounded had been evacuated by Romanian transports since the beginning of the war.

When 3rd Army began its 1942 summer offensive into the Caucasus on 25 July, the FARR provided it with Escadrila 2 (Do 17M) for reconnaissance and Escadrile 112 and 114 (Fleet 10G) for communications. The subordinate Cavalry Corps' rapid thrust to Anapa on the Black Sea was accompanied by Escadrila 17 (IAR 39), while the Mountain Corps in the Crimea and Caucasus was supported by Escadrila 16 (IAR 39). By late October the air force was maintaining transport flights with Escadrila 105's Ju 52s as far as Nalchik in the Caucasus, where 2nd Mountain Division was fighting. Escadrila 15 (IAR 39A) accompanied VI Corps' advance with 4th Panzer Army on Stalingrad during the summer of 1942.

The FARR's contribution to the 1942 campaign, including the army co-operation squadrons, was designated the Grup Aerian de Lupta (GAL). Its HQ was at Rostov. Its main combat element, the Corpul Aerian, was based further forward. It was largely composed of the most recently delivered models of aircraft types used in

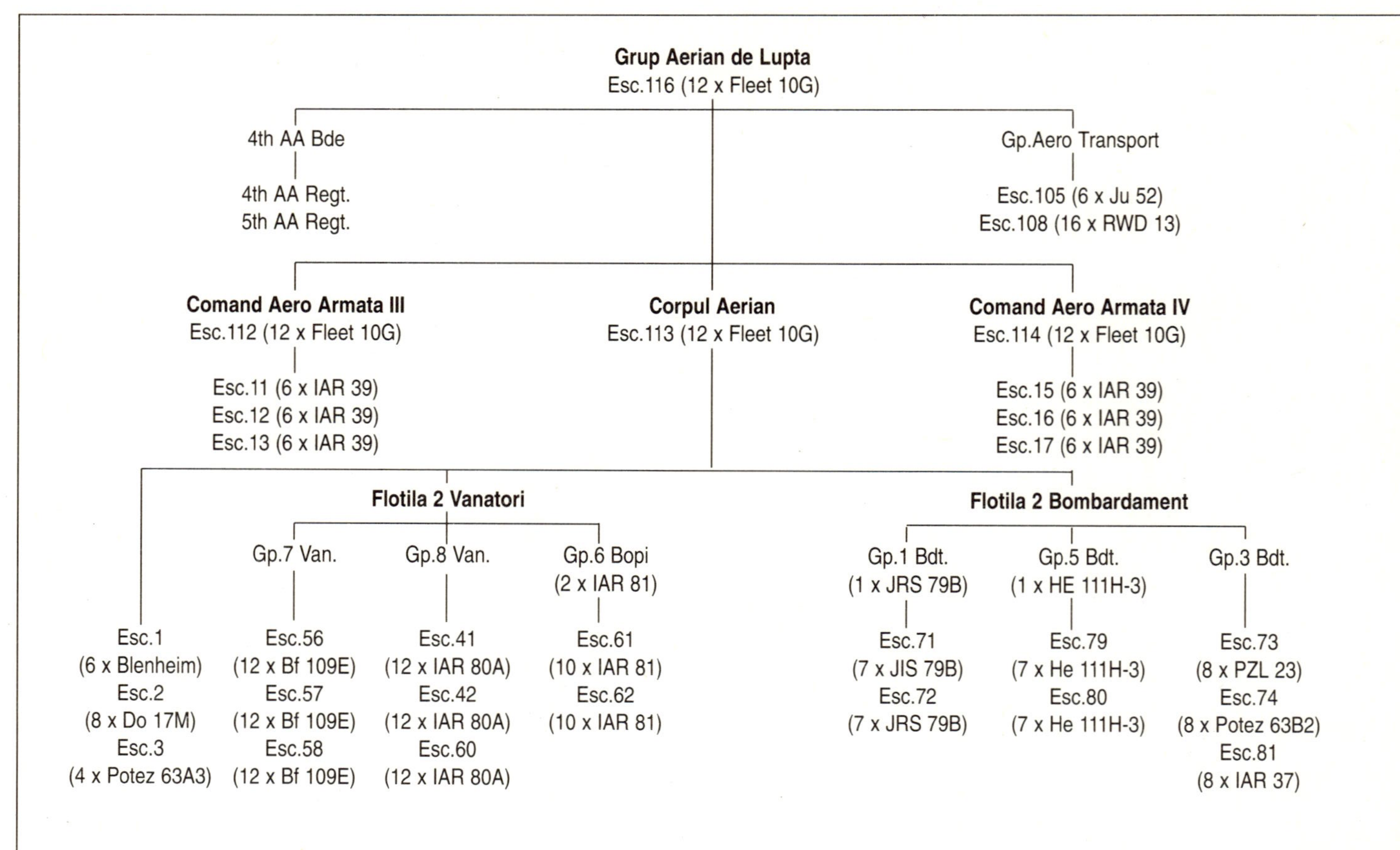
Grup Aerian de Lupta
Esc.116 (12 x Fleet 10G)
4th AA Bde
4th AA Regt.
5th AA Regt.
Gp.Aero Transport
Esc.105 (6 x Ju 52)
Esc.108 (16 x RWD 13)
Comand Aero Armata III
Esc.112 (12 x Fleet 10G)
Esc.11 (6 x IAR 39)
Esc.12 (6 x IAR 39)
Esc.13 (6 x IAR 39)
Corpul Aerian
Esc.113 (12 x Fleet 10G)
Comand Aero Armata IV
Esc.114 (12 x Fleet 10G)
Esc.15 (6 x IAR 39)
Esc.16 (6 x IAR 39)
Esc.17 (6 x IAR 39)
Flotila 2 Vanatori
Gp.7 Van.
Gp.8 Van.
Gp.6 Bopi
(2 x IAR 81)
Flotila 2 Bombardament
Gp.1 Bdt.
(1 x JRS 79B)
Gp.5 Bdt.
(1 x HE 111H-3)
Gp.3 Bdt.
Esc.1
(6 x Blenheim)
Esc.2
(8 x Do 17M)
Esc.3
(4 x Potez 63A3)
Esc.56
(12 x Bf 109E)
Esc.57
(12 x Bf 109E)
Esc.58
(12 x Bf 109E)
Esc.41
(12 x IAR 80A)
Esc.42
(12 x IAR 80A)
Esc.60
(12 x IAR 80A)
Esc.61
(10 x IAR 81)
Esc.62
(10 x IAR 81)
Esc.71
(7 x JIS 79B)
Esc.72
(7 x JRS 79B)
Esc.79
(7 x He 111H-3)
Esc.80
(7 x He 111H-3)
Esc.73
(8 x PZL 23)
Esc.74
(8 x Potez 63B2)
Esc.81
(8 x IAR 37)

1941. Thus, although they were more serviceable than the older aircraft would have been, their relative performance exhibited only marginal improvement at a time the Soviets had introduced a new generation of aircraft. Furthermore, the logistical strain of operating so far from home meant that the scale of the Romanian air effort at Stalingrad had to be below 1941 levels.

On 16 September Grup 7 Vanatori began operations from Karpovka as part of the German VIII Fliegerkorps, with ten days of Bf 109E operations in support of German assaults on Stalingrad. The rest of the Corpul Aerian began arriving on airfields in the Don bend shortly afterwards. On 27 September Grup 5 Bombardament began bombing missions with its He 111H-3s, to be joined by Grup 1 Bombardament's new JRS 79Bs and JIS 79Bs and Grup 8 Vanatori with its IAR 80As on 4 October. The initial raids were aimed at Soviet rail communications north-west of Stalingrad, and were designed to reduce the flow of supplies to the Soviet units defending the city against the German 6th Army.

On 10 October the Romanian 3rd Army HQ took over the front line north-west of Stalingrad with eleven fresh divisions from Romania. It was accompanied by Escadrile 2 and 112 and was allocated the Corpul Aerian as its combat air element. Escadrile 16, 17 and 114 were transferred from the Caucasus to join Escadrila 15, and were attached to the newly forming Romanian 4th Army of seven divisions south of Stalingrad. 4th Army fell under the umbrella of the German VIII Fliegerkorps. The Corpul Aerian was charged with interdicting Soviet communications north-west of Stalingrad, supporting 3rd Army on the ground and maintaining local air superiority on its front. On the 14th Escadrila 1's Blenheims and Escadrila 2's Do 17Ms began reconnaissance missions on 3rd Army's front, and by 20 October were beginning to detect local Soviet attack preparations on 3rd Army's front. Also on the 20th, Grup 3 Bombardament (PZL 23, Potez 63C2, IAR 37) and Grup 6 Bombardament in Picaj (IAR 81) began operations.

In late October and early November the Corpul Aerian's operations were designed primarily to support the last German assault on Stalingrad, but thereafter the growing threat to 3rd Army took priority. On 13 November reconnaissance revealed at least 103 Soviet monoplanes on five airfields opposite 3rd Army. As the Soviets were putting up very few daylight sorties in opposition to GAL operations, this was taken as a further indication of Soviet preparations for an attack. The Soviet South Western and Don Fronts opposite 3rd Army had actually built up their air strength to 790 aircraft by 20 November. Furthermore, by restricting their operations during the build-up, they had 82 per cent operational on that date, compared with the 50 per cent or less the Soviets usually managed. Owing to continuous operations, Luftwaffe availability was well below the Soviet figure at about 60 per cent, and the FARR percentage was below that.

GAL operations were averaging 75 sorties a day by mid-November, but on the 15th, 17th, 19th and 20th bad weather grounded all aircraft. This was doubly disruptive, as on 11 November the powerful, if rather exhausted, VIII Fliegerkorps had begun to turn its attention from Stalingrad, where the German attack had finally stalled, to the Soviet concentrations opposite 3rd Army. Unfortunately, the Soviet attack on 3rd Army began on 19 November and that on 4th Army on 20th November, providing both the Red Army and Romanian defenders with two days of immunity from air attack. Given that VIII Fliegerkorps was undoubtedly the most experienced exponent of ground attack in the world at the time, this situation was very much to the Soviets' advantage. On the 21st a full day of operations was possible, and considerable damage was done to Soviet cavalry formations by the Corpul Aerian and Luftwaffe, but by then the Red Army had already decisively broken through both 3rd and 4th Armies.

Bad weather again intervened on the 22nd and 23rd, and few combat missions were flown. On the 22nd five Ju 52s of Escadrila 105 flew food, fuel and ammunition to the Romanian Lascar group of divisions isolated by Soviet forces and flew out 60 wounded. Escadrila 13, based at Perelazovskii with V Corps, had to fly out to Morozovskaia as Soviet tanks approached its airfield. The other army co-operation squadrons helped establish contact with elements of the Romanian 1st Armoured and 15th Infantry Divisions and the German 22nd Panzer Division which broke out to the River Chir across the rear of the Soviet spearheads on 25/26 November.

Grup 7 Vanatori, attached to VIII Fliegerkorps and based at a German airfield close to Karpovka, near Stalingrad, found itself cut off with the German 6th Army. On 22 November two JRS 79Bs evacuated twenty of the group's personnel to Tazinskaya, but a similar mission by five of Escadrila 105's Ju 52s the following day had to be aborted because the Soviets had the airfield under fire. On the ground, the Romanian ace Alexandru Şerbanescu, a former officer in the Mountain Rifles, organised the Romanian ground defences and evacuation. Romanian-built Vickers 75mm AA guns here engaged Soviet tanks for two days. On the 23rd Grup 7 Vanatori's serviceable Bf 109Es took off under direct fire with spare pilots crammed into the cockpits. Three were shot down, but sixteen escaped to Morozovskaia and Tazinskaya, where they temporarily shared the ground facilities of Grup 8 Vanatori and Grup 6 Bopi. The group's unserviceable aircraft were lost on the ground, and the surviving ground services and AA crews were pulled back to Pitomnik, nearer Stalingrad.

Fliegerkorps VIII's combat sortie rates declined drastically in late November owing to the loss of its forward airfields. As the bulk of the GAL's airfields had been well to the rear of the front, they now became the most advanced landing grounds not to have been overrun by the Red Army. At this time of critical Luftwaffe weakness the GAL continued to maintain an average sortie rate of 50 a day, weather permitting, to the end of November. Thereafter the Corpul Aerian's squadrons found themselves marginalised on their own airfields around Morozovskaia and Tazinskaia by a massive influx of German combat aircraft falling back from the lost airfields near Stalingrad and transport aircraft brought up from the interior to supply the surrounded German 6th Army by air.

By the end of November the ground situation had stabilised, and the Corpul Aerian flew few sorties in the first week of December while it too reorganised. Grup 3 Bombardament was ordered back to Romania on 2 December as its obsolete PZL 23s, Potez 63s and IAR 37s presented a serious maintenance problem which resulted in such low availability that they could not justify their presence on the crowded airfields at the front. Escadrila 105 flew supply missions into the Stalingrad perimeter at Pitomnik and evacuated Grup 7 Vanatori's ground crews and Romanian wounded until 8 December. It was then transferred to the Caucasus, where 2nd Mountain Division was out on a limb at Nalchik. As Grup 7 Vanatori had lost half of its Bf 109Es and most of its ground services at Karpovka, it was withdrawn to Novocherkassk until early January, when new ground services could be organised. Escadrila 2's unreliable Do 17Ms were withdrawn and their crews sent to Escadrila 1, which continued to operate three more-familiar Blenheims. The army co-operation squadrons of 3rd and 4th Armies soldiered on with ever-decreasing availability.

As the bulk of the German 9th Flak Division had been trapped inside Stalingrad, the Romanian 4th AA Brigade assumed considerable importance as the main AA defence of the supply airfields outside the pocket (Morozovskaia, Tazinskaya and Zverevo). When the Red Air Force switched its attacks to the German air transport effort, Romanian AA batteries claimed at least nine Soviet aircraft confirmed and eight probables between 8 and 11 December.

Operations for the remaining aircraft reached a new intensity on 12 and 13 December, when 57 and 68 sorties were flown in support of the German counteroffensive from Kotelnikovo, designed to relieve Stalingrad. At this time the need for ground support was so pressing that the IAR 81s of Grup 6 Bopi were used as dive-bombers. They had previously been used for ground attack, but this was possibly the only period in which the IAR 81 was used in its dive-bomber role, as the GAL's records otherwise record IAR 81 missions as fighter sorties.

On 18 December the focus of GAL operations had to be switched to the front of the Italian 8th Army and army detachment Hollidt, through which the Soviets had broken. However, on 24 December this Soviet advance overran Tazinskaia airfield, and all serviceable aircraft had to be withdrawn to Novotcherkassk. The unserviceable aircraft abandoned on overrun airfields in late December represented the FARR's greatest single loss in 1942. Elements of 4th AA regiment forming part of the ground defences of Tazinskaia claimed the destruction of five Soviet tanks with their Vickers 75mm AA guns before retreating with the loss of five guns.

The Corpul Aerian resumed operations from its new airfields on 26 December, but its strength and operational readiness were now much reduced and the average daily sortie rate for the rest of the month fell to a little over twenty. On the same day it was decided to withdraw the remains of 3rd and 4th Armies from the front. Their army co-operation squadrons and the Corpul Aerian followed in January, the latter's last bombing operations on 15 January being directed against the final Soviet offensive on the encircled German 6th Army in Stalingrad, near Grup 7 Vanatori's old base at Karpovka. Although Grup 7 Vanatori's Bf 109Es resumed operations on 6 January as part of an independent mixed group with the surviving He 111H-3s, they were reduced to only three serviceable aircraft by the time they retreated to Stalino on 20 February. Then they too were withdrawn.

THE 1942 CAMPAIGN: CONCLUSION

Between 16 October 1942 and 15 January 1943 the units of the GAL flew more than 3,900 sorties, including at least 339 army co-operation, 149 reconnaissance, 1,345 fighter and 1,306 bomber sorties. About 2,000 tons of bombs were dropped. At least

61 Soviet aircraft were claimed, 39 of them in air combat. This relatively low figure is probably explained by the fact that the much larger Luftwaffe contingent near Stalingrad, which maintained a strength varying between 500 and 900 aircraft, dominated the Red Air Force for most of the campaign, and the Soviets were usually reluctant to engage Axis aircraft. FARR casualties were 538 dead, wounded and missing, mostly among technical staff and AA crews caught up in the ground fighting, and 79 aircraft were lost. Aerial losses appear to have been about 26 aircraft, the cause in almost all of the known incidents being AA fire, while the remainder were unserviceable aircraft overrun by the Red Army.

The overwhelming presence of VIII Fliegerkorps makes it difficult to establish any distinctive operational impact by the FARR in 1942. However, a similar phenomenon to 1941 can be observed in the increasing reliance on Romanian-built aircraft as the campaign progressed, so that during December 1942 the GAL was most

Romanian Aircraft Losses*, 22 June 1941 to 1 June 1943

Origin	Type	6/41-12/41	1/42-12/42	1/43-6/43	Total
Romanian Designed	SET 7K	2	2	1	5
	IAR 37	3	-	-	3
	IAR 38	13	9	1	23
	IAR 39	25	11	2	38
	IAR 80/81	20	37	12	69
Romanian Built	JRS 79B	-	9	-	19
	Fleet 10G	23	17	4	44
	PZL 11F	18	6	-	24
	PZL 24	3	-	-	3
Italian Types	SM 79B	10	-	-	10
	Cant Z501	4	2	-	6
Polish Types	PZL 11C	2	-	-	2
	PZL 23	2	2	-	4
	PZL 37	4	4	-	8
	RWD 13	-	2	-	2
German Types	He 112B	5	1	1	7
	Bf 109E	9	20	1	30
	He 111H-3	7	8	1	16
	Fi 156	-	3	-	3
	He 114	-	2	1	3
	Ju 52	-	-	3	3
French Types	Potez 63	6	3	-	9
	Bloch 210	4	-	-	4
British Types	Hurricane	2	1	-	2
	Blenheim	11	3	-	14
Total		173	142	27	342

* Including accidents

FARR Combat Operations, 22 June 1941 to 10 October 1943

	Recon.	Bomber	Fighter	
Combat Sorties	5,750+	8,476	17,324	
	In Air	**AA**	**Ground**	
Combat Victories	617	429	161	
	Recon.	**Bomber**	**Fighter**	**Comms**
Combat Losses	65	53	80+	25

truly a Romanian air force. Eighty per cent of its combat sorties were flown by Romanian-designed IAR 37s, IAR 38s, IAR 39s, IAR 80s and IAR 81s or Romanian-built JRS 79Bs. Only Grup 5 Bombardament's He 111H-3s (and a few H-6s just arriving) represented a significant foreign contribution, and their continued availability was probably due to the fact that there were sufficient spares for their engines because the Romanians had ordered 210 Jumo 211D-1 and 211F engines for the JRS 79B and B1 in 1939. Although December 1942 was a difficult and unrewarding period for operations, the mere presence of the FARR at the front in any strength, however limited its effect, owed far more to Romania's development of its own aircraft industry than to tardy German deliveries.

FARR Combat Aircraft Holdings 1941–1944 (and Romanian-built trainers)

Builder	Type	Total 8/7/41	Total 31/8/42	Total 1/4/43	Total 1/2/44	Serviceable 1/2/44
Romanian	(Fleet	144	?	191	177	136)
	(IAR 27	28	?	72	69	64)
	*(NARDI	51	?	98	106	48)
	SET 7K	43	?	42	42	36
	IAR 37	47	34	33	32	19
	IAR 38	70	54	50	44	29
	IAR 39	74	117	107	158	111
	*PZL 24	29	?	19	19	19
	IAR 80/81	±57	152	188	} 302	} 207
	IAR 81 Bopi	-	48	33		
	*JRS/JIS 79B	-	40	43	52	41
Polish	PZL 11A	10	?	4	4	?
	PZL 11B	34	?	24	22	17
	PZL 11C	29	?	25	18	16
	PZL 11F	80	?	39	39	19
	PZL 7P	13	?	7	2	?
	PZL 23	21	13	11	9	4
	PZL 37 A/B	22	10	10	10	8
	RWD 13	12	?	18	18	15
British	Blenheim	34	27	21	20	10
	Hurricane	9	10	10	10	5
German	Fi 156	15	?	22	25	23
	He 112	29	21	21	21	17
	Do 17M	-	10	9	8	6
	He 111	31	29	24	20	18
	Bf 109E	50	53	42	40	26
	Bf 109G	-	-	-	12	8
	He 114	-	9	9	13	13
	Ju 52	-	?	14	21	20
Italian	S 55	5	3	-	-	-
	S 62bis	5	3	3	-	-
	Cant Z501	8	5	4	3	3
	SM 79B	22	?	14	14	4
French	Bloch 210	8	?	3	3	1
	Potez 63	18	33	19	16	9
	Potez 543	6	?	5	5	4
	Potez 651	6	?	3	3	2

* Included some Italian or Polish production

RE-EQUIPMENT, 1943

Of the ex-Allied combat types, only Escadrila 76 with the PZL 37 and the amalgamated Escadrila 1/3 with the Blenheim remained fitfully available during 1943, and only the latter was employed operationally, on long-range reconnaissance over the Black Sea. Apart from Escadrila 108's RWD 13s, none of the other ageing Polish, Italian, French or British types remained active.

Romanian production continued at a respectable pace throughout 1943. Grup 4 Bopi (Esc.45, 46, 49) was re-equipped with the IAR 80C and Gp.9 Vanatori (Esc.43, 47, 48) with the IAR 81C. In addition, Grup 1 Vanatori (Esc.63, 64) and Grup 2 Vanatori (Esc.65, 66) were formed with the IAR 81C over the winter of 1943/44. Grup 2 Bombardament (Esc.82, 83) was formed with the JRS 79B1. There was reasonable hope that these Romanian types could continue to have some combat effectiveness on secondary sectors of the Eastern Front as long as the quality of Soviet pilots remained low and they were unable to realise the full superiority of their latest aircraft. However, their loss rates were likely to be high, and the FARR command was cautious about risking its irreplaceable experienced aircrew in increasingly second-rate aircraft.

By mid-1943 all of Romania's German combat aircraft were also growing obsolescent and had been superseded in Luftwaffe front-line service by more advanced types or models in previous years; the Do 17M and He 111H-3 by the Ju 88D-1 and A–4 and the Bf 109E by the Bf 109G. Furthermore, the number of serviceable German combat aircraft available had shown a decline since the outbreak of war, and most of the ageing survivors were now badly worn and their serviceability was in serious decline. Early 1943 was thus a time of crisis for the FARR.

By 1943 the Luftwaffe was increasingly short of aircrew but was beginning to enjoy growing deliveries of aircraft, whereas the FARR had numbers of trained aircrew flying obsolete types. It thus became advantageous for Germany to supply Romanian aircrew with new aircraft. During spring 1943 Corpul 1 Aerian's Escadrila 2 was supplied with the Ju 88D-1, Grup 7 Vanatori (Esc.56, 57, 58) received the Bf 109G, Grup 5 Bombardament (Esc.77, 79, 80) the Ju 88A–4, Grup 3 Bombardament (73, 81, 85) the Ju 87D-3 and D-5 and Grup 8 Asalt (Esc.41, 42, 60) the Hs 129B.

However, the Germans suspected that the Romanians would try to hoard modern aircraft at home in preparation for the anticipated clash with Hungary, so all the combat aircraft used by Corpul 1 Aerian during 1943–44 were only lent by the Luftwaffe and did not belong to the FARR. All were delivered directly to the Romanian units at the front by Luftflotte 4, which was also responsible for major repairs and replacements. Furthermore, the bomber units had German aircrews attached. Their role, ostensibly, was to teach tactics and provide liaison with German troops on the ground, but there was no doubt that they were also there to ensure that the Romanians performed with due determination. Relations between them and Romanian aircrew were generally correct, but varied between ill-concealed resentment and genuine warmth, depending on the degree of tact with which the Germans interfered in any particular Romanian group's operations.

The Germans could not exert the same control over existing Romanian aircraft or new deliveries from Romanian factories, and the FARR became functionally split in two. While the new German aircraft and mobile ground services re-equipped Corpul 1 Aerian, the bulk of Romania's older types or new Romanian IAR 81Cs and JRS 79B1s were held back on prepared airfields in Transnistria or Romania in static defence of the north-west Black Sea or homeland.

Some German deliveries did continue directly to Romania. Previously, German aircraft had been delivered under bilateral contracts between the Romanian government and German aircraft companies which had been the subject of ponderous commercial negotiations. However, from mid-1943 a more responsive direct government-to-government agreement, the Clodius-Antonescu Protocol, began to speed up transactions. More Ju 52s allowed Grup Aerotransport to form Escadrila 107, and new IAR 39-towed DFS 230 gliders equipped Escadrila 109. A dozen Bf 109Gs were sent in mid-1943 to equip Escadrila 53, and Grup 7 Vanatori's old Bf 109Es were inherited by Escadrila 51, which was apparently retrained in German 'Wild Boar' night-fighter tactics. These two units formed Grup 5 Vanatori and were allocated to the defence of Constanţa. Nine Bf 110C-3s and F–4s formed Romania's first true night-fighter squadron, Escadrila 68, although this unit was also subordinated to the Luftwaffe.

Thus the Romanian 1942–43 aviation plan for 69 squadrons came reasonably close to fulfilment in late 1943, but the raw statistics disguised the facts that the aircraft under direct Romanian control were largely obsolescent, and the modern aircraft received from Germany were largely on loan and held under German operational command, and therefore not freely at the disposal of the FARR.

MARCH 1943 TO APRIL 1944: CORPUL 1 AERIAN IN THE UKRAINE

Romanian air activity fell to a low level at the front from February to April 1943. Only Escadrila 20 (IAR 39) and Escadrila 43 (IAR 80A), which had been attached to the Germans on 7 October 1942 to provide reconnaissance and fighter cover over the Kerch Straits, remained at the front and took part in the air fighting over the Kuban Bridgehead in February-April 1943. 3rd Army HQ retained a squadron of IAR 39s in the Crimea.

The first Romanian unit re-equipped with loaned German aircraft in 1943 was Grup 7 Vanatori, which converted to the Bf 109G at Dnepropetrovsk during March. It operated with the German Udet Group from 29 March to 1 July. As the Romanians' aircraft were only on loan, the Udet Group wanted them to fly under German insignia, but the Romanians insisted on flying under their own colours. Goering had to intervene in the ensuing row, and the Romanians had their way.

This period was regarded by the Romanian fighter pilots as their most profitable because, for the only time in the war, there were no Romanian bombers present at the front to tie them down to escort duties. As a result, the leading Romanian aces added substantially to their scores, at least fourteen gaining more than five confirmed victories. The high point probably came shortly after Grup 7 Vanatori was transferred to Corpul 1 Aerian, when, on 17 and 18 July, 23 Soviet aircraft were confirmed destroyed over the heads of the grateful German army defending the River Mius.

Corpul 1 Aerian became operational again on 16 June 1943. Its new HQ was at Mariupol with Grup 7 Vanatori, Grup 3 Picaj and Escadrila 2. Other sub-units still

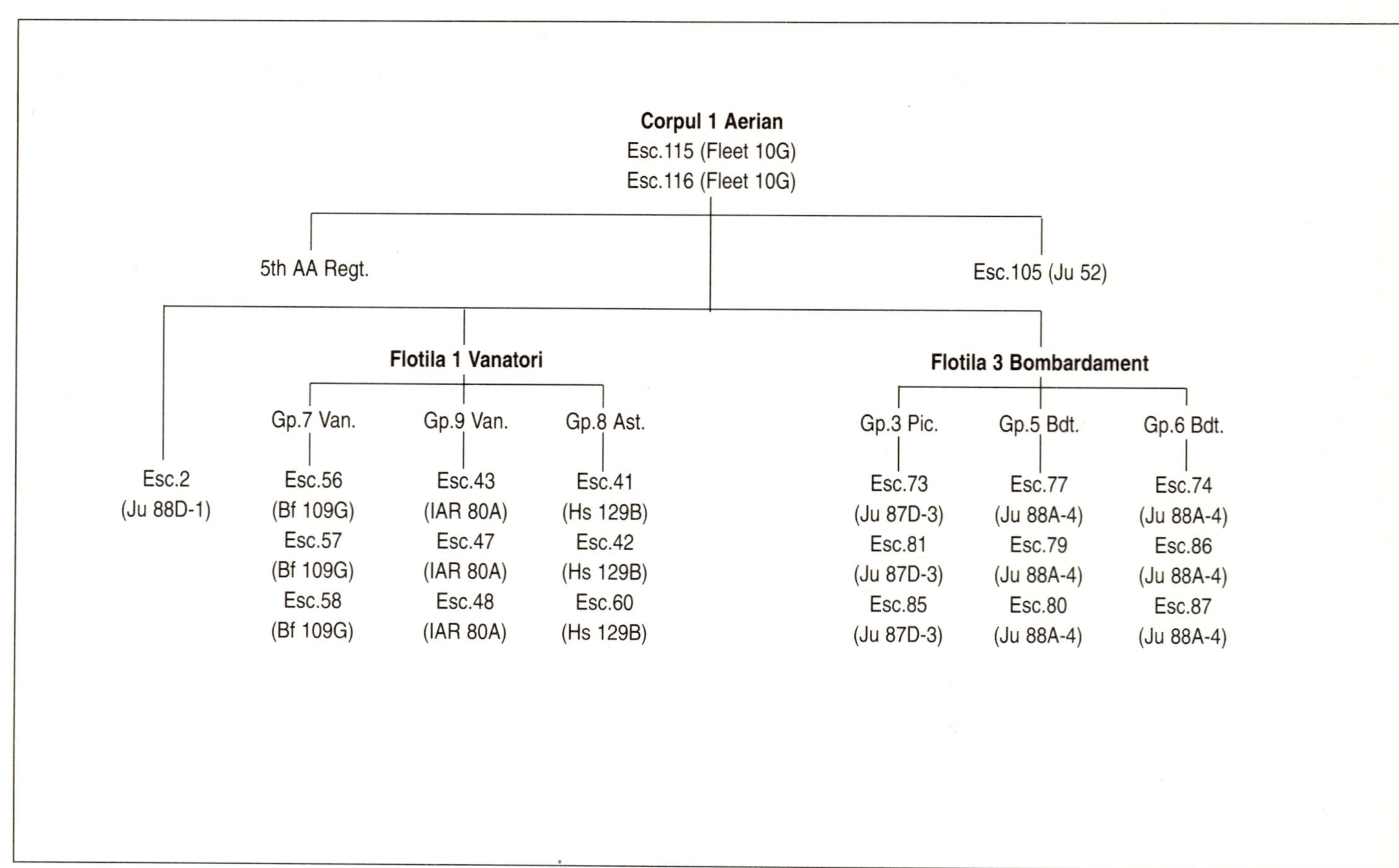
Corpul 1 Aerian
Esc.115 (Fleet 10G)
Esc.116 (Fleet 10G)
5th AA Regt.
Esc.105 (Ju 52)
Flotila 1 Vanatori
Flotila 3 Bombardament
Esc.2
(Ju 88D-1)
Gp.7 Van.
Esc.56
(Bf 109G)
Esc.57
(Bf 109G)
Esc.58
(Bf 109G)
Gp.9 Van.
Esc.43
(IAR 80A)
Esc.47
(IAR 80A)
Esc.48
(IAR 80A)
Gp.8 Ast.
Esc.41
(Hs 129B)
Esc.42
(Hs 129B)
Esc.60
(Hs 129B)
Gp.3 Pic.
Esc.73
(Ju 87D-3)
Esc.81
(Ju 87D-3)
Esc.85
(Ju 87D-3)
Gp.5 Bdt.
Esc.77
(Ju 88A-4)
Esc.79
(Ju 88A-4)
Esc.80
(Ju 88A-4)
Gp.6 Bdt.
Esc.74
(Ju 88A-4)
Esc.86
(Ju 88A-4)
Esc.87
(Ju 88A-4)

converting on German airfields were distributed there and at Zaporozhe and Kirovgrad. They were initially dedicated to supporting the German forces struggling to hold the River Mius. This allowed the Germans to redeploy experienced Luftwaffe units north to support their doomed attack at Kursk in early July. As a result the FARR was to provide the main Axis air contingent at the southern extremity of the Eastern Front through much of the late summer and early Autumn of 1943. Squadron strength in Corpul 1 Aerian (though not the FARR as a whole) was now standardised at twelve aircraft for all combat types, giving a total of 36 per group. There were also, theoretically, nine replacement aircraft per group.

Grup 3 Picaj (Esc.73, 81, 85) had begun conversion to the Ju 87D-3 at Nikolaiev on 1 April 1943, and became operational in mid-June. After a few weeks on the Mius line, Grup 3 Picaj was transferred on 6 July to the Kerch Peninsula, where it remained for several months as the only Axis bomber unit available to support the German and Romanian divisions in the Kuban Bridgehead. It broke up several Soviet ground attacks on the Blue Line, earning commendations from the German 97th Division, Fliegerkorps I and 17th Army. It also laid mines off the coast and strafed Soviet gunboats. By 9 August 31 of its 44 available aircraft had already been damaged, six by fighters and the rest by AA fire, but none had been lost. Grup 3 Picaj's tour at Kerch was arguably the most effective Romanian bombing performance of the war, and might well have been the best direct support the German Army received from another Axis air force throughout the war.

Grup 3 Picaj made a second tour of the Crimea from 4 November 1943, after the Soviets had cut off the peninsula from the main German front in late October. Based at Karankut, it provided close air support for the counterattack by the Romanian 3rd Mountain and 6th Cavalry Divisions which wiped out the Soviet landing at Eltigen in early December 1943. It was withdrawn to Romania in mid-April 1944, after the Red Army had broken into the Crimea.

Grup 5 Bombardament (Esc.77, 79, 80) was re-equipped with the Ju 88A-4 at Kirovgrad in May and returned to operations in June, supporting German troops on the Mius line. However, it was apparently committed prematurely, possibly owing to the pressing need to replace German units transferred to Kursk, and therefore lost a quarter of its crews before training was completed by the end of July. When the unit was committed against Soviet positions across the Mius on 4 August, the Germans described the results as 'impressive'. One consequence of Grup 5 Bombaradament's early losses was that Grup 6 Bombardament at Zaporozhe, which was also forming with the Ju 88A-4, had to relinquish its aircraft and crews to Grup 5 Bombardament after only a few missions.

Grup 8 Asalt (Esc.41, 42, 60) was formed at Kirovgrad on 7 May 1943 by the conversion of Grup 8 Vanatori to the Hs 129B-2. The German decision to issue the Hs 129B-2 to the Romanians was undoubtedly influenced by the aircraft's temperamental Gnome-Rhône 14M 4/5 engines, which were related to the IAR 14K, for which the Romanians already had experienced mechanics. Operations began from Kramatorsk on 12 August 1943, and by the 16th the Germans were already intercepting Soviet radio traffic attesting to the effectiveness of the unit's initial operations. This drew the congratulations of General Mackensen, whose 1st Panzer Army successfully held a major Soviet offensive across the River Donets. Field Marshal von Kleist of Army Group A was later to commend Grup 8 Asalt for its 'excellent support' of a German counterattack which threw the Soviet spearheads back from Krivoi Rog on 2 October.

Escadrila 2 converted from the Do 17M to the Ju 88D-1 in the Crimea, and resumed reconnaissance missions on 17 June. It photographed extensively behind Soviet lines, pinpointing assembly areas and communication centres, and often set up Romanian air strikes, such as several successful attacks in November on new Soviet airfields between the Crimea and Dnepr estuary, from which the Red Air Force was threatening the supply convoys to Sevastopol. From the Romanian army's point of view, Escadrila 2's reconnaissance flights over the Soviet-held ports on the north and east shores of the Sea of Azov were particularly important, as the Cavalry Corps was on anti-invasion watch on the north coast of the Crimea opposite them throughout the winter of 1943/44. One of its aircraft deserted to the Allies in Syria at this time.

Grup 9 Vanatori was to form a second Bf 109G group, and began conversion at Tiraspol in Transnistria. However, aircraft attrition in Grup 7 Vanatori was high, and many Bf 109Gs were diverted to keep it up to strength, delaying Grup 9 Vanatori's conversion. Then, on 1 August 1943, the USAAF carried out its first major raid on Ploieşti, highlighting the need to reinforce home fighter defences for the inevitable onslaught to follow. As a result, Grup 9 Vanatori replaced Grup 7 Vanatori at the front in September 1943, exchanging its IAR 80As for Grup 7 Vanatori's Bf 109Gs. Grup 7 Vanatori was withdrawn into Romania, and flew IAR 81Cs over the winter until the delivery of new Bf 109G-2s during March 1944. Thirteen of Grup 7 Vanatori's leading pilots remained at the front with Grup 9 Vanatori. Thus Romania's best fighter pilots were now divided, facing the Red Air Force with Grup 9 Vanatori and preparing for the onset of the USAAF with Grup 7 Vanatori.

During the summer and autumn of 1943 the FARR contingent on the Eastern Front, Corpul 1 Aerian, was at its best. Its aircraft were for once new, comparatively modern and available in reasonable numbers, while the selected aircrew had two years of operational experience behind them. Corpul 1 Aerian soldiered on through the winter and spring of 1943/44, hopping from airfield to airfield across the Southern Ukraine just ahead of the advancing Red Army but with ever-decreasing availability as losses and damage outpaced German replacement and Romanian repair facilities. On 6 September Corpul 1 Aerian abandoned the Mariupol region and fell back to Melitopol, and then shortly afterwards through Genichesk, Dnepropetrovsk, Kherson and Nikolaiev. In late October much of Corpul 1 Aerian had to fall back even further to airfields in Transnistria, often sharing airfields with the Comando Aero Marina. By early 1944 most groups had few more aircraft serviceable than a full-strength squadron. On 2 March 1944 Corpul 1 Aerian had been reduced to the level shown in the table at the top of the next page.

However, the Corpul Aerian was now better trained and equipped than in 1941 or 1942 to move its supporting ground services with a quickly shifting front, and operational availability was less restricted by this factor. Furthermore, it was falling back on prepared airfields and a shortening supply line in a well-practised routine. In early March the surviving Ju 87s and Hs 129s were still flying an average of three

Corpul 1 Aerian, 2 March 1944		
Corpul 1 Aerian HQ	Tiraspol	—
Gp. 9 Vanatori	Dalnik (Odessa)	12 Bf 109G
Gp. 3 Picaj	Karankut (Crimea)	17 Ju 87D-3
Gp. 8 Asalt	Nikolaiev	13 Hs 129B-2
Gp. 5 Bombardament	Odessa	12 Ju 88A-4
Esc. 2	Odessa	5 Ju 88D-1

missions each per day. On 10 April the Soviet advance reached Odessa, on 12 April Tiraspol fell, and by mid-May the Crimea had been evacuated. Corpul 1 Aerian now fell back into Basarabia, within Romania. By 27 March Grup 3 Picaj, Grup 8 Asalt and Grup 9 Vanatori were operating from Galaţi, and Grup 5 Bombardament and Escadrila 2 Recunoastre were at Tecuci. On 29 April Grup 7 Vanatori was returned to Corpul 1 Aerian at Gheraeşti, and on 20 May the newly Ju 87-equipped Grup 6 Picaj (Esc.74, 87) rejoined Corpul 1 Aerian at Huşi, beginning its operations on 30 May. Grup 6 Picaj was completed by Escadrila 86 on 16 July.

Although the combat commitment of most Romanian aircrew was not in question, higher Romanian authorities on at least one occasion placed restrictions on operations after particularly heavy losses, a luxury the resentful Luftwaffe could not afford. Where Romanian troops were directly threatened, however, Romanian air support was not stinted. It is noticeable that Grup 3 Picaj's successful operations in the Kuban and Crimea, for which the entire surviving aircrews were awarded Iron Crosses, had a direct influence on the fate of the Romanian Mountain and Cavalry Corps, and that the highest sortie rate of the war was to be achieved once Romanian soil was directly threatened in 1944.

Despite some Luftwaffe reservations, the German Army had reason to be grateful for the presence and performance of Corpul 1 Aerian, and its commander, Major

Aircraft Delivered to Corpul 1 Aerian, 16 June 1943 to 23 August 1944	**Esc.2**	**Gp.3 Picaj**	**Gp.5 Bomb.**	**Gp.8 Asalt**	**Gp.7&9 Van.**	**Gp.6 Picaj**	**Total**
	Ju 88 D-1	Ju 87D-3 & D-5	Ju 88A-4 & A-14	Hs 129B-2	Bf 109G-2 & G-6	Ju 87D-3	
Deliveries							
By 16/6/43	12	29	25	35	31	24	156
Later, New	7	83	59	122	132	27	430
Later, Repaired	1	1	-	84	27	4	117
Total Deliveries	*20*	*113*	*84*	*241*	*190*	*55*	*703*
Losses							
Missing	5	3	5	14	9	6	42
Destroyed by Enemy	1	10	13	23	27	3	77
Accident	2	3	3	6	10	2	26
Total losses	*8*	*16*	*21*	*43*	*46*	*11*	*145*
Damaged and Returned to Germans							
By Enemy	3	26	21	83	26	7	166
By Accident	5	46	26	83	100	10	270
Total Damaged	*8*	*72*	*47*	*166*	*126*	*17*	*436*
Disposable 23 August 1944							
Serviceable	4	18	10	16	11	21	80
Unserviceable	-	7	6	16	7	6	42

General Emanoil Ionescu, was awarded the *Ritterkreuz* on 10 May 1944. The deployment of Corpul 2 Aerian and the Soviet suspension of offensive operations at the southern end of the Eastern Front between June and August 1944 gave Corpul 1 Aerian time to rest and rebuild. On 16 June 1944 Corpul 1 Aerian had completed a year of continuous operations, in which time it had flown 18,227 operational sorties, dropped 7,312 metric tons of bombs and claimed the destruction of 401 Soviet aircraft, mostly by Grup 7 Vanatori and Grup 9 Vanatori.

BLACK SEA OPERATIONS, 1942–1944

	Mid-42		27/5/43		2/3/44	
Airfield	**Esc.**	**Type**	**Esc.**	**Type**	**Esc.**	**Type**
Constanţa/Ciocarlia/Carol I			78	He111H-6	78	He 111H-6
					½45	IAR 80C
Mamaia	101	SM 55, 62, Z 501	102	He 114	101	He 114
	102	He 114			102	He 114
Jibrieni	44	PZL 11F			½46	IAR 80C
Cetatea Alba	50	PZL 11F	49	IAR 80C	½45	IAR 80C
Odessa/Dalnik/Tiraspol	3	Blenheim	1/3	Blenheim	1/3	Blenheim
	20	IAR 39	22	IAR 39	22	IAR 39
	43	PZL 11F			½46	IAR 80C
Saki/Eupatoria			20	IAR 39	49	IAR 80C
					20	IAR 39
Tecuci	74	Potez 63B2	82	JRS 79B1	82	JRS 79B1
	75	JRS 79B	83	JRS 79B1	83	JRS 79B1

From late 1941 the FARR's Comanda Aero Marin took primary responsibility for the aerial protection of the coastal convoy routes in the north-west basin of the Black Sea which it was to maintain until early 1944. As the front advanced, Romanian aircraft were progressively deployed on a string of coastal airfields. At the outbreak of war the airfields at Ciocarlia, Mamaia and Carol I near Constanţa were in use to protect the Romanian coast. During late 1941 and early 1942 airfields at Jibrieni, Cetatea Alba (Akkerman) and Odessa came into service to protect coastal convoys to Odessa against naval and air attack from Sevastopol. In late 1942 airfields at Feodosiya and Kerch were used to protect Axis shipping around the Kerch Straits, and during 1943–44 Eupatoria, Saki and Nikolaiev were all used to protect supply convoys and the air bridge from Odessa to the isolated Crimea. A couple of squadrons of medium bombers were usually held in support at Tecuci.

The ageing Italian seaplanes of Escadrile 101 and 102, based at Mamaia, provided coastal reconnaissance from the Bulgarian border up to Sulina and escorted Sevastopol-bound convoys to the limit of their range. In 1940 Romania had ordered twelve German He 114C-1 floatplanes, but the Germans took over the aircraft on the production line for use in the Baltic in mid-1941, and only after the opening of the increasingly important Black Sea convoy routes did they begin delivery to Escadrila 102 in 1942. All of the surviving Italian seaplanes were concentrated in Escadrila 101. More He 114s gradually replaced the remaining Italian types in Escadrila 101 during 1943. Three HD 42 floatplanes (Nos.1-3) were also bought to replace Romanian-built SET 4Hs for training and communications.

The FARR began the war with no dive bombers or torpedo aircraft (if one discounts the obsolete SM 55), and had thus been unable to interfere with the Soviet convoys to and from Odessa in 1941. There were still none available in December 1942, when Soviet naval raids on convoy routes off the Romanian coast were spotted by reconnaissance aircraft. On this occasion, command confusion and low cloud prevented any air strikes being launched anyway. However, these raids led to the last He 111 squadron (Esc.78) being redeployed in the anti-shipping role. It had by now received He 111H-6s with the capacity to carry torpedoes, but it is not clear whether these weapons were actually carried. They were certainly never used, because Stalin suspended naval raids in October 1943.

In 1943 the Romanians requested torpedo-armed He 115 floatplanes, which also had the range to escort convoys all the way between Constanţa and Sevastopol, but delivery was refused even though the type was being withdrawn from Luftwaffe service. In early 1943 Romania also displayed an interest in the torpedo carrying Fi 167A-0, which had been designed for the aircraft carrier *Graf Zeppelin*, but none were received. The Germans also offered 48 ex-French Latécoère 298s, but again none were delivered. In 1944 the Germans promised six Ar 196s, whose 45° dive-bombing capability made them much more potent than the He 114 against submarines, but none were delivered before Romania's defection.

Coastal reconnaissance east of Sulina was provided by IAR 39s. Escadrila 20 at Kerch in the winter of 1942/43 was the most forward such unit, and also engaged in anti-partisan operations in the Crimea's Yaila mountains. Long-range reconnaissance between Sulina and Cape Tarkhan was conducted by the Odessa-based Escadrila 1/3, an amalgamation of the remaining Blenheims of Escadrile 1 and 3.

Until mid-1942, coastal fighter cover against possible attacks from Sevastopol was provided by the Constanţa-based He 112Bs and Hurricanes of Grup 5 Vanatori (Esc.51, 53) and the Odessa, Cetatea Alba and Jibrieni-based PZL 11Fs of Grup 3 Vanatori (Esc.43, 44, 50) – types with either low serviceability levels or limited combat potential that precluded their further deployment at the front. In mid-1942 Escadrila 53 and Grup 3 Vanatori apparently received IAR 80s or IAR 80As, possibly passed on from Grup 8 Vanatori. Grup 3 Vanatori's Escadrila 43 was based as far east as Kerch, and fought over the Kuban Bridgehead in early 1943. Grup 3 Vanatori was then relegated to advanced fighter pilot training at Ghimbav, and was superseded on operations by the new IAR 80Cs of Grup 4 Bopi (Esc.45, 46, 49). The IAR 80C had initially been designed as the IAR 81B dive bomber, and still retained the attachment points for two underwing 50kg bombs. This gave it some anti-submarine potential, although no sinkings were recorded.

On 27 September 1943 the Soviet front was close enough for them to launch their first speculative torpedo attack on Constanţa. It failed, and three Soviet aircraft were shot down. However, at the end of October 1943 the Red Army broke through to the north-west basin of the Black Sea between the Crimea and the mouth of the Dnepr, isolating six German and seven Romanian divisions in the Crimea. The Red Air Force immediately established airfields there, and from 23 November began regular attacks on the vital Axis supply convoys from Odessa and Constanţa to Sevastopol. On 25 November the first Soviet dive bombers appeared.

Grup 4 Bopi's IAR 80Cs at Saki and Odessa scored a number of victories over Soviet bombers attacking coastal convoys, and Corpul 1 Aerian made several attacks on their advanced airfields with some success, but was unable to suppress them indefinitely. Grup 5 Vanatori (Esc.51, 52), now equipped with a mixture old Bf 109Es and IAR 80s, was reportedly brought forward to Nikolaiev on 20 December to cover the particularly vulnerable section from Odessa to the coast of the Crimea. This system worked well during the following winter and spring, and Axis ship and transport aircraft losses remained bearable until the last days of the Crimea evacuation in early May.

On 17 November the Romanian Air Force HQ, in conjunction with the Luftwaffe, had set up an air bridge between Odessa and the Crimea. The Romanian component included Escadrile 105 and 107, each with nine Ju 52s. In reserve for transport duties were some surviving SM 79Bs, Bloch 210s, Potez 543s and Potez 65s, possibly organised into Escadrila 106. Supplies were flown to the Crimea, and more than 3,056 wounded had been evacuated by air by the time the peninsula was lost in early May. Escadrila 49 lost most of its equipment at Saki, but its rescued personnel went on to man the core of the last new IAR 81C unit to be formed, Escadrila 67.

PRODUCTION AND RE-EQUIPMENT, 1944

In 1944 Romanian production of the IAR 81C, Bf 109G, IAR 39A, Fi 156C-3 and JRS 79B1 was barely adequate to replace natural wastage, and was disrupted by USAAF bombing. The first 90 IAR 80s and IAR 80As were by now relegated to training, and work began on converting 100 later IAR 80As and IAR 81s into 20mm Mauser-armed IAR 80Ms and IAR 81Ms even before production of the IAR 81C finished in July 1944. A new batch of IAR 39As began to replace older IAR 39s in some squadrons, but plans to re-equip Escadrila 84 with the JRS 79B1 had to be abandoned owing to losses in Escadrile 82 and 83 and the destruction of several airframes in US raids on IAR-Braşov.

With the Red Army approaching Romanian soil, increasingly desperate measures were taken. Old IAR 37s were reissued to Escadrile 17 and 18, and most PZL 11Cs, Nardi FN 305s, IAR 27s and PWSs were fitted with light bomb racks, in addition to the surviving PZL 24s and PZL 11Fs already so equipped. However, only the IAR 37s were to see operational use, as there were insufficient trained pilots to man the other types on the night nuisance raids for which they were intended.

The continued loan of German aircraft to Corpul 1 Aerian kept its existing groups operational and allowed Grup 6 Picaj (Esc.74, 86, 87) to re-equip with Ju 87D-3s during May-July. In March-April 1944, German deliveries agreed under the Clodius-Antonescu Protocol enabled Grup 7 Vanatori to re-equip with the Bf 109G-2 during the first USAAF raids. Under the protocol the Germans also delivered a squadron of old Hs 129Bs, which formed the new Escadrila 38. However, Escadrile 39 and 40, which were to have completed Grup 11 Asalt, were never formed. The other direct German deliveries were of obsolete He 111E-3s, Ju 86Es and W-34s for training or transport.

It was planned to re-equip all eight fighter groups with IAR-built Bf 109G-4s in 1944/45. Although this aircraft was no longer the best in German service, it was a significant improvement on the IAR 81C. However, USAAF raids on IAR-Braşov in April damaged four Bf 109G-4 airframes, and only six Romanian-built Bf 109G-4s could be delivered by August 1944. Thus, when most Luftwaffe units were transferred out of Romania to shore up the fronts in France and Byelorussia in June and July 1944, the Germans were obliged to replace them with supplementary deliveries of Bf 109G-6s under the Clodius-Antonescu Protocol. However, although about 50 further Bf 109Gs had been delivered by August 1944, only Grup 6 Vanatori and Grup 5 Vanatori had had time partly to convert to them.

The first paratroop company had been founded by the FARR on 10 June 1940, the second in 1942 and a third, support weapons company, in 1943. They formed the 4th Parachute Battalion, and were hidden amongst the numerical sequence of barrage balloon units. However, by October 1943 only 215 men were fully trained, and an impatient Antonescu therefore ordered a mass induction of picked troops from the army to bring the unit up to a regimental strength of 2,877. Although 1,300 paratroops had been trained by the time the Soviets ordered the unit's disbandment in February 1944, only 4th Parachute Battalion (861 men) had reached operational status by August 1944. It required 54 Ju 52s for a battalion drop – a total never available. However, by using Escadrila 109's DFS 230 gliders, LARES airliners and old bomber types, a full drop was technically possible. In 1944 the army also organised an air transportable battalion similar in structure to a mountain rifle battalion.

BASARABIA, SUMMER 1944

By November 1943 it was obvious that Romania's garrison in Transnistria, III Corps, was soon going to be engaged with the Red Army, and it was allocated Escadrila 22 on 14 November. As the Red Army approached the Romanian frontier a new 4th Army was deployed north of Iaşi, and it was allocated Escadrila 19 on 17 March and Escadrila 15 and 112 on 12 April. Their base was Bacau.

The arrival of the Red Army on Romanian soil also led to the operational deployment of the squadrons equipped with Romanian-built or older foreign types that had previously been held back in Romania or operated over the Black Sea. They were formed into Corpul 2 Aerian on 1 April 1944, and concentrated in the zone Ianca-Tandarei-Feteşti-Urziceni-Buzau. Corpul 2 Aerian did not have the same mobile ground services as Corpul 1 Aerian, but it was based on long-established Romanian airfields where the necessary static facilities were already in place. Operations began on 25 April, and 200 missions were being flown daily by 3 May.

In the opinion of the commander of Corpul 1 Aerian, Emanoil Ionescu, Corpul 2 Aerian was too weak to be considered a full air corps. Quite apart from the obsolescence of most of its aircraft and their low serviceability, its army co-operation squadrons were short of observers, its fighter squadrons lacked reserve pilots and its bomber squadrons were short of both crew and aircraft. The Grupul Grenadier, consisting of old Polish aircraft fitted with anti-personnel grenade launchers, was intended for night nuisance raids, but most of its crews were not yet trained for night operations and it was never fielded. The shortage of aircrew was due to Corpul 1 Aerian's appetite for replacements.

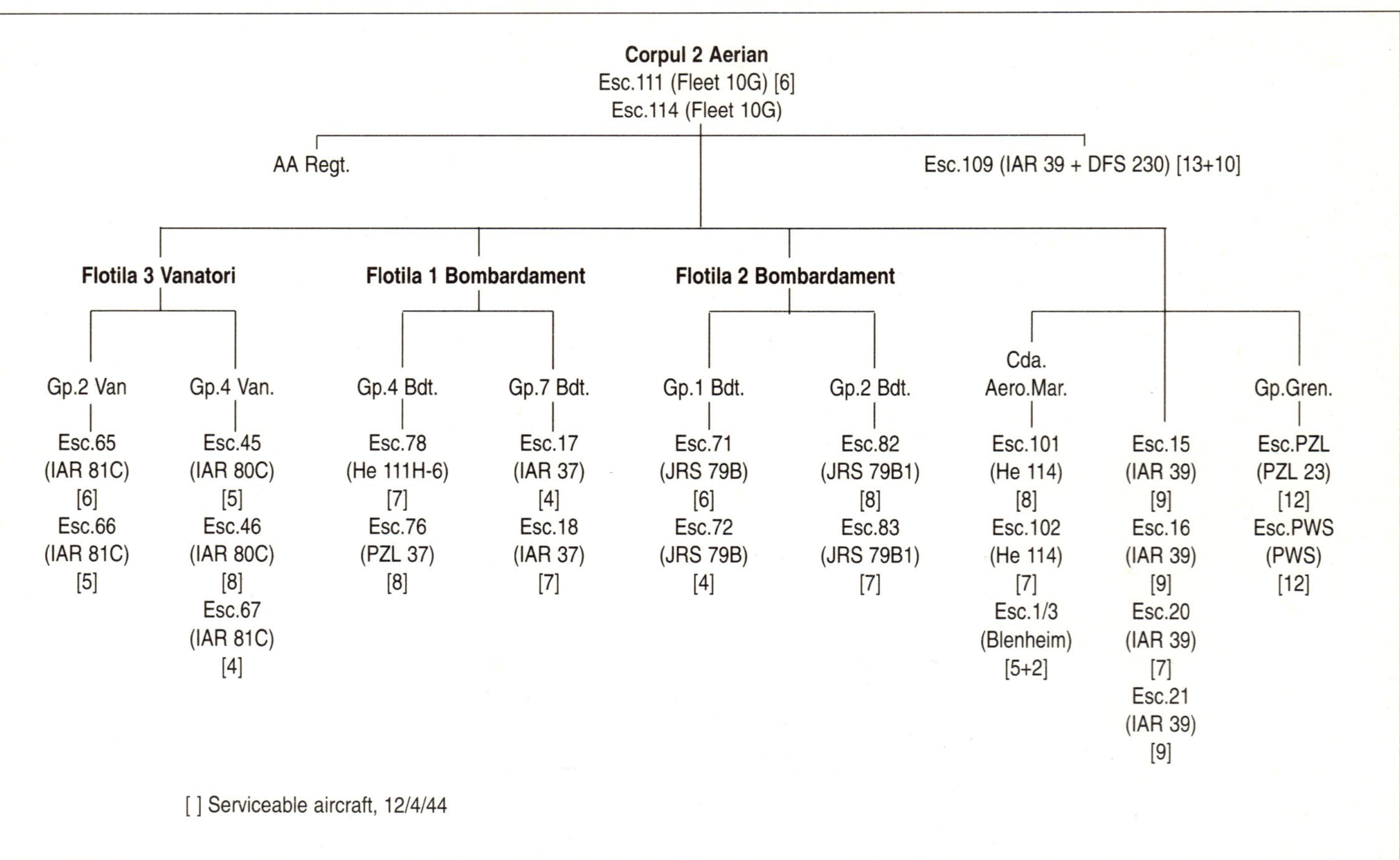
Corpul 2 Aerian
Esc.111 (Fleet 10G) [6]
Esc.114 (Fleet 10G)
AA Regt.
Esc.109 (IAR 39 + DFS 230) [13+10]
Flotila 3 Vanatori
Flotila 1 Bombardament
Flotila 2 Bombardament
Gp.2 Van
Esc.65
(IAR 81C)
[6]
Esc.66
(IAR 81C)
[5]
Gp.4 Van.
Esc.45
(IAR 80C)
[5]
Esc.46
(IAR 80C)
[8]
Esc.67
(IAR 81C)
[4]
Gp.4 Bdt.
Esc.78
(He 111H-6)
[7]
Esc.76
(PZL 37)
[8]
Gp.7 Bdt.
Esc.17
(IAR 37)
[4]
Esc.18
(IAR 37)
[7]
Gp.1 Bdt.
Esc.71
(JRS 79B)
[6]
Esc.72
(JRS 79B)
[4]
Gp.2 Bdt.
Esc.82
(JRS 79B1)
[8]
Esc.83
(JRS 79B1)
[7]
Cda.
Aero.Mar.
Esc.101
(He 114)
[8]
Esc.102
(He 114)
[7]
Esc.1/3
(Blenheim)
[5+2]
Esc.15
(IAR 39)
[9]
Esc.16
(IAR 39)
[9]
Esc.20
(IAR 39)
[7]
Esc.21
(IAR 39)
[9]
Gp.Gren.
Esc.PZL
(PZL 23)
[12]
Esc.PWS
(PWS)
[12]
[ ] Serviceable aircraft, 12/4/44

Although the Soviets had been halted just inside the Romanian border by the Germans, with the support of the newly re-fielded 3rd and 4th Romanian Armies, both Germans and Romanians expected the Red Army shortly to renew its attack into Romania proper. In fact the Soviets intended to attack the German Army Group Centre in Poland, but as part of their deception plans they feigned the preparation of a major offensive on the Basarabian Front in late May and early June 1944. Convinced that these were genuine preparations to overrun Romania, Corpul 1 Aerian and Corpul 2 Aerian responded with their heaviest sortie rate of the war.

On 30 May, 4 reconnaissance, 129 fighter, 83 Hs 129 and 260 bomber sorties were flown on the Eastern Front for the loss of four Ju 87s, three JRS 79Bs and an IAR 81. The following day a further 300 sorties of all types were flown on the Eastern Front and dozens of fighter sorties were put up against a major US air raid on the interior. The tempo remained high into early June, when the Soviet threat subsided. Corpul 2 Aerian saw a serious decline in serviceability during these operations, especially among its vulnerable medium bombers.

During the remainder of June, July and most of August 1944 the Basarabian front was quiet, and it was used as a rest area for IAR 81C units depleted in opposing USAAF bomber raids on Romania. Encounters with the Soviets became occasional as the Red Air Force was largely redeployed to Byelorussia and the FARR was being conserved to oppose the expected final Soviet offensive on Romania. However, they did prove that well-handled IAR 81Cs could still hold their own against the more modern Soviet fighters. For example, on 6 August four IAR 81Cs intercepted a mixed formation of twelve Lagg-5s, Yak-9s and Il-2s, and although they only claimed one probable and a damaged, they also suffered no loss themselves and broke up the raid. It thus became clear in the summer of 1944 that, although the IAR 81C could not expect to gain air superiority over more modern Soviet fighters, it could still contest the air with them on secondary fronts, and it continued to enjoy occasional success against Soviet bombers.

However, the strategic situation was changing rapidly, and the German air fleet charged with air operations over Romania, Luftflotte 4, which had had 845 aircraft at the time of the Soviet feint in early June, had been reduced to only 200 by July as its units were transferred to shore up the fronts in France and Poland. This made the FARR the largest Axis air formation in the theatre. On 30 June Corpul 1 Aerian was allocated to the defence of Southern Basarabia in support of Army Group Dumitrescu, which included the Romanian 3rd Army. Corpul 2 Aerian was redesignated Corpul 3 Aerian and assigned to support II Corps, which was charged with the defence of the coast and Danube Delta. Flotila 1 Vanatori was by now regularly engaged in putting up over half of the Axis sorties flown against the mass US air raids on the interior. The Luftwaffe provided most air support for the Romanian 4th Army.

By late July the Soviets were finally preparing their offensive into Romania opposite both 3rd and 4th Armies. August was used to rest Escadrila 2, the Ju 88D-1 long-range reconnaissance squadron, and it flew only two operational sorties during the first nineteen days, but by mid-August IAR 39s were flying about ten tactical reconnaissance sorties a day and fighters about 25, and Soviet preparations were confirmed well before they launched their offensive on 20 August.

In response, the FARR flew 161 sorties on the Eastern Front on 20 August, rising to 304 on the 21st (11 army co-operation, 159 fighter, 72 bomber and 62 by Hs 129) and 305 on the 22nd (10 army co-operation, 133 fighter, 116 bomber and 46 by Hs 129). By contrast, the Luftwaffe apparently flew 230 sorties on 20 August and declined thereafter. By 23 August the Soviet advance had forced Corpul 1 Aerian to abandon its forward airfields and it had fallen back on those occupied by Corpul 3 Aerian. As a result of this and the political confusion surrounding Romania's defection from the Axis, only 56 sorties were recorded that day, although considerably more were certainly flown.

The opposing Soviet air presence, 1,760 aircraft strong, was numerically overwhelming, and on the 21st put up 1,569 sorties. On the 20th more than half of the Romanian fighter sorties resulted in combat with the Soviets, three-quarters of the engaged Romanian fighters being IAR 81Cs and the remainder Bf 109Gs. They had great difficulty breaking through the large numbers of Soviet fighters to reach their bombers and ground-attack aircraft, but three Lagg-3s, a Yak-7 and an Il-2 were claimed for the loss of two IAR 81Cs. Romanian bombers also had difficulty penetrating to their targets, and a Ju 87, a Ju 88 and an Hs 129 were lost as well. On the 21st nine Soviet aircraft were claimed in air combat, but one fighter and three Ju 87s were lost supporting 1st Armoured Division. The Romanian records for the these and the following days are incomplete, and there are no records of Romanian AA claims for the period.

ROMANIAN ACES

Romania's leading aces had built up significant scores with the Bf 109 on the Eastern Front without serious losses amongst themselves. Indeed, the highest-scoring ace lost before 1944, Tiberiu Vinca (16+ victories), had reportedly been shot down in error by a German Ju 88 he was joining as escort in November 1943.

Unfortunately, Romanian fighter pilots are such individualists that to this day they cannot agree a definitive list of aces. Furthermore, their scores are somewhat confused owing to two major changes in scoring. From evidence of Soviet losses gained after the fall of Odessa in 1941, it became apparent that Romanian pilots were being consistently over-credited with victories. A far more demanding system of confirmation, stricter than that employed by the Germans, was in force during 1942 and 1943, but during 1944 a new system of crediting victories was introduced to encourage Romanian pilots to press home their attacks on USAAF bombers. This awarded one victory for a single-engined kill, two for a twin-engined kill and three for a four-engined kill.

The new system was applied retrospectively, with the result that two different league tables of Romanian aces are possible. It seems that, at the time of his death on 18 August 1944, Capitan Alexandru Şerbanescu, commander of Grup 9 Vanatori, may have downed the highest number of opponents, 45, but that this seems to have registered as 52 under the 1944 scoring system. Capitan 'Buzu' Cantacuzino of Grup 9 Vanatori seems to have scored 43 confirmed victories (registered as 56 under the 1944 system) and 10 (14) probables by 26 August 1944, and several more afterwards. Cantacuzino's unique distinction may be that he was the only pilot to become an ace against the USAAF, Red Air Force and Luftwaffe.

The third-ranking aces seem to have been Sub-Locotenent Milu and Dan Vizante, whose 32 victories by July 1944 apparently registered as 40 and 39 respectively under the 1944 system. Vizante, the commander of Grup 6 Vanatori, had the further distinction of having scored most of his victories flying the IAR 80. Other aces, all from Grup 9 Vanatori (with their unadjusted scores as at July 1944), included Adjutant Mucenica (24), Locotenent Greceanu (20) and Capitan Popescu-Ciocanel (12). There were undoubtedly several other Bf 109 aces with more than ten victories. A considerable, but indeterminate, number of pilots gained between five and ten victories, at least two of whom flew Hurricanes.

When comparing the scores of Romanian and German aces on the Eastern Front, it is as well to recall that the Germans consistently received more-advanced aircraft earlier than the Romanians, spent longer deployed on more active battle fronts and were less often given constricting escort missions.

JUNE 1942 TO AUGUST 1943: EARLY USAAF BOMBER RAIDS

Pressurised by Germany into a display of Axis solidarity with Japan, Antonescu had declared war on the USA on 12 December 1941. The Americans did not reciprocate until 6 June 1942. Six days later Romania discovered why. On 12 June 1942 Romania had the doubtful honour of being the recipient of the first American air raid of the war in Europe, when twelve B-24s of Halpro Force bombed Ploieşti from Fayid in Egypt. No aircraft were lost, but on their return flight, to Habbaniya in Iraq, four of the bombers ran out of fuel over Turkey and were interned there. The surprise raid was primarily a propaganda exercise, equivalent to the Doolittle raid on Japan, and damage was negligible. However, it meant that just as the imminent fall of Sevastopol was about to eliminate the Soviet bomber threat to Ploieşti, the USAAF renewed the attacks. As a result the Romanians and Germans had to continue to extend the defences of Bucharest and Ploieşti throughout the war, and most of the newly-forming IAR 81C groups became tied down defensively. The next USAAF raid paid the price.

The Halpro operation was not immediately repeated because there were no Allied air bases within practical range. However, by mid-1943 the occupation of nearer airfields at Benghazi in North Africa made a more serious raid possible, and on 1 August 1943 178 B-24s attacked Ploieşti at low level. Fifty-three B-24s were lost, eight of them being interned in Turkey, and 55 were damaged. It was proportionally the most expensive major Allied air raid of the war, and was the last operation mounted by the battered US Ninth Air Force in the theatre. The Romanians put up 59 sorties from Escadrile 61 and 62 (IAR 80B), Escadrila 45 (IAR 80C), Escadrila 53 (Bf 109G) and Escadrila 68 (Bf 110), and claimed twenty confirmed or probable victories for the loss of one IAR 80B and one Bf 110. Romanian AA guns claimed a further fifteen. German losses from 89 sorties were five aircraft. If optimistic, the Romanian claims were clearly not outrageously so, and compared favourably with the sevenfold-plus exaggerations which USAAF bomber crews were to claim on this and subsequent raids. Oil production was not irrecoverably damaged, but took eight months to restore fully, at which point USAAF raids really began in earnest.

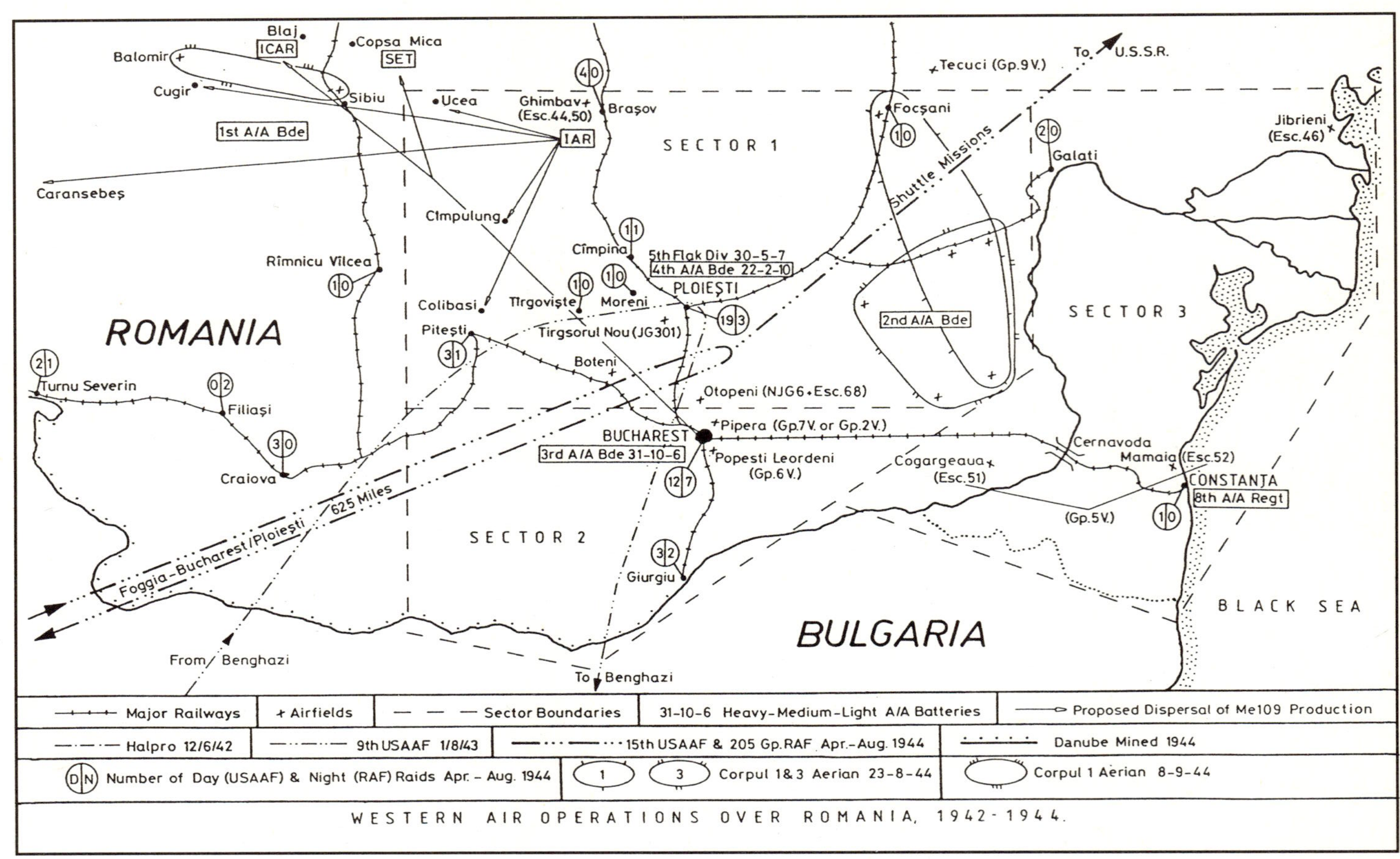

WESTERN AIR OPERATIONS OVER ROMANIA, 1942-1944.

ROMANIAN HOME DEFENCE PREPARATIONS, 1943–1944

As the Germans controlled the Balkan radar defences, they were in effective operational control of Romania's fighter defences. On 8 March 1944 they agreed to the immediate delivery of twenty Würzburg radar sets to the Romanians, and crews were trained in their operation, but it is not clear whether any became operational. Night-fighter cover was provided by the German NJG6 (Bf 110), based at Otopeni, to which the Romanian Escadrila 68 (Bf 110C-3 and F–4) was attached.

In 1943–44 home defence was divided into three sectors. Sector 1, in immediate defence of the Ploieşti oilfields so vital to the Reich, was largely German and had JG301 permanently based at Tigşorul Nou and usually a second fighter group on satellite airfields. It could also call upon the old IAR 80Bs and IAR 81As of Escadrile 44 and 50 (formerly Grup 3 Vanatori) at the Romanian fighter school at Ghimbav, and the factory defence squadron at IAR-Braşov. Sector 2, focused on Bucharest, the capital, was exclusively Romanian. In early April 1944 its Grup 6 Vanatori (Esc.59, 61, 62) was based at Popeşti-Leordeni, while Grup 7 Vanatori (Esc.53, 57, 58) was at Pipera. Both were experienced IAR 81C units, but the latter had begun a rapid reconversion to the Bf 109G-2 in mid-March which was completed during April.

Sectors 1 and 2 were mutually supporting against western raids, but Sector 3, covering Constanţa and the Danube Delta, was more orientated towards the Soviet bomber threat. Constanţa was covered by Grup 5 Vanatori (Esc.51, 52), based at Jegalia and Mamaia with a mixture of old Bf 109Es and IAR 81s, while the remains of Grup 4 Bopi (Esc.45, 46) covered the Danube Delta with its IAR 80Cs from Jibrieni and Leipzig (in southern Basarabia). From April 1944 various Luftwaffe and Corpul 1 Aerian fighter units facing the nearby Eastern Front were also periodically on call, especially against the shuttle raids the USAAF mounted back and forth between Italy and the USSR in June, July and August.

The Germans and Romanians also shared AA defence. The German 5th Flak Division (30 heavy, 5 medium and 7 light batteries on 23 August 1944) was concentrated around Ploieşti. However, half of its manpower was Romanian, and it served beside the Romanian 4th AA Brigade (22 heavy, 2 medium and 10 light batteries in October 1943 and stronger by August 1944), which was fully equipped with modern German 88mm, 37mm and 20mm AA guns. Ploieşti was thus the third or fourth most heavily defended target in Axis Europe after Berlin and Vienna or the Ruhr. Bucharest was defended by the Romanian 3rd AA Brigade with 31 heavy, 10 medium and 6 light batteries.

In August 1944 2nd AA Brigade (14 heavy and 15 medium and light batteries) was responsible for the defence of the airfields of Corpul 1 Aerian and Corpul 3 Aerian, and 8th AA Regiment defended the port and naval base of Constanţa in the east of the country. The 1st AA Brigade's responsibilities in the west of the country included the defence of the IAR factory at Braşov. Owing to the importance of Ploieşti to their war economy, the Germans had trained and equipped 4th AA Brigade more intensively than any other part of the Romanian armed forces, and its standard was high. 1st, 2nd and 3rd AA Brigades were less effective because they were largely equipped with older Romanian-built Vickers 75mm and Rheinmetall

37mm AA guns or imports and captures. By August 1944 the Romanian AA artillery had 101 heavy batteries and 74 medium and light batteries manned by 36,741 men.

APRIL TO AUGUST 1944: THE FINAL ALLIED BOMBER OFFENSIVE

The occupation of still nearer bases, around Foggia in southern Italy, was necessary before regular Allied raids on Romania could begin. From January 1944 invulnerable South African Mosquitoes began a comprehensive photo-reconnaissance of Romanian targets. Then, between 5 April and 19 August 1944, the US 15th Air Force flew nineteen heavy bomber raids totalling 5,479 sorties against oil targets around Ploieşti, and several thousand other heavy bomber sorties in 22 raids against railway yards, railway bridges, oil pipelines, oil storage depots and industrial targets across the rest of the country – Bucharest being hit particularly often. The raiders were accompanied by thousands of fighter escorts. The IAR-Braşov factory building was severely damaged, but the dispersal of the aircraft industry prevented serious loss of plant. Although production was interrupted, it was never completely halted.

Simultaneously, the RAF's 205 Group conducted fifteen night bomber raids from Italy over Romania with similar target priorities to the USAAF day bombers, and additionally laid about 1,400 magnetic mines in the Danube above the oil loading terminal at Giurgiu on two other missions. In just one month the mines reportedly sank 39 small vessels and barges and increasingly paralysed river traffic. In 1,057 sorties the RAF lost 44 bombers to AA, night fighters and accidents. Escadrila 68, as the junior Axis night fighter unit available, was apparently given secondary tasks by the German controllers, and claimed no victories at night.

By August Romanian oil production was reduced to 20 per cent of capacity, and the movement of even this was paralysed. However, this success was not achieved cheaply. Raids on Ploieşti in 1944 alone cost the USAAF 223 heavy bombers – a proportional loss higher than that suffered over Germany, which was recognised by the award of more Medals of Honor than for any other target. When bomber losses over other Romanian targets and fighter losses are added, the total USAAF losses probably exceeded 300 aircraft in 1944. By 23 August 1944 at least 2,829 US aircrew had been lost and 1,123 of them taken POW by the Romanians. The prisoners alone totalled more than the FARR's total front-line aircrew.

As over half the AA and air defences were Romanian, a similar proportion of US losses are reasonably attributable to them. Romanian fighters claimed 197 victories, which is probably more than twice their actual total, and the AA at least 76. However, such a level of overscoring compares favourably with US overclaims over Romania. Romanian fighter losses between 5 April and 19 August, including a few on the Eastern Front, were at least 45 and may have exceeded 50, and approximately twice as many were damaged. Yet the USAAF claimed 41 Romanian and German fighters over Romania on 5 April alone. Although the USAAF and RAF did not bomb Romanian population centres in the deliberate way they did in Germany, their inability to achieve pinpoint accuracy when attacking specific industrial and communications targets within Romanian cities led to the deaths of 7,693 civilians and the wounding of another 7,809. In Ploieşti alone, 23,260 were made homeless. The result was a counterproductive hardening of attitudes in a population largely sympathetic to the Western Allies.

However, serious as the overwhelming USAAF raids on Ploieşti were for the German war economy, of more immediate concern to the Romanians was the imminent threat of Russian invasion. Thus on 20 April, when USAAF air raids were already under way, most of the Bf 109Gs of Grupul 7 Vanatori (Esc.53, 57) were transferred to the threatened Eastern Front. They were replaced at Pipera by the largely inexperienced Grup 2 Vanatori (Esc.58, 65, 66). Thus, until early June, the IAR 81Cs of Grupuri 2 and 6 Vanatori were the main Romanian defence against the USAAF. Only Escadrila 58 flew the Bf 109G.

Grup 2 Vanatori Sorties against the USAAF, 1944

			Claims			
Date	Sorties	Attacking	Victories	Probables	Losses	Damaged
21/4	34	13	4	-	4 IAR 81C	-
24/4	27	25	6	1	-	2 IAR 81C
5/5	25	21	10	3	1 IAR 81C 1 Bf 109G	3 IAR 81C
6/5	23	18	11	3	-	3 IAR 81C
7/5	22	22	2	1	-	4 IAR 81C
18/5	16	16	2	1	1 IAR 81C	1 IAR 81C

What was remarkable was not the somewhat exaggerated successes claimed by the two groups, but the fact that so few of their outclassed IAR 81Cs were downed in these actions. Nevertheless, their cumulative losses were considerable in the unequal contest. Therefore, once the expected Soviet ground assault on Romania had proved to be a feint, it was decided to withdraw the remaining IAR 81Cs to the less demanding Eastern Front. On 30 May Grup 2 Vanatori, less Escadrila 58, was transferred to Corpul 1 Aerian at Bacau-Gheraeşti (where it was joined by Escadrila 67) in exchange for the return of the Bf 109Gs of Grup 7 Vanatori (Esc.53, 57), to which Escadrila 58 was added. Grup 6 Vanatori began conversion to newly delivered Bf 109G–4s and G-6s. Grupuri 7 and 6 Vanatori carried the main burden of interior air defence during June and July, supported increasingly from 6 June by interventions against US shuttle missions to and from the USSR by the élite Grup 9 Vanatori (Bf 109G-6) facing the Eastern Front at Tecuci.

Grupuri 6 and 9 claimed eighteen victories between them on 10 June when they bounced a low-level raid on Ploieşti by 46 bomb-carrying Lightnings and their 48 Lightning fighter escorts. This was probably the IAR 81C's finest hour, for Grup 6 Vanatori managed to ambush and shoot down several Lightnings as they strafed their airfield at Popeşti-Leordeni. US losses that day were 22 Lightnings from all causes, including AA and the Luftwaffe. US pilots claimed 23 aerial victories, but the Romanians lost only a single aircraft on 10 June. However, on 23 June the ace Tudor Greceanu (20+) of Grupul 6 was downed and wounded.

On 22 July the USAAF began a series of fighter-bomber shuttle missions to and from the USSR. On that day 58 P-51s and 76 P-38s strafed Romanian airfields around Buzau, en route to Russia. Grupul 9 Vanatori at Tecuci was in the direct path, and claimed six Lightnings without loss – a score which agrees with known American losses. On this day, American claims of 21 confirmed and probable victories bore no relation to Romanian reality. On 26 July sixteen Bf 109Gs of Grupul 9 Vanatori intercepted 98 returning American fighters and claimed a further ten US aircraft, but lost seven themselves. On the same day the Americans claimed 20 victories but lost only two aircraft themselves. On this occasion it was Romanian claims that bore little relation to American reality. The anomalies on both sides may partly be accounted for by unknown Luftwaffe claims and losses, but it seems probable that there remained considerable overclaiming on both sides.

Although only one Romanian pilot was killed outright on 26 July, several of the country's best pilots were wounded, including the aces Captain Popescu Ciocanel (12+ victories), who later died of his burns, and Adjutant Mucenica (24+ victories). Grupul 9 Vanatori was commended by the Germans for its determination in these two actions. On 3 August the group, now down to only thirteen serviceable aircraft, was transferred to Popeşti-Leordeni in the interior. This was ostensibly to face the American heavy bombers, but the timing also coincides with Antonescu's preparations to prevent a German coup during his last visit to Hitler.

As a result of its move, Grup 9 Vanatori missed raids by a second American fighter-bomber force of 77 aircraft operating from the USSR. On 4 and 6 August they attacked Axis airfields around Buzau and Focşani to soften-up air defences before the final Soviet assault on Romania later that month. Only one of the twelve American aircraft lost on 4 August was claimed by Romanians. The rest fell to the Luftwaffe, which was badly hit itself. The Americans' return flight to Italy on 8 August appears to have been virtually unopposed by either the FARR or Luftwaffe, and they claimed only one Axis aircraft. Unfortunately this seems to have been Romania's third highest-scoring ace, Ion Milu (32+ victories), who was wounded.

The American independent fighter-bomber missions of 10, 22 and 26 July and 4, 6 and 8 August had been expensive for all concerned. On 8 August the Americans called off such missions over Romania because, '...strafing attacks are made too costly by battle damage and losses'. They seem to have been unaware of the serious damage they had done to the cream of the FARR and the local Luftwaffe.

On 5 August Hitler admitted to Antonescu that the Luftwaffe could not guarantee to regain air supremacy over Romania. Probably as a consequence, the Romanian Air Ministry secretly ordered a suspension of fighter operations against the Americans on 7 August because irreplaceable losses of senior pilots were being incurred with no reasonable prospect of breaking through the US fighter screen to cause serious disruption of their heavy bomber formations. Aircrew were to be conserved to oppose the imminent Soviet offensive. The American raids on Ploieşti on 10 and 17 August therefore met no effective Romanian (or German) fighter opposition.

Because Grupuri 7 and 9 Vanatori had been so conspicuously active earlier, Gerstenberg soon detected the change in Romanian policy. Failing to persuade the air ministry, he appealed directly to the sense of honour of Grup 9 Vanatori's charismatic commander, Alexandru Serbanescu. As a result, the Romanians and Germans put up 27 and 19 sorties respectively on 18 August in a last-ditch effort. However, the wisdom of the earlier suspension was confirmed when Serbanescu was shot down and killed. The last USAAF raid on 19 August was unopposed by either Romanians or

Germans, and on the following day the operations of Grup 7 Vanatori and Grup 9 Vanatori were switched back to the Eastern Front to oppose the Soviet breakthrough on that day.

Although they added US aircraft to their scores in 1944, Romania's leading Bf 109 aces were shot down themselves one by one. The superior performance of the Mustang and the enormous numerical superiority of the USAAF made their task virtually impossible. The task of the less experienced IAR 81C pilots was virtually suicidal, although they did have some success against Lightnings at low level and their aircraft were still sufficiently well armed to shoot down heavy bombers on the increasingly rare occasions when they managed to break through the fighter screens. Neither the Luftwaffe nor the FARR were able to cause significant disruption to the American heavy bombers over Romania in 1944, but they did have the consolation of mauling several American low-level fighter sweeps.

THE FARR ON 23 AUGUST 1944

On 23 August the FARR, exclusive of the AA artillery, was 37,196 men strong and was organised as tabulated overleaf.

1st Army on the western frontier with Hungary had available only Escadrila 111 with ten Fleet 10Gs and Escadrila 20 with twelve IAR 39s. The latter had been engaged in spotting groups of Tito's Yugoslav partisans who had been using Romanian territory as sanctuary from German drives. Also in the region at the Fighter School at Ghimbav were Escadrilas 44 and 50 with 35 mostly unserviceable IAR 80Bs and IAR 81As between them.

In the interior were a further 1,094 training aircraft, many of them obsolete combat types. These included Grup 4 Bombardament's Escadrila 75 with Potez 63B2s, Escadrila 76 with PZL 37s and an unnumbered squadron with ten PZL 23s. Under the Statul Major al Aerului were the communications Escadrila 115 and the Escadrilas 105 and 107 of the Grup Aerotransport. Also in the interior was Grup 11 Asalt's Escadrila 38, forming with the Hs 129.

AUGUST 1944: SECURING BUCHAREST

Late on 23 August Romania left the Axis and sued for peace. Confusion reigned for several days, and fighting gradually broke out between Romanian and German personnel on shared airfields. Luftflotte 4 later calculated that it had lost 376 aircraft and 1,723 aero engines in Romania. The Romanians captured 228 Luftwaffe aircraft in various states of repair, but 161 Romanian aircraft were also lost. Most of the latter were non-combat types, but among them were 27 of Grup 6 Picaj's new Ju 87D-5s and Escadrila 68's eight Bf 110s on German-held airfields at Focşani and Otopeni.

However, most of Corpul 1 Aerian was on its own airfields, and in a desperate effort to secure or sabotage all of the German aircraft in its inventory the Germans planned to land a Ju 52 loaded with seventeen Brandenburg commandos by surprise at each of its four main airfields, including Ivesti (Grup 3 Bombardament, Grupuri 7 and 9 Vanatori) and Ianca (Grup 8 Asalt, Esc.78), in the early afternoon of 24 August. In the event, Brandenburgers only disembarked at Tandarei (Grupuri 1, 2

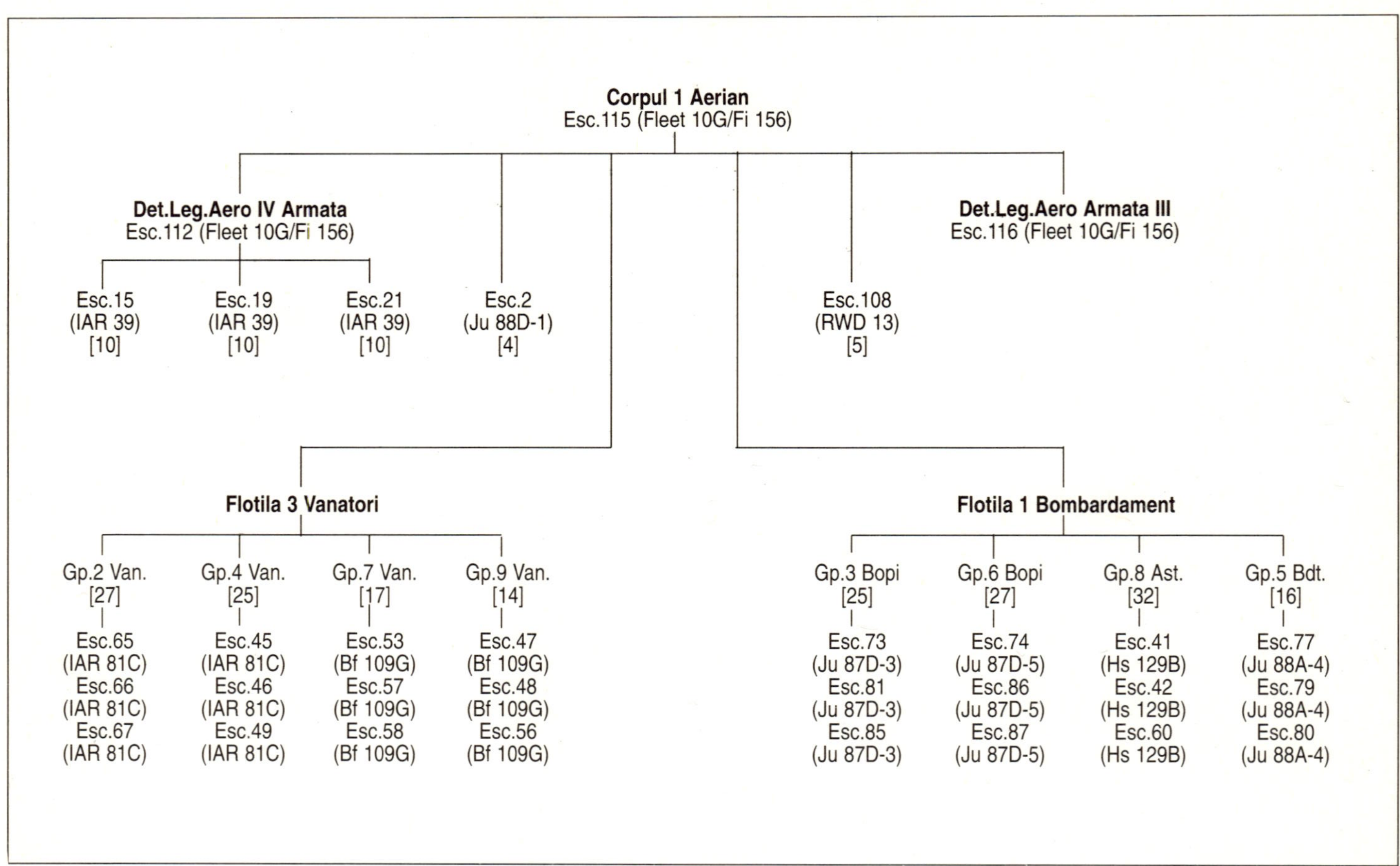
Corpul 1 Aerian
Esc.115 (Fleet 10G/Fi 156)
Det.Leg.Aero IV Armata
Esc.112 (Fleet 10G/Fi 156)
Esc.15
(IAR 39)
[10]
Esc.19
(IAR 39)
[10]
Esc.21
(IAR 39)
[10]
Esc.2
(Ju 88D-1)
[4]
Esc.108
(RWD 13)
[5]
Det.Leg.Aero Armata III
Esc.116 (Fleet 10G/Fi 156)
Flotila 3 Vanatori
Gp.2 Van.
[27]
Esc.65
(IAR 81C)
Esc.66
(IAR 81C)
Esc.67
(IAR 81C)
Gp.4 Van.
[25]
Esc.45
(IAR 81C)
Esc.46
(IAR 81C)
Esc.49
(IAR 81C)
Gp.7 Van.
[17]
Esc.53
(Bf 109G)
Esc.57
(Bf 109G)
Esc.58
(Bf 109G)
Gp.9 Van.
[14]
Esc.47
(Bf 109G)
Esc.48
(Bf 109G)
Esc.56
(Bf 109G)
Flotila 1 Bombardament
Gp.3 Bopi
[25]
Esc.73
(Ju 87D-3)
Esc.81
(Ju 87D-3)
Esc.85
(Ju 87D-3)
Gp.6 Bopi
[27]
Esc.74
(Ju 87D-5)
Esc.86
(Ju 87D-5)
Esc.87
(Ju 87D-5)
Gp.8 Ast.
[32]
Esc.41
(Hs 129B)
Esc.42
(Hs 129B)
Esc.60
(Hs 129B)
Gp.5 Bdt.
[16]
Esc.77
(Ju 88A-4)
Esc.79
(Ju 88A-4)
Esc.80
(Ju 88A-4)

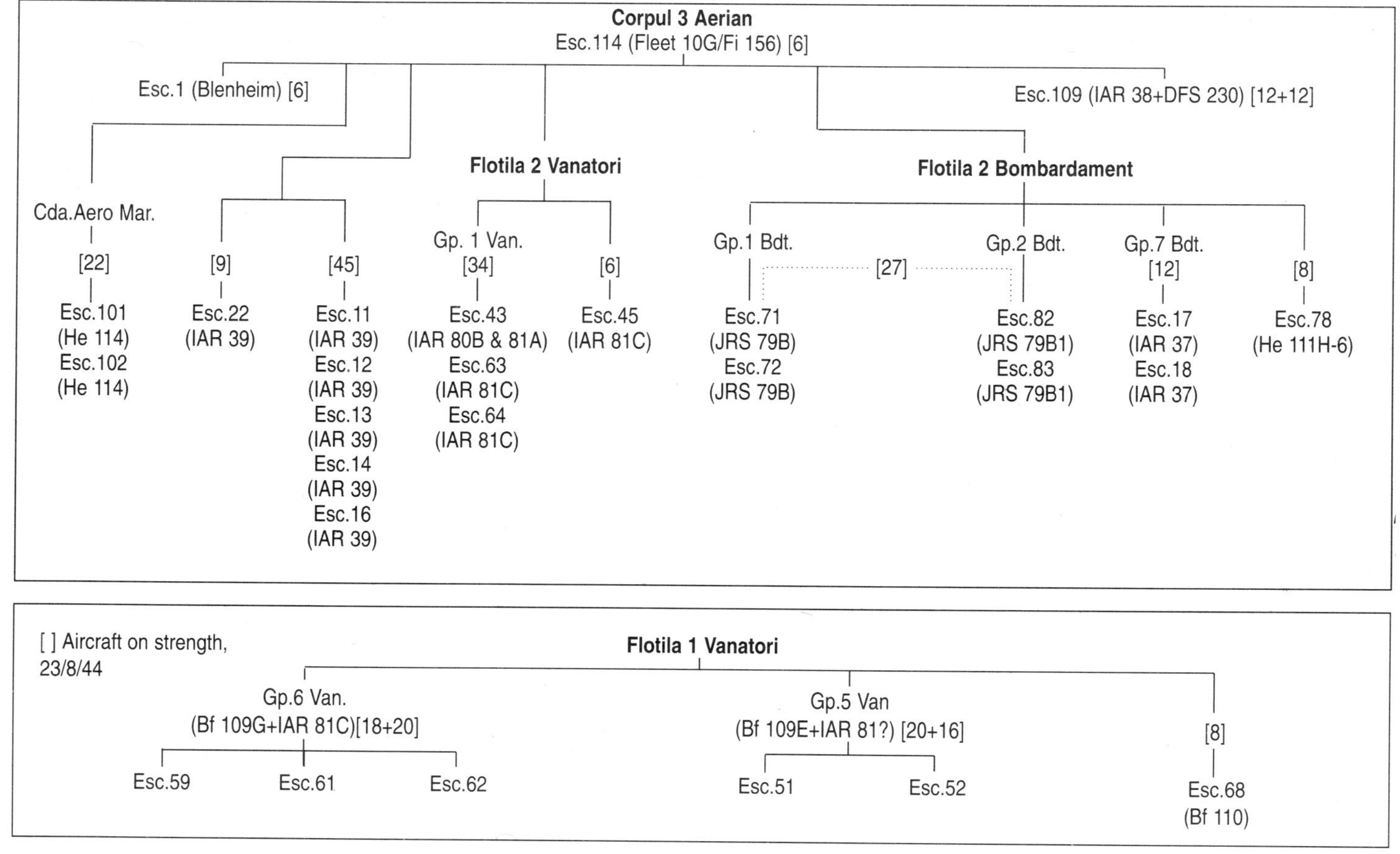
Corpul 3 Aerian
Esc.114 (Fleet 10G/Fi 156) [6]
Esc.1 (Blenheim) [6]
Esc.109 (IAR 38+DFS 230) [12+12]
Flotila 2 Vanatori
Flotila 2 Bombardament
Cda.Aero Mar.
[22]
Esc.101
(He 114)
Esc.102
(He 114)
[9]
Esc.22
(IAR 39)
[45]
Esc.11
(IAR 39)
Esc.12
(IAR 39)
Esc.13
(IAR 39)
Esc.14
(IAR 39)
Esc.16
(IAR 39)
Gp. 1 Van.
[34]
Esc.43
(IAR 80B & 81A)
Esc.63
(IAR 81C)
Esc.64
(IAR 81C)
[6]
Esc.45
(IAR 81C)
Gp.1 Bdt.
Esc.71
(JRS 79B)
Esc.72
(JRS 79B)
[27]
Gp.2 Bdt.
Esc.82
(JRS 79B1)
Esc.83
(JRS 79B1)
Gp.7 Bdt.
[12]
Esc.17
(IAR 37)
Esc.18
(IAR 37)
[8]
Esc.78
(He 111H-6)
[ ] Aircraft on strength,
23/8/44
Flotila 1 Vanatori
Gp.6 Van.
(Bf 109G+IAR 81C)[18+20]
Esc.59
Esc.61
Esc.62
Gp.5 Van
(Bf 109E+IAR 81?) [20+16]
Esc.51
Esc.52
[8]
Esc.68
(Bf 110)

and 5 Bombardament, Esc.2) and Boteni (Grup Aerotransport), and all were quickly killed or captured without inflicting any significant damage.

However, as the Red Air Force continued to attack Romanian aircraft and shot down two unarmed HD 42s, most of the FARR was grounded until co-operation arrangements could be made. Consequently, few bombing missions were flown for the rest of the month. Exceptions were Grup 7 Bombardament Usor's IAR 37s at Ciocirlia, which repeatedly bombed German vessels retreating up the Danube lest they tried to sabotage the vital Cernavoda railway bridge carrying the 9th Infantry Division to the aid of the capital, and Escadrila 78, whose He 111H-6s bombed German vessels higher up the Danube.

Within Romania the German 5th Flak Division managed to secure the two main German airfields defending the oilfields, the night fighter base at Otopeni, north of Bucharest, and the day fighter base at Tirgşorul Nou, near Ploieşti. Through these they were initially able to supply both of their two main pockets of troops in the interior. From them they also began bombing Bucharest early on 24 August. Although the Romanian AA response in opposing both German air and ground attacks was energetic on 24 August, Romanian aerial response was almost non-existent until the 4th Parachute Battalion and air force security companies could secure the vital airfields around the capital by rounding up their German technical, administrative and AA complements.

By 25 August some airfields were secure, and Grup 7 Vanatori and Grup 9 Vanatori were deployed immediately to Boteni and Popeşti-Leordeni for the defence of the capital. Captain Buzu Cantacuzino, the highest-scoring Romanian ace, shot down three German He 111s in the following days, before being sent to Italy on the 27th to liaise with the USAAF on the air evacuation of their POWs. On 25-26 August the parachute battalion of the Brandenburg Division was flown in to Otopeni to join General Gerstenberg's ground attack on Bucharest, but lost entire platoons when some of its transports were shot down by Romanian fighters and AA. The following day Otopeni airfield was recaptured by the Romanians, and Gerstenberg's force was doomed. Tirgşorul Nou airfield also fell on 27 August, cutting off the Ploieşti pocket. Both pockets surrendered within days.

Although prompt and energetic, the German response had been weak and, with few surviving aircraft left in the theatre and their local air bases falling quickly to Romanian ground forces, the Luftwaffe threat to Bucharest had subsided by the end of August. The Luftwaffe later calculated its losses at about 125 flying personnel, 4,500 ground staff, 8,565 AA personnel and 2,944 signals staff. The Brandenburg Division also lost an entire battalion in this ill-prepared operation.

By the time the front had stabilised near Romania's western border on 7 September, the Romanians had claimed 24 aerial victories, most of these being bombers or transports shot down near Bucharest in August. A further 35 were claimed by AA. Romanian combat losses are recorded as only four in the air and three on the ground, but to this must be added the very large number of aircraft lost in the ground fighting. Fifty-five of the 228 German aircraft captured were soon made airworthy, and were issued to Romanian units. However, most were those awaiting repair in Luftwaffe workshops. The Soviets confiscated others, including nine airworthy Fw 190s.

1944–1945: THE WESTERN CAMPAIGN

In early September Corpul 1 Aerian was rushed west to oppose the German-Hungarian offensives on the southern Carpathian passes. By 7 September Corpul 1 Aerian had emerged from the confusion with 210 operational aircraft based at Sibiu and Balomir:

The logistical problems facing the FARR were now enormous. Almost all of its most modern (though by no means state-of-the-art) combat aircraft had only been on loan from the Germans, so Romanian repair facilities and stocks of spares for them were limited. Fortunately most of Luftflotte 4's repair facilities and stocks of spares fell intact into Romanian hands, including much of its reserve of 1,377 new aero engines. Despite this windfall, modern German types necessarily came to form an ever-decreasing proportion of operational aircraft, and a succession of unit amalgamations had to take place. Grup 7 Vanatori was absorbed into Grup 9 Vanatori, the remains of Grup 6 Picaj was absorbed into Grup 3 Picaj, the incomplete Grup 11 Asalt waş absorbed into Grup 8 Asalt, Grup 5 Bombardament accepted the remaining operational He 111H-6s, and the two Ju 52 transport escadrile were combined. By 1945 Grup 3 Picaj and Grup 8 Asalt had to be amalgamated and Grup 5 Bombardament dissolved, its last Ju 88A-4s going to Escadrila 2 for reconnaissance and its last He 111H-6s going to the Grup Aerotransport.

Against this trend, Grup 1 Vanatori was converted from the IAR 81C to the Bf 109G over the winter. This was possible because of the large German Bf 109G-6 deliveries shortly before Romania's defection, the numerous damaged Bf 109Gs captured in August 1944 and the resumption of some Bf 109G production at IAR-Braşov, using the stock of new DB605 aero engines captured from Luftflotte 4 in August. Most of Grup 1 Vanatori's pilots were recently converted IAR 81C pilots, and were not accepted as equals by the seasoned veterans of Grup 9 Vanatori. The SET and ICAR factories also managed to produce small numbers of IAR 39As and Fi 156s, the latter also probably using captured engines.

Thus, whereas on 7 September German aircraft still comprised about 50 per cent of Corpul 1 Aerian's strength, they formed only about 30 per cent of its reduced force by 12 May 1945. All other foreign types were obsolete and lacking spares, so none returned to operational service. This once again threw the air force back on to the same ageing Romanian-built types that had been obsolescent as early as 1942. Although there was now no immediate possibility of producing new IAR 81Cs or JRS 79B1s, many IAR 80s and IAR 81s were overhauled and reissued, and sufficient JRS 79Bs and JRS 79B1s were refurbished to allow Grup 1 Bombardament (absorbing Grup 2 Bombardament) to join Corpul 1 Aerian later in 1944. By the end of the war about 70 per cent of the Corpul Aerian was Romanian-built.

Although AA fire was a continuing threat, Luftwaffe and Hungarian air activity was generally weak, and relatively few combats occurred. Sometimes IAR 80s still managed to hold their own, such as in an inconclusive clash between six IAR 80Bs and IAR 81As of Escadrila 44, a unit including several skilled instructors, and eight much superior Fw 190s on 7 September. However, on 25 September 1944 the true weakness of the IAR 81C was proved when, in three separate combats, a total of 26 of Grup 2 Vanatori's aircraft met seventeen German Bf 109Gs and lost five aircraft without making any claims themselves.

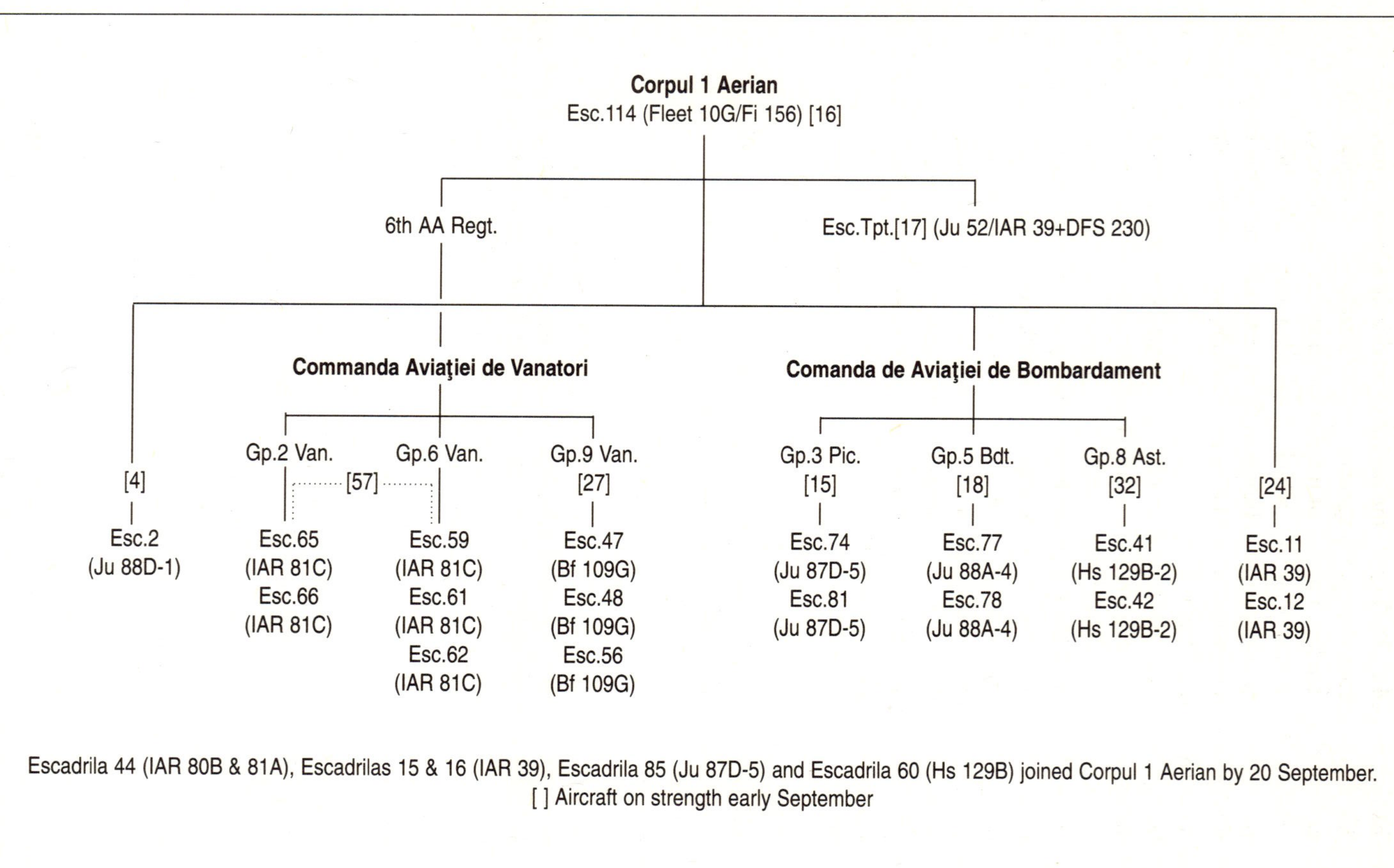
Corpul 1 Aerian
Esc.114 (Fleet 10G/Fi 156) [16]
6th AA Regt.
Esc.Tpt.[17] (Ju 52/IAR 39+DFS 230)
Commanda Aviaţiei de Vanatori
Comanda de Aviaţiei de Bombardament
[4]
Esc.2
(Ju 88D-1)
Gp.2 Van.
Gp.6 Van.
[57]
Esc.65
(IAR 81C)
Esc.66
(IAR 81C)
Esc.59
(IAR 81C)
Esc.61
(IAR 81C)
Esc.62
(IAR 81C)
Gp.9 Van.
[27]
Esc.47
(Bf 109G)
Esc.48
(Bf 109G)
Esc.56
(Bf 109G)
Gp.3 Pic.
[15]
Esc.74
(Ju 87D-5)
Esc.81
(Ju 87D-5)
Gp.5 Bdt.
[18]
Esc.77
(Ju 88A-4)
Esc.78
(Ju 88A-4)
Gp.8 Ast.
[32]
Esc.41
(Hs 129B-2)
Esc.42
(Hs 129B-2)
[24]
Esc.11
(IAR 39)
Esc.12
(IAR 39)
Escadrila 44 (IAR 80B & 81A), Escadrilas 15 & 16 (IAR 39), Escadrila 85 (Ju 87D-5) and Escadrila 60 (Hs 129B) joined Corpul 1 Aerian by 20 September.
[ ] Aircraft on strength early September

For the FARR there were five identifiable phases of campaign to the end of the war. The first was 24 to 31 August, the period immediately following the defection, when 336 fighter sorties were flown against German attacks on the capital. The second was 1 to 19 September, a period of reorganisation and reorientation of the Corpul 1 Aerian to western Romania which involved a mixture of offensive and defensive fighting against German-Hungarian counterattacks across the borders. A total of 1,220 sorties were flown and 177 tons of bombs were dropped, almost all in support of 4th Army in Transylvania.

The third phase was the liberation of Transylvania between 21 September and 24 October, which, as it concerned national territory, elicited a particularly high offensive effort from the FARR and considerable resultant attrition. A total of 2,420 sorties were flown and 340 tons of bombs were dropped. The subsequent campaign in Hungary (26 October to about the end of the year), saw a significant decline in Romania's air effort while much of the air force was refurbished at home over the winter. Only 805 sorties were flown and a mere 74 tons of bombs dropped. The Corpul Aerian was much strengthened by the time the final campaign in Czechoslovakia began in February 1945, but continuous operations led to a gradual decline in strength to the end of the war:

Date	Squadrons	A/C	Date	Squadrons	A/C
7 September	20	210	20 December	14	161
21 September	18	197	18 February	20	239
25 October	14	173	12 May	20	189

The organisation of the Corpul Aerian remained static throughout the Czechoslovak campaign, and by 12 May 1945 it had the strength shown in the diagram overleaf.

During the war against Germany in 1944–45 the FARR flew 8,542 sorties and dropped 1,350 tons of bombs; 176 aircraft were lost from all causes, in addition to the 161 lost on the ground in late August 1944. Personnel losses were 729 men, mostly during ground fighting in August. A total of 126 Axis aircraft were claimed in the air, on the ground or by AA, in addition to the 228 German aircraft captured on the ground in August 1944. Operations were greatly inhibited by the necessarily low serviceability of the increasingly cannibalised German types that formed the backbone of the bomber force, and the risks of flying Axis types alongside the Russians, with whom several clashes occurred. However, because the availability of foreign types once more declined as the campaign progressed, the importance of Romania's own aircraft industry was yet again emphasised.

CONCLUSION

Romania's rearmament in the 1930s had particularly emphasised the aircraft industry, and during the war years a considerable degree of self-sufficiency was achieved. Almost all army co-operation aircraft and trainers, most fighters and a significant proportion of medium bombers were locally designed and/or produced. Thus Romania probably had the distinction of having the smallest air force to achieve this level of self-sufficiency over an extended period during the Second World War.

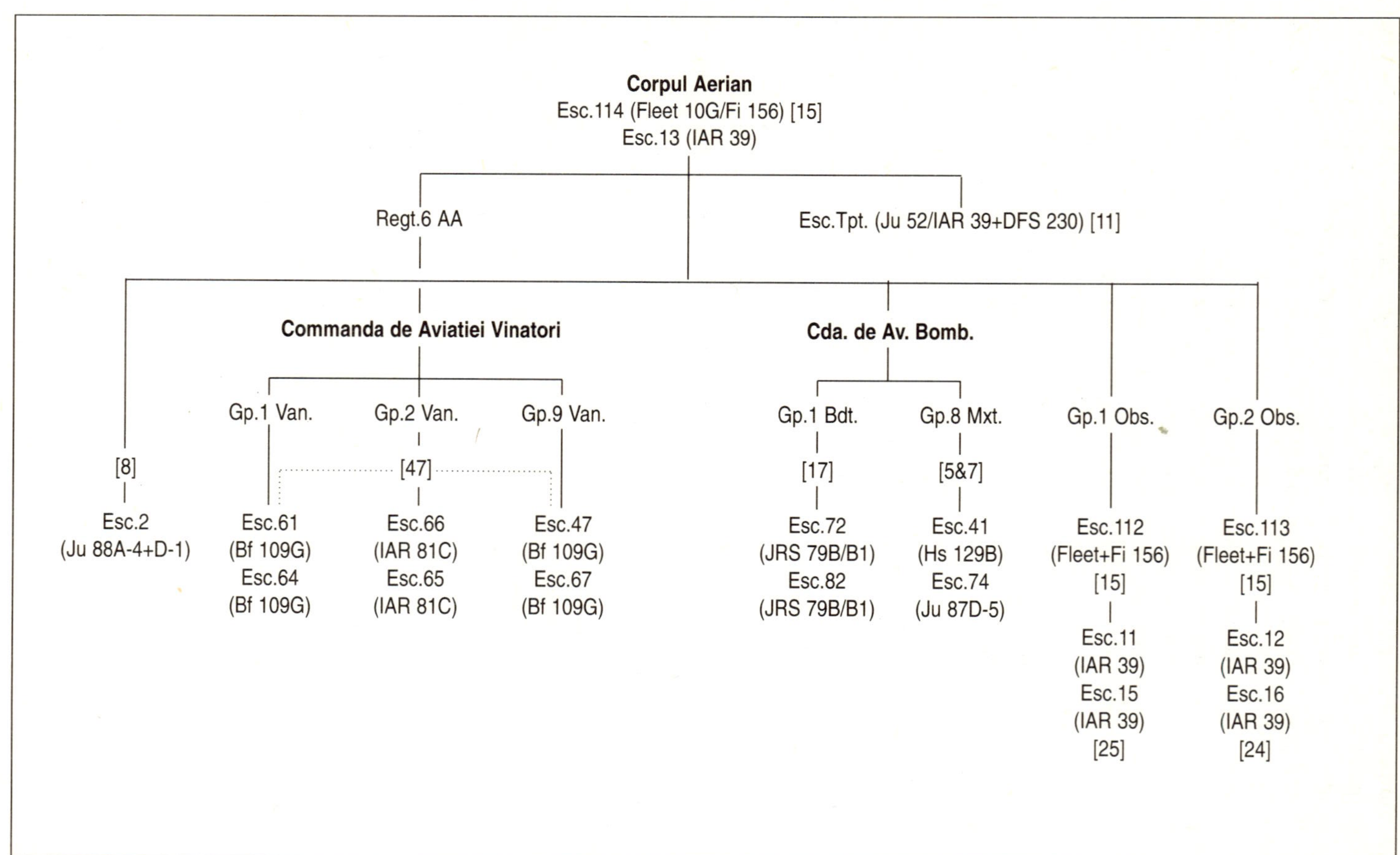
Corpul Aerian
Esc.114 (Fleet 10G/Fi 156) [15]
Esc.13 (IAR 39)
Regt.6 AA
Esc.Tpt. (Ju 52/IAR 39+DFS 230) [11]
Commanda de Aviatiei Vinatori
Cda. de Av. Bomb.
[8]
Esc.2
(Ju 88A-4+D-1)
Gp.1 Van.
Gp.2 Van.
Gp.9 Van.
[47]
Esc.61
(Bf 109G)
Esc.64
(Bf 109G)
Esc.66
(IAR 81C)
Esc.65
(IAR 81C)
Esc.47
(Bf 109G)
Esc.67
(Bf 109G)
Gp.1 Bdt.
[17]
Esc.72
(JRS 79B/B1)
Esc.82
(JRS 79B/B1)
Gp.8 Mxt.
[5&7]
Esc.41
(Hs 129B)
Esc.74
(Ju 87D-5)
Gp.1 Obs.
Esc.112
(Fleet+Fi 156)
[15]
Esc.11
(IAR 39)
Esc.15
(IAR 39)
[25]
Gp.2 Obs.
Esc.113
(Fleet+Fi 156)
[15]
Esc.12
(IAR 39)
Esc.16
(IAR 39)
[24]

However, although its prewar designs were initially comparable with those of the major powers, Romania's small aircraft industry was unable to keep pace with the great advances in aircraft technology made during the war years, and its own types became increasingly obsolescent from 1942. Nevertheless, they retained some operational potential on secondary fronts to the end of the war.

Despite their relatively deteriorating performance, Romanian aircraft provided a vital underlying continuity in the FARR order of battle throughout a war in which it was first cut off from its traditional foreign suppliers, Poland, France and Britain, in 1939–40, then forced into an alliance with a Germany that only briefly in 1943–4 would lend, but not sell, significant numbers of comparatively modern aircraft, and finally left entirely to its own meagre resources by the unsupportive Allies in 1944–45.

The quality of Romanian aircrew remained consistently higher than that of the Soviets, this alone allowing them to continue operating their older types on the Eastern Front in the face of the large numbers and progressively improving performance of Soviet fighters. The considerable scores of the leading Romanian aces, mostly achieved on the Bf 109, attest to this, but they were eventually to be swamped by the massed USAAF raids of 1944. Despite its best efforts, the initial ability of Romania's medium bomber force to provide close ground support was limited. Only in 1943, when German dive-bomber and ground-attack types were lent to it, was the FARR able to influence the ground battle significantly, but by then mostly in support of German troops. The FARR's anti-shipping potential was always minimal.

Nevertheless, the FARR provided both the largest and most readily available allied aerial support for the Germans on the Eastern Front, and on three occasions, the late summers of 1941, 1943 and 1944, it was numerically the largest Axis combat contingent at its southern extremity. The FARR initially lacked the mobile logistic support, repair and maintenance facilities to operate in strength on a distant front all year round, and especially through the winter, but by mid-1943 this weakness had been partly rectified and continuous operations by Corpul 1 Aerian, if not the entire FARR, were thereafter possible.

FARR pilots and AA artillery claimed well over 1,500 Soviet aircraft, about 270 western aircraft and some 350 German aircraft (mostly on the ground) during the war. Even allowing for substantial exaggerations this was a considerable figure. Furthermore, it is also worth noting that most aircraft attrition does not occur in actual combat, but is a result of irreparable battle damage, accidents, lack of spares, obsolescence etc. Thus the very presence of the FARR at the front induced an unquantifiable, hidden toll on its immediate opponents. The reverse was also true, as downed aircraft represented only a small proportion of the total number of aircraft that passed through the FARR's hands in 1939–45.

If the FARR's general efficiency and operational results seldom approached German levels, it must be borne in mind that it laboured not only under the same well-attested difficulties as the Luftwaffe, but under many additional ones as well.

CHAPTER 10

BLACK SEA NAVAL OPERATIONS 1941–1944

INTRODUCTION

The Royal Romanian Navy had been founded in 1860 as a river flotilla on the Danube. It was French-trained, but operated under the Russian flag for convenience during the War of Independence against the Turks in 1877–78. In the following decades it expanded to embrace the embryo of a seagoing Black Sea squadron. In 1895 the government also founded a state merchant marine, the Serviciul Maritim Roman (SMR). Its acquisitions over the following two decades included the Mediterranean mixed passenger/cargo steamers *Regele Carol I*, *Romania* and *Dacia* and the merchantmen *Bucegi*, *Carpaţi* and *Durostor*.

In the First World War the most important element of the navy was still the Danube Flotilla, with the four river monitors *Catargiu*, *Bratianu*, *Kogalniceanu* and *Lahovari*, built in Italy in 1907–8, and eight vedettes built in Britain. The navy had on order four new destroyers and a submarine from Italy, but delivery was delayed by the war and its Black Sea squadron had to rely mainly on armed merchantmen of the SMR. The navy's role was very secondary, and its main success was the mining of an Austro-Hungarian river monitor on the Danube. Its own losses were light. War booty included three Austro-Hungarian river monitors, renamed *Ardeal*, *Basarabia* and *Bucovina*, and in 1921 four Italian-built vedettes (Nos. 1–4) were bought. These additions made Romania's Danube squadron the most powerful such river fleet in the world for two decades.

With the Danube thus secured, the Romanian Navy now turned its attentions to developing the Black Sea arm of its fleet, and in 1920 a naval college was founded at Constanţa, Romania's main Black Sea port. That same year, two of the previously ordered Italian-built destroyers, *Maraşti* and *Maraşesti*, were finally delivered and four ex-French gunboats, *Stihi*, *Dumitrescu*, *Lepri* and *Ghiculescu*, were acquired. Seven ex-Austro-Hungarian torpedo boats were received as war reparations, three of which, *Naluca*, *Smeul* and *Sborul*, saw service in the Second World War. The SMR received the steamer *Oituz*. In 1926 Romania ordered two new destroyer leaders, *Regele Ferdinand* and *Regina Maria*, the submarine depot ship *Constanţa* and the submarine *Delfinul* from Italian yards. All were received between 1930 and 1936. In 1932-33 the SMR bought the ex-German freighters *Ardeal*, *Peles*, *Alba Julia* and *Suceava*.

In 1936 a separate Naval and Air Ministry was formed, and in the following year a major rearmament programme was begun. This was to have included a cruiser, four destroyers, three submarines, four minelayers and twelve MTBs. A major new dry dock was to enable the later vessels to be constructed under licence at Galaţi, and a sail training ship was ordered in Germany to begin preparing cadets for the expanded fleet. However, the navy had a lower rearmament priority than the Army and Air Force, so only the minelayer *Amiral Murgescu*, the three British-built MTBs *Viforul*, *Vijelia* and *Viscolul* (delivered in February 1940) and the sail training ship *Mircea* were received by the outbreak of hostilities. Plans to build nine more MTBs under licence were abandoned as relations with Britain deteriorated from mid 1940. Two of the submarines, *Rechinul* and *Marsuinul*, which were of German design, were completed later in the war. The rest were cancelled; the minelayer *Cetatea Alba* after she had already been laid down.

The naval dockyard at Galaţi on the lower Danube was completed and the first major Romanian-built warships, *Amiral Murgescu*, *Rechinul* and *Marsuinul*, were constructed there. All of the river monitors underwent modernisation in 1937–43, the *Basarabia* and *Bucovina* undergoing almost complete rebuilds. Two of four armoured gunboats previously ordered from the Czechs, *Vedeta No.5* and *Vedeta No.6*, were eventually delivered by the Germans. The SMR also bought two new passenger liners, *Basarabia* and *Transilvania*, from Germany in 1938, and the four new freighters *Balcic*, *Carvarna*, *Mangalia* and *Sulina* from Italy in 1939/40.

The above-mentioned vessels formed the main elements of the Romanian Navy and SMR at the outbreak of war in 1941. Many were old and in poor mechanical condition, and were to place a heavy burden on Romanian technical and engineering staff and facilities during the war when, owing to operational demands and damage repairs, not a single seagoing vessel could be spared for a major refit.

There was very little cross-transference of personnel between the Black Sea and Danube squadrons because the nature of their operations was completely different. The main guns of the river monitors usually acted more like army heavy artillery, using forward fire controllers to range indirect fire on to land targets. These controllers were protected by a specialist company of marines. The seagoing vessels usually engaged in direct fire against naval targets within view of their onboard fire directors.

In early 1940 the SMR had seventeen vessels totalling 72,149 tons of shipping. Romania also had a fourteen-ship private merchant fleet totalling 55,067 tons and large state- and privately-owned tug and barge fleets on the Danube totalling 157,232 tons, some of which could also be used in coastal waters. Including port and dockyard workers, the navy could mobilise 12,533 men. Of these, 1,060 were sailors from the SMR, 919 were from the private fleet and 1,021 were from the state river fleet.

PREPARATIONS FOR WAR

From Romania's admission to the Axis in November 1940, her entry into the war became increasingly probable and preparations against the Soviet Union began. The Soviet Black Sea Fleet was overwhelmingly powerful. It possessed a battleship, three medium cruisers, three light cruisers, three flotilla leaders, eight modern destroyers, five old destroyers, two large torpedo boats, forty-seven submarines and a host of minor and auxiliary vessels. Supporting their navy, the Soviets had a 119-vessel merchant fleet in the Black Sea. The Soviet Black Sea Fleet also had 600 aircraft – more than the entire FARR. During the first year of the war Romania could oppose this with four destroyers, three gunboats, three torpedo boats, one submarine, three MTBs, a minelayer, three auxiliary minelayers, fifteen minor auxiliaries and twenty seaplanes. Thus Romanian preparations at sea were necessarily mostly defensive.

As far as possible, SMR vessels were recalled to the Black Sea before hostilities. However, the *Mangalia* was then in the USA and was sold there. The large and expensive modern liners *Basarabia* and *Transilvania* were no longer able to operate commercially in the Mediterranean and were of little operational value, so they were sent to neutral Turkey for safety. Two SMR vessels, *Balcic* and *Alba Julia*, were in Italy at the outbreak of war, and subsequently worked in the Adriatic with the Italians.

Only two privately-owned Romanian vessels were available to the Axis during the war, the steamer *Danubius* in Romania and the tanker *Campina* in Italy. Two vessels had been lost in the war before Romania entered it. Five vessels whose owners were not Romanian were re-registered as Greek or Panamanian in 1940–41, one was sold in the USA in 1941 while that country was still neutral, one was interned by the Argentines and sold to them in 1942, and five were interned by the British in late 1941 before war broke out between the two countries on 6 December. All eleven British, American, Greek and Panamanian controlled vessels, totalling 44,321 tons, came to serve the Allies, a total not far short of the fifteen vessels totalling 55,396 tons available to the Axis. Twelve of the latter, totalling 43,064 tons, were in the Black Sea; the remainder were in Italy.

In late 1940 the small river steamer *Aurora* was converted into an auxiliary minelayer to work in the shallows off the Danube Delta. In January 1941 the Soviet Union staged aggressive demonstrations on the frontier and *Aurora* laid her first minefields to protect Sulina, the main Romanian port at the mouth of the Danube. Unfortunately a marker buoy indicating the limit of the previous day's minelaying drifted overnight, and *Aurora*'s escort, the gunboat *Lepri*, ran on to a Romanian mine and sank on 11 January. Ironically she was the largest regular Romanian warship lost during the war.

The use of mines was seen as the most practical way to conserve the Romanian fleet in the face of the enormous Soviet naval superiority, and the completion of the *Amiral Murgescu* was hastened. She finally joined the fleet on 15 May, 1941. To reinforce her, the steamer *Regele Carol I* was armed and converted into an auxiliary minelayer. The Romanian Navy was given a few days warning of the German invasion of the Soviet Union on 22 June 1941, and between 16 and 19 June these two vessels laid four protective mine barrages in an arc off Constanţa against surface attack. *Amiral Murgescu* laid Romanian-built Vickers mines, while *Regele Carol I* laid German UC mines. *Aurora* simultaneously mined off Sulina. Security within the Constanţa barrages was maintained by a flotilla of four tugs for anti-submarine duties, two tugs as forward anti-aircraft pickets and a minesweeping sloop. After the outbreak of war German UMC anti-submarine mines were also laid. No Soviet submarine ever penetrated them.

THE DANUBE CAMPAIGN, 1941

The defence of the Danube was the responsibility of the Romanian river fleet of seven river monitors, six vedettes, two armed barges and thirty minor auxiliaries. It

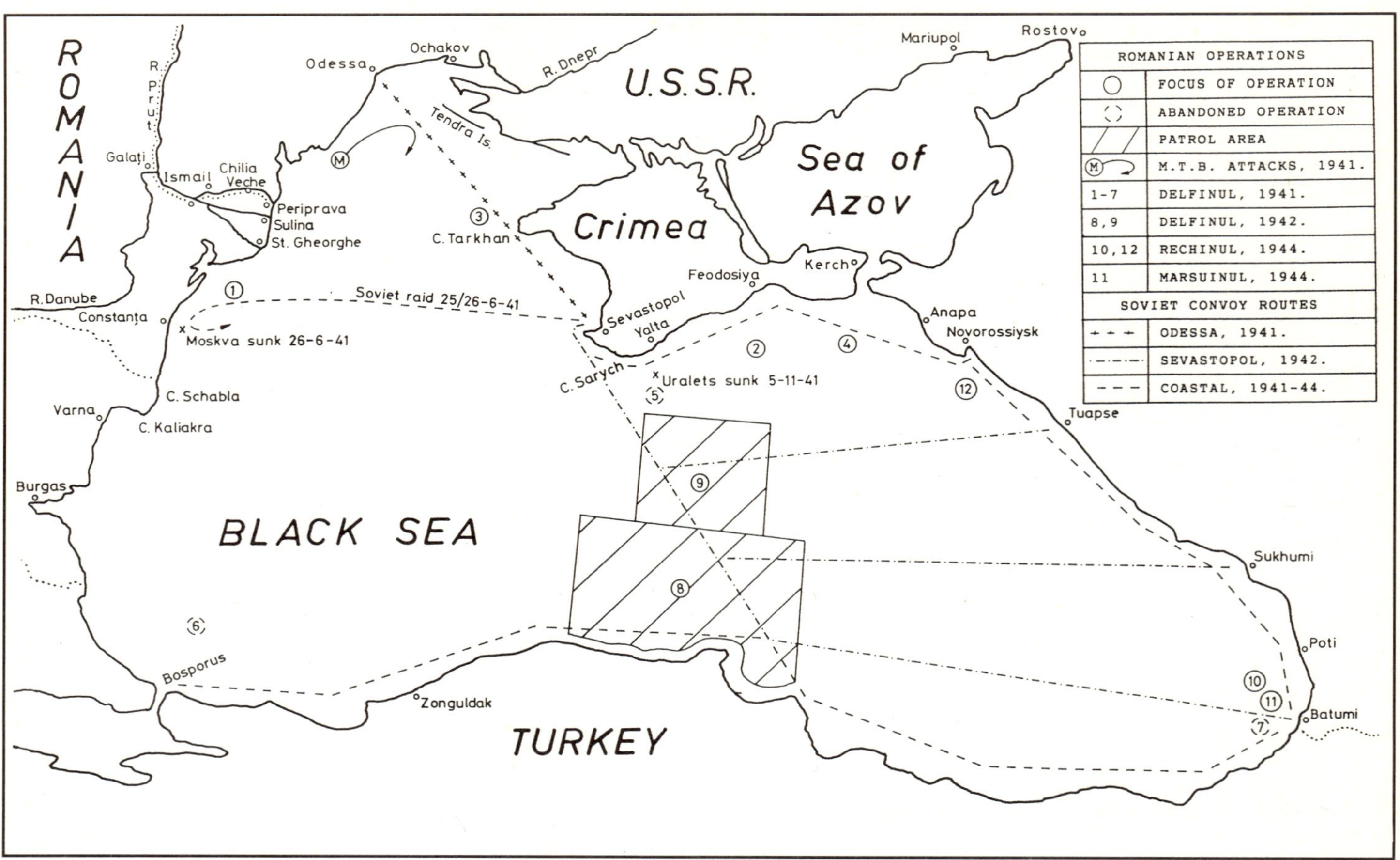
ROMANIAN OPERATIONS
FOCUS OF OPERATION
ABANDONED OPERATION
PATROL AREA
M.T.B. ATTACKS, 1941.
1-7 DELFINUL, 1941.
8, 9 DELFINUL, 1942.
10, 12 RECHINUL, 1944.
11 MARSUINUL, 1944.
SOVIET CONVOY ROUTES
ODESSA, 1941.
SEVASTOPOL, 1942.
COASTAL, 1941-44.
ROMANIA
U.S.S.R.
Crimea
Sea of Azov
BLACK SEA
TURKEY
Rostov
Mariupol
R. Dnepr
Ochakov
Tendra Is.
Odessa
C. Tarkhan
Sevastopol
Yalta
C. Sarych
Feodosiya
Kerch
Anapa
Novorossiysk
Tuapse
Sukhumi
Poti
Batumi
Zonguldak
Bosporus
Burgas
Varna
C. Kaliakra
C. Schabla
Constanța
R. Danube
Galați
R. Prut
Ismail
Chilia Veche
Periprava
Sulina
St. Gheorghe
Soviet raid 25/26-6-41
Moskva sunk 26-6-41
Uralets sunk 5-11-41

faced the Soviet Danube Flotilla of five monitors and twenty-three BKA armoured gunboats at Ismail. The Romanian flotilla was tasked with preventing the Soviet monitors from interfering with the Romanian army's planned up-river crossings, while the Soviet flotilla's aim was to prevent a Romanian crossing of the lower Danube. As a result of their mutual defensive tasking there was little active fighting between the two. However, a Soviet armoured gunboat, probably *BKA-114*, was damaged by *Vedeta No.3* and fled on to Lake Kagul, where the crew beached her and ineffectually attempted to burn her. She was later captured and put into service as *Vedeta No.7*. The Romanian opinion was that this Soviet type was too noisy and made too much smoke for a river craft.

The three battalions of the Romanian Marine Regiment guarded the Danube Delta. The regiment was comparatively recently formed and was poorly equipped with obsolete weapons surplus to army requirements. The Soviet Danube Flotilla would have to pass the positions of its 15th Battalion at Chilia Veche and its 17th Battalion at Periprava if it was to secure its retreat to the Black Sea. On 26 June, in their only successful attack on to Axis soil in 1941, the Soviets crossed the Danube and enveloped Chilia Veche. 15th Battalion was ill prepared, as it had no artillery capable of penetrating the armour of the Soviet gunboats and many of its positions had been flooded by an unusual rise in the Danube. Most of the battalion was wiped out. The Soviets tried to follow up with an assault on Periprava, but 17th Battalion had some 47mm AT guns and they were thrown back.

This repulse was significant because, when the Soviet Danube Flotilla finally withdrew on 11/12 July, it had to pass under the guns at Periprava. While the armoured gunboats attacked Periprava, the larger monitors passed behind them under cover of smoke and escaped along the coast to Odessa. The Soviets are believed to have lost four gunboats, including *BKA-111*, *BKA-113* and *BKA-134*.

THE DEFENCE OF CONSTANŢA, 1941

The Russians had bombarded Constanţa's oil terminal when it was in German hands during the First World War, and the Romanians correctly anticipated that they would repeat the operation. The Soviet flotilla leaders *Moskva* and *Kharkov* attacked at dawn on 26 June. The Soviet vessels apparently passed through the Romanian minefields without incident and successfully shelled oil storage tanks and an ammunition train. To avoid incessant Soviet air attacks, the Romanians had taken to dispersing their ships outside the port area but within the minefields. The destroyers *Regina Maria* and *Mara*ş*ti*, hidden against the dark coastline, opened fire on the larger Soviet vessels, which were silhouetted against the dawn, and may have brought down *Moskva*'s rear mast. Upon then coming under fire from heavy German coastal artillery, the Soviet warships began to retire east under a smokescreen. In passing back through the minefield *Moskva* apparently struck a mine and blew up. Romanian MTBs picked up 63 survivors. The *Kharkov*, after suffering a temporary loss of control owing to a near miss from a German aircraft, escaped to the protection of the cruiser *Voroshilov*, which herself suffered slight damage when one of her escorting destroyers detonated a nearby mine in its paravanes.

Following the repulse of this raid, the Soviets began to blockade Constanţa by air and by submarine. At least eighteen air raids were launched, but their effects were limited as Constanţa was well defended by light anti-aircraft guns which forced most bombers to fly high. However, the tug *Amarilia* was sunk on 1 July. Romanian aircraft were to claim 51 victories, German aircraft 69 victories and AA 25 victories over Constanţa in 1941.

The Soviet submarine blockade was equally unsuccessful. The Romanian Navy remained at Constanţa but posted permanent anti-submarine pickets at the southern and northern entrances to the Constanţa minefields. On 9 July *Naluca* and the three Romanian MTBs reported sinking a Soviet submarine (*Shch.204*?) as it tried to break through. A Soviet air raid on Sulina did sink the auxiliary minelayer *Aurora* on 15 August. However, she gained a posthumous revenge when the submarine *Shch.206* was probably sunk in one of her minefields off Sulina in late September.

The period of confinement in Constanţa was used to prepare for the start of convoy operations. All vessels were degaussed and received the first of a succession of dazzle camouflage schemes. The *Dacia* was converted into an auxiliary minelayer. German rangefinders, firing techniques and signals equipment were adopted, and an exhaustive series of battle drills were practised under German supervision. Merchant ships had twin AA towers constructed fore and aft, and four, six or eight 20mm AA guns were mounted there and in the superstructure. Their AA gunners and a supernumerary signaller and navigator were German, but the officers and crew were Romanian.

Although the Germans regarded the Romanian destroyers as suitable for other operations, they did not consider them to have either the mechanical reliability or battle training to undertake surface actions against the heavy odds they were likely to encounter. As a result, the Romanian Navy was to be given the leading role in the defence of the western basin of the Black Sea, and Romanian surface warships were not usually to operate further east than Cape Sarych in the Crimea.

THE SIEGE OF ODESSA

Pressure on the Romanian coast was eased in early August when the Soviet Black Sea surface fleet became tied down in supporting their isolated garrison in Odessa, which was under siege by the Romanian 4th Army. The Soviets lost an old destroyer (1,100 tons), a gunboat (1,100 tons), an auxiliary minelayer (3,880 tons), a minimum of nine merchantmen (26,187 tons+) and numerous small craft in supporting or evacuating Odessa between July and October 1941. However, most of these losses were attributable to the occasional intervention of the Luftwaffe, as the Romanian Navy's major surface vessels could not be risked against the far larger Soviet Black Sea Fleet, and one operation by the submarine *Delfinul* and seven by the MTBs *Viscolul*, *Viforul* and *Vijelia* against convoys were unsuccessful (see below). The FARR lacked either torpedo or dive bombers suitable for anti-shipping strikes, although repeated medium bomber raids on Odessa harbour probably had some effect on moored vessels.

However, the Romanian 4th Army's siege of Odessa certainly forced the Soviets to risk naval operations that exposed their vessels to successful attacks by the Luftwaffe and on withdrawal obliged them to scuttle several merchantmen to block

Odessa harbour and delay its reopening by the Axis. Soviet naval preoccupation with Odessa, although ensuring a successful defence and withdrawal, also allowed Axis sea movements to the Bosporus to resume.

SECURING THE BOSPORUS CONVOY ROUTE

The sea route from Constanţa through the Bosporus was of considerable strategic importance to the Axis, as the bulk of the Romanian oil used by the Italian Navy passed through it. The Italian Navy was that country's only competitively equipped and armed service, and its operations in the Mediterranean were severely constricted by lack of fuel. The Bosporus convoy route was therefore put into operation as soon as possible, and the Soviets promptly concentrated their submarine operations against it. On 14 August the Romanian steamer *Peleş* was sunk by *Shch.211*, and on 16 August the Romanian steamer *Ardeal* was attacked unsuccessfully. On 25-26 August the Soviet submarine *L.4* laid mines off Varna which claimed the Bulgarian merchantman *Schipka* on 15 September. On 14 September the Italian tanker *Superga* had been attacked while en route to Constanţa, and on her return voyage she was torpedoed and sunk by *M.43* on 29 September.

The Germans organised a movement plan that required merchant vessels to make the normally day-long open-sea journey between the Bosporus and Constanţa in seven coast-hugging hops over two weeks. However, this did little to reduce the danger and wasted valuable time. It was therefore decided to lay flanking mine barrages of German UMC anti-submarine mines down the coastal route as protection, and the task was allocated to the Romanian Navy. Between 5 and 16 October a series of barrages were laid south from Constanţa via Cape Schabla, Varna and Burgas to the Bulgarian-Turkish border. *Amiral Murgescu* would use sonar initially to select the exact site of the minefield. Then, with destroyers as anti-submarine cover and gunboats sweeping ahead of them for Soviet mines, *Amiral Murgescu*, *Regele Carol I* and *Dacia* would lay their mines. However, although the gunboats swept four of *L.4*'s mines, *Regele Carol I* struck a fifth off Varna on 10 October and sank in thirteen minutes. She was an old vessel without bulkheads, and the blast killed 23 men at lunch in the forward crew room. The orderly evacuation was commended by the German liaison staff aboard.

The new barrages soon began to claim Soviet submarines. On 25 October *Shch.212* was damaged off Kaliakra. On 12 November *S.34* was sunk off Burgas and bodies recovered. In November and December *Shch.211* and *M.34* both went missing off Cape Schabla, their losses being attributed to mines. *Shch.205* was also believed damaged on 4 December off Varna. However, the coastal route was still not entirely safe. On 6 November the Italian tanker *Torcello* was sunk by *Shch.214* on the Turkish-Bulgarian border after missing a rendezvous with Romanian destroyers at the Bosporus, and in December the *Oituz* was slightly damaged by *M.58*. However, losses reduced Soviet submarine activity, and they scored no further successes in the winter of 1941/42. On the fall of Sevastopol in July 1942 they lost their last naval base in the western Black Sea, and Soviet submarine operations there were reduced. This enabled the Axis to reopen the faster open-sea route between Constanţa and the Bosporus.

OPENING THE ODESSA CONVOY ROUTE

From the moment Odessa fell to the Romanian 4th Army on 16 October 1941, the opening of a convoy route to supply the overextended German front in southern Ukraine became paramount. Sea transport was of particular importance, because the overstretched railway system could not alone carry the massive supplies needed by the German southern front. However, the Soviets had comprehensively demolished and blocked Odessa harbour and extensively mined the approaches, and some time was needed to secure the route. The minesweepers included the Romanian Flotila Usoara de Dragaj, consisting of the four hired German 200-ton tugs *Amsel*, *Brusterort*, *Drossel* and *Forsch*. Each was fitted with a 20mm AA gun, depth charges and sweeping gear for conventional and magnetic mines. After clearing up to Odessa they continued east to Ochakov, where *Brusterort* and *Drossel* were lost on mines.

On 9 November one of the first shallow-draught convoys, consisting of the Hungarian river vessels *Tisza* and *Ungvar*, was despatched towards Odessa with aviation fuel and bombs aboard. They were escorted by the Romanian MTBs *Viscolul*, *Viforul* and *Vijelia*. Six miles short of Odessa *Ungvar* struck a mine and blew up. *Viforul* and *Vijelia* were apparently sunk by debris or mines as they approached to pick up survivors. As a result, convoy operations were suspended again while further clearance work was done. However, in their first successful counteroffensive of the war the Soviets recaptured Rostov from the Germans on 28 November, and the German Army Group South pressed for an immediate opening of the convoy route to the larger seagoing Romanian merchantmen before it was closed by winter ice.

On 30 November three merchant vessels, the Romanian *Carpaţi* and *Carvarna* and the Bulgarian *Zar Ferdinand*, left Varna in Bulgaria, and at 0700 the following morning they met their escort of *Regele Ferdinand*, *Regina Maria* and *Maraşti* off Cape Schabla. Almost immediately, *Regina Maria* noticed a periscope to starboard of the convoy and turned to attack. As the Soviet submarine fired her torpedoes ineffectually at the convoy it briefly bobbed to the surface only 400m ahead of *Regina Maria*, which dropped a pattern of depth charges at a shallow setting. *Regele Ferdinand* crossed the same spot immediately afterwards, dropping her depth charges at a deeper setting. Debris was seen, and aerial reconnaissance observed an oil slick over the same spot for several days. The submarine sunk was probably *M.58*.

After the convoy had been joined by the merchantman *Cordelia* and Romanian gunboats from Constanţa, it reached the limit of the known Soviet minefields south of Odessa on 2 December, and the destroyers turned back, leaving the gunboat *Stihi* as escort. The convoy had been delayed by bad weather, and a rendezvous with German minesweepers from Odessa was missed, so it had to begin picking its way slowly through the minefields in line astern. The *Carvarna* hit a mine and the benzene aboard exploded, killing 31 Romanian crewmen and 20 German AA gunners. *Carpaţi* anchored immediately, but *Cordelia* touched another mine, exploded and sank. *Carpaţi* later reached Odessa, but *Zar Ferdinand*, which was lagging behind with *Dumitrescu* as escort, had to be diverted to Sulina.

In a final effort to get supplies through to Odessa before winter, a convoy consisting of the Bulgarian *Zar Ferdinand*, the Hungarian *Tisza* and *Kassa* and several German MFPs, with a total of 8,000 tons of supplies, left Constanţa on 16 Decem-

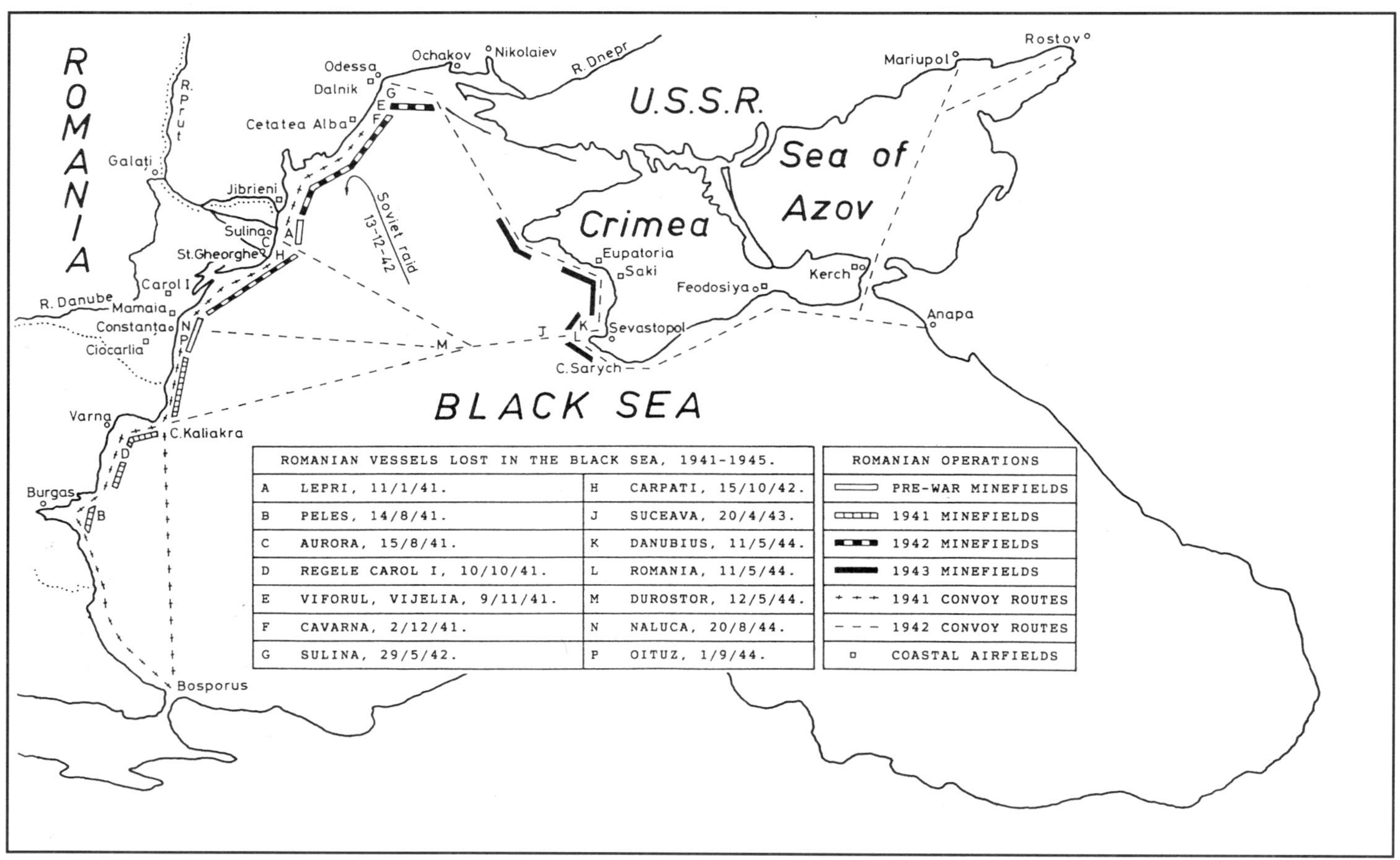
ROMANIA
U.S.S.R.
Crimea
Sea of Azov
BLACK SEA
Rostov
Mariupol
Anapa
Kerch
Feodosiya
Sevastopol
C. Sarych
Eupatoria
Saki
R. Dnepr
Nikolaiev
Ochakov
Odessa
Dalnik
Cetatea Alba
Jibrieni
Sulina
St. Gheorghe
R. Prut
Galati
Carol I
Mamaia
Constanta
Ciocarlia
R. Danube
Varna
C. Kaliakra
Burgas
Bosporus
Soviet raid 13-12-42
ROMANIAN VESSELS LOST IN THE BLACK SEA, 1941-1945.
A LEPRI, 11/1/41.
B PELES, 14/8/41.
C AURORA, 15/8/41.
D REGELE CAROL I, 10/10/41.
E VIFORUL, VIJELIA, 9/11/41.
F CAVARNA, 2/12/41.
G SULINA, 29/5/42.
H CARPATI, 15/10/42.
J SUCEAVA, 20/4/43.
K DANUBIUS, 11/5/44.
L ROMANIA, 11/5/44.
M DUROSTOR, 12/5/44.
N NALUCA, 20/8/44.
P OITUZ, 1/9/44.
ROMANIAN OPERATIONS
PRE-WAR MINEFIELDS
1941 MINEFIELDS
1942 MINEFIELDS
1943 MINEFIELDS
1941 CONVOY ROUTES
1942 CONVOY ROUTES
COASTAL AIRFIELDS

ber, escorted by *Regele Ferdinand*, *Regina Maria*, *Stihi* and *Dumitrescu*. They were joined by *Sborul* and *Smeul* off Sulina. Off Jibrieni *Regele Ferdinand* spotted a periscope in an attacking position. She turned towards it, and torpedo tracks were observed passing down either side of her. These gave a perfect bearing on the submarine, and *Regele Ferdinand* and other vessels made eight attacks. Oil and debris soon surfaced. The stricken Soviet submarine was probably *Shch.204* or *M.59*. Soviet submarine attacks on the coastal convoy route were extremely hazardous because the waters were shallow and gave submarines little scope for evasive manoeuvres. The convoy reached Odessa without loss. The winter of 1941/42 was long and heavy, and coastal traffic to Odessa only resumed after the ice had dispersed in April 1942.

OFFENSIVE SUBMARINE AND MTB OPERATIONS, 1941

The submarine *Delfinul* conducted seven cruises in 1941 and two in 1942. Her first (22-27 June) was as a defensive picket 60km off Constanţa, but she was recalled after failing to detect the Soviet raid of 26 June. Her subsequent missions were all offensive, in co-ordination with the advancing land operations. As the only Axis submarine in the Black Sea in 1941, *Delfinul* had a significance out of all proportion to any tonnage she might have sunk, because as a ship-in-being she forced the Soviets to tie down numerous aircraft and ships in convoy protection across the whole Black Sea. As a result of this, her poor mechanical condition and her crew's initial inexperience, the German naval command in the Black Sea recommended that she should not attack escorted vessels.

Delfinul's second mission (10 July-20 July) was against the Soviet Sevastopol-Novorossiisk convoy route, the third (10-20 August) was against the Soviet convoy route from Sevastopol supplying the besieged garrison of Odessa, and the fourth (3-19 September) was off the Caucasus coast. Despite a number of sightings, including the old Soviet cruiser *Komintern*, no eligible targets were spotted.

At last, on her fifth mission (2-7 November), to intercept traffic off the entrance to the Sea of Azov, *Delfinul* sank an unescorted merchantman, the *Uralets* (1,975 tons), south of Yalta on 5 November. Throughout the day *Delfinul* survived a series of depth charge attacks before having to abort the rest of the mission owing to mechanical problems. Mechanical problems similarly forced the premature curtailment of *Delfinul*'s sixth (30 November - 3 December) and seventh (6-15 December) cruises off Batumi in the Caucasus. Consequently, *Delfinul* was withdrawn from operations over the winter and underwent five months of repairs. Her eighth (18-30 May 1942) and last (25 June - 3 July) missions were as part of the blockade of Sevastopol, south of the Crimea, but were without surface sightings.

Throughout her operations *Delfinul* was forced to dive several times a day by Soviet aircraft, and on a number of occasions she was bombed ineffectually. This had the benefit of making her presence felt throughout her zone of operations. The Soviets had more than 44 submarines in the Black Sea, all bar three of them more modern than *Delfinul*, and at least one always lay in wait off Constanţa, where *Delfinul* had to surface to negotiate the mine barrages. On at least three occasions she ran into them, but escaped each time. In the late summer and autumn of 1942 three (later six)

German U-boats were transferred to the Black Sea overland and reassembled at Romanian dockyards. Thereafter *Delfinul*'s importance diminished. Thus, when her long-standing mechanical problems finally incapacitated her in July 1942, she could be withdrawn to Galaţi on the Danube as a training ship for the new submarines *Rechinul* and *Marsuinul*.

The three Romanian MTBs made 22 sorties in 1941. Ten were anti-submarine patrols near Constanţa, and included a possible submarine sinking with *Naluca* on 9 July. Seven were offensive sorties against the Soviet convoy route supplying Odessa, but five of these were without contact. However, on the night of 18/19 September two MTBs fell in with a Soviet convoy by surprise. Four torpedoes were launched from about 200m, but it is believed that they may not have had time to arm, and therefore any hits would not have exploded. The Soviets apparently thought they were under air attack, and responded with AA fire. On the night of 26/27 September a Soviet vedette was spotted, but combat was avoided as she was mistakenly believed to be the escort for a larger target. The MTBs also conducted four escort missions in 1941, but after the loss of *Viforul* and *Vijelia* on 9 November the surviving *Viscolul* made only a couple of coastal night sorties in early 1942 before becoming the training boat for a new flotilla of six ex-Dutch MTBs.

1942

During 1942 and 1943 the main Romanian operational task was to be the protection of convoys in the western Black Sea. All Axis naval operations in the theatre came under the German Black Sea commander, Admiral Brinkmann. His transport staff organised all convoy vessels, including the Romanian merchantmen, while the Royal Romanian Navy allocated the major escorts. The convoy commander was the senior Axis naval officer present; usually the Romanian commanding the largest escort vessel. However, all vessels, including Romanian warships, carried German supernumerary navigators and signallers to improve co-ordination.

As a general rule, convoy escorts on the longer Constanţa-Bosporus route were mostly Romanian destroyers. On the Constanţa-Sevastopol route the Romanian gunboats and German R-boats were also used. The Romanian torpedo boats, operating with German R-boats, were usually restricted to the coastal Sulina-Odessa route. Romanian escorts operated in pairs of the same class where possible.

The winter of 1941/42 was used to organise spring convoys. Of approximately 34,000 tons of Axis seagoing shipping still available in the Black Sea, 24,825 tons was Romanian. It included *Durostor*, *Danubius*, *Oituz*, *Sulina*, *Carpaţi*, *Ardeal* and *Suceava*. In addition, the coastal convoys included the Romanian tugs *Oltul*, *Elena* and *Arlon*, each towing a 500-ton barge, and increasing numbers of German MFPs, Danube tugs and barges with R-boats as escorts. The Romanian Navy was to escort 459 Axis vessels during the year.

The Axis coastal and river vessels were of shallow draught and made difficult torpedo targets for Soviet submarines, and it was the larger, predominantly Romanian merchant ships which were most at risk. Owing to the small number of these precious vessels available in the Black Sea, their slow speeds and the potentially large number of Soviet submarines hunting them, the convoy escorts on open-sea routes usually outnumbered their charges, but on the coastal route it was at times possible to put through barge traffic unescorted.

To protect the coastal convoy route, *Amiral Murgescu* and *Dacia* began by laying a flanking barrage between Sulina and Sfintu Gheorghe in early April 1942, twice surviving Soviet air attacks. On 15 May they extended the barrage across the northern mouth of the Danube Delta, and on 19-20 May they completed it up to Bugaz. The section from Bugaz to Odessa was simultaneously laid by the *Romania*, which had been converted into an auxiliary minelayer over the winter and transferred to the Germans in March. However, Soviet submarines circumvented the barrage to the east and continued to enter Odessa Bay. On 29 May they sank *Sulina*, and on 11 June *Ardeal* was torpedoed and had to be beached. She was out of action for seven months.

On 24-27 June a 24-vessel Romanian-German squadron under the Romanian Comandor Marcellariu closed this gap by extending the flanking barrages east from Odessa to Tendra Island. Air cover against Soviet interference was provided by the FARR. On 24 August the Soviet submarine *M.33* was mined and sunk off Odessa, and on 27 September *M.60* suffered the same fate. The Soviets subsequently moved their submarine operations further south-west along the coast in search of a weak spot in the mine barrages.

They found one. On 18 October *M.118* torpedoed and sank the German steamer *Salzburg* off Budaki, but was herself sunk by the escorting Romanian gunboat *Ghiculescu*. On 11 October the unescorted Romanian tug *Oltul* was sunk by *M.111*. Then on 15 October *Shch.216* torpedoed and sank *Carpaţi* off Sfintu Gheorghe and *M.35* sank the German tanker *Le Progree* off Sulina. Both were under German escort at the time. These incidents revealed that the Soviets had found a gap in the mine barrages north of Sulina, probably where *Aurora*'s early barrages had drifted, and on the night of 5/6 November *Amiral Murgescu* and *Dacia* sealed it.

After Sevastopol fell to its German-Romanian besiegers in early July, a direct open-sea Constanţa-Sevastopol convoy route serviced by the larger Romanian merchant vessels and the Romanian destroyers and gunboats was opened in October 1942. It was ice-free, and operated throughout the following winter without loss. The capture of Sevastopol seriously damaged the strike potential of the Soviet submarine fleet, as its most common type of boat, the coastal M Class, did not have the range to operate for long in the western Black Sea from bases in the Caucasus. Romanian shipping losses fell accordingly.

In December the Soviets conducted three surface raids. In the first, between 29 November and 3 December, a cruiser and two destroyers shelled Serpilor Island but broke off prematurely when the destroyer *Soobrazitelny* detonated a mine in her paravanes. Two other destroyers ineffectually shelled some fishing boats between Capes Shabla and Kaliakra on 1 December.

On 13 December two Soviet minesweepers attacked the Constanţa-Odessa convoy route, and two other minesweepers simultaneously approached Serpilor Island. They were supported by destroyers over the horizon. Several groups of Soviet vessels were spotted from the air, but the day was overcast and tracking them proved difficult. Furthermore, there was a breakdown in communications which left a coastal convoy consisting of the steamers *Oituz* and *Zar Ferdinand*, escorted by the Romanian torpedo boat *Smeul* and four German R-boats, unaware of the approach of the minesweepers *T–407 Mina* and *T–412 Arseni Rasskin* until they came in sight.

The Romanian convoy commander ordered the steamers back to Sulina while *Smeul* and the R-boats continued on their original course, laying smoke until the superior Soviet vessels found their range. *Smeul* returned fire, but the range was beyond her guns and she and the R-boats then fell back into their own smoke. By repeatedly foraying out from behind *Smeul's* smokescreen in feigned torpedo attacks, they kept the Soviet vessels out of range of the slow steamers from 1037 to 1315, at which point the enemy broke off the action. The Soviets had displayed great strategic daring in mounting the raid, but their tactical timidity and the bold front of *Smeul* and the R-boats deprived them of any success. A final raid by four Soviet minesweepers and two destroyers off Jibrieni between 26 and 29 December was abortive.

During 1942 the privately-owned Romanian tanker *Campina* was reportedly sunk by a British submarine at the entrance to the Dardanelles while en route to Romania. On 14 November the German tanker *Ossag* was torpedoed and damaged off the Bosporus as she was being met by *Regele Ferdinand* and *Regina Maria*. The Soviet submarine *L.24* was probably lost on mines off Cape Kaliakra on 30 December, also while trying to interdict the Bosporus-Constanţa convoy route.

In 1942 the Romanian Cavalry Corps had taken the ports of Jeisk (9 August), Primorsko-Akhtarsk (11 August) and Temriuk (24 August) on the eastern shore of the Sea of Azov, and captured a number of light Soviet vessels in various states of damage and disrepair. These included the small tug *Andre Marti* in Jeisk, an unidentified vessel mounting ten assorted guns in Primorsko-Akhtarsk and the hulk of the 600-ton gunboat-tug *Dnestr* in Temriuk. In December, two damaged Soviet TKA torpedo boats were washed ashore near Anapa and captured. A few of the lighter vessels were briefly manned by the Cavalry Corps, but the bulk were handed over to the Germans.

1943

By the beginning of 1943 Romania still had the five seagoing merchant ships *Durostor*, *Danubius*, *Oituz*, *Ardeal* and *Suceava*, totalling 16,889 tons, in the Black Sea. However, during the year the total tonnage of light German ferry traffic on the coastal route probably began to exceed this. The Romanian Navy escorted 739 Axis vessels during the year.

To reinforce the coastal convoy route when it reopened after the winter ice had broken up, the *Amiral Murgescu* and *Dacia* laid four flanking barrages between Odessa and Constanţa in April 1943. The coastal route had now extended to its maximum, and Romanian barge traffic reached as far east as Mariupol on the Sea of Azov. However, larger Romanian vessels did not normally go further east than Cape Sarych, although on occasions when rendezvous with German escorts were missed the destroyers and gunboats could reach Feodosiya. Combat near the land front in the Crimea and Caucasus was conducted by light German and Italian naval forces. Romanian army units provided the bulk of coastal protection forces in the Caucasus and Crimea during 1943–44, and sank a number of light Soviet craft in repulsing raids and landing attempts.

On the night of 20 April, in the best-conducted Soviet submarine attack of the war in the Black Sea, *S.33* torpedoed and sank the largest surviving Romanian transport, the *Suceava*, off Sevastopol while she was under the escort of *Regina Maria* and light German vessels. Other Axis vessels also lost in 1943 on the Sevastopol route while under mixed Romanian/German escort were the *Kharkov* (9/10 August), *Varna* (20 August), *Santa Fe* (23 November) and *Volga-Don* (24 November). The tanker *Thisbe* was likewise lost on the Bosporus route on 30 August while under Romanian destroyer escort. By 1943 the oil traffic to Italy had cost so many tankers that it had become intermittent.

During mid-1943, Romanian destroyers claimed three possible, but unconfirmed, submarine sinkings off the Crimea; by *Marasesti* on 16 April (probably *M.31*), by *Maraşti* on 7/8 July and by *Regele Ferdinand* on 16 September (possibly *Shch.207*). Success against submarines was much more difficult to achieve and confirm on the open-sea Constanţa-Sevastopol and Constanţa-Bosporus routes than on the coastal routes because the waters were deep and gave Soviet submarines much more scope to evade the rather rudimentary detection systems of the Romanian destroyers. As a consequence, the *Regele Ferdinand* and *Regina Maria* were fitted with the more advanced German S-Gerät sound location system in late 1943.

As most of the submarine attacks were now taking place off the Crimea, *Amiral Murgescu*, *Dacia* and *Romania* laid three mine barrages off Sevastopol and down the western Crimean coast between mid-September and mid-November. These fields probably claimed *Shch.203* off Cape Tarkhan in September 1943 and *L.23* off Eupatoria on 17 January 1944.

The gradual advance of the Soviet land front in the southern Ukraine in late 1943 brought the resumption of co-ordinated air attacks in the western basin of the Black Sea. From 5 September torpedo aircraft began to attack convoys to the Crimea for the first time. From 11 September the Red Air Force began to drop British magnetic mines in the lower Danube. On 27 September Constanţa harbour was bombed, and in late October Soviet dive-bombers were used against merchant shipping for the first time.

However, the FARR provided systematic fighter cover for coastal convoys from 7 September, and effective air strikes on the forward Soviet airfields from late November. As a result, Soviet aircraft had little success against Axis shipping over the winter of 1943/44. Constanţa's AA defences were similarly effective. The Romanians had created a river minesweeping flotilla on the Danube in 1941, and for two years this had had success against occasional Soviet conventional mines. However, the new magnetic mines were initially invulnerable and sank the largest Romanian river liner, *Mihai Viteazul*, the large river liner *Ismail* and a number of barges. In response, the Romanians re-equipped three armoured vedettes and six tugs to sweep magnetic mines, and brought the threat on the lower Danube under control.

The *Alba Julia* successfully returned to Romania from the Mediterranean shortly before Italy's surrender in September 1943, but the *Balcic* was bombed and sunk by the Germans during subsequent fighting with Yugoslav partisans for control of the port of Split on the Adriatic.

WARTIME SHIP ACQUISITIONS

Despite considerable expansion plans, few new vessels were received during the war. On 9 May 1940 the Santierul Naval at Galaţi (SNG) tendered for four minesweepers and a base ship for the Black Sea Squadron and four armoured gunboats and ten armoured sloops for the Danube Squadron, all to its own designs. The base ship was subsequently cancelled, but on 15 October 1941 SNG tendered successfully for four German Type 40 minesweepers and the fourteen Danube vessels. In 1942 the Germans invested heavily in SNG and took effective control. Apart from rebuilding the monitors *Basarabia* and *Bucovina* and completing the Romanian submarines *Rechinul* and *Marsuinul*, SNG was used to assemble or repair much of the German shipping introduced into the Black Sea during the war, including six U-boats.

The fate of the fourteen Danube vessels ordered from SNG is unclear, but it is possible that under the Oil Pact the Germans delivered ten ex-Polish vessels to replace them. At the time of Romania's defection to the Allies in August 1944, the four Type 40 minesweepers were in an advanced stage of construction at Galaţi. However, Soviet armistice conditions meant that they were not completed until long after the war. Plans to follow them on the stocks at Galaţi with two modern destroyers and to buy ten E-boats, ten R-boats and three 450-ton U-boats from the Germans in 1943/44 apparently came to nought, as did a German proposal in late 1943 to use the Romanian-occupied Odessa dockyard to construct Type XXIII coastal U-boats.

However, some minor German-sourced vessels were acquired. The loan of four 200-ton German tugs to the Flotila de Dragaj Usor in 1941-2 has already been noted. In late 1942 the Germans sold Romania the six ex-Dutch Gusto Power MTBs Nos 4-9 (*Vedenia*, *Vantul*, *Vijelia*, *Viforul*, *Varteјul* and *Vulcanul*), but they never became available for offensive operations because the Dutch had removed a vital shaft coupling for which the Romanians were unable to find a high-specification substitute. Consequently they could develop a maximum speed of only 20-25kt, so they were fitted to carry four or six depth charges and used defensively for coastal submarine patrols. Their Rolls-Royce Merlin engines were the same as used in Romania's Hurricane fighters, and several of these aircraft were reportedly cannibalised to provide spares.

Romania received three MFP armed transport barges from the Germans in 1943 which became 'Pontoanele de Transport Armate' *PTA–404*, *PTA–405* and *PTA–406*. In early 1944 the three German anti-submarine armed trawlers *KFK198*, *KFK199* and *KFK270* were also acquired and redesignated 'Vanatori de Submarine' *VS1*, *VS2* and *VS3*. They operated as an independent anti-submarine section on the coastal convoy routes.

In late 1943 the Romanians had a windfall of five Italian CB miniature submarines. The Romanian Navy had historically had a close relationship with the Italian fleet, and when Italy defected to the Allies in September 1943 the Italian crews deliberately surrendered their vessels to their fellow Latins rather than to the Germans. The Romanians formed their Second Submarine Squadron on them. However, only two could be made serviceable, and although they made practice dives in Constanţa harbour in 1944, neither became fully operational. According to some reports Romania also took over seven ex-Italian MAS Type 500 MTBs in August 1943, but there is no evidence of their use.

1944

The Romanians began the year with the seagoing merchant vessels *Durostor*, *Danubius*, *Oituz*, *Ardeal* and *Alba Julia*, totalling 16,879 tons, available in the Black Sea. In 1944 the Romanian Navy was to escort 233 Axis vessels, including 88 evacuation convoys from the Crimea in April and May. The Soviet advance to the mouth of the Dneipr in late October 1943 had cut off seven Romanian and five German divisions in the Crimea, and over the winter all Axis naval activity was devoted to their maintenance. Between 28 March and 10 April further Soviet advances on the mainland forced the evacuation of Odessa, the terminal of the coastal convoy route to Sevastopol. In addition to German vessels, this involved the Romanian gunboats, torpedo boats, *Amiral Murgescu* and many Danube tugs and barges. A total of 24,855 Romanian and German troops were embarked in 25 convoys without significant Romanian naval losses, despite fourteen air attacks, twelve submarine attacks and the last vessels coming under direct artillery fire.

Romanian Naval Evacuation Capacity, 1944

Vessels	Manpower Capacity	Total	Vessels	Manpower Capacity	Total
*Alba Julia, Ardeal**	1,000	2,000	*Durostor*	300	300
Dacia, Oituz, Romania**	700	2,100	Four destroyers, *Murgescu*	200	1,000
*Danubius**	500	500	*PTA 404, 405, 406*	150	450
Thirteen tugs + barges	500	6,500	Three gunboats	60	180
			VS1, VS2, VS3	20	60
* Allocated to the Germans			Theoretical single lift capacity		13,090

The fall of Odessa now threw the entire strain of supplying the Crimea on to the open-sea convoy routes from Constanţa to Sevastopol and the Sulina to Sevastopol route. The more robust coastal and river vessels were diverted to the latter. The Romanian strength in the Crimea by early April 1944 had fallen to 64,000. They had already prepared a contingency plan, code-named 'Operation 60,000', for their evacuation. However, only after the Red Army had broken into the Crimea and the German/Romanian defenders were being forced back into a constricted perimeter around Sevastopol did Hitler agree to an evacuation. As a result, 'Operation 60,000' had to be accelerated, and vessels sometimes left overloaded four- or fivefold. Between 14 and 27 April 20,799 Romanian troops, including 2,269 wounded, were evacuated, as well as 28,394 Germans, 15,055 Russian auxiliaries, 3,748 civilians, 2,559 prisoners and 723 Slovaks. Despite numerous air, submarine and MTB attacks, only about 500 Romanians and a similar number of other evacuees were lost to them.

To disrupt the convoys at source, the Red Air Force attacked Constanţa on 11, 17 and 18 April, but without success, as the AA defences had been reinforced by guns evacuated from Odessa. On 18 April *Alba Julia*, overloaded with 1,456 troops, was bombed 120 miles from Constanţa. Half of the 1,000 men who jumped overboard were drowned, but other vessels rescued the remainder. *Regele Ferdinand*

and *Regina Maria* were rushed to the scene to mount overnight guard and put aboard a skeleton crew to maintain *Alba Julia*'s pumps and stabilise her. On the following day two tugs towed her into Constanţa. On 26 April the Romanian MFPs *PTA–404* and *PTA–406* were also bombed and damaged at Sevastapol. Late in the month a convoy escorted by the gunboat *Ghiculescu* was attacked at night by Soviet MTBs. *Ghiculescu* illuminated them while light German craft engaged and destroyed two of them.

On 27 April, when the Romanians still had the bulk of the Mountain Corps ashore, Hitler suspended the evacuation, and few men were retrieved over the following fortnight. The Germans demanded that the Romanians prepare the fast liners *Transilvania* and *Basarabia*, then in neutral Turkey, for use on the Constanţa-Sevastopol route. However, this would have been a breach of neutrality, and their departure was halted when Turkish police seized vital engine parts, possibly at the behest of Romanian officials opposed to risking them. However, supply convoys continued without loss on the Romanian part until 8 May, when a last Soviet assault on Sevastopol forced Hitler to concede a belated final evacuation.

Between 8 and 13 May virtually every available Axis vessel in the Black Sea was sent to Sevastopol – a total carrying capacity well in excess of the troop numbers still ashore. *Regina Maria*, *Dumitrescu* and *Durostor* sailed twice, and *Regele Ferdinand*, *Mărăşeşti*, *Amiral Murgescu*, *Ghiculescu*, *Stihi*, *Dumitrescu*, *Dacia*, *Oituz* and *Danubius* once each. However, operational conditions had deteriorated in the previous fortnight, as the Soviets had now established forward airfields near Sevastopol and the surviving German and Romanian aircraft had been evacuated or overwhelmed and their airfields brought under artillery fire. Furthermore, the final Soviet advance increasingly brought Sevastopol's sea approaches and loading points under artillery fire.

The *Regele Ferdinand* had the narrowest escape, and her experience is representative. She arrived off Sevastopol with *Stihi* and the German-manned auxiliary minelayer *Romania* at 0200 on 11 May. The Soviets were using searchlights and flares to illuminate the approaches, and blind artillery fire where these were not available. At 0330 she took aboard mixed German and Romanian troops ferried out by barge, and then resumed a constant zig-zag course off Sevastopol against submarine attack. At 0600 she was two miles offshore when the first air raids began. As the most prestigious target available she attracted a disproportionate share of air strikes, suffering 30 or 31 attacks by torpedo bombers, dive bombers and assault aircraft by 1030. The assault aircraft caused havoc among the troops on the crowded decks and superstructure with cannon and anti-personnel bombs, the exposed AA gunners suffering particularly heavily. The bridge was also badly hit and two officers were killed. A blaze was started in the after cabins and some charges for No.4 gun were ignited, but both fires were successfully extinguished by damage control parties. Most serious was an unexploded bomb, which caused an unrepairable leak in the port oil tank.

At 0930 *Regele Ferdinand* was bracketed by Soviet shore-based heavy artillery, but suppressed it with counter fire. At 1030 she zig-zagged further out and reported her damage to Constanţa. Simultaneously, another fifteen-aircraft attack destroyed the radio post and caused damage to the starboard fuel lines. In view of the heavy oil loss, the captain broke off the action and headed for Constanţa, surviving submarine scares en route. Oil eventually had to be passed hand to hand by bucket chain, but at 0200 on the following morning *Regele Ferdinand* ran out of fuel just short of Constanţa and had to be towed into port. Twelve crew had been killed and 28 wounded, and a higher number of casualties had been suffered among the evacuated troops, but several Soviet aircraft had been shot down. The *Romania* was less fortunate, having been bombed and sunk on her return voyage on 11 May, but *Stihi* survived.

The last Romanian convoy to arrive consisted of the *Regina Maria*, *Amiral Murgescu*, *Dacia* and *Durostor*. The last two were damaged by bombs on the 11 May, and *Durostor* was sunk by a torpedo from the submarine *A5* the following day. The other three vessels managed to rescue 800 men on the night of 11/12 May. Other losses were the merchantman *Danubius*, which was bombed and sunk on 11 May, and the two 500-ton Danube barges *Banat* and *Basarabia*. *Ghiculescu* was damaged. The last Romanian ships to straggle back to Constanţa were *Dumitrescu* and *Oituz*, on 14 May.

Between 28 April and the last evacuation early on 13 May, 13,812 Romanian troops and 1,266 wounded were retrieved, and 28,992 Germans and 3,755 others were also uplifted. However, the delay imposed by Hitler led to the avoidable deaths of about 4,000 Romanians and 7,000 Germans on the ships lost, and the abandonment of at least 10,000 Germans and several battalions of Romanian mountain troops. According to Romanian figures their navy had uplifted 38,168 Romanian and German troops during the evacuation. This is less than a thousand below the total of Romanians rescued by sea, indicating that the Romanian Navy bore its full share of the evacuation. In recognition of this, the Germans awarded the *Ritterkreuz* to the Romanian naval commander, Rear Admiral Horia Marcellariu, on 21 May. Marcellariu was in the best of professional company, as the only other non-German naval recipient was the Japanese architect of Pearl Harbour, Admiral Yamamoto.

The crisis in the Crimea precipitated the first operations by the new Romanian submarines *Rechinul* and *Marsuinul*. The Germans were nervous that Turkey might take advantage of their loss of the Crimea to enter the war, and at the beginning of her first cruise (20 April to 15 May) *Rechinul* was sent to spot potential submarine targets in the bay of Zonguldak, on the Turkish coast, before finishing a quiet patrol off Batumi. *Marsuinul* also patrolled off Batumi from 11 May to 27 May without incident, apart from being attacked in error by the German-commanded Croat U-jaeger flotilla on her outward leg. *Rechinul*'s second cruise (15 June to 29 July), off the north Caucasus coast, was also unproductive. Traffic was scarce, and the six German U-boats in the Black Sea also had little success at this time.

After *Amiral Murgescu* and *Dacia*, escorted by *Regina Maria*, *Mărăşeşti*, *Sborul*, *Smeul*, *Viscolul* and *Vedenia*, had laid a final minefield on the night of 25/26 May, closing the gap off Sulina previously used by convoys to Sevastopol, the Romanian Navy retired behind the protection of its coastal minefields and Constanţa's AA defences. The only forays were by *VS1*, *VS2* and *VS3* to escort three Jewish refugee ships out through the minefields.

From April 1944 the British began to mine the middle Danube. This was far more serious than the earlier Soviet mining operations on the lower Danube, as it threatened oil supplies from Giurgiu to the Reich and overwhelmed the capacity of the River Command to clear them. On occasions, oil traffic up the river and army supply traffic down it was brought to a complete halt.

AUGUST 1944

In concert with their final land assault on Romania, the Soviets launched heavy air attacks on Constanţa on 20 August which at last broke through the AA defences. The Romanians lost the torpedo boat *Naluca*, three of the ex-Italian miniature submarines and the river tanker *Aries* sunk, and the *Regele Ferdinand*, *Mara*ş*e*ş*ti* and *Stihi* were damaged. The *Dacia* was also damaged while the ships were dispersed off Constanţa the following day. On 23 August Romania capitulated to the Allies. The German vessels were ordered to leave Constanţa, but before they had done so the Soviets launched another heavy air raid on 24 August which sank the Romanian tug *Basarabia.*

On the same day the Romanian Danube monitors were instructed to cease fire, remove the vegetal camouflage which had hitherto kept them completely hidden from the Red Air Force, and make their way down river to meet Soviet naval forces. Unfortunately, several were then attacked by Soviet aircraft, and in two separate incidents *Kogalniceanu*, *Catargiu* and *Vedeta No.2* were sunk. Only the monitor *Bratianu*, which alone broke orders and returned fire, survived these attacks. Romania declared war on Germany on 25 August, and the naval command immediately sent the remaining monitors in pursuit of a large German convoy trying to escape up the Danube. The tail of the convoy was captured, but just as the remainder was about to be engaged the Soviets recalled the monitors, apparently fearing their possible defection. Soviet reports that Romanian artillery sank a Soviet gunboat at Galaţi as late as 26 August are suspect and unconfirmed. Altogether 430, mostly riverine, vessels were captured and handed over to the Soviets. Another 60 were sunk or scuttled.

On 30 August Romanian MTBs led the first Soviet ships into Constanţa. The Soviets ordered the Romanians not to move any of their vessels, but when the steamer *Oituz* was sunk at her moorings in Constanţa harbour by a German submarine on the same day they were allowed to undertake security patrols. However, when the Soviet minesweeper *T–410 Vzryv* was torpedoed by a German submarine while in company with the *Amiral Murgescu* on 2 September, the Soviets made accusations of treachery and used these as the excuse for seizing the entire Romanian fleet on 5 September.

At that date the Royal Romanian Navy, including its shore-based Marine Regiment (expanded to six battalions), Coastal Artillery Regiment (28 batteries) and Engineer Regiment, had 858 officers, 1,417 petty officers and 18,741 men on strength. Including its most minor auxiliaries it possessed 122 vessels divided between its Black Sea, Coastal and River Commands. However, of the regular Black Sea warships only the destroyers *Regina Maria* and *Mara*ş*e*ş*ti*, the gunboats *Dumitrescu* and *Ghiculescu*, the minelayer *Amiral Murgescu* and the MTBs *Viscolul*, *Vedenia* and *Viforul* were still fully seaworthy. Manpower losses against the Soviets had been 231 dead, 334 wounded and 1,220 missing. The majority of the latter were from 15th Battalion of the Marine Regiment in 1941.

1944–1945

The Romanian Black Sea vessels were soon removed to Caucasian ports. The only part of the Romanian fleet of immediate use to the Soviets were the river vessels. The five surviving monitors were put under the Soviet flag and given Soviet commanders and gun crews, but retained their Romanian technical staff. They campaigned up the Danube with the Red Army as far as Vienna. Most of the state and private Danube merchant fleets were impressed by the Soviets to supply their army.

The Danube was an important supply line for the Soviet advance into Hungary and Austria, and they initially seized all Romanian mine clearance vessels. However, their sailors were unable to maintain the unfamiliar magnetic mine clearing equipment, so they soon reinstated the Romanian crews while keeping them under the Soviet flag. However, the Soviets had broken the equipment, so the Romanian crews had to improvise. Their technique was for a degaussed tug to tow an undegaussed

The Romanian State Merchant Fleet, 1941–1944

Name	Tons	Dimensions (ft)	Launch	DWC	Speed Original	Speed 1940	Fate
Passenger Liners							
Basarabia	6,672t	405.0 x 57.7 x 26.9	1938	2,200t	25.7kts	21.5kts	Interned in Turkey 1941–45
Transilvania	6,672t	405.0 x 57.7 x 26.9	1938	2,200t	24.5kts	21.5kts	Interned in Turkey 1941–45
Mixed Cargo/Passenger Vessels (Auxiliary Minelayers)							
Dacia	3,418t	356.9 x 41.9 x 27.5	1907	1,500t	18kts	14.2kts	b&d BS 21/8/44
Romania	3,152t	356.9 x 41.9 x 27.5	1904	1,500t	18kts	13.6kts	to Germans 1942, b&s BS 11/5/44
Regele Carol I	2,369t	350.0 x 42.0 x 18.5	1898	1,400t	17kts	13.3kts	m&s BS 14/10/41
Cargo Vessels							
Alba Julia	5,700t	409.8 x 53.9 x 23.7	1922	7,840t	10.5kts	9.6kts	b&d BS 18/4/44
Ardeal	5,695t	409.8 x 53.9 x 23.7	1922	7,840t	10.5kts	8.0kts	t&d BS 11/6/42
Peleș	5,700t	409.8 x 53.9 x 23.7	1922	7,840t	10.5kts	9.0kts	t&s 14/8/41
Suceava	5,710t	409.8 x 53.9 x 23.7	1923	7,840t	10.5kts	9.6kts	t&s BS 20/4/43
Bucegi	4,330t	375.8 x 52.2 x 25.5	1913	7,200t	10.5kts	7.4kts	captured by British, 1941
Carpati	4,336t	375.8 x 52.2 x 25.5	1913	7,200t	10.5kts	8.0kts	t&s BS 15/10/42
Balcic	3,600t	360.9 x 50.8 x 23.5	1940	5,000t	13.0kts	13.0kts	b&s Adriatic 15/10/43
Carvana	3,600t	360.9 x 50.8 x 23.5	1940	5,000t	13.0kts	13.0kts	m&s BS 2/12/41
Mangalia	3,600t	360.9 x 50.8 x 23.5	1940	5,000t	13.0kts	13.0kts	sold to USA 1941
Sulina	3,600t	360.9 x 50.8 x 23.5	1940	5,000t	13.0kts	13.0kts	t&s BS 29/5/42
Oituz	2,686t	291.3 x 44.0 x 23.7	1905	4,205t	10kts	7.4kts	t&d BS ?/12/41
Durostor	1,309t	217.0 x 34.0 x 21.4	1911	1,395t	8.5kts	7.4kts	b, t&s BS 12/5/44

Total: 17 Vessels of 72,149t

DWC: Dead Weight Capacity is the weight of cargo, supplies and fuel carried. Cargo tonnage alone is therefore slightly less.

t = torpedoed b = bombed m = mined d = damaged s = sunk BS = Black Sea barge to set off the magnetic mines. This was hazardous, and three tugs, three motorboats and 36 sailors were lost in the process. Once the Germans also began to mine the upper Danube the minesweepers became the only vessels returned to serve under the Romanian flag against the Axis. They were engaged in keeping the Romanian stretch of the Danube clear up to Turnu Severin until the end of the war. The Danube was finally cleared in late 1945 by the FARR, using a captured Ju 52 mine clearance aircraft.

CONCLUSION

The Royal Romanian Navy began the war with very little experience and a preponderance of obsolescent vessels to oppose a more modern and numerically overwhelming, if not very efficient, Soviet Black Sea Fleet. Thus significant surface offensive operations were never possible. Fortunately, the advance of the German-Romanian armies in the Ukraine, Crimea and Caucasus deprived the Soviets of their naval and air bases in the western Black Sea. Furthermore, Luftwaffe anti-shipping strikes, and to a lesser extent Romanian air cover over the western Black Sea, kept the Soviet fleet's surface elements on the defensive and away from the Romanian coast for much of the war, and largely relieved the Romanian Black Sea squadron of its heaviest defensive commitment. This also limited the results of the Romanian submarines, which found very few targets after 1941, although they did tie down considerable Soviet resources in defence. The operations of the Danube squadron were very limited because the land front rested only briefly on the river.

The intelligent use of limited resources enabled the Romanian Navy to conduct a successful anti-submarine mining campaign which imposed sufficient losses and caution on Soviet submarine operations in the western Black Sea to enable Romania to fulfil its two main naval obligations to the Axis; the maintenance of some vital oil traffic to the Mediterranean via the Bosporus and supply traffic to the

Romanian Registered Private Merchant Vessels, 1940–1944

Merchantmen		
Elise	1,986t	Re-registered as Greek, 1940
Virginia	2,041t	Re-registered as Greek, 1940
Max Wolf	6,700t	Sunk by Germans in error in France, June 1940
Jiul	3,127t	Sunk in accidental explosion in Greece, June 1941
Inginer N. Vlassopol	3,610t	Captured by British, 1941
Moldova	4,100t	Re-registered as Panamanian, 1941
Oltul	4,328t	Interned and bought by Argentina, 1942
Prahova	3,609t	Re-registered as Panamanian, 1941
Siretul	3,638t	Re-registered as Panamanian, 1941
Starstone	5,702t	Captured by British, 1941
Danubius	1,489t	b&s BS 11/5/44
Oil Tankers		
Oltenia	6,394t	Captured by British, 1941
Campina	3,032t	Sunk by British in Mediterranean, 1942
Steaua Romana	5,311t	Captured by British, 1941

Total: 14 Vessels of 55,067t

German/Romanian land front in southern Russia. The navy's role in the maintenance and rescue of the garrison of the Crimea in 1944 was also indispensable.

Although the Royal Romanian Navy suffered considerable damage during mid 1944, its warship losses in escorting approximately 2.5 million tons of Axis shipping in the Black Sea and on the Danube during earlier years were remarkably light. However, neither it nor the light German forces in the Black Sea had enough adequately equipped vessels to provide impregnable convoy protection. The consequent losses of Romania's state merchant fleet were devastating; every available ship being sunk or seriously damaged. Romania's private merchant fleet completely disappeared during the war, and the Soviets confiscated most of the river fleet.

State of the Romanian Merchant Fleet, 22/6/41

2 vessels of	9,827t	were war losses before 22/6/41
5 vessels of	15,374t	were re-registered abroad in 1940/41
5 vessels of	25,347t	were interned by the British in 1940/1
1 vessel of	3,600t	was sold to the USA in 1941
1 vessel of	4,328t	Argentine from 1942
2 vessels of	13,344t	were laid up in Turkey in 1941–45
3 vessels of	12,332t	were in Italy on 22/6/41
12 vessels of	43,064t	available in Romania on 22/6/41
Total	127,216t	

'R' Class Destroyers: *Regele Ferdinand* (1928), *Regina Maria* (1929)

Built	Disp.	Dimensions	Speed	Range	Crew
Italy	1,850t	101.9m x 9.6m x 3.5m	37kts	3,000 miles at 15kts	212

Armament: 5 x 120mm, 1 x 76mm, 2 x 37mmAA, 4 x 20mmAA, 2 x 13.2mm twin AA, 6 x 533mm TT, 40 x depth charges or 50 x mines.

The 120mm piece in No.2 turret was replaced by an 88mm AA gun in 1944. The 'S' Gerat submarine detection system was fitted in 1943.

'M' Class Destroyers: *Maraşti* (1917), *Mărăşeşti* (1918)

Built	Disp.	Dimensions	Speed	Range	Crew
Italy	1,723t	94.4m x 9.5m x 3.5m.	34kts	1,700 miles at 15kts	139

Armament: 4 x 120mm, 2 x 37mmAA, 2 x 13.2mm twin AA, 4 x 450mm TT, 40 x depth charges or 50 x mines.

During the war four 20mm and two 37mm AA guns were added. *Marasti* had a cracked shaft and could not exceed 22-24kts.

Gunboats: *Stihi* (1916), *Dumitrescu* (1916), *Ghiculescu* (1917), *Lepri* (1917)

Built	Disp.	Dimensions	Speed	Range	Crew
France	±400t	60.9m x 6.9m x 2.5m.	15kts	3,000 miles at 10kts	50

Armament: 2 x 37mmAA, 2 depth charge launchers.

The after 37mm AA gun was replaced by an 88mm submarine gun, and a 20mm AA gun was added to the rear superstructure later in the war. *Lepri* was mined and sunk by accident on 11/1/41. Tonnage varied between 350t and 450t.

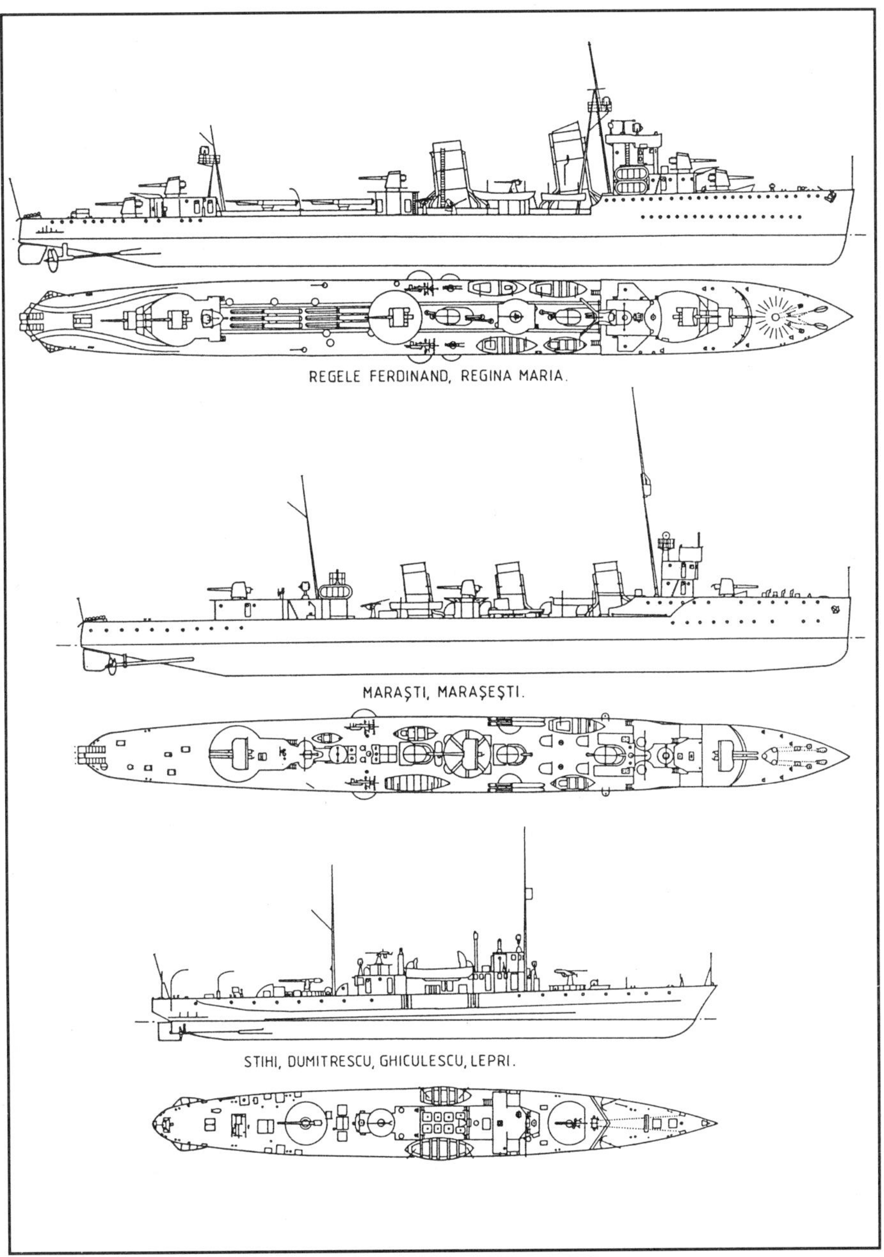
REGELE FERDINAND, REGINA MARIA.
MARAŞTI, MARAŞEŞTI.
STIHI, DUMITRESCU, GHICULESCU, LEPRI.

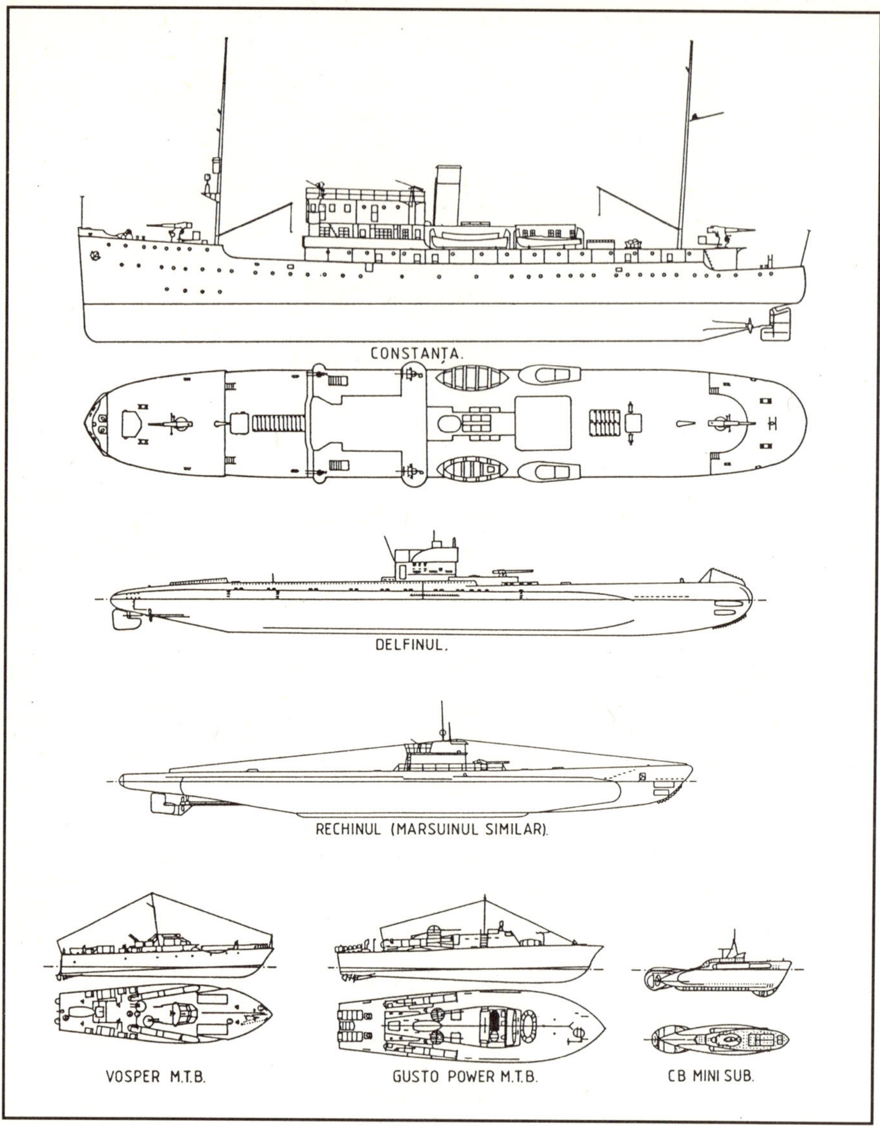

Submarine: *Delfinul* (1930).

Built	**Disp.**	**Dimensions**	**Speed**	**Range**	**Crew**
Italy	650t	68m x 5.9m x 3.6m	14kts/9kts	2,000 miles/15 days	40

Armament: 1 x 102mm, 6 x 533mm TT (4 bow, 2 stern, no reserve)

Delfinul was a poor design, poorly built and in poor mechanical condition.

Submarine: *Rechinul* (1941).

Built	**Disp.**	**Dimensions**	**Speed**	**Range**	**Crew**
Romania	585t	58m x 5.6m x 3.6m	17kts/9kts	7,000 miles/45 days	45

Armament: 1 x 88mm, 1 x 20mm AA, 10 x 533mm TT (4 bow, 2 stern, 4 reserve)

A Dutch/German design related to the German Type IA U-boat and *Marsuinul.*

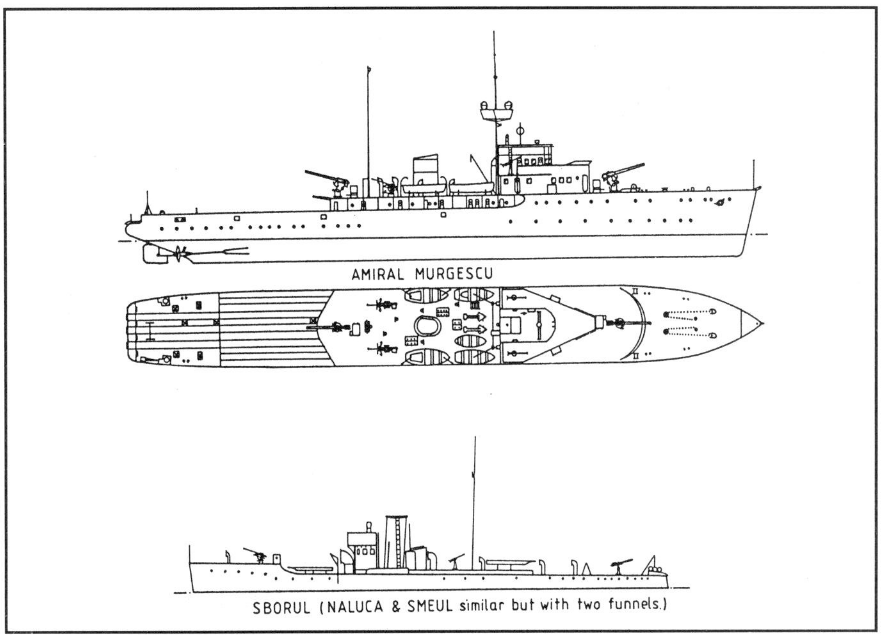

Submarine: *Marsuinul* (1941).

Built	Disp.	Dimensions	Speed	Range	Crew
Romania	508t?	68.7m x 6.5m x 3.6m	16kts/9kts	8,000 miles/45 days	45

Armament: 1 x 88mm, 1 x 20mm AA, 10 x 533mm TT (4 bow, 2 stern, no reserve)
A Dutch/German design. Originally to have been a minelayer, but never used as such.

Vosper MTBs Nos 1-3: *Viforul, Vijelia, Viscolul* (all 1939)

Built	Disp.	Dimensions	Speed	Crew
U.K.	47t	23.3m x 6.4m x 0.9m	40kts	14

Armament: 2 x 533mm TT, 4 x depth charges.
Viforul and *Vijelia* were sunk by debris from a mining on 9/11/41.

Gusto MTBs Nos 4-9: *Vedenia, Vantul, Vijelia, Viforul, Vartejul, Vulcanul* (all 1940)

Built	Disp.	Dimensions	Speed
Netherlands	57t	28m x 7.6m x 1.2m	34kts

Armament: 2 x 533mm TT, 2 x 20mm AA, 6 x depth charges.
Ex-German war booty. Lack of a suitable shaft coupling prevented 20-25kts being exceeded.

Torpedo-Boats: *Sborul* (1914), *Smeul* (1914), *Naluca* (1914).

Built	Disp.	Dimensions	Speed	Range	Crew
A-Hungary	±260t	57.4m x 5.8m x 1.5m.	24kts	±1,000 miles at 16kts	38

Armament: 1 x 66mm, 1 x 37mmAA, 1 x 20mm AA.
Sborul, which was not an identical sistership, retained two 450mm torpedo tubes. *Naluca* was bombed on 20/8/44.

Minelayer: *Amiral Murgescu* (1939).

Built	Disp.	Dimensions	Speed	Radius	Crew
Romania	812t	76.9m x 9.1m x 2.5m	16kts	3,400 miles at 12kts	80

Armament: 2 x 102mm, 2 x 37mm AA, 4 x 20mm AA, 2 depth charge launchers, 135 mines.
A Dutch design. A sister ship, *Cetatea Alba*, was laid down but abandoned.

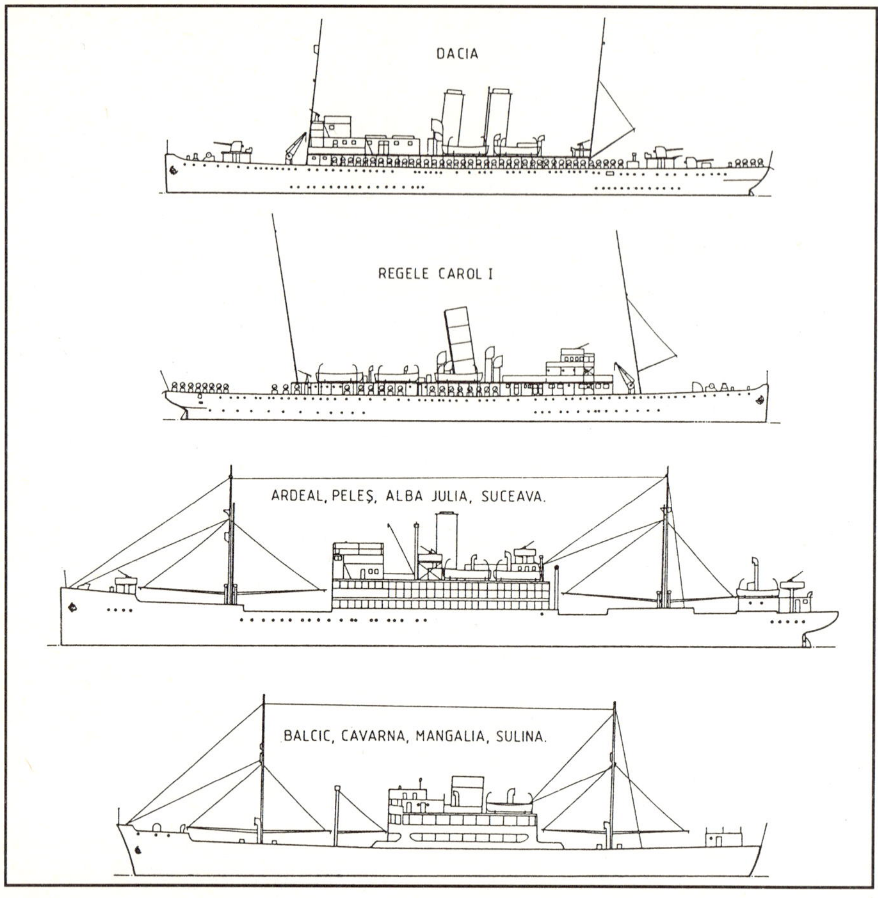

River Monitors: *Kogalniceanu* (1908), *Bratianu* (1907), *Lahovary* (1908), *Catargiu* (1907)

Built	Disp.	Dimensions	Speed	Crew
Italy	680t	±62m x 10.2m x 1.6m	12kts	110

Armament: 3 x 120mm, 3 x 37mm AA, 1 x 13.2mm twin AA.

Completely modernised and up-gunned in 1937. Later replaced the 13.2mm AA gun with another 37mm AA piece and added four 20mm AA guns. *Kogalniceanu* and *Catargiu* were bombed and sunk on 24/8/44.

River Monitor: Basarabia (1914)

Built	Disp.	Dimensions	Speed	Crew
A-Hungary	550t	62m x 10.5m x 1.3m	12kts	100

Armament: 4 x 120mm, 2 x 37mm AA, 4 x 20mm AA.

Basarabia was completely rebuilt with new turrets and up-gunned at *Galati* in 1942-43, and later added four more 37mm AA pieces.

River Monitor: Bucovina (1915)

Built	Disp.	Dimensions	Speed	Crew
A-Hungary	550t	58m x 10.5m x 1.3m	12kts	100

Armament: 4 x 120mm, 3 x 37mm AA, 2 x 20mm AA, 1 x 13.2mm twin AA.

Note: *Bucovina* was completely rebuilt and up-gunned at *Galati* in 1942-43. Her new after turret was *Basarabia*'s old forward turret.

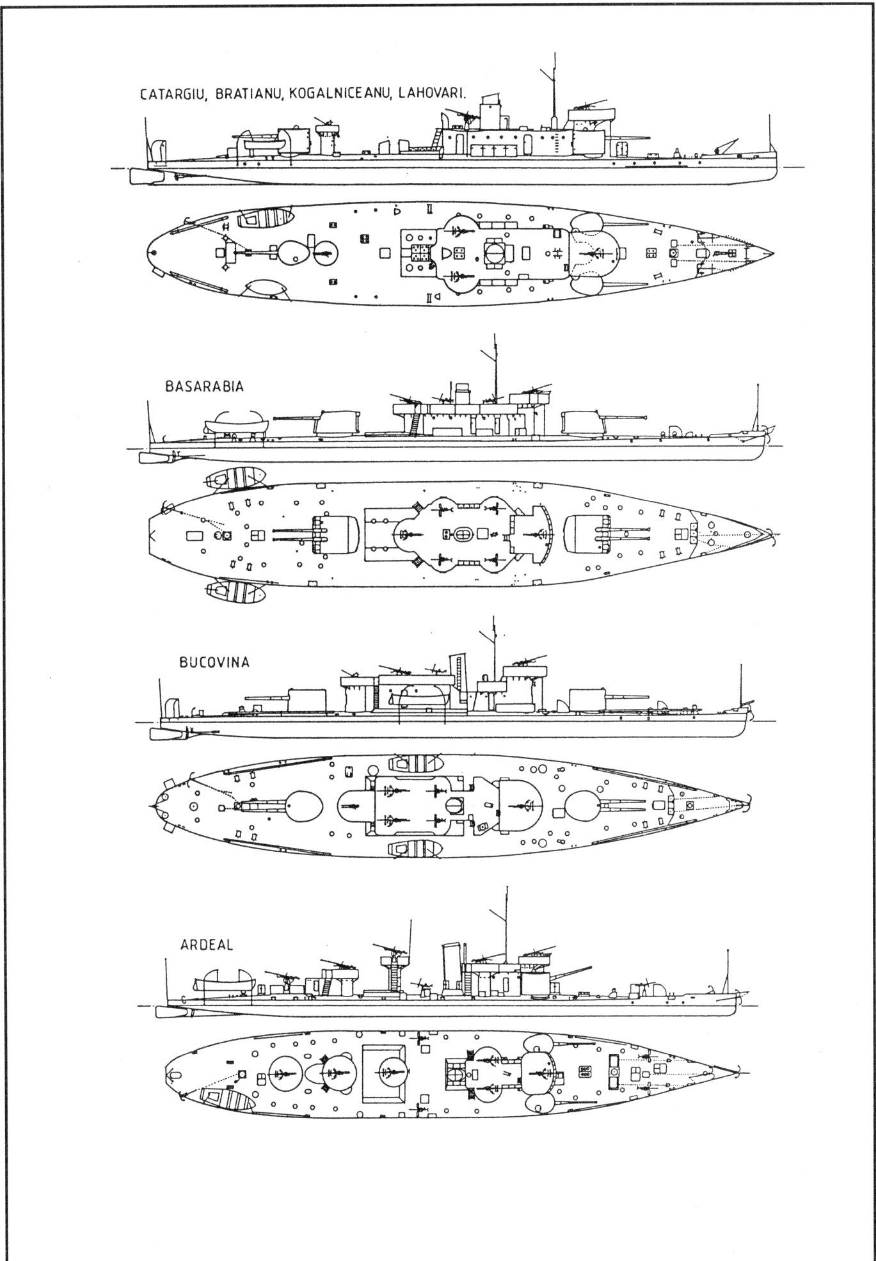

River Monitor: *Ardeal* (1904)

Built	Disp.	Dimensions	Speed	Crew
A-Hungary	440t	56m x 9.5m x 1.2m	10kts	100

Armament: 2 x 120mm, 6 x 37mm AA, 4 x 20mm AA.

Completely modernised and up-gunned in 1937–38, when the after turret was removed.

SELECT BIBLIOGRAPHY

PRIMARY SOURCES

This book is primarily based on Romanian military archive material. The most significant documents have been microfilmed and are held by the Ministry of Defence in Bucharest. However, a huge stock of original material is outhoused at Pitesti and this still includes a great deal of importance.

Microfilms:

FI.1.373, FII.1.1187, FII.1.1193, FII.1.1195, FII.1.1208, FII.1.1217, FII.1.2292, FII.1.2351, FII.2.334bis, FII.2.828-9, FII.2.957, FII.2.1224, FII.2.1249-52, FII.2.1492-3, FII.2.1499, FII.2.1518, FII.2.2018, FII.2.2026-7, FII.3.759-60, FII.3.1060, FII.3.1080, FII.3.1098, FII.3.1137-45, FII.3.1154, FII.3.1157-60, FII.3.1165-6, FII.3.1170, FII.3.1176, FII.3.1179-81, FII.3.1516, FII.3.1529-34, FII.3.1541-2, FII.3.1569-70, FII.3.1572-3, FII.3.1616-17, FII.3.2021-2, FII.3.2024-6, FII.3.3889, FII.3.3899, FII.3.3900, FII.5.2048-9, FII.5.2064, FII.5.2083, FII.5.2197, FII.5.2219, FII.5.2230, FII.5.2254, FII.5.2330, FII.5.2342-3, FII.5.2396, FII.5.2398, FII.5.2443-4, FII.5.2446-8, FII.5.2450-1, FII.6.445-7, FII.6.507-9, FII.6.512, FII.6.521-2, FII.6.525, FII.6.537, FII.113.1170

Operations Diary of Air Force GHQ:

1377/130 (22/06/41-31/07/41); 1377/131 (01/08/41-31/03/42); 1377/132 (01/04/42-10/09/42); 1377/133 (15/09/42-15/01/43); 1377/134 (16/01/43-31/08/43); 1377/135 (01/09/43-23/08/44); 1377/136 (24/08/43-31/12/44); 1377/137 General

SELECTED PUBLISHED WORKS

Wartime secrecy meant that, except for propaganda, there was very little opportunity to publish anything of substance on military matters in the years 1941–44 before the Communists took over. However, during those years some solid articles were published in specialist journals of restricted circulation:

Romania Militara, 1941–45; *Revista Cavaleriei, 1941–44*; *Revista Infanteriei, 1941–44*; *Revista Artilleriei, 1941–44.*

Under Communism virtually all military books were published by the Editura Militara (Military Publishing House), under collective authorship. These concentrated almost exclusively on the campaign of 1944–45. Because they had to adhere to the line that the Communist Party was entirely responsible for a uniformly successful war effort, they consistently exaggerate Communist influence, exclude the stronger nationalist and royalist sentiments in the army and ignore the wide popular support enjoyed by the traditional political parties. They also exaggerate military successes, gloss over occasional reverses, and ignore the very serious problems caused by the 'fraternal' Soviet Union. Thus these books are usually slanted. Nevertheless, they are often detailed, and judicious reading between the lines is productive for 1944–45. However, for the most part they simply ignore the years 1941–44 completely:

23 August 1944. Editura Stiintifica si Enciclopedica, Bucharest 1984. English account of Romania's defection.

Armata Romana in Razboiul Antihitlerist. Editura Militara, 1980. Military Atlas for 1944–45.

Cronica Participarii Armatei Romane la Razboiul Antihitlerist. Editura Militara, 1971. Daily record of war effort, 1944–45.

Documente privind Istoria Militara a Poporului Roman. Editura Militara, 1984–6. Seven volumes of documents covering 1944–45.

Gudju, I., Iacobescu, G. and Ionescu, O. *Romanian Aeronautical Constructions, 1905–1970.* Editura Militara, 1970. English language chronological survey of Romanian-built aircraft with basic three-view drawings and a photograph of each.

Istoria Aviaţiei Romane. Editura Stiintifica si Enciclopedica, 1984. History of Romanian Aviation.

Romania in Razboiul Antihitlerist. Editura Militara, 1966. Standard single-volume work for 1944–5.

Romanian Military Bibliography, 1944– 84. Editura Militara, 1985. English language edition listing 528 titles.

Tudor, G. *Forţa de Şoc.* Editura Militara, 1982. A history of Romanian Armour.

Towards the end of the Communist period a number of books began to make some references to the years 1941–44 without, however, being significantly more balanced about 1944–45:

Romania in Anii celui de-al Dolilea Razboi Mondial, Vols. 1, 2, 3. Editura Militara, 1989.
Istoria Militara a Poporului Roman, Vol 6. Editura Militara, 1989.

Since 1990 the Editura Militara has been hit by financial restrictions. As a result, very little on 1941-44 has yet been published under its auspices. However, the new material is often promising and more will follow:

Pandea, A., Pavelescu, I. and Ardeleanu, E. *Romanii la Stalingrad*. Editura Militara, 1992. Well documented description of Romanian participation at Stalingrad.
Revue Internationale d'Histoire Militaire, No. 77. Bucharest 1992. English edition. Articles of varied quality on the 1941, 1942 and 1944–45 campaigns.
Spaţiul Istoric şi Etnic Romanesc, Vols 1, 2 and 3. Editura Militara, 1992–93. Reproduction of an historical and ethnic atlas prepared for Antonescu in 1941–2. Important for its graphic representation of Romania's perception of its role in European history then and, indeed, now.

Independent publishers are now entering the military field with books of increasingly high production values:

Aviaţia Romana pe Frontul de Est şi in Apararea Teritoriului. Editura Tehnoprod, 1993. Collected memoires of Romanian aircrew blended with operational records from the archives. With photographs. Further volumes to follow.
Safta, I., Jipa, R., Velter, T., and Marinescu, F. *Decoraţii Romaneşti de Razboi, 1860-1947*. Editura Universitaria 1993. Romanian military decorations.
Duţu, A., and Retegan, M. *Ostaşi, Va Ordon: Treceţi Prutul*. Editura Globus, 1993. A day-by-day account of the liberation of Basarabia in 1941 from original sources. The authors hope that this will be the first volume in a series covering the entire war.

There is, as yet, no balanced biography of Antonescu, but a number of more or less pro-Antonescu books have appeared:

Dragan, Josif, *Antonescu, Mareşal Romaniei si Rasboaiele de Reintregrire*. 2nd edition, Bucharest 1990.
Mareşal Antonescu in Faţa Istoriei, Vols 1 and 2. Iasi 1990. Mostly compilation of references to Antonescu by other authors.
Antonescu-Hitler, Vols 1 and 2. Cozia Editura, 1991. Documents on their correspondence and meetings.

PERIODICALS

Revista de Istorie Militara, 1990– . Bimonthly journal of the Ministry of Defence. Numerous short articles introduce latest research by leading military and naval historians.
Magazin Istoric. Monthly general history magazine with numerous articles on 1941–44 period since 1990.
Aeronautica, 1991– . Bi-annual magazine of the Muzeul Aviatiei. Includes biographies of aces and operational memoires of the Second World War.
Revista Muzeului Militar National, 1991– . Annual of the National Military Museum. Main source for indigenous small-arms and artillery.
Modelism and Modelism International, 1982– . High-quality quarterly modelling magazine covering military, civil, land, sea and air subjects. Close print and highly refined drawings often provide exceptional detail. Many back-numbers are still available.
Modelism International has begun to produce a series of 48-page photo-booklets under collective authorships in the style of Squadron/Signal which will eventually cover all major types of Romanian combat aircraft and warships:
Blindatele Dunarii. 1993. River Monitors. Exceptional drawings.
O Misiune Irepetabila: Tidal Wave. 1993. The first description to have access to Axis and Allied sources.
Hidroaviaţia Romaniei. 1994. Seaplanes over the Black Sea.
Aviaţia de Asalt-G8. 1994. Hs129B in Romanian service.

Since 1990 a number of useful articles by Modelism's contributors have appeared in English language publications:

Serbanescu, H. *The Romanian Army of WWII*. Osprey, London 1991. Uniforms: colour illustrations and photographs.
'The Romanian Army, 1941–1945' in *Militaria* No. 8, September 1994, Colour uniform photographs by Horia Serbanescu.
Air International, Vol. 38, No.5. May 1990. IAR80/81.
Air International, Vol. 46, No.4. April 1994. IAR39 by Liviu Morosanu and Dan Antoniu.
Craciunoiu, Cristian, 'Romanian Minelayers in WWII' in *Warship 1991*. Conway, London 1991.
— 'Romanian Submarines in WWII' in *Warship 1992*. Conway, London 1992.

INDEX

INDEX OF ARMY FORMATIONS.

German Army Formations:

INDEX OF ROMANIAN AIR FORCE FORMATIONS: